D1570974

Indian Tribes
of Aboriginal America

Indian Tribes
of Aboriginal America

Selected Papers

of the XXIXth International Congress of Americanists

Edited by

SOL TAX

COOPER SQUARE PUBLISHERS, INC.
NEW YORK • 1967

Published 1967 by
Cooper Square Publishers, Inc.
59 Fourth Avenue, New York, N. Y. 10003
Library of Congress Catalog Card Number: 67-18219

SPECIAL ACKNOWLEDGMENT

This volume, *Indian Tribes of Aboriginal America*, together with two previously published, *The Civilizations of Ancient America* (University of Chicago Press, 1951) and *Acculturation in the Americas* (University of Chicago Press, 1952), constitute the published proceedings of the XXIXth International Congress of Americanists, which was held in New York City, September 5–12, 1949.

The Executive Officers of the XXIXth Congress take this opportunity to acknowledge with thanks the many institutions and individuals who have contributed to the preparation of these volumes. They wish to express appreciation for the work of the Committee on Publications, and in particular, for the time, knowledge, and skill so generously offered by the editor, Dr. Sol Tax, and his faithful assistants.

The Officers also wish to offer special acknowledgment to the Wenner-Gren Foundation for Anthropological Research, Inc., New York (formerly The Viking Fund, Inc.), for its exceptionally generous support not only of a large part of the meetings of the Congress but also of these publications containing the important results.

A. L. KROEBER, *President*
A. V. KIDDER, *Secretary*
W. C. BENNETT, *Treasurer*

PREFACE

The greatest event of discovery in western history, which doubled the size of its world, gave us its greatest mystery. Who were these Indians? Where did they come from, and when? How did they reach such varied ways of life, from "savagery" to civilization? From the seventeenth century the mystery has engaged explorers and missionaries, philosophers and theologians, journalists and scientists. In the past hundred years anthropologists have added careful first-hand study of the cultures, languages, and characteristics of the surviving Indians, painstaking archeological and historical investigation, and application of scientific knowledge of all of the natural sciences, to come to answers that are ever more satisfying.

This book brings together some of the latest of these answers.

The problem of the American Indian has been the focus of a group of scholars calling themselves Americanists, who since 1875 have met together periodically to compare their findings. This book contains selected papers read at the XXIXth International Congress of Americanists, in New York City in 1949. Other selections are published in *The Civilizations of Ancient America* and *Acculturation in the Americas*. An account and history of the Congress itself is contained in the official *Proceedings* published in the latter volume.

The present volume takes one to the heart of the Americanist problem. It deals neither with the flowering of American Indian culture in the great civilizations of Middle and South America, nor with what has happened to the Indians since their development was interrupted by Europeans. It centers attention instead on the roots from which the civilizations grew. Who were the Indians, and what their origin, and their basic cultures in all their variety— these are the questions asked. The answers demonstrate the central unity of the discipline of anthropology, for they require the concerted attack by subjects as diverse as linguistics and physical anthropology, archeology and folklore. These diverse disciplines were indeed brought together in response to these questions, and their unity gives to anthropology its traditions and distinctive character.

Distinguishing cultures by their complexity, and societies by their size, anthropologists sometimes speak of "civilizations" as complex cultures which tie together large societies that extend over great territories, as differing from the cultures of small and independent tribes. In general the Indians of nuclear America, from the Valley of Mexico down through the Andes to Northern Chile, lived in pre-Columbian days as parts of civilizations; all of the others, in North and South America and the Antilles, lived in tribes, in varying degrees confederated or mutually hostile. The papers in this book refer almost exclusively to people of such tribes, "marginal" to the great civilizations of ancient America.

Robert Lowie's paper comparing the marginal cultures most broadly therefore serves to introduce the volume. In general the papers thereafter are arranged by the geographical locus of their subject matter, from North to South, beginning with the Eskimo, where emphasis is on problems of relations with the Old World, and ending with lower South America where the problems of origins are again paramount. There are no subdivisions in the volume—no classification of the chapters because they so easily grade into one another, in terms either of the region treated or the method of anthropology illustrated. Nevertheless, it will be noted that most of the specific archeological papers concern North America, while most on physical anthropology discuss South American problems; and whereas papers on arts and crafts and on religious subjects for the most part come from North America, those on social organization have more southern subjects.

The XXIXth Congress was sponsored by the Wenner-Gren Fund for Anthropological Research, which also has made possible publication of this volume. To it and to the University of Chicago, which provided my time and the use of its facilities, thanks are due. Mrs. Constance Shimbel helped in the initial editorial stages. Mr. Manning Nash became my assistant when work was begun on this volume. With help from others, particularly Dr. Betty Starr (who edited the Spanish and French papers), Mr. Nash contributed the intelligence, energy, and devotion necessary to bring the enterprise to fruition.

SOL TAX

UNIVERSITY OF CHICAGO
December 10, 1951

TABLE OF CONTENTS

ix

THE HETEROGENEITY OF MARGINAL CULTURES

Robert H. Lowie

In accordance with American usage (49, p. 329; 248, p. 837; 86, pp. 434–37)[1] I identify "marginal" with backward peoples—hunters and gatherers or farmers whose cultivation, rudimentary or vestigial, remains ancillary. It is an often repeated proposition that man spent well over ninety per cent of his existence "by catching and collecting what food nature happened to provide" (71, pp. 12–17). The suggestion is one of drearily uniform "parasitic" existence through endless aeons until pastoralism and agriculture ushered in the glorious "food-producing" economy.

I realize that even Professor Childe does not consistently adhere to the dogma of otiose stagnation. Nevertheless, his comparison of the human gatherer with "any other beast of prey" obscures early man's extraordinary achievement; and I regard as vicious the antithesis of food-collectors and of food-producers. In the present paper I shall first, by a series of ethnographic commonplaces, illustrate the heterogeneity of marginal American economies. Next I shall adduce evidence for the creation of these economies by the marginal peoples themselves. Finally, I shall extend the inquiry to non-material aspects of culture, largely confining myself for reasons of time limitation to the South American moiety systems.

I

To begin with the Arctic zone, the Eskimo hunt sea-mammals and caribou, travel in kayaks and in sledges, burn blubber in lamps, and wear snow-goggles. To an Iglulik, fish mean little, vegetable fare less. On the Pacific littoral and among the Western Déné, however, salmon are the staff of life, and berries are "not by any means unimportant" (41, p. 235; 333; 302, pp. 203–8). The Canadian taiga-dweller lacks much of the Arctic equipment, but by way of compensation he uses snowshoes, toboggans, birchbark canoes, and birchbark cooking vessels.

In the Plateau, Basin, and California plant foods become vital; even the Klamath, who subsist mainly on fish, rank pond-lily seeds next in importance. Groups that do not cultivate and are not primarily hunters or fishermen are inevitably collectors, which puts them into a different category. The pine-nut harvesting Cahuilla who depends on some sixty plant species for his fare is not a variety of "hunter" who somehow falls under the same head as an Iglulik sealer and a Haida fisherman: he lives in a distinct cultural universe.

1. Numbers refer to items listed alphabetically in the Bibliography at the end of the volume.

Correspondingly, the Haida, secure from want in his permanent villages of substantial houses, is far more like the Pueblo than like the roving Paiute forced into a "gastric" orientation (Steward) by his eternal fear of famine. Even collectors conform to no single type. Kroeber properly minimizes "the positive similarities of the Basin and Columbia-Frazer areas" and points out that for a desert Californian "the seed beater is more important than the digging-stick" (449, pp. 145, 160; 244, p. 694; 246; 461).

Again, Plains Indian buffalo-hunting constitutes an economy that differs qualitatively from the root-digging of the Plateau, the seed-gathering of the Basin or California, the fishing of the Northwest Coast, or the chase of cetaceans in the Arctic.

In South America Kirchhoff has demonstrated at least two distinct marginal forms of adaptation to the Venezuelan llaños. The Guahibo live largely on armadillos, wild roots, and palm fruits; on the other hand, the Yaruro rarely pursue land animals, depending on fish, crocodiles, turtles, and wild vegetable fare. Minor specializations within the region include the chase of the manatees by the Guamo (233).

As for Eastern Brazilians, we have come to realize that the traditional picture of their extreme backwardness must be revised. Notwithstanding the lack of pottery, weaving, and canoes, both the Gê and their neighbors are not uniformly so rude as ethnographers once assumed; as early as 1930 Ploetz and Métraux pointed out their diversity. The Aweikoma and the Botocudo seem really to have lacked farming aboriginally, whereas Kamakan agriculture corresponds to the Tupian level, the Apinayé astonished early observers by the extent of their manioc plantations, and the Eastern Timbira, though largely hunters and gatherers, nevertheless grew a respectable number of cultivated species (341, pp. 87, 91, 93, 94; 342; 343, pp. 57–74; 368, p. 227).

Finally, in the extreme south, the Ona and the Yahgan differ to such an extent from each other that intermarriage becomes unpractical. The Ona men hunt guanacos with dogs or, regionally, dig out burrowing rodents (Ctenomys). By way of contrast, no Yahgan would go after game in protracted cross-country walks. On the other hand, a Yahgan woman pries loose the mussels that form the staff of life for her household, and paddles her husband's canoe when he goes after seals. Her Ona sister, ignorant of swimming and paddling, would be of no use as a Yahgan's helpmate (158, I, 192, 245, 269, 279, 288, 300; II, 236, 365–626).

II

Every one of the economies just sketched rests on a large number of observations and logical inferences, whose sum total in all of the societies jointly must be reckoned enormous. But are not these varied sets of adaptations due to more advanced neighbors? That some of them are so derived is undeniable: the Navaho did not come to diverge from proto-Athabaskans by independently domesticating maize. But such influences are not to be exaggerated. First of all, every advanced civilization was at one time of marginal level. Secondly, as Tylor pointed out (500, p. 175), an invention found in a particular district and nowhere else is reasonably assigned to the natives among whom it occurs; and there are many cases of this type. The vaulted snowhouse, e.g., "has never been observed in Asia," hence must be credited to the Eskimo (215, p. 208). What is more, innumerable adaptations are inconceivable except as a response of backward tribes to their local circumstances.

Patent deficiencies must not mislead us into belittling marginal achievement. The Fuegians are a case in point. Their scant dress and inadequate habitations have repeatedly been held up to scorn, but Gusinde's illuminating treatises reveal unsuspected aspects of the situation. A Yahgan does not expect to be kept warm by his skin cape; for that end he relies upon his fire, which is truly indispensable, and on the grease he applies to his body in exceptionally cold weather. As an observer remarked in the 1890's, "Had the early explorers imitated instead of despised the Yahgan, they would have had fewer tales of suffering to tell" (158, II, 410).

The fire-making process of the Ona and the Yahgan with its accessories must be a local invention. Whence could percussion have been introduced to Fuegians? As Lothrop notes, the Tehuelche, Pampas Indians, and Araucanians *drill* fire. One has to go as far afield as the Eskimo, Beothuk, and southern New Englanders to find a parallel. The idea that these Northerners diffused strike-a-lights to Fuegia or that the ancestral Fuegians preserved knowledge of the process during their millennial southward trek through regions which lacked the prerequisites of percussion strikes me as fantastic. In Fuegia itself, though pyrites occurs in various spots, flint is scarcer, forming a favorite article of trade. On Tierra del Fuego it is found only on the south coast, in the valley between Ushuaia and Lapataia, where Thomas Bridges vainly looked for the traditional quarry in 1884. Assuming the advent of an immigrant horde familiar with percussion, how likely is it that they would at once discover a source of supply? My guess is that prior to such an event they would freeze; that the earliest invaders came with the fire-drill, discovered percussion by some lucky fluke, and came to prefer the innovation, ultimately excluding the rival technique. Ancillary adaptations to local conditions arose: as a protection against the humidity the apparatus was carried in a pouch; the canoeing Yahgan learned to maintain fires while on the water without having holes burned into the boat; and so forth.[2]

The Fuegian canoe invites similar considerations. Nordenskiöld and Lothrop agree that it is a thing *sui generis*. It is certainly different from any other known form. The woodskin of Guiana, e.g., made from a single strip of purpleheart bark, bears not the slightest resemblance to the Yahgan boat sewn together from three pieces. The very selection of a suitable tree for barking,

2. Percussion is also ascribed to the Alakaluf (345, p. 125; 30, p. 70). However, Gusinde (157, pp. 145, 214) describes fire-drilling and pictures an Alakaluf in the act. See also S. K. Lothrop, 277, p. 64; 158, II, 329, I, 207; 522, p. 78; 122, p. 34).

the traditional preference for *Nothofagus betuloides,* one of the three available species of the antarctic beech, indicates a local origin.

An analysis of the pursuit of whales, the hunting of cormorants, even of the methods used in collecting mussels, would lead to the same inference: these activities rest on observations and adjustments *in situ;* no hypothetical culture-bearer from Peru or emissary of ancient Egypt could conceivably be responsible for the adaptations implied. As Gusinde aptly remarks, man exploits his habitat, creating within it "eine bestimmte Wirtschaftsform, die früher oder später als harmonievolles Zusammenwirken von Mensch und Natur jedem genauen Beobachter vor Augen tritt" (158, II, 511, 625; 277; 345; 402, p. 615).

Even where diffusion is established, it is necessary to discriminate and discover precisely what has been diffused. Some Gê tribes grow manioc and maize, and no one suggests that they invented the cultivation of these plants, which they either borrowed from more experienced farmers or, as Professor Lévi-Strauss suggests, retained as elements of a more advanced economy which at one time they shared. So far, so good. But the Gê also raise a xerophilous creeper (*Cissus* sp.), whose starchy tendrils they bake in earth-ovens. This plant is known neither to Whites nor to any other Indian stock: by Tylor's criterion, then, its domestication is a local achievement (343, p. 59). Like more advanced populations, the Gê do not passively take over new cultural elements, but also creatively add to the loan or heritage.

At all events, the heterogeneity of marginal economies results, not entirely, of course, but in large measure, from a vast number of independent responses to distinct environments.

III

Ecological heterogeneity is paralleled in the realm of supernaturalism, though in this department a different kind of mentality manifests itself. It is one thing to cope with what Vischer calls "the malice of objective reality" (*die Tücke des Objekts*), quite another to give rein to free associations. The igloo is a "marvel of Eskimo technique"; yet the same people believe that a boy who has not yet caught a bearded seal would get his fingers entangled in the harpoon line if he played at cat's cradle. Thirty sizable pages are filled with descriptions of comparable taboos and prescriptions (302, p. 118; 377). Their conception involved no intellectual feat, though their existence adds to the complexity of Iglulik culture.

Eastern Brazilians illustrate differentiation in the sphere of religion. The Northern and Central Gê presumably had at one time a common stock of beliefs, with Sun and Moon as outstanding figures in myth and worship, yet how differently these tribes have worked out their relations with their deities! The Canella collectively invoke them for the common good, but very rarely for individual blessings; and theophany, even in dreams, is lacking. The less worldly-minded Apinayé venerate, above all, the Sun, who reveals himself to natives on lonely hunts. Both tribes definitely subordinate the Moon. This does not hold in the same sense for the Šerénte. Though they, too, give precedence to the Sun, they also greatly revere the Moon. They link the two luminaries each with one moiety, whose members may directly commune not with the solar and lunar gods themselves, but with their satellites, such stars as Mars and Venus. In other East Brazilian stocks resemblance naturally wanes. In Bororó myth Sun and Moon are essentially tricksters, another pair—twin heroes— appearing as exemplars and transformers; and belief here centers in cults of the dead and of evil spirits. Distinct again is the supernaturalism of the Botocudo, who derive extraordinary power from a race of benevolent anthropomorphic sky-dwellers and do not worship ghosts (343; 341, pp. 132–38; 342; 344; 78).

Social organization and custom are often affected not only by free associations, but by external circumstances that require no cerebration whatsoever. A tribe is divided into three clans; one of them becomes extinct; two remain— the basis of a moiety system. One people overruns the territory of another; the consequence is subordination of the conquered, potential stratification.

Scholars I esteem (263, pp. 37–47; 161; 375, p. 162) hold that such a phenomenon as the dual organization did not arise among backward peoples, but spread to them from a higher level, or that the marginal tribes are in a state of decadence, retaining moieties as part of the higher estate from which they have otherwise fallen. Specifically, as the Gê and Bororó borrowed what agriculture they have from Tropical Forest neighbors (or clung to fragments of an agricultural complex once shared with such neighbors), so they borrowed (or retained) a social system that arose on a plane intermediate between their present condition and the Andean civilizations.

I recall incidentally that not even the whole of Gê agriculture is due to a higher source. However, I maintain that even if it were otherwise it would not affect the issue. The domestication of the humblest wild species of plant or animal is a feat of the very first order; the frills of Gê sociology have no bearing on tribal welfare and no more exemplify intellectual power than do Iglulik taboos. They are consistent with any level of cultural complexity. I do not, indeed, dogmatically deny that, say, Arawakans or Tupians originated the moiety scheme. I deprecate merely its *a priori* derivation from such a source on the score of supposed marginal disabilities. The view seems to me to rest on a confusion of extent of cultural inventory with creativeness.

But the matter should not be debated in the abstract, and here the heterogeneity of our marginal peoples becomes significant. There is no model— Arawakan, Tupian, Cariban, Andean—from which we can derive what is found among the Gê or Bororó. We must at once brush aside the Andean *saya* and the Terena moieties, for these were endogamous units. There is evidence in various parts of the world for the loss of exogamy, converting exogamous into agamous moieties, but the positive prescription to marry within one's own unit eliminates that unit from the category of unilateral descent groups. Rivers justly protested that the Toda moieties could be classed with Melanesian ones only by "dependence on a wholly superficial character," the number 2. It would be hardly more artificial to regard our political two-party system as a sample of duality (390; 407, pp. 254–55; 349, pp. 27, 32, 33). In short, the exogamous schemes of the marginal tribes can be connected only with exogamous, or at most, agamous schemes of more advanced peoples.

Let us consider three of the best known marginal schemes, the Bororó, the Canella, and the Šerénte. Common to all three is the spatial segregation of the complementary moieties within the village, but they differ in the rule of descent, patrilineal for the Šerénte, matrilineal for the two other tribes. Further, the Canella moieties are undivided, whereas the Šerénte and Bororó also have clans. Is there, then, a direct affinity between the two latter systems? The Kejara Bororó have a secondary dichotomy, an axis perpendicular to the course of the Rio Vermelho creating an Up-stream and Down-stream division over and above the primary halves assigned to the northwest and the southwest parts of the settlement. To this refinement there is no parallel among the Šerénte. On the other hand, a special bond unites a Šerénte clan with its opposite in the complementary moiety as localized in the village circle. The Bororó clans have each exclusive privileges, a type of labret, bow decorations, certain dances, certain personal names. Except for two anomalous units of comparatively recent accession and in some respects co-ordinated with the moieties, the Šerénte clans, save for festive ornaments, have "neither corporeal nor incorporeal property." The designations of the Bororó clans are largely derived from species of plants and animals; the Šerénte clan names that are translatable denote fire and cotton decorations. Unlike the Šerénte, the Bororó do not associate moieties with the great celestial luminaries and their retinue in religion. Nor must we forget the contrast in the rule of descent. As for the Canella, they have not one, but three, supplementary dichotomous schemes, making four in all. Embracing both sexes there are exogamous moieties and an agamous dual division that holds during the rainy season; further there is a male dual grouping into ceremonial units; and a similar grouping of the four male age-classes. Intimately connected with these schemes are the popular Gê races with heavy logs. Although both Gê tribes practice this pastime, a Šerénte father arbitrarily assigns his son to either of two teams for permanent affiliation, whereas matrilineal kinship determines a Canella boy's membership in one of the agamous moieties. If we assume, reasonably enough, that the Gê systems have diverged from an ancestral prototype and concede that the Bororó shared in this parental scheme, we must concur in Kroeber's judgment that the backward East Brazilians have done an enormous amount of remodeling, innovating, and experimenting (284; 285; 248, pp. 395-98; 342, pp. 16–23; 341; 343; 314; 261).

Turning now to the known dual organizations of Forest and Andean tribes, we find no evidence for the complexities just enumerated in part. The features known only from the Šerénte or the Canella or the Bororó must, on Tylor's criterion, be credited to the natives among whom they occur and to no one else. If, further, as is actually the case, the marginal moiety schemes as a whole are far more elaborate than those of the silval peoples, the argument for that center of dispersal collapses. Such superficial features as the "Lower-Upper" nomenclature may well have a single origin in South America, but they may go back to a period when the intermediate or higher cultures were themselves only on a marginal plane; or they may even have been borrowed by the higher from the simpler peoples. At all events, the same system of naming may hold for units of utterly different character; in the western Plains of North America bands of certain tribes bear the same type of nicknames as the clans of others. The case for the genetic unity of the units themselves must rest on stronger grounds.

Lest I be misunderstood, I should like to emphasize that metaphysically Lévy-Bruhl's and Haeckel's assumption remains a possibility. Conceivably the moiety organization first did take shape on intermediate levels and either spread thence to ruder tribes or persisted among otherwise decadent ones. But we should clearly visualize the empirical implications of that hypothesis. Here is the dilemma. If the Šerénte and Canella independently achieved the elaborations observed, then they were also capable of creating a simple dual organization. If their systems are merely the replica of an earlier silval or Andean pattern, then the ancestral Munduruku or Parintintin or Palikur or Aymará system possessed features of which not a rack remains. Further, since the observed marginal patterns are not only different from one another, but in part manifest contradictory traits, these cannot all go back to a single source. Specifically, we must demand an explanation of how the several rude tribes acquired, respectively, matriliny and patriliny in connection with their moieties. These are formidable difficulties.

Such difficulties do not arise if we cease regarding moieties as abstruse creations of the intellect and see them as the simple unplanned results they appear to be from Lévi-Strauss' own Nambikuara observations, from Rivers' discussion of the Toda, from Hutton's of the Naga.

IV

To conclude: The ecological adaptations of marginal peoples reveal an astonishing inventiveness. The religious, magical, and social aspects of their cultures exhibit comparable heterogeneity without, as a rule, requiring comparable imagination and logical power. *A fortiori*, the occurrence of items belonging to these categories need not arouse our amazement. Specifically, the origin of the dual organization of East Brazilians may very well be referable to these natives or to peoples of a similar technological stage.

PRESENT STATUS OF THE ESKIMO PROBLEM

Kaj Birket-Smith

In the history of science much controversy and many misunderstandings arise because students do not at the outset make it sufficiently clear what the issue is. This is also true of the problem of Eskimo origin. Hrdlička once drew up a list of different authors' opinions on it. His list is rather uncritical; important contributions are ignored or nearly so, whereas it includes a lot of purely casual remarks of authors lacking first-hand knowledge of the Eskimo; but in spite of all its deficiencies the list shows that few of the statements are really clear. Do they apply to the Eskimo racial components, their linguistic relationship, or the origin of their culture—and in the latter case, do they mean the culture as a whole or its individual elements?

In the following discussion it will therefore be advisable to keep the different aspects of the problem apart, and I shall start with a summary of the culture, because in recent years intensive archeological activity has added so many facts that it is now possible to give an approximately accurate account of the cultural growth, even if many details are still obscure.

I

Jochelson certainly overshot the mark in his criticism of Dall's alleged stratification of the Aleutian shell heaps by concluding that the earliest inhabitants of the islands possessed a culture practically identical with the one found by the Russian invaders. Investigations, by Hrdlička, Quimby, and Helge Larsen, have shown certain differences between the earliest and latest phases of Aleutian culture, but the fact still remains that there is a remarkable uniformity throughout all periods. The same applies to the regions farther east on the Pacific coast. In Cook Inlet Dr. de Laguna was able to distinguish three periods of cultural development, called Kachemak I–III, but the difference between the stages is very small. The last period we also found, in nearly identical form, in Prince William Sound, but most traces of earlier occupation seem to have been washed away by the sea because of a recent sinking of the shore line.

Both on the Aleutians and on the Pacific coast the early inhabitants obtained their staple food by hunting sea-mammals and fishing. They lived in semi-underground, sod-covered houses with open fire places. Oval stone lamps were used for illumination. Weapons and tools were made of chipped stone, and decorative art consisted in rather crude, linear designs. In the course of time a few new elements were introduced, e.g., pottery and fishing nets; polished slate replaced chipping, and there was some development in art, cul-

8

minating in certain remarkably sculptured stone lamps characteristic of the Kachemak III period. About the same time the first faint traces of metal make their appearance, and at least in Prince William Sound there is a slightly growing Indian influence.

In Alaska north of the Pacific coast the earliest Eskimo remains seem to be those belonging to the Ipiutaq culture, first discovered by Rainey and Helge Larsen at Point Hope but afterward found also on the Seward Peninsula and at Kuskokwim Bay. Both seal and walrus were hunted, but—what is of paramount importance—whaling was apparently entirely unknown, and the enormous amount of implements made of caribou bones and antler testify to the great importance of land hunting. The dwellings were semi-underground earth lodges with hearths similar to those which are still found on Nunivak Island. Flint chipping had reached a high degree of perfection, but polished stone implements are very scarce. Other remarkable traits are the highly developed animal art and numerous specimens of enigmatical, twisted bone carvings.

In time, the Ipiutaq culture gave way to other cultural types. In the region around Bering Strait we find archeological evidence of the so-called Old Bering Sea culture, characterized by an art different from, although related to that of Ipiutaq. The scroll-like patterns are unique among the Eskimo, and it is clear that they are far from being primitive. An early stage of this art has been described by Rainey as characteristic of what he has termed the Okvik phase preceding the Old Bering Sea proper, while Collins, to whom we are indebted for a detailed analysis of the latter, has traced the development of the rich and variegated style through an intermediate stage, the Punuk, to the more degenerated art of the modern Eskimo.

Apart from the difference in art and the gradual change due to development of old types and certain new elements filtering in, the general aspect of these cultures is remarkably uniform. Seal and walrus were hunted by harpoons provided with floats, either from kayaks or from the ice-floe in winter. Umiaks were also known and used for whaling. The question has been raised whether dog sleds were known, because trace buckles and other appurtenances for dog harnesses are missing. But the great number of dog bones can hardly be explained if dogs had not been employed for traction. It should be remembered that the present Central Eskimo very seldom use trace buckles, and their dog traction would scarcely leave any demonstrable archeological vestiges at all. The houses were of a somewhat simpler type than those of Ipiutaq. Pottery was used for the manufacture of cooking pots and saucer-shaped lamps. Stone implements were both chipped and polished, but in early times chipping predominated.

At Point Hope there is no evidence of the Old Bering Sea culture, which seems to be a rather local development. Here the Ipiutaq was succeeded by the Birnirk culture, the remains of which are found over large parts of North Alaska and as far as the mouth of the Kolyma on the north coast of Siberia.

Here again we have evidence of a maritime life where whaling played a considerable part, clay lamps and pots, polished slate implements, etc. The Birnirk culture was gradually transformed into the Western Thule, which in its turn passed into a late prehistoric phase called Tikeraq. The last cultural stage in North Alaska is characterized by a revival of Thule types with a few elements of eastern origin like stone lamps instead of earlier pottery ones. I shall revert to this fact presently and in the meantime turn to the archeology of the eastern Arctic.

There the earliest prehistoric phase is the Dorset culture to which Jenness called attention in 1925. It has been found on Baffin Island, Labrador, the northern part of Newfoundland, in North Greenland, and as far west as King William Island. As in Ipiutaq culture, seal and walrus were hunted, but caribou were of equal importance, and whaling was not known at all. In other respects it recalls Kachemak I: the lamps are small, oval or triangular, and decoration consists of crude, linear patterns. Stone chipping instead of polishing is characteristic of both Dorset, Ipiutaq, and Kachemak I, as is also the lack of pottery. Peculiar to Dorset are gouged holes instead of drilled ones.

The following period is distinguished by a spread of the Alaskan Thule culture eastwards as far as Labrador and Greenland. Both whaling, seal nets, polished slate implements and other traits were thus introduced. Pottery reached as far as Hudson Bay, but is not known from the regions farther east. The Dorset culture, however, persisted for some time during the Thule period, and some elements of the eastern Thule which do not occur in its early phase in Alaska probably date from this period of contact. I refer for instance to the broad, semilunar soapstone lamps, the soapstone cooking pots, the snow knife, and probably also the fully developed snow hut and breathing-hole hunting, all of which apparently originated under severe arctic conditions similar to the Northwest Passage and the coasts of Hudson Bay.

In Greenland, Thule culture underwent a further development resulting in the Inugsuk stage, which, besides some local features, also shows signs of medieval Norse influence. In the central regions, however, it succumbed to an advance of inland tribes. This is the reason why the modern culture here has an unmistakable continental stamp. On the other hand, analysis of its elements shows that it also includes a rich inheritance from the Thule period. It looks as if the immigrants, while retaining as much of their original culture as possible, took over from their predecessors on the coast all elements necessary to their new maritime way of living. The before-mentioned revival of Thule elements in North Alaska must undoubtedly be due to this advance of inland tribes who drove some of the Thule Eskimo back to the west.

After this brief survey of the cultural development within the Eskimo area the question of how the results should be pieced into a coherent picture arises. I have already called attention to some connecting links between the apparently oldest phases, i.e., Kachemak I, Ipiutaq, and Dorset. Here whaling is entirely absent, and in the two latter cultures caribou hunting occupies a prominent position besides sealing. It is evident that these culture types have a much more pronounced inland stamp than the later forms. On the other hand, both the Okvik, Old Bering Sea, and Birnirk Eskimo were whale hunters and thus much more adapted to the sea than their predecessors. The Thule culture is mainly an off-shoot of the Birnirk, just as the historic cultures in northern Alaska and in Greenland are slightly modified continuations of the Thule. Whaling forms a connecting link between all these cultures from Okvik and onwards, and it will be seen immediately that they correspond closely to what Steensby once called the Neo-Eskimo layer. If this is the case, Ipiutaq and Dorset, with their unmistakable half-coast, half-inland stamp, must be termed Paleo-Eskimo. The position of Kachemak I is not quite clear, because it is still very imperfectly known. It is certainly closely attached to the sea, but on the other hand whaling hardly existed. The question is the more difficult, because the Neo-Eskimo complex is very atypically developed on the Pacific coast.

In some respects, however, Steensby's conception of the Paleo-Eskimo culture must be modified. He was of opinion that it originated in the central regions as an adaptation to coastal life, and he considered breathing-hole hunting and the blubber lamp as its very foundations. We have now seen that the early Eskimo knew only small lamps for illumination and not for cooking. We cannot be sure whether they knew sealing at the breathing holes, but the probability is that they did not. One thing and another indicate that sealing and walrus hunting at the ice edge are older than hunting at the breathing holes. This is in accordance with Old World conditions where there is abundant evidence of ancient seal and walrus hunting not only from Northeast Asia, but also from regions as distant as the Yamal Peninsula and the coasts of Kola and Norway. Still more significant is the close relationship which Helge Larsen and Rainey have pointed out between Ipiutaq and Scytho-Siberian animal styles. Thus the Paleo-Eskimo culture has so many affinities to the Old World that a connection between them cannot be dismissed.

The Neo-Eskimo stage is primarily characterized by whaling with harpoons and floats as well as by certain other elements such as sealing with nets, ground slate implements, pottery, etc. Steensby supposed that its original home was at Bering Strait, and there is no reason to doubt the correctness of his view. The superiority of the Neo-Eskimo culture enabled it to spread eastwards. The situation of the Thule ruins in the central region furthermore shows that it was favored by a land submergence which gave large aquatic mammals better living conditions than today, and possibly by a milder climate.

It has already been stated that the modern culture of the Central Eskimo was brought to the coast in fairly recent times, i.e., within the last few hundred years, by an advance of tribes from the inland. Thus a new, so-called Eschato-Eskimo culture layer developed subsequent to the Neo-Eskimo culture. The Eschato-Eskimo expansion must almost certainly be associated with the uplift of the land which took place towards the end of the Neo-Eskimo period. It is due to this movement that the ruins and tent-rings from the Thule culture are lying up to 15 m. above the present sea level. The rising of the land has restricted the area of the large aquatic mammals, particularly the whales, and must therefore have weakened a culture that principally rested upon hunting of these animals.

The culture of the inland Eskimo still remains to be explained. The most typical inland dwellers are the Caribou Eskimo on the Barren Grounds, although another large group is living around the Colville and Noatak Rivers in northern Alaska. A third group is at the Yukon-Kuskokwim delta, and there are some inland bands in Labrador. An inland culture seems to be so utterly strange to our ordinary conceptions of Eskimo life that it must necessarily be brought into relation to the cultural development at the coast. We are here confronted with three possibilities: *either* both ways of living are equally old, some of the primeval Eskimo bands keeping inland while others preferred to stay at the coast, while still others, perhaps, shifted from a coastal to an inland existence according to the seasons; *or* the tribes of the interior are an offshoot of an original coast population; *or* vice-versa. Although we actually know of some Arctic peoples like the Chukchi and Koryak who are divided into coastal and inland groups, it seems difficult to imagine a "double" culture of this type as a really primitive stage. On the other hand, we have undisputable archeological evidence, both in the Ipiutaq and the Dorset cultures, of a stage where coast and inland hunting were of equal importance. As to the two other possibilities, Mathiassen once maintained the view that the Caribou Eskimo were descendants of Thule tribes who had left the coast attracted by the caribou herds, whereas I pointed out that a great number of their culture elements were more primitive than the corresponding Thule types, for which reason I preferred to consider the Caribou Eskimo the last remnant of the primeval Eskimo that had remained on the tundras when the main part of the people had adapted their life to the sea. Our discussion took place before the archeological investigations had brought the early phases of Eskimo culture to light. At present it is evident that the Caribou Eskimo should be compared with the Ipiutaq and Dorset stages and not with the Thule culture.

Here, however, we meet with very great difficulties, because we know absolutely nothing of the archeology of the Caribou Eskimo. Therefore we have only their recent culture to start from, and however primitive its general character may be, it has, of course, changed a great deal during the centuries that separate it from the Ipiutaq and Dorset periods. One important thing should not be overlooked, however: the small lamp used for illumination only, which in this respect recalls the Dorset lamps. At least it seems to indicate that the inland culture is related more closely to the Paleo-Eskimo layer than to that of the Neo-Eskimo, but on the other hand it does not decide the question whether it is earlier or later than the Paleo-Eskimo. Nevertheless it seems to me that two or three traits may suggest the precedence of the Caribou Eskimo, viz., the type of dwelling, the exposure of the dead instead of regular burial, and perhaps also their almost complete lack of decorative art. Time forbids me to enter upon details, and the full answer can only be given by archeological finds in the future. It may well be, however, that the Caribou Eskimo culture, in spite of all modifications, represents a lower level of development than the Paleo-Eskimo stage or, in other words, that it should be considered Proto-Eskimo. It is highly probable that this also applies to the inland culture in northern Alaska, and it may—although this is a mere guess— even be true of the culture of the lower Yukon and Kuskokwim.

If this be so, there has once been a Proto-Eskimo inland population right from Alaska to Hudson Bay, and we can now reconstruct the prehistory of the Eskimo in terms of an increasing adaptation to the sea. Steensby, who also believed that the Eskimo were originally an inland people, was of opinion that the change to coastal life was the result of a local adaptation in the central regions. This view cannot be maintained now we know of the close affinities of the Ipiutaq to the Old World cultures. It is more likely that the first adaptation to the sea, i.e., seal and walrus hunting, was introduced from the Asiatic coast and spread eastwards, giving rise to both the Ipiutaq and Dorset cultures. This is the Paleo-Eskimo stage. Afterwards a new cultural wave, the Neo-Eskimo characterized by whale hunting, spread in the same direction. The Okvik, Old Bering Sea, Birnirk, and Thule cultures enter at this point. Finally, in the central regions, there was a new advance from the interior leading to the formation of the last or Eschato-Eskimo layer. Just because the inland dwellers had remained stationary at such a primitive level, the superposition of the Eschato-Eskimo layer on top of the Neo-Eskimo stratum necessarily resulted in the culture re-assuming a primitive tinge. It is the Eschato-Eskimo migration which has made the situation so difficult to interpret before the archeological excavations were started, because it resulted in an inversion of the sequence.

II

I believe that by now the main outlines (but only the outlines of course) of the growth of Eskimo culture are pretty well established, but a series of important problems still remains to be solved. In the first instance, how is the cultural development to be correlated with the somatological facts?

In spite of numerous measurements and observations on the physical anthropology of the Eskimo, the material at hand is really rather limited. In many cases the available data comprise very small groups of individuals. However, making comparisons with measurements comprising ten to twelve persons is not merely futile, but something still worse: it is directly misleading, because we have not the slightest guarantee that such series of measurements provide even an approximately reliable expression of the actual average values. It is the same with material that is chronologically unclassified. From a scientific point of view a number of chronologically unclassified skulls are almost useless. It will be readily understood, therefore, that many questions must be left open.

Hrdlička has shown that the population of the Aleutians and Kodiak in historic and late prehistoric times differed physically from all other Eskimo tribes and should be classed with the Tungid race of eastern Siberia. A single skull brought back from Prince William Sound may indicate that the Tungid element was spreading eastwards, although as a whole the population there was more Eskimo-like. In the cultural development of these regions there is no indication of a sudden immigration, but nevertheless we are nearly forced to assume that it has taken place. The most obvious hypothesis would be that it proceeded from Kamchatka to the Aleutians, but the distance here is no less than 270 sea miles, and so far it has been impossible to find traces of early occupation on the Commander group, that forms the only natural stepping stone between the Asiatic coast and Attu Island. On the other hand, if the migration had crossed Bering Strait it is inconceivable that it should have left no traces there. Under these circumstances a direct spread from Kamchatka may, in spite of all, be the most probable solution, the more because some cultural facts point to the same direction.

Apart from the Tungid element all other Eskimo are so closely related physically that they must be considered as belonging to one race, although with three or four sub-types. If we keep to the tribes east of the Mackenzie, including the Caribou Eskimo, the marked similarity between them will be apparent at once. In all cases we encounter sub-medium stature, mesocephalic skulls with a tendency towards dolichocephaly, mesoprosopic faces, and leptorrhinic or slightly mesorrhinic noses. In the northern Upernavik District, West Greenland, dolichocephaly is particularly strong.

On turning to the western Arctic we find much more heterogeneity. That the basis is essentially the same as farther east is scarcely to be doubted, but in the Mackenzie delta there is an "extreme" Eskimo type with a very long and narrow skull, whereas in Alaska an unmistakable increase in breadth of the head has taken place. Among the Point Barrow, Kotzebue Sound and Seward Peninsula Eskimo it is least conspicuous. On the other hand the tribes on the Colville River, the Asiatic Eskimo, and the tribes south of Norton Sound are all on the border of brachycephaly. It is probable that at least to some degree, particularly as far as the inland dwellers are concerned, this is due to mixing with the surrounding Indians and Paleo Asiatics, both of which groups are markedly brachycephalic; but whether this is the whole truth is a question to which I shall revert presently. I may add here that the distribution of types observed when head and face forms are concerned does not quite correspond to the distribution evinced by stature, but as stature is inclined to vary more with environment than the relatively constant head and face forms, it will be justifiable to attach the greatest importance to the latter.

It is extremely difficult to form any opinion of the significance of the sub-types just mentioned. Shapiro called attention to the likeness between the population of Seward Peninsula on the one side and the Copper and Polar Eskimo on the other. He is of opinion that they form one unit and adds: "When this unit is eliminated the other groups fall into a more clearly marked sequence characterized by a decrease in head length and an increase in head and face width as one approaches Alaska." In this connection it should be borne in mind that the measurements of the Polar Eskimo are so few in number (eleven individuals!) that it would be more than reckless to rely on a mean calculated from them, and furthermore the matter is not as simple as Shapiro imagines. I therefore believe that at the moment it will be wisest to ignore completely this combination of Seward Peninsula, Copper, and Polar Eskimo.

So much for the physical characteristics of the present Eskimo, and now to consider the types of earlier times. According to Hrdlička the early prehistoric population of the Aleutians and Kodiak belonged to a dolichocephalic race related to the Siouan and Algonkian types of the Central and Eastern United States. Locally, a similar type also occurs among the prehistoric Indians at Shageluk Slough off the middle Yukon, Alaska. Collins has pointed out, however, that although they are not identical, neither the early Aleut nor the early inhabitants of Kodiak can be dissociated from the South Alaskan Eskimo whom they resemble. It seems that a similar type prevailed up to recent times at Prince William Sound, which probably means that until the arrival of the Tungid element the entire Eskimo population south of Norton Sound must have been fairly uniform.

Unfortunately our knowledge of the early population of North Alaska and the eastern Arctic is very deficient. Fischer-Møller has shown that, as far as one can judge from the somewhat sparse skeletal material from Repulse Bay, the Thule culture Eskimo there closely approached the present population of Point Barrow. If this is true, it means that on the whole we can point to no essential difference between the bearers of the Thule culture and the basic Eskimo type. From the Birnirk period at Point Barrow we have a number of very narrow skulls which Hrdlička compared to the Greenlanders. Inasmuch as in both cases these are distinctly Eskimo types, this is of course correct. But actually only the "extreme" type in the northern Upernavik District (which Hrdlička did not seem to know) gives rise to the supposition of any closer relationship, and even this cannot be decided with certainty. In contradistinction to Hrdlička, Seltzer places the Birnirk skulls together with the present-day Mackenzie Eskimo. It is not improbable that he is justified in doing so; at least the Mackenzie region is much nearer to Point Barrow than is Greenland.

The skeletal remains that can be definitely ascribed to the Old Bering Sea period are extremely few. According to my knowledge they are so far restricted to a single mesocephalic and two markedly dolichocephalic skulls, and consequently further speculation on the racial affinities of the bearers of the Bering Sea culture is really futile for the moment. As to the Paleo-Eskimo periods we are faced with the regrettable fact that Dorset remains are completely lacking. On the other hand, important skeletal material has been found in Ipiutaq graves. Shapiro's account must be awaited with interest.

If finally we try to gather the diffused details we shall scarcely make much more progress than the following: Apart from the late Tungid element on the Aleutians and Kodiak, the Eskimo form one somatic unit, though of course there are local and chronological deviations from the basic form. These sub-types include the Birnirk and present-day Eskimo of the Mackenzie delta and the northern Upernavik District, all of whom stand out by marked dolichocephaly, but it remains for the future to show if there is any close relationship between them.

Regarding the other Eskimo one conspicuous fact is that the western tribes are rather more mesocephalic and on the whole less specialized than the easterly tribes. Two explanations have been offered. One is that the increase in the width of the head is a purely secondary feature due to Indian admixture; the other point, held by Hrdlička, says the relatively unspecialized Alaskan type is the earliest, and specialization has grown under the influence of new surroundings and a changed mode of life as the Eskimo spread east. Against this Jenness has rightly observed that there is no essential difference between the western and eastern Arctic in either geographical or cultural environment. It may also be added that the Caribou Eskimo, for cultural reasons considered descendants of the Proto-Eskimo, belong to the specialized type, and that both Shapiro and Seltzer found close conformity between the latter and the Cree and Chipewyan. On the other hand, two facts speak in favor of regarding the unspecialized type as the earlier. One is that it existed on the Aleutians and Kodiak in remote times; the other that it is probably more closely related to wide-spread Indian types (eastern Algonkians and Siouans), than is the specialized Eskimo type. We cannot arrive at a solution of the problem until much more information is available about the racial characteristics of the early Eskimo stages.

There is, however, a third possibility which cannot be completely ignored. The Norton Sound border line, which is so well defined linguistically, less plainly racially and culturally, may, perhaps, date back to Proto-Eskimo times, which means that the Proto-Eskimo of North Alaska and farther east even at that early period belonged to a somewhat more specialized type than their southern kinsmen. It might be objected that by accepting this hypothesis, the whole race problem is pushed further back without bringing it closer to solution. But, before answering a question we must always gather all relevant details and take all possibilities into account. There is another and more serious objection. As mentioned before, the inland tribes of North Alaska are the most brachycephalic of all Eskimo. Now they have certainly lived in more intimate contact with the brachycephalic Indians than any other Eskimo group, which may account for much. There are also a few cultural traits, like house type, that link them with the comparatively broad-headed Eskimo south of Norton Sound. It is possible that a more thorough study of this particularly interesting group may solve the riddle.

III

If we are confronted with considerable difficulties when treating the race problem of the Eskimo, we are no better off when we turn to linguistics. There is no doubt that the Aleutian language occupies the most aberrant position within the whole stock. As I understand it, the general opinion is now that besides the genuine Eskimo element the vocabulary also includes a foreign, non-Eskimo component. It is, of course, tempting to correlate this fact with the immigration of the Tungid race element in late prehistoric times and with the occurrence of certain Asiatic traits in their culture. In order to decide the question it will be necessary to make a comparison with the Paleo-Asiatic languages, in particular Kamchadal.

For the Eskimo language proper the most conspicuous demarcation line runs along Norton Sound. North and east of this line as far as Greenland and Labrador the dialects are almost as closely related to each other as are the English dialects. On the other hand, mutual understanding between the Eskimo of Seward Peninsula and the Yukon delta is impossible, for the languages differ as much as do English and German. On the whole the phonetics of the western dialects are the most primitive. Thalbitzer has shown that a so-called retrogressive uvularization has taken place in the eastern area, and in addition a retrogressive labialization occurred in Greenland. However, there has also been a special development in South Alaska resulting in the dropping of a short "i" in many unaccentuated syllables.

Of course the old-fashioned form of the Alaskan dialects does not necessarily mean that the language has spread from west to east. There is no justification whatever for believing that the primordial home of a language is the area where the less developed form is spoken today. In order to trace the history of the Eskimo tongue it would be of paramount importance, if anything could be said of the language of previous periods. We may take it for granted that the Neo-Eskimo, including the bearers of the central Thule culture, spoke a northern Eskimo dialect, because dialects of this type occur wherever Neo-Eskimo culture prevails at present, i.e., in northern Alaska and Greenland. As pointed out by Collins the great conformity of the dialects in both places is partially explained by the Thule backwash to North Alaska in late prehistoric times. It is probable that the Paleo-Eskimo of Alaska spoke some kind of Eskimo dialect, in so far as the South Alaska groups, except for the Tungid immigrants, can be considered rather direct descendants of Paleo-Eskimo ancestors. Of the linguistic affinities of the Dorset people there is no evidence. But both the Northwest Passage and the inland tribes speak Eskimo dialects. This at least suggests that both the Dorset and the Proto-Eskimo languages belonged to the same stock.

However, if the supposition is correct that the inland tribes of North Alaska and the Barren Grounds are modern representatives of the Proto-Eskimo, then why do they speak dialects of the northern type, i.e., more closely related to those of the Neo-Eskimo than to those of the southern type? It is just possible, of course, that the Noatak and Colville tribes, who have lived in close contact with the coast dwellers, adopted their present speech from them. This is extremely unlikely for the Caribou group, because its culture is nearly uninfluenced by the Neo-Eskimo. Thus we are, perhaps, led to the conclusion that the Thule backwash does not suffice to explain the Norton Sound linguistic boundary, or in other words that the Proto-Eskimo comprised two different though mutually related groups, one in the Yukon-Kuskokwim area and another one farther north on the tundras around the Noatak and Colville Rivers, with bands of the latter roaming as far east as the Barren Grounds. As mentioned before, the difference in physical type and cultural development may point into the same direction.

Here we arrive at the question I once raised in relation to the Pacific Eskimo and which has recently been revived by Dr. de Laguna for the Eskimo as a whole, viz., whether they all spring from the same stock, or whether they were originally several distinct groups which in the course of time were welded together. This, however, is a question that must be left open for the present, as must also the problem of the possibility of linking the Eskimo language with other stocks such as the Uralian and Indo-European.

DISCUSSION

Frederica de Laguna

It is a real pleasure and an honor for me to follow on this program Dr. Kaj Birket-Smith, my former expedition comrade in Alaska, from whom I have learned so much in the field.

In this paper he has presented a clear, well-argued discussion of Eskimo origins and development. Furthermore, he has suggested some directions in which new researches can most fruitfully be pursued. He has given us a map, a compass, and sailing directions, and wished us God speed on our voyages of discovery.

I confess that some details of this map of the Eskimo problem remain a bit obscure to me and that I cannot quite orient myself. In other words, on a few points I cannot quite agree with Dr. Birket-Smith. I do not mean that I disagree with him, but rather that I am not yet prepared to accept all of the implications of certain particular points that he has made. I shall speak of these problems first.

The first problem involves the relationships between the Okvik-Old Bering

Sea and Ipiutak cultures, the oldest Eskimo cultures known from western and northwestern Alaska. As I understand it, "Okvik" is really the early phase of Old Bering Sea. The name "Okvik" refers to the art style rather than to the total culture; Okvik art is the same as Old Bering Sea style 1. This style, while ancestral to Old Bering Sea styles 2 and 3, has, I believe, relationships with Dorset and probably also with ancient Pacific Eskimo-Aleut art. On the other hand, Ipiutak art seems to me to be more closely related to the developed Old Bering Sea styles 2 and 3.

I am not sure that I can accept the Ipiutak culture as ancestral to Old Bering Sea (using the latter name to cover the Okvik-Old Bering Sea). I personally feel that Ipiutak and Old Bering Sea share more in common than do, say, Ipiutak and Dorset, or Ipiutak and Kachemak Bay I. There is a good deal more that I should like to know before defining the precise relationship between Old Bering Sea and Ipiutak. For example, we have, as Dr. Birket-Smith has pointed out, practically no skeletal material from Old Bering Sea and obviously know equally little about their burial customs. Did the Old Bering Sea Eskimo have an elaborate death cult, a feature which is one of the outstanding characteristics of the Ipiutak?

In any case, I believe that there are so many cultural traits which cross link Ipiutak, Old Bering Sea, Dorset, and Kachemak Bay I (or Pacific Eskimo I), that in default of accurate methods of dating, we may consider these four distinctive Eskimo cultures as roughly contemporary. In other words, I would be happy to see them all assigned to Dr. Birket-Smith's Paleo-Eskimo stage— or should I say, Paleo-Eskimo age, that is, to an ancient Eskimo era.

Another problem is the extent to which whaling was practiced in the Old Bering Sea culture. I would hesitate to call them "great whalers," since I understand that only about 3 out of some 1,000 Old Bering Sea harpoon heads are big enough for whaling harpoons. There is, of course, no question but that the Punuk culture, which developed out of the Old Bering Sea largely because of cultural enrichments from Siberia, as well as the Thule culture, were both great whaling cultures. Perhaps it would be safe to say that the translation of the Paleo-Eskimo cultures into their Neo-Eskimo forms was just beginning to get under way as the Old Bering Sea was ending.

And then—to what extent is whaling the most important criterion for defining an Eskimo culture as coastal? The introduction of whaling certainly does mean a fuller utilization of maritime resources, but this could produce different results for different Eskimo groups. For some it could mean a reorientation towards the sea, but for others it might mean an expansion of population or well-fed leisure for greater ceremonial activities without necessarily involving neglect of such mainland resources as caribou fur and antler. In other words, does adoption of whaling involve a different way of life or simply a more abundant life?

These are the questions to which I would like to learn the answers.

We cannot overstress the importance of studying other inland Eskimo groups as thoroughly as Dr. Birket-Smith has done for the Caribou Eskimo in his classic monograph. If these studies are made, will we find a fundamental uniformity in the cultures of the Caribou Eskimo, the inland Labrador bands, the northern Alaska interior groups, and the Yukon-Kuskokwim peoples? Or will we find various different inland ways of life? Off hand I would expect significant differences, since, for example, the Yukon-Kuskokwim Eskimo enjoy the great salmon runs from Bristol Bay and also trade with their Athabaskan neighbors. I have also heard that there was considerable population exchange between northern Alaskan coastal and inland groups through intermarriage and through family visits which might last a year or two or a generation. If this is correct, the situation is different here from that in Canada, where the Caribou Eskimo seem to be much more isolated from their coastal neighbors. And certainly, as Dr. Birket-Smith has stressed, fully to understand these inland cultures we need the time perspective of archeology.

I would not be surprised if the Proto- or beginning Eskimo culture stage involved what Dr. Birket-Smith has called a "double culture"—i.e., the coexistence of both inland and seashore phases, with contacts between the two. This would be a situation in which neither party had perfected an adaptation to a single, perhaps restrictive or demanding environment, and needed the resources of both. But then, as you know, I have played with the idea of multiple origins for Eskimo culture, and still find this idea too interesting to abandon without further experimentation, although it may be unnecessarily elaborate and mistaken.

Among the various suggestions which Dr. Birket-Smith has made and which I wish he had had time to expand because of their very valuable implications was the sketch he has given us of the mutual enrichment of Thule and Dorset cultures. I would like to see research specifically devoted to that problem.

Another stimulating suggestion was that of an ancient series of inland tribes extending from Alaska to eastern Canada. If these peoples had semi-coastal counterparts or successors might not this series explain how there come to be such curious links between Dorset and Pacific Eskimo I—links which do not involve Old Bering Sea or Ipiutak?

Dr. Birket-Smith has made some particularly illuminating observations on Eskimo somatology. In particular he discussed the significance of the recent physical type on Kodiak and the Aleutians which submerged an earlier population. This earlier population was essentially southern Eskimo, and the intrusion cut off the Prince William Sound Eskimo from their more northern brothers. This intrusive element Hrdlička called "Tungid," though I personally distrust his identifications. In any case, he believed that this element came from the Alaskan mainland, because it seemed to be a little older on the eastern Aleutians than on the central islands and was lacking on the westernmost. If his archeology is correct, I would be inclined to associate the intrusive population on the Aleutians and Kodiak with the recent movement of Athabaskans from Cook Inlet.

But whoever these newcomers may have been or wherever may have been their original home, I am convinced that there were contacts of great cultural importance between the Aleuts and the Kamchadal. I am therefore delighted at Dr. Birket-Smith's failure to be daunted by this ocean crossing. If he cannot get his immigrants through the "Ellis Island" of the Kommandorskis, he does not hesitate to bring them into the New World without a stop-over.

The suggestion of comparing Aleut with Kamchadal in an endeavor to discover the source of the foreign elements in the Aleut language is one which I hope some able linguist will attempt, reserving a check on Ainu as a further possibility, in case the first comparison yield negative results. Proof of linguistic contamination of Aleut from the Asiatic side of the north Pacific would be peculiarly welcome to me since it would support some of my own pet theories of cultural exchanges. But more seriously, Hrdlička's failure to find archeological sites on the Commander Islands during a visit of five days when the Russians entertained him so royally that he did practically no digging, cannot be taken as evidence that they do not exist. The Russian sea-otter farm personnel told him that they knew of no sites—but were they competent to recognize them (especially if they were only the camping places of travellers, perhaps obscured or mutilated by movements of sea level); and if they did know of any sites, would they necessarily reveal them?

This paper has been so packed with interesting points, each suggesting further discussion and elaboration, that I have been tempted to speak longer than is appropriate perhaps for a discussant. I can only plead your indulgence since it has been such a pleasure once more to see my old friend and to talk with him about the Eskimo.

THE IPIUTAK CULTURE: ITS ORIGIN
AND RELATIONSHIPS

Helge Larsen

As early as 1914, Steensby pointed out the possible existence of two layers of Eskimo culture, an early Paleo-Eskimo layer which he thought originated in northern Canada and a later, the Neo-Eskimo, which, according to his theory, originated in the Bering Strait region. Steensby's theory was later elaborated by Birket-Smith who added a third layer to Steensby's two, the Eschato-Eskimo which is represented by the present-day Central Eskimo.

The theories of Steensby and Birket-Smith were mainly based upon ethnological indications and despite increased archeological activity during the decade following the appearance of Birket-Smith's theory, no find seems to substantiate the validity of the theory of two culture layers. Nearly all diggings, whether in the eastern or the western part of the Eskimo territory, revealed cultures which showed some relationship to the Thule culture discovered by Therkel Mathiassen on the Fifth Thule Expedition and which, according to Birket-Smith's theory, represent the Neo-Eskimo culture layer.

The Thule culture, or the Arctic Whale Hunting culture as Rainey and I have called it, was a pronounced coastal culture, the economy of which was based upon sea-mammal hunting, primarily whale hunting, and which is otherwise characterized by permanent settlements consisting of solidly built semi-subterranean houses of sod, stone, wood or whalebone, the use of stone or earthenware lamps and cooking pots, of ground slate implements and baleen. Only two Eskimo cultures did not conform to this general picture, the Cape Dorset culture and the Kachemak Bay culture.

In 1939, a party consisting of Froelich Rainey, Louis Giddings, and myself began excavation at Point Hope, Alaska. The Neo-Eskimo culture is here represented by the modern village of Tikeraq, Old Tikeraq (the abandoned western part of the village), and an earlier site at Jabbertown—five miles east of Tikeraq. Meanwhile, in addition to these, we found evidences of earlier inhabitants, the culture of which did not follow the pattern of the Neo-Eskimo culture, and that is the Ipiutak culture.

Near the north shore of Point Hope, at a place called "Ipiutak" by the local Eskimo, about one mile from the Tikeraq village, five of the gravel bars, of which the entire Point Hope spit is built up, are virtually covered with shallow, rounded depressions, some of them with a smaller oblong depression extending westward. Excavations proved that each of the rounded depressions represents a house. We counted 575, but the total number of houses is undoubtedly much larger as the northernmost row has been partly covered by drifting sand.

The seventy-two house pits we excavated gave us an idea about the ground plan of the Ipiutak house, but since very little wood was preserved, the excavations did not reveal much regarding the superstructure. In order to form an opinion about the Ipiutak house, we had to use a house type with similar ground plan as a model, and we found this in the house of the Nunatarmiut, the inland Eskimo of arctic Alaska. The Ipiutak house differs from the house of the Neo-Eskimo in ground plan as well as in superstructure. While the former had heavy sod walls which supported the roof, the roof and the slanting walls of the Ipiutak houses were supported by four posts placed inside the house and presumably connected by a square frame on top. The rafters leaning against this frame and forming roof and walls were probably covered with thin moss turf and dirt.

Instead of a main platform or a sleeping place at the rear of the house with floor space in front, the Ipiutak house had platforms on three sides surrounding a floor with an open fireplace in the middle. Some houses had a wooden floor, but the low platforms usually consisted of gravel which had been covered with willow twigs. Most houses were about four meters square with rounded corners. The entrance to the house had been in the west wall, but it is uncertain whether there was an entrance passage; if so, it must have been short and did not enter the house below floor level. As already mentioned, not all houses had the oblong depression or a culture layer in front. Hence the question of an entrance passage is still unanswered.

Ipiutak houses with solid walls of logs lying horizontally were found last summer at Platinum, Kuskokwim Bay, and this summer at Deering.

One of the major differences between the Arctic Whale Hunting culture and the Ipiutak culture is the absence in the latter of lamps and cooking pots of stone or clay. All phases of the Arctic Whale Hunting culture are known to have possessed these two culture elements, but not one potsherd or fragment of lamp was found in the more then seventy houses excavated at Ipiutak. Considering the abundance of potsherds in other Alaskan sites, we are convinced that the Ipiutak people were unable to make pottery and, until otherwise disproved, we must assume that an open fire was their only source of heat and light. This naturally leads us to the question of fuel, which is of paramount importance, especially in the Arctic. Driftwood is the only answer since Point Hope is far away from timbered areas. It is true that driftwood is plentiful in places along the shores of the Arctic Ocean, but it is not likely that there would be enough at Point Hope to supply a large village, such as Ipiutak, with fuel and building materials—at least not for any length of time. A priori one would not consider a people dependent on wood for fuel as fully adapted to life at the Arctic coast, and since a number of traits in the Ipiutak culture point toward an inland habitat, we have come to the conclusion that Ipiutak was not a permanent village, but one inhabited only during the spring and summer months by a people who spent the rest of the year inland. This would also explain the numerous house pits, because people would not necessarily use the same spot for a temporary dwelling year after year, especially since there were ample building grounds at Point Hope.

Well drained gravel bars seem to have attracted the Ipiutak people and peoples with a related culture in other parts of Alaska as well, which investigations during the last two summers have borne out. The main attractions of Point Hope, however, were the spring seal and walrus hunting, and the abundance of flint and related minerals which furnished excellent material for weapon points, knives, and scrapers. Judging from the bones found in the houses, seals were the main source of food and the walrus must have been highly valued on account of its precious ivory. Seal and walrus were hunted from the edge of the ice and in leads in the ice with harpoons of the familiar Eskimo type; whereas open-water hunting from kayaks was probably not practiced. This assumption is based not so much upon the lack of any trace of boats as on the absence of float accessories in the find. The lack of floats also eliminates whale hunting, at least in its arctic form where the whales are actually caught, which is another significant difference from the Arctic Whale Hunting culture.

As mentioned before, we believe that the Ipiutak people were seasonal migrants who spent the fall and winter in the interior. This assumption is based upon certain traits in their culture, of which I have already mentioned the open fireplace. Another trait is the importance of caribou hunting. Judging from the finds, especially from the burials, the bow and arrow seem to have been the favorite weapon of the Ipiutak people, and bows and arrows were primarily used for caribou hunting. Twenty-two per cent of the total find are artifacts used in connection with archery, while only three per cent were parts of gear used for sea mammal hunting; only eighteen burials contained hunting gear for sea mammal hunting, compared to seventy-two burials with parts of bows and arrows. Of even greater significance is the fact that antler was the preferred material for tools and weapons rather than ivory, of which they seemed to have had plenty. As another inland trait, I might mention that birchbark was used for vessels. That the Ipiutak people actually spent some time inland is proven by the find of Ipiutak specimens in a cave on Seward Peninsula, 35 miles from the coast.

One of the most conspicuous features of the Ipiutak culture and one which definitely differentiates it from the Arctic Whale Hunting culture is its flint industry. Except for adze blades, which in both cultures usually are made of a hard, silicified slate, the Ipiutak people would use flint, jasper, chalcedony or other cryptocrystalline minerals where the Arctic Whale Hunters would use slate. Only adze blades, whetstones and some kind of a chisel are polished, all other stone objects are merely chipped. The Ipiutak flint industry distinguishes itself by quantity as well as by quality. More than half of the total number of specimens found at Ipiutak are made of flint, comprising several types of arrowpoints, insert blades, knife blades, scrapers and gravers. The blades have been chipped on two surfaces, scrapers and gravers on one only. With a small bone hammer and a flaking tool consisting of a handle and a bone point, the Ipiutak men managed to shape the hard flint into extremely thin, slender points and blades. Noticeable is the frequent use of thin blades inserted as cutting edges in arrowheads, lance heads, daggers and knives.

The great number of flint implements in the Ipiutak find definitely leaves the impression of a Neolithic culture and yet the use of iron was not unfamiliar to the Ipiutak people. Only one tiny piece of iron was found, inserted in an engraving tool, but most of the knife handles of antler and ivory had so small a blade slot that they could only have held a metal blade. These knife handles, which are almost bisected and clasped the blade firmly, were probably invented for the purpose of holding a small blade, an indication of the scarcity of iron. The familiar Eskimo composite knife handle, consisting of two halves lashed together, is probably a later development of this Ipiutak type. The iron has been analyzed and proved to be wrought iron and not of meteoric origin, which means that it can only be of Asiatic probably Siberian origin.

Most tools used by the Ipiutak people do not deviate from the ordinary Eskimo types except in decoration. Some common Eskimo types, like the bow drill, needle case and thimble holder, do not occur in the Ipiutak find. This might, of course, be accidental although it is not very likely in a find of almost 10,000 specimens. Regarding the bow drill, it is significant that most holes were cut or gouged and not drilled. The round holds that occur may have been made with hand drills.

Although not found at Ipiutak, I believe that basketry should be added to the Ipiutak culture elements. Excavating a house at Platinum, Kuskokwim Bay, last summer, I found several pieces of charred grass baskets and matting of twined as well as coiled weave. The house, which had been exposed to fire, contained among other Ipiutak types many chipped flint blades identical with those found at Ipiutak, and even if the presence of stone lamps, drill rests and a single slate ulo blade seems to indicate a later stage of the Ipiutak culture, there are good reasons to believe that the Ipiutak people at Point Hope made basketry too.

One of the most characteristic features of the Ipiutak culture is the art. The Ipiutak people have expressed their artistic sense not only in their unique ivory carvings, but also in the delicate shape and ornamentation of implements used in their daily life. The Ipiutak find contains more decorated artifacts than any other find of Eskimo culture, and even if the decoration is often limited to a few straight or curved lines, it is always well adapted to the shape of the artifact. Four parallel, equally spaced, longitudinal lines are so common that they could be called the trademark of the Ipiutak culture. Curved lines, circles and other forms of closed round motifs are also frequently used in addition to spurs and combinations of light and heavy lines. As well as the purely geometric designs, the Ipiutak people often used realistic motifs, such as schematic human faces and animal heads, and there are many examples of originally realistic motifs which have been transformed into geometric designs.

The Ipiutak surface decoration is very similar to that of the Okvik and Old Bering Sea phases and is, in a few cases, difficult to distinguish from the two; but as a whole the Ipiutak patterns are more simple in composition, thus forming a definite Ipiutak style of decoration.

It is the sculptural art, however, that particularly distinguishes the Ipiutak culture. In their unique carvings in walrus ivory and antler, the Ipiutak craftsmen have combined the highest technical skill with a vivid imagination. Animals, and in particular animal heads, were their favorite motifs, and they did not limit themselves to the local fauna but went far beyond that into the realm of fantastic animals, or combined parts of various animals into one. Zoomorphic motifs also form one of the elements of which the strange, so-called openwork carvings are composed, which make us believe that the use of animal motifs is not purely decorative but may have some religious significance also. In addition to the animal figure, two other elements—a chain and a swivel—may be found in these openwork carvings of which no two are exactly alike but which occur in a multitude of fantastic, indescribable forms. We have interpreted them as shamans' regalia on account of their resemblance to the carvings attached to the Tlingit shaman's costume and because all three elements of which they are composed occur in metal on Siberian shaman costumes. We believe that the swivels, like the ivory chains, are imitations of similar metal objects and that the Ipiutak people, lacking sufficient quantities of iron, have used ivory as material for the various symbolic objects with which their Siberian colleagues adorn their garments. Virtually all the openwork carvings were found in surface burials that also contain arrowheads and daggers which, on account of their shape, could not have been used as such, but must have had a symbolic or ceremonial significance.

Other burials, with grave furniture similar to the finds from the houses, consisted of a log coffin, often deeply buried, which usually contained one skeleton which was extended and supine, with the hands on the pubic region. The grave furniture indicates elaborate burial customs, like adornment of the deceased with artificial eyes, nose plugs and a mouth cover, all carved out of ivory—undoubtedly in order to prevent evil spirits from entering the body. Another indication of ghost cult are the many animal carvings with the spine and ribs incised on the back and probably representing spirits. A loon skull with similar artificial eyes, a dog buried in a log coffin and many examples of animal heads with the same tattoo marks as are on human heads show that the Ipiutak people had the same conception of the relationship between animals and humans as most boreal peoples. Judging from the loon skull and many carvings representing loon heads, the loon must have played an important role in the spiritual life of the Ipiutak people. Another boreal trait is the bear cult, indicated by the presence of pierced brown bear jaws in graves.

When the report on the investigations at Point Hope was completed, all evidence seemed to point towards Asia, more specifically Siberia, as the original home of the Ipiutak culture. Even if the entire flint complex, one of the most characteristic features of the Ipiutak culture, was not known from any Asiatic site, most of the types of flint implements occur in the Old World and the frequent use of side blades in particular seemed to indicate an Old World origin. The iron point, which could only have come from Asia, the knife handles with a slot for an iron blade, the chains and other indications of a knowledge of iron pointed in the same direction; so also did the burial customs and the shamans' paraphernalia, if we were right in our interpretation of the fantastic ivory carvings.

In addition to these arguments in favor of an Old World origin, we had another very characteristic feature of the Ipiutak culture, the animal motifs which dominate the sculptural art and which must be the Scytho-Siberian animal style transferred to American soil. This is obvious when we look at an ivory figure representing a young walrus, on the hips of which is a pear-shaped boss accentuated by a surrounding groove with raised edges. Similar bosses on hips or shoulders of animal figures form one of the fundamental elements of the Scytho-Siberian animal style and are widely distributed in the Old World. In addition to the bosses, the walrus figure has the skeleton design, another element of the animal style. A metal figure from the Perm District in Russia has both elements and a diamond-shaped head not unlike some Ipiutak animal carvings. Two small Ipiutak heads, one of antler and one of jet, have a curved beak, eyes and ears, and undoubtedly represent the eared bird of prey or the griffin, another common element in the animal style and equally widely distributed as the pear-shaped boss. In Siberia in particular, heads like these frequently adorn knives and other implements. Still another characteristic motif of the animal style, a bear head between the two front legs, which occurs on metal brooches from Pyanobor in the Perm district, is found on two rake-like implements, one from Ipiutak itself and one from an Ipiutak grave at Point Spencer, Alaska. Crudely cast bronze objects which may have been sewed on shamans' costumes and which, more than anything else, are reminiscent of the Ipiutak openwork carvings, have been found in East Russia and West Siberia, a region from which also other less obvious parallels with the Ipiutak culture are known.

The fact that so many Ipiutak culture traits occur in this region has led us to the belief that it was the original source of the Ipiutak amiliarity with iron, the animal style, and the models for the openwork carvings. Knowing that peoples with an Eskimo-like culture living on the arctic coast have been in close contact with this culture center by way of the rivers Ob and Yenisei and their tributaries, it seemed natural to look for the original home of the Ipiutak people at the mouth of these rivers.

Meanwhile, James L. Giddings found at Cape Denbigh, Alaska, a culture layer below and separated from layers with an Ipiutak-like culture by sterile clay. The deepest layer contained, among other things, arrowpoints and insert blades shaped like the corresponding Ipiutak types, but thinner and of a still finer workmanship. Not only has Giddings now found much more of this culture which is definitely pre-Ipiutak, but in 1949 I found what I suspect to be the same culture in a cave in the interior of Seward Peninsula and under similar stratigraphic conditions as Giddings' find. I did not find the Ipiutak-like arrowpoints and insert blades, but lamellar flakes as at Cape Denbigh and slender arrowheads of antler with grooves for blades in each side. These finds show that the idea of using flint sideblades was introduced to America long before the Ipiutak culture flourished at Point Hope, and that the Ipiutak flint industry consequently could be a further development of an ancient American tradition. In other words, is the Ipiutak culture originally an American culture or did it come from Siberia as we have suggested?

If Shapiro, from his study of the Ipiutak skeletal material can prove that the Ipiutak people were natives of America and not immigrants from Asia, we must consider the Ipiutak culture as an American culture which has received very strong impulses from Siberia. If on the other hand the question of the origin of the Ipiutak people is left open, I still consider a migration from Asia at the beginning of our era as a strong possibility. In the first place, the pre-Ipiutak culture discovered by Giddings has undoubtedly existed on the Asiatic side of the Bering Strait as well as on the American side; secondly, it is almost inconceivable that so many and such significant culture elements could be transferred from one people to another merely through contact. This, of course, does not exclude the possibility that Giddings has discovered a very early form of Eskimo culture or even a Proto-Eskimo which gave rise to other forms of Eskimo culture, as for instance the Dorset culture.

With the recent finds of pre-Ipiutak culture it becomes more evident than before that the Ipiutak culture represents an early form of Eskimo culture, and that we are justified in identifying it with Steensby's and Birket-Smith's Paleo-Eskimo culture. The Paleo-Eskimo differ from the Neo-Eskimo in being seasonal migrants rather than sedentary; their economy is based upon caribou hunting, seal hunting and fishing, and not whale hunting; they use a different type of house, and chipped stone implements rather than ground-slate implements. Among other traits, lamps, pottery and bow drills were lacking in the Ipiutak culture.

Meanwhile the Ipiutak culture is not the only Paleo-Eskimo culture, and it appears that some cultures which we identify as Paleo-Eskimo possess one or more of the three culture elements just mentioned. The best criterion for a Paleo-Eskimo culture seems to be the prevalent use of chipped stone implements as opposed to ground slate. One of these cultures was found on the Point Hope spit mingled with true Ipiutak burials. This culture which, for lack of a better name, we called Near-Ipiutak, is a modified Ipiutak culture with stone

lamps and probably thin, paddled pottery. It also contained whaling harpoon
heads and a few pieces of ground slate, indicating contact with a Neo-Eskimo
culture or the beginning of it. Far to the east the Cape Dorset culture has
Paleo-Eskimo culture traits like chipped flint tools, caribou hunting and sealing,
and lacks whaling, bow drill and pottery; hence there is good reason to believe
that it belongs to the same culture complex as Ipiutak.

To the south of Ipiutak we have the same prevalence of chipped flint implements in the first period of the Kachemak Bay culture and in the earlier culture
layers in the Aleutian Islands. The latter seems to be more closely related to
Near-Ipiutak and the Dorset cultures than to the Ipiutak culture proper, having
oval-triangular stone lamps in common with both, a few types of implements
in common with Near-Ipiutak and a style of decoration reminiscent of that of
the Dorset culture.

Hoping to bridge the gap between Point Hope and the Paleo-Eskimo cultures of South Alaska and the Aleutians, I made a field trip to the Kuskokwim-
Bristol Bay area last summer. I found three sites with chipped stone implements
in the Kuskokwim Bay area. Two of these, at Chagvan Bay and Nanvak Bay,
also contained pottery, while the site at Platinum had oval-triangular stone
lamps, but no pottery. The pottery just mentioned is not of the ordinary
Eskimo type, but of a finer ware and with check stamped and paddled striated
decoration. A culture with the same kind of pottery and flint implements was
found the same summer at Cape Denbigh in Norton Sound by Giddings, and
this summer I found two different phases of the Ipiutak culture at Point Spencer
and a true Ipiutak site at Deering.

It thus appears that the Ipiutak culture is not an isolated phenomenon but
is widely distributed in Alaska, either as Ipiutak culture proper or culture
phases closely related to it and belonging to what we believe is a Paleo-Eskimo
culture complex. We also believe that descendants of the Paleo-Eskimo are still
to be found among the present-day Eskimo. As Paleo-Eskimo we consider the
Caribou-Eskimo, the Nunatarmiut of arctic Alaska and other Alaskan Eskimo
who originally lived the same semi-nomadic life and had caribou hunting as
their main occupation like the Nunatarmiut. Most of these have been so
strongly influenced by the Neo-Eskimo that it is now impossible in most cases
to distinguish between Paleo- and Neo-Eskimo.

The Ipiutak culture is closely related to the Neo-Eskimo culture, or Arctic
Whale Hunting culture, especially to its earliest stage, the Okvik phase. We believe that the Neo-Eskimo culture developed in the Bering Strait region on the
basis of a Paleo-Eskimo culture, which might be the Ipiutak culture proper.
On St. Lawrence and Diomede Islands the abundance of sea mammals and
absence of caribou resulted in a greater adaptation to life at the arctic coast and
abandonment of the inland side of the culture. Some of the new culture elements like whaling with floats might be of local origin, while others like pottery, ground slate objects and the bowdrill may have been introduced by new

immigrants from east Asia. Such an immigration would explain the definite difference in physical appearance between the Alaskan coast and inland Eskimo. Much investigation has to be done before the question of the origin of the Eskimo culture is solved, but the discovery of a pre-Ipiutak culture by Giddings opens up new possibilities of finding the culture which lies back of all Eskimo cultures.

DISCUSSION

D. JENNESS

I feel some embarrassment in discussing Dr. Larsen's paper [or rather the comprehensive report on Ipiutak which he and Dr. Rainey have published (252) and which his paper summarizes], because the war sharply interrupted my anthropological studies and I am no longer fully abreast of recent developments. It seems to me, however, that Eskimo archeology is following the same pattern as atomic research; each fresh discovery opens up new and alluring vistas, but only deepens the principal mystery. Similarly, while the excavations at Ipiutak carry us one step farther back along the path of Eskimo prehistory, they do not yet reveal its earliest stages.

We can hardly doubt that the Ipiutak complex is an Eskimo one. Whatever the physical type or types of its inhabitants may have been—and this we may know soon when the skeletal remains have been examined—its dwellings and household furniture, its tools and weapons, all bear an unmistakable Eskimo stamp. Dr. Larsen offers good reasons for believing that it was a spring and summer settlement, vacated in winter when its inhabitants, probably Nunatarmiut or Inland Eskimo, roamed the hinterland in pursuit of caribou. In the spring of 1914 I spent several days with a band of such Nunatarmiut Eskimo who had hunted the previous winter on the south side of the Endicott Mountains, then in spring, before the rivers broke out, they moved northward to the Arctic coast of Alaska, about 100 miles west of the International Boundary, to hunt seals and to carry on a little trading. In the summer of the same year I excavated a large settlement at the eastern end of Barter Island which had been a spring and summer camp like Ipiutak, though very much more recent.

The most striking features of the Ipiutak complex are its chipped flint industry, its ivory carvings, and its apparent lack of certain elements that are present in the Okvik or earliest phase of the Old Bering Sea—or, as Dr. Larsen renames it, the Arctic Whale Hunting culture. Because of its numerous resemblances to the Kachemak Bay I remains unearthed by de Laguna in Cook Inlet, and to the Dorset culture of the eastern Arctic, he suggests that Ipiutak may have been the earliest Eskimo culture in America, and that from it came all later ones, including the Arctic Whale Hunting culture and the Dorset.

I find several difficulties in this theory. In the first place the Ipiutak complex can no longer stand as the earliest known culture in the Bering Strait region, for in 1948, under an ancient house site at Cape Denbigh, Giddings uncovered two layers of stratified clay that contained chipped flint implements, but none of polished slate (138). The implements in the upper layer resembled Ipiutak types, but they were accompanied by pottery, which Dr. Larsen believes was not known to the inhabitants of Ipiutak.[1] The second clay layer at Cape Denbigh, two to six inches below the upper, contained no pottery, and its flint implements were smaller than those in the upper, and of different types. Many of them were lamellar flakes, or retouched from lamellar flakes, a feature little developed at Ipiutak but common in the Dorset culture, whose chipped stone implements are also smaller than Ipiutak ones. Indeed, the specimens that Giddings illustrates from his lower layer seem identical with specimens from Dorset sites in the eastern Arctic. Does this not suggest that there was a culture in Alaska earlier than the Ipiutak, a culture that was even closer to the Dorset of the eastern Arctic and therefore more likely than the Ipiutak to have been ancestral?

Quimby's investigations in the Aleutian Islands appear to support this hypothesis. He points out (373) that it was the middle period of Aleut art, not the early one, that most resembled Ipiutak art. The early period had its closest parallels in Dorset.

Still a third argument weighs against Dr. Larsen's theory. If Dorset culture stemmed off from Ipiutak, we would expect to find in the former not only the same types of flint implements, but other Ipiutak traits such as labrets, composite flint-flakers, squirrel-tooth engravers, chain rings, and open-work carvings. Of course, some of these elements might have dropped out in the long migration eastward. No such argument, however, will explain why only the simplest and rarest form of Ipiutak harpoon-head (Larsen's Type Ia) recurs in Dorset remains (where it is exceedingly common), and that other Dorset harpoon-head types cannot conceivably have evolved from Ipiutak ones.

All in all, therefore, I suspect that the Dorset culture of the Hudson Bay region is not the lineal descendant of the Ipiutak, but that it stemmed off from some earlier culture in the western Arctic. The numerous parallels between Dorset and Ipiutak[2] suggest that this unknown parent culture did not long predate the Ipiutak; but only the future can decide whether or not it was the microlithic one uncovered by Giddings at Cape Denbigh.

In seeking an origin for his Ipiutak culture Dr. Larsen naturally turns to Asia, the only possible source for the iron that was used in some of the knives and drills. He notes a resemblance between the mask-like set of carvings found

1. The five small potsherds he found there, in two burials, he considers intrusive.

2. To the parallels listed by Dr. Larsen I might add the ice-creeper (which was not actually discovered at Ipiutak, but is known from the Okvik phase) and the carved human heads (Larsen and Rainey 252, Pl. 52), which recall the human heads carved on antler that Rowley found near Iglulik, at the north end of Hudson Bay, and Learmonth on the coast of Boothia Peninsula (see *American Anthropologist*, XLII [1940], 490–99). Learmonth's specimen is in the Royal Ontario Museum, Toronto.

in an Ipiutak grave and ancient Chinese art; and he mentions some other parallels with Chinese neolithic and Han dynasty remains. Nevertheless, traces of an Eskimo-like people on the Arctic coast of Siberia, especially on the Yamal Peninsula, and certain resemblances between Ipiutak open-work carvings and Scytho-Siberian metal work of the first millennium B.C., incline him to minimize the Chinese parallels, to favor instead an ancient cultural connection with the Urals, and to seek around the lower Ob and Yenesei Rivers for the remains of the ancestors of the Ipiutak people.

This theory, too, leaves me frankly uneasy. From the Ural Mountains to the mouths of the Ob and Yenesei, and from there to Bering Strait, seems an inordinately long distance for iron to travel, becoming scarcer and more precious, as it must have done, at every stage of the journey. A southwestern source— the Amur River or even China—would certainly be shorter, and this direction rather than an Arctic coast one is suggested by the use of iron-bladed knives on St. Lawrence Island during the earliest phase of the Arctic Whale Hunting culture, which Dr. Larsen considers to be partly contemporary and partly subsequent to Ipiutak. One may add, too, that the use of birchbark vessels at Ipiutak hardly favors a long migration along the Arctic coast of Siberia, where birch trees are few and in many places lacking. Again, considering the great conservatism of the Eskimo language, which displays only minor variations from Bering Strait to Greenland, we might reasonably expect some kindred tongue to survive on the Arctic coast of Siberia if the Ipiutak people, who presumably spoke an Eskimo dialect, did not leave the Yenesei region until the second half of the first millennium B.C. It is true that a few scholars, particularly Sauvageot and Uhlenbeck, do find parallels between Eskimo and the Ural-Altaic tongues, notably Finnish; but the correspondences they cite, even if significant, seem much too tenuous and remote to support any migration of Eskimos from a Ural-Altaic environment as late as four or five centuries before the Christian era. Finally, although I am not familiar with Scytho-Siberian art or competent to assess its correspondences with Ipiutak, those that are listed by Dr. Larsen seem to me rather too weak to carry the superstructure of theory he builds on them.[3] Instead, I would give more weight to the analogies he notes with ancient China, such analogies as the jade eye-protective amulets of Han dynasty times, which resemble the artificial eyes at Ipiutak. Certainly, after looking at the old Chinese bronzes and jades and bonework in the Royal Ontario Museum in Toronto, I cannot help feeling that there is no need to search as far afield as western Siberia for analogies with Ipiutak art, but that even its open-work ivory carvings could have been inspired by twisted metal objects from the Chinese world.

Dr. Larsen does not believe that all the Eskimo stemmed from the Arctic coast of Siberia. The Ipiutak people did, he thinks, and brought their peculiar culture with them; but soon after their appearance the Bering Sea region re-

3. The pear-shaped boss on the hip of his walrus figure (252, Fig. 31) which he calls "the first American example of one of the fundamental elements of the Scytho-Siberian style," recalls to me the "eye" design employed by Pacific Coast Indian carvers to represent joints.

ceived some immigrants from northeastern Asia, immigrants who carried with them new culture elements, some of Chinese origin, and who contributed the eastern Asiatic strain in the present Eskimo population. This latter immigration—from northeastern Asia to the Bering Sea—I am tempted to accept, although the evidence for it remains still dim and shadowy. Even the earlier one, eastward along the Arctic coast of Siberia to Ipiutak, does not seem at all improbable when we remember the Eskimo-like remains on the Yamal Peninsula and elsewhere. For even if the strange religion and art of Ipiutak received their stimulus from China rather than from Western Siberia, as I have suggested, it would still be possible that, of the Ipiutak people themselves, some at least entered Alaska from the Arctic shores of Asia rather than from its northeast coast. Dr. Larsen has shown that Ipiutak was not a permanent village occupied throughout the whole year by a single Eskimo group, but a spring and summer camp that was abandoned at the approach of winter; and while most of its inhabitants were probably inland natives, signs were not lacking that it had been occupied contemporaneously by more than one people. We may reasonably assume, therefore, that it was a trading center similar to others of later date, e.g., Kotzebue at the head of Kotzebue Sound, Neqleq at the mouth of the Colville River, and, in the middle of last century, Barter Island and Demarcation Point near the International Boundary.

Now the probability that Ipiutak was primarily a summer trading center has some significance in relation to its age. A few of its houses and burials contained harpoon heads and other objects identical in type with Okvik specimens from the Bering Sea; but there was no indication that whaling was practiced, and other important elements of the Arctic Whale Hunting culture, such as slate implements, pottery and sleds, seemed lacking. Dr. Larsen has therefore concluded that the Ipiutak complex predates the Arctic Whale Hunting one, even though on the Ipiutak site itself the two cultures slightly overlapped; and he adds: "We must assume that Okvik and with it the entire Arctic Whale Hunting culture must have had a special development on an original foundation of the Ipiutak complex" (252, p. 151).

I wonder whether we are justified in drawing these two inferences. Because Point Hope and other settlements within the Arctic Ocean are not accessible to the Bering Sea Eskimos before the month of July—weeks after the bowhead whales have passed northward to spend the summer in the Chukchee and Beaufort Seas—there would be no reason for the southern natives to carry winter sleds or whaling equipment on a trading expedition to Ipiutak, even after whaling had become their regular occupation during the spring months. Even their newly acquired pottery they could well have left behind as being too fragile and precious to risk on a long boat journey over what can be quite a rough sea. Hence, because whaling equipment and some other Okvik traits are absent at Ipiutak, it does not necessarily follow that the Ipiutak culture preceded the Okvik (though I think this not unlikely); still less does it follow that the Ipiutak developed into the Okvik. The two cultures may have evolved from a common base and been broadly contemporary; but the northern one may have developed more slowly than the southern, and, in the realm of art, a little differently, perhaps because it was more remote from the vivifying influences of northeastern Asia.

It seems wiser, then, to withhold judgment concerning the exact relationship between Ipiutak and Okvik until future discoveries settle the issue. Meanwhile we can be fairly sure that Ipiutak stood at the dawn of a great revolution in the Bering Sea region and Arctic Alaska, a revolution whose repercussions were to be felt right across the top of America to Greenland. If Ipiutak's death masks, its chains, and its open-work carvings so suggestive of metal forms were among the earliest products of that revolution, as I rather suspect, then, so far from being local, they should be found on the coastline farther south, and perhaps also on the shores of Siberia opposite. For Dr. Larsen himself observes that the death masks have undeniable resemblances with ancient Chinese art, and that some of the open-work carvings recall certain bone ornaments of the Tlinkit Indians on America's northwest coast.

The parallel with Tlinkit Indian art introduces a larger question, viz., whether we can associate the revolutionary impulses that gave birth to the Arctic Whale Hunting culture with the passage into America of some of our North Pacific Coast Indians, who in appearance are the most Mongoloid of all Indians and who retain so many links with the so-called Americanoid natives—the Koryak, Kamschadal and others—of northeastern Asia. It is hardly possible to deny a connection between Eskimo whaling with detachable harpoon-heads and inflated bladders, and the similar whaling technique of the Nootka and other Indians on the British Columbia coast; and one may fairly ask whether it was the Indians who taught the Eskimo and not vice-versa. Could the same Indians have brought labrets to the Ipiutak people, and the East Asian semilunar knife which the Indians still use for cutting fish; for both labret and knife were unknown, apparently, to the Dorset Eskimo. And what about the pottery, unearthed in near-Ipiutak graves, that seems to resemble pottery found on the Amur River? Did the Indians introduce that too, and later discard it in favor of wooden cooking-boxes? From whom did the Alaskan Eskimo derive their slat armor, and was it unknown to them before Punuk times? These and a number of other questions cry out for answer. And when that answer is at last forthcoming I for one would not be surprised if it revealed that the Eskimo were in direct contact with the forefathers of our Pacific Coast Indians 2,000 or 2,500 years ago. For the centuries immediately preceding the Christian Era seem to have witnessed great maritime activity and strong population movements all along the east Asian coast from Java to Japan; and it does not seem impossible that, contemporary with the more southern movements, there should have been a migration in the far north, one that brought our Indians by boat along the Kamschatka Peninsula and through the Bering Sea to colonize at last the eastern shore of the Gulf of Alaska and the north Pacific Coast.

A SURVIVAL OF THE EURASIATIC ANIMAL STYLE IN MODERN ALASKAN ESKIMO ART

CARL SCHUSTER

In their recent study of Ipiutak, a prehistoric Eskimo culture discovered at Point Hope on the arctic coast of Alaska (252, pp. 126, 159), Larsen and Rainey call attention to a number of sculptured motives which are obviously derived from the bronze- and iron-age animal style of the Eurasiatic steppes. The authors lay special stress on the engraved markings of an ivory animal, on which the ribs are indicated and the hip is emphasized by a pear-shaped boss surrounded by a groove with raised edges (Fig. 12) (252, fig. 31). They point out that these two features occur together in metal representations of animals from places as widely separated as the Urals (Fig. 13), Finland (Fig. 14) and Denmark.[1] Other motives of the Eurasiatic animal style recognized by Larsen and Rainey in their Ipiutak material include griffins' heads, the representation of the fore-part of a bear with outstretched paws seen from above, and certain general traits, which they summarize as "the frequent use of realistic and fantastic animal heads as a terminal decoration of many kinds of artifacts, the use of inlays, and the combination of various animals or of zoomorphic and anthropomorphic motives on the same object."[2] This startling series of correspondences undoubtedly justifies the authors' statement: "there can be little doubt that the sculptural art [of Ipiutak] is a branch of the Eurasiatic or Scytho-Siberian animal style, which has, for the first time, been recognized in the New World" (252, p. 145). The discovery thus heralded is bound to have a bearing of great importance on the study of ancient and modern Eskimo art, and perhaps even wider consequences which can not yet be foreseen. In this paper we wish to call attention to the correspondence between a modern Eskimo design and a type of motive well known and widely distributed in the ancient animal style of the Eurasiatic steppes—and then to draw certain inferences which may be of help in understanding features of the prehistoric art of the Eskimos.

1. Our Fig. 14 is from the source cited by Larsen and Rainey (252, p. 126, n. 3). Our Fig. 13 is from Spitsyn (456, Fig. 397): a bronze "toad" from Perm. Spitsyn dates it eighth to ninth century.

2. Larsen and Rainey, 252, p. 145. Possibly this list can even be extended. For example, the detached animals' legs or hoofs (252, Pl. 51, Fig. 7; Pl. 52, Fig. 12) may be likened to the detached hind quarters of animals, which are a recognized, if still enigmatic, entity in Scythian art (Borovka, 53, Pl. 19). Again, the manner of carving the ends of antler tubes with animals' heads in Ipiutak art (252, Figs. 28, 45; Pl. 26/17, Pl. 76/11) is sufficiently like a similar treatment of the ends of curved bone objects or boars' tusks in Scythian art (53, Pl. 31, *B;* and especially 487, Fig. 13) to deserve special mention, even though this correspondence may be subsumed under the heading of the "general traits" listed by Larsen and Rainey.

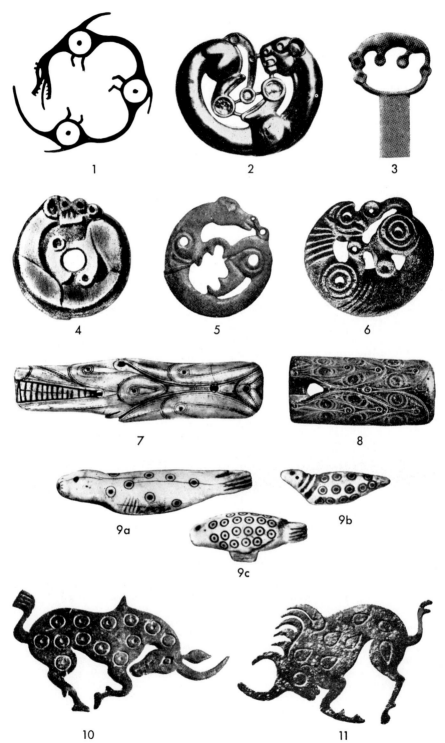

FIGS. 1–11

Figure 1 represents a design commonly painted on the inside of wooden dishes by the modern Eskimos inhabiting the lower Yukon valley and the Alaskan coast between the mouths of the Yukon and Kuskokwim Rivers (338, Fig. 155). This six-legged monster is regarded by the natives as an extinct beast of prey with habits like those of the crocodile. How such legends became associated with the design is an interesting problem, but one which does not concern us here. Our interest centers in the purely formal correspondence between this design and the type of the coiled animal (*animal enroulé, Rolltier*) which occurs in cast metal throughout the whole vast area once dominated by the animal style: from the northern shores of the Black Sea and the western slopes of the Urals to Western Siberia (Fig. 2), the Minusinsk basin of the upper Yenisei (Figs. 3–5), and the Ordos border region between Mongolia and China (Fig. 6).[3] Though from region to region the metal examples of this motive vary somewhat in style and in detail, they show an obvious and fundamental uniformity of conception. The type seems to appear almost simultaneously in all of the areas mentioned, and probably also in China proper, around or just before the middle of the first millennium B.C.[4] Each of the five examples here illustrated shows a beast coiled up in such a way that its snout touches, or almost touches, its tail. The body is so stretched that the flexed legs, which sometimes end in rings, generally form an interlocking pattern in the enclosed space. Of special interest in the light of the Eskimo analogy are the concentric circles marking the shoulder and hip of the Ordos beast (Fig. 6) and the perforated bosses in the same position on the Minusinsk bronze (Fig. 5). These have their obvious counterpart in the first two round expansions on the body of the Eskimo beast. It seems very likely that the third bodily expansion of the Eskimo beast arose through a misunderstanding (at some undetermined point in the trans-

3. Our Fig. 2 is from 53, Pl. 45; Fig. 3 from Merhart (311, Pl. 8/5); Fig. 4 from Klements (236, Pl. 8/18); Fig. 5 from Tallgren (486, Fig. 68); Fig. 6 from Salmony (410, Pl. 15/9).

Most comprehensively, perhaps, the motive of the *animal enroulé* has been treated by Tallgren (487, pp. 10–20). Most recently, the theme has been handled again by Kiselev (234, pp. 142–44).

We have included among our illustrations the knife-handle, Fig. 3, because its animal seems prototypic for those of the plaques, Figs. 2, 4–6, in that the circular form is completed by the animal's tail rather than by its inordinately extended body. In date, however, despite Brehm (57, p. 42), it seems that this knife is hardly appreciably earlier than other representations of the coiled animal (311, p. 128). In Teploukhov's classification it falls in the second phase of the Minusinsk Kurgan Culture (136, Pl. 19, Fig. 87); thus presumably not earlier than the sixth century. Our Fig. 4 is regarded by Kiselev (234, p. 142) as antecedent to our Fig. 5, which most authors (234, p. 142; 311, pp. 128 f.; 57, p. 43) seem to agree is "relatively late." The Siberian gold plaque, Fig. 2, is dated by most authors in the sixth century B.C. As for the Ordos plaque, Fig. 6, it is one of those cited by Kiselev (234, p. 142, n. 80) as being "a late Han variant" of a "late Tagar" type characterized by ornamental treatment—i.e., one from the last phase of the Minusinsk Kurgan Culture, presumably approaching the beginning of the Christian Era. However, the dating of Ordos bronzes is still controversial. See Karlgren (223, pp. 97 ff.).

4. On the early occurrence of the "coiled animal" in China proper see Loehr (275), and compare Karlgren (233, p. 101, No. 9).

mission of the motive) of the ring-like expansion which occurs either at the tip or the base of the animal's tail in all of the illustrated metal examples (and, in Fig. 2, also in the middle of the tail). The third pair of legs in the Eskimo design has no analogue among metal prototypes of the Old World; and we may assume that they represent a fanciful addition by the Eskimos.[5] Certain features of the Eskimo design raise puzzling questions, which we cannot answer in terms of the metal prototypes here assembled, but which should be stated as problems awaiting solution. Thus the wing-like protuberance extending outward from each bodily expansion of the Eskimo animal, and the rudimentary horns on its head, have no counterpart in the "animal style" of the steppes: they suggest the possibility of a Chinese prototype of dragonesque form, which, if it existed, must have been under the influence of, or closely analogous in conception to, the steppe type of coiled beast.[6]

Now, it may be said that there are two possible ways of understanding the occurrence in modern Eskimo art of a design obviously derived from the ancient animal style of the Eurasiatic steppes. Either we have here an isolated freak of survival; or the Eskimo animal is an integral part of a larger inheritance, which has been thoroughly assimilated into Eskimo tradition. The observation made by Larsen and Rainey of extensive influences from the animal style upon the ancient Eskimo art of Ipiutak clearly restricts our choice to the second alternative—and thus forces upon us an interesting and, I believe, significant conclusion. Undoubtedly the most striking feature of the Eskimo animal is the series of round expansions of the body at the points where the limbs are attached. On the one hand, as we have seen, these expansions have their counterpart, or prototype, in the joint-markings of animals similarly represented in the Eurasiatic animal style; but on the other hand, they show the form of a distinctive, ancient, and typical Eskimo design—that of the nucleated circle. If the whole design is inherited from the animal style, then it is hardly likely that the nucleated circles, which form an integral part of it, are derived from any other source; and if these particular nucleated circles are derived from prototypes in the animal style, the question automatically arises whether the Eskimo motive of the nucleated circle *per se* is not simply a part of the same inheritance—in

5. It must be mentioned that the Eskimos who painted the coiled animal of Fig. 1 also paint a much larger version of the same six-legged creature in straight form along the sides of their sea-going *umiaks* (338, Fig. 156). This raises an interesting question. As the Eskimo coiled animal is certainly derived from an ancient Asiatic prototype, one might be led to assume that the straight version of the six-legged creature was also inspired from the same source. However, until and unless we find such a prototype in the Siberian animal style (which is very unlikely), we seem forced to the conclusion that the Eskimos themselves straightened out the coiled beast, extra legs and all, for application to their boats.

6. As a possible explanation of the "wings" of the Eskimo coiled animal, Fig. 1, it may be mentioned that certain Ordos bronzes, and certain Chinese bronzes under the influence of the animal style (275, Fig. 3), show the coiled animal viewed from *above*, with the two left legs projecting inward and the two right legs projecting outward from the periphery. It seems, however, rather unlikely that the "wings" of our Eskimo beast are to be explained in terms of such outer limbs.

other words, whether the motive of the nucleated circle, so deeply rooted and widespread in Eskimo tradition, did not come to the New World originally in the form of a joint-marking on representations of animals. If this is so, it would obviously give us a valuable clue to the understanding of much that is now enigmatic in both ancient and modern Eskimo art.

Let us examine the evidence for an Old World derivation of the nucleated circle as a joint-mark in Eskimo art. It may be said that a good deal of attention has been paid to the motive of joint-markings in various phases of the Eurasiatic animal style, but often without a clear appreciation of their specific character. In the more sophisticated or more "naturalistic" phases of this style, the joint-mark often appears as a mere decoration, and is generally so understood by art-historians. Actually the motive of the joint-mark has a very ancient prehistory, stretching back several millennia before the rise of the animal style of the steppes.[7] And throughout this long prehistory, as well as in the relatively late style which here more especially concerns us, the joint-mark has a tendency to be either rationalized as a superficial spotting of the animal's skin, or treated inorganically as an incidental and fanciful decoration. The underlying symbolic quality of the joint-mark—what we may call its indispensability to the theme of animal representation (or perhaps even its magic significance)—has been obscured throughout its history by the rationalizing tendency of an art under the more or less direct and constant domination of the early urban civilizations of the Ancient East—an art forever bent upon naturalistic representation. The fact that the motive of the joint-mark nevertheless persisted, in ever-changing form, for several thousand years throughout so many phases of Near Eastern and Mediterranean art suggests that there must have been a more primitive strain of artistic expression, unaffected by the civilized ideals of the great urban centers, probably flourishing contemporaneously in remote and peripheral areas (perhaps in the far north, or in various Asiatic mountain regions), in which the motive of the joint-mark was more closely integrated with and more obviously inseparable from the animal representation. This popular strain of art remains unknown to us archeologically because of the perishability of the materials in which it was expressed. It is from such a primitive and conservative tradition, underlying the "animal style" as known to us largely in metal remains, that we may presume our Eskimo design to be derived. Though we must hypothecate such a tradition, we cannot "pinpoint" it or the culture which carried it. We can only refer to the obvious relationship between the Eskimo design and the whole widespread group of *animals enroulés* in metal, while noting that the closest congeners of the Eskimo motive, in respect to the essential feature of the joint-marks, seem to occur in certain bronzes of Minusinsk

7. On the prehistory of the animal joint-mark in the early civilizations of the Ancient East and the Mediterranean, see, among others, Bossert's (54) remarks in explanation of his Fig. 55; Kantor (22), and especially Christian (72, p. 15). His Fig. 19 shows a stone steer from Uruk with deep depressions for colored inlays on the shoulder and hip.

and the Ordos.[8] Presumably these metal representations are not the immediate prototypes of the Eskimo design, but themselves go back to prototypes in wood, bone, birchbark, felt, or other such materials. The fact that the Eskimo design is painted in itself suggests the general character of its probable prototype.

Now that our attention has been called to the important role of the joint-mark in the relationship between Eskimo art and the Eurasiatic animal style, we may examine certain other possibilities of relationship between the two arts in terms of this feature. In pointing out metal analogues for the Ipiutak walrus (Fig. 12), Larsen and Rainey dwell upon the shape and double outline of the "pear-shaped boss" on the animal's flank, thus stressing a stylistic criterion of comparison. We wish to shift the emphasis now to what might be called the concept rather than the form of the joint-mark, and to re-examine the material in these terms. Besides the pear-shaped boss in the region of its flank, the Ipiutak walrus (Fig. 12) shows a number of perforations—one for the eye, another for the ear, one 'just below the shoulder, and one on each paw. Some of these holes are slotted, evidently, as the authors say, to accommodate thongs for attaching the object, perhaps to a shaman's clothing. Several of the holes obviously correspond to anatomical features of the animal; but one of them, the hole under the shoulder, whatever function it may have served, can hardly be explained in terms of normal anatomy. We suggest that this hole is, in fact, the somewhat misplaced and misunderstood joint-marking of the shoulder, just as the "pear-shaped boss" is the joint-mark of the hip. This becomes clearer in the light of comparison with the analogous representation of a polar bear from the Old Bering Sea phase of ancient Eskimo culture (Fig. 15) (80, Fig. 7). Here there is no representation of the ribs, and the backbone, a prominent feature of the Ipiutak walrus, is reduced to a short "ladder" near the rump. The "pear-shaped boss" with multiple outline here appears, without marked protuberance, a little higher on the back of the animal, in the region of the kidneys. The eye-holes are perforated clear through the head; a number of other holes at various places on the body were probably plugged originally with inlays of baleen or wood. The holes in the rudimentary legs evidently communicated with slots for attachment—analogous to the slots in the flippers of the Ipiutak walrus (80, p. 49). What interests us especially in this animal is the presence of a hole for an inlay behind the shoulder—and the decorative embellishment of this hole with a certain arrangement of lines characteristic of Old Bering Sea art. In view of all the other similarities between this bear and the Ipiutak walrus, it is obvious that this hole, despite its slightly different position, corresponds to the hole on the fore-flank of the Ipiutak walrus—and in all probability, like the latter, represents the joint-mark of the animal's shoulder. This is an important circumstance, for it means that on at least one relatively natu-

8. The occurrence of joint-marks on the coiled beast is, however, not confined to Minusinsk and the Ordos. It occurs also west of the Urals: for example, on a well known plaque from Anan'ino (53, Pl. 64, *D;* 487, 1932, Fig. 10) and on a fragmentary specimen found in 1936 at Turbino, near Perm (371, Fig. 15/3), the latter showing perforations at the hip and shoulder.

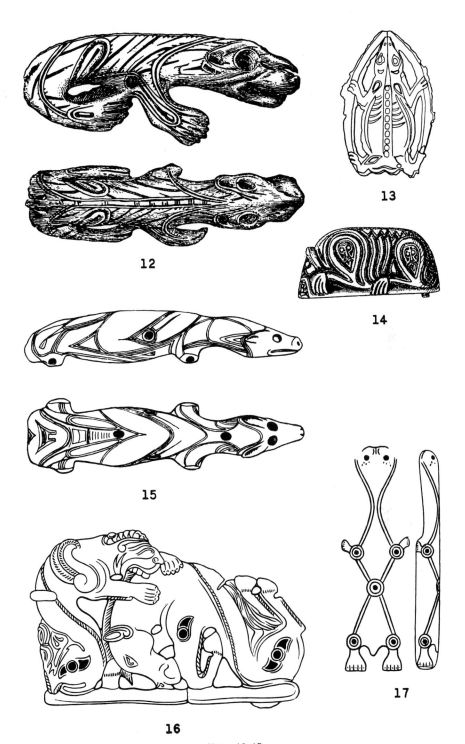

12

13

14

15

16

17

FIGS. 12–17

ralistic carving of the Old Bering Sea art we have a characteristic eye-like motive or ocellation, serving pretty clearly as a joint-mark. The essential features
of this typical marking are a disc or pit surrounded by one or more concentric
grooves, from which in turn more or less triangular spurs project outwards.[9] It
is difficult to speak of such markings without referring to them as "eyes" (80,
pp. 51, 76, 298)—and I believe it can eventually be shown that that is precisely
what they are.[10]

Now, let us compare the inlaid and outlined eye-shaped joint-marking of the
Old Bering Sea polar bear (Fig. 15) with the joint-markings on a well-known
Siberian gold plaque in the collection of Peter the Great (Fig. 16).[11] Disregard-
ing superficial differences of style, it is obvious that the joint-marks of this
plaque show the same essential features as the shoulder-marking of the Eskimo
bear: a circular pit for an inlay, surrounded by a contour line, and flanked by
two triangular "spurs." That these spurs are inlaid on the gold plaque but without inlay on the Eskimo carving may be regarded as a minor and unessential
difference between the two markings.

Here again we have a clear prototype in the Eurasiatic animal style for an
important feature of Eskimo art—and this time the parallel is with ancient
rather than modern Eskimo art. The second analogy confirms the first, and
serves to emphasize the importance of the joint-mark as an essential feature
of the primitive animal style which found its way from Asia to the New World.

Drawing together the inferences from these two comparisons, we believe it
justified to conclude that the Eskimo motive of the nucleated circle, in all its
stylistic variants, both ancient and modern, and in all its variant usages, is
really derived from a joint-marking, as practiced in a primitive strain of art
presumably underlying the Eurasiatic "animal style." Since the nucleated
circle is one of the most important motives in Eskimo art,[12] it follows that the
debt of Eskimo art to the "animal style" is even greater than Larsen and Rainey
first proposed.

Though it is, of course, true that in both ancient and modern Eskimo art the
nucleated circle occurs in a great many contexts other than as a joint-mark on
animals, the analogies here cited strongly suggest that the motive must have
been transmitted originally as a joint-mark, and that it then gradually became

9. For variants of the eye-like motive in Old Bering Sea art see Collins (80, Fig. 15).

10. Though I cannot attempt to justify this interpretation here, I may mention two circumstances which seem to me to support it—first, the occurrence of a naturalistic eye-motive
as a joint-mark in the art of the Pacific Northwest Coast and, second, the undoubted occurrence of eyes as joint-marks on *human* figures from a number of areas around the Pacific
(see Carl Schuster, *Joint-Marks*, Communication XCIV. ["Publications of the Department
of Cultural and Physical Anthropology," No. 39.] Amsterdam: Royal Institute for the
tropics, 1951).

11. After Borovka (53, Pl. 46, *A*). Recently a number of objects bearing this type of joint-
marking has been brought together and identified as a group (see Salmony, 411).

12. On the present-day distribution of the nucleated circle in the New World, among the
Eskimos and elsewhere see Smith and Spier (436).

dissociated from its original function and developed into an independent element, which has at various times been more or less freely used in various styles of Eskimo decorative art. Though we cannot trace the process of dissociation step by step, we are not entirely without clues as to the way it took place. Figure 7 shows an ancient Eskimo ivory carving, presumably from the same phase of the Old Bering Sea style as the polar bear (Fig. 15).[13] In this carving we can sense the transition from a naturalistic animal representation to pure decoration. The species, so cleverly portrayed in the carving of the polar bear (Fig. 15), can no longer be recognized. Only the exaggerated teeth and the conventionalized reduction of the backbone to a "ladder" misplaced along the middle of the side suffice to establish the animal origin of the design and enable us to recognize one of the several nucleated circles as representing the animal's eye, and a hole behind the eye as representing its ear. Apart from these features, the rest of the carving is made up of delicately outlined ovoid panels, each containing a nucleated circle with spurs like that of the animal's eye. It would hardly require a great many transitional examples to establish the derivation of these supernumerary eyes from an ocellated joint-mark like that on the flank of the polar bear (Fig. 15). In fact, it is difficult to see how else these "eyes" can be explained except as the irresponsible multiplication of such an originally symbolical marking. A carving like Figure 7 may well represent the beginning of the process which led eventually to the typical designs of the following phase of the Old Bering Sea style (OBS III), in which the animal disappears altogether and there remains only a network of panels containing eye-like nucleated ovals, as we see them in Figure 8.[14]

Fortunately, this development has an instructive analogy in the Eurasiatic animal style. Karlgren has shown very clearly that the pear-shaped, or sometimes circular, markings on the flanks of beasts have a tendency, at an early date, simultaneously throughout three widely separated provinces of the animal style (South Russia or Scythia, the Ordos, and the Huai or Late Chou style of China) to multiply so as to form a pattern all over the body of the beast (223, pp. 102–12). We show only two characteristic examples of this development, from the flat relief decoration of Chinese bronze vessels of the Huai style (Figs. 10, 11).[15] Though Karlgren does not use the expression, we propose to designate this development a multiplication or proliferation of joint-marks, and to see in it a close analogy to the process which takes place in the Old Bering Sea art of the Eskimos—and which may well have taken place also in other ancient Eskimo art styles. Thus, the Eskimos took over from the animal style not only the motive of the joint-mark, and the coiled beast as one of the char-

13. From a photograph kindly supplied by Dr. H. B. Collins, Jr. Published by Collins (80, Pl. 15/3).

14. From a photograph kindly supplied by Dr. Collins. Published by Hrdlička (195, Pl. 21).

15. Details of photographs kindly supplied by Dr. Alfred Salmony. For the complete originals (vases of the *hu* type) see, respectively, Kelley (226, Fig. 6), Visser (508, Pl. 28), or Karlgren (223, Pl. 59/2) (Stocklet Collection).

acteristic carriers of this motive, but they obviously must have absorbed also the tendency toward a decorative multiplication, or proliferation, of the joint-marks, from whatever phase of the Eurasiatic animal style it was to which they were exposed. It is perhaps unnecessary to emphasize that this development in Eskimo art led to very different results than in the parent animal style—that it led, in fact, to the evolution of a distinctive and characteristically "primitive" decorative style, which, apart from significant exceptions, seems very quickly and thoroughly to have lost all traces of its Asiatic ancestry.

In addition to the motive of the coiled beast with joint-marks (Fig. 1), we must call attention to at least one other survival of the motive of the nucleated circle as a joint-mark on animals in modern Eskimo art. Figure 17 (42, Fig. 15) shows the engraved decoration on an ivory effigy of a seal. This is no isolated example: the nucleated circle appears quite commonly in the position of a joint-mark on figures of seals, otters and walruses from the same Alaskan region where the coiled beast of Figure 1 makes its home.[16] On many of these effigies, moreover, we notice, as in Figure 9,[17] the same tendency toward decorative multiplication of the circular joint-mark as we observe, for example, on the Late Chou beast (Fig. 10). Thus in Eskimo art, while on the one hand the motive of the nucleated circle early became dissociated from animal representations (Fig. 8), it also persists in certain phases of Eskimo tradition in its original context—either as a joint-mark, or in multiple form as a decoration all over the bodies of animals—both manners of treatment clearly having their prototypes in the ancient Eurasiatic animal style.

Finally, we wish to make some observations about the possible spread of certain traits of the Old World animal style to the south of Alaska. In this connection it must be regarded as significant that the eye-motive (which we believe to be, in effect, the same as the Eskimo motive of the nucleated circle with spurs) is regularly used in the art of the Northwest Coast Indians as a joint-mark (40, p. 175). We will not attempt to answer the question whether this usage is directly traceable to Eskimo art. Obviously the art of the Northwest Coast represents a different stylistic development—but the fact nevertheless remains that one of its fundamental usages is identical with a fundamental usage of Eskimo art.

A second point, which perhaps involves even more difficult questions, is the fact that what appear to be typical joint-markings occur on animal representations among Indian groups living still farther to the south. In Figure 18 an ancient Ipiutak representation of a polar bear (252, Fig. 30) is juxtaposed with

16. E.g., Boas (42, 1908, Pl. 30/2–5); Hoffman (186, Pl. 56/3, p. 815); Nelson (338, Fig. 111); and many specimens in the U.S. National Museum and doubtless in other museums.

17. Fig. 9, a, b, c: ivory effigies of seals in the U.S. National Museum, cat. Nos. 33618, 48219, and 48642, respectively. Fig. 9, a from St. Michaels; 9, b from Sledge Island; 9, c from Kotzebue Sound. All collected by E. W. Nelson. Fig. 9, a = Hoffman (186, Pl. 43/4); Fig. 9, c = Hoffmann (186, Pl. 56/4). Photographs from the Smithsonian Institution, through the courtesy of Dr. H. B. Collins, Jr.

the painted representation of an otter (Fig. 19) on a modern Blackfoot Indian tipi.[18] The Indians regard the spots on the hind quarters as representing the animal's kidneys, which, together with the tongue, throat and heart, are considered sources of the animal's supernatural power.[19] Are we to dismiss this explanation as a local rationalization of a motive whose origin had been forgotten (for the same animal carries joint-marks on its knees), or does the Blackfoot Indian perhaps give us an insight into the still more ancient origin of the joint-

Fig. 18

Fig. 19

mark itself as the representation of a vital internal organ—such as is known to us in paleolithic animal representations of the Old World? If the latter explanation is correct, we shall obviously have to examine anew in the light of this possibility the whole background and prehistory of the Eurasiatic animal style.

18. After the original, preserved in the American Museum of Natural History, New York. Length, 110 cm. Body black, shaded areas green, white areas red in the original.

19. Information kindly supplied by Mr. John C. Ewers, of the U.S. National Museum. The original informant was a Piegan Indian, and the reference was to the figure of a deer, rather than an otter. But on the Piegan (Blackfoot) lodges, both creatures are provided with similar markings.

ANATOMICAL STUDIES OF THE EAST GREENLAND ESKIMO DENTITION

P. O. Pedersen

Greenland, a Danish colony, is the largest island in the world. The greater part of the country is covered with ice. The ice cap completely separates East Greenland from West Greenland. Greenland has only 20,000 inhabitants, of whom approximately 1,300 live on the eastern coast. There are no inhabited areas outside the immediate vicinity of the coasts.

During the greater part of the year East Greenland is isolated from the outside world by an almost impenetrable ice girdle. All the natives of East Greenland live in the territories around the trading stations of Angmagssalik and Scoresby Sound. The Eskimos at Angmagssalik were contacted in 1884, when the tribe was discovered by an officer of the Royal Danish Navy. In 1894, the Danish Government established a trading station at Angmagssalik in order to prevent the natives, rapidly on the decline at that time, from perishing. The Scoresby Sound area became reinhabited in modern times—as late as 1924—by emigration of Eskimos from Angmagssalik. The Eskimo of East Greenland are practically without European admixture.

On the other hand, West Greenland had early European contact and Danish colonization was firmly established more than two centuries ago. The western coast of Greenland is more easily accessible than is the eastern coast and European influence is more predominant. The natives, among whom are a large number of European-Eskimo mixture have to no small extent settled down under urbanized conditions.

Under the joint sponsorship of the Royal Danish Government, the Royal Dental College in Copenhagen, and the Anthropological Department of the Copenhagen University Institute of Anatomy, extensive studies of native dental conditions in East and West Greenland were made during the past thirteen years. The principal purpose of this work was that of contributing to the knowledge of dental disease, especially dental caries. Eventually, however, it became clear that the Eskimo dentition, besides displaying an interesting pathology, exhibits several features showing marked racial characteristics. Accumulating evidence to that effect was the exciting factor of the present study, the principal aim of which was that of scrutinizing the East Greenland Eskimo dentition for such features.

By limiting this report to the permanent dentitions of Eskimo of unmixed East Greenland descent, we reduce our total Greenland material from 3,300 living Greenlanders and 525 skulls to 702 modern East Greenland Eskimos

46

above 6 years of age and 52 adult East Greenland Eskimo skulls examined in East Greenland in 1937 and in the Copenhagen Anthropological Museum, respectively. Of all Eskimos living in East Greenland in 1937, 96 per cent were examined. Besides routine records of all cases, 150 casts of Eskimo dentitions and 2,000 roentgenograms of the teeth of modern and ancient Eskimo were analysed and described. Metrical studies were made of the dentitions of the skulls.

Here are some of our principal findings:

1. The crowns of the molar teeth are superior in size (as indicated by the module) to those of whites, whereas the crowns of premolars, canines and incisors are not. This is noteworthy in so far as it indicates that the proportionate size of the crowns is not necessarily the same within the dentitions of all modern ethnic groups.

2. The teeth, in general, are of a blunt mesotaurodont shape being without a well-defined neck and having short, straight, and moderately divergent roots. In West Greenlanders, as in whites, the necks of the teeth are more marked. In West Greenlanders the roots are prone to be slender and divergent and also to exhibit bends and crooks.

3. Congenital absence of mandibular incisors and the molars is more frequent than in whites. Congenital absence of maxillary lateral incisors and mandibular premolars is less frequently met with than in whites. The third molar is congenitally missing more often in the East Greenland Eskimo than in any other group on record. The third molar is vestigial in a very high proportion of cases. In the West Greenlanders the incidence of vestigial and congenitally missing third molars is decisively lower.

4. Shovel-shaped incisors are almost universal.

5. Cusp numbers and occlusal pattern of the molars come closer to conditions found in fossil apes such as *Dryopithecus* than do cusp numbers and occlusal pattern in other modern populations and ethnic groups hitherto studied. The lower second molar is quintitubercular in a high percentage of cases.

6. Carabelli's cusp—present in about 75 per cent of whites if we include the pitted type—is almost entirely absent in the East Greenland Eskimo. In West Greenland hybrids about one-third of upper first molars exhibit Carabelli's cusp or pit.

7. Paramolar tubercles of Bolk, i.e., supernumerary buccal cusps on third and second molars, are frequent.

8. There is a tendency for the Eskimo to develop small pearl-like excrescences on the occlusal surfaces of premolars and molars as well as on the lingual aspects of the canine cusps.

9. Buccal pits and grooves on lower molars are frequent and quite often pronounced. They may be surrounded by an area of hypoplastic enamel.

10. Enamel extensions from the gingival margin opposite root bifurcations and grooves (originally described by Leigh in American Indians, Eskimos and

Polynesians) are normal in the Eskimo of Greenland. They are frequently present to an extreme degree. They are closely related to enamel drops (or nodules), which are found on upper third and second molars in a much higher percentage of cases than in whites. As many as 25 per cent of maxillary third molars exhibit enamel nodules distally and/or mesially. This seems to be far the highest incidence recorded for any group.

11. Average root height is reduced during lifetime to a striking degree. In many cases root resorption of vital incisors occurs even during adolescence. More or less pronounced resorption of the apical part of the roots with hypercementosis of the remaining part of the roots seems to be an almost normal occurrence in the adult primitive Eskimo. This is probably due to the excessive demands the Eskimo puts upon his dentition and should be kept in mind when data on root heights are evaluated. Generally speaking, it is felt that more attention should be paid to secondary changes of root height by students of tooth dimensions. This is especially true when heavy attrition of the crowns indicates strenuous function of the teeth. In fact, little if any attention has been given to this very considerable source of error so far.

12. Supernumerary roots are frequent. On the mandibular first molars distolingual roots are found ten times as often as in whites (Bolk). High incidence of this root has been reported by Tratman of Singapore in peoples of Mongoloid stock living in Malaya.

13. "Fusion" of root branches is common. Such failure of the roots to divide into branches resembles conditions found in certain specimens of early man in Europe.

14. The pulp cavity is large during childhood and young adult age and, in fact, remains large, but in mature individuals secondary deposits of dentine, including enormous pulp stones, are widespread. Some of these pulp calcifications are suggestive of vitamin-C deficiency.

The following features of the East Greenland Eskimo dentition are suggestive of Mongoloid affinities and ancestry of the Eskimo: (1) High incidence of shovel-shaped incisors, (2) very low incidence of Carabelli's cusp, (3) high incidence of three-rooted mandibular molars, (4) characteristic pattern of congenital absence of teeth, and (5) high incidence of congenital absence of third molars.

In addition, the East Greenlanders display the following dental characteristics supposed to be prevalent in Mongoloid stock, (6) high incidence of pronounced enamel extensions on the molars, and (7) high incidence of enamel nodules on the molars.

Conditions in the East Greenland Eskimo dentition generally considered primitive are (1) frequent retention of remote ancestral cusp numbers and crown pattern (*Dryopithecus* pattern), (2) large size of the pulp cavity and moderate taurodontism.

Conditions in the East Greenland Eskimo dentition generally considered advanced or late in evolutionary respect are (1) reduction in size of the posterior molars, (2) high incidence of vestigial third molars, and (3) very frequent congenital absence of third molars.

The significance, if any, of the other dental conditions mentioned in this report is obscure.

There are some indications that dental anatomy is not identical in all Eskimo groups, but further studies are needed especially of Eskimos from the American Continent, before conclusions may be drawn.

From the present study[1] no decisive support can be lent to the view that the Eskimo be either very primitive or very far advanced in evolutionary respect. What is definitely borne out by his dentition, however, is confirmation of his Mongoloid ancestry.

The attempts of analysing the Eskimo dentition here demonstrated in gross outline, are in fact attempts of approaching the highly interesting and important question of the origin and antiquity of the Eskimo from an angle heretofore little considered by students of Eskimo anthropology. However, the scope of such studies is felt to be wider in so far as they seem to have been successful in demonstrating the significance of the dentition as a bearer of racial characteristics in modern man. Hence future anthropological studies of human races will not be complete without expert dental scrutiny.

Finally, it is obvious that studies—including dental—of the influence of population mixture, such as may be made on comparison of East and West Greenland natives, will probably be able to yield information of importance from the point of view of human genetics. Hints to that effect were already given by Birket-Smith, and the present study tends to support his views.

1. Full details of this study may be found in *Meddelelser om Grønland*, Vol. CXLII, No. 3 (1949). This official Danish bulletin on Greenland is published by Reitzel in Copenhagen.

POSSIBLE EARLY CONTACTS BETWEEN ESKIMO
AND OLD WORLD LANGUAGES

W. Thalbitzer

I

Much work has been done in attempting to relate Eskimo to other languages. This article will cover the results of some of the comparisons made between Eskimo and Asiatic languages and Eskimo and North American Indian languages. It will then take up some of the more recent and promising work done in comparing Eskimo and Indo-European.

Eskimo does not seem to be related to its Asiatic neighbors. There are a few Eskimo words and elements which may be compared with corresponding ones in Koryak, but there is apparently no genetic relationship between the two. The same is true of Eskimo and Chukchee, a language which Vladimir Bogoras has shown to be related to Koryak. There are only a few cases of what may be called loan-words from Chukchee-Koryak to Eskimo or vice versa.

Resemblances between Eskimo and neighboring Asiatic languages:

I. *Concrete resemblances:*
   Eskimo: *niviaq* 'young unmarried maid'
   Koryak: *neven* 'wife'; *nevek* 'daughter'
   Kerek: *nivi, nevek* 'daughter'
   Chukchee: *ne, new* 'daughter'
   We may recognize the same stem in Samoyed: *ne* or *nee; neä* 'woman' and *nebea* or *nevea* 'wife'
   Finnish: *nainen* 'woman'; *neito* 'unmarried woman'
   Lapp: *neiete (neiti)* 'maid, daughter'

   Eskimo: *imaq* 'sea, ocean' and *imeq* 'fresh water'
   W. Eskimo: *moq* 'fresh water'
   Compare Koryak-Chukchee *mimel, mimal; mimil* < **iml.*
   The initial *m* in W. Eskimo is = *imoq* (E. Eskimo *imeq*), thus showing a marked resemblance to *mi-, im-* in Koryak-Chukchee words. The similarity, however, is not convincing as evidence of a relationship between Eskimo and its nearest Siberian neighbors.

II. There is another sort of resemblance to be considered if we take such a word as Eskimo *inuk* 'human being, man, Eskimo,' plural *inuit* 'men,' derivative *inuiait* 'people, peoples, nations.' A similar word in Koryak is *inug* 'sea, ocean.' Is this a real or fortuitous resemblance?[1] The Eskimo stem *inu-* suffixed with *-qati-* 'comrade, fellow' plus *-gi(ng)-* 'mutually combined, belonging together,' gives the total meaning: '*inuit* belonging together, *inuit* of the world' with the ablative ending *-nit-* 'from.' But if we compare the single case endings of Eskimo

---

1. We may call it a "fallacious resemblance" as long as we do not have any reasonable explanation of the formal similarity of the two words in question.

with the corresponding ones in Koryak-Chukchee, we find no concrete resemblances. The same is true of the possessive endings of both languages.
III. *General systematic resemblances:* These are of a formalistic character, and although they are interesting, they tell us nothing about genetic relationships.

There seems, therefore, to be no relationship between Eskimo and neighboring Asiatic languages, at least not the kind of relationship found among Indo-European languages. There is probably not even as much affinity between Eskimo and neighboring languages as that postulated between the Indo-European and Finno-Ugric languages, although this postulated genetic relationship between Indo-European and Finno-Ugric, despite Collinder's arguments, is not yet supported by a sufficient body of evidence. However, there is a *general formal resemblance* in nearly all the languages of Europe and Northern Siberia, including Eskimo. There are common trends in the formation of systematic noun declensions, verb conjugations, and suffixal morphemic derivation.

Throughout the past fifty years I have sought for Eskimo loan-words or inner resemblances in other languages, first in those of the North American Indians and next in reports about more distant peoples in Asia, e.g., the Ainu, Japanese, Turkish, Tungus and even more distant peoples than these. Unfortunately, the results have been so meager that I concluded that *Eskimo is not related to any other language in the world.*

I will present a few samples picked out of a synoptic list which I had made:

1. Eskimo *qaiaq*, plural *qainnat* (irregularly formed) 'kayak'
   Turkish (Yakut): *qajiq* 'kayak'
2. W. Eskimo: *tuŋra* 'spirit of a shaman'
   Turkish: *teŋri* 'deity of the heaven, sky-god, shaman spirit'
3. Eskimo: *Asiak* 'deity of rain, the melter or dissolver of snow and ice'
   Aztec: *Asiak* 'rain-god'
4. Eskimo: *Sila* 'deity of the air and weather, the source of force; mind, intellect'
   Old Bulgarian: *sila* 'force, strength'
5. W. Eskimo: *qajige, qadjige* = E. Eskimo *qashge (qagsse)* 'festival house, temple, club, men's house'
   Ainu: *kashi* 'hunting lodge'
   Japanese: *kaji, kashi*
   Ostyak: *xat, kot* 'tent'
   Finnish: *koti*
   Lapp: *kāote, kāohte*
   Magyar: *ház* 'house'
   Old Cymric: *cûdd;* Danish-Norwegian: *hytta;* German: *hütte* < Old German: **hōdian, *hudjōn*
   Old Irish: *kattia* < Indo-European: **keudh-*
6. W. Eskimo: *iayaq* 'tambourine (in the holy language of the shamans)'
   E. Greenland: *eajāq* (id.)
   Kerek: *jajarit* 'drum'; koryak: *yayai* 'shaman's drum'
   Sanskrit: *yājati* 'to glorify a god by religious rites'
7. Eskimo: *inuk* 'man'
   Algonkin (Pequot): *in*, plural *inug* 'man'
   Narraganset: *nnin* 'man'

8. Eskimo: *tupeq* 'tent'; W. Eskimo: *tupîgaq* 'mat made of straw'
   Dakota: *ťi'pi* < *ťi* 'dwelling'
   In *ťi'pi* (ti-pi) 'they dwell' *ťi-* is the stem, *-pi* plural.
9. W. Eskimo: *qadjige* 'festival house, temple, club, men's house'
   Déné of British Columbia: *kōskōnōn kazhga*
10. Eskimo: *uŋa(si-)* 'long distance'
    Déné: *yu* 'farthest away, the longest distance'
11. Eskimo: *ssît* 'willow'
    Tlingit: *ssit* 'Sitka fir tree.' But salix in Tlingit is *schat* 'willow, salix'

Such isolated word resemblances serve, at most, as an indication of contact between peoples during the course of their history. Although they present clues for our studies, we must be very careful in using them as evidence for language relationships or culture contact without more detailed investigations.

II

The different lines of more recent investigation may lead, however, to a reconsideration of the conclusion that Eskimo is not related to any other language in the world. Let us consider some of this evidence.

In the Southwest Greenland dialect a small number of Danish and Old-Icelandic loan-words have come in and are used to this day. *Pellese* (nowadays spelled *palase*) and *puluke* mean 'priest' and 'pork' respectively. W. Greenland *kuáneq* (angelica Archangelica, an edible plant) seems to be a word of Old-Icelandic origin: *hvannir* (plural), dialect *kvanner*, meaning the same plant.

Along the North Pacific coast south of the Bering Straits, we have on the American side the Aleuts, and on the Siberian side the Kereks, a maritime branch of the Kamchadal-Koryak peoples. In the language of the former there is undeniably an Eskimo substratum,[2] in the latter seemingly another kind of stratum which we may call a hybridism—a mixture of Eskimo and Koryak.[3] There are several striking coincidences between Kerek and Eskimo. We find, for example (in Radlinczky's list of words), the Kerek verb *pivok* 'to wound oneself.' Compare this to Eskimo (Greenlandic) *pivoq* 'he lost his life by upsetting in his kayak.' This cannot be a mere coincidence; it indicates common origin, etymologic identity.

Another line was followed long ago by Rask, who found that Old-Icelandic could not be derived from the *Grønlandske sprog* (Greenland Eskimo), but rather that Eskimo seemed to be connected in certain respects with Finno-Ugric and even with Aleut. Sauvageot has argued for the same hypothesis, but his peculiar way of dealing with the problem did not lead to any acceptable results (418, pp. 296–97).

We also have to consider the cultural features common to the groups in question. Ethnographic and sociological evidence reveals a number of striking

2. C. C. Uhlenbeck (502) has proposed some new terms besides "substratum," viz., "superstratum" and "adstratum."

3. For some of my former investigations on this, see 490, 491.

correspondences between all the Arctic peoples directly west from Scandinavia via Siberia to East Greenland. I called attention to some of these "parallels" many years ago at the Sixteenth meeting of Scandinavian scholars of natural sciences at Oslo and later, in augmented form, at the Twentieth Congress of Americanists at Rio de Janeiro, 1922 (490).

Again, linguistically the results were meager:

COMPARISONS WITH FINNO-UGRIC

Eskimo: *qipik* 'feather bed, eider-down' Samoyed: *kufu;* Finnish: *kupo*
Eskimo: *kamik* 'boot' Lapp: *kama* (*kapma-*) 'boot, shoe'
Eskimo: *siko* 'ice (frozen salt water)' Lapp: *jeēŋna* (Magyar: *jég*) 'ice'
Eskimo: *sermeq* 'hard frozen snow, inland Lapp: *čarava;* Zyrian: *tšarom;* Yenesei:
ice' *sir-*

A far more fertile field was opened by Uhlenbeck, who suggests an age-old connection between Eskimo and Indo-European (491). Uhlenbeck saw that Eskimo *oqaq* 'tongue' might be compared with the Indo-European root *$*wek^w$* 'to speak,' which is the same as Latin *vox* (genitive *vocis*) 'voice.' Likewise he would find Eskimo *aųssaq* 'spring, summer' in Latin *ver* and Old Norse *vár:*

ESKIMO	INDO-EUROPEAN
aųssaq 'spring, summer'	Latin: *ver;* Old Norse: *vár;* Danish: *vär*
< **qu—*	
qōroq 'valley, cleft'	**ker-* (*sker-*) 'to cleave'
tōrpā 'thrusts at it'	**(s)teug-, (s)teuk-*; (Latin: *tundo*)
tutivā, 'treads on it'	**(s)teud-*; (Latin: *tundo*)
tupigā 'is surprised at it'	**(s)teup-*; (Latin: *stupeo*)
tunivā 'gives it (him)'	**(s)teup-*; (Latin: *do*)

We note a whole series of corresponding vocalic and consonantal transitions—leading even to an explanation of that somewhat troublesome stem of Latin *do* 'I give' which may be derived from a verb meaning 'to thrust something over to some other person.'

Uhlenbeck reckons that Eskimo *oqaq* 'tongue, word' has lost an initial consonant (cf. Indo-European *vox* > Eskimo *ok-*) and that the same is true of some few other stems:

ESKIMO	INDO-EUROPEAN
arnaq 'woman'	*$*g^u nā-$*; German: **kwennôn* < **kwenn-*
erneq 'son'	*$*g^e nē-$*; German:**ken-*, **koni-* < **ĝenos* 'kin'
orpik 'tree' < **or* and *-pik* 'true, genuine'	*$*u^e r-$*; cf. Old Norse: *ǫlr;* Norwegian: *or* (older); Indo-European: **el-*, **ol-*
ule 'flood, highwater'	*$*u el-$*; Sanskrit: *vrnóti*
aᵇʰla, *aλa* 'another'	**al-*; Latin: *alius, alter;* Greek: ἀλλος
áipā 'the other (of two), his companion'	Sanskrit: *ápara;* cf. Gothic: *aba* 'husband'

ESKIMO	INDO-EUROPEAN
aner(poq) 'breathes'	Sanskrit: *ániti* 'breathes'
anore 'wind'	Sanskrit: *ánila* 'wind'
ai(voq) 'goes'	*ei-* (Greek: *εἶμι* 'I go')
aglu(voq) 'is poor'	Gothic: *agls* 'disgraceful'; cf. *aglo* 'poorness, grief'
milug(poq) 'sucks'	*miluks;* Latin: *mulgeo* 'I milk'
mini(pā) 'passes over him at a distribution'	Sanskrit: *minóti* 'diminishes it'
sana(voq) 'works'	*sen-*; Sanskrit: *sánati* 'he works'
tikeq 'index, forefinger'	*deik-*; Greek: *δεικ-* 'points at, shows'

Uhlenbeck has been very cautious in claiming that such convergences or correspondences indicate *Urverwandtschaft* or fundamental intimate relationship. He seems to be content with the view that the similarities are due to an ancient borrowing, i.e., that they are loan words. He does not tell us in which direction the borrowing occurred, but when he will compare, for instance, Eskimo *ingneq* 'fire' with Latin *ignis*, Slavic *ognĭ*, Sanskrit *agnĭ-*, I must maintain that the true origin of the word is found by examining the etymology of Eskimo *ingneq*. This is a contraction of **ikineq* 'result of kindling.'

mingneq	**mikineq*	*-neq* is an affix of verbal
angneq	**angineq*	abstract and adjectival
tangneq	**takineq*	superlative

*Ikineq is a verbal infinitive form (also used as superlative abstract) which means: the superlative result of *iki-* 'the drill-boring in a wooden block to produce fire.' The Indo-European word for fire (Latin *ignis*) may be derived from the Eskimo word for fire-drilling.

This example may be considered characteristic of a series of correspondences between Eskimo and Indo-European as made by Uhlenbeck and myself. The etymologies of the common bases seem to be explained in the Eskimo forms of the words. These Eskimo forms may be considered as the more primitive by virtue of their etymologic transparency.

I should like to state that we might be justified in considering the remarkable language of the *Inuit* race as a residuum of the Indo-European proto-language. It is possible that early in the populating of the Arctic regions some isolated migrating people from inner Asia may have gone up by way of the Baikal Sea and the Amur River to the narrowing corner of Asia from where they were able finally to step over to the Alaskan peninsula to discover America a long time before Columbus.

I am cognizant of the tentative nature of my remarks concerning the similarities in the general character of Eskimo and Indo-European and of the single words so far paired. Are they like hidden footprints in the grass, remainders of an old path that was once trodden in past times—or are they like will-o'-the-wisps? Can we rely on them? My task in this article has been only to ask, not to answer.

THE EARTH-DIVER AND THE RIVAL TWINS: A CLUE TO TIME CORRELATION IN NORTH-EURASIATIC AND NORTH AMERICAN MYTHOLOGY

EARL W. COUNT

More than fifteen years ago, I was struck by certain basic similarities between the Earth-Diver stories of the American Indians and those told by the Slavs. It appears that, setting aside the latter-day spread of Christianity, the cosmogonic notion of a primal sea out of which a diver fetches material for making dry land, is easily among the most widespread single concepts held by man. It stretches from Finland across Eurasia—roughly, over the USSR, the Balkans, Mongolia and Turkestan; it even appears in India and southeastern Asia; and it covers most of North America, excepting the Eskimo, the Northwest Pacific coast, the Southwest and most of the Southeast. Over this area, numerous other peculiar mythological ideas occur, often in conjunction with the Earth-Diver motif itself.

I have assembled from the literature about 230 specimens of the tale. Their scrutiny quickly broadens into a far greater study, one of a comparative mythology as yet scarcely touched. This study awaits the combined efforts of a host of scholars who would view the mythological systems of northern Eurasia and of North America simultaneously and comprehensively, noting the similarities and differences of *total pattern*, and relate the mythopoea to the social processes and religious and political evolution of the peoples on these two continents. This study would work from the hypothesis that mythology is the cultural philosophy of the folk, expressed symbolically and pragmatically, and therefore it is an integral part of their culture.

The present study has had to be set aside repeatedly, particularly during the war and its aftermath. A recent Viking Fund grant has been providential: the study may now go forward to completion.

I

The history of Earth-Diver studies indicates most American scholars have not been aware that the motif occurs outside the North American continent. European scholars, particularly Slavic and Finnish, from the mid-nineteenth century on have become acquainted with a limited number of American versions; but, with few exceptions, they have not been included in their analyses. There is a respectable literature on the Eurasiatic versions, in French, German, Finnish, Magyar, and especially in Russian.

55

Study of the Earth-Diver in Eurasia concerns itself with two main problems: time and place of the origin of the motif itself and, where, how, and when did the striking dualistic complexion attach itself to at least the majority of the tales?

The second of these problems has been the more fruitful. Briefly, there is hardly room for doubt that the dualistic dress stems from the Middle Ages, when the various Gnostic and Irano-Chaldean religious systems were competing for the allegiance of the inner-Asiatic folk—Finno-Ugric, Turko-Mongol, eastern Slavic. The systems which have left their most striking impress have been: Mazdaism, Zervanism, Manicheism, Bogomilism, Nestorianism, Buddhism, eastern Christian Orthodoxy—all *selon le cas*. Repeatedly it is possible to recognize, even in the very names of the *dramatis personae* (Satanail, Shaitan, Burkhan, Shulumys, Anromori, Khurmuzta, Zorvan, Mai-tere) more than one of these influences in one and the same story.

The dualistic climate of the Near and Middle East (hereinafter called Levant for brevity) in the early Christian Era had back of it centuries of socio-religious thinking in mankind's busiest habitation. What irradiations from those centuries of thought passed continuously over the highlands of Asia into its Northland, belong largely to the unwritten record. Possibly we should ascribe to that age the migration to North America of such motifs as the great turtle-atlas, the world-tree and the world-rock, the Cosmic Womb, the color-symbolism of the earth's four quarters, perhaps even the primal ocean itself with or without its earth-diver. To these we might add, from perhaps another and later time, the set of world-periods in which one of them is destroyed by a fiery flood; and more important than this, the superior world composed of several storeys. The issue is this: Undeniably, many earth-diver tales in both Eurasia and North America contain dualistic notions; are they genetically connected, or are they unrelated parallelisms?

European scholarship has chosen either to treat them as parallelisms, or else to consider that, for practical purposes in accounting for the origin and spread of the dualisms in the Eurasiatic tales, the American versions could be safely ignored. One bold exception has been Dähnhardt, who, as far back as the early twentieth century declared the American dualisms to be offshoots of the Medieval Eurasiatic. However, Dähnhardt's work hardly proved his case; we still are faced with the question whether the American dualisms are derived from the Eurasiatic, or whether they are autochthonous upon this continent. We are forced, then, to begin by first becoming acquainted with the dualistic intellectual climate of Eurasia in the early part of our era; second, we must follow through its effects upon the mythologies of the Eurasiatic folk; third, we must seek, in the American tales, not merely basic and general notions, but numerous details which correspond to the Eurasiatic, not only in form but in location. If successful, we should have a fairly definite dating for their passage from the Old World to the New, plus a limitation upon the time for the acculturative modifications. Let us carry out these three operations.

II

EURASIATIC DUALISMS

In the early Christian centuries, the Levant was in a philosophical turmoil over the nature of God, and the kind of universe and man which must follow logically from that nature. Specific issues were: Are the Good and Bad Principles coeval? If so, how may the Good be stronger than the Evil? Must not the Good, if it is really to be good at all, logically demand the existence of Evil? Is there an Absolute which is beyond and above both Good and Evil? In a dichotomy of Good and Evil, what is the nature of the Material in contradistinction to the Spiritual? Is Matter good or bad? How reconcile the presence of the spiritual man within a material body? Granted the presence of evil in both world and man—what scheme is there for eliminating the evil, so that the universe may ultimately be purified?

It is such thoughts which become expressed finally in the tales which make of Ormuzd and Ahriman a pair of twins fathered by Zorvan upon a primal mother; so that Ormuzd, who should be the older and more powerful, is born *viâ vaginâ*, while his evil brother bursts through his mother's side and so becomes the elder. However, which is really the elder? This is the age which produces the tradition, finally to be enshrined in the Bundahish, that Ormuzd is full of light and goodness and wisdom, and makes all things well; while his dark, evil, and ignorant brother, Ahriman, perverts or evilly caricatures Ormuzd's good works. Ahriman has his short day of a few thousand years; at last the two appoint a day of conflict, and Ahriman is defeated forever. The Christian and semi-Christian sects are also involved in these issues in many ways. There are stories in which Jesus Christ and Satan are twins, with Satan often the older; or, by a confusion of one archangel with another, Satan is replaced by Gabriel.

To Hebrews, orthodox Christians, and orthodox Mazdans the world was not inherently evil; the good creation had merely been marred by the evil principle. On the other hand, to the Gnostic sects and to the Iranian heretics, material was itself evil; and purification of the spiritual must ultimately involve annihilation of matter. There were many concrete expressions of these ideas. Was it God or the Devil, Ormuzd or Ahriman, who created man's body? This gives play to such notions as, that Satan made the body, but was powerless to animate it; God animated it. Or, God made the body and Satan sullied it while God was temporarily away, looking for a soul to animate it.

So also with the creation of the world itself. The Levantine notion of a primal sea is, of course, thousands of years older than the period we are dealing with. The idea that *terra firma* is condensed out of the primal waters is also very old; but it does give room for the play of fancy in this period. There still exist tales in the Levant which are manifestly part of the general "earth-diver pattern," yet where the earth is *condensed out of sea-foam* instead of being first fetched from the depths. Moreover, the evil Adversary—by whatever name he may be called—may in the Earth-Diver tales supply the matter, at God's command, while God applies the magic to it. The Adversary is often clever, but outwitted by circumstances; or he may be stupid. He may demand or beg a share of the created world and men; all that he receives is what the point of his staff rests upon; yet this is enough to give him a passageway to the nether world, which he peoples with monsters—reptiles, for instance. That he gains control of the dead as his share in mankind, sometimes turns out to be a shrewd business deal; and God has quite a hard and expensive time breaking the contract.

Many Eurasiatic details are interesting because they have replicas in some American earth-diving tale, and occur in the same position in it. Let me mention a few. Satan emerges from a bubble of foam on the primal ocean, to become God's companion; God being lonesome; a white raven is sent out to inspect the growth of the earth for its size; it eats corpses, and so is turned black. After the Creator has made the earth, a formidable antagonist appears, holding a staff, and demands a share of the creation. One trait must be cited particularly: the primal creative spirits are often ornithomorphic, either permanently or temporarily. As far west as the Ukrainian Christmas carols, they perch on a solitary tree which projects from a primal ocean; they dive for the earth. The tree can be equated with the luminous world-tree. In some of our tales, it is replaced by the central, primal rock, or by a mountain; or by a pillar.

III

A. EURASIATIC VERSIONS

Gypsy (Magyar).—When there was nothing on earth anywhere, except a vast quantity of water, God decided to make the world, only he did not know how to begin the job. As he was disgusted because he could not find a way and still more because he did not have a brother to consult with, he threw into the water the stick on which he leaned when he walked on the clouds. As soon as the stick struck the water there grew up immediately in that spot a gigantic tree, the roots of which reached down to the depths of the sea. On one of the branches of the tree sat the devil, who at that time was white, like the man God later created.

"Dear God, dear brother," cried the devil, and smiled, "I am really sorry for you. You have no brother nor companion. All right, I will be your brother and companion."

"Oh, that cannot be," answered God, "you cannot be my brother; no one can be my brother. Be my companion." . . . (There follows the earth-diving, and the devil's trickery in connection with it.)

Ukrainian.—At first, in the beginning of time, everywhere there was one great water. God flew over this water, and with him his faithful chief angel. And the Lord said to the angel, "Dive to the bottom and seize slime in your hands; it is time there were an earth." (After an unsuccessful trial, the angel finally obtains slime; God sows it; it grows; but the angel has hidden some of it in his mouth. He sows it and it forms topographic features which are barren and accursed. Wherefore God curses the angel, changes his name to Satanail.) "God flew higher and farther away, towards the sunrise, and Satan down and westward. From God's sowings came good people and lands, but from the devil's, evils and all unrighteousness and sin. Since then Satan with his retainers keeps himself usually over the water, in mill-ponds and fords; things that are of the water are all his children."

Yezids (Near East).—In the beginning the world was an ocean, in the midst of which was a tree created by divine power. God lived on this tree in the form of a bird, for many centuries. . . .

After that, the Lord created from his own reflection the Archangel Gabriel, also in the form of a bird, and placed him beside himself on the tree. After a little he asked him, "Who are you and who am I?" Gabriel answered, "You are you, and I am I." With this proud answer the archangel wished to give God to understand that each of them had a special importance and that he, Gabriel, could consider himself the peer of his creator. When the Lord heard Gabriel's answer, he became angry, he pecked the archangel and drove him from the tree. Gabriel flew off and began to cut the air with his wings.

He wandered into every part of the world. He flew for several whole centuries, but finally he tired and returned to alight again on the tree. . . .

Cheremiss.—The Cheremiss of the Kazan country believe in two chief and coeternal deities: the good Yuma and the evil Keremet, who appears as the younger brother of the other; but he is just as eternal as the other. In the beginning of the world Keremet wished to do just as did Yuma, but because of his lack of power he was able only to mar what his older brother created. When Yuma desired to create dry land, he instructed Keremet, who was swimming upon the sea in the form of a drake, to fetch from below the water a handful of earth. . . . Yuma breathed upon the handful of earth and commanded it to cover the surface of the water. . . . Then Keremet began to spit forth the portion of earth he had hidden; and wherever he spat there appeared mountains and rock-morasses. . . ." (Then Yuma creates man's body; while he is gone to get it a soul, Keremet bespittles it.)

Kuznetsk Tatars.—When as yet there was no heaven and earth, but only water, Ulgen descended to the water to create land. He thought and thought and did not know how to begin. There came then a man to Ulgen; Ulgen asked him, "Who are you?" "I too have come to create land," said he. Ulgen became angry and said, "I myself cannot create, how then can you?" And the man answered, "I will find something to create land immediately." (He finally dives, finds the mountain at the bottom of the sea, breaks off a piece and brings it up. He and Ulgen both strew, but Ulgen's land is good, while his is evil. So they quarrel.) "The man had a stick, on which he leaned while he stood and listened while the god abused him. At last Ulgen said, "You shall not be allowed on this land." He heard Ulgen and said to him, "Let me have as much of a place as the end of my stick will take up." Ulgen said, "I won't give even that." The man stood and cried. Then Ulgen relented and said, "Well, take that place. What will you do with it?" At these words, the man sank through the land he had asked for, and was gone. . . .

Mongolia.—In the beginning there was heaven and water, but the earth was not yet. Ochurmany lived in heaven, and he wanted to sit down somewhere. On conceiving the idea of creating the earth, he began to wish for himself a companion; there came Shagan-Shukuty, and immediately they started to dive into the water. . . .

B. NORTH AMERICA

Yokuts.—The whole earth was once covered with water, and there were no living creatures, save an eagle and a crow. There was a stump of a tree that projected above the surface of the watery expanse, and upon this the two birds were wont to stand and hold converse. Finally they became weary of the solitude, and between them they managed to create a duck, which swam about the stump. One day the duck dove to the bottom and brought up some earth on his bill. This struck the eagle and the crow as worth looking into, since they had never seen anything like it. They were very tired of having nothing but the stump to roost on, and as the mud brought up seemed promising, they entered into an agreement to keep the duck constantly employed diving for it. They could not agree, however, as to where the mud should be deposited. So they divided the world into two portions. (While the eagle was absent, the crow took for himself a larger half of the mud. When the eagle returned, they quarreled; the eagle seized the piles, and reversed their positions; hence the present position of the high Californian Sierras, and the low coastal range; also, why the eagle is honored and the crow despised.)

Crows.—The earth was all covered with water. Old-Man Coyote alone was going around on the water. Then a little coyote met him. "I am alone, I am looking for a companion, I'll meet one," he said. Then they met. There was no living thing then. They went around together. "We are alone, it is bad; let us make the earth." "All right, how shall we make it?" After some time ducks came flying. "You dear younger brothers, dive here," he said. "How shall we do it?" "Dive into the water, bring earth, we'll make the world," he said. They brought some. "Is there any?" "Yes." "Go, bring some." Four times they brought some, he took it and made the earth. . . .

Wahpeton Dakota.—Wakantanka, the "Great Spirit" came down from above in a rainbow before there was any earth—all was water under the heavens. As the rainbow neared the water, it rose up to meet it, and Wakantanka stood there upon the water.

(He makes two monsters—unktehi—one male, one female, out of right and left ribs respectively. He commissions them to be leaders of the Indians' festivals.)

There was no land whatever—all was water, and the two monsters, the unktehi, were in the midst of it. "We shall have to get soil and make land," they said. So they called two birds and two mammals to them. . . ."

Tuscarora.—(The tale begins with the lower, dark world with its primal ocean; the fall from the upper world by the woman pregnant with twins; the earth-diving; the placement of the earth upon the back of the turtle; the woman coming to rest upon the earth. She comes to her travail.) "While she was in the limit of distress one of the infants was moved by an evil opinion, and he was determined to pass out under the side of the parent's arm, and the other infant in vain endeavored to prevent his design." (The mother dies in the travail; the twins are self-sustaining, and grow up.) "The good mind was not contented to remain in a dark situation, and he was anxious to create a great light in the dark world; but the bad mind was desirous that the world should remain in a natural state. (The good mind now creates various natural features and bodies, vegetation and animals. At this point, some of the language and details indicate recent Christian influence. The bad mind follows after the good, and creates evil topography and reptiles; so that the good mind has to go back over it and rectify.) "The bad mind proceeded farther in his motives, and he made two images of clay in the form of mankind; but while he was giving them existence they became apes; and when he had not the power to create mankind he was envious against his brother; and again he made two of clay. The good mind discovered his brother's contrivances, and aided in giving them souls. . . . (At last) the bad mind offered a challenge to his brother and resolved that who gained the victory should govern the universe; and appointed a day to meet the contest. . . . On the day appointed the engagement lasted for two days . . . the good mind gains the victory. The last words uttered by the bad mind were, that he would have equal power over the souls of mankind after death, and he sinks down to eternal doom, and becomes the Evil Spirit. . . . (The details of this read startlingly like the Bundahish itself, and like the Zervanite story of the rival twins.)

IV

Surveying the entire area over which the Earth-Diver occurs, in Eurasia and North America, several very significant over-all features emerge. First, these two portions of the world contain a single distributional area; presumably, tales on both sides of the Pacific have a common origin. Second, the *dualisms* are very likely to have had a common origin; if so, they can be dated from the early centuries A.D. on the basis of the analyses done by European scholars. I am not, however, ready to commit myself as to whether the Earth-Diver is older than a dualistic overlay, or whether the Earth-Diver motif itself did not reach Inner Asia before the coming of the dualisms there. I say it this way, because earth-diving tales are known from ancient India, but without dualisms. In the third place—in spite of the area being basically a continuum from the present standpoint—there is a distinctive American pattern too, just as the rest of American culture has a distinctiveness.

Whatever the reasons for this distinctive culture, in the case of the Earth-Diver we are seeing reflected the distinctiveness in social, religious, and political patterns between Eurasia and North America. The cultures and empires of Inner Asia drew their integrating philosophies from out of the sophisticated religious systems which sent them missionaries. The empire-builders imported their religious systems, and attempted to make them serve as the philosophical support of the socio-political edifices they were erecting. Sophisticated religions, moreover, are book-religions. Among the folk themselves, "high" or literate traditions were imperfectly assimilated, and transmuted in their lore.

In America, there was no way for these things to happen. We can say confidently that no missionary of Asia's book-religions has ever left a trace of activity on this continent. The Eurasiatic dualisms could never have been carried over here as systems.

If the Asiatics made something of a potpourri out of the influences that flooded their world, then it was only a potpourri that they could transmit. The dualistic earth-diving motif could hardly have reached this continent only once. Every Asiatic who passed it on to an American had his own particular antecedents; and he embodied the fact that over the centuries, religious emphases in Eurasia changed. We must *not* expect to find that all American dualistic Earth-Diver tales will, when probed, converge upon one *souche* prototype.

The Americans, instead of importing book-religions, could do nothing but build their own systems. We find them doing something with the Earth-Diver for which, among the Eurasiatics, as far as I know, there was no necessity. I refer to the fact that some of the American Indians incorporated the tale into the recitative side of the rituals. The most striking illustrations of this are the Arapaho and Dakota Sun-Dance, and the periodic, formal public recitations by the Iroquois chiefs. Never, as far as I know, in Eurasia is the Earth-Diver called upon to perform such a heavy cultural duty. Earth-Diver undoubtedly is of lowly, folk-origin, and still is so after accepting the garb of the sophisticated dualisms. In Eurasia he even moves up, on occasion, to the literary dignity of becoming ensconced in such religious works as the Russian monastic "Bundle of Godly Books" (*Svitok Bozhestvennykh Knig*); but he never enters into a ritualization.

This, I think, is cardinal to remember when we turn to America. The simplest, least formalized Earth-Diver tales, those most nearly like some of the Asiatic, all things considered, are from Central California. There are others which are marginally aberrant and individualized, wherever there is a cultural frontier. The northern Athabascans seem to have the simplicity of impoverishment. The Plains area is tribally individualistic. The eastern Algonkians and the Iroquoians have some peculiar traits in common, but also some peculiar differences, and they have much remodeled their materials. Again, the Iroquoians also approach the Siouans. The Iroquoian Five Nations seem to have been on the way to elaborating a somewhat standardized version which was differentiating away from the versions told by the Huron-Wyandot. These remarks are made as much in a suggestive vein as in an assertive one.

V

CONCLUDING REMARKS

Over the area we have treated, North American mythology cannot ever be understood in terms confined to this continent alone, because much of it is a part of a larger area which includes so much of Eurasia; and the cultural tide has been prevailingly from west to east—Eurasia the donor, North America the recipient.

By corollary, whenever we can determine the time, place, and evolution of some Eurasiatic ideas whose presence in North America can also be established, we have begun to set in order the chronology of American culture-history, both relatively and absolutely.

The Jesuit missionaries to the Algonkians were somewhat dismayed by what they thought were perversions of Biblical truth which seemed to have gotten to this continent ahead of them. It is true that later tales collected from the Indians often have shown Christian graftings; but I think that sometimes even scientific investigators have been too ready to assume that certain of the similarities were such graftings. A little more study may convince us that some of the similarities are due to the fact that, when we crossed the Atlantic, we who swim in the westward stream of the Levant were confronted with the eastward-flowing stream from that same source. Although it was far less formal, it had traveled farther and faster.

NOTE.—Full references to the versions of tales from which excerpts are quoted in this paper will appear in the completed monograph.

THE "SEAT OF HONOR" IN ABORIGINAL DWELLINGS OF THE CIRCUMPOLAR ZONE, WITH SPECIAL REGARD TO THE INDIANS OF NORTHERN NORTH AMERICA

Ivar Paulson

In his recent survey of the North Eurasian primitive dwellings, Professor Dr. Gustav Ränk (374), my compatriot and former academic teacher at the Estonian University in Tartu (Dorpat), has pointed out the importance of a combined structural and functional analysis in dealing with the ethnological study of dwellings (*Hausforschung*). Certain parts of human habitations have their particular place (significance) in the economic, sociological and religious system of the native inhabitants. As always in primitive cultures, the "practical" and the "idealistic" aspect of the complex are inextricably interfused. This, for example, is well illustrated by the manifold uses of the so-called "bloody door" (*varr-lips*) in the rear of the ancient Lapp tent (187). Through this opening, which lies opposite to the common entrance, the Lapp man goes to his hunting trips and brings home his game, from which the epithet "bloody" seems to be derived. No woman is allowed to touch this sacred entrance through which the ceremonial rites for the family gods behind the tent are carried out. In connection with this holy door the whole rear part (*posjo*) of the tent is generally regarded as a holy place where the weapons, the house idols, and the magic drum of the shaman are preserved. It is the sitting-place of adult male members of the family or of honored male guests. Similar taboos as in the case of the "bloody door" obtain for women with regard to the "seat of honor."

A similar "seat of honor" is known to various peoples of Siberia, Central Asia and Northeastern Europe (374). The popularly known "holy corner" in the peasant home of the Orthodox Russians and other East European peoples has, as Professor Ränk stipulates, its primitive counterpart and historical background in the aboriginal dwellings all over North Eurasia.

The location of this "seat of honor" is adapted to the architectural character of the dwelling. In the four-cornered block-houses of the East European peasants as in the similar buildings of certain Turcs and Mongols in Central Asia and the Yakut and Amur peoples (Manchu, Gold, Gilyak, Ainu) it is one of the rear corners as seen from the front entrance of the house. In the circular tents of the nomads and migratory peoples of North Eurasia it is the rear part of the habitation which lies opposite to the common entrance in the front of the tent behind the central tent fire (374).

Sociologically the "seat of honor" stands in essential connection with the family and sib system and the division of sexes in their labor and their valuation. With the mainly patriarchal peoples of North Eurasia, the seat of honor per-

tains to the male family members, their economic occupations and the patri-
linear house gods (374).

If we now proceed across the Bering Sea to the New World, we find a kindred
phenomenon among the Indians of northern North America. As a special paper
considered by this Congress will bring fuller data on the subject, some illustrative examples with a brief summary of comparative results may be included
here.

In northern North America the "seat of honor" complex has quite the same
manifestations as in the Old World. It lies "in the rear" (without allowing a
nearer definition) in the circular tents of the various Athapaskan and Algonkian
tribes of the great subpolar interior area in Canada. Turner's monograph on the
Naskapi of Labrador (497) includes under Folklore a narrative "The starving
Indians" with a reference to the Indian custom of depositing most honored or
preferred objects (here a new suit of clothes) in a place in the rear of the tent,
opposite to the fireplace. It is there that the "seat of honor" for guests is found
in the Eastern Cree tent (429). In the dome-shaped and conical lodges of the
Northern Saulteaux (Ojibway), the honored place for guests was called wêk-
wondésen or "the center of the side," and was at the back of the lodge opposite
the door and as far away from it as possible (429, pp. 112–19).

In the elaborate Northwest Coast house the sleeping quarters of the owner's
family were at the far end of the house, the more desirable location generally
enclosed by a partition (plank wall) (148). At the rear, on the right, there was
often a similar enclosure for the safe-keeping of ceremonial objects, which
served also as a dressing room when ceremonies were in progress. So we have
here a New World counterpart to the four-cornered houses of North Eurasia
with the "seat of honor" or "holy corner" in one (here the right) corner of the
rear part of the building.

The third aspect of our phenomenon has a more restricted area of expansion
in both the Old and New World. In the so-called roof-door houses of certain
peoples in the outermost Northeast of Siberia (Kamchadal, Koryak, ancient
Chukchee) as in the northwest of northern America in the "Behring-Sea house"
of Jochelson (215), there is regardless of the adopted layout of the interior
another focal place of "holiness" and "honorableness." It is the top opening,
the entryway with a ladder for entrance. One can find vestiges of such an
"upward direction" of veneration also in the movable circular tent of the Cir-
cumpolar Zone, where the main tent pole is considered sacred as the "owner of
the tent," the "ladder to heaven" (in shamanistic rites) and is modified in the
mythology of North Eurasia into the "world pillar" motif under influences
from more southern ancient centres of civilization (188).

That our phenomenon is not restricted to northern North America alone (as
it also occurs in Eurasia) is borne out by instances of the Southwestern kiva,
the location of the sanctuary in Mexican and Central American temples and the
tipi of the Plains, where the heads of the family usually sit near the rear facing

the door (524). It seems that only one form of locating the "seat of honor" in a rear corner of an angular four-cornered structure, which is widely distributed in the Old World, appears in America at the Northwest Coast as so many other interesting cultural traits of this unique area in the New World.

To sum up the results of this study, of which the present paper is only a brief abstract with some illustrative examples, we may say that in northern North America as in North Eurasia the following common traits prevail:

1. The veneration of a particular place in the habitation is closely related to the structure of the dwelling. In circular shelters the "seat of honor" lies in the rear part behind the central tent-fire opposite to the door entrance. Angular houses have their "holy corners" in one of the rear corners. Roof-door houses have another "concentration point" of veneration in the entrance on the top of the house and the entry ladder.

2. From an economic point of view this home sanctuary stands in intimate connection with the main food-getting activities of the inhabitants. In our region it is primarily hunting as a masculine function.

3. Sociologically it is therefore the man who reigns supreme in the "holy place" and ousts the women toward the doorside.

The rear part of the dwelling, especially in the circular tents of the migratory peoples of the great Northern Interior Area, thus assumes the character of a "male side." But in America this trait is far less distinct than in North Eurasia, where patriarchalism is more strongly developed.

4. The magico-religious aspect of our problem is perhaps the most interesting but surely the most complex one as well. The primitive conception of "purity" quite materialistically understood, lies at the bottom of this phenomenon, as I understand it. The "purity" is a quality of all that is one's "Own," i.e., that belongs to one's own group (family, sib) and especially to its consanguineous members. In our region the male element of the unity is contrasted to the alien, the "dangerous," which manifests itself not only in strangers but also in their own "outsiders," the female members of the group. The aspiration for "purity" or "luck" in one's own home and particularly among the male adults of the house and in their economic occupation as the basis of livelihood for all the group naturally emerged from a fear of a magic "infection" through everything alien and strange. The "dangerous" (since unknown) is an idea so typical of the primitive mind generally. Only honored guests are allowed to share the holy place with the fathers of family.

Our bird's-eye view of this hitherto rather neglected subject may finally serve to show how universally interwoven with various aspects of human life is even such a simple thing as a certain revered place in a primitive dwelling. But after all we must not discard a simple psychological aspect of our phenomenon. Most of us chose a comfortable corner place in the train and, I think, any one of us would prefer to sleep in a bed standing near the wall of the bedroom rather than in its middle.

PETROGLYPHS AND PICTOGRAPHS IN BRITISH COLUMBIA[1]

Gutorm Gjessing

It is quite obvious that the distinction between petroglyphs and pictographs (i.e., between carvings and paintings) amounts to something much deeper than merely a difference in technique. While petroglyphs are practically confined to the coastal region, pictographs strongly predominate in the interior. Marked differences are also discernible as far as the choice of motives and style is concerned, even between petroglyphs and pictographs within the same area, as is the case in, say, the Kwakiutl or in the Coast Salishan territories. Finally, no petrographs have as yet yielded definite proof of European influence whereas pictographs very often show conclusive evidence of having been executed in post-contact times.

Consequently it is possible at once to substantiate a chronological difference between the two groups, the petroglyphs by and large being older than the pictographs. Thus it is not probable that the petrographs of the coastal region, as suggested by Harlan I. Smith, have diffused from the interior through the Bella Coola valley (439). Obviously the process must have been a much more complex one.

A motive occurring very frequently on pictographs from the Kwakiutl, Bella Coola, and Tsimshian territories, is "coppers," of which I have found in all one hundred and three specimens from twenty-one different panels (Fig. 1). On petroglyphs, however, "coppers" are extremely rare; in the material avail-

1. In the following discussion of some problems concerning petroglyphs and pictographs in British Columbia, I am indebted to the National Museum of Canada for the almost incredible friendliness and readiness to help which the staff in general and Dr. Douglas Leechman, chief curator of archeology, in particular, showed me during my visit to the Museum in January and February, 1947. I am also deeply indebted to Dr. Diamond Jenness, who readily and generously put his rich material at my disposal, and to Dr. Marius Barbeau for much valuable information. Any mention of Canadian petrographs (the term "petrographs" including both petroglyphs and pictographs) must begin with the name of the late Mr. Harlan I. Smith, who published on a number of different sites and also a list of all petroglyphs known up to 1927 (438), but whose greatest merit is undoubtedly the collection of an impressive, comprehensive body of data comprising notes, sketches, tracings, photographs, and maps. Even though Mr. Smith personally visited a large number of sites, this material had to a great extent been compiled and conveyed by amateurs. Nevertheless, the material is extraordinarily valuable, and I am deeply indebted to the National Museum for having been allowed to exploit this rich source. The illustrations accompanying the present paper are my own sketches and tracings based on this material. Consequently, this is not what I would call first-rate material; but, having had the opportunity to compare sketches, tracings, and photographs, I have been able during my work with this material to make quite a few emendations and supplementations.

able they are known from only two sites, one on Meadow Island in the Kwakiutl territory, published by Philip Drucker (111), and one in Elcho Harbor in
the Bella Coola territory (Fig. 2). Aside from one or possibly two "coppers,"
the latter petroglyphs represent a human figure wearing a mask, reminiscent of
the square-shouldered so-called "head-hunters" known from petroglyphs from
Pueblo I or II period in Utah (382). The figure is very closely related to some

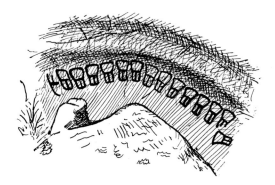

FIG. 1.—Nass River. Tsimshian Territory. Pictographs. Copied from photograph

FIG. 2.—Elcho Harbor, Bella Coola Territory. Drawn from photographs. Petroglyphs

mask-wearing human figures found at the mouth of Swallop Creek (Dean
Channel) in the Bella Coola territory (Fig. 3).

"Coppers" are generally assumed to be post-contact origin, although no
plausible European or Asiatic prototypes have been found. The recent dating of
some pictographs representing "coppers" is also evident from a panel on Petley
Point, Kingcome Inlet. This panel consists of one stratum executed in red pigment representing a Kwakiutl canoe, a series of "coppers," and the number
1921, and an additional black layer representing a Japanese fisherman's boat
with the name "Sutsuma" painted below, a "copper," a series of quadrupeds,

and the number 1927 (Fig. 4). Another panel on Petley Point represents two "coppers" and a European brig.

As far as I can see, however, there is no serious objection to the assumption that "coppers" may have been manufactured as early as prehistoric times. In olden times they were always made of native metal, and even after imported raw materials had come into use the specimens made of native copper were considered by far the most valuable. Presumably the "coppers" should be regarded as the result of the prehistoric transit-trade in native metal from Copper River in Alaska. They were mentioned by early travellers like Lisiansky in 1804 and Dunn in 1834 (339). Hence, I do not see sufficiently strong grounds for

FIG. 3.—Swallop Creek, Bella Coola Territory. Petroglyphs. Drawn from photographs and tracing.

accepting "coppers," as such, as conclusive proof of a post-contact origin of the petroglyphs concerned.

The pictographs on Petley Point show another motive typical of pictographs but entirely absent on petroglyphs: boats. Pictographs representing boats occur both in the coastal and the interior regions, and are not confined to British Columbia. Among pictographs on a panel at Mereworth Sound in the Kwakiutl territory, some represent a number of canoes and a European sailing-vessel, and a panel near Karlukwee on Turmour Island, also in the Kwakiutl territory, represents a man in a wagon drawn by a horse, a sun disk, two steamers with sails, a schooner, etc., probably from the last few decades of the nineteenth century (Fig. 5).

This is evidence that pictographs were clearly being executed on the northern North-west Coast up to modern times. Besides "coppers" and boats, the most

Fig. 4.—Petley Point, Kwakiutl Territory. The left part of the panel is executed in red pigment, while the part to the right is painted in black. Pictographs

Fig. 5.—Karlukwee, Turmour Island. Kwakiutl Territory. Pictographs. Copied from sketch by Fr. J. Barrow, slightly revised after photographs

common motives are human figures and human heads, often with large circular eyes, angular marked eyebrows, and circular or oval mouths.

The pictographs found in the Gulf of Georgia region which was occupied in historical time by Coast Salishan tribes, are executed in a markedly different style, partly representing other motives, and showing no evidence of European influence. While, strangely enough, marine animals are entirely absent on northern pictographs, salmon, sharks, and cetaceans as well as canoes, human figures, etc., are very common on those from the Salishan region (Fig. 6). A motive occurring only on pictographs from this region is a double-headed horned snake (Fig. 7) resembling the type known from petroglyphs in the South-west (383). It is obviously related to the *sisiutl*, or double-headed snake of the Nootka, Kwakiutl, and the ivory charms of Tsimshian sorcerers.[2] Even if European influence connot be ascertained, the pictographs of the Gulf of Georgia region are actually of quite recent date. This is substantiated by stylistic identity with the representations on the painted power boards used in the great winter ceremony of the Indians around the Puget Sound, especially of those from the central Puget Sound, the Squamish, Duwamish, etc. (Fig. 8). These power boards are apparently of the same kind as those grave boards "carved and painted with rude representations of men, bears, wolves and animals unknown. Some in green, others in white and red, all most hideously unlike nature," which Ross Cox reported to have seen in 1811 (518).

While the stylistic gap between the pictographs of the northern and southern parts of the North-west Coast is fairly great, the southern style is much more like the style of the pictographs of the interior Salishan region. Judging by the material available, pictographs are by far the most common in the area inhabited by the Shuswap Indians, but they are also found among other tribes such as the Lillooet and Thompson Indians, and also among the Okanagan and Kootenay. In the Athabascan territories, however, pictographs have as yet only been found in the regions inhabited by the Chilcotin and Carrier Indians occupying the south-eastern part and thus being the neighbors of the Salish-speaking Indians. The motives are, of course, partly different from those along the coast, quadrupeds such as mountain goats, mooses, deer, bears and bear paws playing a much more important role. A motive very typical of inland pictographs both in British Columbia and Washington, is a human figure with two smaller human satellites standing within a rounding or below an arc provided with rays or spurs at the upper side—obviously some mythic figure (Fig. 9). Outside the territory of the interior Salish, this figure is apparently unknown. Its stylistic character, however, does not differ very much from that of the Coast Salishan pictographs, as can be seen for example from the way in which salmon or human figures are depicted (Fig. 10). It is approximately the same style that characterizes the pictographs in other parts of Canada and the United States. We have no means of determining the chronology of these inland pictographs except

2. Verbal information from Dr. M. Barbeau, Ottawa.

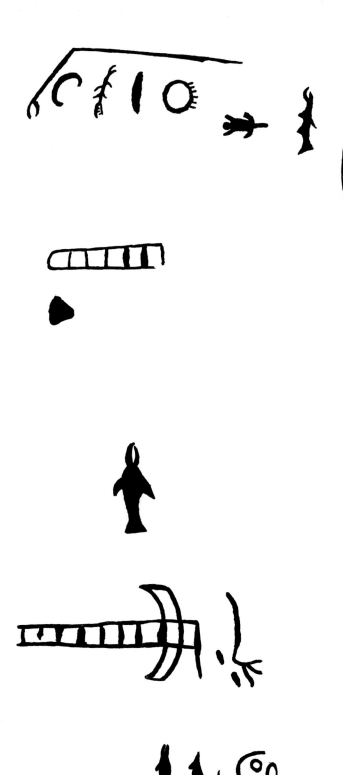

Fig. 6.—Sakinaw Lake. Coast Salish Territory. Pictographs. From sketch by Fr. J. Barrow, revised after photograph

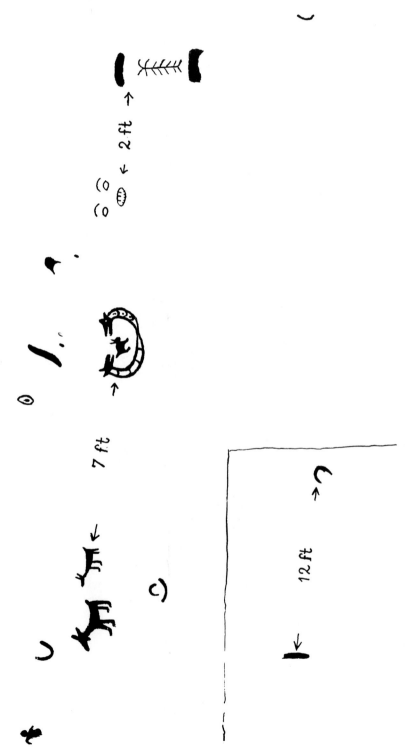

Fig. 7.—Salmon Arm. Coast Salish Territory. Pictographs. From sketch by Fr. J. Barrow

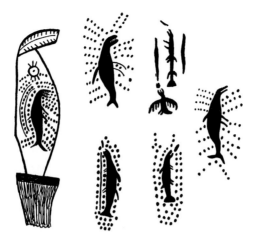

Fig. 8.—Representations from painted power boards. Puget Sound. Redrawn after Waterman.

Fig. 9.—Pictographs from two different localities at Mara Lake. Shuswap Territory

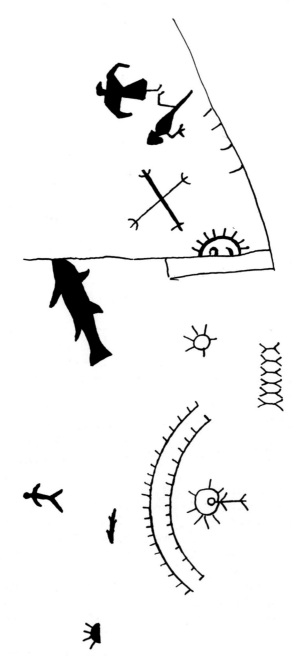

Fig. 10.—Sicamour. Shuswap Territory. Pictograph. Sketch revised after photograph

74

through the stylistic conformity with the Coast Salishan material. In discussing the chronology of North American petrographs, however, we must always take into consideration that the rate of style change certainly has been accelerated in post-contact times, in other words, the styles were more static before the culture contacts deeply penetrated Indian life.

Proceeding to the petroglyphs, we should recall that Boas suggested a northern origin of the classic North-west Coast style. In his opinion, this style was introduced into Kwakiutl territory comparatively late, and it was preceded by the characteristic art style, primarily known from war clubs, of Western Vancouver Island and particularly of the whole Gulf of Georgia area (47). Specimens collected by Captain Cook, Vancouver, Captain Magee, and other early travellers, indicate that this was the prevailing style among the Nootka and the Coast Salish at the time of the first contact. The petroglyphs support Boas' theory in so far as the classic style is beautifully represented on the southeastern Alaska petroglyphs published by Emmons (Fig. 11) and Keitahn (116). It rarely occurs in Kwakiutl territory (Fig. 12). But as long as the chronology of the petroglyphs is so uncertain, it is not possible to determine whether these Tlingit petroglyphs are contemporaneous with or more recent than the Tsimshian, Kwakiutl, and Bella Coola panels. The introduction of the classic style into the Kwakiutl territory must have begun at least as early as the latter half of the eighteenth century, since Cook collected ceremonial masks decorated in this style in 1778. The chronology of the North-west Coast style is, however, not yet fully known. Since no petroglyphs show any evidence of European influence as pictographs frequently do, it seems reasonable to suggest an earlier dating for petroglyphs in the classic style.

In the territories inhabited by the Coast Salishan tribes the petroglyphs are stylistically rather heterogeneous. Some of them are executed in the typical style of the war clubs (Figs. 13 and 14, *d*, *f*, *g*), while others are characterized by figures, mostly animal, decorated with horizontal, often undulating, parallel lines (Fig. 15, 16). This trait probably belongs to the same stylistic milieu, possibly representing an older phase. Similar parallel lines or zigzag lines are found on some of the war clubs. On the other hand, some of the petroglyphs representing human figures with faces of the war club style, have semi-naturalistic bodies (Fig. 13), reminiscent of some rather naturalistic petroglyphs which in all probability are late (Fig. 17). These are never associated with animals decorated with parallel lines, which, however, are sometimes found on rocks together with human figures with circular eyes and mouths, reminiscent of the majority of petroglyphs (and also many pictographs) from Kwakiutl and other northern territories. However, a motive very common in the latter region, non-outlined human faces with large, circular eyes and oval or triangular mouths, is entirely unknown in the Gulf of Georgia region, where the faces are always outlined. Still there seems to exist a relationship between these types of human faces.

FIG. 11.—Petroglyphs from S.E. Alaska. Tlingit Territory. Redrawn after Emmons

FIG. 12.—Bella Coola River. Bella Coola Territory. Petroglyphs

Fig. 13.—Hornby Island. Coast Salish Territory. Petroglyph

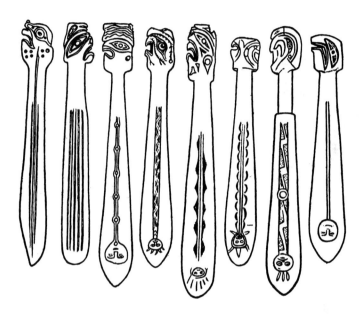

Fig. 14.—War Clubs. Coast Salish. Redrawn after Boas and H. F. Smith

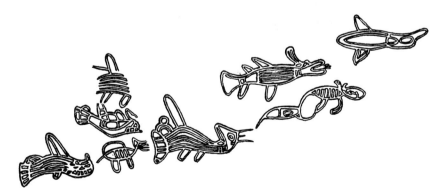

Fig. 15.—Sproat Lake. Coast Salish Territory. Petroglyphs. Redrawn after H. F. Smith

77

FIG. 16.—Nanaimo. Coast Salish Territory. Petroglyphs. Redrawn after H. F. Smith

FIG. 17.—Hornby Island. Petroglyph

78

Related to these faces is also a human head carved on a big boulder at Nanaimo on South-eastern Vancouver Island in Coast Salishan territory (Fig. 18). It is more elaborate, though, with an angular nose, tattooings, teeth, and hair or some headdress. According to an unsigned article in *The Daily Province* of May 26, 1926, this boulder was found fourteen feet below the surface and ten feet beneath the roots of a gigantic cedar tree. The annual rings showed that this cedar was more than a thousand years old, just how much more could not be determined owing to decay of the inner part of the trunk. If this information is reliable the carving must presumably be at least fifteen hundred years old!

Consequently we have to consider the possibility that these faces, outlined or non-outlined, with large circular eyes, which are found all over the Pacific world,

Fig. 18.—Nanaimo. Coast Salish Territory. Petroglyph. From photograph

represent the oldest substratum of petroglyphs in the whole North-west Coast area.[3] They were partly superseded in the south by the style of the war clubs, in the north by the classic style. But if this is actually the case, these types of human faces have survived the coming of the new classic style, because they are common on pictographs of the northern group.

In a short paper like this it has been possible only to touch very lightly on a few of the many problems involved. A closer study of the material will reveal interesting evidence of diffusion which, however, cannot be treated here. Likewise, it is impossible to deal with the important problem of the significance of the petrographs. In a discussion of these problems the petrographs cannot be viewed in isolation, but must be looked upon as an integral part of the whole cultural pattern of prehistoric and historic times.

3. This view might perhaps be supported by the prehistoric carvings in bone from the Dalles-Deschutes region, published by W. Duncan Strong, W. E. Schenck, and J. H. Steward, *Archaeology of the Dalles-Deschutes Region* (478).

CULTURE AREA AND CULTURE DEPTH: WITH DATA FROM THE NORTHWEST COAST[1]

Marian W. Smith

I. INTRODUCTION

It is not necessary for the readers of this paper, composed largely of anthropologists, to be reminded of the importance of historical reconstruction. No anthropological problem, even in such realms as culture and personality, can ever be adequately explored on a single time level. Cultural problems, by practice as well as by definition, carry the investigator into an examination of the relationship of present to past, an examination which too quickly, in the absence of full historical data, must shift to the relationship of "here" to "there." As Linton has aptly phrased this latter phase of our work: "The only universally applicable approach to . . . historical reconstruction is that of the study of trait distributions and the subsequent analysis of these distributions" (271, p. 367).

In modern studies of diffusion made by American scholars, wide distributions of single traits are slighted and attention tends to center upon clusters of associated traits. Both in archeology and ethnology, recent work has emphasized proportionate trait figures in attempts to arrive at definitions of cultural wholes. All American anthropologists working in the field of historical reconstruction insist upon keeping within the limits of reasonably controllable time spans and space boundaries. And, although the culture area concept has been variously criticized in recent years, these anthropologists also depend upon mapping techniques to classify their distributional data and they often point up their conclusions by redefining area limits or by reducing recognized areas to subareas.

One cause of dissatisfaction with culture area designations as they now exist is the fact that they classify data in a sort of artificial timelessness. All available data are lumped together and the main effort is to be as inclusive as possible. In Wissler's use of the concept he delineated his areas first on the basis of particular kinds of data, arriving at food areas, areas drawn from textile arts, work in stone and metals, social groupings, mythology, etc. Where a number of these overlapped, showing a distinctive syndrome of traits, he placed the centers of his culture areas. The tribes falling within such limits were called "typical" of the area. Acceptance of the major points of Wissler's classification has been so general, and followed his phrasing so immediately, that American anthropolo-

1. All my work on the Northwest Coast owes its greatest debt to the financial assistance over a period of years of the Columbia University Council for Research in the Social Sciences.

gists have tended to regard his areas as *faits accomplis*. Refinements have occurred, first, through efforts to correlate culture areas with areas drawn from
other data, notably with "natural" areas, and second, through attempts to
arrive objectively, even statistically, at more adequate definitions of the syndromes of central or typical traits. Yet any careful reworking of diffusion data,
such as Ray's "Cultural Relations in the Plateau," has returned to Wissler's
original method of mapping separate items of culture. Refinements have taken
such a method for granted and have accepted Wissler's basic assumptions as to
the historical relevance of distributional data and the necessary retention of
discrete data within integrated cultural wholes. American anthropologists have
consistently frowned upon any method which tears a trait from its context.

A third elaboration in Wissler's culture area technique has grown out of discussions of the relative merits of the diffusion and invention of traits. Emphasis
in these discussions has been overwhelmingly placed upon process. Kroeber,
to whom many of the refinements in the culture area concept are due, has, for
instance, relied upon a dynamic feeling for process when he has suggested such
useful expressions as "stimulus diffusion" and when he has changed Wissler's
focus from culture "center" to culture "climax." It is this preoccupation with
process which can be seen to underly recent studies of culture change and the
most self-conscious of these have evolved into the new field of "acculturation"
studies. Through careful control of culture change, especially under conditions
of culture contact, students of acculturation have demonstrated the great
multiplicity of factors which may account for the acceptance, rejection, integration or redefinition of traits and complexes. Working largely within the frame of
known history, these are the students who are most impatient with the inadequate treatment of time depth afforded by the culture area technique. They are
fully conscious of the magnitude of the changes which may occur even in short
time spans and are justly critical of the deceptive ease with which historical
reconstructions may blossom overnight out of the juxtapositions of relatively
static culture areas.

It is the purpose of this paper to point out how, in one region, the values of the
culture area concept in the dimension of space may be retained without slipping
into overgeneralization in the dimension of time. By keeping rigidly to the distributional data *per se*, it becomes possible to map several "areas" which can be
seen to fall into relative positions on a time scale. To characterize these it is
necessary to bear processes of diffusion in mind. In particular, then, I shall make
use of newly published data to set up a partial sequence of culture areas in the
Northwest Coast of America, and I shall distinguish certain diffusion processes
through which areas may be variously designated.

II. THE SALISH, THE PLATEAU, AND CALIFORNIA

Wissler's first plotting of distributions in western North America revealed a
Salmon Area which included the territory surrounding all the streams draining

into the Pacific Ocean from San Francisco Bay to Bering Straits. The "historical tribes" of this large area he further divided among four culture areas, the Plateau, California, the North Pacific Coast, and the Eskimo Area. The north and south extremes of this region Wissler recognized as culturally aberrant, grouping the Alaskan Eskimo with an Arctic distribution of traits rather than with North Pacific Coast (523, p. 229) and placing northern California with the area of that name although isolating it from other parts of the state on the basis of similarities between it and North Pacific Coast (523, p. 226). For cases such as these he used the term "intermediate." Retaining the Plateau as a unit, with its center among the Interior Salish, he classified areas within it only on the basis of the intrusion of Plains traits from the east. The North Pacific Coast he "treated under three subdivisions: (*a*) the northern group, Tlingit, Haida and Tsimshian; (*b*) the central group, the Kwakiutl tribes and the Bella Coola; and (*c*) the southern group, the Coast Salish, the Nootka, the Chemakum and some Columbia River groups" (523, p. 227). He held the Coast Salish to be typical of the southern group and saw a progression between the three subdivisions in terms of artistic and ceremonial features which thinned out as one moved southward. It should be particularly noted that, although he made no very great point of it, Wissler allows for historical depth in his area scheme by arranging separate areas on an archeological level. For the region under discussion, these archeological areas parallel the cultural ones with the exception of substituting "Columbia Basin" for Plateau. This serves to shift the center in the central and southern groups from the upper Columbia to the middle and lower reaches of the river for the earlier period loosely described as "archeological."

As early as 1895 Mason had spoken of four northwestern areas: the North Pacific Coast, the Columbia Drainage, the Interior Basin, and California-Oregon. In 1907, he changed the second of these "ethnic environments" to include the Fraser drainage and called his new area the Columbia-Fraser Region (246, pp. 6–7; 301, p. 428). The Interior Basin, home of the Shoshoni, is now often treated as a separate unit related to the Californian area which is normally extended into southern Oregon. Mason left the area of our interest, therefore, in two divisions: the North Pacific Coast which included all the tribes from the Tlingit to the Coast Salish, and the Columbia-Fraser Region which covered the western section of Wissler's Plateau.

In 1924, Goddard dealt with the coastal strip from southern Alaska to south of the Columbia, popularizing the North Pacific Coast under the designation, now so widely accepted, of the "Northwest Coast" (148). In this treatment Goddard handled all the tribes as though they represented slight variations upon a basic pattern and Wissler's overlapping distributions were lost sight of in a concentration of traits which lacked not only a temporal dimension but also any clearly drawn spatial dimension.[2]

2. It should be added in justification of Goddard that, in view of the nature of the handbook series, it is difficult to see how he could have done otherwise. The series furnishes excel-

In 1939, Kroeber reviewed North American culture areas in checking them against natural areas and reduced their number from nine (north of Mexico) to six. Under these conditions, the Northwest Coast is somewhat larger than Goddard's area of the same name. It covers a Northern Maritime region corresponding to Wissler's northern, a Central Maritime corresponding to Wissler's central and including Kwakiutl and Bella Coola, four other subdivisions among which is divided the territory of Wissler's southern, and a seventh, the Lower Klamath, covering northwestern California. The southern extreme of Wissler's Salmon Area is thus placed directly within Northwest Coast limits. The second culture area of interest here is called by Kroeber the Intermediate and Intermountain and includes three major subdivisions: the western portion of Wissler's Plateau under the designation of the Columbia-Fraser Plateau, the Great Basin, and California in which only central California remains (246, pp. 28–31, 49–59; 248, pp. 785–89). This noticeable elaboration and realignment of the southern parts of the area west of the Rockies seems to reflect two factors: an increased amount of detailed information for these regions, for recent work has centered here, and also a real complexity and localization of cultural traits. This is likewise an "intermediate" region, to use Wissler's term, and consequently more difficult to classify within standard culture area boundaries.

A recent résumé of the archeology of this southern region underlines its cultural complexity (444) and the emergence of a new area, the Middle Fraser, further complicates the picture of cultural relations. The lower reaches of the Fraser River are clearly intermediary between the Gulf of Georgia (21) and Puget Sound Salish (441) and it had previously been assumed that a similarly simple transition between Interior and Coastal Salish occurred in the neighborhood of Yale on the Fraser. The Middle Fraser, covering the Fraser drainage area from Yale to Mission, has been distinguished in the last few years on the basis of mythology (76), house form (442), and physical type (77) and, although it seems to mark the bilingual transition usual in the region from east to west, the evidence for considerable cultural uniqueness and continuity cannot be overlooked.

Ray's intensive work in the Plateau has distinguished a center of "older and more fundamental traits" among the Southern Okanogan, Colville, Sanpoil, Lower Spokane, and Columbia (379, p. 149) and he also points to a western, longitudinal subarea extending the entire length of the Plateau from Carrier to Klamath. A similar longitudinal subarea lies along the eastern border of the Plateau and is characterized by the intrusion of Plains traits. Whereas this eastern border region is marked "by a distinct temporal aspect" (379, p. 147)

---

lent short summaries of bewildering masses of data and is invaluable for laymen and beginning students but, through its oversimplification within culture area bounds, it has brought the culture area concept somewhat unwarranted criticism from many scientific sources. It is interesting to note that Wissler's Plains volume, the first of the series, is the one to have received sharpest critical evaluation.

which reflects the recent introduction of Plains influence, the western subarea, including many of the Interior Salish, is not so "temporally qualified." Cultural contacts between this eastern Plateau region and southern Northwest Coast are very striking. The southern parts of the western Plateau bear clear resemblances to Puget Sound and the cultural complexities of the Fraser suggest old and continued contacts over the whole of its drainage.

Following Kroeber's lead, and utilizing the new material available since his formulization was made, Ray's western longitudinal subarea may be included with the Northwest Coast. The reasons for including northwestern California (Lower Klamath) seem equally valid for this western mountain strip. Four areas have been distinguished in Puget Sound: the Puyallup-Nisqually, Central, Northern, and Inland Puget Sound (441, pp. 203–6). The last of these parallels the Cascades along the upper reaches of the streams and I should like to suggest at this time that Ray's western longitudinal band be incorporated with Inland Puget Sound and the Middle Fraser to form an eighth subdivision to Kroeber's present seven Northwest Coast areas. This subdivision might conveniently bear the name of the Interior, Foothill, or Upriver region. Ray also describes three lateral subareas in the Plateau: a northern Athabascan group, the Canadian or northern, and the American or southern. These north-south divisions he believes to be "the most definite and distinctive of any in the Plateau." It is an open question whether the far northern one should be included in our Interior or Upriver area. But the Canadian Plateau is reflected in the Middle Fraser and the American Plateau in Inland Puget Sound. These two west-of-the-mountain areas bear the same sort of striking difference to each other remarked by Ray for the lateral areas of the Plateau, and north-south divisions within the Interior area may be taken as highly significant. To the south, the Interior or Upriver area would adjoin Kroeber's Lower Klamath to form a continuous Northwest Coast culture area.

Such a reallocation of Wissler's western Plateau would place Mason's Columbia-Fraser Region in the Northwest Coast and remove much of Kroeber's Columbia-Fraser Plateau from the Great Basin and California. I am in complete accord with Ray's insistence upon the unique character of his Plateau material which in many key complexes is amazingly unlike classical Northwest Coast. But in these same key complexes Puget Sound is also unlike classical Northwest Coast except for a thin veneer of traits which never reached the Inland Puget Sound region at all. The Plateau subterranean house occurs in the Middle Fraser and the Plateau mat lodge on Puget Sound, but it is in the realm of social traits, such as pacifism and the slight importance given to rank, that the Interior area shows its greatest cohesion. Future work may determine that our Interior or Upriver area belongs south with Kroeber's Great Basin and California instead of west with the more southern areas of Northwest Coast, and it may show the existence of two separate, and narrower, longitudinal bands in the Plateau: the westernmost of which belongs with the western foothills to form a truly Foothill or Interior area and a central, truly intermontane, strip which includes Ray's center of old and fundamental traits. North-south divisions will certainly remain important. Whatever future elaborations there may be, the evidence for the unity of these regions east and west of the watershed of the Cascades and Coast Ranges seems difficult to avoid.

I confess to some dissatisfaction with the classifications I have just presented. Of course the distributions should all be replotted, but my discontent goes deeper than any simple review of the data could satisfy. Having recognized a continuous distribution of traits in the Interior, Foothill, or Upriver region, it does not seem to me of prime significance whether it is retained within the Plateau as Ray might wish, handed over to the Great Basin and California as Kroeber might conceivably desire, or placed with the Northwest Coast as I have done here. It certainly has distributional ties in all of these directions. Yet under our present arrangement of culture areas, historical reconstructions must rely upon exactly this type of decision, and to beg the question of final placement of an area is to beg the whole question of its historical relations. This seems quite unnecessarily cut and dried. But before turning to further development of this theme, I should like to review briefly another region within the Northwest Coast.

III. THE BELLA COOLA AND THE KWAKIUTL

All culture area arrangements agree in placing the Bella Coola with the Kwakiutl despite the fact that the Bella Coola are a Salish-speaking people, isolated from other Salish, and the Kwakiutl speak a language classified with that of the Nootka as "Wakashan." Wissler places only the Bella Coola and the Kwakiutl in his central group of North Pacific Coast. Goddard treats the Bella Coola and the Salish of Vancouver Island among the typical Northwest Coast tribes along with the Kwakiutl, Nootka, and more northern tribes. He omits from this unit the Coast Salish of the mainland and the more southerly Salish groups (148, p. 14). Kroeber follows Wissler by placing the Bella Coola with his Central Maritime and further identifies them with the Kwakiutl by grouping the two tribes together to form the northern subtype of the Central Maritime, the southern subtype including the Nootka and seaward tribes of Washington.[3] In looking at the ethnological data, one sees obvious similarities in material culture, in art, in ceremonial detail and in ceremonial organization which certainly link the Bella Coola and the Kwakiutl. Whole blocks of Bella Coola ceremonial life can be duplicated among the Kwakiutl. Since these are just the cultural fields in which Northwest Coast development has been most spectacular and which are most characteristic of the area, it was inevitable that our present use of area designations should place the two tribes together.

For many years, knowledge of the Bella Coola was dependent upon Boas'

---

3. In view of the importance of the east-west longitudinal areas given for the Plateau, it should also be noted that these two "subtypes" run as much east-west of each other as they do north-south.

work of 1897 (50). Now, fortunately, the recent publication of McIlwraith's data (304) offers opportunity for a reappraisal of their position. First, it should be noted that Goddard's map of Northwest Coast tribes carries Bella Coola territory closer to the open-water islands of the Pacific than Boas' data indicated (for revised boundary of Bella Coola see Fig. 1). McIlwraith's definition of Bella Coola territory agrees in every important detail with Boas' and it can now be stated with great surety that although the Bella Coola are often referred to as a "coastal" people, they actually lived at the upper heads of deep-set salt water estuaries. Like many Coast Salish, they were a people of inland waters.

Much of their total relation to their environment and to their neighbors can also be duplicated farther south. Although no complete comparison of Bella Coola and more southerly Salish can be attempted here, the Bella Coola villages, like other Salish villages as far south as Puget Sound, formed autonomous units tied only through common territory, common cultural practices and commonly recognized linguistic similarities. Three general groups were granted loose kinship by these factors but, before the remnants of population joined at the mouth of the Bella Coola Valley drainage, no common name applied to them all. The Tälio, at the mouth of a river of the same name, lent their name to the eight or more villages of South Bentinck Arm; the Kimsquit villages numbered about the same and were called after the drainage of the Kimsquit River which empties into what is now Dean Channel; the Bella Coola proper occupied at least twenty-six villages scattered the full length of the Bella Coola Valley and took their name, as did the entire drainage, from a village at the mouth of the river. Each village within these groups retained its own local autonomy. A second river, the Dean, flows into Dean Channel and this was formerly occupied by Bella Coola who were supplanted by Carrier (304, p. 16); the lower sections of Dean Channel were occupied by a people speaking a variant Bella Bella (Kwakiutl) dialect and forming a link between Bella Bella and Kimsquit (304, p. 21); and Kwatna Bay was held by Bella Bella although at least one village was practically bilingual (304, p. 19).

Strangely enough these conditions sound more like Puget Sound than like Gulf of Georgia Salish. The bilingual villages, the evidence of prolonged and gradual contact through intermarriage, the pressure of a foreign language group moving west along the rivers (in this case the Carrier, on Puget Sound the Sahaptin), the emphasis upon drainage systems, the lack of any political organization even such as might have been expected to stop the Carrier advance— all of these factors can be duplicated on Puget Sound. Even more striking is the fact that Bella Coola villages were strategically located for fishing; each village controlled the site either of what McIlwraith calls a major "salmon weir" or a "fish trap." The villages seem to have been identified with a local means of subsistence in a manner reminiscent of Puget Sound but *not* of Gulf of Georgia and Fraser River Salish (441, pp. 199–202).

The independence of each village unit with its often unfriendly, but never

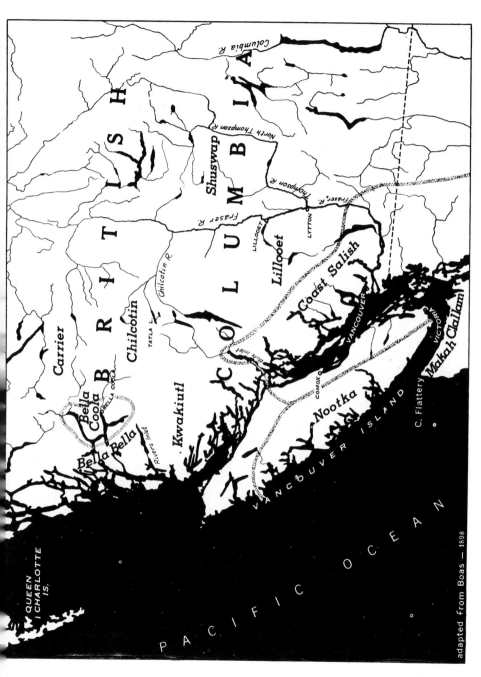

FIG. 1.—Revised map of Bella Coola territory, showing their southern neighbors

adapted from Boas — 1898

militantly organized, relations to its neighbors again reflects Puget Sound rather than the Gulf of Georgia. On the short Samish drainage system just north of the present Swinomish Reservation, the Upper Samish spoke a Salish similar to that of the Lower Skagit and other groups to the east and south, while the salt-water Samish spoke a Lhungen dialect like the Salish to the west and north. Animosities between these two groups occurred within the historic period and it seems clear that the Upper Samish represent the former population of the entire drainage system which had been driven back by Lhungen speakers. The displacement on the lower and salt water sections of the drainage seems to have been completed by the early part of the nineteenth century (81, pp. 152–53). But the Lhungen are a Gulf of Georgia and Fraser River people and this is the farthest south their inroads went. Among Puget Sound Salish one cannot find a parallel for this type of aggressive advance. There were fights and aggressive acts, but territory was actually taken over only through a kind of seepage due to intermarriage.

"Pacifism" is a trait cited by Ray for the Plateau and the same type of contrast in emphasis on rank which he notes between Plateau and "Northwest Coast" is now given between Bella Coola and Kwakiutl. The Kwakiutl apparently laugh at the Bella Coola, saying that among them "all are chiefs." Despite all the attention paid to privileges of rank and inheritance, status among the Bella Coola was achieved, and McIlwraith makes the flat statement that "any Bella Coola can rise to a position of importance" (304, p. 170). McIlwraith also furnishes an example of a dog for which a potlatch was given and which became, consequently, a "chief." This was how foreign to political power or leadership was the chieftaincy acquired by the Bella Coola! With the economic validation of the potlatch and all the paraphernalia of ceremonial rank, with supreme personal arrogance, yet the Bella Coola manage to seem amazingly unlike the Nootka and the more northern Northwest Coast tribes.

All such social traits suggesting eastern and southern provenience could be greatly overrated for the Bella Coola. Their importance, however, must be viewed against the fact that Boas, largely on linguistic grounds, saw the Bella Coola as migrants from the Fraser River (50, pp. 122–23). Again on purely linguistic grounds, a recent study of Salish distributions makes the following reconstruction: "The Lillooet in their original location must have filled the intervening space between the Bella Coola and Shuswap. The Bella Coola owe their isolation from other Salish groups to the intervention of the Chilcotin moving southward (pushing the Lillooet before them) and of the Kwakiutl moving inland from the coast" (481, p. 166). According to this, Salish-speaking peoples once extended in an unbroken line from the Fraser to the Bella Coola. Other data support a southward movement of Chilcotin, although an inland movement of Kwakiutl seems less well documented. The Bella Coola River rises in an open plateau which renders travel possible for long distances, and Chilcotin as well as neighboring Carrier descend through the valley. Various headwaters of the Chilcotin River, which is a tributary of the Fraser, are thus within relatively easy reach of the Bella Coola drainage. This is the route by which Boas himself entered Bella Coola territory from the Fraser in 1897. And it may well have been the one used by the Bella Coola at some earlier period.

As new evidence accumulates, it seems fairly certain that the closest ties of the Bella Coola are via the interior river systems to the upper or middle Fraser River rather than via the lower reaches of their own drainage system to present day salt-water Salish of the Gulf of Georgia and the lower Fraser.

Boas had also earlier pointed out a number of striking similarities between the social organization of the Kwakiutl and the Bella Coola. The Bella Bella and the Bella Coola both favor a form of local endogamy and both live in basic village communities with a prevalence of paternal descent (46). McIlwraith reaffirms endogamy for the Bella Coola and it is interesting, although probably not directly relevant, that endogamous villages are also now reported from the Puyallup-Nisqually (440, p. 42). Boas points out the existence of a transition between the northern tribes with their clearly marked maternal and paternal lines, the weak clans of the Bella Bella, and the strong village community of the Kwakiutl which is not, as in the north, subordinated to the exogamic clan but which is identical with that of the Coast Salish of the Gulf of Georgia. He found kinship terminologies reflected a basic bilaterality for the Bella Bella, northern Kwakiutl, Kwakiutl proper and for the Bella Coola. It has since been determined that Puget Sound terminologies reflect the same quality. This contrasts sharply with the unilateral northern systems and the total effect of Boas' comments was to establish two basic areas of social organization on the Northwest Coast—a northern and a southern, with the Kwakiutl tribes as transitional between them reflecting clan practices particularly in the inheritance of rank and privilege.

Murdock's recent, detailed study of kinship terminologies (337) makes the same basic bifurcation of the Northwest Coast into northern and southern halves although he adds some interesting elaborations. He derives his four Salish samples "from an ancestral Hawaiian structure." (It should be remembered that Murdock's terms are type names, they do not refer to necessary historical connections. Thus, "Hawaiian" is the type to which the Hawaiians also belong, not a type derived from that of the Hawaiians.) The Flathead, Klallam and Sinkaietk still preserve organizations of this type, while the Eskimo structure of the Quinault contains intimation of a derivation from the Hawaiian type (337, p. 350). Since the Kwakiutl are analyzed as Patri-Hawaiian from Normal Hawaiian (337, p. 338), they can be classified with the Salish on this score. The Haida and Tlingit are both classified as Avunco-Crow from Normal Crow, and the Tsimshian as Avunco-Iroquois (through three steps), so that they fall well outside any Hawaiian type organization.

It is unfortunate that Murdock's Salish sample is so small, only about a third of available material is included, but what there is identifies Clallam with

Kwakiutl and corroborates the recent southern migration of these people which is strongly attested by other data. A second interesting result is to point up the relative historical complexity of Quinault as compared to Clallam-Kwakiutl. This agrees with other suggestions that Quinault link through the Chehalis with southern and central Puget Sound where an old and integrated culture seems to be represented.

Although the Bella Coola seem to have clear-cut ties with the Interior region of the Fraser, despite their ceremonial ties to Kwakiutl, the Kwakiutl, for their part, seem to have a number of traits of social organization in common with the Salish. This reminds one of Sapir's postulated linguistic relationship between Wakashan and Salish, which has recently been revived. The period of unity of the two language families has actually been assigned a tentative dating of "1,500 or more years" ago (481, p. 162). Certainly, fully developed Kwakiutl and Bella Coola ceremonial life has nothing like this venerable an age. All data point to a relatively recent development of many of the traits of Kwakiutl artistic and ceremonial life under stimulus from the north, probably in the protohistoric period.

To set the Kwakiutl and Bella Coola together in one subdivision of a culture area does small justice to the complexity of the diffusion picture in this southern region of the Northwest Coast. At least three levels can be distinguished: a period of cultural continuity in the region which is represented today by similarities in language and in social organization; then a period when the Kwakiutl developed characteristics of their own, especially of a social nature; and, finally, the period of intensive Kwakiutl-northern contact during the latter part of which Kwakiutl and Bella Coola were also in contact and during which developed the peculiar and startling Kwakiutl ceremonial and artistic life as it is known historically. As it happens, detailed archeology is very insufficient for this region and serves only to document the relative recency of Kwakiutl-northern contacts. Whereas the third and most recent of these periods is reflected in culture area subdivisions placing Kwakiutl and Bella Coola together in the "central" Northwest Coast, the first, and oldest, of the periods is generally given no consideration in culture area designations. Yet distributions of this early period indicate a twofold division of Northwest Coast, with the Kwakiutl and Bella Coola falling south with the usual "southern" tribes, and recognition of this composite southern region, distinguished as it is from the regular northern subdivision, is of major importance in historical reconstructions of the area.

Even the brief summary of obvious distributions given here suggests that the Northwest Coast can best be described in terms of several layers of culture designations each representing a different level of culture depth. The ethnological data in this one region take on the character of the superimposed strata of an archeological site. There seems to be no necessary sequence involved here in the greater apparent age of linguistic and social organization traits: other regions might yield quite different culture depth sequences and the inclusion of other distributions here would yield additional levels and, hence, additional sequences. Particular traits, such as whaling among the Nootka and Makah of western Vancouver Island and the Olympic Peninsula, offer special problems which fall outside the range of this study. But I see no reason why the earliest level represented in our material should not have included purely maritime adaptations as well as adaptations to inland salt-water regions such as existed in those Salish areas we have examined. To use single traits, even such spectacular traits as whaling, to characterize whole cultures seems to me a most hazardous procedure. Theoretically at least it should be possible to reconstruct entire cultural wholes for each of the levels distinguished in an area.

IV. DIFFUSION AND PROCESS

Arrangement of culture areas in sequences representing culture depth can, admittedly, only be accomplished in few regions of the world today, and even in these the sequences must be understood to be partial and tentative. Although archeologists have done more along these lines than ethnologists, I cannot see that the basic diffusion phenomena studied by both differ in their essentials. Different types of material are often examined by specialists in the two fields of anthropology but they have always been clearly recognized as mutually contributing to historical reconstruction. Largely because of the fact that ethnologists work with more or less even distributions of traits, and archeologists with concentrations of traits at particular sites, the culture area technique developed mainly as an ethnological tool. Yet this distinction also seems to be one of convenience and archeologists do, of course, plot their distributions in good culture area fashion. Recent studies in acculturation likewise furnish grist to the mill, for they are simply extreme elaborations of the diffusion process on the recent level. Their normative aspects are really nothing more than a valuable by-product.

Since the arrangement of culture areas in sequences according to culture depth is a formidable task, it would be helpful to have some means of distinguishing between "culture areas" which would point toward the eventual achievement of our goal as well as afford in the meantime more accurate descriptions of diffusion data. If such means could be found, our task would be immeasurably lighter. Actually, the concepts are already at hand in processes of diffusion which, although they may seldom be explicit, are implicit in most anthropological reconstructions. There is relatively little disagreement on many of these diffusion factors and they have been in use in diffusion-time studies for many years. Our means for clarification are, therefore, available. They only need to be isolated and labeled, and possibly expanded as the knowledge of diffusion processes increases. The following paragraphs may call for considerable revision but there seems little doubt that some such schema for defining and distinguishing culture areas would prove exceedingly valuable.

The term "marginal area" is frequently used and elaborate historical reconstructions have been drawn which employed the marginal area as a key concept. Different authors tend to define the term, however, in somewhat different ways. For instance, Kroeber stresses that marginal areas are "retarded because of their peripheral or marginal position in geography" in relation to a cultural climax (248, p. 418), and Herskovits, while following this at least in regards to a cultural center where the greatest clustering of traits occurs, further adds that a marginal culture is simply "one where traits from a neighboring area are to be discerned" (177, p. 198). Marginal may also mean economically or culturally less developed and, although economies may differ widely under these conditions, Linton speaks in this vein of "marginal survivals" (271, p. 329). He also distinguishes between the "problem of establishing common origins for two or more culture continuums and that of establishing common origins for elements within different cultural configurations" (271, p. 389). Significant as such variations in statement may be, each of these men, and other anthropologists as well, are actually aware of the full range of the concepts involved and would employ any or all of them in reconstructing the history of a given area. Under these circumstances, it might prove useful to limit the term to more restricted and more exact situations, and to apply other terms to variations in the diffusion picture.

Marginal area carries in its very name the implication of being "marginal to" a climax, center, or region of higher culture. It is on the margin, or edge, of a higher culture and, although it shows fewer or less well integrated traits, these may be seen to relate back to the region to which the area is marginal. It well illustrates the process of diffusion from a known center or climax and, as Kroeber has indicated (248, p. 421), applies rather to total cultures than to separate or isolated traits. A variant to this phenomenon may occur in situations in which the marginal area actually occupies a place within the region of the higher culture, thus forming a kind of cultural island. Such cases might conveniently be referred to as internal or island marginal.

Survival areas are also generally marginal to, or on the edge of, central areas but in these cases there is no proof of dissemination from the centers. The traits can best be seen as survivals from an earlier cultural continuum which included the region of the center but has since disappeared from it. Kroeber speaks of the "perpetuation of ancient practices at the remote margin" of a distribution which may be assumed to have been continuous at one time. Such survival is clearest in single, often isolated, traits or complexes and must be carefully checked against the possibilities of independent invention. Survival areas are most easily distinguishable when two or more regions exemplify the same traits and are separated from each other by a region of historic cultural vitality. Survival traits are always older than the superseding traits of the intervening territory, and places like Tasmania, which most anthropologists regard as having held survival traits (or absences of traits), are so ancient as to have survived even longer than their companion survival areas. Such cases are fortunately rare. They cannot be easily demonstrated but, when they are convincing, survival areas are often regarded as one of our surest indications of age. The center of dispersal, and even the direction of dissemination, of survival traits can seldom be proven, though they may be hypothecated.

Cultural substrata offer the same form of cultural continuum which is assumed to have existed between survival areas but in these cases the evidence for the continuum is present. The distribution of traits through the region is more or less even. The term is borrowed from archeologists who can in their materials often discern an "underlying substratum" of traits and they usually seem to apply the concept to whole cultures or cultural syndromes rather than to isolated traits. The word "basic" is sometimes used to refer to certain "basic traits" or traits of a "basic culture" but the aura of primacy and necessity which it carries gives it an unfortunate connotation. Distributions *per se* seldom reveal any more than "underlying" cultures. Whether some phases of these are "basic" or not is largely a matter of judgment.

Climax vividly describes the situation in which an underlying cultural substratum blossoms into a higher level of achievement. This may occur because of invention, the introduction of new traits by borrowing, or further development of existing traits through secondary circumstances such as greater natural resources in one section of the area covered by the common culture of the substratum. Whatever the causes, and they are generally multiple, climaxes are essentially self-developing and almost inevitably serve as important centers of dispersal. They are the areas to which outlying regions become "marginal." The climax is naturally more recent than the substratum from which it derived and older than its marginal areas.

Peripheral areas may be conveniently distinguished from the situation just described by the lack of any clear cultural dominance such as that wielded by the climax. Areas of relatively the same cultural status may remain in contact with each other for long periods and, although each retains its identity, there may be considerable borrowing and lending of traits between them. Peripheral areas are peripheral to each other and they are largely contemporaneous. The duration of their contact is often most difficult to determine. In some areas such as parts of the Middle East one can best speak of peripheral "cultures," for sedentary and nomadic peoples have here retained their identities for as long as historical records are available, yet there has for all of this time been regular contact between them. The Pueblos and Navajo-Apache furnish a similar example and there are reasons for believing that the possibility of this type of diffusion situation has too often been overlooked in historical reconstructions.

Intermediate areas represent fusions of culture from two directions. They are intermediate between areas the cultures of which differ from each other. Such areas may show considerable cultural vigor but they may be distinguished from incipient climaxes by the fact that their outlying regions are not alike. Their cultural fusion does not rest upon a common substratum but upon an even-handed borrowing from two unlike groups. Invention and virtuosity also play relatively little part in comparison to the climax situation and the intermediate area itself often acts as a kind of buffer region between the two areas from which it has borrowed.

Culture area and *culture sphere* may also be distinguished from each other. Each represents continuous distributions. But, whereas the one has been used most successfully in regions of relatively simple cultures where cultural and natural areas coincide in large part, the other refers most aptly to the spheres of influence of more highly developed economies with greater control over their environments. Asiatic and European civilizations offer excellent examples of the latter type. Culture spheres can, however, be distinguished as early as historical records can be traced and it may well be profitable to draw a parallel between the area of the culture sphere and the region embraced by a climax, its marginal areas and the outlying sections which represent the farthest spread of the climax traits. Such instances apparently occur on all levels of economic development. Any such limitation of the referent of the parent term seems undesirable. "Culture area" may best be kept as fluid as "culture" itself to stand for any continuous or semi-continuous distribution irrespective of the processes by which it has been built up.

Acculturation areas are frequently very extensive. Today they may be said to be world wide. But, again, there seems little reason to believe that the diffusion processes involved are of more recent vintage than in any other type of diffusion phenomenon. Many acculturation areas are associated with extensions of political or military dominance. In any case, one of the contacting cultures exerts control over the other. This control may be actual and self-conscious as in empire building, or it may come about through the sheer weight of recognized cultural superiority, the latter happening most frequently when civilizations with more efficient tools, better transport means, superior armaments, etc., come in contact with underprivileged groups. Total cultures are involved in these situations and tensions are often great. The distributions are frequently exceptionally spotty, for the acculturation area is geographically defined by movements of persons from the region of the dominant culture and these may cover great distances depending upon transportation routes. "Acculturation" studies today generally deal with situations of the sort described here but they often also include diffusion phenomena which can be better understood in terms of one or the other of the preceding categories.

In arranging culture areas in order of culture depth, it is clear that any one region may be differently classified at different time levels and that even on one time level diffusion processes are often complex enough to warrant classification of the cultural whole in different categories when viewed from different points of view. Thus, the historic culture of the Middle Fraser is peripheral to both the Gulf of Georgia and the upper Fraser, and marginal to the Kwakiutl climax. In this case at least, the integrity of the culture (which leads the area to be distinguished at all) seems to rest upon the fact that it represents the region of an old climax. The vigor of a true cultural climax is probably not easily, or quickly, dispersed.

The historic culture of the Plateau has most often been viewed as intermediate between Northwest Coast and Plains. I would follow Ray, however, in describing the Plateau, in the terms we have used here, as marginal to the Plains in the recent period, and peripheral to Northwest Coast.

If our diffusion categories are to be of value, they should help to illuminate historical development as well as assist in describing areas in their relation to other areas. The difficulty here, as in so many of our investigations, lies in our incomplete control of the data. We simply do not know enough yet to draw the necessary conclusions. What are the ties of the Northwest Coast with the natural Salmon Area described earlier by Wissler? The correspondence between the two is striking and has been further underscored by Kroeber's extension of the Northwest Coast into California and by our inclusion of the Interior region, which is still within the country of the salmon streams. How long has such a correspondence existed?

The earliest level of Northwest Coast culture discernible at the present time seems to be a substratum of traits with Arctic affiliations. In so far as such traits derived from the Arctic, or were adaptable to the Arctic, they could not be essentially based in salmon fishing. However, it is still possible that a substratum with certain common food-gathering techniques existed over these climatically varied regions. It is also possible that this substratum extended across the northern Pacific into Asia. The distribution of traits across the northern Pacific unequivocally attests to contacts between Northwest Coast and northeastern Asia. The parallels in these regions are specific, unlike those rather shadowy and unsatisfactory (though intriguing) trans-Pacific parallels which are sometimes suggested for more distant areas, but any details as to the exact nature of the contacts which brought them about remain obscure. The bulk of the evidence from the Northwest Coast, however, leads one to suppose that the period of the majority of these contacts corresponds with the area of a cultural substratum covering Northwest Coast, in its largest definition, and portions of the Arctic and of northeastern Asia. Although the data cannot be reviewed at this time, the existence of such a substratum is variously shown in both traits and complexes. Bearing these factors in mind, one may conclude that the correspondence between the cultural area of the Northwest Coast and the natural Salmon Area of North America is later than the northern Pacific substratum.

The culture of the northern Pacific substratum seems to have become locally adapted to the Salmon Area and to have reached a climax on the Fraser River.[4] Other climaxes within the substratum can be discerned in what is now Alaska but these fall beyond the scope of our inquiry. Probably as the Fraser climax waned, the northern and southern sections of the Northwest Coast, the antecedents of Kwakiutl being grouped as southern, became peripheral to each other. This is the earliest of our levels discussed above. Keeping only to the data discussed here, there then seems to have been a period of intense localization during which Nootka-Kwakiutl, Puget Sound and Middle Columbia set up as separate peripheral areas, and this was followed by a general intensification of the northern cultures, which again saw Asiatic contacts, and a final climax in Kwakiutl. The most doubtful element of our reconstruction concerns the relation of this climax and the northern groups but there is no doubt that the region south of Kwakiutl was in many respects marginal to the north in the historic period.

However many changes may subsequently be made in the history I have briefly reconstructed, the use of culture area concepts in relation to culture depth seems fully justified and the suggested diffusion terms seem also to aid in clarifying the picture.

4. For fuller discussion of this climax see Marian W. Smith (444).

THE ROLE OF THE DEAD IN NORTH-
WEST COAST CULTURE

Joyce Wike

The culture area of the Northwest Coast of America presents some interesting problems in the field of religion. Various sociologists have differentiated folk or primitive culture from modern, industrialized society on the basis of the rather unique and intensive secularization of the latter. In most societies man's relationship to the supernatural is of fundamental importance both in the ordering of interpersonal relations and as a significant reflection of them. We do not describe a people without describing their gods yet we have omitted them to a considerable degree in the classical picture of Northwest Coast culture.

The main feature of "characteristic" Northwest Coast culture that has been placed in a primarily religious category are the secret societies.[1] In the area of their greatest complexity, among the Kwakiutl, secret society activities seem to have been in the nature of historical pageants dramatizing a period when man did, indeed, have supernatural powers; the extent to which these powers are still active and meaningful is not very explicit.[2] Reasons for these performances or the native rationale behind them have not been made clear in the emphasis upon their theatrical function as vehicles for the display of wealth and hereditary prerogatives.[3]

This seeming lack of religious orientation in Northwest Coast culture is even more paradoxical when we consider the functional correlations between religious organization and other aspects of social structure which can be established elsewhere. In the culture sequence of both the Old and the New World, organized religious systems seem to appear in intimate association with hierarchical social structures and class stratification and these religious systems vividly operate to consolidate and to support the hierarchical status quo. On the aboriginal Northwest Coast the position of an hereditary aristocracy does not seem to have been maintained by the customary impressive, strong, and organized supernatural sanctions. Since this is the one area where we can document a class structure with economically important slavery on a hunting and

1. And they by no means uniformly characterize the whole area; the Haida do not have them and they are unimportant and "recent" among the Tlingit, as see 107.

2. Their function in warfare was indicated by Boas (39, pp. 425 ff., 664), and, of course, warfare was moribund when these customs were recorded.

3. Lopatin (276) has interpreted their function among the northern Kwakiutl speakers (Haisla or Kitamat) to be an intimidation of the lower class by the chiefs.

gathering subsistence foundation, it is possible that Northwest Coast culture could be "aberrant" in many respects. Both Boas and Sapir, for instance, have derived this social structure from a simple expansion of family organization, a derivation which is explicit in native traditions (39, p. 334; 414).

The fundamental simplicity of this social structure, however, does not mitigate against the fact that it has expanded to encompass extremes of status differentiation and economic advantage, and that it has elaborated within on the principle of hierarchical ranking. Developed with this social structure are impressive achievements in traditional art and ceremonialism; here, again, achievements normally found in the sphere of religious activity. On the Northwest Coast, therefore, one seems to be faced with what would appear to be a high degree of secular, formalized organization in combination with an extremely weak and insignificant, or chaotic and individualistic religious ideology.

As one resolution of this paradox we will consider the possibility that we may have been in error in relegating religion and religious attitudes to an insignificant place in the lives of these people. There is not the space here to reconstruct their total religious life; I will confine myself to a presentation of some of the evidence for the existence on Northwest Coast of widespread, important, and systematized beliefs concerning the relationship of the living to the dead.

A continuity in the relationship of the dead to the living is one important reflection of the familiar Northwest Coast emphasis upon inherited position, ancestral pride, and the recording of genealogies. The nature of this continuity is structured by the belief that the rewards and the status rankings of real life are maintained or intensified in life after death. Existing along with these beliefs, and it is possible, rather independent of them, are ideas that physical and ritual contacts with the dead will insure personal successes.

Archeological evidence suggests that these beliefs may have considerable antiquity. Strong has interpreted archeological material from the· Lower Columbia River as an indication of some sort of "death cult" (477). Far to the north at Point Hope, the prehistoric remains of Ipiutak are dramatically characterized by elaborate burial customs which include differential burial, grave goods, peculiarities in the decoration and handling of the dead.[4] At the historic level in cultures which may have partially derived from Ipiutak we find an emphasis upon death objects and rituals described by Lantis, the Alaskan Whale Cult (250).

The whole problem of reconstructing religious beliefs in functioning Northwest Coast culture may be complicated by the effects of European trade and colonization in this area. A sweeping shift in cultural emphases may have been an important consequence of this trade and colonization, starting in the nineteenth century and accelerating with the effects of depopulation from epi-

4. See Larsen, this volume, pp. 22–34.

demics and widespread prostitution, with the introduction of wage labor, and with disturbances in the aboriginal balance of power which heightened the disruptive consequences and casualties of warfare. The aboriginal economic foundation of the hereditary chieftainship and the normal responsibilities and controls vested in that office were destroyed in this period by the terrible reduction of personnel[5] and by the introduction of opportunities to gain wealth outside of aboriginal productive relations (304, p. 243; 369, pp. 313–14). It would not be surprising in this situation if the religious functions of the chieftainship were modified.

Wealth of itself did remain among the people in this period. This exceptional fact in combination with the fundamental pragmatism of their religion may account for a seeming reversal of the usual effects of European contact on native religions. While other embattled American Indian groups responded with religious revivalism those of the Northwest Coast emphasized the manipulation of wealth.[6] That this manipulation was an earthly manifestation of supernatural power and related to supernatural power was lost sight of.[7]

Not only were the supernatural sanctions for privileged secular status minimized but the religious functions of privileged status were weakened in a general setting of the undermining of inherited power. In this respect, therefore, late Northwest Coast culture may well be moribund; the interpretation of this period as a "Golden Age" (117, p. 26) appears to be based upon the fact that these people "had money to burn." Such an interpretation is best understood as a reflection of our own cultural values.

On the Northwest Coast of the late 18th century we know that although the chiefs quarreled, boasted, and made ostentatious display of wealth and gifts, they also prayed. A rather detailed and idealized description of a priest-chief comes to us from the observations of the distinguished Mexican naturalist, Moziño, on the West Coast of Vancouver Island.[8] According to Moziño, the Nootka chief, Maquinna, held his inherited position by virtue of his successful spiritual intercession with the supernatural who controlled the food supply (336, p. 20). Another observer from this period understood that it was the dead

5. For example, in the 1860's a Nootka "tribe" had 14 warriors, 3 of whom were hereditary chiefs (59, p. 22); another Nootka hereditary chief had a total of 11 subjects (59, p. 24).

6. Although the Prophet Dance and later movements were both geographically and ideologically accessible to Northwest Coast proper (451), they do not seem to have taken hold. It is my impression that this reservation would hold for the later Shaker Cult, which originated in Puget Sound, and that it was not well received or was rejected by groups emphasizing the potlatch complex.

7. There are some interesting parallels here with the Pawnee Ghost Dance Hand Game (260), although the Pawnee retain supernatural elements.

8. Much of the idealization in his account seems to come from the chief who served as his main informant. Moziño's observations (336) are the basis for the general descriptions of Espinosa y Tello (117) and for much of the general discussion of Nootka culture in de Roquefeuil (401).

who were most important in controlling the food supply (117, p. 65), but in Moziño's account the noble and chiefly dead simply communicated with the living by their control of various forces of nature (336, p. 20).

A ceremonial house belonging to this chief was visited which differs little from that described by Boas (401, p. 102; 48, pp. 261–69); the latter contained mummies of children and adults, guardian skulls, beds of skulls that were slept on,[9] and whale effigies. The visitor was told that Maquinna went to the house after a successful whale hunt for rites that included offering his ancestors a part of his catch (401, p. 102).

The missionary, Father Brabant, who lived in this vicinity in the 1870's gives additional details of the use of these ceremonial houses. One contained, "human skeletons, especially those of ancient chiefs and famous hunters. To these skeletons he (the Hesquiat chief) would speak as if they were alive and order them to give him 'whale.' Each of the skeletons had its turn, and in addressing himself to them he would give due credit to those of the number, who he had reason to suspect, had been granting his request" (335, p. 50). A few months after this very chief died he was given the credit for a beached whale: "For the Indians say that their chiefs do not forget their friends and subjects when they reach the other world. . . . Konninah sent the dead whale as a token of good will" (335, pp. 49–50).

Brabant had the impression that Nootka re-burial practices were partially designed to prevent the relics of the kin dead from being stolen by outsiders since, "The skull of the dead was used to become a successful hunter, warrior, or shaman" (335, p. 60). It may be of more than passing interest that Lantis suggests the possibility of a skull cult in western Alaska in her study of Alaskan Eskimo ceremonialism (251, p. 18). To return to the Nootka. Brabant apparently saw a seal hunter rub his own eyes with the eyes of a corpse to improve his vision on the seal hunt (335, p. 72); a similar use of parts of the dead in hunting other than whaling was recorded from the modern Quinault (350, p. 148).

It seems likely therefore, that ritual observances in bones houses, and the use of skeletal parts and corpses which are important elements of the whale cult can be placed in the wider context of other hunting practice (251, p. 44), warfare, shamanism and religion in general, both among whalers and non-whalers on the Pacific Coast (250, pp. 440–45). The rationale behind these customs appears to be the idea that the possession of such relics or ritual contact with them gives one access either to the intervention of the general dead, or to powers possessed by the specific dead involved. Somewhere in this framework we may someday more meaningfully place such customs as cannibalism and head-hunting.

When the role of the dead in the potlatch is considered it is found that an

9. Meares (306, p. 125) also reports a "bag of skulls" used as a pillow by a Nootka aristocrat.

active relationship to the kin or ancestral dead is reported to be the core of the potlatch and associated ceremonies among certain Northern and Central Maritime tribes (246, p. 29), as well as groups on the Gulf of Georgia. The return of the dead is the central feature of the Bella Coola potlatch (304, pp. 184–86). Among the Tlingit reverence for the dead is the motivation behind all of the potlatches and the dead are thought to be present as is true for the Cowichan and Songish memorial potlatches (483, p. 413; 87, p. 72; 520). The Tlingit, Tsimshian, Haida, Bella Coola, Klallam and Squamish feed the dead, usually through the medium fire at mourning feasts and in some groups, upon other occasions (483, p. 413; 135, p. 240; 485, pp. 34–35; 304, pp. 109–10; 155, p. 296; 183, p. 478). Property which is burnt goes to the dead among most of these peoples as well as among the Kwakiutl (45, pp. 711, 1329). Each blanket which the Tlingit distributed at a potlatch was given in the name of a dead relative who received a spiritual counterpart (483, pp. 431, 462).

The potlatch and associated customs such as the destruction and burning of food and property may, therefore, be given a religious rationale emphasizing the establishment of good relations between the living and the inhabitants of the after world, particularly the kin dead, along with the possibility of establishing a secure after-life for the living participants.[10] The potlatch, of course, also had the secular and legal functions which have been assigned to it. I simply wish to emphasize that in common with similar institutions elsewhere in the world, the potlatch had its spiritual as well as its worldly aspects. Again it is of more than passing interest that these essentials: the placating of dead relatives and the raising or maintaining of prestige by property distributions, are the very essentials of the Great Eskimo Feast of the Dead on the Bering Sea coast from the Kuskokwim approximately to Point Hope.[11]

In the case of that most important legal aspect of the potlatch, the assumption of an hereditary chieftainship, the property distributions might serve a dual spiritual function. This was one occasion in which the incumbent gained the support of his powerful ancestral predecessors, which support he needed in order to discharge his responsibilities for the welfare of his group. In addition, property distributions on this occasion helped to insure that the titleholder would join these ancestral dead as a powerful chief, himself. On the west coast of Vancouver Island this latter contingency was stated to be a most important factor in assuring an hereditary chief of the support and co-operation of his people (336; 117, p. 110). Although these people, the Nootka, may be aberrant in this regard it is also true that from them we have the earliest and most intimate observations of functioning Northwest Coast culture.

Two general aspects of life after death seem to have been important to the

10. This is not to say that food and property were not "sent" to other supernaturals.

11. Lantis (251, pp. 21–27, 110–11). A more southern extension of these customs than was briefly noted by Lantis by no means contradicts her evaluation of their indigeneous character in the area of her study.

living. In the first place, life after death is pictured as a reflection of life in this world and the dead demand that the living take a share of responsibility for maintaining the spirit-land status quo (483, pp. 461, 431; 304, p. 109; 485, p. 35; 135, p. 240). The living are also concerned with assuring themselves of a respectable or comfortable position in an afterworld in which the status ranking of this world was continued.[12]

The reported consequences of a disequilibrium in relations with the dead vary from the Quinault and Nootka extremes that the dead could stop fish runs (171; 350, p. 142) to the Bella Coola idea that the dead simply indicated their displeasure by "causing stomach aches and other ailments" (304, p. 110). The Haida seemed to have a happy reversal of the Tlingit practice of sending property to the dead for "When living relatives were poor, the souls sent them property. Men still aver that they have received property in this way" (485, p. 35).

Naturally, we would anticipate real inconsistencies of this type; we do not claim that attitudes toward the dead formed a unified theology over this wide territory nor one with complete inner consistency in any given locality. That there is evidence of an ancient tradition granting importance to the dead cannot be denied; this tradition appears to have been organized to give more spiritual depth to Northwest Coast status striving, inheritance, and the potlatch, some rather needed supports for Northwest Coast hereditary chieftainships, and a rationale connecting customs as diverse as the whale cult, headtaking, cannibalism, bones houses, and burial practices. Unfortunately, we have not had the space to consider the importance of the dead in shamanism, the widespread use of effigies of the dead and their characteristic style, and in speaking of "the dead" as such we have violated some extremely elaborate concepts concerning the organization of the soul and body which tie in with ideas of reincarnation.

The fact that this religious structure gives meaning to Northwest Coast culture is not, of course, scientific proof of its validity. On the basis, however, of the very scattering of accounts of potentially related beliefs in diverse localities by diverse observers over a period of a century and a half, we can say that this aspect of Northwest Coast religion must possess more vigor than has been recognized, especially when we consider that we are speaking of the rationalizations for customs that have either a wide, or a wide and uninterrupted distribution. This temporal and spatial distribution sug-

12. A Nootka chief who did not make the proper religious observances did not join his ancestor nobles but was relegated to a darker world inhabited by commoners (336; 117, p. 109). The darker commoner afterworld is also mentioned by Martinez (229). Status after death dependent upon worldly achievement is also reported from the Chinook (126, pp. 334–35) and the Bella Coola (304, p. 97), who thought potlatches would "smoothe the way for the giver after death," (304, p. 186) and for the non-aristocratic Nootka (171, p. 65); but the Massett Haida anticipated no distinctions of rank after death except for shamans (485, p. 37).

gests that these beliefs may have been lost to us in the intervening periods and localities as a result of inadequate records,[13] or that they were actually lost to most of the members of the culture as a consequence of a shift toward secularization, in particular, the increasing emphasis upon the economic aspects of the potlatch, post mid-19th century.[14] Even at this late date additional field studies in this area may provide us with a more definitive answer to this problem.

13. Brown discusses the difficulties that he and Sproat experienced in attempting to get religious data from the Nootka in the 1860's because of their secrecy (59, p. 217), as does Swan for the Makah (482, pp. 61–62). Some of the problems involved in obtaining Kwakiutl religious concepts are demonstrated in Boas (48, pp. 170–79).

14. This was one hypothesis advanced by McIlwraith (304, p. 242) to explain the absence of the return of the dead in the potlatch of groups other than the Bella Coola.

SOUL LOSS ILLNESS IN WESTERN NORTH AMERICA

William W. Elmendorf

This study deals with the widespread primitive disease theory that illness may be caused by loss of the soul, as found among the native peoples of western North America. The area examined in detail is that covered by the University of California's Culture Element Distribution Survey; roughly, North America from southeastern Alaska to Mexico west of the Rocky Mountains. Basic data are drawn from the Culture Element Distribution trait lists, supplemented by other ethnographic literature.[1]

The steps in procedure followed are: (1) definition of the exact areas of occurrence and absence of the soul loss concept in western North America; (2) analysis of the data on soul loss for component traits and groupings of traits; (3) examination of the distribution of these traits and their associations with each other and with some other features of native culture outside the soul loss complex; (4) consideration of the findings of these procedures in their bearing on the theory of unitary origin of the soul loss concept, the theory of Asiatic origin of North American soul loss, and the possible courses of development of soul loss theories and associated practices within the area treated.

In this brief summary a number of other problems cannot be considered. Such are the possible psychological bases for the idea of soul loss illness, the functional relations of this notion to various shamanistic curing methods, and its relations to other primitive disease theories. It is hoped that the present study may furnish a basis for later approach to these topics.

I. DISTRIBUTION IN WESTERN NORTH AMERICA

Loss of the soul is recorded as a theory accounting for at least some types of illness among the majority of the native groups covered in the Culture Element Distribution lists.[2] Many supporting or additional references are forthcoming from other ethnographic sources, though these alone, apart from the trait lists, do not provide a very full distributional picture and are generally deficient in negative information, i.e., the recording of definite absences.

Using the two types of sources conjointly we find that soul loss occurrences group in two large continuous areas (Fig. 1) and a third smaller and possibly

1. Nineteen element list groups (published and in MS) contain pertinent information. Two of the groups of lists, on the Yana and Pomo, have no material on this subject; the rest yield material of varying degrees of completeness. Lists used: 112, 22, 156, 381, 211, 20, 106, 118, 511, 2, 105, 165, 108, 110, 143, 466, 463, 462, 465.

2. See map for areas of recorded presence and absence. Out of 279 lists, 130 groups (allowing for duplication of a few lists) are entered as definite positives for the traits, 59 as definite negatives, 13 as having soul loss but no cure (here treated as negative).

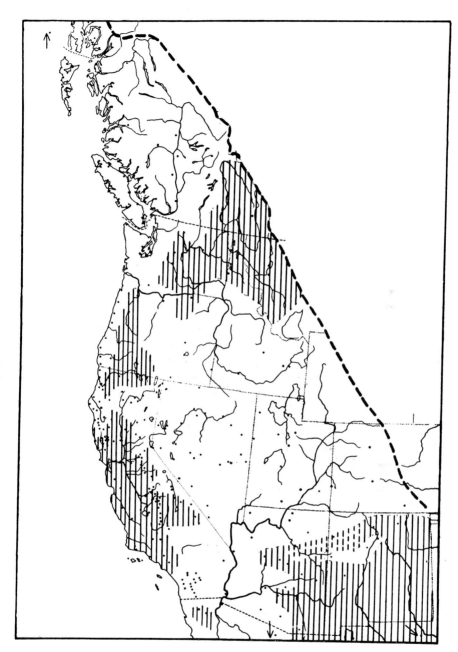

Fig. 1.—Soul Loss in Western North America. Unshaded area, recorded presence. Shaded areas, recorded absence. Dotted shading, doubtful absence. Dotted boundary delimits area surveyed.

isolated one. Of the principal positive areas, one comprises the Northwest Coast–Oregon coast–northwest California, the other centers in the Great Basin with outliers on the Colorado River, in extreme southern California, and in northeastern California. In addition, the pueblo of Zuni and several Keresan pueblo groups show a somewhat special type of soul loss belief.[3]

The two main areas of soul loss occurrence—Northwest Coast and Basin—are nearly separated from each other by a belt of negative areas in southern and central California, in extreme northern California and western Oregon between the coast ranges and the Cascade Mountains, and in the southern and central Plateau. Most of the southwestern Athabaskan peoples are also recorded as lacking soul loss, and these nearly surround the puebloan positive area.[4] Contacts between the two positive areas centering on the coast and in the Basin occurred only on two very limited fronts, one in north central California,[5] the other in north central Oregon, between eastern Oregon Shoshoneans and the Sahaptin Tenino.

The Plateau cases, here counted as negative, are peculiar. Outside the Fraser River drainage, the northernmost part of the Plateau, and two groups on or near the lower Columbia adjacent to coastal influences (Klikitat and Tenino), other Salishan and Sahaptin peoples of the area are listed by Ray as believing that loss of the soul invariably causes death. This of course precludes shamanistic curing and associated ideas and procedures in such cases. No cause of soul loss is given in these cases except for the Kutenai—theft by ghosts. Apparently while these peoples believe that the soul may be lost, such loss does not entail a curable disease. Rather the circumstance is regarded as a fatal accident, much like falling off a cliff, though presumably more lingering. I have not counted these cases as true soul loss illness, in this agreeing with Ray (379, pp. 100–102).

It should be noted that the areas of soul loss presence and absence here defined apply only within the part of western North America here examined. In the wider context of continental distribution, the larger Northwest Coast area of positive soul loss is not delimited to the north or east throughout its northern half, in fact it here probably represents only an extension to the Pacific coast of a huge northern region of soul loss presence which includes all the Eskimo and a great part of the Mackenzie Basin areas.[6] The eastern border of the Great Basin positive area is quite indefinite, being here represented only as the limits of the Culture Element Distribution survey, though soul loss does not seem to be an obtrusive notion in much of the Plains area.

3. Information on these cases has been drawn from 359 and from references cited there.

4. Definition of these negative areas emerges from material in the following trait lists: 2, 105, 106, 108, 110, 143; 165, 211, 381, 511. Some supporting references from other literature are: 378, pp. 169, 203; 452, p. 244; 449, pp. 100–101; 413, p. 40; 99, p. 469; 127, p. 63; 245, p. 343; 104, p. 197; 142, pp. 309, 316.

5. Through the northern Sacramento Valley Wintu (113, pp. 104–5).

6. See maps in 73, p. 227; 400, p. 563.

As mapped, the areas of soul loss absence appear peripheral, or better, internally marginal, within the larger area considered.

II. ANALYSIS OF COMPONENT TRAITS

The scheme of analysis here proposed appears to stand the test of distributional consistency fairly well. All reported cases of soul loss within the area treated vary as to elements under five constant categories of traits. These categories are: (1) nature of entity lost; (2) general cause of loss; (3) specific agent causing loss; (4) destination of lost entity, or from where recovered in case of cure; (5) curability. Under these may be subsumed, for western North American data:

1. Entity
   Soul (variously described or defined)
   Guardian spirit
   Other entities (heart, luck, etc.)
2. Cause
   Fright
   Fall or jar
   Wandering (spontaneous, or in dream)
   Theft
   Snared
3. Agent
   Dead (ghost)
   Shaman
   Witch
   Dangerous being (earth dwarfs, coyote, etc.)
4. Destination (recovered from)
   This world
   Abode of dangerous beings, etc.
   Trail to land of dead
   Land of dead
5. Curability
   Recoverable
   Irrecoverable

Each case examined throughout the area can be described in terms of one item under each of these categories. When a plurality of type cases of soul loss illness occurs among the same people, as, e.g., in western Washington, the significance of this is not obscured under this scheme of description, as might be the case if the traits of each particular kind of soul loss were lumped together in a single list.

Distributional plotting of these elements also yields a picture of historical value. It can be shown that certain traits, particularly under the categories of cause and agent, are often found in areas where soul loss disease does not occur. A number of elements of the complex are not peculiar to it, but occur with the same linkages among them in other contexts within the area treated. A case is seen in California where fright by ghosts causes a conceptually vague illness in parts of central California (127, pp. 63, 66). In northwest California the same cause and agent operate but the illness is specifically soul loss. Yet further north and in coastal Oregon ghosts more often cause soul loss by theft, though cases of both types occur. Our analysis here enables us to discern clearly a marginal displacement of elements.

The above traits will be examined as to their geographical distribution as components of the soul loss complex and in their occurrence and relation to similar traits outside that complex.

III. DISTRIBUTION OF COMPONENT TRAITS

1. *Entity lost.*—Following the analysis suggested above we find that in most recorded cases the spiritual entity involved in the type of illness considered is the soul. This term covers a variety of concepts and native terms throughout the area—"breath," "life," "mind," "shadow," "health," etc. All indicate a separable, spiritual part of a human individual which continues to exist after the death of the body. The basis of the soul loss concept is simply that departure of this entity from the body causes lingering illness, rather than immediate death, and that death in such cases can be averted by recovering the soul and restoring it to the body of the patient. This notion is coincident with the area of positive soul loss, defined above.

In parts of the Plateau, in western Washington, and among the Kalapuya of western Oregon, a similar type of loss illness may be caused by loss of the guardian spirit.[7] The latter is among these peoples, as generally in North America, an entity quite distinct conceptually from the soul. In western Washington illness from loss of the guardian spirit coincides in distribution with true soul loss; among most central and southern Plateau tribes, as among the Kalapuya, the latter notion is absent.[8] I agree with Ray that guardian spirit loss in the Plateau is old, and that the few peoples of this region who have soul loss have received it by diffusion from the coast (379, p. 102). Both concepts seem well-integrated and complex in western Washington, and the Kalapuya and Plateau instances of spirit loss may be ultimately peripheral to a Puget Sound center of loss-illness elaboration.

A number of Pueblo groups are noted as having a peculiar and specialized form of loss illness, the entity concerned being the "heart" or "breath-heart." This may be stolen by witches and is recovered from a river by curing society

7. See 211; 350, pp. 142–43; 518, p. 131; 160a, p. 250; 74, p. 169. These items supplement Ray's trait list entries (381) and his earlier discussion of Plateau spirit loss (379, pp. 98–100).

8. In Puget Sound belief the guardian spirit may be stolen by a shaman or the dead; among the Kalapuya and Sinkaietk by shamans only, as generally in the Plateau. The Puget Sound cases coincide with certain soul loss cases among the same groups in regard to traits: theft by ghosts, shaman; destination land of dead when ghosts steal; ceremonial recovery in event of ghost-theft. Contrary to Benedict's erroneous assumption (25, p. 80), this probably represents a reinterpretation of guardian spirit notions in terms of soul loss and recovery, rather than vice versa. The beliefs and shamanistic practices associated with loss illness (soul and guardian spirit) in this western Washington region are very complex.

doctors who dramatize their struggle with the thieving witch, catch the heart with a bear's paw, and represent it by a corn grain or rag doll in restoring it to the patient. This entire Pueblo complex appears to be a locally specialized development without recent connections with, or influences from, other forms of loss disease.[9]

2. *Cause of loss and agents.*—Loss of soul due to fright occurs in three areas separated by no-data gaps; two of these areas are possibly continuous. Fright is one of several causes in the Gulf of Georgia, western Washington, and coastal Oregon.[10] It is the typical cause in part of northwest California, on the margin of or south of the area showing cultural influence from the lower Klamath River. Finally, three lower Colorado and Gila River Yuman tribes are noted as having the concept. These are flanked south and east by negative cases which also include Yuman groups.[11] Fright as a cause of soul loss is probably a reinterpretation in terms of loss disease of a more widespread but more vaguely defined disease cause. This seems certainly the case for northwest California, where fright illness, without defined loss of spiritual entity, centers south of the area of soul loss, among such groups as Pomo and Patwin.[12]

On dislodgment of the soul by a fall, and on its loss by wandering, we have only scattered and meager data. Fall, as a soul-loss cause is recorded only for northeast California, but I have noted it, rather tentatively for the Twana, and Olson mentions something similar for the Quinault, both western Washington

9. For this Pueblo heart loss complex see 359, pp. 63, 136, 423, 425, 532, 708, 711–12, 719–21, 900, 940, 1111, and references cited there; further, 459, p. 144. Groups represented include Zuni, Laguna, Cochiti, San Felipe, Nambe, Isleta, Sia. Theft by "evil spirit" at Laguna (359, p. 711; 357, pp. 118 ff.) may connect with an eastern Basin belief, coyote (spirit) steals souls. Recovery of lost heart from river in all pueblo cases may be compared with Luiseno belief, water spirit (in river) steals souls (445, p. 210). I am indebted to Professor Leslie White for the information that this "breath-heart" represents a true soul among most puebloans.

10. The Skokomish (western Washington) are, however, negative for fright-loss both in Gunther's list (156) and in my field notes. The positive distribution is continuous down the coast to the Tolowa, who show negative in Barnett's list (20). This list is, however, more divergent generally than ethnographic knowledge of the Tolowa would lead one to expect. It was recorded from field notes of Drucker, not direct from informant.

11. The positives here are Mohave, Maricopa (110), and Yuma (124, p. 191). The neighboring negatives for the trait are Cocopa (141, p. 306), Akwa'ala, Papago, Pima, Yavapai, Walapai, and Shivwits (110).

12. Fright sickness without soul loss is a well developed disease concept in central California south of Round Valley (the southernmost point reached by soul loss). From the Freeland example (127) and personal communication from Driver, it is apparent that the usual method of cure is refrightening of patient by an "outfit doctor" costumed as a ghost. In Essene's list (118) Kato, Kalekau, and Yuki "soul loss doctors" are entered as curing soul loss cases by "refrightening" patient. The neighboring Lassik have the same type of soul loss cause but do not cure by refrightening. It is to be noted that the Lassik were without the Kuksu cult (Essene, personal communication). The refrightening technique by ghost-costumed doctors seems actually a curative feature of the Kuksu cult which has become attached to a few southern marginal cases of soul loss in this part of California. The type of cure here has nothing originally to do with soul loss. North of Round Valley soul loss from ghost-fright is "probably general in the area" (106, note to trait 2464). On the Oregon coast ghost-theft is a more common cause of soul loss than ghost-fright, though the latter is not unknown (109, p. 275).

peoples.[13] For loss by wandering (spontaneously, in sleep, or as result of specific dream) we have presence indicated for Tsimshian, Bella Coola, and two Basin Shoshonean groups. The trait probably has a wide distribution, both in association with soul loss and as a separate illness cause, but no definite summary can be based on present information.[14]

Theft of souls has a wide distribution, occurring over most of the soul-loss area, and even in certain cases where the concept of soul loss as a curable illness is absent. Cases of theft are most conveniently considered in connection with the types of agent with which they are linked. These are most commonly spirits of the dead, or malignant shamans, but various other sorts of potentially evil beings occur as soul stealers: witches, "evil spirits," earth dwarfs, etc.

For theft by the dead there are two areas of occurrence, possibly continuous: (1) Northwest Coast (Bella Coola to southwest Oregon), Plateau (in part), northern and western Basin;[15] (2) Lower Colorado and Gila Rivers.[16] Outside these areas only negatives for the trait are recorded.[17] This ghost-theft concept occurs independently of soul loss in several cases (Kutenai, Clackamas, Kalapuya, Klamath), and does not occur in other areas having forms of soul loss (northwest California, eastern Basin).[18] Like fright-caused illness, stealing of

13. This trait is listed only by Voegelin (511), and it may be questioned whether the general silence of ethnographic literature outside the limited area of her survey means much. It seems one of the simplest and most obvious explanatory notions to account for dislodgment of the soul. Within northeastern California there is a confirming reference for the Achomawi (11, p. 356). Quinault case is noted (350, p. 173).

14. The positives are 44, p. 588; 35, p. 421; 356, p. 41; 463. The literature otherwise supplies largely scattered negatives. A possible Duwamish instance is noted by Dorsey (101, p. 236), adjacent to the three western Washington negatives of Gunther's list (156). The curious cases of Northfork Mono (140, p. 52), and Friant Yokuts, Auberry and Northfork Mono, and Indian Diggins Northern Miwok (2), where (bodily) "wanderers" are "called by spirits," may have some resemblance to soul-wandering.

15. Positive occurrences are: Bella Coola; Kwakiutl; Gulf of Georgia tribes; Makah, Klallam, Skokomish; Lummi; Snohomish; Duwamish; Quinault; Chinook; Clackamas; Tillamook; Alsea, Siuslaw, Tututni, Galice Creek; Lower Carrier, Shuswap, Lillooet, Kutenai; Thompson; Klikitat; Nez Percé; Klamath; Lemhi and Fort Hall Shoshoni, Bannock; Paviotso; Southern Nisenan; Friant Yokuts, Auberry, and Northfork Mono; Owens Valley Paiute. See n. 1 for trait list references.

16. For this area the trait is positive for: Mohave, Maricopa; Yuma; Cocopa; Cahuilla; Kamia; soul-theft, not clear whether by shaman or dead.

17. These apparently exclude it from the eastern Basin and the Southwest east of the Maricopa and hint its absence in northwest California. Basin and Southwest negatives include Skull Valley and Deep Creek Gosiute, Promontory Point and Grouse Creek Shoshoni, Shivwits, Walapai, Yavapai, and Pima. The Yavapai are noted by Gifford as having theft of child's soul by the dead (irrecoverable) and otherwise no soul loss. The Akwa'ala of Baja California are also listed as negative by Drucker. In California the Lockford Plains Miwok and Tolowa lack the trait. The extension of ghost-theft down the Oregon coast probably does stop at Tolowa; as remarked above, though the ghost agent is present in northwest California soul loss cases, it causes the loss through fright, not theft, while ghost-fright sickness without soul loss extends still farther south to the Pomo and Patwin.

18. Linking of ghost-theft with loss of child's soul only for Nez Percé and Yavapai. The notion that the soul of the living may fall into a new-dug grave is widespread in the Northwest; e.g., Flathead and Upper Chehalis.

living souls by the dead may be a more widespread and possibly older notion which has become secondarily an explanation of soul loss or of certain cases of soul loss. General concern with the affairs of the dead is particularly intense in the southern Northwest Coast and parts of the Plateau, as Spier has demonstrated, and may well have afforded a basis for fitting the already present notion of soul loss illness to a specific fear of the dead.[19]

Occurrences of theft of the soul by shamans are widespread but discontinuous. Neither the Culture Element Distribution lists nor the ethnographic accounts provide a complete distributional picture for this trait. With the data at hand we may distinguish three positive areas: (1) Northwest Coast (south to Columbia River), northern Plateau, Willamette Valley (guardian spirit theft); (2) Northeastern California; (3) Chemehuevi and Mohave in the Southwest.[20] In general stealing of souls by shamans only occurs where loss disease is positive, in contrast to the ghost-theft trait. Unlike the latter shaman-theft does not occur, i.e., has not diffused independently of the idea of curable soul loss. There may be a functional basis for this circumstance in the very nature of the concept: what one shaman has wrought, another shaman can cure.

Several rather heterogeneous and areally more limited agents causing soul loss by theft appear in addition to the dead and shamans. Such are "earth dwarfs" (western Washington), coyote spirit (southern Basin), and witches (Zuni and Keresan pueblos). Illness caused by coyote spirit in the Basin does not appear always to constitute true soul loss.[21]

Snaring of the soul by means of a looped string snare is a peculiar and localized cause of soul loss in northwestern California. In some cases the snaring technique seems to constitute mere harmful imitative magic without the concept of soul loss entering in.[22]

3. *Destination of soul.*—Three alternative traits under this category appear to be distributionally significant. These are recovery of soul from this world, recovery from trail to land of dead, and recovery from the land of the dead. More than traits under previous categories, these elements correlate significant-

19. As between Northwest Coast and Plateau as possible originating centers for soul loss caused by ghost-theft, priority must be given the former (specifically its southern British Columbia–western Washington portion). Concern with the dead is not everywhere intense in the Plateau. Soul loss is atypical or absent in much of the Plateau.

20. In the Willamette Valley the trait is linked to loss of guardian spirit, not the soul, as is also the case with the Plateau Sinkaietk. Barnett gives a single negative for Gulf of Georgia (Klahuse), but the informant "lacked confidence" (22, p. 223) and in this case was probably in error. Eyak and Tsimshian have the trait, which is probably general in the northern Northwest Coast.

21. Examples of coyote as soul-stealer are all in Stewart (466). Other instances of malignant coyote or coyote spirit as illness causer are Paviotso (355, p. 40), Northfork Mono (140, p. 52), Chemehuevi (227) (coyote sent by shaman to *bite* victim), Lassik (118), Wintu (113, "malignant werebeast"). Only the Lassik among these last instances seems connected with soul loss.

22. The groups reported are Kato and Lassik (118), with the former "apparently unaware that the method is soul-capture" (118). Driver also reports snaring for Chilula and Hupa; a connection with soul loss in these cases is very uncertain (see 106, note to element 2466).

ly with different types of curing procedures. Comparison with type of cause and agent shows that recovery from this world coincides with all forms of cause, recovery from trail to the dead links with wandering or (more usually) theft by the dead, while recovery from land of the dead seems almost always correlated with ghost-theft.

The three items also show an interesting and nearly concentric distribution. Recovery from this world is virtually concurrent with the total area of (recoverable) soul loss.[23] Recovery from trail to dead is more limited: southern Northwest Coast, northern Plateau, northern Basin.[24] Recovery from the land of the dead is yet more restricted areally. Its occurrence comprises the Fraser River (northern Plateau), Gulf of Georgia, part of western Washington, and northwest Oregon. It lies entirely within the area occupied by cases of recovery from the trail to the land of the dead. These traits are not only concentric, they are concurrent. All three soul destinations are recognized in individual cases of soul loss in western Washington.[25]

4. *Curability.*—Under this category we have two possibilities: recovery of the lost soul, on which depends a variety of shamanistic curing procedures; and irrecoverability—the soul once lost by whatever cause, whatever its destination, cannot be returned to its owner. Both possibilities occur as traits, linked to other categories of the complex as here analyzed. Recoverable cases have throughout this study been equated with true soul loss, i.e., a curable illness. Irrecoverable or incurable cases lack the entire complement of curing procedure by a shaman, though diagnosis is often present. Since the elements of the loss complex are usually present, such cases can hardly be other than historically related to the more prevalent type of loss-recovery illness, yet the lack of possibility of cure introduces a fundamental difference.

The main body of irrecoverable instances are from the central and southern Plateau. Other cases, apart from doubtfully interpreted trait list entries, occur well to the south—a few groups in southern California and in the Yuman-Piman area (Papago, Yaqui). All sure cases appear peripheral, the Plateau ones to the Northwest Coast, the few California Yuman and southern Arizona instances to the Great Basin-Colorado River area of solid soul loss.[26]

23. Portions of the area for which this trait is not recorded (e.g., eastern Basin) are simply outlying sections without pertinent data.

24. In cases outside the area of recovery from land of dead the present trait carries as a corollary irrecoverability if the soul has actually reached the land of the dead.

25. Driver reports recovery from land of the dead for Hupa in northern California. The trait also occurs, quite isolated from the western Washington center, on the lower Colorado River among the Mohave, Yuma, and Maricopa.

26. Definite recordings of loss of soul without possibility of cure occur for the following: Masset Haida (112; seems distributionally doubtful, and the informant seemed overfond of negatives); Umatilla, Kittitas, Wenatchi, Sanpoil, Chilcotin (?), Kutenai, Flathead, Coeur d'Alene; Serrano, Western Diegueno of San Pascual; Papago, Yaqui (Drucker, 1941, n. 3024); Yavapai (142, p. 309). This last group is negative for soul loss in 110. Ray's recording of incurable soul loss for the Chilcotin is contradicted by recent field work with this group by Mr. Robert Lane.

IV. CONCLUSIONS

Suggestions as to the comparatively recent diffusion of soul loss as a disease concept into the New World from Siberia, where it has long been known to be the dominant theory of disease, were made by Lowie in 1925, with subsequent discussion in 1934 and a revision of opinion in the light of new South American material in 1948 (280; 281; 282; 286, pp. 356-57). Until Clements' work on primitive disease concepts, soul loss was thought to be confined in the New World largely to northwestern North America with a few sporadic cases in South America (280, p. 547). Clements found the concept widespread in North America and covering large areas in South America.[27] On the basis of this distribution he concluded that all American, as well as Old World, cases are historically related, but that the connection is a very ancient one, going back to Upper Paleolithic times. Clements' distributions however hardly bridged what Lowie had termed "the gap yawning between the southernmost North American and the northernmost South American occurrence of soul loss" (280, p. 340).

Actually, a good case might be made for a nearly continuous distribution of soul loss from the southwestern United States to Panama. The Yaqui, Tarahumare, Tepehuane, Aztec, Zapotec, Chontal of Tabasco, Tzeltal, Maya of Quintana Roo, and Cuna all entertain the concept, and the list here is a more or less random one, with no pretence to completeness. The hypothesis of a single origin may be strengthened by this connecting series of Mexican and Central American occurrences, but the probability of a recent American derivation from Asia seems considerably lessened.[28]

Yet the possibility remains, even if the single origin theory be accepted, that certain cases of North American soul loss have had a comparatively recent diffusion from northeast Asia. Such an explanation is at least suggested by the emphasis on this concept and its relatively great elaboration both in Siberia and on the Northwest Coast. I conclude that the present known distribution of soul loss makes recent transfer of all American cases from Asia highly unlikely, but that diffusional influence from Asia in northwestern North America is quite possible, accounting for the seemingly universal Eskimo, the widespread Mackenzie Athabaskan, and the universal Northwest Coast cases.

When we turn to the results of the present analysis within a more limited area, we are confronted with the fact that several types of soul loss illness existed in western North America, with probably differing local histories. The particular conclusions in this regard which I think emerge from this study may be summarized as follows.

27. See map (73, pp. 227, 193-97).

28. Rogers (400, p. 563) presents a map, revised from Clements, in which no North American occurrences of soul loss are shown south of southern California in the western, or of Ontario in the eastern, part of the continent. Rogers (400, p. 564) does not consider soul loss as necessarily a "younger" concept than, say, object intrusion. On this point I am in closer agreement with him than on his distributions. On the improbability of recent American soul loss diffusion from Asia see Park (356, p. 137).

Western North America shows two large areas of positive soul loss occurrence, nearly separated by areas of absence in California, western Oregon, and the Plateau. The geographical centers of these areas are, respectively, the Northwest Coast and the Great Basin.

Centers of elaboration, i.e., of complexity of soul loss traits occur in the southern Northwest Coast (western Washington and southern coastal British Columbia), on the lower Colorado River, and among some of the puebloan peoples. The southern Northwest Coast has been an originating center for at least the traits of ghost-theft (as connected with soul loss), and recovery from the land of the dead and the trail thereto. The greatest variety of type cases also occurs in this region.

The Mohave and possibly the Yuma show more traits of the complex than do any neighboring peoples, and have a number of traits otherwise lacking in the region but common much farther north; such are fright-cause, ghost-theft, shaman-theft, recovery from the land of the dead.

Pueblo heart loss represents an old, locally developed complex. It is probably historically unconnected except in its most general features with other forms of loss disease.

Many traits now found associated with soul loss in western North America seem to have had long and separate histories within the area, and some seem accretions to the soul loss complex from other magico-religious contexts. Such are probably fright (particularly that caused by ghosts), snaring of soul, and even theft by ghosts. Guardian spirit loss in the northwest (Plateau, western Washington, western Oregon) seems, on the other hand, a transfer of ideas originating in the soul loss complex to a spiritual entity of a different type.

Within the area considered the concept of soul loss illness has probably been gaining ground in recent times at the expense of the negative areas in western Oregon, California, and the Southwest.

If such areal and typological diversity exists for this seemingly simple concept within a limited part of North America, its total range of diversity over the entire New World, from the Eskimo to the Yahgan, must be great. If soul loss really does go back to a single origin, that point must be temporally very remote, and hardly discoverable by any method of purely ethnographic analysis.

THE OLD-WORLD DRAGON IN AMERICA

Marius Barbeau

During the Crusades, a Bavarian monk recruiting soldiers to free the Holy Land, enlisted the peasant Udo, but failed with Wolf von Wolfenstein, an intrigant villager. Both these young men courted Maria, a virgin, whose preferences leaned towards the crusader. During his prolonged absence far away from home, Udo was believed to have perished at the hands of the infidels. Wolf, who had spread this false rumor, hoped now to gain Maria's favor. But she resolved to yield herself to the Dragon, who annually carried off a maiden to his lair. On the morning of her approaching doom, a knight in shining armor mounted on a white steed—no other than Udo returning home—galloped to the mountain side and slew the monster. Wolf fled in disgrace, and Udo wedded Maria. They lived happily ever after.

Here in its German form, this ancient myth of Perseus and Andromeda, of Hercules slaying the Hydra, of the Dragon with Seven Heads, and of the Great Dragon and the Harlot in the Apocalypse, was commemorated in 1947 at Furth in an annual festival the beginnings of which are lost in prehistory (296a). Other traditional tales and survivals of the same type are familiar to us. They stud the mythology of Europe, Asia, and America.

These ageless themes merit study by Americanists as soon as they are noted in the New World either as truly native tales or as diffusions after the landing of the white colonists in the sixteenth century. And if I single out the Old-World Dragon, it is because its features and career belong to this continent as well as culturally older lands (437, pp. 83–86, 89, 91, 93, 104; 519; 492; 493; 494).

The arid Southwest—Arizona and New Mexico—at once comes to mind, with its Plumed or Horned Serpent and its rain gods. Overwhelmingly predominant, they are helpful sky monsters controlling the waters and thunders. They are deities among the Apache, the Navaho, and the Pueblos. And Mexico, as if its cue came from Egypt, included them in its pantheon. In Egypt, Osiris at night became an evil dragon, identified with Set, and could be propitiated only by human sacrifices (437). The pyramids of Mexico are surrounded by hundreds of Dragons, carved out of stone, with their mouths gaping wickedly and their foreheads surmounted by horns or plumes.

The subject is too vast and intricate for full development here. Only two fields in North America can be outlined: the Huron-Iroquois on the Atlantic sea board, and the Nootka, Kwakiutl, Haida, Tsimsyan, Tlingit, and Déné in the Northwest. Both these territories were once ridden by the Dragon, which had sown its teeth everywhere in the sea, lakes, and rivers, as well as on the

115

mountain tops. Not all this breed, whose remote origin was in the Old World, was evil and deadly; some could be harnessed, by ritual and propitiation, for occasional service to man.

The Huron-Iroquois were staunch believers in the Horned Serpent, whose habitat was the lakes and the many rivers in their woodlands. Varied tales, now being recorded, are still current among their "acculturated" descendants. The so-called "pagan" Iroquois of Grand River speak of the destruction of a whole village once, long ago, by a huge Serpent whose mouth was a cave entrance. The dirge songs arising out of a heap of human bones inside, were learned by some hunters wandering in the vicinity. They were handed down to posterity— eighty-four songs or more in all—and became the core of the *Ohkiwe* or Festival of the Dead, held every autumn in the Long-Houses near Ohsweken, Ontario. The *Ohkiwe* may coincide in scope and date with the pageant of the Dragon at Furth in Bavaria. In the past month, I have recorded for the National Museum of Canada, the larger part of these mythic chants which commemorate the destruction of a tribe and the slaying of the monster at the hands of heroes whose equivalents, in European lore, are Siegmund, Beowulf, Sigurd, Arthur, Tristam, and Lancelot. Dr. William N. Fenton and Mrs. Gertrude Prokosh Kurath have been working in the same field.

The Wyandots (an Iroquoian nation) formerly of the Great Lakes, later dispersed in northeastern Oklahoma and at Indian Lorette near Quebec, also propitiated or worshipped the Great Serpent, which was a striking duplication of the Iroquoian monster. At one time the Wyandots had a Snake clan guarded by a Snake similar to the classical Hydra of the Old World, that is: a head surmounted by a pair of pronged deer horns, a cavernous mouth with serrated teeth breathing deadly fumes and flames, large rolling eyes, a huge body covered with fish scales shining like polished brass, a reptilian tail—the forked tail of the Devil. Its Algonkian name at Lorette was *Carcajou* or Wolverine (a native devil). It was credited with digging the course of the St. Charles river below the waterfalls and through the canyon. It could change into a Lion or a Dwarf. The Jesuits once exorcized it, forcing it to drag its enormous bulk through the village, where it left a gully behind. Reluctantly it sought a belated hiding place in Lake Tantare in the Laurentians. Recently, so they say, the monster was seen in the gulf of St. Lawrence. Last year, a CP newspaper item, dated Detroit (in the former Wyandot country) July 23, 1948, reported: "While men yelled and one woman fainted aboard the passenger liner City of Detroit III, a sea serpent slithered through Georgian Bay. That was the report of an eye-witness, Bess Munroe, of Pinconning, Mich., the ship's social hostess. She described the serpent as a 60-foot, green-and-purple scaly monster with a huge horned head. The description was confirmed by more than a dozen passengers and several of the ship's crew. . . ."

The myths of origin of the Snake clan among the Wyandots—which I recorded in 1911–12 in Oklahoma (17, pp. 313–49, Pls. X, XI)—are of a few different types. The most important one tells how a maiden of the Deer clan underwent her puberty training in the forest. Her grandmother would not have her accept the visions of animals which visited her in her dreams as would-be guardian spirits for a lifetime. Too ambitious, the matron coveted only the most powerful spirits. One morning, the Great Snake rose out of the lake (Ontario), its body curled round that of the maiden, who was changing into a snake up to the waist. Soon both of them had finished digging up a lake for their new home. The water rose, and Hinon, the Thunder, roared while black clouds obscured the sky. A dart of lightning or, according to other versions, hunters armed with magical weapons, killed the monster of the deep, but not before he had yielded some of his precious blood, or his antlers, or his copper-like fish scales. These charms became possessions of the Snake clan.

We learn from other accounts that the Snake-men (for the snake could assume the form of a young man embracing the maiden) wore on their heads deer antlers, the very panache of the Chinese dragon. These regalia also suggest the horns of Cerastes, the ancestral Dragon of Egypt and Babylonia (437, p. 91).

The Great Snake of the Huron-Wyandots taught the members of its clan fifteen ritual songs, and required them to hold an annual feast in commemoration.

The personal names of members of the Snake clan surviving as late as 1911–12 in Oklahoma contain Snake and Dragon references. These names and words are explained in recently recorded narratives of a Dragon tradition in Ontario and the state of New York.

Some features picked out of Iroquoian myths and tales for comparative purposes are:

Out of Wyandot-Huron narratives (17):

"The huge Snake, the husband, surged out of the lake with large forked antlers on his head, like those of a Deer. His bride composed a song and said: 'Sing it every year!'

"While she was combing her hair she changed into a snake up to her breast and began to crawl. The monster Snake came up and both dived into the lake, henceforth their abode.

"The Snake husband appeared with white antlers, his bride, with blue antlers.

"Many people knew about the Great Snake, and communicated with it, because it was their protector, their advisor as to the future.

"From the heads of the Flinty Giants which had been cut off, serpents grew to an enormous length, and followed the Wyandots in their migrations. They plagued them for ages, while dwelling at the bottom of the Great Lakes. When, at times, the waters boil over during the storms, the people make offerings to the Snake. The rivers adjoining the great inland waters are only the worn trails of these monsters from one lake to another.

"Near the present Sandwich (on the Detroit River), a huge Horned Serpent,

Tijaiha, appeared out of the boiling water, with distended jaws and flaming eyes." Its home became the Huron River (Michigan).

The Iroquois of Oka, St. Regis, and Caughnawaga in the neighbourhood of Montreal, did not forsake all their tribal recollections because of their new and diluted Christianity. Their Sulpician missionary, Arthur Guindon (154, pp. 47-48) bears this out (translated from the French):

"Long ago, an immense Serpent bearing horns (*encorné*) devastated Lake Ontario. The Sun and the Moon witnessed the extinction of the Indians, swallowed up one after another by the monster. In the end not a canoe was left on the water, not a lodge on the lake shores. But one day the beast ventured too near the falls (Niagara). The Thunder god slew it with a bolt and left its body floating on the water like a chain of rocky spurs.

"The Double-headed Serpent (*le Bucéphale*) emerged from the lake and made captive within its coils a Tsonnontouan (Seneca) town. There it slowly poisoned its people with its deadly breath. . . . In the end, only a few survivors were left. A boy, one morning, came smiling out of a cabin, went up to the monster, and shot at its body a magical dart [of red willow]. Transfixed, the reptile mowed the forest with its tail, then loosened its coils, and slid into the lake, its abode thereafter."

"Serpents with four legs and human hair on the heads" were known to exist at various points in Ontario (154, chap. xii).

The Niagara itself owes its name to the Great Serpent. Here is how Charles A. Cooke, of Mohawk extraction, interprets it:

'*o'ña''ga're'*: serpent-roar (*-o''ña:* serpent; *ga're'*: sound, noise, roar).

Significantly coupled with the Snake is the Lion, in Iroquoian, Tsimsyan, and Asiatic mythology. Just as in the Apocalypse (*The Revelation of St. John the Divine*), the "great red dragon, having seven heads and ten horns stood before the woman, . . . and the woman fled into the wilderness," and the beast, "like unto a leopard . . . , and his mouth the mouth of a lion (chap. 12), and the dragon gave him his power," the Lion or the Panther of the Great Lakes formed a supernatural pair with the Snake. Called *Yenrish* (American puma, in Wyandot), its name in Mohawk is *Genreks*, which has been deformed into Erie.

The great White Lion, according to a Wyandot narrative (17, pp. 95-97, 342-43) "lived in Michigan, beside a Wyandot settlement, on the Huron River. Its home was in the water, and whenever anything out of the usual was to happen, the water boiled and foamed, and the Lion came out." Twelve songs were left to commemorate the battle with and defeat of the Lion. These songs became part of an annual festival.

These sacred songs were recorded among the surviving Wyandots in Oklahoma. Their words and the ritual they accompanied follow the same Lion pattern. They must be their contemporaries. They mention the appearance of the Lion, the virgin its captive, the bow and arrow, never used before, that killed it, and the new leather bag which held its blood before it dried up into a charm.

The slaying of the Lion, like that of the Dragon, by the Iroquoian warriors armed with bows and arrows, is a humanized version of the fight described in the Apocalypse (chap. 12).

Among the four monsters around the throne, in the Apocalypse, beautifully illustrated in the Angers tapestries (French, fifteenth century), the third is the flying Eagle. Like the other beasts, the Eagle had six wings "full of eyes within"; its power was in its mouth and in its tail, "for their tails were like unto serpents; they had heads" (chap. 4); and "seven thunders uttered their voices (chap. 10)."

This inspired description of the Flying Eagle also fits the Thunderbird of North-American mythology in general, no less than those of the Iroquoians and of the Pacific coast Indians. Hinon, the Thunder spirit of the Huron-Wyandots, is a kindly sky god who assisted the warriors in their destruction of the Dragon. And the great Thunderbird of the North Pacific Coast, a helpful spirit, is one of the two or three leading totems of the North Pacific and Alaska.

Like the Dragon and the Lion, the northwestern Thunderbird is a mythical concept of the same ageless extraction as Zeus or Jupiter the divine Eagle, the Hydra or Osiris of the waters, and the winged monster half eagle and half lion. Myths in Europe, Asia, and America, tend to confuse the features of these animals and assimilate them into one or to sunder them into related parts.

Thus among the Dénés of the Northern Rockies, an Oblate missionary not so long ago was moved to interfere with his neophytes, because they were conjuring the Dragon swallowing the moon, during an eclipse.[1] But an earlier missionary of the same order, among a northern tribe of the same stock, had already recorded the myth of the Woman wedded to the Serpent, whose reptilian children dwelt in a hollow tree. They were all destroyed by the hunters who had discovered their haunt, and their remains, reduced to ashes on a pyre, changed into insects and mosquitoes (361, pp. 19–12).

On the North Pacific Coast, from Oregon as far north as the Aleutian Islands, the Dragon and the Thunderbird reign supreme among the great totems of the sky and the salt waters. In every tribe we find varied forms under many names and features, but ever recalling the same mythological tree, the roots of which are deep in more than one continent. Here again the Dragon at times has more than one head; for instance, the *Heiltlik* of the Nootka, the *Sisiutl* of the Kwakiutl, and the *Larah'wœs* of the Tsimsyan. Chain-like in its trans-asiatic diffusion from tribe to tribe, it appears among the Koriak of Northeastern Siberia as a monster with several heads (216).

The *Heiltlik* of the Nootka, on western Vancouver Island, is believed to be

1. In the Carrier tribe on the Bulkley River, a tributary of the Skeena.

the Mountain Snake. Double-headed, it reminds the people of olden times, when brave ancestors attacked the fierce monster in its lair. This reptile is still supposed to be the maker of lightning, when it associates with the Thunderbird. The Kwakiutl of Cape Scott, just north of Vancouver Island, give a striking account of the *Tsiakish* or a Hydra-like monster living beneath the sea and swallowing canoes with all aboard. When, one day long ago, a chief was walking eastward close to the sea shore, he met Kosa, a young girl, and bade her go and fetch water for him to drink. She refused, because of the dreaded monster with a huge mouth guarding the spring and swallowing all intruders. As soon as she agreed to obey, she put her *Sisiutl* belt on, and the vampire instantly killed her. The chief, a wizard, sang an incantation which caused the beast to burst open and disgorge all the people it had devoured. Coming back to life, they limped forward or tripped sideways; their bones were all mixed up. But the chief soon sorted them out, and they became the present Koskimo tribe.

Among the northern tribes of the Pacific Coast—Haida, Tsimsyan, and Tlingit—this myth assumes another form under various names: these names are *Wenaamaw* or Woodworm (Haida), *Rhtsenawsuh* or Single-headed Caterpillar and double-headed *Larah-wæse* (Tsimsyan), and *Tlugurh* or Scrub-Worm (Tlingit). Here in this group, the theme of the Hydra is at its best; it prevails in the wood carvings, and shares some of its features with Asiatic and European prototypes.

The Dragon, among the Tsimsyan and their neighbors, has become a charm in the sacred bundles of the medicine-men. Made of ivory, it is either single or double-headed; the heads being placed back to back. It appears in wood carvings which stand inside the houses as corner posts, or in front as totem poles.

The Tsimsyan know the Caterpillar (*Rhtsenawsu*) very well; its home formerly was Krhain island, where the town of Prince Rupert now stands. Double-headed, it was like the *Larah-wæse*. Even to-day, the Indians at Prince Rupert point to the dented depressions in the mountain behind the town as the segments of the double-headed monster.

The Haida of Skidegate on the Queen Charlotte Islands know the same tale with minor differences. One night, an old man lying down in his lodge heard something gnawing wood. The next morning, his boxes of candle-fish oil were empty. The people, on the alert because all the oil boxes had run dry, discovered a great worm hiding underground and gorging on the people's food. As they were about to kill it, they learned that it was the pet of the head-chief's daughter. When it was still small, she suckled it when it would stick its mouth up from its burrow. Then it had begun to pilfer the food caches everywhere in the village. The warriors, with large knives tied on to long shafts in the manner of spears, fought the huge worm. They found it difficult to pierce its body. It was covered with scales like those of a large fish. Had they failed, it would have destroyed the whole tribe.

A Stikine River version of the same story, recorded among the Haida of Massett, concludes otherwise. After the people had banded together to overcome the enormous worm, they decided that the chief's daughter, because of her baneful fancy for her pet, should refrain from marrying. She stayed in hiding behind the village. When late in life she married an old recluse, her husband, to celebrate the event, gave away a great deal of food. But it all changed into snails, worms, and frogs.

Among the Tsimsyan of the Skeena River, the Dragon is once more associated with the Lion. At one time a monster, the *Hawaao*—resembling a puma or mountain lion, but supernatural—ascended the river, destroying people wherever he met them. It became a totem, and its carved wood monument is still standing on a platform at Kitwanga.

The symbolism of these world-wide myths of the Hydra or Dragon, the Thunderbird and the Lion, are clearly brought out in a Tlingit version recorded by Dr. J. R. Swanton (484, pp. 151-52).

The chief's daughter at Ququarhdun in Alaska had a wood worm (*tluqurh*) for a pet. She fed it at her breasts, then out of the food boxes of her parents. When it reached the length of a fathom, she composed a cradle song: "It has a face already. Sit up right here!" Another day, her song was: "It has a mouth already. Sit right up!"[2] After her people had heard the same songs ever so often, they began to wonder, and her mother spied on her. She saw a frightful worm between the boxes in the seclusion hut, and became alarmed.

Meanwhile the people in the village found their oil boxes empty, as the big worm had been stealing the oil. The chief tried to induce his daughter to come out of her seclusion. Her aunt, who was very fond of her, he said, wanted to see her, for she needed her help. That day, the song she sang to her pet was: "Son, I have had a bad dream." To her mother she asked, "Give me my new marten robes." Then she walked out of the hut with a rope tied like a belt round her waist, and sang a new song: "They have begged me long enough to come out. Here I am, just as if I were about to die. Parting with my love means death."

A great uproar broke out. She cried, for she knew that the people were slaying the great worm which she had fed at her breasts. After a long struggle had ended, she heard that the monster was dead. She cried out mournfully:

"I had to leave you, my son, and they have killed you. I was blamed for bringing you up. It could not be helped, it was not my own doing. Now, you shall be heard of all over the world. You shall be claimed by a large clan as its own, and be looked upon as great."

Indeed, the Caterpillar or the *Sisiutl* of the North Pacific Coast, elsewhere known as the Dragon or the Hydra, or the Great Horned Snake, or the Feath-

2. These songs have become traditional and were later used in rituals.

ered Serpent, has been claimed by many natives the world over as their sacred emblem. The subject of myths and tales, it has been illustrated countless times in the plastic arts of at least three continents. "It has been heard of all over the world," as in the Tlingit song. In places on the seacoasts of America, the blinking of the monster's eyes produced thunder; elsewhere, its breath gushed out like poisonous flames; and its voice was thunder. Another Tlingit myth, also quoted by Dr. Swanton, concludes with a variant:

A girl once had offended the Snail. The next morning the people saw her at a distance, as she stood on the face of a high cliff with the big snail coiled about her. Her brothers, bent upon rescuing her, carved wings, dressed up like birds [Eagles], flew up to her, and brought her down. But henceforth they remained birds. They were the Thunders (18).

MATRIARCHAL DANCES OF THE IROQUOIS*

Gertrude Prokosch Kurath

The ceremonial importance of Iroquois women corresponds to their social prestige as agriculturalists and mothers.

Social function.—They perpetuate family lineage, for they bear and raise the children and continue in them the maternal clan. Traditionally they provide the main food staples, cultivate, gather, and prepare vegetable foods, roots, fruits, and berries. They honor the ancestral spirits of the clan and tribe; formerly they officiated at the re-interments held every twelve years, when the bones of the dead were transferred from their exposed tree platform to the cemetery.

The ancient economy has changed. The aboriginal occupations have to a large extent been supplemented by jobs in canneries, gypsum mines, and the Erie Railroad. Tractors are replacing ploughs. Hunting and warfare are virtually extinct, and these men's dances have been converted into medicine rites. Men buy the beef for the ceremonial feasts. But women continue to grow vegetables for the family and feasts, and to rear children. The corresponding ceremonies have been preserved and are, if anything, gaining ascendency over male roles.[1]

Ceremonial function.—The regular cycle of seasonal rites concerns the planting, growth, and harvesting of foods. The chief matrons govern the feasts addressed to the food spirits—the Planting, Maple, Strawberry, Raspberry, String Bean, Green Corn and Harvest festivals. The tribal chiefs govern the Thanksgiving and Midwinter festivals addressed to all beneficial spirits ruled by Haweniyo and particularly to animal spirits. The matrons also sponsor their own medicine rites and the men's False-Face rite. At all gatherings they are in charge of the final distribution of food, whereas the men offer the introductory and concluding prayers, the tobacco invocation, and most of the musical accompaniment.

For the major ceremonies the people gather at the tribal longhouse and observe a sequence of events which, despite local variations, is essentially the same at different longhouses. Participation is democratic and usually open to all present, including children and visitors. But each sex and moiety occupies its prescribed position on the benches long the wall, near the stove pertaining re-

* The research upon which this study is based was supported by a grant from the Wenner-Gren Foundation for Anthropological Research.

1. The descriptions are from observations at Allegany Seneca Reservation, New York, and Onondaga and Sourspring Cayuga Longhouses at Grand River Reserve, Ontario. Dr. William N. Fenton's generously proffered field notes furnished supplementary facts, texts, and translations; and his collection of recordings formed the basis of musical transcriptions.

Research is still in progress on all the ceremonies and has barely begun on the Four Nights dance.

spectively to men or women. Each sex fulfills specific ceremonial assignments and enters the dances in a prescribed order, according to moieties—men and officials ordinarily in the lead. Following the leader, an increasing crowd circles the central singers' bench in a counterclockwise direction. Social dances pair the sexes; most ritual dances segregate them in a line, either by separating them or by excluding members of the other sex.

Women monopolize the *Ęskänye, Tǫwisas, I'yondatha-De'swadęyo, 'Ohgi'we'*, and *Geiniwašǫndaje'*, though men are drawn into assistant participation. Women start off two social dances—*gasgaiǫda'dǫ* (Shaking-the-Bush) and *dagä'e'o'enǫ* (Chicken), the men later joining as partners (Fig. 1, *9*).

The *Ęskänye* is the women's special shuffle dance, not a complete rite. *Ęsi'da'gänye* means "they shuffle their feet." Its tutelaries, Corn, Beans, and Squash, the three life-sustaining sisters, join in the dance. In concept and song texts the women are identified with corn and the fickle bean plant. The traditional Iroquois (and Cherokee) method is to plant two bean and two squash seeds in each hill of corn; so the beans climb up the stalks and on reaching the top, stretch over to the next one.

One of the six to eight male singers on the benches plays a small water drum; the others strike horn rattles with the right hand against the palm of the left or on the knee. According to the occasion, there are three kinds of song cycles—

1. *Ęskänye gainǫ·gaiyǫ·ka'* or old time *ęskänye* of twelve to fifteen archaic ritual songs, subdued in scale and tonality (Fig. 1, *1*).[2]

2. *Ęskänyego'owah* or great *ęskänye*, of twenty-five to thirty similarly ancient ritual songs (Fig. 1, *2*); five introductory chants by men, ten with the women in unison an octave higher, as they stand facing the men, then a dozen or more dances to men's singing. In the difficult step the women shuttle their feet back and forth with sideward twisting, heel accents, and knee flexion, sidling right with face to the center of the circle. Inferior performers and little girls just shuffle back and forth or merely walk around. Experts counter the foot rhythm with horizontal swings of the forearms, wrist rotation, subtle head tilting, jumps and pivots from side to side or completely around.

3. Modern *ęskänye* (Fig. 1, *3*), with the same steps but recently composed songs. These contrast with the old type in their extended form, free scale, bold descent, and abandoned, even strident vocal quality.

This dedication to the Three Sisters threads through all of Iroquois ceremonialism exclusive of men's rites and so-called Stomp dances. The women use the step in the *ganeo'ǫ* or Thanksgiving dance, in the False-face round, *deyosidǫdi'has*, in the cross-over double line dance *waienǫe'* or Striking-the-Stick, and authentically in the five forms of the *gędzo'enǫ ka·* or social Fish dance type. It marks climactic moments of the *'Ohgi'we'* and *Geiniwašǫndaje'*. It has a definite place in a set succession at all of the food festivals, which varies

---

2. Owing to lack of space, the vital element of musical interpretation can receive only passing reference.

somewhat between longhouses; for instance, at Soursprings—Feather dance, *ęskänye, ga'da'čot* Stomp, Corn, Bean, and Shake-the-Pumpkin. It is inserted at will in all post-ritual social evenings, and constitutes special "sings" by three to twenty men.

The concept of the life-giving corn mother also reaches over into ritual forms which do not use the *ęskänye* step.

The *Tǫwisas* (meaning women) chants of the women planters regularly form part of the Green Corn festivals and sometimes, as among the Cayuga, of the Planting celebration. Tradition speaks of a Cherokee origin, of transmission by two female Iroquois captives who escaped from the Cherokee.

Though not spectacular, the ceremony captivates by its archaic and hypnotic songs of three or four reiterated notes. The poetic words concern ancestry, progeny, and sustenance in a broad concept of fertility.

The members of the society occupy two vis-à-vis benches in the southwest corner of the longhouse; the men gather at the north wall. The four parts are as follows:

1. All are seated. Thanksgiving prayer made by the leading matron. Introductory antiphonal chants are intoned by the leader and echoed by the chorus to the rhythmic shaking of a small box turtle hand rattle, "brought from the South." One song says "Throughout the earth the turtle is stirring"; for the earth rests on the back of a turtle. Another says—"I have begotten grandchildren. They are coming creeping on the ground." Another refers to the sun, our elder brother, and to grandmother moon, *et so·t*, who sings to her grandchildren (Fig. 1, *4*).

2. All stand. Individual thanksgiving prayer and chant made by each woman, first the two leaders, who belong to opposite moieties, then each in turn in counterclockwise order, with accompaniment of turtle rattle, paddle, or broomstick. One song is translated:

> The fruit on the bushes in all the forests
> It is hanging ripe with fruit; in all the forest.

Another:

> In fair fields I am walking
> Along the meadow's edge I am walking.
> It's a nice garden that is planted
> It shows nice ears of corn [Jemima Gibson, Onondaga].

3. Jokingly, any man may approach the chanters with his own individual *adǫwe* thanksgiving chant, to the men's explosive "he-he" and the women's handclapping. The *tǫwisas* try to capture him and sing one of their songs, under peril of having his face streaked with soot by a paternal joking relative or *agadoni*.

4. The *tǫwisas* march around the women's stove, gradually followed by all female members of the audience, each holding an ear of corn. The leader chants:

> Now I am marching. Thanks I am saying.
> They have fulfilled. They have participated. Our children.

Fig. 1

The Corn Dance, *Oneǫnt'oenǫ,* belongs to the women, though they do not monopolize nor even lead it. This is a single short dance, distinct from the three-day Green Corn festival. It is included in the food spirit festivals and in social evenings of "songs of all kinds." It ties up with the *ęskänye* by concept but not by its step, which is a forward shuffling trot or stomp. Men follow the two singing leaders and the ladies join in various ways, among the Cayuga at the end of the line, among the Seneca in alternation, among the Onondaga in double-file with their left arm hooked in the male partner's right. The Seneca leader may wind the whole queue back and forth between the benches and stoves in a serpentine path.

Thus not only the corn, but the bean, too, is symbolized by the clinging action of the women and again by the representation of the tortuous growing habits of the plant.

The rare *Geiniwašǫndaje'* or Four Nights dance is unique among the Iroquois in the use of pantomimic gesture. In fact, this is probably due to its transmission from the Tutelo that settled on Grand River. Sometimes it is added to the minor one-day Green Corn feast of the Onondaga, as on August 16, 1949. The duration has now dwindled to a couple of hours.

FIG. 1.—Matriarchal Dances of the Iroquois

1. *Ęskänye gainǫ·ga'iyǫ ka',* ninth song in a cycle of 17 songs recorded by Joseph Williams, Seneca Longhouse, Six Nations Reserve, Ontario.
   haney'o weheya; wahaneya weheya; weya waheya'a haweyo
2. *Ęskänyego'owah,* twenty-fourth of 27 songs rendered by Chancey Johnny John of Coldspring Seneca Longhouse, N.Y.
   honiwayo wado'niyǫn (repeat) yoho
3. *Modern ęskänye,* first of 7 songs by Ed Curry, Coldspring Seneca.
   heya haiya howie yoheho (repeat); ga'en hawiya heya; ho
4. *Tǫwi'sas,* first of 7 songs recorded by Fannie Stevens, Coldspring Seneca.
   o·ya'ahi (o·ya'ahi); oyahi yawę ho' (o·ya'ahi)
   berries are ripe
5. *I'yonda·tha',* thirtieth of 34 songs by Chancey Johnny John and Albert Jones.
   guna huya hawiyaha; guna guna wiiyehe; ho
6. *Deswadęnyǫ,* twenty-third of 42 songs by Chancey Johnny John and Albert Jones.
   haniho yoho yahene (repeat); yohahahęnǫ
7. *'Ohgi'we',* thirty-third of 68 songs by Mr. and Mrs. Charlie Jamieson, Onondaga of Six Nations Reserve.
   gayonine nehe; dawenoya; ędawi hoyane'e'e;
   gayo'o ho'o, gayoniine nehe; edane goyane'e'e
8. *Ganadjitga'hǫ,* third of 10 songs by Joseph Logan, Six Nations Onondaga.
   yowe'e yowi hanuye (repeat)
9. *Gasgoi'ǫdadǫ,* second of 7 songs by Chancey Johnny John.
   weyahiyo ya'ane (repeat)

Except for *tǫwi'sas,* the texts are burden syllables or obsolete words. Recordings and text transcriptions by William N. Fenton: musical transcription by Gertrude Kurath.

A long string of females of all ages follows the three costumed leaders round and round the seated assembly of singers, men and boys. While echoing each song as given by the men, the women keep up a pulsating beat of step-brush, step-brush from side to side. Toward the end of the first hour they represent in gestures the hunting of strawberries among the leaves by sweeping the left arm forward and back. Then they enact the husking and winnowing of corn by jerking the hands right and left, first in separating action, then in clasped position.

Finally they speed up to a brief *ęskänye*. Every second dancer faces about and thus takes a partner. Pairs change places and on repetition of the song swap back to their own places.

This pattern is significant, for it terminates the Bear and Buffalo curing rites and constitutes the choreography of the Fish dance type. Thus we have another instance of the unifying motifs of Iroquois symbolism.

The idea of fertility and fickleness also pervades the two women's curing rites, though not by personification of corn and beans. The compound *I'yondatha-de'swadęyǫ* (and Quavering Changing-Ribs) survives among the Seneca, but is virtually extinct at Six Nations. Its members are cured sufferers from lassitude, lame joints, or respiratory ailments. The rite is said to have originated in the marriage of an obstinate bachelor with a semi-supernatural frog woman who later wearied of him. This theme of mating and inconstancy is tossed back and forth in teasing word play between men and women, during Quavering (Fig. 1, *5*). The second part, Changing-Ribs (Fig. 1, *6*), consists of a distribution of cloth to the singers and a forward shuffling round dance by the women.

The *'Ohgi'we'* Death Feast, which shares the cloth distribution and shuffle, has remained an important and elaborate ritual. Not only does it commemorate the spirits of the dead, but, as secondary function, placates these spirits when they have in anger caused neurotic derangements. Usually the patient's home is the scene of a private healing rite, and the longhouse of the communal memorials in the spring and fall. The body of the ceremony consists of two long dances, *'Ohgi'we'* and *Ganadjitga'hǫ*, separated by the distribution of cloth.

1. The *'Ohgi'we'* (Fig. 1, *7*) chants first syncopate the drum beat, then, half-ways of the songs, synchronize. The seated male drummer intones each song, repeats it with his two male assistants and hands it on to the women for two more repetitions. The two singing matrons guide the society members and, later on, additional volunteers, in a slow counterclockwise procession. Sometimes they break the monotonous dragging step with small stamps, kicks, pivots, and elbow waftings. After an hour and a half, the tempo speeds up and a brief *ęskänye* terminates the *'Ohgi'we'* proper.

2. During the intermediary *Ǫdasat'da* the two chief matrons stand facing the male singers on their corner bench and receive pieces of cloth from the female

sponsor. They wave them back and forth in time with the drum beats and reiterated chants, and distribute them to all officials, singers, and dancers. These gifts from participants may be a vestige of ancient sacrifice.

3. *Ganadjitg'ahǫ* (Fig. 1, *8*) (Carry-out-the-Kettle) focuses around the central drum, which is carried out at the finish. In the middle of the room the drummer and four singers of both sexes rotate slowly against the sun. Other women join and later on also men, all hooking arms as in the Onondaga Corn dance, but in arbitrary order. Facing the center they jump sidewards right with a lively hop-kick. A thick group finally winds itself around the musicians, joking and laughing.

4. After the feast an epilogue of social dances resembles the food spirit sequence—on this occasion *ǫskänye, ga'da'čot* stomp, *ǫskänye,* bean, Cherokee stomp.

5. At Onondaga longhouse a strange observance takes place at dawn: an outdoor processional elevation of cakes, which may once have symbolized sacrificial communion and is still attended by bad luck beliefs and omens.

The ritual structure, song tonality, step, and beliefs all point to great antiquity and imply symbols no longer consciously operative:

a) A consistent duality couples male and female functionaries and doubles formal constituents, from songs to the complete ceremonial structure.

b) The dance steps tie up with medicine and food rites, the shuffle with the Bear and Buffalo cures and Corn dance; the *ǫskänye* with the women's special dance, the False-face and Thanksgiving dances; the jump-kick with the Bear, Buffalo and False-face climaxes.

c) The uncoiled '*Ohgi'we*' and coiled *Ganadjitga'hǫ* may echo a half-forgotten myth about an all-devouring earth-serpent.

The prominent role of women as conductors and actors is especially significant in combination with the various associations of fertility, growth, and revival. The women as mothers and agriculturalists are in a position to evoke life out of death, out of the soil where all creatures lie buried. By pleasing the spirits of the departed they appeal to their chthonic powers.

The mothers.—In these various rites the matrons are consciously identified, by tradition and song texts, with life-giving elements—corn, beans, squash; the earth-turtle, the watery frog; the moon whose cycle governs planting and ceremonial timing; and circling against the sun. These attributes are commonly associated with women's ceremonies in other ethnic groups, as well as the Iroquois. They affect the entire choreographic system of agricultural and matriarchal tribes as the Cherokee, in contrast with male-dominated tribes of the Plains, Southwest, and Mexico.[3]

---

3. Verification of this hypothesis hinges on more extensive co-ordination of ethnological and choreographic materials.

Among the Iroquois these features are particularly integrated in the ceremonialism.

Superficially the women seem to tag along behind the vehemently gesticulating male dancers; with decorous and retiring demeanor (notwithstanding their often justified reputation for fickleness), they glide and hop with tiny precise steps, confined arms, downcast eyes; and they sing with gentle, subdued sopranos. Their power, though subtle, is nonetheless real and enduring.

One of their roles, agriculture, is being taken over by men. But it is a safe guess that the process of acculturation will not alter nature's assignment of the maternal function and the perpetuation of the race from past generations through the present into the future.

ARCHEOLOGY IN THE VICINITY OF NEW YORK CITY

Carlyle S. Smith

Archeological sites still exist in the vicinity of New York City, some of them on Manhattan Island itself. In Inwood Park at the northwestern corner of Manhattan several rockshelters and at least one shell heap are present. Specimens from the sites are on display in the American Museum of Natural History. Other sites are to be found in the Bronx, on Staten Island, and on Long Island. The best sites are found on Long Island because the city has not spread far enough to destroy or disturb them.

Typical sites consist of thin deposits of refuse made up of marine shells mixed with stained earth, charcoal, animal bones and artifacts. The refuse rarely exceeds six inches in thickness and usually covers less than an acre of ground. Bowl shaped pits filled with refuse are scattered over the sites. Most of the pits are approximately three feet in diameter and four feet in depth. Some of the historic sites are marked by rectangular earthworks.

All of the people inhabiting coastal New York spoke Algonkian languages. Staten Island was occupied by a branch of the Delaware confederacy. Manhattan, the Bronx and Westchester were inhabited by members of the Wappinger confederacy. The people on Long Island were known collectively as the Metoac but the nature of their tribal affiliations is obscure. Most of the Indians suffered greatly as a direct result of contact with the European colonists and their cultures quickly disintegrated. As a result there are few sites belonging to the period of contact with western civilization.

Despite the fact that the first museum-sponsored archeological explorations in New York State were carried on in the vicinity of New York City the characteristics of the cultures and their sequence in time have been but vaguely known. Skinner (431) presented a paper at the XIXth International Congress of Americanists in which he demonstrated that there are two levels of culture in the coastal area of New York, one without pottery and the other with pottery. He did not attempt to further subdivide the ceramic period except to recognize two divisions, one marked by simple pottery and the other by more complex forms suggestive of Iroquois. Most of the other writers treated their data in a timeless manner, often describing the material from the entire region as though it came from a single site. It has been necessary to re-examine all of the original data, especially the pottery, in order to solve the problem.

Ritchie (387, 388) studied the published accounts and postulated the presence of a Coastal aspect which he divided into two foci called "Early" and "Late." A third focus was designated as Orient. In 1932 I began to make a survey of the archeological resources of Long Island. At about the same time Ralph Solecki and M. C. Schreiner began similar independent investigations. It was not until 1938 that we pooled our findings and started to interpret them. Additional data were obtained by studying collections at the American Museum of Natural History and the Museum of the American Indian. The publication of a series of preliminary reports (432, 433, 434) prompted Rouse to contribute similar data from Connecticut (405, 406).

The archeology of coastal New York reflects certain cultural changes which took place in time throughout the eastern part of the United States. Wherever research has yielded evidence of a cultural complex characterized by the practice of agriculture and the manufacture of pottery an underlying horizon marked by a hunting and gathering economy and the absence of pottery has been revealed. The division of time into periods differing in economic pattern is somewhat blurred on the coast because of the peripheral position of the area in relation to the main centers of cultural development and, probably, because an adequate supply of shellfish, fish, game and wild vegetal food was always at hand. Throughout most of the archeological record hunting, gathering, fishing and shellfish-collecting appear to have remained the principal means of livelihood. In the course of time agriculture and pottery appear and by historic times agriculture had become an important source of food.

Ritchie's division of time for central New York into four major periods, Archaic, Intermediate, Late Prehistoric, and Historic, is applicable to the coast (388). The Archaic period is characterized by a hunting and gathering economy supplemented by shellfish-collecting. Artifacts of stone, especially chipped stone projectile points, are abundant while artifacts of bone and antler are absent or extremely rare.

The Intermediate period is characterized by the addition of agriculture, the probable decline of hunting, and the growth of shellfish-collecting as an important economic pursuit. Pottery is relatively common but artifacts of chipped stone are not as abundant as before. Bone and antler artifacts are present. The rich grave goods of the Orient focus suggest a preoccupation with the burial of dead which is characteristic of the period in central New York.

The Late Prehistoric period is marked by the intensification of agriculture and the refinement and elaboration of the pottery. The collecting of shellfish continued as a major economic activity supplemented by hunting and gathering. Artifacts of chipped stone are less prevalent than in the preceding period and appear to give way to those made of bone and antler. Small round, and probably dome-shaped, houses make their appearance. Mortuary practices are simple and grave goods are rare. In this period the manufacture of wampum begins.

The Historic period is marked by the advent of European explorers and settlers and the consequent disintegration of the native culture complexes. The period is essentially a continuation of the Late Prehistoric as far as the economy and the nature of the artifacts are concerned. Pottery continues in use for some time but most of the other artifacts are replaced by those of European manufacture. The manufacture of wampum reaches its apogee at this time. Many of the villages include a stockaded enclosure for use as a refuge in time of war. Documentary sources indicate the presence of rectangular and round houses. All of the cultures present in the Historic period are identifiable with Algonkian-speaking groups.

In terms of the McKern classification, two archeological patterns, Archaic and Woodland, are present in the coastal area. The Archaic pattern includes the horizon marked by the absence of pottery and agriculture. It is not divided further because of the dearth of adequate data. The Woodland pattern includes all of the cultures which practiced agriculture and made pottery. It is suggested, but not as yet demonstrated, that the Woodland pattern may be made up of two phases, Coastal and Northeastern, in this area. The Windsor aspect may belong to the Coastal phase while the East River and Shantok aspects may belong to the Northeastern phase. Each of the three main cultural divisions (aspects) are further subdivided into foci which, in most cases, are interpreted as temporal levels within each of the aspects.

The Pre-Ceramic horizon is poorly defined because of the dearth of sites producing sufficient data for comparison. The projectile points resemble some of the varieties found in the Laurentian and Windsor aspects so it is postulated that the culture may have been derived from Laurentian and that it contributed to the development of Windsor. At the Dyckman Street site on Manhattan Island the Pre-Ceramic horizon is stratigraphically earlier than Windsor. Spaulding (446) has postulated that the Laurentian aspect came in from Asia by way of Bering Strait. If this is true the archeological record in coastal New York may be linked with that of the Old World.

The Windsor aspect is identifiable in the Historic period as Nehantic in Connecticut but further documentation is lacking. Probably other historic groups in Connecticut and on eastern Long Island will be identified with the aspect when more work has been done. Originally the Windsor aspect had a circum-Long Island Sound distribution, over-lying the earlier Pre-Ceramic horizon, but in its later stages it became restricted to limited areas in Connecticut and eastern Long Island. Its earliest stage, the North Beach focus, is marked by the appearance of pottery in a variety identical with Vinette Type 1, the oldest known pottery found in central New York. The Windsor aspect lasted a long time, extending from the introduction of pottery to the settlement of the area by Europeans.

Documentation identifies the East River culture with the Massapeag subdivision of the western Metoac on Long Island in the middle of the 17th century. The distribution of the sites containing objects of European origin also indicates that the Wappinger confederacy and some groups of Delaware may have been responsible for the culture outside of Long Island. Its advent represents a marked cultural discontinuity because the underlying culture is an early stage in the development of the Windsor aspect, the Clearview focus. The different character of the artifacts in the East River aspect and the survival of the Windsor aspect elsewhere in the area militate against attributing the change in culture to the diffusion of new traits to the coast. It seems to represent an invasion by new groups of people following a different cultural tradition. The East River aspect is limited to the western half of the area under study and is separated from the Shantok aspect by the surviving remnant of the Windsor culture to the east. East River resembles Owasco and Iroquois of central New York.

The Shantok aspect is identifiable as Mohegan-Pequot on documentary and distributional grounds in Connecticut. On eastern Long Island it is documented as the culture of the Corchaug and the Montauk, both subdivisions of the eastern Metoac. The occurrence of one prehistoric site in Connecticut and the documentation of the others on both sides of Long Island Sound as mid-seventeenth century to early eighteenth century in date suggests a date bracket of *circa* 1600 to 1750 A.D. Shantok is limited to southeastern Connecticut and far eastern Long Island. The culture differs radically from Windsor in content but shares a few traits with East River. Shantok resembles the Iroquois aspect in ceramics.

Interpreting the archeological record in terms of the documented identity of the peoples responsible for the culture complexes we find that after the introduction of pottery and agriculture the entire area around Long Island Sound was occupied by the cultural ancestors of the Nahantic and other related groups, identified above with the Windsor aspect. After the Windsor aspect had reached its greatest spread, possibly *circa* 1000 A.D., groups of people who were ancestral to the western Metoac, Wappinger confederacy, and possibly some of Delaware, identified above as East River, invaded the western half of the area and pushed the Windsor culture eastward. The Windsor aspect survived in the eastern half of the area in relative isolation. In *circa* 1600 the Mohegan-Pequot invaded Connecticut and split the Nehantic tribe into two parts, Eastern and Western Nehantic. Diffusion from the Shantok aspect carried by the Mohegan-Pequot caused some of the eastern Metoac, notably the Corchaug and Montauk, to adopt a similar material culture. Impetus was undoubtedly given to the adoption of the Shantok culture by the migration in 1637 or 1638 of a group of Pequot to eastern Long Island after the Pequot War. It is significant that the two sites, Fort Corchaug and Pantigo, attributable to the Shantok aspect on eastern Long Island are documented as having been in use after the Pequot War. Soon after the arrival of the European colonists the native cultures disintegrated. Today there are a few remnants of Shinnecock and Poosepatuck on eastern Long Island and some Mohegan-Pequot in Connecticut.

Coastal New York and the immediately adjacent parts of the mainland of New Jersey and New England still offer opportunities for archeological research. The sequence established on the coast correlates well with that established by

Ritchie for central New York, similar time markers being present. When time perspective has been established in New England and in New Jersey even greater significance will attach to the cultural succession in coastal New York. Important fields for future research lie in the documentation of additional historic sites so that the three cultures, Shantok, East River and Windsor, may be identified with more of the tribal groups which were present in the area in the seventeenth century. It is necessary that more sites attributable to the period prior to the introduction of pottery be found and excavated before we can define the Pre-Ceramic horizon accurately. The salient characteristics of the pottery-using cultures are already clear but further work in Connecticut and on eastern Long Island will clarify matters. Details concerning the archeology of the area around New York City are embodied in my doctoral dissertation which has been published by the American Museum of Natural History (435).

SOME HIGHLY SPECIFIC MIDDLE MISSIS-
SIPPI CERAMIC TYPES

James B. Griffin

In the Mississippi Valley and southeastern United States there is a fairly long ceramic tradition now estimated to have begun roughly 2,000 years ago. For most of this period and throughout most of the area the pottery is, by and large, characterized by relatively simple utilitarian shapes. Other ceramic features, with some exceptions, are also not particularly outstanding and do not suggest inter-areal connections into Latin America or into the Southwest. The major influence in the early half of the use of pottery was apparently derived from northeast Asia.

As the result of stimuli from Meso-America probably around 1000 A.D. a new ceramic orientation entered the southeastern United States. There is also some evidence for cultural connections with the Southwest at about this same time to provide a secondary ceramic contact. The former influence is best identi-fied with the introduction of the pyramidal mound and its associated cere-monial plaza. From these two influences plus carryovers from the preceding period there gradually developed in the middle South as a part of the Mis-sissippi period an impressive and varied assemblage of modelled vessel forms and of painted wares which have been favorably compared with those of other New World centers. It is the purpose of this paper to review the position of some of these ceramic features in time and space. This has been presented in more detail in a forthcoming publication (363).

The human effigy bottle is one of the most common of the modelled forms, has a rather wide distribution in space and is at home in a number of distinctive sub-areas. It has interesting inter-areal connections outside of the Southeast. Some one hundred and seventy examples are distributed from Oklahoma on the west to almost the east Tennessee line, and from lower Illinois on the north to the Gulf Coast region on the south. Within this area there are two major con-centrations, in central Tennessee about Nashville, and in the contiguous portions of southeastern Missouri and northeastern Arkansas. This is probably best re-garded as a continuous rather than an interrupted distribution. Probably ninety per cent of the human effigy bottles in the Southeast have come from this more limited region. There are many minor modifications of shape but generally there is an attempt to model the whole human figure. This bottle is sometimes deco-rated with negative painting in the Cumberland but painting of any other kind even including red filming is very rare. The vessels usually represent a female. Among other features is the emphasis placed in portraying the figure as a hunchback with representations of the backbone, occasional indications of ribs and other resemblances of a skeletonized figure. There are also decorative

136

cross-overs between the human effigy bottle and the head vases. Most of these bottle forms are "hooded." In this treatment they somewhat resemble human effigy forms which are rather common in the Casas Grandes region of Chihuahua. A connection between these two areas has been recognized for some time. It is less well known that in the Anasazi culture human effigy vessels which must certainly have connections to the Southeast are a part of Developmental and Great Pueblo. Such vessels are much less common in the Southwest than in the Southeast.

Closely related to the human effigy bottle is the head vase. This form has a more limited distribution as the fifty examples are confined to northeastern Arkansas which has the Pecan Point, Conway, and Garland variants; and to southeast Missouri where the Charleston variant is at home. The Pecan Point type includes most of the specimens and can be regarded as the "classic" and perhaps original form. These head vases are usually painted in red and white on buff, red-on-buff or are red filmed. The Garland variant has closely spaced wide circular incised lines which links it to the late horizon in the lower Arkansas valley. The Conway variant has the distinctive late hourglass neck of the lower Arkansas and has human facial features placed on a flattened bottle form. The Pecan Point head vase is usually a skillful portrayal of the human face and undoubtedly represents the head of a dead person. These have been well illustrated in a number of publications. The Charleston type has the head modelled on the body of a carafe neck bottle. This variant is sometimes negative painted. In spite of certain stylistic resemblances to Central and South American head vases of various types there are no good connecting links available whereas strong connections can be seen to the head decorations of some of the human effigy bottle forms. This suggests the head vase developed locally in northeastern Arkansas, and perhaps because of its relatively late time position did not have time to spread far from that center.

The stirrup neck bottle is a form with obvious South American and Meso-American connections. Furthermore there is a degree of continuity in its geographic distribution which argues for gradual diffusion from south to north. In the Southeast thirty-four specimens of this vessel shape are concentrated in southeast Missouri and northeast Arkansas. In the prehistoric Southwest there are less than half this number and they are concentrated in the Anasazi culture between Basketmaker III and Pueblo IV. Meso-American stirrup-neck bottles are as early as Tlatilco in the Valley of Mexico Formative period but are most numerous in the "Tarascan" culture in post-Teotihuacan times.

Close to one hundred negative painted vessels can be listed for the Southeast. They are from a number of centers, the earliest of which is Crystal River, Florida. Crystal River Negative Painted is unique in the Southeast both in vessel shape and design. There is no direct evidence that it was ancestral to the Middle Mississippi styles. Nashville Negative Painted is the most abundant style and has its center in the Cumberland area. It is generally a carafe neck bottle. This neck form is associated with quadruped effigies (the so-called "dog pot"), or with a normal body bearing "cosmic symbol" designs, or with other motifs such as the hand and skull that are associated with the Southern Cult. Angel Negative Painted is found most commonly on a high rim plate and has its center at the Angel site in southwest Indiana. Sikeston Negative Painted is concentrated in southeast Missouri and is at times combined with direct painting. It is also associated with a carafe neck bottle and with the Charleston type of head vase. This technique of decoration becomes important about half way through the Mississippi period and lasts until sometime in the seventeenth century. The manner in which negative painting was disseminated into the Southeast is not known but it has been reported from as far north as San Luis Potosí in Mexico.

The tripod bottle is a common Meso-American form which appears for the first time in the Southeast near the mid-point of the Mississippi period. It too is concentrated in the central part of the Mississippi Valley particularly in the St. Francis and Memphis area with some extension into the Caddoan area of southwestern Arkansas, and to the north about the mouth of the Ohio. Records of ninety tripod vessels indicate that the bulbous leg is the most common shape. There is also a high proportion of slab legs, many of which are stepped. Other leg forms are ball shaped, conical and peniform. Tripod vessels have predominantly plain surfaces, and in the area of concentration these are called Neeley's Ferry Plain and Bell Plain. They are also common on Old Town Red, Carson Red-on-buff, Nodena Red on White, and in the Caddoan area appear with Blakeleytown Engraved. There are also Nashville Negative Painted forms but these are rare. All of these variations of the tripod seem to have died out before the full historic period but in some sites must have lasted into the seventeenth century. Tripods are not common in the Caddoan region or in the Southwest. Their precise connection into Meso-America is still not clear.

One of the distinctive forms is the compound bottle or jar. It is also concentrated in northeast Arkansas and the immediately adjacent areas. Compared with the other ceramic groups already discussed, this form is seen to be quite rare as only thirteen specimens have come to my attention. They are all plain shell tempered pottery with one exception which is Nodena Red and white. These vessels have either an opening between two adjoining bodies or are connected at their greatest diameter by a hollow cylindrical rod. They are also joined at the rim by a bar or strap handle. In the Southwest this compound horizontal shape is found in three Anasazi sites of the Great Pueblo period and is more frequent in the Casas Grandes area for there are available references for nine specimens.

This brief paper has presented information on six specific ceramic features. They are all a part of the Middle Mississippi culture and in time fall in the middle to near the close of the existence of that archeological division. They, along with other features of Middle Mississippi have connections to both Meso-America on the one hand, and to the Southwest on the other. This latter areal inkage is as yet not sufficiently developed but is a most promising field.

SOME GEOGRAPHIC AND CULTURAL FACTORS INVOLVED IN MEXICAN-SOUTHEASTERN CONTACTS

J. Charles Kelley

It has long been assumed that certain elements of the aboriginal culture of the Southeastern United States were of Mexican derivation. An economy based on agriculture, specific cultivated plants, agricultural techniques, and perhaps a basic ceramic complex are early Southeastern traits for which a southern origin seems indicated. Subsequently, the appearance in the Mississippi Valley of a complex, presumably of ceremonial nature, involving the construction of truncated earthern mounds serving as temple pediments, probably represents renewed or continued diffusion from the south. It has been pointed out in recent years that a highly specific ceramic complex associated with early manifestations of the ceremonial complex is likewise of Mexican origin. And at least some of the elements of the Southern Death Cult seem to have been introduced into the Southeast from Mexico in late prehistoric times.[1]

Comparatively little attention, however, has been given to the question of the nature of the contacts between the two areas and the routes followed. Simple expansion of the Mexican cultural area is not the explanation, since there exists an archeological hiatus of several hundred miles of territory in the state of Texas in which few or no remains attributable to either of the great cultural patterns have been found. This area, instead, produces abundant remains of the culture of a very simple hunting-collecting group, the Balcones Phase, and such evidence as is available indicates that this cultural pattern has great temporal depth in the area and survived almost unchanged until the late prehistoric period, say 1500 A.D.[2]

Explanations advanced to explain Mexican-Southeastern contacts through this hiatus usually involve either migration, trade, or simple diffusion. All of these processes undoubtedly were operative to some degree, and it is my belief that an examination of the archeological, ethnographical and geographical situation within the hiatus zone in the state of Texas will demonstrate the working of the actual processes of the contact.

Several routes of contact between Mexico and the Southeast have been discussed by various workers. The possibility of connections between the Southwest and the Southeast has attracted much attention, and it may well be that basic agricultural products and techniques were introduced from Mexico into

1. Outstanding papers dealing with the relationship between the Southeast and Mexico include 27, 114, 123, 144, 241, 300, 305, 338, 348, 362, 515.

2. For a recent discussion of this cultural horizon see 249.

the Southeast by this indirect route. Likewise, as the work of Krieger, Kelley, and others has shown there were later influences exchanged between Southwest and Southeast. However, these latter instances of diffusion seem to have been too late to be directly involved in the development of the Southeastern Cultural Pattern (242, 230).

An alternative route, "the Northern Overland Route," from Zacatecas and Durango down the Rio Conchos to the Rio Grande and thence overland across the Edwards Plateau to the Mississippi River Valley looks especially attractive, and indeed an elaborate system of trade and diffusion—best illustrated by the wanderings of the Jumano Indian, Juan Sabeata—developed along the northeastern part of this route in late prehistoric times. Again, however, this development seems to have been too late to be of marked significance (230).

Movements along the Texas Coast, either by land or by boat, must certainly be included in the possibilities, and McNeish has shown that Huastecan culture was indeed slowly spreading northward along this route (305). The area and its cultures are now being intensively investigated by T. N. Campbell and valuable results are sure to materialize in the future.

Gilmore and Krieger have advocated the possibility of the expansion of farming cultures, or, alternately, of the actual migration of Middle American groups northward along the belt of prairies paralleling the Balcones Escarpment on the south and east (243). This "Gilmore Corridor" followed the northern branch of the *Camino Real*, lay within an area of relatively favorable conditions for farming, and gave access to the many large springs which break out along the Balcones fault line. Archeologically, however, much of this territory seems to have been a "shatterbelt" of overlapping local territories and cultures and one not suited for group movements.

But if the lower half of the Gilmore Corridor throughout its southern extent is added to the belt of coastal prairies we have another potential line of movement, which might be termed the "Southern Overland Route." This route runs northward across the Gulf Coastal Plain and eastward to the Mississippi River Valley paralleling and overlapping the Gilmore Corridor proper on the south. This was a direct route along which ran the southern branch of the *Camino Real* and today the modern main highways and railways out of Mexico likewise follow it. A careful examination of the ethnohistorical data indicates that persons, things, and ideas actually traversed this route in the early historic period. This was the territory of the Coahuiltecan Indian bands and closely related groups, an area occupied by many small bands with overlapping territories and characterized by an extremely simple hunting-collecting culture. Archeologically, the basic underlying culture of this Coahuiltecan group is a slightly modified version of one aspect of the old Balcones Phase culture which had occupied the area for many thousands of years, a culture closely related to the basic Archaic culture of the Southeast and the Desert cultures of the Southwest. This culture appears to have filled the entire hiatus between Southeastern and Mexican cultures, and the archeological evidence indicates that at an early period the Huastecan-Mexican outposts on the south and the early Mississippian-Southeastern outposts on the northeast were actually in contact with this low-level neighboring culture (229).

So we have the picture of a simple culture occupying the hiatus and in contact with both the respective major cultural patterns at opposite ends of the area. Could persons, things, and ideas have been transmitted from one area to another through this cultural medium and yet leave it virtually unchanged? The answer is certainly an affirmative one. The detailed account of the Tejas, the Caddoan Hasinai Indians of eastern Texas, basically Southeastern in cultural orientation, given to the Spaniards in Coahuila in 1676 by Coahuiltecan Indians will serve to demonstrate this point: Coahuila, the Spaniards were informed,

has as a neighbor on the north, inclining somewhat to the east, a populous nation of people, and so extensive that those who give detailed reports of them do not know where it ends. These who give the reports are many, through having communicated with the people of that nation, which they call Texas, and who, they maintain, live under an organized government, congregated in their pueblos, and governed by a casicque who is named the Great Lord, as they call the one who rules them all, and who, they say, resides in the interior. They have houses made of wood, cultivate the soil, plant maize and other crops, wear clothes and punish misdemeanors, especially theft. The Coahuiles do not give more detailed reports of the Texas because they say they are allowed to go only to the first pueblos of the border . . . [51].

Here we have relatively detailed ethnographic data transmitted by diffusion and personal travel over six hundred miles or more of the hiatus. And if such detailed accounts of the Southeastern outposts could have been transmitted across the hiatus at this late date there is reason to believe that similar detailed accounts of Mexican culture—accompanied by persons and things pertaining to that culture—could have been transmitted through the same cultural medium, known to have been long in existence, to the nascent cultures of the Mississippi Valley at a much earlier date.

The geographic and cultural picture of the Coahuiltecan-Balcones Phase occupation of the hiatus zone as reconstructed from the reports of such early Spanish visitors as Alvar Nuñez, Cabeza de Vaca, who spent several years there in the early 1530's, and from the archeological record, is instructive as to the actual machinery of the contacts (16, 96, 89, 185). A peculiarity of the regional geography is the tendency toward local, and in part, seasonal concentrations of the plant foods of importance in the regional economies. The great concentration of mesquite (*Prosopis*) lay to the south and west along the Rio Grande and northward along the Balcones Escarpment with a comparatively thin extension northward and eastward into the Coastal Plain itself. Along the Nueces, Guadalupe, Colorado, and Brazos Rivers were great pecan groves, the produce of which could support many people in the late fall and early winter. Between these rivers and especially in the Nueces River region were huge thickets of prickly pear (*Opuntia*), whose fruit, the *Tuna*, was sufficiently abundant in the late summer and early fall to support many people. Aside from these plants, the food supply of the Texas Coastal Plain was inadequate to furnish subsistence for even a moderately large population. Deer or antelope were present and were utilized, but not to any great extent; bison were available in large numbers only in certain years; fish were locally available and locally utilized. In practice, the subsistence level was very low, even for the small population represented, and seasonal, annual, or intermittent starvation seems to have been the rule.

The net result of the lack of dependable food resources and their local and seasonal distribution was the development of an involved system of seasonal nomadism by the various Coahuiltecan bands. The example of the Mariames, a putative Coahuiltecan band who apparently occupied the lower Guadalupe, perhaps the Colorado, River, as reconstructed from the accounts of Nuñez and his associates between 1530 and 1535 illustrates the point.

During the winter the Mariames occupied the lower stretches of the river, living on rats, snakes, insects, dung, powdered bone, roots, and anything else that was even near-edible. This was the real starvation time. In the spring the river overflowed and fish were caught in the overflow pools, furnishing for some weeks a new source of food. As the early summer came on, the group moved slowly down the river toward the coast, eating green *Tunas*, berries, roots, and small game. They then turned southward toward Mexico and followed the coast for some thirty leagues, subsisting *en route* by killing "deer"—perhaps antelope— by running them into the sea.

At the end of this journey the Mariames turned inland for some ten leagues to the great prickly pear thickets—probably those of the Nueces River region— which in the late summer and early fall furnished ample food for all the bands of the region. This period was one of plenty, of feasting; a time when other groups who had come from long distances away—especially from the south— lived side by side with those who came from the north. Group ceremonials were held and trading was carried on. Tribes came from a long distance away to bring bows and arrows—new items on the Coastal Plain in the early sixteenth century—to trade. These are undoubtedly the great Indian fairs so often mentioned in the literature of the seventeenth century in Texas. At this time individuals such as Nuñez, wandering traders, discontented persons or exiles, adventurers, escaped captives, could leave their own bands and affiliate themselves with new ones. When the time came to leave the *Tuna* grounds, a man, or products, or ideas might go with a group returning to the north, although originally they may have been brought to the vicinity from the distant south.

With the waning of the *Tuna* season the various bands returned to their own winter territories. The Mariames marched overland toward the north, eating *en route* the last of the *Tunas*, to their homes on the Guadalupe River. There they arrived in time for the ripening of the nuts in the great pecan groves along that stream. Here again they found many other bands who had come from distant areas—this time from the north and from the east—to partake of the seasonally ample supply of nuts. Here too for a time the various groups lived in close association and when the nut harvest was over an individual who had started out from the lower Rio Grande with one group and transferred to another at the Nueces River, and returned with it to the Guadalupe River, could now join still a third group—or a fourth, or a sixth—and return with it still further eastward and northward to the region of the Colorado or the Brazos River. In less than a year's time—or on a journey spread over several years—persons, things, and ideas could thus move from the peripheries of Mexico to those of the Southeast, just as the detailed description of the way of life of the Tejas had moved southward over the same route. Just so might have moved on an earlier time horizon, bags or jars of maize and beans, and stories of how to raise or manufacture these products; and, later, ideas and paraphernalia of a ceremonial nature, specific pottery types, etc.

Thus, there actually existed a well organized system of diffusion of ideas, of movement of trade products, of transference of personnel along the Southern Overland Route through the medium of the Balcones Phase and the Coahuiltecan bands. The system bears all the earmarks of great antiquity and it is conceivable that it alone—without invoking, as Krieger and others have done, long distance mass migrations (338a)—could explain the resemblances between the Southeast and Mexico. In fact, the very nature of culture materials diffused through this process would tend to produce just that order of vague and generalized similarity between cultural parent and distant offspring actually encountered in this instance.

This of course still leaves the cultural hiatus itself unexplained. If we are to believe that Mississippi Valley tribes heard of a new way of life to the south, borrowed the food products, and along with them, eventually, certain new religious concepts and the associated paraphernalia and techniques, then we must ask why the intervening Coahuiltecan bands themselves, located far closer to the actual stimulus, did not take over this same new way of life. As later occupation of the area demonstrates, a primitive agricultural economy probably could function without difficulty in the region, so simple geographic factors alone can not provide an adequate explanation.

I think that the very nature of the Coastal Plain economic system, based as it was on the peculiar distribution of the wild plant food resources, supplies the answer. Any one group that attempted to maintain itself by maize farming in, say the Guadalupe River valley, would not only thereby interfere with the seasonal food supply of the other tribes who depended for their very survival upon the utilization of the seasonal products of the region, but in turn would have their own stored agricultural products raided by the same half starved bands who seasonally came there for food. Briefly, the economic adjustment for the entire group was too delicately balanced, too close to the bare survival level, to permit successful experimentation with a farming economy by one group which might deprive many groups of their only seasonal source of food. Remove one link in the complex and long established chain of seasonal economic migrations and the entire system would have crashed, as in fact it did at a later date, probably in part as the result of just such causes.

The history of the occupation of the Great Plains of the United States by our own culture provides a comparable example. The cattlemen established an early priority for the utilization of the land by their economic system. When farmers began to penetrate the area, considerable friction developed. The pioneer farmers of a necessity settled in those areas surrounding permanent water and used that resource for their own needs. But the cattlemen needed the same permanent water for the maintenance of their own system and could not tolerate this usurpation by the farmers; to do so simply spelled disaster to their cattle raising economy.

Thus the concept of a sedentary way of life based on farming and all of the associated traits could diffuse through the medium of the Balcones Phase without being adopted by that culture. But in the Mississippi River Valley conditions probably were quite different. Food resources seem to have been much more plentiful and, more important, highly diffuse rather than locally concentrated. Local bands on an Archaic level of culture probably depended upon all the resources of a local area, rather than sharing the seasonal products of several areas with many groups. Here an individual band could experiment with farming over the years, adding farm produce gradually to their other means of subsistence, without seriously encroaching upon the food supply of neighboring groups. Here a true sedentary culture based on agriculture could and did develop. The important distinction apparently lies in the localization of food resources in the hiatus zone and their dispersal in the true Southeast. Unfortunately my knowledge of conditions in the early Southeast is inadequate to allow of further development of this point.

In closing, let me emphasize that the *mechanism* of diffusion here described actually existed in the hiatus zone, and was operative in the early historic period. That it was by this means that the diffuse Mexican traits actually penetrated the Southeastern United States obviously is another question. To me it seems highly likely that it was principally by this means that such diffusion did occur, but obviously the hypothesis must be subjected to testing and to much more intensive study before it can be regarded as more than a hypothesis. In the meantime, however, let me suggest that as a hypothesis it at least has equal status with those theories of Mexican-Southeastern contacts based entirely on *a priori* grounds.

THE GALLINA PHASE OF NORTHERN NEW MEXICO[1]

L. PENDLETON

Northward from Cuba, New Mexico, almost to the Colorado state line, or perhaps beyond, lies an area some 1500 square miles in extent, which in the eleventh, twelfth, and thirteenth centuries A.D. supported a large agricultural population similar to and yet distinct from the Pueblo peoples of the Rio Grande Valley.

The University of New Mexico began work in this area as early as 1933. Before the war excavation work under the direction of Dr. Frank C. Hibben was carried out on a cliff house in Nogales Canyon and a small Pueblo-like group, known as Cerrito, located on a promontory some 400 feet above the Gallina River Valley. The Nogales Cliff House consists of towers and single-roomed units clustered together under a deeply over-hanging cliff. The Cerrito group contained five unit houses, a tower and a pit house.

The towers and unit houses of the Gallina People were usually built as single-roomed noncontiguous structures, separated from each other by several hundred yards of forest. However, beneath overhanging cliffs and on small promontories, wherever space was at a premium, groups of from two to fourteen contiguous rooms are known. The apparently simultaneous use of three different and distinctive types of architecture is one of several problems which confront us in the Gallina region.

During the 1947 and 1948 field seasons it was my privilege to work with Dr. Hibben on the excavation of a Gallina site on Rattlesnake Ridge six miles north of Llaves, New Mexico. The site contains, from surface indications, two pit houses, a unit house and a tower. In addition, there are two reservoirs, a feature which makes this site unique.

Our first season's work was concentrated on the tower. The Gallina towers are usually located on cliff edges, sharp ridges and other defensive situations. They can be either rectangular or circular in shape; are 15 to 26 feet in their greatest horizontal dimension; and probably stood 25 to 30 feet in height. (Their height is, so far, only an estimate based on the cubic content of fallen wall masonry and the thickness of the wall.)

Unit houses are found on low river terraces as well as on cliff edges and ridge tops, although the more defensive positions seem to have been the most popular. They are rectangular with either square or rounded corners. In some the corners are so rounded as to make the room almost round. Inside, the unit houses are 15 to 25 feet in their greatest horizontal dimension and were approximately

1. See 179, 181.

145

8 feet in height. (Again an estimate.) The walls of both towers and unit houses are constructed of large roughly shaped stone blocks and slabs forming a double wall with a rubble fill between.

Pit houses are located in small villages on river terraces or low promontories and on high saddles and ridges where the dirt cover is sufficient. They are roughly circular in shape and 15 to 25 feet in greatest horizontal dimension. (There are surface indications of pit houses 50 feet or more in diameter.) Excavated, the pit houses are 7 to 9 feet in depth. Except for plastered walls, the pit houses were otherwise unlined.

In all three types of structures the interior features are the same—ventilator shaft in the south wall opening into the room at floor level, fire pit near the center of the room, fire screen between ventilator and fire pit. Also on the south

Fig. 1.—Tower before excavation

side of the room adobe walled bins protrude from the east and west walls. The fire screen is sometimes built as a small bin, and bins are often built in the corners of the adobe bankette which runs around three sides of the room, from the bins on the east to the bins on the west. This bankette varies in height and width from one structure to another but is always too high or too narrow or both to serve as anything more than a shelf. Floors are usually finished with neatly fitted flagstones in adobe matrix, but some are simply plastered smooth. Black and red wall murals consisting of two apparently standard patterns with an occasional variation have been found in most unit houses and towers excavated to date. Subfloor cists are found occasionally in the unit houses.

Entrance to the structures must have been through the roof. The tower at Cerrito had walls still standing up to 17 feet with no sign of any doorway. The

Fig. 2.—Interior of round tower after excavation

walls of the Rattlesnake Ridge tower stand 12 feet with no doorway evident. Unit houses with standing walls of 4 to 5 feet show no signs of a doorway.

Just west of the excavated pit house and tower at Rattlesnake Ridge we found a structure previously unknown in the Gallina area. Apparently a storage and work area, it consisted of two small rooms, one rectangular and one **D**-shaped. Upright posts at roughly 18 inch intervals supported the roof. Brush may have been fastened between the uprights to form a windbreak, or the areas may have been left open to the breeze. Apparently the floor was of smoothly

Fig. 3.—Interior of excavated unit house showing firepit, fire screen, bins, bankette, flagstone floor and murals.

plastered adobe, and the roof construction followed the usual Gallina pattern— that is, beams 4 to 6 inches in diameter laid side by side, a thick layer of adobe mud plastered over the beams, and flagstones set in the top of the still damp adobe. This ponderous roof construction seems to have been used by the Gallina people for pit houses, unit houses and towers alike. When the small structure was burned, the roof over the rectangular room apparently pancaked almost completely intact. Excavation revealed it lying directly on, and in contact with the smoothly plastered adobe floor.

The top of the roof of the rectangular room was divided into two large bins. Numerous small mounds of burned corn seemed to indicate that the bins were used for the drying or storage of the grain. In the shallow fire pit in the **D**-shaped room there were two restorable bowls nested upside down.

Most Gallina sites investigated to date have borne evidence of having been subjected to intense heat following the violent death of the occupants. Walls, floors and roof debris are burned to varying shades of pink and orange. Corn and beans in the storage bins are charred. Often potsherds have been reduced to a bubbly froth by the extreme temperature. The charred remains of the occupants have been found with points embedded in their bones. A stone axe was deeply embedded in one skull.

Fig. 4.—Detail of murals showing two standard patterns

It seems possible that such complete firing of the stone and adobe structures could have been accomplished by filling the interior with sage brush which burns even when freshly cut, gives off a tremendous heat and leaves such a small quantity of fine powdery ash that within a few days all trace of the fire's fuel would have been removed by the wind.

Gallina pottery is of two distinct types, and both coiled and paddle-and-anvil techniques were used in their construction. The black-on-white decorated ware, although contemporaneous with Pueblo III, more closely resembles Pueblo II in workmanship. The plain grayish colored utility ware bears a striking resemblance in shape and manner of decoration to eastern Woodland potteries. Frank Hibben (182) has recently published a detailed study of the Gallina pottery, so that a brief outline of its most outstanding characteristics should suffice here.

The decorated ware is made from a fine homogeneous gray paste with a fine grit temper. It is built up by coiling and covered with a thin slip of the same material as the paste. The walls are thinned by scraping and smoothed on the exterior. Decorated wares usually occur in the form of large ollas and water jars, small olla forms with lugs and bowls of small size. Decorations were applied with a black carbon paint in lineate designs, solid figures and hour glass patterns. The vessels were polished over the paint.

Fig. 5.—Typical Gallina decorated ware

Two types of undecorated ware are found in this area. One bears a close resemblance to the decorated ware in paste, form and construction, its only variation being in the use of the paddle-and-anvil in thinning the basal portions of the vessel and the occasional use of a fillet decoration on the rim.

The second undecorated type of Gallina pottery has been referred to as utility ware because of its great profusion in every Gallina site. It is made from dark gray clay with coarse sandy temper. The vessels were coiled and thinned with paddle-and-anvil. Coils were often left on the neck of the vessel in a washboard effect or as flat coils. Often the coils were imperfectly obliterated. The bottoms of these vessels were pointed or semi-pointed so that the lower part of the vessel has a very pronounced conical shape. Constriction at the neck is slight; the rim is flaring, the mouth wide. A fillet was applied on or just below the rim but not completely around the vessel so that a gap, or "spirit opening" was left. Occasionally the fillet was pinched at intervals by way of decoration. Other decorations sometimes found include corrugation, striations formed by short strokes of either a corncob without kernels or a jagged stick, pinching with fingers in wet clay in rows or designs and fingernail marking in designs.

In the Gallina area many of the generally less diagnostic features are quite distinct from their Pueblo counterparts. Axes are all of one type—in general a rather large axe blade tapering to a pointed bit and with three notches so arranged as to form a T-shaped hafting around the body and also around the poll of the axe.

Pipes, too, seem to be all of one type. They take the form of a comparatively large elbow pipe of baked clay. The bowl of the pipe is flaring and bell-shaped, and the elbow is provided with two small projections or legs. Most specimens average around 4 inches in total length.

A distinctive type of knife is also found in Gallina sites. This has a laurel-leaf or semi-lanceolate form with one point blunted. The hafting seems to have been effected on the pointed end, leaving a semi-pointed blade for cutting purposes.

Charred roof supports yield an interesting series of dates from every site excavated. The earliest dates—1085, 1087, 1092 A.D. (O'Bryan)—came from the tower on Rattlesnake Ridge. However, this tower was destroyed twice, and these dates represent only the first building of the tower. Some time later the rubble inside the tower was leveled off about 6 feet above the original floor and a new flagstone floor constructed over the north half of the tower. This floor was then divided into two large storage bins. We were unable to get a date for the construction of the bins. However, I feel that they may safely be assumed to have belonged to the occupants of the unit house which was attached to the side of the tower. This structure yielded the date of 1223 A.D. (O'Bryan)—over 100 years after the tower was first built.

A pit house excavated by Dr. H. P. Mera and dated 1106 A.D. (Mera) stands, so far, as the only dated pit house. We were unable to secure any datable wood from the pit house on Rattlesnake Ridge.

The Nogales Cliff House[2] yielded one date of 1239 A.D. and five later dates— 1256, 1259, 1264, 1266, and 1267. From Cerrito came the date 1240-41 (Stallings), and a unit house excavated by Dr. Mera was dated 1253-54 (310).

These dates clearly indicate a contemporaneity with the great Pueblo III centers of Chaco, Aztec, Mesa Verde and the Rio Grande Valley. Yet the cultural development of the Gallina people lagged well behind. The paucity of evidence indicating trade between the Gallina people and their neighbors may be one explanation of this strange cultural lag in the midst of progress. Dr. H. P. Mera (309) in 1935 reported the finding of six intrusive potsherds in the western

2. Dated by Haury-Scantling.

Gallina (Largo) region. Three of these sherds were unidentified. One was identified as Chaco II; one as Santa Fe Black-on-white; and one as similar to Mesa Verde. Dr. Hibben (182) reported six cord-marked sherds from House VI at Cerrito and two "maize-marked" sherds from Cuchillo. No other trade evidence has been reported.

Geographic isolation is hardly an adequate solution to the problem. The country, although rugged, is quite accessible from any direction to a man on foot.

There is a great deal of work yet to be done before the many strange complexities of this area and their relationships to the other Pueblo peoples can be fully understood.

THE ABANDONMENT OF THE NORTHERN PUEBLOS IN THE THIRTEENTH CENTURY

Deric O'Bryan

Every archeologist interested in the southwestern United States eventually becomes involved with possible explanations for the retreat from—the abandonment of—large and favorable areas by the Pueblo Indians during the later stages of their pre-Spanish development. The problem is particularly challenging in the consideration of the San Juan drainage: this area is thought by many to be the cradle of the Basket Maker–Pueblo culture; peaks were reached by the 12th century inhabitants of the Chaco tributary and by the 13th century cliff-dwellers of the Mesa Verde and Kayenta regions; then, at the height of their prosperity and presumably at the maximum of their strength, they left the San Juan drainage abandoning their large communities in an unhurried orderly manner.

A number of theories and combinations of theories have been advanced regarding particular and general retreats by the pre-Spanish Pueblo Indians. Each theory is substantiated at least by local evidence; to date no theory appears to have general applicability. Briefly, these are the theories and some evaluations of them:

I. The Great Drought, from 1276 to 1299, was determined by Dr. A. E. Douglas, an astronomer, while studying conifer growth in the Southwest. Thinking of the devastating effects of an extended period of deficient rain-fall to Pueblo agriculturists throughout the semi-arid country, Dr. E. W. Haury stated: "It does not seem that crucial periods in both weather and Pueblo history should occur simultaneously through coincidence" (172, p. 14).

The Drought theory is ingenious; it does not stand close scrutiny, although the cluster of dry years may have been the final misfortune to cause the desertion of certain already insecure settlements. In the first place, the 1276 to 1299 drought has no bearing on the evacuation of the great Chaco sites which have terminal tree-ring dates from 1121 to 1135. Some Mesa Verde people were moving south by 1225, judging by the earliest re-occupation date from Aztec National Monument (147, pp. 124–30). Although pertinent tree-ring dates are not available, indicative pottery types found on the Hopi mesas suggest an exodus from the Kayenta region under way before the publicized drought years. Secondly, Gladwin (146) has pointed out that a correlation between tree growth records and annual crop success or failure is doubtful at best. A southwestern conifer adds most of its annual ring in the spring, usually reflecting the amount of winter moisture; corn, beans, and squash planted in the spring sprout if there

153

is sufficient moisture in the soil retained from the snows of the preceding winter, however, their growth to maturity is dependent upon adequate summer rainfall. Finally, an extended drought would lessen stream and spring flow; more often than not the movements of people appear to have been to more arid areas, away from snow-retaining mountains and perennial streams.

II. The Arroyo-Cutting theory was advanced by Dr. Kirk Bryan, a geologist, based on a study of epicycles of erosion and sedimentation in the Southwest. Dr. Bryan stated: "The effect of arroyo cutting is somewhat different from that of a mere drought. The growth of an arroyo takes place by the headward migration of falls. . . . As the falls move upstream, flood-water field after flood-water field becomes useless . . . and the cultivator knows that this year or at least within a few years calamity will overtake him" (60, p. 240). Dr. Bryan's reasoning may present a condition coincidental with the abandonment of the Chaco communities. But why were the largest Chaco colonies, on the Animas and San Juan Rivers—in fertile valleys about 50 miles to the north, abandoned rather than expanded at the same time? If the need of fertile soil was the only governing factor, the inhabitants of the San Juan should have moved to the rich bottom lands along the upper Colorado and upper Rio Grande Rivers.

The Arroyo-Cutting theory has been applied to the Kayenta district: ". . . The abandonment of Tsegi Canyon by the Pueblos is accounted for by the changing conditions of deposition and erosion of its stream" (23, p. 158). This is a conclusive statement which I question: it does not explain the concurrent abandonment of Mesa Verde by mesa-top agriculturists, nor does it take into consideration the many flood-water retaining dams and other evidence of mesa-top agriculture found on both sides of Tsegi Canyon in the heart of the Kayenta region (153, p. 69).

Variants of the Arroyo-Cutting theory are: soil exhaustion, and forest retreat and denudation. Until very recent times, there was little possibility of soil exhaustion through over-cultivation in the Southwest; the limited amount of water available was too unyielding a safety factor until the continuous pumping of ground water augmented local supplies within the last two decades. Soil exhaustion, meaning diminution by erosion, is of course of common occurrence and is the basis of the Arroyo-Cutting theory. Forest fires may have caused the abandonment of small areas for limited times. Dr. E. K. Reed stated: ". . . The forests have been receding upward . . . over the Southwest generally . . . with consequent deterioration of water supply . . . during the period of human occupation of the Southwest" (384, p. 69). Dr. Reed rightly concludes that this slow recession had little to do with "the abrupt abandonment of large areas"; both the Kayenta and Mesa Verde people moved from well forested areas to lower, more barren, country.

III. The Epidemic theory, proposed by Dr. H. S. Colton, has few followers. Dr. Colton believed that the founding of large communities led to unsanitary conditions, increased the infant mortality rate and fostered epidemic diseases, thus depopulating whole areas (82). There is little archeological evidence of epidemics, and no suggestion of population decline during the period in question —before the end of the fourteenth century.

IV. The Warfare theory, the intrusion of hostile nomads, was summarized in part by Dr. A. V. Kidder as early as 1924: "Attacks [brought the hunting tribes] rich stores of garnered corn, and they soon came to realize that by raiding the practically defenseless small towns they could supplement their food supply and so maintain themselves in territory not hitherto open to them because of lack of game. . . . In the northern San Juan the 'unit type' villages began to bunch together to form somewhat larger aggregations" (232, pp. 126–27). A recent proponent of this theory stated: "As the nomads increased in numbers [in the 900's, in the upper San Juan drainage] the area became crowded and the Rosa people were forced to move up on the less desirable but more easily defended highlands" (163, p. 103).

This theory is partly refuted by Dr. E. H. Morris. He reviewed the few instances of calamitous death and concluded: "So few direct evidences of disaster . . . argue against a prevalence of warfare, and indicate marked freedom of attack by predatory neighbors" (334, p. 42). Dr. Morris also stated a variant possibility: "The defensive quality of the great-house style of construction cannot be denied. But the destroyers . . . whom it was thus sought to keep at bay may as well have been groups living under the same culture, as bands of alien raiders" (334, pp. 41–42).

Dr. Ralph Linton also questions the importance of nomadic pressure and advocates internecine warfare: "The assured food supply of the [Pueblo Indians] . . . gave them an overwhelming superiority of numbers, while they were better organized and at least equally well armed and mobile. . . . The cliff-dwellings and fortified pueblos are mute witness that the Anasazi of the Pueblo III period considered themselves in serious danger. If we discard the nomad theory, the only logical explanation seems to be that these defenses were designed to protect the various . . . communities from each other" (272, pp. 28–32).

I wonder why the few remains of violent death should bar the presence of hostile nomads on the one hand, yet support the possibility of internecine strife on the other.

There is general consensus that the formation of large communities, and the construction of towers and other fortifications, in the 12th and 13th centuries were reflections of a hostile atmosphere. (Oddly enough, the same reasoning has not been applied as the explanation of the huge Pueblo I villages of the 700's and 800's, and there is strong although questioned (42) evidence that a large number of round heads filtered into the Southwest at that time and mingled with the established Basket Makers.) Most differences of opinion are over the source or sources of that hostile atmosphere. Some recent publications contain information which supports the theory of attack by nomads as the major condition leading to the abandonment of the San Juan drainage. And I have determined some tree-ring dates for indisputably late Pueblo III fortifications in the area.

The Huschers reported on "The Hogan-Builders of Colorado"; much of their investigation was along the northern edge of the San Juan drainage. They concluded: "Though the actual time of their arrival still is not known . . . most of the pottery finds would indicate a brief occupation sometime around 1,000–1150 A.D. . . . it is certain that by the time the Spanish were on the scene . . . the Southern Athapaskans—now the Apache and Navajo—had spread over and beyond the Pueblo Southwest and had learned about everything the Pueblo could teach them, without forgetting very much of what they already knew" (203).

Hall believed the Gobernador stockaded settlements and certain non-Puebloan material culture accessories to be evidence of an intrusion of nomads in the upper San Juan drainage in the 900's (163).

A curious complex of conical bottomed pottery vessels, antler tools, fortifications, and violent death—mixed with Puebloan characteristics—has been reported from the height of land between the upper San Juan and Chama (western Rio Grande) drainages. Dr. H. P. Mera (310) and Dr. F. C. Hibben (182) have published on this Largo-Gallina Phase. Charcoal from sacked towers, located less than 100 miles northeast of the Chaco centers, has furnished reliable dates ranging from 1085 to 1248. This scene of strife and complex of foreign (possibly Athapaskan) traits are well within the recognized Pueblo area, and the dates have meaning in regard to the abandonment of the adjacent Chaco and Mesa Verde areas.

A number of protected springs, fortified dwellings and watch towers are situated north of the San Juan River, within and around Hovenweep National Monument. These sites are famous as examples of extremely defensive construction. In 1941 I recovered some datable wood from a fortified dwelling locally known as Cutthroat Castle, and from a look-out in Square Tower Canyon within the National Monument.[1] The specimens from the fortified dwelling furnished four bark dates from 1245 to 1266; a single bark date of 1254 was determined for the look-out. The builders of these sites shared cultural characteristics with the Mesa Verde cliff-dwellers—whose southward exodus from their canyon retreat area began in or shortly before 1225.

The Pueblo Indians have deserted villages, groups of settlements, even large areas in historic times and for known reasons. The citing of a few historic examples may throw light on past abandonments, and furthermore suggest that no single cause is the important factor all of the time.

Pecos was the eastern bastion for the upper Rio Grande Pueblos from the 14th century until the early 1800's; the Spaniards reported the inhabitants to be unusually aggressive, and accustomed to withstanding periodic attacks from nomads to the east. Pecos did not prosper under Spanish domination nor from

1. Material in the Gila Pueblo Wood Library.

enemy forays in historic times; however, it remained a powerful center until decimated by an epidemic. The few lingering survivors finally moved to another pueblo—Jemez.

Hawikuh was the richest of the famed cities of Cibola. It, and the other Zuni strongholds, successfully repelled nomadic marauders for centuries before the arrival of the Spaniards. Eventually Hawikuh was destroyed by the "Apaches de Nabaho" (184); the few that escaped joined other survivors in the pueblo of Zuni.

Awatovi, the largest eastern settlement of the Hopi, flourished before and after the coming of the Spaniards. Intra-tribal disputes developed, and internecine warfare abruptly terminated the occupation.

Epidemics, droughts, the erosion of farm land, and many other conditions may have been causes of local abandonments. But I believe the evidence now at hand warrants the attachment of greater importance to the Hostile Nomad theory as the major explanation of the regional abandonment in the 1100's and 1200's. The large, easily defended communities in the Chaco, Mesa Verde and Kayenta areas served their purpose—they were not attacked and razed. But it is not hard to picture the Navajo nomads in the vicinity, burning fields, robbing granaries, killing hunters, and successfully besieging marginal settlements (whose ruins usually are passed over by archeologists in favor of the richer, more diagnostic, and more spectacular culture centers). Finally, I believe that the worried agriculturists of the San Juan drainage, weary of constantly increasing stealthy pressure, joined their kin in less molested locations to the south.

EVIDENCES OF EARLY MAN IN BAT CAVE AND ON THE PLAINS OF SAN AUGUSTIN, NEW MEXICO

HERBERT W. DICK

Bat Cave is situated at the southwestern end of the Plains of San Augustin, Catron County, west central New Mexico, in the northeastern periphery of the Mogollon culture area. It was excavated under the joint auspices of the Peabody Museum, Harvard University, which supplied financial aid, and the University of New Mexico, which furnished equipment.

The San Augustin Plains lie some fifty miles west of Socorro and seventy-five miles north of Silver City, New Mexico, in a region of flat-lying volcanic rocks generally included in the Colorado Plateau physiographic province. The general landscape bears a strong resemblance to the Basin and Range country.

The plains are a typical arid basin with an average rainfall of 13 inches a year. They are surrounded by mountains that rise abruptly from 1000 to 3000 feet above the plains level (370, pp. 346-47). The lowest point in the plains has an altitude of 6,775 feet above sea level. This point is encountered in the middle of the southwestern portion of the basin, directly in front of Bat Cave (370, p. 347).

The cave was formed by the erosive action of lake water, underground water, wind, and perhaps frost action. Lake action against the high volcanic agglomerate cliffs, which form the southeastern border of the plains, was probably the greatest single erosional factor in the formation of the cave.

During the last glacial period, the basin contained a large body of water. According to Powers (370, p. 350), Lake San Augustin at its highest stage of 165 feet (6,940 feet) was a body of water 34 by 11 miles in extent. It had no outlet, but there is evidence of an inlet in the northeastern corner of the basin which drained several other small lakes at a high stage of their history. Antevs' studies of the beaches indicate that the lake culminated some 12,000 to 10,000 years ago.

There is a long gentle slope from the lowest point in the basin to the foot of the talus of the cave; the cave talus then proceeds quite steeply until a gentler gradient is reached at the main floor of the cave, 131 feet (6,906 feet) above the bottom of the basin.

The cave proper is a huge amphitheatre-like rock shelter, measuring 75 by 70 feet. The roof at the springline is 75 feet above the floor. The floor had been disturbed by vandals and guano hunters in every section not covered by roof fall. Four small, narrow side chambers on the east side and in front of the large chamber were found choked with undisturbed debris. These chambers and the

158

talus deposits gave the clearest picture of the cultural and geological history of the site.

Excavations were begun in the talus in front of the caves. Six-foot squares were laid out in a grid system and excavation was carried on there for half the season; then labor was transferred to the small caves for the remainder of the season.

Dr. Antevs'[1] study of the excavated talus slope and cave deposits is as follows:

The sections in Bat Cave show three main beds:

The top bed, mostly 4 to 6 feet thick, stands apart by copious organic matter which occurs as plant debris or trash in the dry recesses and in the form of humus in the outer areas that were exposed to rain and run-off. The color of the bed changes accordingly from yellowish brown to brown in the dry parts of the cave through gray to almost black in the moist areas. In the dry niches the bed is made up of grass bedding with ashes, roof debris, dust, bones, food plants and artifacts of stone, baked clay (in the upper levels), wood, plant fiber, animal hair and skin. In the moist areas the bed consists of rock blocks, spalls, fine fragments, silt and clay from the cave roof and of decomposed organic matter. Only stone artifacts and sherds are preserved.

The middle bed, 1 to 6 feet thick, is similar in recessed and exposed areas of the cave and is distinctive by the lack of organic matter. It is yellowish brown to a gray buff and is composed of blocks, spalls and particles from the cave roof and dust (and sand) which may in part be airborne. It contains infrequent artifacts of stone.

The lower bed, 5 feet and deeper (not explored to bottom), consists of fine to medium coarse rolled gravel—beach gravel. The pebbles have a thin white coating of calcite. No artifacts have been found.

AGE OF THE BEDS IN BAT CAVE

Bat Cave was mostly battered out by successive pluvial lakes when these were at and near their highest stand. The last substantial water body, Lake San Augustin, reached the level of 165 feet deep. The beach gravel, which was exposed by excavation at 6,880 feet altitude (105 feet above the basin bottom and 60 feet lower than lake maximum of 165 feet), was deposited during the subsidence of Lake San Augustin.

The sterile middle bed may derive from the Altithermal age about 5000–2500 B.C., which in the region was warmer and drier, with sparser vegetation, than the present. Solitary stone artifacts and hearths show that man occasionally used the cave.

The top bed with its plentiful vegetable matter and ample evidence of continuous occupance by man, may have begun forming when the climate had become moist enough to supply permanent local water, or at least as moist as today. This may have occurred about 2500 B.C., which is the date of birth of the last water bodies in Owens, Abert and Summer basins, California and Oregon, judging from their salt contents some 50 years ago. The oldest specimens of maize, found a few inches above the base of this bed, may be nearly 4000 years old.

The top bed contained the greatest number of both perishable and imperishable artifacts. The upper 22 inches contained pottery and was somewhat mixed in sections. The deeper strata of the pottery level contained more consistently plain brown ware and red ware. The pottery, identified by Emil Haury, was for the most part Mogollon types and included Alma Plain, Alma Scored, San

1. Personal communication.

Francisco Red, Mogollon Red/Brown, Three Circle Red/White, Kiatuthlanna or White Mound Black/White, Tularosa Fillet-Rim and a plain brown ware, yet undescribed. The pottery level extended from about 500 A.D. to 1300 or 1400 A.D.

Large numbers of bison bones (*Bison bison*) were found concentrated in the pottery level and thinning out in the lower levels. Other mammals found in the top bed, both with the pottery and below it, were two varieties of deer, sheep (wild variety), probably elk, antelope, wolf, and a variety of rodents, including rabbit and porcupine. The mammal bones were sparse below the middle of the top level. No extinct mammals have been identified as yet.

Many of the stone implements in the upper levels had scraps of hair and meat still adhering to them. The implements, scrapers, knives, choppers, hammerstones and grinding tools found throughout the top strata and into the middle strata were in appearance and measurement similar to all types known from the Chiricahua and San Pedro stages of the Cochise Culture of southern Arizona (419, pp. 15-30). They were also similar to those found by Martin in the Pine Lawn phase, an early pottery horizon, of the Mogollon culture at the S.U. Site, located 40 miles west of Bat Cave. Similar artifacts were also found by Martin in the Wet Legget Complex, a variant of the Chiricahua phase of the Cochise industry (297, pp. 39-80) in the same area.

Over 400 projectile points were recovered from the excavations in Bat Cave. These fell into a total of seventeen types, including sub-varieties. A brief summary of the seven most diagnostic types gives a possible clue to the spatial and chronological position of the Bat Cave lithic industries in the prehistory of the southwestern United States.

In stratigraphic order from top to bottom we find the following common types:

1. Small, corner and side notched projectile points, with a triangular or rounded base. These are commonly called "bird points."

2. Large, corner and side notched projectile points, with a triangular or rounded base.

3. Points resembling those of the San Pedro Stage of the Cochise Industry of southeastern Arizona (419, Pl. XVIc).

4. Points resembling a Pinto Basin type (399, Pl. 13, *r, s*) and also resembling projectile points found by Martin in the Wet Legget complex.

5. Points resembling Chiricahua projectile points; these include all types attributed by Sayles and Antevs to the Chiricahua Stage of the Cochise Industry (419, Pl. XI, *b, c, d, f, g*).

6. Augustin projectile points, with a pointed base.

7. Bat Cave projectile points, having a slight indentation below the base, and rounded shoulders.

It is important to note that there is a striking similarity in the grinding tools and other utility implements, such as rough scrapers and knives, to those found in the Chiricahua and San Pedro phases of the southeastern Arizona Cochise

Industry. Also important is the fact that these implements remain the same throughout the stratigraphic column from bottom to top, whereas there is a continual change in projectile point styles. The points tend to decrease in over-all size from bottom to top; and rarely, if ever, do corner and side notched points with a triangular or rounded base appear below the 2500 B.C. date zone.

Perhaps we are on the threshold of an archeological theorem in being able to state that corner and side notched points with a rounded or triangular base did not make their appearance in the Southwest until after 2500 B.C. Also, that from sometime shortly after 5000 B.C. there was a growing tendency for points to diminish in size. This is suggested not only from the evidence of Bat Cave but other archeological horizons in the southwestern United States.

The San-Pedro-like points occur for the most part in the *upper half* of the 2500 B.C.—A.D. 500 date zone. The Chiricahua-like points center for the most part in the *lower half* of the 2500 B.C.—A.D. 500 date zone; a few are found below the 2500 B.C. date line. The Pinto-like points overlap the San Pedro and Chiricahua points and form a pattern *midway* in the 2500 B.C.—A.D. 500 date zone.

The range in style and size of the projectile points named *Augustin points* is great. The term "Augustin point" has been given to facilitate present and future identification of this diagnostic type and to relieve the burden of designating every pointed-base projectile, regardless of situation or appearance, by the over-used term "Gypsum point," a type first distinguished by Harrington and found with extinct mammals in Gypsum Cave, Nevada (168, p. 60). The pointed-base projectile point termed Manzano Point, found in Manzano Cave in north central New Mexico by Hibben (180, p. 36), is neither in size nor in appearance, except in broad generalization, like the Augustin point. Also, the Manzano point has not been isolated satisfactorily enough in the disturbed deposits of Manzano Cave to give it a clear chronological position in early Southwestern prehistory.

It is likely that projectile points similar to the Augustin point have been found in central and southern Chihuahua and Coahuila, Mexico, and might, very tentatively at this writing, be related to the introduction of the first maize into Bat Cave. The Augustin point centers in the *upper fourth* of the 5000–2500 B.C. date zone and extends into the *lower part* of the 2500 B.C.—A.D. 500 date zone. It overlaps to some extent the Chiricahua types.

The Bat Cave points are quite distinctive, with a straight to slightly concave base and rounded shoulders. The middle of the blade is usually greater in width than the base. These points center in the *upper third* of the 5000–2500 B.C. date zone and overlap the position of the lower Augustin points. The deepest projectile point found in the site, a single specimen, is a generalized form of the Bat Cave type. It was found in the *lower quarter* of the 5000–2500 B.C. date zone.

In conclusion, from this preliminary study of the Bat Cave artifacts, we find the two later stages of the Cochise Industry appearing in Bat Cave at a later date than that given by the first finders, Sayles and Antevs, in southern Arizona.

The Chiricahua Stage in southeastern Arizona is dated by Sayles and Antevs (419, Fig. 19) from 8,000 to 3,000 B.C., or about 10,000 to 5,000 years ago. The Bat Cave Chiricahua Phase is found in the lower half of the 2500 B.C.—A.D. 500 period. The San Pedro Stage has been dated as from 3,000 B.C. to 500 B.C./ A.D. 1, or from 5,000 to 2,500/2,000 years ago. The Bat Cave San Pedro Phase is found in the upper half of the 2500 B.C.—A.D. 500 period. It is probable that the later dates for implements of these two stages encountered in Bat Cave are more applicable than the original dates given by Sayles and Antevs, and that they substantiate the later dates given for the industries in Ventana Cave, southern Arizona, by Haury.

The Bat Cave maize has been thoroughly studied by Dr. Paul C. Manglesdorf and C. Earle Smith, Jr., both of the Botanical Museum, Harvard University. Mr. Smith accompanied the expedition as botanist for the specific purpose of studying plant remains from the deposits.

The maize comprised a total of 766 specimens of shelled cobs, 125 loose kernels, eight specimens of husks, ten of leaf sheaths, and five of tassels. Most of the specimens, even those from the lowest stratum, were extraordinarily well preserved.

According to Antevs' estimates, the lowest maize found at the bottom of the top bed may be nearly 4,000 years old.

A brief summary of Manglesdorf's and Smith's studies (292, pp. 243–44) of the maize is a follows:

1. Remains of maize isolated from a cultural deposit in Bat Cave in New Mexico reveal a distinct evolutionary sequence.

2. The maize excavated from the lower strata of the top bed is the most primitive maize so far known. It is both a pod corn and a pop corn. The ear is not enclosed in husks, but is surrounded at its base by an involucre of leaf sheaths.

3. This early maize is clearly not derived from teosinte.

4. Beginning about midway in the sequence, there is a strong evidence of an introgression of teosinte germplasm into maize.

5. There is a progressive increase in cob and kernel size from stratum to stratum.

6. Since ancient types did not disappear completely when new types came into existence, there is a progressive increase in total variability from stratum to stratum. This factor is believed to be of particular significance in the evolution of cultivated plants in general.

7. The problem of where maize originated as a wild plant is not solved by the new evidence.

As a corollary to the excavations in Bat Cave, an extensive survey was made of open sites in the Plains of San Augustin. Twenty sites were located, all on beaches and terraces around the edge of the Plains. All were at levels ranging from 25 to 125 feet above the lowest point in the basin, indicating an extremely low lake level at the time of occupation.

Practically all of the implement types (including projectile points) found in the open sites were also found in the cave. The three principal exceptions were a Sandia-type point found at a site six miles across the basin west of Bat Cave; a Plainview type base eight miles across the basin northwest of the cave; and a Lindenmeier Folsom base at the inlet into the basin northeast of the cave.

It is hoped that through a typological comparison of the implements, particularly the projectile points, from the open sites and from the cave, some progress can be made toward dating the terrace levels on which the open sites were found.

THE ANTIQUITY OF THE FINLEY (YUMA) SITE
EXAMPLE OF THE GEOLOGIC METHOD
OF DATING

JOHN HALL MOSS

The purpose of this paper is two-fold: first, to describe the Finley site near Eden, Wyoming and secondly, to discuss the geologic method of dating as employed in establishing the antiquity of the Finley artifacts. It is fitting that a report on this site should have both an archeological and geological purpose because the work at the site has not only revealed new information bearing on the Folsom "Yuma" problem, it has also provided an unusually clear example of the dating of artifacts by geologic techniques.

The complex problem of the relative antiquity of Folsom and "Yuma" artifacts needs no introduction; it has been puzzling workers in the field of Early Man for many years. Although Folsom cultural implements have been dated by geologic techniques at the Lindenmeier and other sites in the western United States, few well-substantiated dates for exclusively "Yuma" sites have been obtained. There are at least three reasons for this circumstance: first, at many sites "Yuma" artifacts have been found associated with Folsom, precluding dating "Yuma" alone; second, the typologic definition of "Yuma" is so broad and the variety of forms so dissimilar that considerable disagreement has at times arisen over precisely what was being dated; and third, at some sites, not enough geologic evidence was present to determine the antiquity with any certainty. At the Finley site, however, none of these difficulties was encountered. The artifact-bearing sands contained clearly recognizable Eden-Yuma and Scottsbluff-Yuma points, with no admixture of Folsom artifacts, and sufficient geologic evidence was present to establish with reasonable assurance the antiquity of the site.

Geology possesses no method for directly dating artifacts. At many sites, however, geologic investigations have shed light on the antiquity of the sedimentary layer, or layers, in which the artifacts were found. Careful study of the different sedimentary beds at a site may reveal differences in color, texture, structure, sorting, and mineral and organic composition which are indicative of a series of climatic changes extending an unknown length of time into the past. If study of other deposits in a wide area around the site reveals that this record of climatic change has a large geographic extent, it is in all likelihood part of the widely recorded climatic variations of the Pleistocene, which are believed to have been world-wide and synchronous. It then remains to determine the correct relation between the climatic sequence at the site and the Pleistocene

164

climatic chronology. At some localities this can be done by correlating a geologic event at the site with a period of cutting or filling of a terrace on a creek
heading in a mountain range which was subjected to glaciation. It may then be
possible to trace this terrace upstream to a glacial moraine whose position in the
glacial chronology of the mountain range is determinable by detailed field work.
If the glacial record in the mountains is clear enough, a plausible correlation between the mountain sequence and the sequence of advances and retreats of the
continental ice sheets in the Middle West can be established. Although no exact
dating of the maxima of successive continental ice sheet advances has been obtained, many students believe that the late Wisconsin (W3) ice advance, which
is important in dating North American Early Man sites, reached its maximum
approximately 11,000 years ago. Artifacts must be younger or older than 11,000
years depending on whether the sedimentary layer containing them lies on top
of or underneath gravel laid down during this advance. Moving towards the
present, another datable horizon which is often recognizable at Early Man sites
is that which records the so-called postglacial climatic optimum, or period of
greater warmth and aridity than the present. Evidence from many sources
indicates that this period extended from about 5,000 to 3,500 B.C. If the artifacts
lie below the caliche deposits of this age, they must be more than 5,000 to 7,000
years old; if they lie above it, they must be of lesser antiquity. At the Finley
site, deposits of both the climatic optimum and late Wisconsin advance are
recognizable and the dating of the artifacts is thereby greatly enhanced.

The Finley site is situated about 1,000 feet from the western margin of the
Kilpecker dune field, a vast body of sand which stretches over 60 miles in an
easterly direction from the eastern margin of the Eden Valley in central western
Wyoming (see Fig. 1). This valley, lying near the eastern border of a large oval-
shaped structural and topographic depression known as the Bridger Basin, is the
area of confluence of three streams: Big and Little Sandy and Pacific Creeks.
The first two rise amid the high peaks of the intensely glaciated Wind River
Mountains to the northeast, while Pacific Creek, at present, has its origin in the
basin near Oregon Buttes. Although the basin at present has a cold arid climate
and is covered by desert vegetation, the presence of moist-climate soils and
bison bones at the Finley site indicates that wetter climatic conditions must
have prevailed in the past.

At the Finley site are three superimposed wind-blown sands overlying gravel
of glaciofluvial origin. They are here named for convenience: the Lower, Middle, and Upper sands (see Fig. 2). The Lower and Middle sands occur at numerous localities along the western margin of the Kilpecker dune field, but are not
found more than a mile east of the site. The Upper sand, also present along the
western margin of the dune field, increases greatly in thickness to the east
and apparently represents the most intense period of aridity and wind action
recorded in the dune area. This period, also represented by a thick layer of
caliche at the top of the Middle sand, is believed to correspond to the so-called

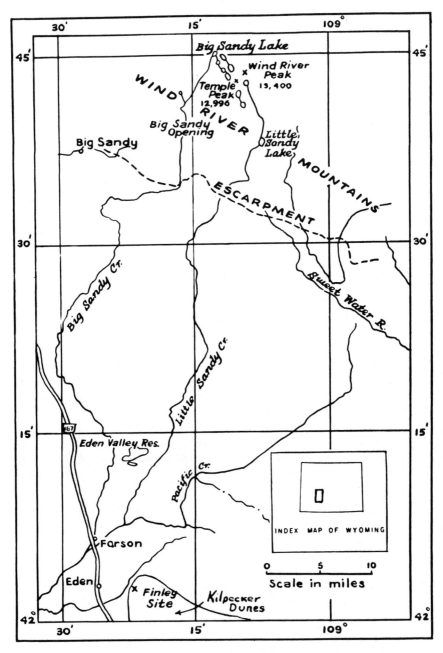

FIG. 1.—Map of the northeastern part of the Bridger Basin, Wyoming, showing the location of the Finley site.

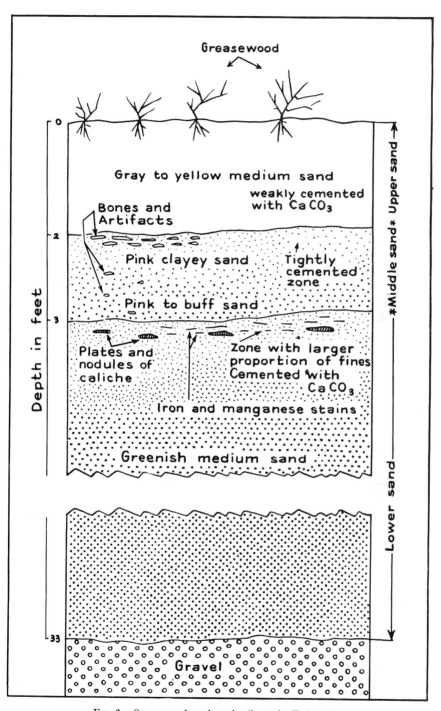

Fig. 2.—Sequence of sands and soils at the Finley site

167

climatic "optimum." The ancient soils reflecting somewhat moister conditions than the present lie at the top of the Lower and Middle sands, and were therefore both formed before the climatic optimum and after the deposition of glaciofluvial gravel. The artifacts and bison bones were found throughout the Middle sand. Their greatest concentration occurred in the soil zone at the top of this sand. Owing to the thickness and impenetrability of this layer, the bones and artifacts could not have been intruded later and therefore must have been emplaced before the "optimum." Accordingly they have an antiquity of at least 5,000 to 7,000 years.

All evidence indicates that the dune field was built up by westerly winds and that the source of sand was either glaciofluvial deposits in the Eden Valley or the sand of the dune field itself. The Lower sand was deposited synchronously with the gravel that floors Washington Draw, an abandoned course of Pacific Creek which borders the dune field on the west. As the glaciofluvial streams deposited their load of sand and gravel in the Eden Valley, the strong westerly winds, during daily and seasonal periods of low water, blew the sand to the dune field. Because the cooler and presumably wetter conditions which produced glaciation in the mountains must also have affected the climate of the basin, the development of moist climate soils was possible. Accordingly, in the dune field this was the time of development of the Lower sand soil in areas where vegetation in places was able to stabilize the sand being blown in from the Eden Valley. Later when Pacific Creek abandoned Washington Draw, the water table was lowered, vegetation lost its hold, and the upper layers of the Lower sand soil were blown away. Caliche was also developed at the top of the Lower sand during this interval and somewhat later, the Middle sand was deposited. Deposition of this sand was shortly followed by a climatic swing to moister conditions during which a "wet spot" existed at the site. At this time, the western margin of the dune field, and possibly much of the basin, was probably covered with grass making them attractive to bison. This was the time of emplacement of the bison bones and artifacts at the site. It was followed by a return to arid conditions, as indicated by the semi-arid characteristics of the Middle sand soil. Subsequently, the climate became extremely arid (climatic "optimum") during which time caliche formed in the Middle sand, the upper horizons of the sand were blown away, and the vast thickness of Upper sand was laid down. The subsequent history of the dune field is contained in minor modifications of the Upper sand. From the above interpretation of the sands and soils at the site, it is clear that the Yuma hunters were in the area principally during the moist period represented by the soil at the top of the Middle sand. It is important to note that this was the second of two moist periods represented in the sedimentary sequence at the site. To determine the antiquity of these moist periods, a correlation with the larger Pleistocene chronology must be made.

Fortunately, climatic change is recorded not only in the complex of sands and soils at the Finley site but also in the succession of glacial advances and retreats recorded in the Wind River Mountains. In the Big Sandy Creek drainage system five tills and four sets of moraines are discernible. The oldest stage, the Buffalo, is represented by deeply weathered patches of till but no moraines, and in all probability corresponds to Blackwelder's Buffalo advance recorded on the Buffalo Fork of the Snake River. Following an interglacial or interstadial period, the ice readvanced to form the Leckie Ranch moraines, which are correlative with the Bull Lake stage on the east flank of the Wind River Mountains. After a subsequent interstadial period, the ice advanced again to Big Sandy Opening where a pair of moraines, the equivalent of Pinedale, were formed. In the upper reaches of the Big Sandy Creek drainage system is a fourth set of moraines, first recognized by Hack and named the Temple Lake stage. These moraines reflect a minor swing to glacial conditions after Pinedale time but still far in the past. The relatively recent Cirque moraines of the Neoglaciation are the uppermost moraines found in the Big Sandy Creek valley. They lie a few hundred feet in front of existing ice masses.

TABLE 1

Name	Height (Ft.)	Moraine
Floodplain	1– 3	Cirque
Parker	4– 8	Temple Lake
Lower Farson	10– 13	Pinedale 2
Upper Farson	15– 30	Pinedale 1
Lower Eden	30– 55	Bull Lake 2
Upper Eden	60– 90	Bull Lake 1
Higher terraces	100–200	Unknown

Connecting the sequence of climatic events recorded in the glacial deposits of the mountains with those at the site are the series of gravel-strewn river terraces standing at different levels above present stream grade, and representing higher levels at which Big Sandy and its tributaries once flowed. Each of these terraces can be traced from the Eden Valley to one of the four sets of moraines in the mountains, indicating that the gravel on them must be of glacial origin. The name of each terrace, its height above stream grade, and the moraine to which it is traceable is given in Table 1. Of particular interest in dating the Finley site is the Upper Farson terrace which forms the floor of Washington Draw and extends under the Finley site. Clearly, the eolian deposits at the site, as well as the artifacts and bison bones, were emplaced after the formation of this terrace. As the gravel on this terrace is traceable upstream to the outer Pinedale moraine (Fig. 3), we know that the artifacts are Pinedale or younger in age. Also, if the oldest moist period is correlatable with the Pinedale, it seems extremely probable that the later moist period represented by the soil zone at the top of the Middle sand is the equivalent of the Temple Lake stage.

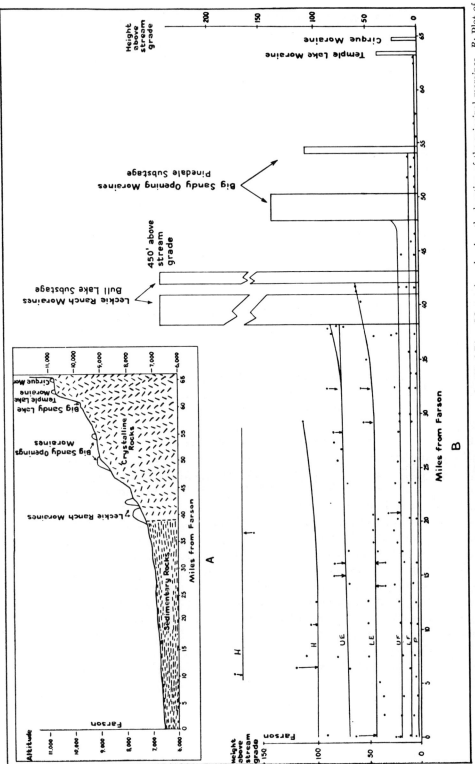

FIG. 3.—*A*: Grade line of Big Sandy Creek from Farson near the Finley site to the Wind River Mountains, showing the location of the principal moraines. *B*: Plot of moraines and terrace remnants on Big Sandy Creek. Each dot represents the height of a terrace remnant above present stream grade. Lines through dots are approximate grade lines of former stream grades during successive glacial substages. *H*, higher terraces; *UE*, upper Eden terrace; *LE*, lower Eden terrace; *UF*, upper Farson terrace;

Although no direct correlation has yet been made between the glacial sequence in the Rocky Mountains and the better-known glacial chronology in the midcontinent region, similarities in degree of weathering of the tills and preservation of morainal topography have caused most workers to classify the Pinedale as late Wisconsin (W3-Mankato). The Temple Lake substage is therefore probably the equivalent of the Long Draw substage in the Southern Rocky Mountains, which Bryan and Ray have correlated with the Cochrane readvance in the midcontinent region.

As the artifacts were found in beds overlying Pinedale gravel and beneath the caliche presumably formed during the climatic optimum, they have an antiquity of between approximately 11,000 and 5,000 years. However, the great concentration of bones and points in the upper part of the Middle sand indicates that the majority of them were emplaced late in this interval. On the basis of the distribution of bison in the last century, it seems unlikely that he would be an important game animal in the Bridger Basin in an arid climate similar to the present. In the 11,000 to 5,000 year interval, the most auspicious time for the bison to be in the basin would be during the Temple Lake advance in the mountains when the basin climate probably became slightly moister and the area more hospitable to grazing animals requiring large quantities of grass. Accordingly, the antiquity of the Yuma artifacts in the Middle sand is probably not greater than approximately 7,000 years.

To those who hold the Folsom culture developed from "Yuma," the results of the geologic work at the Finley site will pose something of a problem. Recent geologic work by Judson at the San Jon site in New Mexico lends further support to the idea that "collateral" Yuma, at least, extends into more recent time than Folsom. At the other extreme are the "Yuma" sites discovered by Schultz and his co-workers in Nebraska. On the basis of the present state of knowledge of terraces in Nebraska, it would appear that the Scottsbluff and Lime Creek sites have an antiquity closer to that of the Lindenmeier site than to the points in the Middle sand at the Finley site. However, more detailed terrace studies linking the Nebraska terraces with glaciofluvial terraces on the upper tributaries of the Platte are needed before it will be possible to compare with much certainty the antiquity of sites close to mountains with those in Nebraska.

As Howard (191a) has pointed out, few sites have produced "Yuma" points in place. The work at the Finley site, therefore, has fulfilled a definite need in the Folsom-Yuma problem, namely the dating of "Yuma" points *in situ*. Although this is only one site and it would be unwise to draw too broad generalizations from one locality, it is quite apparent that the most interesting result of these investigations is the relatively youthful antiquity of the Eden-Yuma points of the Finley site. However, more sites must be discovered and dated if the range of Eden-Yuma culture is to be fully understood.

STYLE AREAS IN HISTORIC SOUTHEASTERN ART

John M. Goggin

The art and material culture of the Indians of the Southeastern United States has been a greatly neglected field. This is perhaps due to the belief of a general scarcity of material, and, in addition, to the thought that the existing material comes from such thoroughly acculturated groups as to be relatively uninteresting. Neither opinion is completely true. Material is indeed scarce but collections do exist, particularly those of the Museum of the American Indian, Heye Foundation, which are very rich in certain types of artifacts. Acculturation too is overemphasized—form is often affected but content may remain the same. As will be shown some art styles may have long histories.

One of the most useful cultural approaches of the Southeastern archeologist has been the comparative analysis of pottery, its composition, form, and decoration. This last trait is extremely important both in chronological and in areal studies. Unfortunately pottery styles were relatively similar and undistinctive in historic times in this region and thus a valuable comparative marker is missing for that period. However, on considering this problem it seemed to the writer that if art styles on pottery were useful for comparative purposes, art styles among other mediums should also be valuable. With this consideration in mind a survey of the material culture of historic Southeastern tribes was carried out.[1]

Four classes of decorated objects were found in sufficient quantity to be of comparative value. These are silverwork, basketry, bead embroidery and woven beadwork, and textiles. However, only the last two groups seem desirable for this type of study. Silverwork is limited in value, because it appears to have been influenced more by introduced designs than any other art medium. Basketry also had to be put aside for this purpose since its designs are too closely tied to the limitations and nature of the medium.

However, in bead embroidery and in textiles we have arts stemming from a prehistoric cultural background, yet arts allowing wide opportunity for variation. Only in woven textiles do we find the medium effecting the design. Moreover, both of these classes of objects were fairly popular and considerable material is available for study. Our greatest limitation is the tribal coverage. For a number of tribes we have abundant material. For others it is scarce.

The study to date has been only introductory in nature, but already it ap-

1. This paper represents a preliminary statement on this research program of the Department of Sociology and Anthropology, University of Florida, aided by a grant from the Viking Fund, Inc. Photographs illustrating this paper were kindly furnished by the Museum of the American Indian, Heye Foundation, New York.

172

pears that two broad style areas, at least in terms of these objects, can be drawn.

Before these are discussed a brief statement concerning Southeastern Indian history is in order. Throughout historic times, and judging from archeological evidence for some hundreds of years previously, there was an unusual restlessness among the tribes in the region. During the period of European observation some tribes or towns are known to have moved hundreds of miles. Such wanderings were not exceptional. Furthermore, archeological evidence indicates that broad religious art patterns, the Southern Cult for example, spread throughout the Southeast.

As a result of this movement and contact there were few isolated enclaves—objects and ideas moved freely and even if not copied, exotic artifacts were obtained and used. Opportunities were favorable then for widespread art styles, and regional art was subject to various pressures. Such style movements did take place, as for example in the case of ceramics. Archeological data are overwhelming in demonstrating a steady movement east and southeast from the Mississippi and Tennessee valleys of ceramic styles which submerged most local forms, except in Florida. In many cases this was perhaps the result of new peoples moving in but that cannot have been the total answer. However, other mediums seem to have differential resistance to the western styles.

As we have noted, preliminary work suggests two major art style areas in certain fields of decoration. These will be briefly discussed in the light of our present knowledge.

The first of these can be called the *Eastern*, typified by the Creek, Seminole, and Yuchi.[2] Their art appears to be basically simple geometric in design, especially in finger woven textiles. Diamonds, V's, and W's are favorite motifs (Fig. 1). Bead embroidery, not so common, appears to represent modified floral and conventionalized designs including the double curve motif. It seems as though these have been dying out in the last 100 years. An examination of the archeological remains in the region shows little similarities in art between either of these styles and ceramics, for example.

In techniques and designs there is considerable similarity to Northeastern Woodland tribes; many of the finger woven sashes would not be out of place in an Iroquois setting. Such other items as the double curve motif are also shared with Northeastern groups.

The second or *Western* group is typified by the Alabama, Choctaw, Chickasaw, and Koasati (Fig. 2).[3] While they do some simple geometric bead weaving, one of their major art expressions is in bead embroidered cloth belts or sashes. In

2. A brief consideration of Seminole art may be found in Skinner (430, pp. 71–72). Yuchi art is discussed and illustrated in unusual detail by Speck (447).

3. Few discussions or representations of their art, in terms of the materials under discussion, have appeared in the literature. Douglass and D'Harnoncourt (103, p. 155) illustrated an old Choctaw belt with a scroll design, noting: "The characteristic regional style based on the scroll. . . ."

a

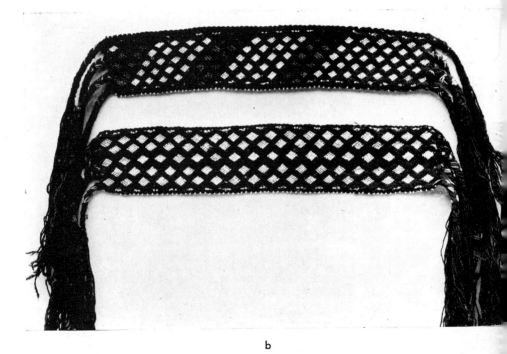

b

FIG. 1.—Eastern style designs. Seminole finger woven belt (A) and garters (B). Specimens are from the Museum of the American Indian.

174

A   B   C   D   E   F   G   H   I   J

Fig. 2.—Western style designs. Bead embroidered cloth belts and shoulder pouch. *A–D*, Koasati, Louisiana; *E*, Alabama, Texas; *F–J*, Choctaw, all Mississippi but *G*, from Louisiana. Specimens are from the Museum of the American Indian.

175

this medium they have a distinctive art style. The design is laid out in a panel with two basic motifs. One is a pair of scrolls connected by a line cutting from one diagonally across the panel to the other (Fig. 2, A, C, D, G, J). This line, the scrolls, and other elements are often bordered by little ticks.

The other basic design centers around a series of rosettes or circles spaced down the panel. They may be enclosed in diamond elements (Fig. 2, E); or a similar effect may be achieved by placing X elements between the two (Fig. 2, B, F, H, I). Variations include added elements such as crescents (Fig. 2, G).

Even the most cursory observation indicates the differences between the *Eastern* and *Western* styles as defined here. The archeologist studying the *Western* type designs is immediately struck by their close similarity to prehistoric pottery types. The second motif has general affiliations in design composition with many types of Middle Mississippian or similar pottery, such as the Fort Walton of Florida. However, the double scroll motif is very similar to that on some forms of "Caddoan" pottery occurring west of the Mississippi. The bordering ticks are a detail shared by both.[4]

Turning to neighboring regions we find little similarity in these art forms although Catlin collected this type of sash with a double scroll up the Missouri River.

In summary we can say that in terms of certain traits and motifs these are two major areas in the Southeast, the Eastern and Western. Moreover, from the little that has been pointed out it can be seen that the history of styles here is not simple. It is also apparent that significant relationships can probably be traced eventually both areally and spatially. This appears to be a valuable tool for more intensive study.

4. Compare Moore (329, various figures, esp. Nos. 34–54).

MATERIAL FROM THE HEMENWAY ARCHEOLOGICAL EXPEDITION (1887–88) AS A FACTOR IN ESTABLISHING THE AMERICAN ORIGIN OF THE GARDEN BEAN

Volney H. Jones

A distinguished member of the VIIth International Congress of Americanists was Ludwig Wittmack, professor of botany at the University of Berlin (528, p. 377). Wittmack attended this congress, held in Berlin from October 2 to 5, 1888, to present a paper summarizing the archeological plant materials from recent excavations in Peru (529). While there he chanced to see an exhibit of archeological materials from Arizona. As he previously had examined archeological plant materials from such sites as Troy, and Ancon, Peru, it was natural that his eyes were attracted by a small sample of charred food plants in the exhibit.

This exhibit was from the collections of the Hemenway Southwestern Archeological Expedition made during the seasons of 1887–88 (173, pp. 3–9). The expedition had operated in the Salt River valley of southern Arizona, in the vicinity of the city of Phoenix. Several sites, including such large ones as the Los Muertos ruin and Las Acequias ruin had been excavated. Edward S. Morse and Sylvester Baxter, officials of the expedition, had been delegated to attend the congress to describe the work of the expedition and to exhibit selected specimens from the sites. A paper by F. H. Cushing, leader of the expedition, was published in the proceedings of the congress (89). The specimen of food plants which interested Wittmack was from the Los Muertos ruin.

The box of charred plant remains from the Hemenway exhibit was removed so that Wittmack might examine the contents more closely. The maize, which was the more abundant material, he passed over lightly but he was not so sanguine when he noted beans mixed in with the maize. But let him speak (528, p. 377): "But who can imagine my surprise when, . . . I inspected the little box containing the maize more closely. In it I found without doubt garden beans. . . ." The significance of this he summarized as follows (528, p. 378): "Prehistoric beans, as far as I know, have not been known in North America before this. Therefore the present find is of universal interest, and it confirms my theory that America is the home of the garden bean." The eagerness with which Wittmack grasped this evidence is indicated by the fact that within fifteen days after the adjournment of the congress he had submitted a paper describing the beans and their importance (528, p. 374). But to appreciate the timeliness and significance of this discovery, and to understand Wittmack's excitement, it is necessary to review briefly the status of research at that time on the origins of cultivated plants, and particularly opinion as to the original home of the garden bean.

177

After the discovery of America there was an exceedingly active, and largely unrecorded, exchange of crop plants between the Old World and the New World. Some three and a half centuries later, when scholars became interested seriously in determining the origins and histories of domestic plants, data were often scanty and confusing (65, p. 447). On the basis of available evidence from botanical, historical, and linguistic sources (65, pp. 8–28; 56, pp. 109–12; 8, pp. 14–21), frequently it was difficult if not impossible to determine even in which hemisphere a particular crop plant had originated. Late in the nineteenth century more or less carefully executed archeological excavations were begun and remains of cultivated plants often were found in these excavations. These offered tangible and definitive evidence of the occurrence of particular cultivated plants in specific areas and at more or less deducible time periods. Such archeological plant materials were instrumental in resolving many problems which had puzzled students of crop plant history.[1]

Wittmack had given particular attention to archeological plant materials and had examined materials from both hemispheres. In materials from excavations in Peru he had found garden beans, while in those from Troy and other Old World sites, garden beans were absent but other cultivated beans were found. This offered a strong suggestion of a New World derivation for the garden bean and, as early as 1879, Wittmack argued that the garden bean was an American plant.[2] This unorthodox suggestion had gained few if any adherents up to the time of the congress in Berlin.

The garden bean, *Phaseolus vulgaris* L., had been known in European botanical literature since the time of the sixteenth century herbalists. Linnaeus (270, p. 723) in 1753 referred it to India, and most authors following him concurred in an origin somewhere in eastern Asia. Candolle (66, pp. 961–62) argued effectively that the garden bean was not known in eastern Asia in early times, and attributed it to western Asia. In this he was followed by Martens (295), who issued the first comprehensive monograph of the garden bean. There was an increasing realization that the garden bean was widely cultivated in many varieties in America, but the possibility of an origin there apparently had occurred to no one until Wittmack made this suggestion in 1879.[3]

In his classical *Origines des Plantes Cultivées* in 1883, Candolle handled the question of an American origin of the garden bean with considerable reserve (65, pp. 270–75). He took cognizance of the archeological material adduced by Wittmack, but held that the pre-Columbian nature of the Peruvian tombs

1. Candolle (65, p. 15) pays high tribute to archeological evidence on the origins of cultivated plants and states a preference for this over other types.

2. Wittmack (528, p. 374; 530, pp. 13–14) presents reviews of his role as protagonist of an American origin and cites the following papers in which he argued this point: 525, 526, 527. In the libraries to which I have had access these papers have not been available, and citations here are based on footnotes in 528 and 530.

3. For data on the history of opinion concerning the origin of the garden bean see 151, pp. 130–38; 65, pp. 338–44; 175, pp. 422–28; 8, pp. 60–62.

producing the garden beans had not been demonstrated satisfactorily. He made numerous concessions of facts which pointed to an American origin (151, p. 135), but did not commit himself. Instead, he placed the garden bean in the category "Species of Unknown or Entirely Uncertain Origin" (65, p. 360). Candolle resorted to this uncertain category for only three of the some 250 plants treated. He allocated other species to a more specific origin than was given the garden bean, on much less convincing data. Ames has recently remarked that Candolle made a clear case for an American origin of the garden bean and proved conclusively that the inhabitants of Europe could not have known it until after the discovery of America (8, p. 60).

The French edition (1883) of Candolle's book was reviewed by Asa Gray and J. Hammond Trumbull and his treatment of the garden bean discussed at some length (151, pp. 130–38). They produced an array of historical data calculated to demonstrate the American origin of the garden bean and considered that the proof of a New World derivation of it was conclusive. There can be no doubt that Candolle saw and gave attention to this review for in the revised English edition of his book (1885) he makes a number of references to it in connection with other plants (65). He chose, however, to ignore them in the case of the garden bean and remained unswayed, leaving the section on the garden bean essentially as it appeared in the original edition (65, pp. 338–44).

The archeological bean material from American sites which had been studied prior to 1885 was entirely from South America. As there was apparently some justification to questioning its pre-Columbian age, the evidence was perhaps inconclusive. Obviously what was then needed to resolve this impasse was clear cut material from other parts of the Americas, and particularly that from definitely pre-Columbian sites. This is precisely what Wittmack found in the Hemenway exhibit at the congress in Berlin. Since the publication of his paper in 1888 (528), the American origin of the garden bean has not been questioned seriously and abundant evidence has piled up to confirm an origin and domestication of this esculent in tropical America.

The Hemenway Expedition was the first well staffed and well equipped expedition to excavate in North America and received wide attention in scientific circles and in the press. The bulk of the materials excavated was exhibited at the Peabody Museum of Harvard in 1894 and later placed in storage there (173, p. 4). Some short papers describing the organization and activities of the expedition were published, but a comprehensive report of the findings of the expedition did not appear until 1945 (173). Thus, little of scientific value accrued from this elaborate expedition for over half a century. The timely and decisive datum on the beans, utilized immediately by Wittmack, seems to have been the earliest scientific dividend from the Hemenway Expedition.

Wittmack describes the beans seen at the Hemenway exhibit as charred and with the seed coats burned away from most, allowing the cotyledons to separate. Apparently a few were still intact, however. The bulk of the beans were small, from 6.7 to 8.9 mm. long, 3.8 to 4.8 mm. wide, and 2.9 to 3.2 mm. thick.[4] He comments that these beans are smaller than those grown in Europe at that time and noticeably smaller than beans from Peruvian graves. A single cotyledon of a bean was conspicuously larger with dimensions of 10.3 mm. long, 6.3 mm. wide, and 2.7 mm. thick. This he considered as being of more normal size and comparable in dimensions and form to the Dwarf French Bean of his day. Wittmack identified the beans of both sizes as garden beans, *Phaseolus vulgaris*.

A sample of beans in the Hemenway Collections at the Peabody Museum of Harvard which I examined in 1946, is quite similar to the lot described by Wittmack. This sample is catalogued as no. H3443 in the Hemenway Collection, and according to the catalogue data and information from an associated exhibit label, is from the burned portion of the Western Temple at Las Acequias. It is, therefore of the same archeological period as the Los Muertos beans of Wittmack (173, pp. 163–72). About sixty beans were isolated from a mixed lot of charred materials. A few of the beans were intact but most had been reduced by burning to single cotyledons. These beans fall into two size groups, with the smaller ones more numerous. The smaller beans are chiefly from 7 to 9 mm. long and from 4 to 5 mm. wide. The larger ones are from 11 to 13 mm. long and from 6.5 to 7.5 mm. wide. On the basis of size, typical kidney shape, and general aspect these larger beans must be identified as garden beans, *Phaseolus vulgaris*. The smaller beans tend less toward kidney shape and in size, form, and general aspect suggest strongly the tepary bean, *Phaseolus acutifolius*. I offer this identification for them and suggest that all of the Los Muertos beans seen by Wittmack, except the one large cotyledon, were also tepary beans rather than garden beans.

Freeman in 1910 obtained a large series of bean varieties from the agriculture of the Pima and Papago Indians of southern Arizona (129). The Indians classified these beans into two distinct types, *frijoles* and *teparies*. Freeman found that the *frijoles* (comprising twenty varieties) were uniformly garden beans, *Phaseolus vulgaris*. The *teparies* (comprising forty-six varieties), however, he discovered to be a distinct type of domesticated bean which had not been called to scientific attention. He described it in 1912 as *Phaseolus acutifolius* A. Gray variety *latifolius* Freeman (129, p. 587). The species *acutifolius* had been described earlier by Gray from an uncultivated bean having its distribution from western Texas through northern Mexico into southern New Mexico and Arizona.

Freeman points out a number of ready distinctions of the garden bean and the tepary (129, pp. 583–85). Most of these are based on vegetative characters and on other features which usually could not be applied to the determination of archeological materials. One fairly consistent and distinctive difference is, however, in the size of the seeds. If it can be established that the size difference

---

4. In Wittmack (528, p. 377) these dimensions are given as "cm."; but this is patently an error, as beans of such size do not occur. I have taken the liberty of correcting these to millimeters.

is sufficiently distinct and constant, this could be applied in the identification of even charred beans in which most other diagnostic features have been obliterated. In the discussion of the varieties of beans and teparies collected from the Indians, Freeman gives the average dimensions of each variety (129, pp. 593–602, 576–82). He presents a tabulation of average and extreme dimensions for the tepary (129, p. 592), and from his figures for individual varieties I have made similar calculations for the garden bean. These are presented in the accompanying tabulation.

	Length*	Width	Thickness	Weight*
	Tepary			
Maximum average for a variety.......	9.78	6.68	4.76	0.22
Minimum average for a variety........	6.93	3.88	2.66	0.09
Average for all 46 varieties...........	8.56	5.68	3.80	0.14
	Garden Bean			
Maximum average for a variety.......	12.9	7.8	5.08	0.34
Minimum average for a variety........	9.6	6.0	4.10	0.18
Average for all 20 varieties...........	11.05	6.85	4.55	0.25

* Dimensions in millimeters and weight in grams.

It is evident that the tepary and garden bean are essentially distinct in size; for instance, only two of the twenty varieties of garden bean have lengths less than 10 mm. (each being 9.6) and only three of the forty-six varieties of teparies over 9.5 mm. (9.54, 9.60, and 9.78). The overlap in dimensions is, therefore, very slight and there would be little risk in classifying archeological beans from the Southwest below 9.5 mm. in length as teparies, and those above 10 mm. as garden beans.[5] Actually, in materials which I have examined the contrast is greater than this, coming nearer the average of about 8.5 mm. for the tepary and about 11 mm. for the garden bean.[6] The data from dimensions can be reinforced with observations on form based on differences listed by Freeman, so that separation of the two species can usually be made with assurance.[7]

5. This does not take into account other beans, such as *Phaseolus lunatus, P. multiflorus*, and *Canavalia ensiformis*, which occur sparingly in the area but which are sufficiently distinctive in their sizes and forms that they would not be confused with the tepary and garden bean.

6. In material from the Winona and Ridge Ruin sites (219a, p. 297) some of the teparies were as small as 5 mm. long, and some of the garden beans as long as 12 mm. For charred cotyledons some allowances must be made for the loss of seed coats. Freeman (129, p. 604) states that the seed coats of the garden bean average 0.13 mm. in thickness and those of the tepary 0.09 mm.

7. Jones (219a, p. 297) to the contrary.

Applying the size criterion to the Los Muertos beans described by Wittmack, it seems quite clear that the bulk of these beans (described as from 6.7 to 8.9 mm. long) fall well within the distinctive size range of the tepary and completely outside of the size range for the garden bean. It seems entirely justifiable to consider them as teparies. Only the one cotyledon (10.3 mm. long) seems to have been actually the garden bean. At that time (1888) Wittmack had no alternative but to consider all as garden beans, as the tepary was not called to scientific attention until 1912. All the beans in the lot fell within the concept of the garden bean existing at his time.

Recognition of the tepary in archeological materials has come about only very recently. I have found no report of archeological teparies published earlier than that by Gilmore in 1932 (145, p. 25). As late as 1941, when reporting teparies from the Winona and Ridge Ruin sites, I was able to discover only two earlier archeological records of the tepary (219a, pp. 297–98). It is evident that all archeological beans from the southern portions of the Southwest identified before 1912 should be re-examined, as the possibility of the occurrence of the tepary could not have been considered before that date. Further, identifications prior to about 1932 or even 1940 are under some suspicion, as there seems to have been little awareness of the likelihood of the tepary up to about those dates. Apparently there is an increasing alertness to discover the tepary in archeological materials, as Carter in 1945 in reviewing the then known archeological distribution of the tepary was able to list fifteen sites which had yielded this species (67, p. 57).

In Haury's publication on the Hemenway materials a brief section is devoted to food materials from the Los Muertos site.[8] Among those discussed are beans which are identified as probably *Phaseolus vulgaris*. No teparies are mentioned. Haury omitted any discussion of the Las Acequias material which I saw in the Hemenway Collections in 1946. He gives no description of the beans, so there is no basis for checking the identifications. Apparently considerable confidence can be placed in it, as Haury indicates that Dr. J. J. Thornber of the University of Arizona is responsible for the identification (173, p. xi). Thornber should be well aware of the distinctions between garden beans and teparies, as he was associated with Freeman while the latter was doing research on the tepary, and is credited by Freeman with giving some assistance in this work (129, pp. 578, 588). I searched in the Hemenway Collection for this Los Muertos material in 1946, hoping to examine it but was unable to locate it.

The three lots of food plants from the Hemenway Collection seen by Wittmack, Haury, and Jones all bear a general similarity in condition and content. All were charred and each contained maize, beans, and mesquite pods. The catalogue and exhibit labels associated clearly indicate that the material which I saw is from Las Acequias, whereas the other two lots are from Los Muertos.

8. Haury (173, p. 162). I found no mention of remains of cultivated food plants elsewhere in the volume.

Haury says that the material exhibited in Berlin, in which Wittmack saw the food plants, was later deposited in the Royal Ethnographic Museum of that city, and states explicitly that he did not see those materials (173). It thus appears that there were three distinct lots, although the possibility remains that the food sample exhibited at Berlin may have been a smaller lot selected from the larger and more varied one discussed by Haury. Although the three lots are not from the same site, they are of the same cultural affinity and time period. Haury considers the Los Muertos and Las Acequias sites to have been occupied contemporaneously and places them both in the Civano Phase of the Classical Hohokam period, which is dated about A.D. 1300–1400 (173, pp. 12–13, 204–13). Wittmack was thus justified in considering the Los Muertos specimens as of pre-Columbian date.

Freeman considered that the cultivated tepary had been domesticated from the wild tepary somewhere in the area of northern Mexico or the southern portion of the Southwest (129, p. 618). Carter recently reviewed the data bearing on the origin of the tepary and offered strong support for this opinion (67, pp. 61–68). Carter further demonstrated that the tepary is apparently closely associated with the Hohokam archeological culture, and ethnologically with the tribes of lower Colorado River and its tributaries. The kidney bean, on the other hand, was associated with the Anasazi archeological culture and ethnologically with the Pueblo peoples of the plateau. The crop plants of the Hohokam and the Anasazi, according to Carter's formulation, were distinct throughout most of their histories, but in late periods after about A.D. 1100 there was some interchange. The Civano Phase, the period from which the three lots of Hemenway material were derived, saw a movement of the Salado people into the Hohokam area (173, p. 205), bringing with them Anasazi traits and presumably the Anasazi crop plant complex. Both the tepary and the garden bean would be expected in the Hohokam area at that time, and both seem to have been present in the Wittmack material from Los Muertos, and in the Las Acequias sample.

Food plant materials are not often recovered from Hohokam sites and the knowledge of cultivated plants associated with that culture is not very full. The discussion and reinterpretation of the Hemenway beans is offered here to aid in filling this hiatus. The maize and mesquite pods also merit some discussion but are outside the scope of this paper. I cannot pass up the pumpkin material without a few remarks, although it is not pertinent to the immediate subject. Haury reports that in the Los Muertos material there was a fragment of pumpkin stem which was identified as probably *Cucurbita pepo*.[9] An exhibit label with the Las Acequias food materials listed "squash seeds" as an item in the material. The catalogue entry did not mention any squash seeds, and care-

9. Haury (173, p. 162). This is referred to in the text as "squash" rather than pumpkin, but, according to modern botanical usage, the term "pumpkin" is preferred for this species (see Castetter and Erwin, 70, pp. 107–8).

ful search in 1946 revealed none in the collection. We can be most certain that in the Los Muertos materials seen by Wittmack there was no evidence of pumpkins. He was as keenly interested in the origins of the pumpkin as he was in the derivations of the garden bean. Part of the paper in which he discussed the Los Muertos beans was devoted to a consideration of the origins of the pumpkin, and he bemoaned the lack of data from North America. After remarking on pumpkin specimens from Peruvian sites, he says (528, p. 379): ". . . to my mind the arguments are so convincing that there can be no possible doubt that the home of many of the pumpkins is America. . . . *It would now be very desirable to find pumpkin seeds in some North American graves,* so that the species could be determined" (italics mine).

Although the Hemenway food plant materials form additional records for the Hohokam, they are in no way particularly remarkable today. This is a commentary on the progress which has been made since 1888, when these were the first archeological mesquite pods and teparies and *Cucurbita pepo* ever found, and the first garden beans from a site north of Peru. One can readily understand Wittmack's excitement at the discovery of the beans which won his point (although on only a single cotyledon of validly identified material!), and can regret that the evidence of pumpkin for which he was so anxious was excluded from the exhibit and did not come to his attention.

TWO CONCEPTS OF POWER

Regina Flannery

An outstanding aspect of American Indian religions is the direct contact of the individual with supernatural beings who give him power to cope with his world in ways which are beyond his natural means. The term "guardian spirit" is commonly used to designate the power-giving supernatural being, and the complex of beliefs and practices associated with the guardian spirit concept has been widely discussed prior and subsequent to Benedict's study (25), which is a landmark in the field.

Although it has been pointed out that in some areas of North America the concept hardly exists, it is recognized as a widespread and many-faceted phenomenon. In some regions the contact of the individual with the supernatural agent may be sought, in others it may come involuntarily to the individual through dreams; it may begin at puberty or before, or it may be vouchsafed only to the mature; it may be limited to a single experience, or many experiences may be required; the experience may be of an auditory and/or of a visual nature, and so on. All of the elements are variable and the situation is an exceedingly complicated one. At the risk of over-simplification I should like to suggest a classification of concepts within this broad over-all guardian spirit concept based on the kinds of power which the supernatural agents are believed to grant to the individual.

The primary distinction rests on the basis of whether the power granted by the supernatural agent is in the nature of an outright gift, which, once it is conferred, the individual may utilize without further direct contact with the power-giving being; or whether the supernatural agent promises aid, is available on call, and a continuing relationship with the supernatural being is involved. Further sub-divisions of this latter concept of power will be made, but first let us illustrate the two major concepts, as they may be identified among three groups: the Gros Ventre of Montana, the Klamath, and the Paviotso.

Among the Gros Ventre, in the private rites and observances—as contrasted with the public rituals—the main wishes they sought to satisfy were for personal prestige through war prowess and wealth, cure of individual illness, success in gambling and in love, and knowledge of distant or future events. Toward these ends, reliance was upon aid imparted by supernatural spirits. There was a differential here, however, in that knowledge of distant or future events depended on immediate help, given in each case of appeal, by an ancestral spirit who was conjured up for that particular purpose by one who had been given the formula by that spirit; whereas wealth, cure of illness, and success in war, love, and gambling depended on supernatural power imparted once and for all by some non-ancestral superhuman being. The ancestral helper imparted to the individual no power of clairvoyance or prophesy; whereas the other supernatural beings conferred actual power which the individual could himself draw upon in order to bring about one or another of the specific results above listed, and without the power-giving spirit being summoned to come each time the imparted power was being exercised.

The type of power which consisted in outright gift was commonly, though not always, acquired by quest after pubescence, and not only was accepted or rejected freely, but was also transferable. On the contrary, the ancestral helper was not sought but more or less forced his services on the recipient, and could not be transferred to another person.

The difference between the two types is quite clear in the Gros Ventre mind and was explained to me by informants in connection with curing. A person who was known to have power to cure was a "doctor" (na‚tʌnehi). By following the instructions given to him by the supernatural spirit at the time of his vision, he was able to remove the object causing illness, to mention only one method of procedure. If a person had been further granted power to perform marvelous feats which he might display as part of his curing rite, or at other times, he would be known as a "holy person" (bi‚tænehi). On the other hand a person who had an ancestral helper would be called a "medium." If, for instance, relatives of an ill person wished to know whether he would recover, the "medium" would be called in. A seance would be arranged at which the "medium" summoned his spirit helper and questioned him. The presence of the spirit at the scene was known because the audience could hear the voice of the ancestral helper, and the tent shook as the spirit entered and then departed on its mission, and again when it re-entered to give the verdict, and so on—the characteristic phenomena associated with the so-called "shaking tent" type of conjuring (121; 85, pp. 50–77). The point here is that informants insisted that the "medium" would never rate as either "doctor" or as "holy person" because the "medium" has no power of prevision of his own. He has to have help. It is really the ancestral spirit who functions; whereas the "doctor" and the "holy person" accomplish their ends by their own powers, i.e., those transferred to them by their spirits (279, p. 307). Thus to the Gros Ventre the distinction between the two types of power does not lie primarily in the classes of spirits involved—ancestral vs. non-ancestral; nor in the means of obtaining contact with the supernatural agent—involuntary acceptance vs. quest; but to them the basic difference was that the one who is befriended, or rather, as the Gros Ventre say "pitied," by the non-ancestral being is given the power of that agent and may then operate on his own, so to speak. The individual who has merely an ancestral helper on call, depends for knowledge of distant or future events on the report of that helper, who retains its power and a continuing relationship with the helper thus is necessary.

Again, the two major concepts, of outright gift on the one hand, and of continuing contact on the other, may be seen among the Klamath. Spier notes that all who were successful in their quest for contact with supernatural beings received continuing powers to carry on the arts and professions or for success and wealth. It is clear, however, that while the power-giving spirits were not invoked by others (although theoretically they might be), for the shaman a continuing contact was involved. In order to cure, the shaman had to conjure up his familiars, who were thought to line up with one foot forward, ready to help. They entered the shaman in turn and it is they who spoke, saw, and acted through him (449, pp. 109, 249–50). The shaman had, it is true, been granted the ability to conjure up the spirits for aid in curing, but he must call upon the spirits each time he wishes to cure, and just as with the Gros Ventre "medium," it is the spirits themselves who are conceived of as actually doing the work, so to speak, and the shaman is powerless without their presence.

As a third illustration of these concepts, we may take the Paviotso. Here, as among the Klamath, it is the type of power acquired by the shaman which requires a continuing contact with the spirits, as against the type of power acquired by others. Park states: "While the shamans who doctor are visited in their dreams by their spirits or can call on them to help in curing, the men who have supernatural power in hunting, gambling or warfare appear not to receive further visits from their powers" (355, p. 104). Although Park specifically states that these spirits watch over the warrior, the hunter or the gambler, as well as over the shaman, and that they are conceived of as guardians, it would seem that only the shaman must invoke his familiar spirits each time he wishes to perform. During the curing rite the spirits may give songs on the spot to the shaman who afterward cannot remember them, and some shamans have the ability to go into trance in order to consult their guardian as to the cause of disease (356, pp. 51–56). The presence of the spirit is necessary but the shaman alone is directly aware of it. He, not the spirit, sings the songs which the audience hears in the curing rite.

If I have interpreted correctly, in the three cultures described, we can see the two concepts, which we have separated on the basis of whether or not continuing contact with the supernatural agent is considered necessary for the operation of the power. In that type of power in which continuing contact with the spirits exists, a further subdivision is necessary. It is clear, from the very examples given, that each typifies a somewhat different aspect of the concept of continuing contact. Among the Gros Ventre, the "medium," who is in continuing contact with his ancestral helper exemplifies in his procedure the basic elements of the conjuring complex, or shaking-tent rite. The Klamath shaman who in curing calls up his familiars which enter his body, is a typical example of inspirational possession.[1] The Paviotso shaman is representative of the kind of contact which we may, for want of a better term, label "secret helper relation-

1. For definition of inspirational possession see 464a, p. 324.

ship." The criterion for recognizing these different aspects of the broader concept of continuing contact is the manner in which the spirits are believed to operate.

From this point of view, the kinds of power or ability granted to the conjuror and to the subject of inspirational possession show similarity. In the case of the Gros Ventre "medium" and of the Klamath shaman when curing, the presence of the spirits is not only a necessity but, in addition, the person who has the ability to summon them remains passive, while it is the spirits themselves who carry out the functions for which they were called in. In other words, in contrast to those in their respective cultures who have the outright gift of power, the "medium" and the shaman are "powerless" in that restricted sense of the word. Furthermore, in both of these cases, the audience is directly aware of the presence of the spirits so that the spirits perform publicly, as it were. The Paviotso shaman, however, differs in that while invocation of the spirits is necessary, it is the shaman alone who is directly aware of their presence. He is the actor who, guided and advised in secret by the spirits, has the ability to cure (356, p. 21).

We have seen from our three examples that the two major types of power may exist side by side in the same culture, that the idea of power once conferred co-exists with the idea of continuing contact, under one or another of its several aspects.[2] The emphasis which each receives varies from culture to culture.

Among the Gros Ventre, certainly the major emphasis is placed on power once conferred, with conjuring in a minor role, as it is apparently for all of the Plains tribes for which it has been reported (85, 79, 380)—so much so, in fact, that our recognition of the conjuring complex in the Plains area is only relatively recent.

In contrast, among the Paviotso, the emphasis apparently lies on the continuing contact type of power at the expense of the outright gift. It is possible that this is characteristic of the whole Basin, whether in its aspect of "secret helper relationship" as among the Paviotso, or under its aspect of inspired possession among at least some of the Southern Paiute (279, pp. 152, 154).

Spier has stressed the importance of what we have interpreted as outright gift for the Klamath and for the whole west coast. Ray, however, takes exception to the generalization so far as it applies to the Plateau. Granting that in the area power or talents may be conferred which are effective without constant spirit presence—corresponding to our concept of outright gift—nevertheless Ray holds that the general pattern for the area is that of specific and necessary invocation—an intimate and continuing contact, which for many of the tribes is apparently what we have designated as the "secret helper relationship," although he does not bar inspirational possession (379). It was he, too, who first

---

2. This is not to say, of course, that both concepts of power have, of necessity, to be found in all cultures of North America in which the "guardian spirit concept" itself exists. It is doubtful whether the outright gift of power is a concept of the Northern Algonquians.

called our attention to the existence of the conjuring complex in the Plateau, among two groups (379). In one of these, the Kutenai, the emphasis in modern times at least, is on conjuring as the most important kind of ability, according to Turney-High (498, p. 174), although in the other group, the Coleville, it apparently plays only a minor part.

Although I am sure that the suggested classification of power concepts is far from complete, it may help toward readier identification of traits such as inspirational possession and the conjuring complex in regions where they have not previously been identified. As a case in point, let us review the power concepts of the Yuman tribes of the Gila River, as described by Spier. The dominant concept is seemingly that of outright gift of power. Everybody dreams, but relatively few are befriended by animal spirits who taught the dreamer over a period of time, and, when the power was considered complete, the individual might then practice—that is, use the powers granted, such as oratorical power, curing, bewitching, marvelous feats, clairvoyance, power in war, etc. If directions were not followed, the power was withdrawn. It is stated that in curing, the spirits were concerned only in that they had taught each shaman his cures. During the cure the shaman was not possessed, nor did he so much as call on his familiar for aid. Nevertheless in at least one of the several methods of clairvoyance described, there are some indications that the continuing contact concept of power may be present. This particular type of procedure was carried out on stormy nights to foretell if enemies were approaching. A little hut was built inside the meeting house and after the shaman had sucked up each of four piles of dirt, he dropped "dead," as the informant put it, and was placed with a rattle in the little hut. Another man, sitting beside the shaman, acted as interlocutor. Spirits of several mountains came into the little hut during a seance, although one left before another entered. The audience felt a draft as the spirits entered. The informant said: "The house might be crowded, yet they could hear the mountain talk in there." Questions were asked regarding the whereabouts of the enemy and the spirits answered. Most significant from our point of view, however, is the belief that the mountains as spirits differed from those of birds and animals in that *they had no powers to grant*, plus the fact that the informant did not know what spirit would have granted ability to a shaman who performed in this manner (450, pp. 252, 292–93). Given the similarity in features of procedure in the seance to the shaking tent type of conjuring, and the clue that among these people, as among the Gros Ventre, where the emphasis is likewise on outright power, the spirits which are summoned have no powers, in that sense, to grant, it is possible that we have here the occurrence of the conjuring complex in an area for which, so far as I know, it has not been previously recognized.

CULTURE HERO AND TRICKSTER IN NORTH AMERICAN MYTHOLOGY

Géza Róheim

A combination or antagonism of culture hero and trickster is characteristic of North American mythology. One of the most widely known of these trickster heroes is Coyote.

In 1931 I wrote down a long Yuma myth of Kokomat and Coyote. Kokomat the creator god is bewitched by his daughter and about to die (incest motive). The cremation is to take place next day. They sent his son Coyote to tell people that the cremation would be tomorrow. He was thinking about the things his father had told him in his life time. "When I die thou shalt take my heart (*iwam me thauka*) and be happy." "Take my heart," meant "follow my ways"— but the people knew that Coyote would take it literally.

Leaving out other important details of this myth we emphasize only the *misunderstood message*.

What Coyote would have to do would be to acquire a super-ego to be like his father. Instead he takes things literally—or should we say on the archaic or phantasy level?

Schizophrenics frequently tell us that they have eaten somebody or somebody is in their inside, but they are not capable of following the ways of their fathers. Freud has described the mechanism of super-ego formation as introjection, i.e., swallowing, eating, having inside (131, pp. 382–83).

In this situation part of the aggression must be turned inwards and part of it sublimated as identification or imitation. That is just what Coyote and similar trickster heroes fail to do; *they are beings without a super-ego*. Coyote tries to imitate his host and fails. Frequently the imitation is associated with feeding guests, i.e., providing for the children and that is where Coyote or Raven fails.[1]

"He first took up the awl. But when Nanabushu seized hold of the lodge pole he was not so successful in his efforts at climbing up and after a long while he was able to get upon the cross-pole. And when taking hold of both his testes with his hands after that he seized a firm grip upon his awl and then "Sank, sank, sank," he said. He aimed at his testes, pierced them and dropped with a thud into the center of the fire—the fall killed him" (219, p. 347).

According to Freud castration anxiety leads to super-ego formation—and here we have the failure to form a super-ego and the regressive step to self-castration and death.

1. For instance, see 88; 44, p. 90.

But this negative definition is only the first step. We know that Coyote and similar mythological personages are characterized by the absence of a super-ego.

According to Reichard, Coyote had helpers who could predict his behavior. When he came to an impasse he summoned them. "None of my informants could (or would?) tell me exactly what those helpers were. They always said 'That's a Coyote word.' The Thompson and other Salish tribes attribute special powers to Coyote's excrements. From linguistic evidence I suspect that the four powers are excrement, testes and penis" (385, pp. 98–103).

The Chiricahua Apache tell the following story: "Coyote has intercourse with a girl who sits on his penis. She picked up a rock and hit Coyote's penis with it. This is the reason the foreskin goes back" (351, pp. 53–54).

It is the phallic hero who liberates the Salmon. He becomes a baby and lets himself be adopted by one of the women who owns a dam. In some of these stories he merely bores a hole into the dam through which the water breaks with the salmon, in others he does the same with the woman who owns the dam, i.e., he has intercourse with her. In a Coeur d'Alene myth Coyote is swimming in a river. He heard the people say that they cannot eat salmon because the dam is closed up and four girls who are cannibals refuse to let the salmon pass.

Reichard enumerates many parallels. The release of the salmon, the infant transformation and coitus with girls who own the dam or coitus across the river from a complex of motives (385, pp. 98–103).

It is evident that the opening of the dam with the salmon swimming out is birth—and who but the phallic hero could break through female resistance and the dam (inhibition) and bring all the good things of this world to mankind!

But the culture hero is also the child. A powerful chief kept daylight, sun and moon in a box and the box was in his house. The Raven wanted to liberate daylight. The chief's daughter came to draw water. He wants to marry her but she refuses him.

Thereupon he changed himself into a pine needle and fell into the water and she drank the water. She became pregnant of the Raven and was delivered of the Raven. The child grew rapidly and its grandfather loved it very much. After some resistance the child got the box that was hanging on the roof. Finally the grandfather allows the child to peep into the box. Then it is opened wider and wider till the child in the shape of Raven flies out with the box (38, pp. 173, 208, 211, 246, 272, 2091).

But if daylight is brought into the world by a small child and this happens when the child hero can open a box and get out of a house we may safely interpret the myth as meaning that every child brings daylight into his own world when he is born. Raven brings daylight, the child sees daylight. Raven (or any other mythical hero) goes around naming places—the child learns the names of places. The mythical hero is the prototype of how things are done. This is the way Raven did it—is the Tlinkit's answer to every problem (239, pp. 253–54). From this point of view the culture hero simply means the process of growing.

Every human being is his own culture hero; that is, he has to grow up to acquire the culture of the group in which he lives.

If we regard the myth of the culture hero as autobiographical we cannot fail to see that the *story of growing up* revolves around three significant motives: (1) the fight with the father, (2) incest, (3) castration anxiety.

In the Chippewa myth Manabozho the Hare (Hiawatha in Longfellow epic) is told by his grandmother that his father the Westwind killed his mother because she died giving birth to him. The well-known battle scene follows. Mudjekeewis is vulnerable through a black stone, Manabozho allegedly by a reed. But the latter is only a ruse and the son drives his father, the Westwind to the end of the world dealing him hard blows with the black stone.

"Hold," cried he, "my son, you know my power and that it is impossible to kill me. Desist and I will portion out to you as much power as to your brothers" (421, p. 135; 422, pp. 18–19).

Somebody might object that the number of myths in which the Father and the Son fight each other is not very great. In Greek mythology we also have only one Laios but many veiled representations of the same theme. In North America these versions are often very slightly veiled. They may have something to do with the joking relationships where the incestuous desires and the antagonism are openly represented with the grandfather or some other substitute and his wife as mother substitute.

In the Iowa version of the myth of Hare the wandering Hare comes upon the Uyo (female organ of the world). "He went home and asked his grandmother what it was." She said, "that is one of your *grandmothers*, keep away from it. Hare disobeyed his grandmother and was sucked in by the evil grandmother. The good grandmother rescues him, he cohabits with her and this is the origin of menstruation" (376, pp. 37, 39, 105, 162).

Since he has relations with his grandmothers it follows that all his enemies are his grandfathers. He kills one grandfather who withholds the tobacco, then he kills the Bear, also his grandfather (376, pp. 96–97). In the Winnebago myth while the Twins rid the world of dangerous monsters their father becomes panic-stricken and flees.[2]

Another "motive" very frequent in North America is the *vagina dentata*. Women had teeth in their vagina, the hero breaks their teeth and makes intercourse possible.

On the Fraser River the story is told about Quals who came to a place where an old woman lived who had teeth in her vagina and killed everybody who had intercourse with her. The sons of "Good Weather" use a hammer and break the teeth. If they had not done so women would still have teeth in their vagina (38).

2. The fusion of the infantile and the phallic is recognized by P. Radin (376; see also 400*a*).

The culture hero's life story is everybody's life story, we all grow up and manage to overcome the Oedipus conflict and castration anxiety.

How is it then that the hero of these stories shows distinct traits that make him a personification of the phallos or libido or Id (38)? The process of maturation is symbolized by the Phallos since genital libido more than anything else helps to overcome the anxieties of the oral or child-mother situation. At the same time mastery of the world around this is also achieved by growing up, by increased ability to show aggression. The Phallos is a weapon and the trickster hero is destructive right from the beginning. Thus we arrive at the surprising conclusion that the culture hero is the Id or the life-principle. Looking upon culture as we generally do as a process of adjustment to society we should expect to find the super-ego in this role. However, the problem becomes easier if we remember that the culture hero is merely a word, and may have nothing to do with the origin of culture which it somehow purports to explain. These mythical beings symbolize the process of growing up in the individual. The characterization of psychoanalysis that it takes a person "from infancy to adultery" is certainly valid for these mythical beings. The question remains unanswered: what is specifically North American about all this?

Why is Coyote the really popular hero? Why is there such a strong element of the obscene, of the unpermissible, or contrary in these beings? And why the vicarious pleasure in those narratives?

The answer is that North American Indians have a very strong super-ego and the representative of the Id as hero is a counterbalance to social pressure.

Now, of course, when I use the expression "strong super-ego" it is meant in a relative sense. They are repressed, inhibited, etc., when compared to Australians, Melanesians, Somali. This is probably not so if we use New England guilt feelings as our yardstick.

The attitude of the parents is different than among other primitive people I have known. The institutions I would like to name as creating a severe super-ego are (a) the cradleboard, (b) the alleged training, (c) speech making.

The cradleboard has recently found champions who approve of the institution. Leighton and Kluckhohn seem to be rather in favor of the cradleboard yet they observed: "After about six months, however, the infant apparently begins to feel the confinement a frustration and will wail to be released" (259, p. 26).

The cradleboard is undoubtedly also used as a punishment and for the convenience of the adults. Grinnell relates how if a Cheyenne mother could not hush the baby she would tie it to a cradleboard and hang it in the bush. Kwakiutl babies were said to be bound to prevent them from having wild and roving dispositions. When they were released from the cradle after a year or so they were as clumsy and helpless as normal babies one month old (361a, p. 12).

On basis of these facts we are tempted to suggest the equation: cradled child —hero as wanderer.

What I call *training* is very different from the usual mild and indulgent or carefree way of other primitive tribes. Among the Lummi:

When the boy grows up the first objective of all education is to develop in the little boy courage and self-confidence in the face of the terrors of nature. He is sent out on very dark and stormy nights to fetch something from an old man who lives at a remote place. He must bathe every morning in the icy waters of the Puge of Sound and often for punishment he is forced to do so again in the evening. He is harshly treated and discriminated against, deprived of good food and given as nourishment only the tail end of the salmon and the backbone of the ducks. The father is so anxious to develop fortitude in the child that at the slightest breach of severe discipline he becomes furiously enraged. The father tests his son's endurance by cutting his body with sharp stones.

After plunging into the icy water of the Sound he rubs sand on his breasts to make them tender or even drawing blood, then amputates his nipples by crushing them between stones [458]. Babies are thrown into the snow very early by the Navaho and probably other tribes. Among the Yuma I found the custom of making speeches and telling the child what sort of a man he should become. I don't think the children like it. Hallowell tells us that the Northeastern tribes are anxious, inhibited and that the ideal is that of strong restraint and control [163].

No wonder then that the real hero of their mythology is the Id—although to preserve the integrity of the ego they pretend to deride their hero.

POWER ANIMALS IN AMERICAN INDIAN ART

Herbert J. Spinden

The word "art" should cover, in general parlance, all of man's expressions and embodiments of use and beauty and not be trimmed down to decorations of a trivial nature and to sensuous enjoyment, likewise trivial. It is true we often restrict the general term in special ways for special reference, as the art of speech, or of architecture, or of self-defense, but after that special usage, we should let the word spring back to its broad general meaning. I say this because some recent publications tend to give art a minor definition. Thus, in the *Handbook of the Indians of South America*, art is used to mean decoration, generally unexplained as to meaning, while esthetics is joined to recreation in a sensuous and holiday sense. Decoration, among primitive people at least, is generally a prayer, and beauty in nature or in man's own products is highly functional, either in a mechanical or in a cultural sense.

Power animals (Fig. 1), as I use the term, are a basic force in the religious art of the American Indians. Indeed, they are found the world around, being one of the first primitive concepts to be examined critically by anthropologists. Belief in power animals led to early tribal organizations of totemic type and to the rise of spirituality and illusion in man's social life.

I think of man as creating an artificial world of his own culture, as an enlightened animal who by innate intelligence and trained imagination managed to set up a series of achievements which roughly parallel the evolution of living forms in nature and, like these, are subject to ultimate and inexorable law.

The power animals of American Indian art, and those of Old World art as well, have contributed valiantly to the formation of gods and philosophies.

A power animal of Indian art in the form of a great eagle flew up from Mexico to Alaska; he dropped plumed snakes in lieu of lightning on whales which he carried inland to devour. Sometimes he put down his burden to help a clan ancestor set up his heavy roof-tree. Now, seeing is believing and believing is seeing: the Kwakiutl have monumental carvings to prove that the Thunder Bird did carry off whales in his talons.

Other traditions exist about Man-Eagle, bird of thunderous wings, flying upward until lost in the sun. First and last he was merely a rapacious bird and therefore equipped to be a patron of war and warriors for Toltecs and Incas no less than for Romans and ourselves (witness the eagles, bearing shields and arrows, on our seals and coins). No doubt the Eagle and Jaguar Warriors of ancient Mexico were chivalrous at heart, but in actual performance imagined

195

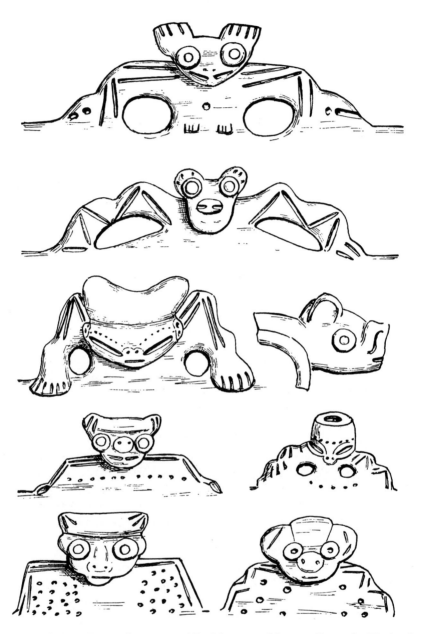

FIG. 1.—Bat motive on the pottery of La Mata, near Maracay, Venezuela. The bat is similarly handled in Porto Rico, Santo Domingo, and eastern Cuba. It expresses a cult of ancestors and cave worship ultimately of Central American and Colombian origin.

force was too strong for good intentions. It was a Jaguar Sun God who asked for blood and what could priests or captains do but yield?

When Tylor wrote on animism and Spencer synthesized the new results of natural science, they disagreed on the matter of wilful souls and thinking gods. Tylor recognized that men around the world believed implicitly in souls and ghosts, immaterial counterparts of their own perishable bodies. These souls, they believed, entered other objects, till the universe was animate, or existed as vague imponderable influences which could help or hinder living men. Magical art was born with the first intentional grave. Mechanical art was already old, for offensive and defensive weapons had been filched from other animals since their claws, teeth and horns could be used by man as clubs, knives and spears. Representative art, sculptures or pictures, was held from the first to be coercive on the thing carved or pictured. Beliefs die but artistic forms, in which they have been expressed sincerely, remain as monuments to their creators and form a human heritage. Our own ceremonial eagles come from Roman sources but similar designs occur in ancient Peru.

Many power animals of American Indian art possess outstanding skills which they are supposed to impart to man. "What animal's sharp sight have I for my sharp sight? The gull's sharp sight I have for my sharp sight," sings the Eskimo woman sewing a garment. The song, then, is sympathetic magic. In great rituals of the Osage, explicit statements exist about help conferred on man by friendly animals. In designs of Central America the pelican is pictured as fisherman's luck, while the crab pulls in fish by hook and line in northern Peru. This principle of outstanding ability accounts for figures of the orca, a whale which kills other whales, in important art of the Pacific coast from California to Alaska. The orca also is found in textile and ceramic designs of southern Peru and less conspicuously in stone figures of New England.

Nomad hunters appeal to the puma or mountain lion, also to the lynx and the wolf for hunter's luck over much of North America.

When proof through amulets and pictures fail, mythology steps in with tales and magic songs to fill gaps in archeological distribution not only for North America but also for South America. A Carib song runs as follows:

> I am the spirit of the lightning eel,
>   the thunder-axe, the stone,
> I am the force of the fire-fly, thunder and light-
>   ning have I created.

The principle of choosing power animals for their skills may be extended to various other associations as when the turtle is asked to assist at childbirth. Also the turtle or the otter bring mud from the lake bottom to create land in cosmogonic tales of North America. In Central America the crocodile appears as earth-animal par excellence—perhaps because it sleeps on watery surfaces like a bit of land protruding. In Mexico, the deer is sun-bearer, while the rabbit, or some other rodent, holds a similar office as regards the moon.

In still other connections animals acquire importance in American Indian art. There are clan animals, guardian-spirit animals and special helpers of shamans. Shaman helpers probably are portrayed on stone pipes of the Mound Builders. At least such representations agree with practices in curing over much of America.

Among the Maya we find early orders of power animals which enter into astronomy and astrology. There are the thirteen animal constellations of the Maya zodiac, upon whose bodies the positions of the planets could be marked. In the Codex Peresianus this zodiac is practically intact: every twenty-eight days the sun is in the mouth of a new bird or beast. Also there are animals which give names and signs to days and months in the calendar. Thirteen gods form a chronocracy which rules over the numerical coefficients of day signs. When this series is applied to the coefficients of time periods there is a doubling over in the sense that numerals above thirteen have the old faces to which death symbols are added. Thirteen is the owl and seven the jaguar; the two combine to make perfect twenty. The place values are frequently pictured as birds.

Animal forms dominate Maya art. The jaguar is most important, changing into a god in human form as the centuries pass. Next comes the serpent which joins with the trogan to produce a god of rain and storm in opposition to the jaguar sun deity: this composite figure becomes associated with Venus as celestial warfare is more and more a religious motive. The peccary, the deer, the bat, the crocodile, the monkey and the owl are all outstanding power animals of the Maya, playing important roles in ceremonial representations. It seems the influence of these creatures was widely felt in ancient America. Proofs have been presented that the Maya cult of the jaguar sun god, with his shield having a jaguar face in the center and serpent rays, passed deeply into South America. If the Jaguar stairway at Copan set a pattern in A.D. 511, which was reflected on the Portal of the Sun at Tiahuanaco, there is hope for an extension of dates: it now appears the Copan assemblage continued among the Maya, the evidence being miniature temples recovered at Jaina.

If persons sensitive to art forms and associations could agree on this and other distributional evidence, affecting the spread of designs, ceremonies and philosophies in ancient America, we might hope for history and chronology covering the entire New World. The pattern of two jaguars supporting a jaguar sun was continued by the Maya in a renaissance of their culture during the Eighth and Ninth Centuries, also. And there were techniques and prepared materials which began to connect North and South America at this time.

Perhaps the most widely distributed power animal in America was the bat which developed into an underworld deity in various combinations in a generalized Cult of the Dead. In late Mixtec codices a demon bat guards the underworld but earlier figures in Maya sculpture are more diverse. Also, there is a bat constellation, a bat month and a bat tribe. As we pass south to Costa Rica we find magnificent bats in jade and in Colombia the common material for bats, in gorgeous variety, is gold. Pottery figures of bats, which may carry off children, occur in Peru where also there are complicated textile designs dealing with this animal. The bat motive in Venezuela is all important again mostly in pottery although large simplified bats in green stone and conch shell occur. Unfortunately these figures are not often recognized by the dirt archeologists who have worked in the field. The bat spreads its wings on pottery of ancient and modern manufacture along the Amazon and well south of it up the Xingu, Araguaya and Madiera rivers. But the most striking expansion of this power animal was over the West Indies in the spread of Arawak culture, later individualized by Taino artists. Only La Borde definitely says the *zemi* are bats, but thousands of bat figures, lightly conventionalized, are broadcast over the islands. Their recognition and association in Taino culture only await a generation of dirt archeologists who will reconstruct designs on the sherds they excavate. The word *zemi* means "tobacco," I think, rather than "bat" in Taino for the figures of this animal served as a model for ghosts and spirits of the dead. At least *zemi* is cognate to *shäma*, an Arawak word for tobacco, and the herb was notable as incense offered to the dead.

The Spaniards saw devil worship in West Indian rites for the simple reason that in Europe the small night-flying animal was a principle incarnation of evil powers.

THE STUDY OF AMERICAN INDIAN CRAFTS AND ITS IMPLICATION FOR ART THEORY[1]

Gene Weltfish

The American Indian has created some of the most remarkable design styles in the world. Nowhere do we find such a variety of geometric arts, with each tribal style possessing its own "classic" beauty. By contrast, the meagerness of our own geometric design, so often limited to the "egg-and-dart" and the "Greek key" provides a sad spectacle.

What are the sources of these creative energies in the American Indian, and the cultural paucity of our own civilization in this field?

I shall use as illustration of the American Indian design styles, two different styles, one from the North American continent and one from South America, with particular attention to the craft of basketry in which the Indians of both continents excel.

The first example is from the Pima Indians of southern Arizona whose design style is most highly developed in their coiled basketry. The baskets are for the most part shallow round trays with black designs on a natural background.

Upon analysis we find a number of standard elements that appear in the designs:

Most striking is a basic figure of a black disc at the center with four arms extending from it which reach about halfway out to the circumference, and in the intervening spaces, four arms extending inward from the rim (Fig. 1, *8, 9, 10, 11*). Other common aspects of the designs are a filling-in of the intervening spaces between the "arms" with a fret figure (Fig. 1, *8, 9*), or various angular lines connecting or outlining the arms (Fig. 1, *10, 11*).

At first these design ideas seem inexplicable. From what conceivable aspects of the experience of the Pima could these designs have been derived? Such forms as the cogwheel, the octopus or other natural objects which might suggest this form are absent from Pima life and could, therefore, not have served as models.

In the past, explanations of the development of art have rested heavily upon the theory of inspiration from Parnassus or some other divine source. In the last century, in the light of archeological discoveries, Gottfried Semper, German architect and art historian, pointed out what an important part the mundane experiences of the artist had upon the designs he created (425). Technical practices, materials used, uses for which the objects were designed, social forces such

---

1. This paper expresses the viewpoint which will be more fully presented in a forthcoming book on art and technology.

as prestige and other such factors, all played a part in the creativity of the artist-designer.

If we examine the technical medium in which these Pima designs appear, the coiling of basketry obviously bears no relation to the designs. The radiality of the lines of the design run directly counter to the circular spiral nature of the technical structure. Moreover, while the spiral framework is sewn round by round concentrically, the design plan is obviously visualized for an entire surface. Such a scheme, containing line elements and a total plan usually suggests painted design on pottery. If we examine Pima pottery, the designs have no relation to the basket style.

The most important method for deriving the dynamics of Pima art style is if possible to range the designs in temporal order. Of course, the most desirable would be stratigraphic archeological material, but even where this is not available, museum collections in the modern period, provide a certain rough time sequence. According to the monograph of Kissell (235, p. 254), who made a special study of Pima basketry in the field, the oldest designs are the most complex and elaborate and have no precedent in the arts of the surrounding peoples or among the Pima themselves (Fig. 2, *12, 14, 15, 16*).

Among the other objects besides pottery that the Pima use, we find the carrying net which served as a model for this design. The carrying net which is used by the Pima women to carry burdens on their backs, has a conical wooden framework of four poles arranged like an inverted tipi, a wooden hoop being placed inside the wide end of the cone to spread the sticks apart and to constitute the rim. Over this framework, a conical net of lace is drawn to keep the burdens that the Pima woman carried from falling through the frame. The design on the lacework is a series of lines which take account of the presence of the four radial poles of the wooden frame (Fig. 2, *17, 18, 19, 20*) (235, Figs. 77–79).

In its interpretation in the basket-design, the hole at the center of the lace net is represented by a black disc at the center of the basket, while the four sticks of the framework are the radial arms that project from the central disc. The four arms that extend inward from the rim represent those aspects of the lacework pattern that are complementary to the radial arms. The black intervening lines on the basket are analogous to holes in the lacework by which the design is delineated (Fig. 2, *12, 14, 15, 16*).

From a more faithful representation of these many details in the earlier baskets, a simplification is developed in the modern work which then takes on its own pattern of elaboration. One of these elaborations is the bending of the radial arms in a leftward whorl effect which is traceable to two influences—one the design style of a neighboring group which the Pima have imitated (Fig. 1, *3*), viz., the peoples of south California, and the other from the technique of coiling itself.

The south California tribes have a whorl as a common theme in their basketry design. However, the whorl usually leans rightward, while the Pima whorl

FIGURE 1

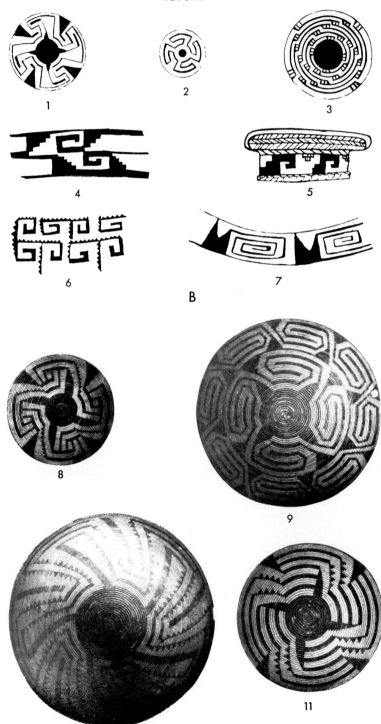

trends leftward (Fig. 1, *8, 9, 10, 11*). This is traceable to a difference in the spirality of the coiling in the two basketry techniques—the Pima being a leftward or counterclockwise spiral, the south California tribes a rightward spiral coil.

As for the fret design itself, this no doubt has its derivation in the Mexican art tradition, as it is a very common motif in the higher arts. Figure 1, *4* and *6*, are motifs in rock relief on the wall at Mitla, the Zapotec burial ground for kings; Figure 1, *5*, is a Maya twill-plaited basket represented in stone sculpture; and *7* is a motif painted on a Huastec pottery vase from Tampico.[2]

But rather than elaborate on this question, I shall turn to another style, that of the Indians of the Amazon River, which throws some light upon the question of the ultimate origin of the fret design itself.

At the beginning of this century, Max Schmidt, German anthropologist, visited the Indians of the Amazon and from his observations of their craft practices propounded a very interesting and much-maligned theory of the origin of certain geometric designs as an outcome of their basket-weaving techniques (420, chaps. xiv, xv). The kind of basketry he considered is twill-plaiting, a technique that superficially appears to have a relation to loom weaving. However, in its operation, the manufacture of twill-plaited basketry is very different from loom weaving. Unlike ordinary textile weaving, in plaiting, warp and weft are identical flat ribbon-like strips; the weaving does not usually begin at the bottom and proceed upward for the whole fabric, but instead a small section is interwoven, the piece is then turned and further wefts are added to the fringe

---

FIGURE 1

A, Basic pattern plan of Pima coiled basket design.

FIGS. *8, 9, 11*.—Coiled basketry bowls of the Pima Indians showing the basic pattern plan of central black disc with four "arms" extending outward from it and four "arms" extending inward from the rim in the intervening spaces; fig. *10* follows the same basic pattern plan with five "arms" instead of four. (Photographed from specimens in the American Museum of Natural History.)

B, Additional design elements superimposed on the basic pattern plan.

FIGS. *1, 2, 3*.—Additional elements of the design are the fret figure (*8, 9*) or angular lines connecting the arms (*10, 11*), and the general leftward whorl effect. Fig. *1* is a diagrammatic version of a common Pima design combining the fret motif with the basic pattern plan. Fig. *2* shows the fret motif alone; (drawn after photograph in Breazeale "basket made by a little girl"). Fig. *3* whorl effect alone; imitated from the south California tribes to the west; (drawn from photograph in Kissell, 235, fig. 60e); it differs from south California version in leaning leftward instead of rightward; this is traceable to a difference in the direction of the spiral coil of the weave between the two groups.

FIGS. *4, 5, 6, 7*.—Different versions of fret motif from the higher arts of Mexico; the Pima fret probably derives from this tradition. *4* and *6*, rock relief on Mitla tomb; *5*, stone sculptured representation of Maya twill-plaited basket; *7* motif painted on Huastec pottery vase from Tampico.

2. Fig. 1, *4, 5, 6*, after Spinden (455); from Joyce (220, p. 198, Fig. 44).

FIGURE 2

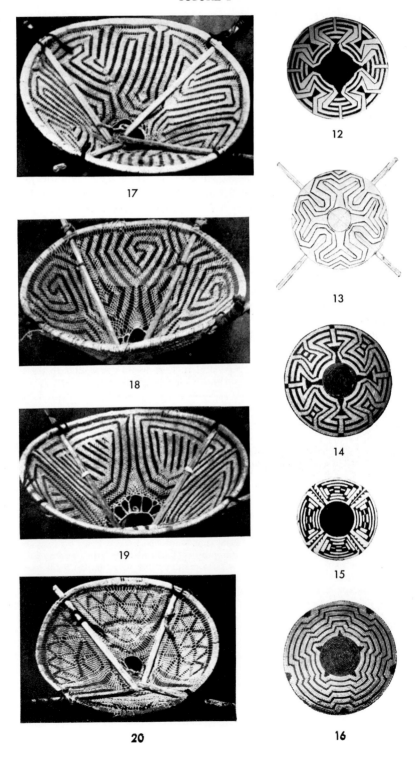

17

18

19

20

12

13

14

15

16

extending out to the left of original sector, then the fabric may be turned again and wefts added to the strands that extend to the right—the fabric thus being built up in sections to equalize the tension of the two sets of threads (Fig. 3, 27). Another method of accomplishing this is to change the direction of the diagonal twill in successive weaving sectors. In Figure 3, 22, two and a half weaving sectors are shown, with the twill shifting from leftward at the bottom, to rightward in the middle, and then leftward again in the upper sector.

As a result of the successive shifts in the position of the fabric during manufacture, and on the different diagonal patterning of each of the weaving-sectors, there emerges a varied total texture pattern. Figure 3, 22, shows a zigzag. Another such pattern is the diagonal fret, with sections illustrated in the diagrammatic sketch of a twill-plaited quiver (Fig. 3, 27). The completed basket is in the form of a somewhat truncated cylinder which was probably woven as a flat fabric and then fastened to a round base. For purposes of illustration I have represented the basket lying down on its side. I have drawn lines across the design extending out beyond the edge in order to indicate the different work-sectors in which either the position of the fabric or the direction of the twill were shifted in the course of the weaving. Because of the unevenness in the size of the juxtaposed sections, the diagonals conjoin to form a fret pattern rather than a zigzag or a diamond.

The designs which originate in the weave mechanics are then copied in other media—pottery, woodwork, and other decorated objects. Illustrated are designs on pottery, one painted (Fig. 3, 26), and one engraved (24), from the Amazon region, in which the diagonal fret pattern is clearly represented. The other illustration is the same design engraved on mammoth ivory from the Upper Paleolithic deposits of south Russia (Fig. 3, 23, 25). Figure 1, 22, shows a remarkable parallel between the twill-plaited head crown made by the Amazon tribes and an ancient fragment of mammoth ivory on which a similar zigzag design has been engraved (Fig. 3, 21). These two pieces demonstrate with some conclusiveness that although no textiles have been found in these very ancient paleolithic deposits, the people must have made plaited basketry and gone through a similar process of design evolution as the peoples of the modern Amazon, but in a

FIGURE 2

Derivation of the basic pattern plan in the Pima carrying net

FIGS. 12, 14, 15, 16.—Early type of Pima basket design showing clearly the derivation of the basic pattern plan from the four-stick framework of the carrying net and the hole in the center of the lacework. Fig. 13, diagrammatic sketch of carrying net. Drawn after photograph in Kissell (235, fig. 76a). Others photographed from specimens in American Museum of Natural History.

FIGS. 17, 18, 19, 20.—Pima conical lacework carrying nets drawn over a wooden frame of four converging poles fastened to a circular wooden rim. Design of the net and the framework have been taken together as a model for the basic pattern plan of the coiled basketry. Photographs courtesy American Museum of Natural History; see also Kissell.

FIGURE 3

remoter period. This throws further light on a controversial question of design evolution: Which originated first—representative art or geometric? The general opinion was that geometric design was a species of degenerated representation. From Aurignacian deposits in France as well as this material which shows a high development of geometric art, it would appear that both lines of art developed in parallel course.

On the Amazon and in Mexico, these designs, once freed from their original technical context become conceptualized and freely elaborated so that whole decorative arts develop around them. In a small way, this is what has also happened with the original Pima carrying-net pattern.

When we consider that even a small tribe of several hundred Indians has the creative vigor to evolve and develop a living style of design, while in our own culture, neither the whole nor the several parts of our one hundred and fifty million people shows an equivalent creative vigor, we must ask ourselves, "Why? How is a national art to grow up in the United States?"

First let us look at the conditions under which decorative design is created among American Indians. There are certain significant contrasts between the design-creative process in our own industrial society and that of the Indians that should be taken into account:

First, most native arts are decorative arts. "Art for Art's sake," equivalent to our portraits, paintings, and statuary, is relatively uncommon. Therefore, artistic effort is pretty well concentrated in this field.

FIGURE 3

Designs derived from the technical mechanics of twill-plaited basket-making and copied in other media

FIG. 22.—The derivation of the zigzag design is shown in the mechanics of the twill-plaiting. The fabric is made in sections, marked off by a change in the direction of the twill. In the bottom section, the twill is a leftward diagonal, while in the middle section, the twill trends rightward. The small sector at the top is again twilled leftward. The weaver apparently felt no need to make these sectors of equal size. Plaited Bakairi headring or crown, modern tribes of the Amazon, after Schmidt (420).

FIG. 21.—Fragment of mammoth ivory bracelet from Upper Paleolithic deposits of the Ukraine; the zigzag pattern shows such a close analogy with the twill-plated texture pattern that there is every reason to believe that these ancient inhabitants of south Russia were also makers of twill-plaited fabrics. Drawn after Macalister (289a).

FIG. 27.—Diagrammatic sketch of a cylindrical basketry quiver from the Amazon (Bahuana tribe, Rio Branco) constructed from a twill-plaited fabric. (The quiver is shown lying on its side to better illustrate the design.) The fabric was constructed in a series of rectangular sectors, each being woven onto the one before as the work progressed. As in fig. 22, the adjacent sectors are uneven in size and as a result of their particular juxtaposition, a diagonal fret pattern emerges (Schmidt).

FIG. 24.—Diagonal fret pattern engraved on a clay hearth, Icana River, northwest Brazil; fig. 26, fret design painted on pottery, black-on-white, Icana River. Both drawn after Koch-Grunberg (238).

FIGS. 23, 25.—Fragments of mammoth ivory bracelet from Upper Paleolithic deposits of the Ukraine engraved with fret pattern, indicating as in fig. 21 that these designs were derived from twill-plaited models as among modern Amazon tribes. Drawn after Macalister (289a).

Second, in native society, it is the industrial craftsman who both invents and carries out the designs, while in our society industrial designer and industrial worker are poles apart. Why does not industrial design come naturally from our industrial worker as it does in the case of the native craftsman?

Explanation has been sought in a false contrast, which has become a common stereotype of our culture, viz., that the craft worker, fired by artistic inspiration, works tirelessly and ungrudgingly, while the industrial machine worker has an inevitably drab work situation and is therefore niggardly of his energies. The craft worker, even though he creates design, also finds the work arduous. Indian women have many times complained to me after a day's craft work, of cramped muscles and general tiredness, as workers do anywhere. But yet, the craft objects may each bear a design that is the individual creation of the craftsman, and this is true, not only of the unusual craftsman, but of all the members of the tribe.

If the work of the handcraftsman is tiring in an analogous fashion to the industrial worker, how then do we explain the fact that the craftsman is aesthetically creative, while this faculty does not appear in our industrial worker?

There are many who believe that the use of the machine prevents the industrial worker from sharing in the design-creative process, while the handcraftsman works under entirely different conditions. But is it the machine alone that differentiates one group of workers from the other? Even among our more craft-like activities, plumbing, carpentering, etc., no special creative impulses make themselves manifest in our workmen. While it is not possible to develop the subject here, I should like to point out that expert craft operations in which context most native designs appear, require a certain automaticity of motion that is in a sense analogous to machine operation, and that the actual difference between the two kinds of industrial work is not as great as has commonly been supposed.

I think one important factor is our general belief that the industrial worker should not aspire to aesthetic creativity. He is divorced entirely from the industrial designer whose aspiration seems to trend toward the pent-house night-club circle, while the design he invents is supposed somehow to edify the mass of people in mass-produced objects. In an attempt to depart from the old Greek fret, egg-and-dart cycle for instance—carrots, suitcase labels, umbrellas, and other familiar objects have found their way into textile and wall paper "moderne" designs. Perhaps such objects seem very appealing to the sophisticate who does the designing, but when we look to the forty million American housewives who have to peel, cut, cook and eat carrots, the subject does not have much aesthetic appeal. One might argue that the carrying net of the Pima Indians which has served as inspiration of their basketry decoration is an equally utilitarian object. But the attitude of the Pima woman toward her carrying net, and that of the American housewife toward carrots differ fundamentally. To the Pima woman, many associations cling to the carrying net—religious associations, social occasions, personal and emotional memories and values, that make it something worth celebrating in design. Out of these associations and the feeling tone and affect that go with them, an art is created that has vitality and the dynamic force to change and develop into new and more beautiful designs. Our industrial designer has no such base to draw on. He is separate from the people who use his objects and separate from the people who make them.

In blaming the lack of aesthetic creativity of our industrial worker on the machine, certain other important elements of his work situation have been overlooked. As any artist knows, speed-up, fear of unemployment and other major anxieties that beset our industrial worker are not conducive to the production of aesthetic values. And it is precisely the absence of these conditions that most clearly differentiates the operations of the native craftsman from that of our industrial worker. I would not, like William Morris, suggest that we revert to the crafts, however.

I think in trying to convince the industrial worker that his work itself is antithetical to aesthetic creativity, or in blaming the various kinds of "negative know-how" of our society upon the machine, we are not facing the real issues. We should face the fact that while the Pima Indian draws from his poor desert-like home and simple crafts a wealth of beauty, we in our civilization, with the greatest material and technical opportunities of all time know how to spread more anxiety and distribute more misery amid plenty than almost any other society that has been known. It is this type of affect that inhibits the aesthetic possibilities that could be realized in our industrial work situation.

We have been dwarfing our artistic stature by ploughing-under the creative energies of our industrial workers beneath a welter of anxieties. Only when our industrial worker breaks through the mist of misconceptions, and learns to struggle for his creative right to satisfaction in his work with freedom from needless anxieties, will we have a national art which we can compare with that of the Pima Indians, the Amazon Indians, and other magnificent craftsmen of the American continent.

Our art will be different from that of the craftsman; it will be an art of a machine industrial civilization, but it will have the same creative quality, for it will come from the maker.

CULTURE AND STYLE IN EXTENDED DISCOURSE

Z. S. HARRIS

This paper will propose a method for analyzing extended discourse, with sample analyses from Hidatsa, a Siouan language spoken in North Dakota.

There are several lines of investigation which might lead one to analyze extended discourse. One such line of investigation is a direct continuation of descriptive linguistics: Descriptive linguistics yields statements about the occurrence of morphemes, words, and the like within a sentence. That is to say, it states how the occurrence of one class of morphemes (or words) is restricted in terms of the occurrence of some other class of morphemes (or words) within the same sentence. Having obtained this result, one might readily ask how the occurrence of one sentence is restricted in terms of the occurrence of other sentences within the larger discourse. It is clear that there is some restriction of this kind; for if we stop short in the course of any text, for example at the end of the present sentence in this paper, the probability that certain particular English sentences will occur next is greater than the probability that certain others will occur. (It is more probable that the next sentence here would contain certain linguistic terms, or English learned words, or that it should have assertion-intonation and be of considerable length, than that it should contain names of automobiles, or specifically colloquial words, or that it should have exclamation-intonation and be short. This has indeed just been the case.) Nevertheless, it has not in general been possible to state how the occurrence of one sentence is restricted in terms of the occurrence of another within the larger discourse. Attempts to find regular sequences of particular sentence types within a text have generally been unsuccessful.

Another line of investigation which might lead one to analyze extended discourse is the distinction between what descriptive linguistics states to be "possible" in the language (i.e., to constitute a sentence in the language) and what is actually said. As is well known, descriptive linguistics states, for example, that a particular sentence type is a sequence of particular morpheme or word classes. However, it is not the case that every member of one of these classes occurs in the same sentence or phrase with every member of the other class. Certain combinations of particular members do not occur, but it would be difficult to use the regular techniques of descriptive linguistics in order to yield efficient statements as to what combinations do not occur. The analysis of extended discourse may provide techniques for such investigations, since, as will be seen below, it deals with the question of what particular members occur within the same discourse.

Yet another line of investigation which might lead one to analyze extended

210

discourse is the correlation between linguistic behavior and other social or interpersonal behavior and relations. Here lies the question of what is the difference between the languages of two different cultures; what is the difference between the uses of language of two communities which have important cultural differences but descriptively or grammatically much the same language. Here also is the question of style—what differences in use of language are to be found in different social groups, different persons, different subject-matters, and so on. If we consider the speech of people who are using different styles, or come from different cultural backgrounds, we find that the individual sentences they use may be different, but in ways that cannot be efficiently stated within descriptive linguistics. Furthermore, many of their individual sentences may be identical, but they may occur in different orders, or intermingled with different other sentences. The problem is therefore not one that can be met by the present tools of descriptive linguistics. Nor can it be met by the tools of culture analysis, since these are much too unspecific and otherwise inadequate to yield precise differentiations in language use. It becomes, therefore, a question of comparing samples of the discourse of one group, person, or subject-matter with that of another. What is needed is a body of techniques that can show precisely what are the differences between one extended discourse and another.

We consider first what type of techniques are available for the analysis of extended discourse. Since an extended discourse differs from a single sentence only in being longer, the type of analysis that is possible is on the whole similar to the type of analysis that can be made of a single sentence. In both cases, the basic requirement is that the elementary parts, say the morphemes, be unambiguously identifiable, so that we should always be able to say whether a particular part is an occurrence of a given morpheme or of another morpheme. In both cases, too, the basic operation is substitution: we ask whether a particular part or sequence of parts is substitutable for another, as the word *political* or the phrase *relatively inconspicuous* are substitutable for the word *scientific* in the sentence *We held a scientific meeting*.

One might ask: If the basic analysis here is the same as that used in descriptive linguistics, how are we to expect further results from applying it to extended discourse? The answer is the difference in the domain of application. In descriptive linguistics this analysis is traditionally used only within the limits of one sentence at a time. Except for certain parts of syntax, the linguist does not seek the relation between some part of one sentence and some part of another. At the same time, however, he obtains his results from all the sentences in his sample of the language. If he sets up a class A which occurs before a class N, that means that this order is to be found throughout his material, except in stated circumstances. Instead of all this, we can take a single body of extended discourse, and analyze it as a separate domain. On the one hand, we would then consider the occurrence of any particular morpheme not only in respect to the other morphemes of the sentence but also in respect to the other morphemes throughout the discourse. On the other hand, we would not consider morphemes as substitutable for each other if they were found to be so in other sentences of the language, but only if they were found to be substitutable in sentences of this particular discourse. We would thus obtain a grammar of this discourse by itself.

When the basic operation of substitutability is applied in this way, much of the analysis will take on a somewhat different form than in descriptive linguistics. The criteria and types of classification will be different, as also the possibilities of interrelation among the members of a class. In somewhat the same way, if we view phonology and morphology as applying the same basic operations, but to short stretches of speech and to full sentences respectively, we will find that these same basic operations yield in phonology types of classes and inter-class relations which differ from those that these operations yield in morphology, as a result of the different domains used in the two cases.

The primary operation in analyzing a text of extended discourse, then, is to set up what may be called context classes, parallel to the phonemes of phonology or the morpheme classes of morphology. Members of a context class are substitutable for each other within the text. That is to say, if in a sentence of our text we replace one word by another word of its context class, we obtain another sentence of our text. For example, if our text contains the sentense *We held a scientific meeting*, and if the words *scientific* and *annual* are members of the same context class (for our text), then our text should also contain the sentence *We held an annual meeting*.

In most texts it is impossible to find many sentence pairs of this kind, which differ in only one word. However, we will frequently find pairs of sentences within a text that will differ only in having different members of two or more context classes. For example, if we set up for our text a context class containing *held* and *heard*, as well as other words, and another context class containing *meeting* and *lecture*, we may find in our text the sentence *We heard an annual lecture*. This method can, of course, be used in such a way as to make very many sentences of a text identical in their context-class composition. Similarly, the classification methods of descriptive linguistics can be used in such a way as to make very many sentences in a given language identical in their structure: for example, all sentences of the major English type can be said to consist merely of an N sequence plus a V sequence. However, just as morpheme classes can be used in a more refined way, to give a greater number of sub-types of English sentences, so context classes can be used in a more refined way, to yield a greater number of differentiated sentence types within the text.

Once we have stated the sentences of our text as particular sequences of context classes, we find that many statements about our text become possible. We may find that many sentences, either successive ones or not, are identical in terms of their context classes. Sentences which are not identical may be partially identical in their context classes. We may then investigate the pattern of occurrence of a particular context class through the various sentences, or through the sentences of a particular type; and we may consider how the occurrence of this context class is restricted in terms of the occurrence of some other context class. We may also consider the order of the members of a context class, in the successive sentences which contain that context class.

From all these investigations, we can obtain a description of this text in terms of its context classes. We may then compare this text with others, to see whether the occurrences of context class are similar (even if the context classes themselves are not). Or we can take various texts of one person, one social group, or one subject-matter, and compare them with texts of another, in order to see what the structures of the first have in common as against the structures of the other texts. Finally, we may wish to correlate that which is common in the structures of the first group of texts with the non-linguistic behavior or relations that are common to the people who spoke or wrote them.

We now consider two Hidatsa texts, the first a narration of a culturally important public event, and the second a casual narration of some private activities of the speaker. (Both were transcribed from recordings made by the same informant, Charlie Snow, in the course of work done by Carl Voegelin and me.)

The first text[1] reports the activities of the Water Buster clan in retrieving their sacred skulls from a museum, so that they might pray to them for rain. The word *wa.'a.htu.'as* (skulls) occurs very frequently, and was taken as the starting point for context-class formation. We denote it by S. We then consider the environments of S, and notice that every sentence which contains S also contains a word ending in -*c*, -*k*, or -*wa* (all clause-enders, meaning final-verb, non-final-verb, and *while it is*, respectively) immediately after (rarely one or two words after, and twice immediately before). These clause-ending words contain *wa* (we) twice, I once, and the various third-person plural overt and covert forms in all other cases. Furthermore, in a few cases the verb is composed of two stems, e.g., *watawa.'a.htu.'as wahku.ci-wa.wa.ha.'ac* (our-skulls we-to-get we-want). If we now compare these two-stem cases with the cases when one or more words intervene between S and the verb, we note a parallel: *wa.'a.htu.'as aru'i.ku.ci se'ehta u.waca'as ri.ha.'awa* (the-skulls to-get for-that money while-they-put). We can say that the last three words here are substitutable for the second stem in the two-stem verbs. In one pair, the two final verbs are the same: *watawa.'a.htu.'as o.kirure iska'ac* (our-skulls to-go-after they-planned); *wa.'a.htu.'as o.kure'e iska.k* (the-skulls an-owner [for them] they-planning).

On this basis, we may form two context classes: the final verb F, which is here removed from S by an intermediate stem or word; and the intermediate stem or word I (which never have the clause-enders above; the stem differs from the word only in having no main stress). The remaining verbs (i.e., words with clause-enders), which occur immediately after S, can be shown to be substitutable for F, and are thus put in the same context class. The sentences containing S thus have the composition S (I) F, the F including a WE, I, or THEY morpheme.

1. This text is published in Lowie, Harris, and Voegelin, *Hidatsa Texts* (287).

We now consider the sentences which do not contain S. Some of them contain *wiripa.ti* (Water Busters) plus a word ending in *-c*, *-k*, or *-wa*. We place these words into one context class; since some of the members are identical with members of F, this class is substitutable for F. Other sentences have the same clause-ending words (or others), but with *ruxpa.ka* (people), *e.c.iri* (everyone), *iha* (others), instead of Water Busters. We put all these in a class W, and all the clause-ending words that occur with them into F. Finally, much the same verbs occur in clauses by themselves, and these too are put in F. The prefix THEY which occurs with these F is substitutable for W + THEY in the clauses that contain W: *wiripa.ta'as e.ca kiruwac.ihka.'ac* (the-Water-Busters all they-gathered); *kiruwac.ihka.k* (they-gathering). Hence the prefixes THEY, WE, and I, which occur with F in the sentences containing S, can also be placed in the context class W. The sentences which contain S now have the composition S (I) W-F; and the sentences which do not contain S have the composition W F, the W being in some cases only a prefix. (A few additional substitutions have to be made in order to bring certain other sentences into the W F form; but these will not be carried out here.)

The only remaining sentences or clauses are *xare.c* (it rained), *wi.k.a.rus.a ki'ahuk* (even-grass becoming-plentiful). These are substitutable for each other in their environments, and may be denoted as R clauses.

Finally, a number of sentences of all types have initial clauses ending in *-ru*, *-k*, *-wa*, and containing words which do not appear in the rest of the sentence: *wa.ra i.piraka.ci e.raha.ru* (years twenty in-the-past); *a.tawa* (in the morning); *se'eruha.k* (then).

The text as a whole is a long series of S(I)W-F clauses and WF clauses, alternating in very short groups or singly, with a few R clauses interspersed toward the end. It may be noted that there are no sentences consisting of just S plus a verb whose subject the S would be (i.e., whose prefix would be part of the S).

We now consider the second text, reporting some personal experiences. Here the majority of words end in *-c*, *-k*, *-wa;* i.e., most clauses consist of just one word, with its prefix and its verbal clause-ending. In the first three clauses the prefix is I; we mark the clauses, with their prefix, stem, and clause-ender, by I. In some of these clauses, words with zero ending (often indicating what might be called a noun) or with *-hta* (to), *-kua* (in) precede the main word; since these words can be replaced by zero, the clauses containing them will also be denoted by I: *hawa se'ehta ware.c* (then there-to I-went); *ware.c* (I-went).

The last I clause in this initial group contains the word *sehi.wa* (Chippewa): *se'eruha.k sehi.wa wa.wasiwa* (then a Chippewa I-hired). The next clause is *wa.hiric* (he works), and for five more clauses the subject of the main word is HE. We denote these six clauses by H. There follow about ten I clauses, half of them having some word in addition to the main one. In the last of these the word is *watawa.karista* (my child). The next five clauses (C) have HE for the prefix, with MY CHILD specified in two of them as the HE in question. Then follow seven I clauses, followed by five clauses (B) with third-person prefix, in the first two of which *wa.hti* (boats) is specified as the subject. Then come fourteen I clauses, in the first few of which there is reference to traveling on the boats. The last of these is *a.tawa wa.ki-waka.'ac* (in-the-morning prayer we-reached; i.e., it was Sunday). The next clause is *wa.pixupa.wa ruxpa.ka akihtia wa.ki'ati ihtiawa wa'as.ak* (on-Sunday the-people many the-prayer-house the-big-one filling). This is followed by three third-person clauses (P) with PEOPLE or OTHERS as subject. Then follow four I clauses, and eight third-person clauses with my children as subject.

We thus have a simple sequence of groups of clauses: I, H, I, C, I, B, I, P, I, C. Every other group is I. The groups are fairly long. In about half the transitions from one group to the following one, a side word in the last clause of a group appears as the subject of the main word in the next group. Various additional features might be pointed out about the order of stems within each of these groups, and so on, but space does not permit.

Even this cursory presentation of the analysis of the two texts shows that considerable difference can be found between them in the way their context classes occur in respect to each other. More detailed analysis brings further differences to light. One cannot, of course, make inferences about the difference between formal and conversational narration in Hidatsa merely on the basis of this material. But if such analysis is carried out independently on a sufficient number of formal narrations, and also on a sufficient number of conversational ones, and if the common features in the structures of the first group were compared with the common features of the second, we might expect to obtain results that could be correlated with the particular social and interpersonal relations involved in these two types of activity among the Hidatsa.

STRUCTURE AND VARIATION IN LANGUAGE AND CULTURE[1]

PAUL L. GARVIN

This paper is an attempt to expand some of the recent thinking on ethnolinguistics in terms of structural rather than situational parallelisms (509a, 510). In essence, our objective is to formulate some of the conceptual tools for dealing with the type of problems usually summarized under the heading of "Language, Culture, and Personality."[2] Our argument is from the basic assumption that in terms of relational variables, there is an essential parallelism between verbal and non-verbal behavior. This parallelism lies not in the specifics of the subject matter themselves, but exists in terms of relevant relationships between the specifics: the Gestalt qualities are of the same type, where the summational qualities differ.[3] We shall illustrate some of our salient concepts with examples from Kutenai language and culture; the linguistic material is taken from our own research, the cultural material from H. H. Turney-High's Kutenai monograph (499).

I

The range of human behavior may be seen as circumscribed by a set of frameworks, subsequently to be numbered I.1, I.2, and I.3.

I.1 is what may be called the total culture, the generic framework of behavior applicable to each member of the group. I.2 is something that many

1. Much of what is presented here is the result of a series of discussions with fellow-linguists and colleagues from other fields at the University of Oklahoma. Aside from colleagues in the Department of Anthropology, Kenneth L. Pike, of the Summer Institute of Linguistics, Drs. Donald H. Dietrich and John Rohrer, of the Department of Psychology, and Professor Gustav E. Mueller, of the Department of Philosophy, have made substantial contributions to our thinking.

2. Advanced as much of the previous thinking has been, most formulations proposed so far may legitimately be considered partial formulations. Thus the trend characterized by Benedict's and Linton's work is concerned with problems of culture and the individual and does not deal much with language. Sapir's earlier work, and especially B. L. Whorf's conception of language as an index of the cultural categorization of reality, deal with language and culture, and so do Voegelin and Harris (509a). Finally, three main lines of approach can be singled out in the treatment of language and personality: Ferdinand de Saussure's early and psychologically rather naïve, though linguistically valid, contrast of individual *la parole* with collective *la langue;* Karl Bühler's (62) more sophisticated differentiation of individual and social speech; and, finally, B. F. Skinner's work, much of it unpublished, along different lines, on the motivation of verbal behavior.

3. The importance of a Gestalt approach to language has long been one of the basic tenets of the Linguistic Circle of Prague; a number of cultural theorists, as well, have stressed the importance of a configurational, rather than atomistic, approach (see Linton, 273; Sapir, 417; Lévi-Strauss, 267; Malinowski, 291).

psychologists have dealt with rather successfully, and some anthropologists have included in their theoretical thinking, namely the role—or roles—of the individual in the culture, which can be considered a sub-framework under I.1. Thus, while total Kutenai cultural and linguistic behavior would fall under I.1, status-determined behavior in terms of sex, kin affiliation (499), or membership in societies (499) would fall under I.2. Finally, individual variations under both I.1 and I.2 constitute I.3.

Framework, in terms of this approach, is equivalent to what most linguists, and some anthropologists, call structure (237). Structure, in turn, is statable in terms of relations between the variables, between the units of the structure. Leaving the definition of units for later, the relationship between units of a linguistic structure, at any rate, can be defined in terms of distinctive contrasts. Again in language, this distinctive contrast is a relation in terms of the peculiar and specific function of language as a sign system. In other structures, relations between units may have to be stated in different terms, but the important point to be made here is that structure is to be stated in terms of relations between units defined in terms of the function of the structure. Another important point is that since I.2 is a sub-framework of I.1, units in I.2 have to agree with those in I.1; they have to be compatible with I.1; they cannot have relations different from those in I.1.

One statement to be made about structural units at this juncture is that they are range values, i.e., magnitudes including all the individual instances falling within the same general contrastive range. Individual instances can, in terms of the Prague Circle terminology, be referred to as actualizations. Each range unit contains a modal segment, upon which falls the statistically greatest number of actualizations and which usually represents the maximum of contrastive value, and limital segments, at which the range gradually peters out or flows over into the next range. In this, the range unit closely approximates the well-known normal curve.

In the Kutenai phoneme pattern, the non-lateral front spirant /s/ ranges from a rather fronted, almost pre-dental point of articulation to a palatal point of articulation considerably further back. The modal segment of the range is around the dental and alveolar points of articulation; the remainder of the range is constituted by the limital segments. The range peters out towards the front limital segment, and flows over into the range of the lateral spirant at the back limital segment, i.e., the latter actualizations of /s/ are in quite a few instances confused with those of /ł/.

Actualizations falling into, or close to, the limital segments of the range are often accompanied by what may be called special effects, that is additional qualitatively different functional involvement of the unit. Finally, actualizations falling completely outside the range may lead to what may be called structural malfunction. In the case of language this is failure of communication, of non-verbal behavior, maladjustment—"being outside the culture," "working against the culture." Thus, in our attempts at speaking Kutenai, we were most often moving in the limital segments of ranges and achieving the special effect of sounding like a "strange foreigner," not to mention the many cases of being beyond the range and incurring failure of communication.[4]

Framework, in terms of the preceding discussion, can be defined as behavior expectancy, i.e., the type of behavior that is expected of a member of a culture group by his fellow members (237; 252). Structural malfunction is then equivalent to not behaving as expected, unpredictability, and hence incomprehension, non-acceptance.

Individual variations within the frameworks of culture and role within the culture fall into two general types: those that may be called situational, i.e., variations dependent upon the situation in which the behavior occurs, and those that may be called individual in the strict sense, i.e., variations depending upon the individual who is behaving. B. F. Skinner has been very much interested in what is here called situational variations; his terminology speaks of verbal behavior and his approach tries to determine the specific motivations of individual instances of speech. In terms of the present approach, each of these individual acts of verbal behavior would have to fall within the framework of the linguistic (i.e., cultural) structure as a whole, and within that sub-framework of the structure which is consistent with the role structures of the individuals involved (i.e., honorific, sex, or other status determination). Within these frameworks, then, individual occurrences may vary dependent upon situational and individual motivation. Another way of putting it is that cultural and status frameworks are "personalized" in terms of the dynamics of the individual (222).

Shifts in range modes, and subsequently in total ranges, can well be envisioned in terms of cumulative individual variations in a given direction; this, at least, seems to be a formulation acceptable to some of the clinical psychologists and not incompatible with the thinking of some cultural theorists.

An interesting example of such shifts in connection with Kutenai kin behavior is reported by Turney-High; it shows the transition from a shift in modes to a shift in total ranges: in order to circumvent the taboo upon gambling between classificatory siblings, younger Kutenais use Christian names instead of kinship terms in speaking to cousins. "With the small and dispersed modern population," says Turney-High, "they often try actually to forget the relationship, and have gone far towards doing so. . . . The result is a tacit passing over of the old brother-sister character of cousinship for purposes of gambling. An unexpected result has been a more than occasional disregard of such relationships for extramarital sex indulgence. . . . The dropping of verbal symbols to accommodate one feature of the gambling complex has caused a weakening of the importance of verbal symbols for another part of the complex—sex" (499).

Variations as discussed above may affect the framework or sub-frameworks to a varying extent; one may then speak of a degree of pattern involvement, in

4. For structural malfunction in non-verbal behavior see Benedict (26) and Linton (273).

stating how much of the pattern is touched by any particular variation. This degree of pattern involvement may be used as a gauge for what some of the psychologists might want to call the "depth" of individual dynamics: certainly it has been used in a common-sense, undefined way as an index of the degree of, for instance, regressions as manifest in speech patterns. The validity of this concept depends to a large extent upon how far segments of the pattern can be defined as more or less basic; inclusion of more basic aspects of the pattern is then greater degree of pattern involvement than inclusion of less basic aspects. A classification of phonemic contrasts as more and less basic has been attempted by Roman Jakobson (212). Jakobson's findings are definitely compatible with the present argument.

Another aspect of the degree of pattern involvement pertains to the relationship of sub-structures in terms of role to the total structure: here, the degree of pattern involvement contingent upon role sub-structuring is an index of the "depth" of role-determined attitude. An example of this is honorific language: in those languages where honorific speech extends over a considerable and basic area of the total linguistic pattern, status-determined respect attitudes are of considerable psychological depth and form an important layer of the total cultural behavior pattern; in languages where honorific speech is limited to a few pronouns and occasional vocabulary items, respect attitudes are culturally much less penetrating. Status-determined involvement may vary individually; the same honorific speech pattern may be used to a varying degree by different individuals, and in different situations, as has been observed by us on Ponape.

II

Structure consists of three types of relationships, to be numbered II.1, II.2, II.3 in the subsequent argument.

II.1 are structural units, i.e., actualizable ranges; II.2 is the internal structure of units, i.e., the contrastive qualities which mark their ranges; II.3 is the integration of units into next larger units, which by many linguists is treated under the heading of "distribution."

The establishment of units arises from the need for choice from the infinite total number of observable individual items. The question is, as Lévi-Strauss puts it, *"quelle est la raison du choix, quelles sont les lois de combinaison?"* (264). The criterion of a structure is its function—for linguistic structure, the sign function; for kinship structure, as Lévi-Strauss states in the above-mentioned paper and elsewhere (267), social cohesion by means of reciprocal exchange. Structural units, then, exist in terms of the function of the structure. As was further pointed out above, the many items to be accommodated in terms of structural units are fixed entities, point values, i.e., actualizations of the units, whereas the units themselves are range values. As for their additional characteristics, they are—as Bühler has said for signaling units (62)—abstractively relevant, i.e., not all of the qualities of the total physical fact mark the unit, but only certain, abstractively relevant ones; and they are distinctively contrastive, i.e., they exist by virtue of the distinctive contrast of their abstractively relevant qualities with each other.

In this respect, our above-mentioned Kutenai range unit /s/ has the abstractively relevant characteristics of being a non-lateral front spirant; the particular point of articulation is variational. The spirant character exists by virtue of its contrast with the stop /t/, the front character by virtue of contrast with the back spirant /x/, and the non-lateral character by virtue of contrast with the lateral spirant /ł/.

In addition, the unit, being a range value, is a potential magnitude, existing in reality only by its actualization, as was recently pointed out in connection with certain phonemic problems by Kenneth L. Pike (365). In the final analysis then, structural units exist only through their place in the structure. Differences within the range of the unit, within its place in the structure, are then non-distinctive variations, falling under I.3 in the first part of this paper; this is where the observable items must be placed, whereas the units themselves are, by the nature of structure itself, abstractions made from many items.

The internal structure of a unit is statable in terms of the qualities, or features, determining the place of the unit in the structure. That is, in terms of those abstractively relevant, distinctively contrastive features which were used to define units above.

Finally, the integration of units into next higher units involves, in addition to their sequential distribution, the Gestalt-like fusion of these sequences. Integrative sequences of units then are not mere juxtapositions of units, but units of a higher order, with Gestalt qualities of their own, and organizable as units on a next higher level of integration, and with varying degrees of integratedness. Thus, Kutenai morpheme clusters such as -s=n=ał- *on from here*, -qa=n=ał- *on from there*, function distributionally as single units within relevant frames of reference, and are not modifiable or dissociable in terms of naïve native speaker's reaction (417, 133). They represent fused units on a level of integration above the morpheme and with a high degree of integratedness. Kutenai words, representing a next higher level of integration, show a somewhat lower degree of integratedness: they are modifiable by paradigmatic manipulation, though not always dissociable, in terms of naïve native speaker's reaction. Naïve native speaker's reaction is, at this juncture, used only as a possible index of the degree of integratedness, and by no means as the sole, or even the most important, determinant.

There are then, in the structure, several levels of integration, depending on the extent of the unit chosen as a point of departure. An integrative sequence of units on the next lower level of integration constitutes a unit on the next higher level. Morphemes, morpheme clusters, words, phrases, sentences, typify units of possible levels of integration of an increasingly higher order in language.

In addition, dependent on the degree of involvement of the function of the structure, there can be various levels of structuring. In language, the two levels of structuring are the phonemic level, with partial involvement of the signaling function, and the grammatical level, with total involvement of that function. The same item may often constitute a unit on both levels of structuring, as in morphemes consisting of a single phoneme. Relations between levels of structuring can be stated when units of one level are stated in terms of units of another level, as is the case in morphophonemics.

Finally, not all of the contrastive relationships of the structure are of equal weight in terms of integration possibilities and relevance for the functioning of the structure, or—in the terminology of the Prague Circle—they have unequal functional load. Thus, in Kutenai, while most all consonantal contrasts have considerable functional load in terms of frequency of occurrence, clustering, as well as differentiating and identifying morphemes, the functional load of the contrast between the spirant lateral /ł/ and the liquid lateral /l/ is very slight; indeed, in several instances the two phonemes are interchangeable, as in ma·łí ∼ ma·lí *Mary*.

Different structures on the verbal, or on the non-verbal level, are not necessarily mutually exclusive: acculturational symbiosis of two patterns is by now a well-known fact in anthropology, and at least on the phoneme level, the fact of coexistent phonemic patterns was recently pointed out by Pike and Fries (133). Hence, in a given instance, two or more coexisting structures are found; their relationship is similar to that of different levels of structuring described above: instead of differing in terms of the involvement of the function, however, they differ in terms of the internal structure and integrational possibilities of their units.

In Kutenai loan words, three coexisting patterns can be discerned: Kutenai, English, and French. Sometimes, the three patterns are found concomitantly in the same segment, as in ča·łí *Charles*, čapaní *Japanese*, where the phoneme č belongs to the English pattern, final stress to the French pattern, and the other characteristics of the segment to the native pattern.

If one assumes that the basic objectives of research are in two directions— that of the isolation of phenomena, and that of the reintegration of isolated specifics into functioning wholes—this approach should prove fruitful in both directions: with regard to the isolation of phenomena, by the insight that the subject matter is composed of units as well as items; and with regard to the integration of specifics from various aspects of the general field, by pointing at some of the outstanding interrelationships, and at the basic likeness of human phenomena from the standpoint of structuring and integration.

LINGUISTICALLY MARKED DISTINCTIONS
IN MEANINGS

C. F. Voegelin

If one is inclined to accept the statements (1) that WHAT a speaker talks about is properly classified as CULTURE, and (2) that the proper study of linguistics is the structure of this talk, then how relevant is a detailed explanation of the iterative aspect, or any other grammatical category, either to cultural anthropology or to linguistics? This is certainly not WHAT speakers are talking about. Nor are the various shades of iterative meaning, one blending into the other, to be confused with the clear-cut distribution of morphemes marking the iterative in a given language. Perhaps humanistic studies which are verbal would be most benefited by precise statements on grammatical categories; we may be certain that humanistic students would be less resistant to statements in linguistics via category than via structure.[1] But the price of precision is acceptance of linguistic structure as a point of departure.

The chief impediment to any discussion of the relationship of grammatical categories to ethnolinguistics or to structural linguistics or to humanistic studies lies in the imprecise ways in which the categories have been stated. While the structures of native languages are being stated with greater and greater precision, the same cannot be said for the associated categories. Statements on meaning are tending neither toward greater nor less precision—such statements are merely becoming fewer. The tendency here is for linguists (who analyze structure) to get along with less and less meaning which is scrutinized again, in the context of whole utterances, by culturalists and semanticists (who do not analyze structure).

One after another, the meaning content of an older generation's use of a category is abandoned, leaving nothing but distribution, that is, position in an utterance or part of an utterance, as a word or phrase. Thus, from the older use of verb (V) as an action word and noun (N) as a thing word, and so on, modern analysts of natural languages use V and N and other parts of speech in a strictly formal sense, divorced from meaning.

In descriptions of American Indian languages, interjections are generally

1. This is impressionistic on my part: that scholars steeped in humanistic studies are resistant or negative—not to linguistics as a whole, but to the structural aspect of modern linguistics. Among the various specialists in anthropology itself, I know physical anthropologists who are more appreciative of structural linguistics than some cultural anthropologists; among cultural anthropologists themselves, I sense that those whose training began in the humanities are more likely to reject the structural approach than those who came to cultural studies from one of the physical or biological sciences.

called particles, together with other words, such as sentence introducers, conjunctions, words called oral punctuation, and so on—in contrast to a wider classification of nouns and verbs than that found in the traditional classification; and some aboriginal languages, as Eskimo, are supposed to lack verbs, while other languages, as in the Salish family, are virtually supposed to lack nouns. We seem here to have a wide range of choice—to take three major form-classes (nouns, verbs, particles) as a possible base for describing previously unknown languages; or to resort to the full panoply of the traditional classification of words; or to combine some categories of the latter, as adjectives and adverbs into attributes; or, indeed, to dispense with major form-classes altogether and to list instead sub-classes on a co-ordinate basis, as de Groot does for Dutch (thus totaling 30 word-classes) (94).

The first effective critic of the traditional classification of words was Herman Paul who found the categories (meanings associated with word-classes) logically non-co-ordinative, and the syntactic criteria of privileges of occurrence (e.g., a noun may occur as a subject) non-distinctive because there is frequent overlapping in a given privilege of occurrence between two different word-classes (not only a noun, but a pronoun or an adjective or another word-class also occur as a subject).[2] Paul's criticism was good; however, his conclusion was negative: it is impossible to segregate sharply WORD-CLASSES AND THEIR MEANINGS. One agrees today with Paul in his criticism but avoids his negative conclusion by distinguishing WORD-CLASSES from THEIR MEANINGS. Then it is possible to segregate sharply one word-class from another word-class in a given language. By applying such purely formal criteria, a word ending in any one of a certain group of suffixes is a verb in Tübatulabal; a word ending in one of another group of suffixes is a noun, although a free translation of such a noun might mark action, as *I've got to go*—or more literally, *my necessary going*. This use of formal criteria is also a matter of privilege of occurrence or of distribution, but as stated above for Tübatulabal, it is a matter of distribution among morphemes within a word (morphology) rather than distribution among words within a whole utterance (syntax); additional description of Tübatulabal would require statements on the relationship of morphemes across word boundaries as well as within the boundaries of a given word. If structural statements virtually begin with a morpheme list (after phonemes are discovered, of course), then the distribution of a given morpheme or a class of morphemes, both within and across word boundaries, may be treated all together. This avoids the dual treatment implied in morphology versus syntax.

Word-classes or morpheme-classes remain as an important feature of description in American Indian linguistics; meanings associated with such classes—one kind of category—are largely abandoned (169). Another kind of category, partly correlated with word-classes, is often treated by such technical terms as CASE, ASPECT, MODE, TENSE. (Perhaps in most American Indian languages, nouns as

2. Paul is cited and discussed by De Groot (94).

well as verbs mark *tense*.) There is a tendency to use technical terms for CASE, as SUBJECTIVE or OBJECTIVE, merely as a short hand reference to certain morphemes without implying that the subjective case always marks *actor*—or that the objective case always marks *goal* (in Boas' Chinook [43] the objective case marks not only the *goal of transitive verbs* but also the *actor of intransitive verbs*, not to mention *gender of nouns*). Here, the case terms have what might be called a high correlation of uselessness, so far as meaning is concerned.

But besides edging away from this latter type of category in this way, some scholars take categories of the case-tense-mode-aspect type seriously and attempt to resolve the difficulty by appealing to dualistic oppositions of categories. If such an attempt were made for Southern Paiute, one might cite what Sapir called the objective case (specifically marked by a suffix), and oppose this to the subjective case (unmarked, or if you wish, marked by zero) (415). Then a subject noun (unmarked for case) may serve as the actor of a verb, and an object noun may serve as the goal of a transitive verb. So far so good. But an imperative transitive verb is not associated with a goal noun to which the objective case suffix is affixed—no suffix is affixed, or as Sapir put it, the object of an imperative verb is a noun in the subject case. Here the dualistic opposition is reversed: the so-called subject case is used as goal. Conversely, the so-called object case, specifically marked with a definite morpheme, may in certain sequences of morphemes serve as an actor (that is, when the object suffix before person markers relates the person marked as possessor of the noun). While the objective case suffix may thus appear in words which serve as either actor or goal, and while a noun unmarked for case (the so-called subjective) may also appear as either actor or goal, there is still another use of the objective case which lacks any kind of dualistic opposition. This is the association of noun with noun in which the noun to which the objective case morpheme is suffixed serves what Sapir calls a genitival relation to the unmarked noun. It would, of course, be possible to set up a zero category parallel to some uses of zero morphemes, and then oppose a genitive to a non-genitive noun. To apply such a system of inevitable symmetry to the human body, we would list two eyes, two ears, two arms, two legs, two breasts; and for the central organs, for example, two noses, the ventral nose and the dorsal nose, the latter occurring on the back of the head and being distinguished as a zero nose.

Dualistic oppositions are not lacking in precision. Their weakness is that they conjure up zero whenever convenient, and thereby conceal asymmetries on the one hand, and also fall short of correlating structure and meaning at all points.

By taking as a point of departure the larger structural operations of natural languages, and correlating these with meanings associated with greatly recurring morphemes (as suffixes or prefixes) or morphemic operations (as reduplication or ablaut or morpheme order), a four way arrangement may be stated which includes: Uniquely Marked, Inferentially Marked, Differentially Marked, and Paradigmatically Marked meanings. This arrangement is extensible (conversely stated, it is not a closed system); and, like all linguistic statements, it applies to a high level of abstraction.

In contrast and by definition, ethnolinguistics is at a low level of abstraction. Here meaning changes with change in the non-verbal part of a situation even when the verbal part of the situation is constant. Bloomfield's example is excellent: *I'm hungry* whether said by a starving beggar or by a well fed child [who wants to put off going to bed] is linguistically the same (= at a high level of abstraction); we add, it is ethnolinguistically different (= at a low level of abstraction.[3]

The missionary workers of a century ago were actively publishing dictionaries. Published descriptions of American Indian languages today generally give us texts and grammars without dictionaries. Material for the latter is difficult to characterize comprehensively. Without ethnolinguistic consideration—reference to the non-verbal situation—many different lexical entries would yield the same single gloss; all such entries, whether or not they include ethnolinguistic commentary, have structural properties (for example, they are organized in terms of word or morpheme-class).

1

UNIQUELY MARKED MEANING is meaning marked by a single morpheme whether the morpheme is an affix, a morphemic tone or stress, or some manipulation of another morpheme, as in reduplication. Here we deal with a single morpheme, a single meaning, and a single distribution (in respect to morpheme class).

A suffix which we number 27 in Tübatulabal uniquely marks meaning, namely *future time*. Suffix 27 occurs after one of two possible forms of the verb, here represented as YV. If YV = *he eats*, then YV + 27 = *he will eat*. The single distribution of suffix 27 is in respect to the sub-class YV. Another suffix is numbered 11, and uniquely marks *causative voice*. But this suffix 11 occurs after either one of the two possible forms of the verb—after XV or after YV. Since XV + 11 = *to cause to eat, to feed*, and YV + 11 equals the same, then we may say that suffix 11 occurs in a single distribution in respect to class V (either XV or YV), just as we say that a group of morpheme alternants count as a single morpheme. Among affixes, only suffixes can be involved in what is uniquely marked in Tübatulabal, for prefixes are lacking.

In Southern Paiute, another Uto-Aztecan language, prefix 33 uniquely marks *far;* it is cited here to illustrate a maximum restriction in distribution. Prefix 33

3. What Bloomfield (33) said about his much cited utterance *I'm hungry* is "Linguistics considers only those vocal features which are alike in the two utterances, and only those stimulus-reaction features which are alike in the two utterances." As given, the two utterances (by the stranger or beggar and by the child) are identical in vocal features, hence linguistically the same; if linguists actually would consider the stimulus-reaction features, they would then come to an opposite conclusion: that the two utterances are different (just as American Indian informants often reply to questions put to them by linguists "Yes, it is the same, but different").

appears only before one morpheme-class, namely nouns, and is found only in sequence with one N out of the total class of N, a N meaning *west;* 33 + N = *far west.* In contrast, suffix 61, uniquely marking *past, former time,* appears after N or after V (N and V thereby constitute a super morpheme-class which is labelled NV). Morphemes which may be suffixed after any of the major word classes are often called enclitics in descriptions of American languages; they may be said to have a single distribution in respect to the most inclusive word class—W.

In Coeur d'Alene (385), a certain phoneme of V, namely a medial vowel, may be replaced by another vowel for marking *causative* (as -u- in kʷul *be red* replaced by -i- in kʷil *dye, make red*). And for a few V, all the phonemes are replaced for marking *plural* (kwin *take hold of one*, čam? *grasp more than one*). Here, as in most other Salish languages, one kind of reduplication and phoneme alternation of N uniquely marks *diminutive* (if N = *man*, RN [reduplication of N] = *boy*), while other kinds of reduplication of N bear other meanings, as *distributive* and *plural.*

For prefixes and suffixes, it is often possible to give the single distribution of what is uniquely marked in terms of relative order (rather than merely with reference to the morpheme classes of base). Most descriptions of Athabascan languages give the relative order of prefixes. Thus in Chipewyan (269), one of the Mackenzie area languages of this family, a group of prefixes which has the common-denominator meaning of 'local and adverbial' (not to be confused with an adverb word class) includes prefix 22 which uniquely marks *up.* Any one of these prefixes, if one of this group occurs in a given sequence, will precede another relative order group of prefixes which includes prefix 31 uniquely marking *iterative aspect.* If prefix 31 does not appear in a given sequence, then prefix 22 may directly precede one of the so-called modal prefixes, say 77, which uniquely marks *local relationship.* In a sequence which includes prefixes 27 (*up*) and 71 (*local relationship*) before V, the 'direction of V' appears to be twice marked, once specifically (*up*) and once generally (*local relationship*). What is twice marked is the common-denominator meaning, that is, the feature of meaning held in common (as 'direction of V') between two uniquely marked meanings which are, as such, distinct (as *up* and *local relationship*). Some reports do not give us the distinction between such pairs of uniquely marked meanings but present the pair as pleonastic—as though each member of the pair marked the same identical meaning.

Thus, in the South American Cahuapana language, the interrogative mode may be twice marked—by prefixes and suffixes. In one and the same utterance, person may be twice marked in many aboriginal American languages. So also, in gender concordance between V and N in Algonquian, animate or inanimate is twice marked. In twice marked meanings, one may be uniquely marked, the other paradigmatically, for example.

For the little known languages of South America—which is to say, for languages known only from little preliminary sketches—much of what is vouchsafed to us about grammatical categories appears to be uniquely marked. Further analysis would show which of the half dozen morphemes marking as many distinct modes in Yunca (166) (*dubitative, obligatory, imaginative, purposive, benefactive*) belong in more than one paradigmatic set (see criteria listed under **4**), and which serve to transitivize certain verbs, and hence exemplify differentially marked meaning (**3**). Further analysis would show which of the morphemes marking *plural* in Timote (by a prefix which may appear twice in sequence before N) (394), in Puinave-Macu (396), in Mataco (167), for example, occur in languages marking the singular inferentially (**2**, below).

In languages with a plethora of bound forms, said by some 19th century scholars, as Horatio Hale, to be characteristic of primitive peoples, there also appears to be much that is uniquely marked: one is faced with long unwieldy lists of meanings marked by separate bound forms (162).

Accepting linguistic structure as a point of departure, the lists become manageable. And uniquely marked meanings between different languages can be interpreted in terms of language distance;[4] thus, the relative order prefixes of Athabascan languages which appear immediately before V might be expected to be reflected in all the sister languages, while some of the meanings uniquely marked in the prior relative orders would yield brief lists in some Athabascan languages, elaborate lists in others. This is similar to research in comparative morphology, with the limitation there that the languages must be related; but the uniquely marked relative order lists of Athabascan affixes could be compared to similar lists in non-related Chinook, as an isolated language; or the Athabascan lists (with all their internal diversity) could be compared to lists showing what is uniquely marked in relative order affix groups of another language family, as Uto-Aztecan (with all its internal diversity).

2

INFERENTIALLY MARKED MEANING is meaning marked by the association of two or more morphemes across word boundaries; or, more indirectly, by associations of morphemes within a word.

The former kind of marking (across word boundaries) is traditionally termed 'inherent': if English *to codify* is 'inherently' transitive, it is because we predict that this verb will appear in an utterance before a goal (*he wants to codify it*); if *to wade* is 'inherently' intransitive, it is because we predict that this verb will appear without goal (*he wants to wade*).

English singular for nouns is inferentially marked (the so-called 'singular' in Turkish is not). Thus, for English there are such associations across word bound-

---

4. This, in turn, could be compared to language distance as estimated by Morris Swadesh (percentage of retained basic vocabulary between two daughter languages).

aries as *wants* with singular N, *want* with plural N: *that child wants to wade while the other children want to swim.* Parallel Turkish constructions are possible but optional. A better contrast is plural N after plural quantifying words in English (*five girls*), but a singular noun after singular quantifier (*one girl*); Turkish plural suffix after N is incompatible with a quantifying word preceding N, whether the quantifier marks *one* (bir kiz) or *five* (beš kiz).

For English it is possible but for Turkish impossible to say that N unmarked for plural means, inferentially, *singular.* American Indian examples by and large resemble the Turkish rather than English picture in forming noun plurals, but with a characteristic difference. Many native American languages have a variety of ways of marking more than singular, resulting in *duals, plurals*, and *distributives* of various kinds. If none of the number markers appear with N in an utterance, singular is not inferentially marked; in many languages *singular* may be uniquely marked (see 1 above).

As shown above, quantifiers (separate words) may precede N unmarked for number. In some American languages such N are found in association across word boundaries with V marking certain aspects (as, *to eat here and there, to graze*); this leads to the inference that the associated N (as *sheep*) is plural.

In Tübatulabal transitive verbs may be marked by suffixes which we number 11 (*transitivizing causative*) and 12 (*transitivizing benefactive*). Thus, intransitive V (*to be silent*) + 11 = *to silence him;* intransitive V (*to gamble*) + 12 = *to gamble for it* (*as money*). Not all transitive verbs in Tübatulabal are so marked by specific suffixes; some are inferentially marked (509), either by association with a goal N (parallel to the English example, above), that is, across word boundaries; or by morphemes within one word. Suffix 12 in sequence with an intransitive V marks single goal (see above); suffix 12 in sequence with a transitive V marks double goal. Thus, transitive V (*to shell it*) + 12 = *to shell it for him.* Whenever a double goal is marked in Tübatulabal by suffix 12, one may infer that the base preceding 12 is a transitive base. So also, whenever a passive voice is marked by a sequence including V and morpheme 17 (the passive suffix), one may infer that V is a transitive V. Thus, V (*to lick her—as a kitten*) + 17 = *she is being licked* (*as by the mother cat*). On the other hand, the sequence intransitive V + 17 is also possible, but instead of a *passive* this sequence marks an *impersonal* verb. Thus, V (*to cry*) + 17 = *there is crying* (*a ceremonial affair*).

3

DIFFERENTIALLY MARKED MEANINGS are alternant meanings which may be distinguished in two or more distributions of one morpheme. Here we have a single morpheme but a double or triple distribution, and two or three meanings.

This is not to be confused with morphemes or groups of morphemes—often lexical items—which are said to have a wide range of meaning—this latter of course refers to the various ethnolinguistic situations to which the same morpheme may be applied. Examples of such a wide range of meaning are found in Southern Paiute where a morpheme may mark a person or thing as merely small (diminutive) or as small and affectionately regarded, or as affectionately regarded though actually not small. Characteristic of such wide range of meanings is the fact that possible ambiguity is actualized when the non-verbal aspect of a situation is unappreciated.

The same morpheme in Southern Paiute in sequence after a sub-class of N (partially reciprocal kinship terms) marks *descending generation*. The *grandparent in descending generation*, or as we say in English, the *grandchild* is neither a term of affection nor necessarily small—an adult *grandchild*, a disagreeable *grandchild*, and a beloved baby *grandchild* are all called by the same term which includes the morpheme marking *descending generation*. This differentially marked meaning is not subject to the ambiguity mentioned above.

So also in Southern Paiute, the *number* category of certain single morphemes depends on the distribution of the morpheme: *dual-number* is marked when the morpheme is associated with a so-called singular stem, *plural number* when the same morpheme is associated with a plural stem. As already noted, what Sapir calls the *objective case* suffix marks contradictory meanings; the contradictions are removed if the meanings of this single morpheme, which we may here label as 21, are stated in terms of the distributions of the morpheme in question. For most syntactic modes, with transitive V before N + 21, 21 marks goal (but imperative mode transitive V is incompatible with a following N + 21); for N + 21 with person marker, 21 marks possession and occurs in a sequence of morphemes with N serving as actor; finally, for N + 21 before N, 21 marks *of*, or as Sapir says, it has a genitive function (*rain-of children = Rain's children*).

The last examples take into account distributions both within and across word boundaries. In South America, the Matako language has one morpheme used as a free form, probably an N class, ka *thing;* but as prefix, ka- means *as if, as though:* a *spoon* is an *as if mussel shell;* a *father-in-law* is an *as though grandfather*. The prefix here would be generally called a deverbal derivative or a by-form of the free form; not all such by-forms distributionally mark distinct meanings. Algonquian and Salish languages abound in examples of such distributionally marked alternate meanings.

Tübatulabal is particularly rich in distributionally marked meanings. What the published account calls the atelic form of the verb we may rename the X base or XV, and call the telic form of the verb the Y base or YV; then the meaning of morpheme 16 depends entirely on its distribution. In the sequence XV + 16, 16 marks desiderative mode (e.g., *to want to eat*); in YV + 16, 16 marks inceptive aspect (*to be on the verge of eating*).

What is often called SPECIALIZED MEANING (an inescapable difficulty when morphemes from the lexicon are considered) is specialized in the sense that the meaning of a particular lexical morpheme is differentially marked in certain sequences. The following examples are Tübatulabal inanimate actor intransitive V in sequence with suffix 11 (*transitivizing causative*): V (*it is ripe*) + 11 = *he cooks it;* V (*it wears out*) + 11 = *he files it;* V (*it fades*) + 11 = *he washes it.*

Much of what is bothersome in accounting for the meanings of compounds is a result of specialized meanings, i.e., differentially marked meanings occasioned when certain lexical items enter into a compound. What little compounding there is in Tübatulabal is highly specialized, as N (*house*) + V (*to sit*) = V (*to visit*); most specialized are examples in which the second member of the compound is V (*to die, to be unconscious*) and which then rather poetically (or is it botanically?) associate *sleepiness* with the *evening primrose*, and reasonably enough *thirst* with the *sun*, and interestingly enough, *hunger* with *father* (rather than with *mother*): N (*evening primrose*) + V (*to be unconscious*) = V (*to be sleepy*); N (*sun*) + V (*to be unconscious*) = (*to be thirsty*); N (*father*) + V (*to be unconscious*) = V (*to be hungry*).

Though going beyond exclusively structural considerations into the extralinguistic world of social role, some speaker-involved meanings are conventionally included in descriptions of languages. Speaker-involved meaning is an analogue of differentially marked meaning in which the difference in meaning of a given morpheme (*honorable* for *plural* below) is determined not by another distribution of morphemes but rather by different relations of speakers to one another. A California visitor speaking Miwok would refer to a single affinal relative of his Miwok friend as *your uncle's wife* or *your mother-in-law's brother*, and to more than one of these relatives as *they, your mother-in-law's brother*, for example. But a Miwok man, making reference to his own relationship to such affinal kin of opposite sex, would prefix morpheme 26 to the kinship terms, saying literally, *they, our uncle's wife*. And a Miwok woman, making reference to her own relationship to an affinal kin of opposite sex, would say *they, my mother-in-law's brother*.

These so-called literal translations are actually incorrect translations. The so-called *plural* markers which are added to kinship terms (in this particular interpersonal relationship) here mark *honorific respect*. If morpheme 26 marks *plural* in most situations, but *honorific respect* when speaker refers to his own affinal kin of opposite sex, then the proper translations for the utterances cited are: *the honorable wife of my uncle*, and *my honorable mother-in-law's brother*.[5]

4

PARADIGMATICALLY MARKED MEANINGS include two or more discrete meanings (marked by a set[6] of morphemes), and a single overriding meaning. We have

5. It is perhaps worth noting that the Miwok, though living in a pre-Columbian marginal culture, were not deterred from using HONORIFICS, which are, to be sure, also found in the languages of pre-Columbian high cultures, as Nahuatl (128).

6. In the older literature, sets of forms were often listed which differed formally but not in meaning. These were sometimes called "paradigms" or "inflections" or "conjugation" but would today be relegated to morphophonemics—regarded as groups of alternants constituting the same morpheme.

two or more morphemes, but a single distribution for each morpheme in the set; we find as many discrete meanings as there are morphemes in the set, and in addition, for the paradigmatic set as a whole, an overriding meaning.

Perhaps no arrangement is more commonly encountered in linguistic literature than paradigms; yet the criteria for what is paradigmatically marked are still open to some question. If a common-denominator meaning is acceptable as the overriding meaning of a paradigm, then a set of suffixes marking several different kinds of *plural number* and also *singular number* would count as a paradigm, with the common-denominator meaning being *number*. Such a set of forms is found in Cuna, a language belonging to the Chibcha family, with sister languages found in both South and North America (189, 190). Listing the morphemes which comprise this paradigm as suffixes numbered 11, 12, 13, and 14, then N + 11 marks *variety in plural number* (if N means *people* or *tribe*, then N + 11 means *different* or *variously assorted people*); N + 12 marks *unity in plural number* (if N means *fish*, then N + 12 means the *fish nation*); 13 marks *quantity (many)—in plural number* in certain sequences [and in others, not relevant to the paradigm, *intensive plural number (much, very many)*]; N + 14 marks *singular number*. In order to satisfy the formal criteria of a paradigm, we must here assume at least that all N may appear before any of the suffixes of the 10 decade (either 11, 12, 13, or 14), and that each suffix in the 10 decade is incompatible with every other suffix; and that no more than one zero suffix occurs in the Cuna example. Suffix 14 is zero, and marks *singular;* if we were able to say that N may appear unmarked for *number*, then the common meaning of suffixes 11, 12, and 13 would be *plural*.

The difficulty with common-denominator meanings is that groups of relative order suffixes, as in Chinook, can just as well have a common meaning ascribed to each relative order group. Boas gives five groups of relative order suffixes after V in Chinook and ascribes some general meaning held in common by each group, though the meanings ascribed are very general indeed. Group 10 he characterizes as *generic*, [and the discrete or specific meanings for the suffixes of this group may be said to be *position* (for suffix 11), *active causative* (12), *passive causative* (13), *directional completive* (14)]; the next relative order group, here numbered 20, is characterized as *local suffixes;* group 30 as *semi-temporal suffixes;* relative order group 40 as *temporal and semi-temporal;* group 50 as *terminal successful completion*. None of these relative order groups of affixes satisfy criteria for sets of morphemes making up a paradigm. A given base, V, would not necessarily be compatible with all the suffixes in group 10, for example; a certain V might appear before suffixes 12 and 14, another V before 11 and 14, and still another V might appear in a sequence which included three suffixes (11, 12, 13) from this one group. This Chinook example as a whole represents various specific meanings each of which are uniquely marked (see **1**, above).

We conclude that each morpheme found in a relative order group may represent uniquely marked meanings, as in the Chinook example and the Chipewyan example already cited (the latter under **1**); and that paradigmatically marked meanings may be also marked by morphemes falling in one or more relative order positions.

Thus, for Chipewyan, prefix 1 + N marks possessor of N for *first person;* 2 + N for *second person,* 3 + N for *single third person possessor,* 4 + N for *paired third person possessor* (occurring in an utterance which contains another third person as actor); 5 + N for *indefinite person possessor,* and so on. These are some of the specific meanings of this paradigm; the overriding meaning of the paradigm is *possessor relation to N.* For plural person, one morpheme or morpheme cluster designated as 2 + 7) + N marks either (a) *first person plural,* or (b) *second person plural possessor of N;* here we say that both (a) and (b) are paradigmatically marked; and the distinction between the two [(a) vs. (b)] is inferentially marked across word boundary (see **2,** above), just as zero is inferentially marked even though occurring in a paradigm.

To obtain an overriding meaning in this sense implies that a given language will show at least two sets of forms with parallel or analogous specific meanings, but with contrastive overriding meaning. In Tübatulabal, the parallel or analogous specific case meanings are *actor, goal, genitive* (and some *localizing cases*); the overriding meaning for what is paradigmatically marked is *absolute* (N unrelated to person as possessor) versus *relative* (N related to person as possessor, whether or not specifically marked by a subsequent person paradigm).

Some languages yield more than a dualistic contrast in overriding meanings for what is paradigmatically marked. In Chinook, the parallel or analogous specific meanings in three person paradigms are: *first person (singular; dual* vs. *plural exclusive; dual* vs. *plural inclusive); second person (singular, dual, plural); third person singular (masculine, feminine, neuter); third person without gender (dual, plural, indefinite as to number); vocative.* These numerous specific meanings are marked by three sets of forms, hence three paradigms, which we may number pdg. 100, pdg. 200, pdg. 300. Then in the sequence pdg. 100 + transitive V, pdg. 100 marks *actor.* Since pdg. 100 occurs only in this sequence, there is no further problem here. But pdg. 200 appears both in the sequence (a) pdg. 200 + transitive V; and in sequence (b) pdg. 200 + intransitive V. We might say the difference between overriding meaning (a) and overriding meaning (b) is differentially marked (see **3,** above), because in sequence (a) pdg. 200 marks *goal of transitive V,* while in sequence (b) pdg. 200 marks actor of *intransitive V.* Or we might say that the same common overriding meaning is paradigmatically marked by pdg. 200, and that the apparent difficulty resides in translating into English because English distinguishes goal forms in first and third persons (*me, him*) from actor forms (*I, he*), while Chinook merges the two, perhaps in the sense of having impersonal passives (*there is running by me, by him,* etc.) instead of having intransitive V of the English type (*I run, he runs*). But in still another sequence, (c), pdg. 200 + N, the overriding meaning of pdg. 200 is *gender (including number) classifier of N,* not to be confused with the paradigmatically marked *possessor* of pdg. 300 + N (the overriding meaning of pdg. 300 is always *possessor of N* just as the overriding meaning of pdg. 100 is always *actor of transitive V*).

Pairs of these three paradigms appear in single sequence, as when a transitive verb marks both *actor* (by pdg. 100) and *goal* (by pdg. 200); and when a noun marks both its *gender* (by pdg. 200) and its *possessor* (by pdg. 300).

Any of the numerous forms for marking specific third persons of pdg. 200 may mark *gender* and *number* in sequence 200 + N (or 200 + 300 + N, when the N is also possessed). It has been suggested that third person should be regarded as though marked by zero in Chinook, and that the forms in question here mark only *gender* and *number;* but zero marks *vocative*, and it is impossible to distinguish between the meanings of two zeros in one paradigm.

As the Chinook example shows, we attest overriding meaning by contrasting parallel sets (each with a series of discrete or specific meanings); and besides this find that overriding meanings may be further marked differentially (cf. 3).

The specific or discrete meanings in a given paradigm set are easy enough to abstract when they are each marked by single morphemes, but we need special consideration for pairs or clusters of morphemes which, juxtaposed in a fixed order, mark more than the sum of the meanings of each. Each such morpheme pair or cluster may be treated as a single juxtapositional morpheme, and the total meaning of the juxtapositional morpheme may then be treated as a single discrete meaning.

Our most elaborate example is from Southern Paiute. Person suffixes or enclitics are found in association with transitive V, in clusters having fixed orders, as follows. A variety of morphemes marking *third person* (and *visible* or *invisible;* and *singular* or *plural* or *dual-plural animate;* or *inanimate* without specification of *number*) always precede one or more morphemes marking *first person* (*singular* or *dual inclusive;* or if *plural, inclusive* or *exclusive*): the resulting meaning is either *third person actor* with *first person goal*, or vice versa, *third person goal with first person actor*, irrespective of the fixed order of the morpheme clusters. Parallel in position-point to these amazingly complex morpheme clusters is a single morpheme (in other distributions marking *second person objective*) which here marks *first person actor* with *second person goal;* but the converse in meaning, *second person actor* with *first person goal*, is again marked by morpheme clusters, as are the meanings for *second person actor* with *third person goal*, and vice versa. One cluster of the last set appears with morphemes marking *second person* before morphemes marking *third person* (the full meaning is: *you plural actor* with *invisible third person animate dual-plural*); all other clusters in this set appear with morphemes for *third person* before morphemes for *second person* irrespective of which person is marked as actor and which as goal. In *third person actor* with *third person goal* identical morphemes may be juxtaposed in clusters.

NOTES ON THE THEORY OF POPULATION DISTRIBUTION IN RELATION TO THE ABORIGINAL POPULATION OF NORTH AMERICA

Stanley D. Dodge

The geographer who studies the distribution of population may only work with surety in those areas for which there are censuses. He depends, that is, primarily on censuses taken by minor civil divisions—by counties, towns, or districts; by departements, communes, or arrondissements; or by barrios. Then only are his data adequate. Where there are no censuses, he may, as a second best, use maps of the distribution of houses, villages, towns, and cities. Where there are neither proper censuses nor proper maps, he may proceed only by probabilities, making use of the principles of the distribution of population. The latter course is the only one open to the student of the pre-Columbian distribution of population in the Americas.

So little is known of the distribution of pre-Columbian Indians that the geographer is practically helpless when working in most of North America. Perhaps three major divisions may be distinguished in each of which the degree of uncertainty is different:

I. In some places, counts of the people were made shortly after the conquest, and these may be used to indicate the possible distribution before the conquest. But, it must be remembered, the conquest itself, even the peaceful penetration of the wilderness for the purposes of trade, so dislocated the structure of the aboriginal distribution that there are no certain grounds for believing that early censuses really show anything of the pre-Columbian distribution.

II. A second region of the continent may be recognized in the arid and semi-arid parts of the southwest, where numerous pueblos have been preserved. Their size may be proportional to the density of their population. They may be used as a fairly accurate index after proper account has been taken of the relations between economy and numbers and between numbers and the sizes of pueblos.

III. However, throughout the vast humid regions of the continent the *wooden* villages have disappeared, and only the accidental discovery of artifacts makes their identification possible. A few exceptions may be noted. The mounds of the Ohio and Mississippi valleys may be clues to the distribution of population, and middens like that at Damariscotta, Maine.

The distribution of population is not only a function of space, that is, of area, but also of time, for the local numbers of people vary from time to time. Deductions from the known distribution of villages, therefore, are invalid, unless it can be shown that the villages were occupied simultaneously. Furthermore, deduc-

234

tions from the post-Columbian distribution of villages are vitiated by the fact that the whole distribution of Indian population was disarranged by the European conquest and by European settlement. In some places, the local Indians were killed, either by the arms of the conquerors or by the diseases which the conquerors introduced. The relatively easy settlement of New England by the Pilgrims and the Puritans was probably owing to the fact that many Indians had died from scarlet fever (?) introduced into Maine in the first decade of the seventeenth century. When the Atlantic shores of America had been occupied by Europeans, and when the Indians had recovered from the immediate effects of the occupation, they regrouped themselves in villages, but not necessarily on the same sites or in the same numbers.

In view of the uncertainties surrounding the pre-Columbian distribution of the Indians, the most reliable course for the student to follow would seem to be that of inference from the distribution of trails and of resources.

Inference from resources suffers the same disabilities as those affecting inferences from villages. The quarries, mines, and fields used by the Indians, like their towns and villages, may often be discovered only by accident. It may be unknown, too, when they were used, and the temporal difficulties may prevent an accurate description of the distribution of Indians on the basis of resources, like copper, flint, and shells for the manufacture of wampum.

The surest method of deducing the distribution of the Indian population may be suggested by the following thoughts. The general theory of the development of roads has been worked out by Hilaire Belloc. He uses the word *road* in a broad and general sense to cover any travelled way, whether it be path, trail, railroad, canal, or road proper. His principle may be stated thus: In the course of its development, the road tends to become as short and straight as the circumstances of the land will permit. The principal circumstances preventing short and straight roads are mountains and marshes. Now mountains and marshes are permanent features of the physical geography of many lands. Low hills may be razed, but instances of razing are few. Marshes and swamps may be drained, but only the most assiduous labor prevents their reforming. In the course of ages, therefore, nearly straight roads tend to be developed, and even with changes in economy and in engineering ability, the same courses of roads, paths, and trails, tend to be followed.

When nearly straight roads are found, like that between Boston and Hartford, the presupposition is that it represents an Indian trail. When it is known that it was the route followed by Hooker on his migration to the site of Hartford, it becomes a certainty that it is an old Indian trail. It was the easiest way through the wilderness of eastern Connecticut.

The network of trails in Ohio has led to the discovery of the sites of numerous Indian villages, but the network itself is a clear indication of the distribution of Indian population, even though no precise figures may be given. That population tends to be distributed along roads and especially at the junctions is a principle too well substantiated to be doubted. Road junctions are the obvious places for people to congregate, whether the junction leads to the establishment of a drug-store, the building of a hamlet, or the flourishing of a metropolis like Paris or New York. Where junctions are many, either there are many villages and so many people, or there are many resources to which paths lead, and so many people to make the paths.

Ullman's recent map of the railroads of the United States, though not complete, shows how clearly routes of travel indicate the principal concentrations of population between Chicago and the east. Those who are familiar with it will recognize that the rail net of Manitoba, Saskatchewan, and Alberta does the same thing, and that the rule is general.

A like relation between a network of roads and relatively dense population may be thought of as existing in Ohio. Where trails are many, Indians were many; where trails were few, the Indian population was sparse. Since the trails are as nearly straight as hills, fords, marshes, and swamps will allow, they may be thought of as providing a long-lasting framework for the distribution of the Indian population.

Near the junctions of paths and trails many Indian villages have been discovered already. More may yet be discovered. Straight roads are the beginning of investigation, and, although accuracy may never be attained, the straightness of roads in relation to permanent features of the land is somehow a guarantee that, in spite of temporal difficulties, the network of roads is an index to the distribution of Indian population. Numbers may have changed from time to time, but however they changed the people were always distributed along a network of nearly permanent routes of travel.

There are, in addition, ways of checking the distribution of population, again proceeding with caution by the way of probabilities. When a sufficient number of village sites has been discovered, one may note the resources on which they seem to have depended, and then work out the distribution of the resources. This method may only be used to supplement conclusions drawn from the network of roads, for it must be remembered that geographical theory in no way supports the notion of a positive relation between numbers of people and resources. A developed mine or quarry does not necessarily indicate any great concentration of people. There are more people concentrated about Paris, New York, and Chicago than there are in the mining areas of France and the eastern United States.

Though resources are not a reliable index to the distribution of population in Europe and America, they may be such for people living under the primitive economy of pre-Columbian America. Indeed, theory would suggest that it was so. Where people depend wholly on farming, areas of fertile soil are likely to be more densely populated than infertile ones. Where people depend wholly on hunting, the margins of areas with abundant game are likely to be more densely populated than areas where game is scarce. The meadows of the Connecticut

River attracted the first migrants from Boston into the wilderness of New England. The Puritans used them to pasture their cattle, and the Indians would appear to have had their villages near them, because they were grazing grounds for deer. Many a New England town has been planted on the site of an Indian village. Shores where shells were abundant attracted a few Indians for the manufacture of wampum, but it does not appear that the distribution of shells either affected or could have affected the distribution of population to any great extent.

Though mines and meadows may be used as checks on already discovered facts about the distribution of Indian population, it would appear that the trails leading to them would be a surer guide. In the end, therefore, I would say that the first attack on the distribution of the aboriginal population must be made through the mapping of trails. Then, if theory be sound, the distribution of population may be deduced with some degree of certainty. But, always, of course, difficulties will remain because of our inability to know that the trails and villages discovered were in use at the same time throughout the network, and because it may not always be possible to know whether a road or path, even if it were straight, was indeed an Indian trail.

DISCUSSION

Jan O. M. Broek

The starting point for most studies on the native population has usually been the collection and evaluation of accounts by early white observers. For North America the tabulation by James Mooney has been generally accepted, be it with local modifications, as Kroeber's for California (328). With all respect for Mooney's monumental pioneer work it appears to have two weaknesses. First— a minor one—the bibliography as published with his posthumous essay contains, despite its length, a relatively small number of firsthand accounts, except for areas in which Mooney was particularly interested. Secondly, the reliance on written reports inevitably puts the date level at the period of direct contact with the whites. As H. J. Spinden suggested years ago, is it not likely that European diseases, introduced by 1500, had already depleted the native population by the time the white man, in 1600 or even as late as 1750, appeared among them? (454).

Whatever the explanation, the question remains whether the figures of Mooney, relating to dates of contact with Europeans, have not been accepted too rashly as *the* ("normal") Indian population. They are, obviously, the only kind of figures on which we can pin a date, but they do not necessarily give us a picture of number and distribution in the pre-Columbian era, or any part of it.

If we abandon these figures, it will be said, we are left with mere speculation. I do not mean that we should ignore them, rather that we should not be hypnotized by them. If one takes Mooney's or similar counts at face value, one has to cut the pattern of Indian economy to fit these measurements. In Professor Kroeber's study (246, pp. 148–50) it would seem that his acceptance of Mooney's data colored his exposition of the mode of life of the Eastern Indians.[1]

There will be general agreement that we should use all possible approaches to arrive at the best possible estimate. We might take figures like those of Mooney as a starting point, and probably as a minimum. At the other end of the scale should come an evaluation of the maximum Indian population density in each area, under a certain social and economic organization and level of technology. In addition there are the remains of former settlements, burial mounds and other artifacts, that should throw further light on the problem.

Professor Dodge now proposes that we give priority to the examination of Indian trails as the most reliable guide to population distribution. This suggestion is novel as well as interesting. Like all new ideas his is certain to be resisted; I myself am a doubting Thomas.

Every road is the expression of a type of culture; the road is a function of society. It is, therefore, dangerous to apply the concepts of our commercial economy to the almost self-sufficient way of living in pre-Columbian North America. But I take it that Professor Dodge's case does not rest on analogies with the road pattern around modern New York, Chicago or Paris. The basic questions are:

a) Was there a positive relationship between roads and population distribution in aboriginal North America?

b) Even if so, do we have—or can we achieve—adequate knowledge of the Indian trails?

There is no simple yes or no to these questions. It seems best to point out some of the characteristics of the Indian Road (used as a generic term). The road—any road—can be viewed from three angles: (1) its *function*, or the purpose served by the road; (2) its *course*, or route; and (3) its *structure*, or form and degree of improvement.

First of all we must distinguish between buffalo roads and Indian trails. The early explorers usually made a clear distinction between the two (198). The buffalo had obviously his own goal in mind when he traveled, be it fresh pastures, salt licks or wallows. Parts of these well-trodden pathways certainly served the Indian as well as later the white man (198). No doubt wagon roads and perhaps even railways followed the routes blazed by the buffalo herds. The point, however, is that these trails, even where used by the Indians, are in themselves no index to the distribution of population.

1. *Function of the road.*—Coming now to the Indian trails, what were their functions? There were the trails to the hunting, fishing and gathering grounds for food, and to quarries, mines and beaches for flint, copper, clay, shells and

---

1. Kroeber (246) explains brilliantly why the eastern United States had a low density of population (according to Mooney's data) when compared to California, in spite of its more advanced type of economy. But what period do we wish to consider? On p. 149 he speaks of "the Mound Builder days of heavier population" and continues "If there were such days, and it seems there were. . . ."

such. Together we may call these resource trails. Some of these were long distance, serving often for seasonal treks; many were short distance routes.

Then there were trails serving social travel, as for ceremonial meetings of clans or tribes; these trails were mainly between the villages of a tribe and did not necessarily coincide with the resource trails.

At first sight Professor Dodge's thesis appears correct for these kinds of trails: the denser the population the more numerous the paths of travel. But what of another function of the road, the well-known warpath? The mode and frequency of warfare is a function of society at a given historical period. The density of warpaths does not necessarily give a clue to the density of population. Moreover, it seems unlikely that population would have been concentrated along the warpaths.

Finally, there is the trade function. Commerce certainly is a prime mover in gathering people along roads, especially at nodal points, as examples of modern countries show. But trade was a minor matter in most of aboriginal North America. I do not know of any Indian settlement before the advent of the white man that can be called a trade center. What exchange there was appears to have been subordinate to other activities, often connected with the social-ceremonial visits as an exchange of gifts.

So much for the various functions of the trails. Supposing we knew the trails, how shall we determine which were warpaths, and therefore unreliable as indicators of population density? More serious is the next difficulty. Indian settlements were far from permanent. As the community moved to another spot, the trails radiating from the village necessarily moved too. I will return to this point a little later. Now let us look at

2. *The course.*—First of all I must point out an obvious restriction on the usefulness of Professor Dodge's suggestion. In the eastern half of North America the rivers were an essential part of transportation. Hulbert (198, p. 63) points out that water routes were not as predominant as is often assumed, and enumerates their limitations (such as ice, low water, obstructions). However, the wide use the Indians made of canoes cannot be denied, and the numerous portages attest to the significance of water traffic. It appears that in many parts of the country the population was concentrated near streams and estuaries (246, chap. ix; 327). On the other hand it has been argued that the Mound Builders preferred upland locations. Probably it depended on the type of economy practiced. However that may be, the point is that reliance on the distribution of land trails would give us a very lopsided picture of population distribution.

Returning now to the land routes, it is well to summarize here the relevant argument of Professor Dodge. Accepting the principle of Hilaire Belloc, he states that a network of nearly straight trails, or modern roads following these nearly straight trails, indicates a long-lasting framework for the distribution of Indian population. I must take issue with the principle, ascribed to Belloc, that "every road tends to become as short and straight as the circumstances of the land will permit." Certainly, the statement should include reference to the level of technology as another conditioning factor. Even so, one wonders if the principle has validity. I was unable to find the reference in Belloc's writings, but I did find a statement by this author that expresses perfectly my own views.

The straight road results from design, from planning by a central authority; otherwise the road "just grows" in a haphazard fashion. And Hilaire Belloc says: "It may be urged that the discovery of advantages as time goes on gradually improves the road, and in this way half-conscious development will always give you the best road in the long run. . . . But History is against this view. Europe is full of roads thus established haphazard, confirming themselves by use and by expenditure . . ." (24, pp. 7–11).

The Indian tried, like anybody else, to find the shortest route between two given points with the minimum expense of energy. That implies, however, that often straightness was sacrificed to other savings in energy by avoiding—in our eyes—minor obstacles, and to safety from attack. Reports from many explorers and early settlers mention the "twisting," "winding," "sinuous" courses of Indian trails (198, pp. 16, 33).

Speaking of "given points," how many of these had permanency enough to cause a well-defined impress of the trail on the landscape? It would seem that only passes—be it through mountains and marshes or fords across rivers—and perhaps quarries and mines had the qualities of permanent objectives. We may stretch the "point" literally to include portages. On the other side of the ledger, as said before, we must consider that Indian settlement sites shifted frequently and to some degree the same was true of areas of resource exploitation. Thus trails were also shifted. One must conclude that most trail routes were temporary affairs, except for stretches near passes and quarries.

There is little doubt that the white man used the Indian trails wherever they were to his advantage. Friederici (132) has pointed out that the exploration of America owed much of its rapid advance to Indian guides who, of course, led the paleface along the trails they knew. Also, stretches of these trails later became actual roads. But between the Indian and the white man there was such divergence in purpose and thus in direction of the road that the trajectories of most trails proved of little value beyond pure frontier conditions.

3. *The structure.*—Finally a word on the structure of the road. It has been said that every road is in answer to a need; the greater the need, the better the road—always, of course, within the limits of a given technology. The roads of the Inca Empire demonstrate the point by their excellence. On the other hand, the Indian trails of North America indicate that needs were few. They were transient, narrow paths, and as a rule not improved in the technical sense of the word. Their tenacity of imprint was much less than that of the buffalo traces which by comparison were wide highways. The mapping of the Indian trails will therefore be an arduous task.

As Professor Dodge admits, even if all Indian trails were mapped the resulting network would in no way mean that all parts were used at the same time. In view of these difficulties, one wonders if the method proposed is any more reliable than others used so far, and if the preliminary work required would not be disproportionately large in relation to its value for disclosing the distribution of population.

SUMMARY

a) The proposed method takes no account of water routes.

b) Buffalo traces, although used for Indian travel, must be disregarded.

c) Warpaths are no reliable indicators of population distribution.

d) Trails serving economic and social purposes have value. However,

e) Their practical use as indicators is limited because (1) they were shifted frequently, and (2) there is no certainty that discovered trails formed a contemporaneous network.

f) The slight imprint of the trails impedes adequate mapping.

I may have been unduly critical. Actual investigation may prove the errors of my deductive reasoning. Research on the much-neglected topic of roads should be encouraged, for its own sake as well as for the clues it may give to the distribution of population. I hope that the paper of Professor Dodge will provide the needed stimulus.

AN ANTHROPOMETRIC STUDY OF RETURNED
MEXICAN EMIGRANTS[1]

Gabriel Ward Lasker

The cultural effects of intra-American migration have received a great deal of attention. Much less is known about its physical influences. Indeed, the scientific study of change in residence as a factor in biological change is relatively recent.

In several previous studies it has been shown that, among various groups immigrant to the United States, those who have lived in this country during their childhood differ in respect to several physical dimensions from those who have been brought up in the country of origin. The most notable of these changes is a general increase in size which is manifest particularly in an increase in stature and in the dimensions most closely correlated with stature. An analysis of the previous studies has led to the concept of an "environmental growth factor" (253). The most thorough studies of the physical anthropology of migrants, notably the investigations of Shapiro (428) and Goldstein (150), give evidence that individuals brought up in the United States tend to be taller and to differ also in other characteristic respects from the population of the region from which they have come. In these studies the migrants tend to be intermediate in size between their American-born offspring and the "sedentes," as the stay-at-home individuals of their own group are called. This has led to speculation concerning a "selective" factor which might single out particular physical types for migration. The interpretation of these differences is further complicated by the fact that a gradual increase in size is also a general phenomenon which has been observed both in this and in other parts of the world.

In Goldstein's study, Mexican immigrants and their children, including adult offspring, were measured in the United States, and other Mexican families were measured in those parts of Mexico whence the migrants had come. This study shows that the younger generation of sedentes is taller than the older, and that the first generation of migrants is taller than the sedentes. But the general secular increase in size—whether evolutionary or not—and physical selection of migrants—whether conscious or accidental—do not suffice to account for the extent of the augmentation in stature of United-States-born Mexicans. At least a part of the difference is probably best explained as a result of some factor in the environment during the growth period of the individual.

My own recent study was undertaken to test the relative importance of en-

1. Aided by a grant from the Viking Fund, New York.

vironmental and selective factors in a parallel situation. On the present occasion I shall speak more especially of those findings that have to do with stature. In any case, previous study has shown that stature serves as a satisfactory index of size and of factors affecting size. The data on twenty-five other measurements and additional observations will be published elsewhere.

To make the most useful comparisons between migrants and non-migrants, it seemed desirable to deal with individuals from a single community and from the same families. By comparing sedentes in such a community with several classes of returned emigrants, one could eliminate some of the variables which may have affected similar comparisons in previous studies. A small community where climate, diet, and other conditions of life contrast with those which the migrants meet in the United States would be suitable.

Paracho, Michoacán, Mexico, is a town of some 3,000 persons of Tarascan and Mestizo descent. It is in the heart of the Tarascan Sierra region at an elevation of about 8,000 feet and was relatively isolated until recently. Although inbreeding is apparently not close, most of the people measured were traceably related to each other by common descent or marriage. About one-third of the adult population were measured. Virtually all of the parents of these 480 persons were reported to have been born either in the town itself or in the immediate region.

No one seems to have migrated from this town to the United States before about 1904. The man who first did so soon returned home and again went to the United States with several other youths from the town. Since that time a large proportion of the townsmen have been in the United States either as semi-permanent migrants or as contract laborers. Most of them have gone as industrial, railroad or agricultural workers to the Middle Western, Central and Western States.

Very few women from the town have been in the United States. Virtually all of them have been measured. The stature of these 22 women is significantly greater than that of the female sedentes. Over one-half of the female migrants had first gone to the United States before the age of seventeen. The average age at the time they first went was 16.7 years. The female migrants also tend to be larger than the sedentes in respect to all the other measurements taken, except for some dimensions of the head and face.

For the purpose of this analysis the male migrants have been subdivided into several groups (see Table 1). Those who had first gone to the United States before the age of seventeen and who had stayed two years or more might be expected to show the effects of any factor in the environment which operates during the growth period. Those who first migrated between the ages of seventeen and twenty-seven and who stayed for two years or more might also reflect any such factor, but its influence in their case could not be expected to be as great. Those who migrated after the age of twenty-seven, when epiphyses are closed and linear growth is complete, could hardly be expected to show any direct response to such environmental factors. Likewise, those who had spent less than two years in the United States could not show the same degree of response to the environment as those who had been longer in this country.

On the other hand, if American employers or officials showed a preference for big men, for instance, this would be a factor primarily affecting the selection of adult men and not that of the wives or minor children who might accompany them to the United States. Of course, such a factor might also favor the migration

TABLE 1

STATURE OF ADULTS IN PARACHO, MICHOACÁN, MEXICO, IN RELA-
TION TO AGE AT FIRST MIGRATION TO THE UNITED STATES AND
TOTAL DURATION OF RESIDENCE IN THE UNITED STATES

AGE AT FIRST MIGRATION	DURATION OF STAY IN THE UNITED STATES (YEARS)	NUMBER	MEAN STATURE (MM.)	STANDARD ERROR OF THE MEAN
		Male		
Never (Sedentes).....	0	109	1,618.0	± 5.6
Less than 17........	2 or more (mean = 16.0)	29	1,642.7	±11.2
17–27·.............	2 or more (mean = 8.3)	65	1,635.6	± 6.4
27 or more..........	2 or more (mean = 6.9)	13	1,610.2	±15.8
27 or more..........	1	43	1,615.1	± 8.8
15–27.............	1	30	1,633.1	± 8.9
		Female		
Never (Sedentes)....	0	155	1,512.3	± 3.8
Various*...........	2 or more (mean = 7.7)	22	1,532.9	± 8.7

* Less than 17, 11; 17 to 27, 6; 27 or more, 3; born in the United States, 2.

of early-maturing boys, for small, young-appearing youths are known sometimes to have been turned back at the border. In general, individuals who display late growth tend to converge towards, or even to exceed in eventual stature, those whose principal growth occurs at an earlier age. Selection of those with more precocious growth would therefore have little effect when, as here, the stature of adults is considered. Now, the most interesting of the statistical findings is that the males who went to the United States youngest and stayed longest—those who were less than seventeen when they went for the first time and who have stayed for two years or more—are the tallest of the migrants and significantly taller than the sedentes. They are larger than the stay-at-homes also in respect to all the other 25 measurements. Those who have migrated to the United States for the first time between seventeen and twenty-seven years of age and who have stayed two years or more also are significantly taller than the sedentes. These individuals, that is those who have migrated at an age near the end of the growth period, are intermediate in respect to virtually all dimensions between the sedentes and those who left home at a younger age. Those individuals who have first migrated at the age of twenty-seven or over closely resemble the sedentes in stature and other measurements.

These facts accord well with the hypothesis that there is an environmental stimulus to growth which affects those who go abroad for considerable periods of time during their growth period, and not those who first emigrate at an older age.

On the other hand, if selective factors were responsible for the differences found, one would expect to see their influence manifest in those who were physically mature at the time they left home. But those who were over twenty-seven years old when they left show no such tendency. And among those who went between the ages of seventeen and twenty-seven the increase of stature and other measurements is less than in those who migrated at still earlier ages. In short, those who first migrated before the age of seventeen are the tallest group, although they would not be expected to show as much evidence of selection as those who first migrated at a later age.

Were this the total evidence, it would appear that selection plays no appreciable role, but that the environment during the growth period may affect virtually every dimension. It should be noted, however, that each of the migrant groups so far considered averages more than ten years older than the sedentes. This concentration of the sedentes in the younger age levels probably means that many of them are actually pre-migrants rather than non-migrants. To that extent the full effects of any selective factors affecting other communities might be absent in this case. On the other hand, stature seems to decrease slightly with increasing age in these series, so that any correction for the differences in age would further slightly augment the stature of the migrants when compared with the sedentes.

There is one further piece of evidence which may bear on the question of selection. Another group of those measured consists of men who migrated to the United States when relatively young (fifteen to twenty-seven years of age), but who stayed for only one year. They, too, exceed the sedentes in stature. Because of the small size of this series, the difference is not statistically significant, but the trend is suggestive, especially because the tendency to exceed the sedentes in size extends to practically every measured dimension. The mean age of this group of migrants who went abroad at relatively early ages for short periods is the same as that of sedentes. These individuals, who migrated for periods possibly too brief to have their growth much affected directly by the northern environment, are on the average very similar to other individuals who emigrated when young but stayed longer in the United States.

While, therefore, it is possible that the differences found between returned migrants and sedentes are in small part caused by some undiscovered selective influence, it can be said that residence in the United States did stimulate physical growth. This finding supports the results of previous studies. The question still to be answered is, just what environmental factors are specifically responsible for the enhanced growth.

CÁLCULO DE LA TALLA DE MEXICANOS DEL VALLE DE MÉXICO A BASE DE LA LONGITUD DEL FÉMUR

Juan Comas

Se trata de una investigación a base de 102 fémures depositados en el Depto. de Antropología del Museo Nacional de México, correspondientes al Valle de México. He aquí su distribución:

> ♂ prehispánicos, 32 (17 der. y 15 izq.)
> ♀ prehispánicos, 27 (11 der. y 16 izq.)
> ♂ modernos, 29 (13 der. y 16 izq.)
> ♀ modernos, 14 (9 der. y 5 izq.)

Lo reducido de las series no ha permitido obtener más que la media.

Independientemente del deseo de conocer la estatura de los indígenas que habitaron el Valle de México antes y después de la Conquista, sentimos curiosidad por comparar los valores obtenidos utilizando distintos métodos:

1. Ante todo se recurrió a la técnica y tablas de Manouvrier (298, p. 1069; 196a, pp. 174-75).[1]

2. Luego se hizo el cálculo aplicando las fórmulas de Pearson (298, p. 1070) a base de la longitud *total* del fémur (♂ = 81.306 + 1.880 × long. total del fémur; ♀ = 72.844 + 1.945 × long. total del fémur). Es lo que en lo sucesivo denominamos Pearson I.

3. En los casos en que no se haya tomado directamente la longitud máxima del fémur, Pearson propone obtenerla sumando a la longitud fisiológica 3.2 mm. para ♂ y 3.3 mm. para ♀ (298, p. 1071). Hemos calculado pues también la talla en esta forma, y la denominamos Pearson II.

4. En fin, en el clásico trabajo de Manouvrier (293, p. 351) dicho autor expuso claras, y a nuestro juicio convincentes y acertadas, razones para utilizar en el cálculo de la estatura la longitud fisiológica del fémur en vez de la longitud máxima propuesta por Topinard. En efecto, "une même longueur maximum de fémur peut entrer dans la stature suivant des proportions différentes," ya que la oblicuidad del fémur varía considerablemente en función de la anchura de la pelvis, de los ángulos cóndilo-diafisario y cuello-diafisario, etc.

Por estas razones nos pareció interesante aplicar también las fórmulas de Pearson a base de la longitud fisiológica del fémur y ver los resultados compara-

---

1. Incidentalmente, debe subsanarse el error tipográfico que a ese respecto aparece en Hrdlicka (196a), última línea de la p. 174: dice "2 mm. from . . ." y *debe decir* "20 mm. from. . . ."

247

tivos. Dicha modificación de método es lo que designamos en este ensayo como Pearson III.

El resumen de los resultados obtenidos de acuerdo con estas 4 técnicas son:

VALOR MEDIO DE LA ESTATURA EN EL VALLE DE MÉXICO
A BASE DEL FÉMUR (EN MM.)

	Pearson I	Pearson II	Pearson III	Manouvrier
Prehispánicos:				
♂ der........	1602.37	1600.75	1593.94	1584.82
♂ izq........	1619.23	1618.84	1612.38	1604.38
	1609.93	1608.86	1602.21	1593.58
♀ der........	1476.90	1475.90	1469.00	1449.18
♀ izq........	1483.38	1482.18	1475.44	1460.00
	1480.74	1479.63	1472.88	1455.59
Modernos:				
♂ der........	1616.50	1616.83	1609.75	1604.17
♂ izq........	1615.94	1616.43	1610.06	1601.81
	1616.18	1616.60	1609.92	1602.82
♀ der........	1495.38	1494.37	1486.50	1477.00
♀ izq........	1524.00	1525.25	1518.25	1512.25
	1504.92	1504.66	1497.08	1498.75

Y he aquí ahora algunas de las deducciones que pueden hacerse:

A. Menor estatura en las series prehispánicas que en las modernas, en los dos sexos: ♂ = 1593.58 y 1602.82 respectivamente. ♀ = 1455.59 y 1488.75 respectivamente. Estos valores corresponden al cálculo con las tablas de Manouvrier; pero el fenómeno se observa igualmente en las medias obtenidas con las técnicas de Pearson.

B. Como norma general de cada grupo, los cálculos a base del fémur izquierdo proporcionan valores de talla *más elevados* que los obtenidos con los fémures derechos, cualquiera que sea la fórmula o técnica utilizada. Como única excepción están los Modernos ♂ izquierdos que en un caso se comportan como la generalidad (Pearson III), en otro su valor se equipara al de los fémures derechos (Pearson II), y en los dos casos restantes se ofrecen valores invertidos (Pearson I y Manouvrier).

C. La media de la talla, dentro de cada grupo, y con las 4 técnicas utilizadas presenta una gradación uniforme: los más altos valores corresponden a Pearson I; siguen los obtenidos con Pearson II; en tercer lugar aparecen los calculados con Pearson III; y en último lugar, o sea los valores mínimos, son los deducidos con las tablas de Manouvrier.

D. Si comparamos la talla de las series ♂ y ♀ modernas con la obtenida en el vivo en grupos similares, como son los Aztecas medidos por Starr, Hrdlicka y especialmente por Siliceo Pauer (ya que este último realizó su investigación precisamente en el Valle de México) observamos que los valores medios 161.9 para ♂ y 147.7 para ♀ (83, p. 38) no señalan variación sensible digna de tenerse en cuenta. Se confirma de este modo el incremento de la estatura observado a partir de las series prehispánicas.

E. En consecuencia no parecen ser de aplicación a los indígenas prehispánicos ni modernos del Valle de México las observaciones de Stewart respecto a la disminución de la talla de los indios en los últimos siglos, basado en los datos de su investigación entre los Eskimales de El Labrador y Cakchiqueles de Guatemala (467, pp. 61–65, 84–87; 468, pp. 28, 30 y 32). Por el contrario nuestros datos concuerdan mejor con las observaciones de tipo mas general, hechas por múltiples autores en copiosísima bibliografía, y que parecen indicar la tendencia a un incremento mundial paulatino de la talla humana.[2]

F. Evidentemente las tablas de Manouvrier y las fórmulas de Pearson, confeccionadas para grupos blancos, no son en muchos casos aplicables para calcular la talla en series humanas cuyas proporciones corporales difieren de las europeas. En efecto el poseer extremidades inferiores relativamente más cortas que el busto, traducido en un elevado índice skélico, o braquiskelia, trae como consecuencia que la talla calculada a base de la longitud del fémur dará valores inferiores a la estatura *real* del individuo. En ese sentido son justas las observaciones de Stevenson y las del propio Stewart haciendo resaltar que los valores medios de estatura obtenidos con las fórmulas de Pearson para Chinos y Eskimales de El Labrador (braquiskélicos) deben ser incrementados con 3 cms. para que correspondan a la realidad.

G. Sin embargo, estos hechos están en contradicción con lo investigado en los Aino, a los cuales pudo aplicar Pearson sus fórmulas con todo éxito (467, p. 61), aunque los Aino son también braquiskélicos (298, p. 339).

H. Stewart generaliza las afirmaciones anteriores respecto a chinos y eskimales diciendo "que la fórmula de Pearson se ha demostrado que falla por unos 3 cms. en la reconstrucción de la estatura de los pueblos *mongoloides*" (468, p. 28). Si interpretamos bien las ideas de nuestro distinguido colega, esta explicación le sirve para justificar los valores obtenidos en la reconstrucción de la talla en los Cakchiqueles de Guatemala; y en tal caso debemos preguntarnos: ¿qué entiende Stewart por mongoloides?, ¿incluye en ese grupo a todos los aborígenes americanos? Porque el hecho evidente es que existen numerosos grupos amerindios que son *meso* y aun claramente *macroskelos:* para comprobarlo basta con echar una ojeada a las recopilaciones estadísticas de Martin (298, p. 339), Comas (83, pp. 62, 63 y 79) e Imbelloni (209, p. 235).

---

2. Sobre este interesante tema véase la excelente exposición y revisión hecha por Imbelloni (209, pp. 196–243).

I. Las mínimas diferencias de resultados entre Pearson I y Pearson II nos autorizan a dar como válida, por lo menos para las series mexicanas estudiadas, la técnica que permite obtener la máxima longitud femoral añadiendo a la longitud fisiológica o bicondílea 3.2 mm. para ♂ y 3.3 mm. para ♀.

J. En fin por lo que respecta al ensayo hecho de la Técnica Pearson III, queda patente que sus resultados divergen de los de Manouvrier mucho menos que Pearson I y Pearson II. Seguimos creyendo válidas las razones que se dieron en el apartado 4); pero desde luego sería prematuro deducir conclusiones ni siquiera provisionales. Damos a conocer la experiencia, confiando que algunos colegas hagan ensayos similares a fin de acumular los suficientes datos estadísticos para que en un futuro más o menos próximo pueda decidirse por la técnica más exacta en cuanto a cálculo de la talla con ayuda del fémur.

LIVING ARCHEOLOGY OF THE BRIBRI AND CABÉCAR INDIANS OF COSTA RICA

Doris Stone

The Bribri Indians today are found in two distinct zones of Costa Rica, in the southeastern portion of the Sixaola valley along three tributaries of the river: the eastern bank of the Coen, the Uren, and the Lari, and on the Pacific side of the Talamancan range, at Salitre of Buenos Aires. They were placed here in the eighteenth century by the Costa Rican government as punishment for the massacre of Franciscan priests and the burning of their missions.

The Cabécares are located in four sections of eastern Costa Rica. They are found along the western bank of the Coen river, the Chirripo river, and the upper Estrella valley, but there is also a colony on the Pacific side, at Ujarras of Buenos Aires, where they were transplanted at the same time and for the same reason as the Bribri.

Space does not permit a detailed picture of their culture, nor is it the purpose of this paper. We are interested in describing certain elements of their pattern which we feel might be of use to the archeologist as well as the ethnologist working in the region of southern Costa Rica and Panama.

To begin with, we have grouped these people together because culturally one has been dependent upon the other for many hundreds of years. Before the Spanish arrival, the Bribri conquered the Cabécar and the result was that the temporal head of both groups was Bribri while the spiritual head was Cabécar. Today, the temporal head has disappeared, but the medicine men, who serve as priests, are still trained by the Cabécar and the best doctor-priests are found among this group.

Both tribes are organized on the basis of matrilineal clans. The ancient burial custom was to make bundles of the dead and to leave these in thorny bushes to protect them from rapine birds or animals, for one year. The bundles were then collected and buried in a deep shaft grave, each clan having its own. The Costa Ricans have tried to prohibit this custom with the result that only in remote places, such as Chirripo, is this still carried out, and, of course, in deepest secrecy. The burial bundle, however, is commonly used today, whether or not secondary burial is practiced. Food and artifacts are wrapped with the body. Cacao paste in leaf packages or in small gourds, a form of totaposte often of pejivalle, tobacco if available, a piece of cotton and household utensils if the deceased is female, or bow and arrows if male, accompany the corpse and are wrapped in the white bijagua leaves (*Calathea insignis* Petersen) which take the place of a coffin.

251

Each clan, in addition to having had its own grave, had, and frequently still has, an emblem or nahual. The physical form of this is a pre-Colombian gold *huaca* or figure. The emblem of the clan is secret and is preserved by a medicine man or elder. Its history or significance has its roots in the very theology of these peoples. In addition to this, many of these gold figures have a legend connected with them. Some of the explanations which demonstrate this theological significance and are still accepted by the Bribri and the Cabécares are in all probability a continuation of the pre-Colombian beliefs. Here are a few examples.

The eagle.—Many gold so-called "eagles" have been found in prehistoric graves. The Cabécares claim that these are not "eagles" but buzzards. When

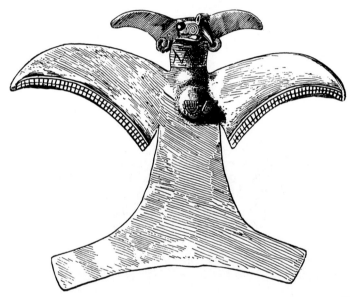

FIG. 1.—Gold "eagle" with a collar. After MacCurdy (290, fig. 353, p. 206)

Sibu, as they term God, visited the earth, he frequently took the form of a buzzard and often wore a collar. (Many of these gold figures have a collar, Fig. 1). In particular, this was the manner in which Sibu appeared when he taught people how to dance.

The crab.—Gold crabs (Fig. 2) are often found in Costa Rica and Panama. The crab is one of the symbols used by the Usegrə clan of the Cabécares which is second in rank only to the Rey clan. The significance of the crab in the ideology of the Usegrə clan is evidenced by the belief this group have that the crab is responsible for bringing water to them. They say that the crab went to a dry place and entered the earth. When he came out of the hole, water followed him. Therefore, the Usegrə have the crab as one of their protectors.

The beetle.—Gold beetles are found in the south of Costa Rica (Fig. 3). The Cabécares and Bribri believe that the beetle is important as he was sent by Sibu to teach man how to dig holes so that he could bury his dead.

The armadillo.—Gold armadillos are occasionally found (Fig. 4). This animal at one time supposedly did not have a shell. He was sent by Sibu as a guardian to protect the grains of corn from which man was later to be created. In spite of the fact that the armadillo has no teeth, Sibu caught him collecting in a large shell some of the grains to eat. Sibu was furious and clamped the shell on the animal's back, and threw him from the sky to the earth. The weight of the shell

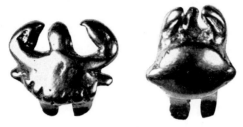

FIG. 2.—Gold crabs from the "Linea Vieja," Costa Rica. (Actual size)

FIG. 3.—Twin beetles in gold from the general valley, Costa Rica. (Actual size)

FIG. 4.—Gold armadillo from Palmar, Southeastern Costa Rica. (Actual size)

and the force of the blow made a large hole. The armadillo went on digging deeper from fear, but Sibu made him come to the surface so that he could serve man as food.

The monkey, the crocodile, the whale and many other animals have legends connected with them and are used, or have been used, as clan emblems.

PASCUAL DE ANDAGOYA ON THE CUEVA OF PANAMA

Hermann Trimborn

The first Spanish settlement on the mainland was founded at the Gulf of Urabá in 1509. Vasco Núñez de Balboa became the leading figure there. In 1514 Pedrarias Dávila was appointed governor of Castilla del Oro. He first resided in Darién, and in the year 1519 he founded the city of Panama. With Dávila came a number of scholars to the "Indies." They were good observers and writers and left to posterity an account of their times. Among these scholars the most outstanding were Gonzalo Fernández de Oviedo and Pascual de Andagoya. Andagoya recorded his impressions and experiences, and together with several brief articles, later combined them into his widely known historical account, *Relación de los sucesos de Pedrarias Dávila en las provincias de Tierra firme o Castilla del oro, y de lo ocurrido en el descubrimiento de la mar del Sur y costas del Perú y Nicaragua*, first published by Martín Fernández de Navarrete (119a, pp. 393–456).

Historians of the conquest praise Andagoya as having been a good friend of the Indians. This fact might have played a role in his appointment as *visitador general de los Indios*. Andagoya, however, not only gave the Indians sympathy but also scientific attention. Like the young Cieza who wrote his impressions at the campfires of the Spanish mercenaries, Andagoya did actual field work. This seems especially noteworthy since Andagoya was at this time very young. This interest in scientific observation of the land and the people has found expression in extensive chapters of his account. These descriptions are, together with Oviedo's and later Lionel Wafer's the most valuable sources for our knowledge of the culture of the Indians of the Isthmus.

Leaving aside the contributions of other authors and concentrating on Andagoya's statements is the best way, we think, to do justice to his authentic and early description of the Cueva.

Andagoya showed less interest in landscape then in people. Nevertheless, the different localities were described by him clearly, if briefly. He pictured Darién, the first Spanish settlement on the mainland, as partly mountainous, partly plain, and subject to inundation. He credited the parts of the Isthmus that extend toward the Southern Sea with a healthier climate. The coast of Nombre de Dios, where Nicuesa had tried to found settlements, was reported as ill suited for human occupation; even in pre-Columbian times, Andagoya relates, the area was sparsely populated. In contrast Andagoya praised the rest of the Isthmus, with its valleys, fields and evergreen trees; deer and naval hog (peccaries), wild birds, and fish which furnished food for the colonists and settlers. The woods were inhabited by puma and jaguar, three to four other feline varieties, and a

254

small kind of marsupial, described as being smaller than a fox and as stealing chickens from farmhouses, as well as carrying its young in a pouch.

Andagoya gave brief sketches of some countrysides. On the Río de la Balsa, the fertile lowlands of the mountainous flank were suited for bread cereal farming. The mountainous center of the Isthmus was reported to have a healthier climate than the Darién coast; this was true for Careta, as well as Acla and Comogre. For a traveler coming from the east the open savannah begins in Comogre. West of Panama there was Tobreytotra, a cool mountain covered richly with oakwoods. Chiru and Nata were stretches of lowland which were farmed extensively. Another fertile region lay between Burica and Huista in the western part of the present day Panama.

On the Isthmus the difference between night and day during the entire year is only half an hour. The dry season, from the beginning of December until the beginning of May, is called summer. Northern and northeastern winds bring cool air. During these months illness is almost absent. The winter lasts from the beginning of May until the end of November. South-southwestern winds bring the heat and thunderstorms during August and September. During this time people are subject to illness.

The coast of Panama up to the Gulf of San Miguel has a mounting tide said to flow in places one-quarter to one-half Spanish miles into the mainland. All rivers into which the tide flows carry "that kind of snake which we call lizards," i.e., the Kaiman—a formidable fighter in water, but rather helpless on land.

The density of population varied with the character of the land. The Darién coast and the shores of Nombre de Dios were only sparsely peopled, but the higher regions of the Isthmus were more densely populated—this was true of the mountains between Darién and the Mar del Sur and of the valleys of the Río de la Balsa.

Comogre or Pequeo were once as heavily populated as the regions from Pocorosa towards Chame. In Nata, also, there were many settlements.

The origin of these peoples is difficult to trace. Their own tradition offers little evidence as to when they came, so that Andagoya thought that they were indigenous, except for a few later migrations.

The main part of the population of the Isthmus can be divided into two related groups. The first group Andagoya calls, adequately, Cueva. The region of the Cuevas included the Province Pocorosa near the Northern Sea and Comogre. From there the Cueva area stretches over Peruqueta to the Gulf of San Miguel, including the Pearl Island and the region the settlers called "Behetrías," meaning land without lords. This is probably the area between the Coast of San Miguel and the Río de la Balsa. One people speaking one language lived in this large territory—from the Northern Sea to the Southern Sea across the Isthmus. Another idiom, called by Andagoya Coiba, was spoken in the territory west of Peruqueta, starting probably with Paruraca and reaching as far as Chame, a distance of 40 Spanish miles; Coiba differed only dialectly from Cueva, and

Andagoya expressly stated that they were the same language, only Coiba being a refined court version. In the regions west of Chame reaching to Burica, the frontier of Costa Rica, each ruler spoke his own language. So Chiru, Escoria and Paris are linguistically differentiated, although their culture was fairly uniform.

Andagoya was fairly exact about the distances between the realms of single tribes and rulers. His information is exceedingly valuable for conclusions about

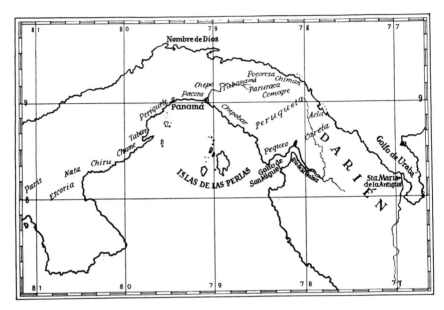

the more ancient topography of the ethnic groups on the Isthmus. These data of the distances can be arranged as in the accompanying tabulation (consult map):

	Miles		Miles
Darién—Careta	More than 30	Panamá—Nata	30
Careta—Acla	5	Panamá—Periquete	4
Peruqueta—(Ade) Chame	40	Periquete—Tabore	4
Comogre—Chiman	2	Tabore—Chame	4
Pocorosa—Paruraca	2	Chame—Chiru	7, also 8
Paruraca—Tubanamá	4	Chiru—Nata	4
Tubanamá—Chepo	8	Chiru—Escoria	8
Chepo—Chepobar	6	Nata—Escoria	6*
Chepobar—Pacora	2	Nata—Paris	12
Pacora—Panamá	4		

*This distance seems to be too long by comparison with previous figures.

These data justify a correction of Markham's plan, as has been attempted in the attached map (294a).

In the regions we deal with there are found occasional hints of more recent migrations, i.e., traces of foreign immigration. Besides, beginnings of a native historical tradition can be observed. The Chuchure are cited by Andagoya as being one such foreign element speaking their own language. They came on boats from Honduras crossing the sea and landing at the coast of Nombre de Dios.

Andagoya also talked about the ruling class in Escoria. They were supposedly pleasing to look at—superior in body and performance, so much so that all other inhabitants seemed dwarflike by comparison.

Andagoya also appreciated the relatively high cultural standards of the Cueva Indians. Compared with the unusually primitive inhabitants of the coast of Santa Marta, these Indians were on a much higher social level ("de más policía"). Outstanding in this group were the Coiba both as to their refined language and to their dignity.

Dress and almost all other factors of culture were uniform. The women were dressed in draped cotton blankets reaching to the feet, but leaving arms and breasts uncovered. The greater part of the male population went nude. The Spanish noticed, however, that the men wore a strange penis cover made of well-shaped, colored seashells and attached with loin straps. This cover held only the penis and seemed to provide for its wearer great freedom of movement. In the Coiba region even the covers were absent and the male population went entirely naked. Coiba women's garments had colored designs on them. In the western part of what we today call Panama, men were nude and women wore loincloths.

Village settlement prevailed. In contrast to the Mexico and Maya regions the complete absence of town foundation is striking. Family groups lived spread out in the villages, each in their own cabin on their own farm land. The cabins were fenced in and closed at night to ward off pumas and jaguars. Intricately worked cotton hammocks were used as bedding.

A survival of what may be called the hunting economy met the need for meat. An abundance of good fish made fishing near the coast and in the rivers profitable. The indigenous fauna—deer, peccaries, tapir, leguan, two varieties of turkey, turtledove, and pheasant—made extensive hunting possible. The peccary, described by Andagoya as a tailless hog which does not grunt and having a kind of navel on its back, was hunted by grassfiring and killed by flint bladed missiles hurled from slings. In the western part of Panama up to Burica they were hunted with thick thistle rope nets into which they were driven before being lanced. The boars also provided sport for the noblemen at large summer hunts. Male hunting and fishing was supplemented with food gathering by the women. We are unsure, however, if the fruit trees from which fruit was gathered were wild or planted trees. At any rate their output was less important than agricultural production. The rest of the information is lacking in detail. We know, however, that not only the people of Nata were, according to Andagoya, industrious cultivators, but that large corn plantations existed everywhere.

This cereal not only furnished the principal food but also intoxicating beer for a festive beverage. Of other utility plants the following were mentioned: cotton plant, sweet potatoes, melon, berries (*coccoloba uvifera*), and manioc.

As in Darién, gold was mined on the Isthmus in pre-Columbian times. The precious metal was also used by the craftsmen for making jewelry. The warrior nobility of Escoria wore chains fashioned of single gold links. When gold was not found locally the noblemen procured it by exchange from neighboring tribes. The Indians were not unfamiliar with other trading. The people of Acla and Careta furnished the rare shells, used for penis pouches, to the people of the interior.

River communication was by boat. The Chuchures of the coast of Nombre de Dios reputedly came by boat to the shore where they lived.

The Indians of the Isthmus had marriage customs and incest and exogamy rules. They chose their own mates. Unions with one's own sisters and daughters were forbidden. Among the nobles polygamy often prevailed, but with a chief wife who had to be of noble family. The ranking son of the first ranking wife could inherit wives of his father, excepting his own mother. The first ranking wife was called "espobe." For the lesser wives there was no wedding ceremony. The chief wife and the lesser wives were co-resident, with the latter being subordinated to the main wife. Contrary to the ideal that harmony and lack of jealousy should prevail among wives, intrigues often developed. Andagoya reported a case from Pocorosa where one of the wives of a chief killed the main wife.

Among commoners property went to the sons; for the princes, the sons of the chief wife inherited. Sons of the lesser wives did not inherit, but were provided for by the sons of the ranking wife as children of the household.

From the preceding it has already become clear that there existed different social levels. The so-called "Pirarailos" were a class of nobility by birth, distinct from the free-born commoners. The Pirarailos were noted for heroism in warfare. There also was a nobility based on merit; a man who slew an enemy or was wounded in battle was promoted to the rank of "cabra." He received an estate as a fief, together with people to serve on it. From this we may conclude that serfdom existed; presumably serfs were taken from prisoners of war. In Escoria, the nobility was of an alien people. This gentry was proud of its military superiority, and its members wore chains and ornaments on their chests and arms.

The highest social rank, however, was held by the lords or chieftains, the so-called "Tiba" (the word is reminiscent of "cipa" in the related language of Muisca). In Careta and Acla, two adjoining regions, two brothers reigned; their mutual claims for sovereignty over the entire region resulted in wars between them. Such small lords were found in the whole region from Comogre to the west; their realms were often only one or two (Spanish) miles in extent. Thus a system of small principalities was characteristic of the Cueva country; it forms a striking contrast to the large states of Mexico and Peru.

These particular principalities were mentioned: in Pocorosa there ruled a cazique; in a region called Behetrías and located presumably on the Río de la Balsa, there was no common overlord, only chieftains of small local units, maintaining friendly relations among themselves; in Tobreytrota, west of Panama, three or four lords ruled; independent princelets reigned in the region extending from Tobreytrota to the border of modern Costa Rica; Nata and Escoria had caziques; and the lord of Paris, called "Quitatara" or Cutatura had brought under his rule the caziques of Quema, Chicacotra, Sangana and Guarare and certain Ubsagano.

The princes were both feared and loved by their people. Each prince had three to four residences within his realm, according to his political power. Because of the smallness of the political units, these residences lay more or less in sight of each other. The princes relied on the labor of their subjects from such services as house-building, fishing, work in the fields, and gold mining, where such mines existed. The princes were apparently the leading merchants of their lands, indulging in the gold traffic.

The Spanish conquerors always claimed that the pagan "savagery" of the Indians justified suppression.

This claim is certainly not based on the Cueva, for Andagoya stated that they lived under the rule of some kind of law, although it was common or "natural" law rather than a written code. Primitive forms of statute law existed—the chieftains pronounced certain rules. The lords conducted and decided lawsuits in person; therefore, there were no professional judges. A kind of constable who arrested malefactors and took part in the execution of sentences was known.

In a suit both parties appeared before the cazique to present their cases. Witnesses were not summoned, and a lie in court was punishable by death. The decision of the Tiba was final—there was no appeal. Manslaughter, adultery, and theft were death meriting offenses. Sodomy, a rarely occurring crime, was also punishable.

Public assessment seems to have been absent, even as taxes paid in kind. But a levy for labor in house-building, work in the fields, and fishing, was made by the Tiba. The Tiba also exacted service in war, but it is suprising that he maintained the warriors at his expense.

For obvious reasons we are better informed about the military activities of the Indians than about other aspects of their life. Although we are not here concerned with the details of the wars with the conquerors, it is noteworthy that the conquistadores did not disrupt a state of general peace among neighbors; on the contrary, warfare had been common among the native peoples.

On the issue of sovereignty between the lords of Careta and Acla a fierce battle had been fought prior to the advent of the Europeans. The ferocity of the battle was reflected in the name of the battlefield—Acla, which means human bones. As a consequence of this battle the populations of these areas were disorganized.

The inhabitants of Nata and Escoria were embittered enemies. The Kazik of Paris had conquered the neighboring regions of Quema, Chicacotra, Sangana, and Guarare, and he was on poor terms with his rival in Escoria. In an engagement the Escorias broke into Paris and for eight days fought a daily battle losing nearly the entire warrior nobility of Escoria. In this bloody engagement, when all arms were exhausted hand to hand combat ensued, and the Escorias, physically superior, using arms and teeth virtually "bit" their way out of the country and to victory. On the march to their own land the Escorias left many dead en route. Andagoya saw "silos" or depots where the dead had been collected; he also saw a street plastered with human skulls and a tower built of enemy skulls so high that a man on horseback could not be seen over it.

Two years before Andagoya's arrival there had been an attack on Paris from the direction of Nicaragua. These invaders were described as being so fierce that everyone in their line of march submitted to them and met all their demands. They were cannibals. Encamped in the nearby Tauraba they had young boys brought to them as food from the surrounding villages. They were, however, attacked by a disease with which was connected severe attacks of diarrhea, forcing them to retire toward the coast. Quitatara of Paris attacked them in their weakened condition, slaughtered them and even took rich booty.

This scanty information on indigenous historical warfare is supplemented by general observations of bloody feuds between small states about fishing and hunting grounds and boundaries. Especially known for continual strife was the region of Tobreytrota. The villages there were protected by trenches and palisades. The palisades were made of a special thistle plant entwined in such a manner so as to form firm walls.

Nata had a standing armed force for defense against attacking neighbors. This force fought with spears, clubs, the "tiradera," and the Macana, a wooden club wielded with two hands. Spies were used.

Still, on the whole, war had rather the aspect of being a tournament conducted according to certain rules. Thus, for instance, we read that Quitatara met the Spanish on a plain for the final settlement of their hostilities.

Perhaps to nullify the accusation of idolatry, Andagoya stated that the Indians had neither cults nor fetiches. Closer to the truth, however, is his observation that simple people do not discuss these things.

The "tequina," a kind of priest who conferred with the "devil" that is their God Tuira, was known to Andagoya. A cult house of a small, doorless cabin was the place where the priest conferred, cajoled or influenced Tuira. After a night session in the cult house the priest repeated Tuira's revelations to his superiors.

In addition to the official "tequina," male and female magicians received from Tuira recipes for ointments made of various herbs. By virtue of these ointments the magicians "practiced." Tuira appeared to the magicians as a beautiful child so that human beings would not be frightened of him. Tuira's hands and feet were said to be armed with three griffin claws, concealed from human sight. This apparition accompanied the magicians when they performed rites. Andagoya was firmly convinced that one of these witches had been seen in two different places at the same time.

Certain food taboos, noted by Andagoya, apparently had magic import. In Paris, for example, the warriors, unlike the rest of the populace, abstained from meat, eating only fish and leguan.

Besides Tuira, there was at least one other god—Chipiripa, god of the heavens and controller of rain and atmospheric events. Also, a beautiful woman, living with her child in the heavens, played an important part in Indian mythology. Andagoya found in this tale some analogy to Christian legend. He also drew attention to narrations of a flood in which an Indian "Noah" and his family escaped in a boat.

From his own experience, Andagoya gives a rather full picture of the burial customs of the nobility. When a chief died his wives of lesser rank who claimed to love him dearly were buried with him so as to serve him in the world beyond. But professions of affection notwithstanding, if the deceased nobleman had decreed that his wives should accompany him, their burial with him was compulsory.

The corpse was adorned with golden ceremonial arms and clothed in some of the deceased's best garments. The heir and the family of his father's house and the nobility of the land assembled. The corpse was put in a sitting position by binding the body with straps. Numerous braziers were put around the body to dry it. The fat or drippings from the corpse were collected in two leather containers. The completely dried body was then hung up. During this process twelve noblemen, clad in black garments from head to foot and concealing the face, watched. No one but the twelve was admitted. The twelve met watchmen, one of whom had a drum which he pounded at intervals. A chant and chorus response began, waxing so loud that two hours after midnight Andagoya and his fellows rose from their camp and armed themselves. Then there was a sudden silence—then drum beating which sounded like bell clanging, and then there was sudden laughter and drinking. The twelve watchmen were excluded from the merriment. Andagoya, attending the burial of Pocorosa, learned that the "prayer" for the dead was nothing but the recital of the deeds of the dead chief—a kind of ballad to glorify the hero.

After a year had passed a celebration, on the same day as death occurred, in memory of the dead was held. The deceased's favorite dishes were assembled near the dried out corpse; his arms and small, wooden imitations of his boats were also assembed. The assemblage was then carried to a place, cleared for the occasion, and burned to ashes so that the smoke could reach the chief in heaven.

These yearly commemorative feasts to a deceased lord were a standing practice and usually entailed a banquet.

PERSISTENT ELEMENTS IN SAN BLAS CUNA
SOCIAL ORGANIZATION

D. B. Stout

The Cuna of eastern Panama have been influenced by various Euro-American societies for nearly four hundred and fifty years and by Negro slaves and their descendants for a somewhat lesser period. As a consequence, the Cuna have undergone many social and cultural changes. It is not the purpose of this paper to chronicle all these changes in detail but rather to draw attention to certain persistent elements in social organization which have survived.[1] Although the present-day Cuna cannot be positively identified to the satisfaction of every ethnologist with the Cueva or Coiba in eastern Panama of the early years of the Conquest, we do have continuing references from the beginning of the 17th century and sufficient comparative cultural detail from the 16th century to assume safely that if they are not directly descended from the Cueva-Coiba, they are at least very closely related.

In social organization, the Cuna of the early period were marked by a stratified structure which embraced: (*a*) chiefs and nobles who were polygynous; (*b*) commoners who were mainly if not exclusively monogamous; and (*c*) captive women, who were secondary wives and servants, and a few captive males, who became slaves. With each of these strata there were associated cultural differences, the most marked of which were those pertaining to the chiefs and nobles. They, for instance, practiced intensive warfare in which special titles were won; they wore special clothing and ornamentation; chiefs were accorded elaborate funeral rites which included the burial of retainers and wives with them, and their status was expressed in a number of material forms of esthetic and technological complexity such as elaborate gold ornaments. These social and cultural elaborations rested on an economic and technological base, in the patterns of which the commoners were full participants. This base can be generally characterized as similar to the pattern found in the tropical forests of South America but with certain emphases and specializations, such as more intensive farming (at the expense of hunting and fishing). The above are given as mere illustrations, and are to be taken as such; a full characterization can readily be found elsewhere (464).

In common with other tribes of the Circum-Caribbean culture type, as designated by Kirchhoff and Steward, the Cuna underwent a process of deculturation or down-grading in cultural complexity as a consequence of the Conquest, with the end result that the Cuna now resemble the Tropical Forest tribes of South

1. Data on which this paper is based have been previously published in Stout (476).

America in general pattern of culture more than they once did, and indeed, the Cuna culture, as we know it from the 19th and 20th centuries, is mainly that of the commoners in Cuna society of the late 15th and 16th centuries. That this should be so is readily understandable if it is remembered that the distinguishing features, once participated in and maintained by the chiefs and nobles, were destroyed by the Conquest and the following colonial periods. This is, as Steward has pointed out (464, pp. 8–11), the only hypothesis that accounts for the apparent discrepancy between demonstrated cultural complexity for the pre-Columbian period, as revealed in the archeology of Panama, and the known relative simplicity of ethnological fact for Panama of the last two or three centuries. It is a far cry from the descriptions of Oviedo, Andagoya, or even Adrian de Santo Tomas, to the accounts given by various 19th century canal-route explorers or the descriptions provided by 20th century ethnographers.

Yet, through all the shifting detail of cultural change there appear at least three persistent principles of social organization which carried through from the original stratified society to the present simplified, "deculturated" situation. These persistent principles are: an emphasis on seniority among males as a determinant of succession of authority in the family and household; an emphasis on achieved statuses among the specialties practiced by and open to males; and a preference for village or local community endogamy.

The first principle, that of seniority, is borne out by the early references to inheritance from which it is quite clear that oldest sons inherited the position and title of chief and in the instances of polygyny, the son of the first wife was the heir. Now, despite many years of changing situation and a very probable shift from patrilocality of marriage, at least for the chiefs and nobles, to independent residence upon marriage, and finally to the matrilocality that obtains today, there is evident the same principle. For, at present, it is the oldest son-in-law in a matrilocal household who inherits the position of authority and leadership in that household. This position of authority, it should be noted, is independent of the inheritance of property rights, as they have developed in recent times (475). Its main expression is in the allocation of work among the men of a household and the planning of household activities. This may not seem of great moment, but it looms large in the estimations of a young Cuna man who must not only choose a wife but who must also weigh the characteristics of a potential father-in-law, under whose direction he must work co-operatively and whom he may in time succeed as household head. The seniority principle is also reflected in the hierarchy of women in a household, but in a much milder fashion, for it is assigned for them on the basis of marriage to the household head, by marriage to the male next in line of succession, and so on down to the most junior of unmarried girls in the household.

The second element, that of the relative emphasis on achieved statuses, is clearly evidenced in the early accounts. Nobles, who could rise from the status of commoners, won their status and title through conspicuous bravery in warfare, and though their sons inherited the title, they had to validate it by devoting their life to military exploits. In addition, special titles were accorded to commoners, as well as nobles and chiefs, who had distinguished themselves in one of the crafts or as medicine men. It is, in short, evident from the early sources that, along with the ascription of status on the basis of the social class into which one was born and which tempered the rules of succession of authority, there was a series of opportunities for the achievement and improvement of status through personal action. This principle of social organization is a marked feature of recent San Blas Cuna society. Now, nearly all statuses open to males (except the relative position of authority and succession within households) are determined almost exclusively on the basis of achievement. This is true for the statuses of two of the three grades of medicine man, ceremonial leaders and their assistants, chieftainship and lesser political posts, and a number of minor specialties. The one exception is the status of *nele*, the highest of the three grades of medicine men. Persons born to this status are determined by certain signs at the time of birth, but they must validate their position through long study and demonstrated ability. This emphasis on experience and ability is, in fact, a clue to the very persistence of Cuna culture itself through the centuries of varied contacts with other societies, for it has often been the men with experience in the world beyond the Cuna boundaries who have returned to the tribe and occupied positions of political authority and have been instrumental in the initiation of cultural changes which became effective by virtue of their wider experience.

To turn now to the third principle, that of a preference for village endogamy, we must invoke evidence of a different order, namely that of genetics. Aside from the knowledge that captives were taken in the 16th century (and presumably were involved in interbreeding), we have little data on the rules of endogamy or exogamy obtaining at the time of the Conquest. But from 1620 onwards we do have frequent reference to the occurrence of albinos among the Cunas; from 1681 we have an estimate, made by a man with medical training, of an incidence of 1 in every 200 or 300; from 1925 there is the estimate by a geneticist of an incidence of .69 per cent (or about 1 in every 150) and for 1940 a percentage of .47 (or about 1 in 200) (474). Now, as is well known, albinism is a recessive genetic factor; such a persistence of high incidence (the usual expectation among peoples of the world is much less, being about 1 in 10,000) can be accounted for only on the basis of a long continued inbreeding, which in cultural anthropological terms means village or local community endogamy. This degree of endogamy, it should be noted, could be sustained only in a society composed of communities of non-kin groups (that is, in this case matrilocal households) which have been noted as one criterion of the Circum-Caribbean culture type. And a society of non-kin groups comprising each village, in turn rests on an economy that encompasses techniques of agriculture that are intensive enough to support fairly large community populations.

No one of the above three elements of social organization is especially significant and certainly is not unique in itself; but their persistence as a combination makes them useful historical criteria. Lacking as we do the opportunity for making a direct cultural comparison between the remnant peoples of Panama and the inhabitants of the same area for the 16th century, our recourse has been to seize upon three significant elements and attempt to demonstrate, independently of the Circum-Caribbean hypothesis proposed by Steward, that his interpretation of culture history in this area is essentially correct. Each element has been shown, within the limitations of space at our disposal, to have survived from pre-Columbian to recent times, although during this period other aspects of the society and its culture have been changed so radically that the original affinities of Cuna cultural patterns are obscured. Unfortunately, Murdock's (377) important analysis of social structures appeared too recently for an application of his interpretations and hypotheses to this data. The account given above should be reexamined, and perhaps rephrased, in the light of his illuminating studies.

THE PHYSICAL WORLD, THE WORLD OF MAGIC, AND
THE MORAL WORLD OF GUIANA INDIANS

C. H. DE GOEJE

I. DREAMS

In any Indian tribe, the visions, the dreams of medicine-men, the myths, and the magical practices form a unified whole. Several myths are simply a popular tale of a neophyte's initiation dream while he is in a trance. Information about the hereafter comes from the same source.

Before the neophyte can withdraw from the world of sense and enter into the world of spirits and be judged by them, he must sanctify his body and soul. He abstains from sexual intercourse, observes food and drink taboos, drinks a potion of the holy tobacco-plant or some other plant and vomits. In North America purification is often by sweat-bath.

In a Musquakie myth (354) the purification is projected into the trance-dream in the divine twins episode. Thus, "The divine Twins Hot Hand and Cold Hand saw an antelope. All day they ran after it. It jumped over a ravine and was gone. The Brothers jumped; they fell into the ravine; they fell through the bottom of it into a cave. The cave had in it the Ancestors (ancestral animals). . . . Make them *ma-coupee* (full of magic, fetish) said the Animals. . . . The Animals smoked in turn, Grandfather Racoon last. He offered the pipe to Cold Hand. Cold Hand said, 'To him first, he is Elder Brother.' Hot Hand had it first. He passed it in his right hand across his left to Cold Hand. He fell down asleep. At the first whiff, Cold Hand trembled; at the second he was faint; at the third he was blind, and at the fourth he was breathless. He handed back the pipe as he was falling. He slept.[1]

"The Animals cut out the Brothers' hearts, livers, lungs, stomachs, bowels; they purified all with water and the smoke of medicine; they returned them to the bodies. The Brothers slept a moon (twenty-seven days). They had dreams. . . ."

The Arawak dreams of taking a far journey and seeing many good and bad things. In the dream a wide road opens that he has to follow. Then he sees a group of withered trees, which fall across the road one after the other, and this makes him afraid, but he says to himself, "I shall take courage and go on," and he loses all fear. Next he comes to a big swamp on which a wooden bridge is floating. He must pass that bridge, but it bobs and tosses on the water. In this swamp he sees many kinds of man-eating fishes and dangerous water-animals. When he has crossed the swamp, he sees, in the middle of the road, a swarm of

1. For Australian parallels see 488, p. 525.

big bees. Again he gathers courage and passes by. Going further, he reaches a place where many poisonous serpents and insects try to bite him. Next, he comes to a place where there is a huge tiger who wants to catch him. Again he is afraid, but he takes heart. The tiger approaches him, opens its mouth, but instead of biting licks his face. Continuing, he comes to a great many pigeons who fly to him crying, "Come let us peck out your eyes!", but he passes on. Then he sees a witch whose breasts hang down to her feet to make him laugh, but he remains serious.

Now he comes to a beautiful, flower-strewn road leading to the country of the tobacco-spirit. There he sees many lovely tobacco-plants with blooms and seeds. The tobacco-spirit teaches him how to cure illness (91).

In myths the divine twins have similar adventures. The Tupi tell how the supreme god tested the twins in this manner to find out if they were really his children (312, p. 37).

We would call such dreams nightmares, indications of something amiss with the body or soul. In the Maya myth some of the demons that put the twins to the test bear the names of diseases (240). According to Indian conceptions, illness is often the wrath of the spirit of an animal species, provoked through a personal insult by excessive consumption of his creatures.

II. THE MAGIC WORLD

Maliwiayu, a Kaliña, has given a detailed description of his initiation to A. Ph. Penard (360; see also 10, 92, 93).

After a long preparation with dances, Maliwiayu had to swallow two cupfuls of strong tobacco-mash. He became extremely dizzy, and suddenly found himself in spirit land. A marvellous light was pouring down on him from above. He saw a naked redskin standing before him. It was *Tukayana* (a king-vulture spirit), who kindly said to him, "Come with me, neophyte, you will be taken up to heaven up the stairs of *Tukayana*. It is not far."

The *Tukayana* in one step brought Maliwiayu to his winding-stairs. Already another *Tukayana* stood waiting there for him. Maliwiayu was given over to the protection of the new *Tukayana*, in whom he had full confidence. They cautiously mounted the stairs and safely reached the first floor of heaven.

Maliwiayu was taken successively through the settlements of the animal-spirits, the heavenly forest, and the heavenly savannah. He saw the spirits of tools and the settlement of the spirits of the various parts of the body. They then arrived on the heavenly beach, home of crab and shellfish spirits.

Maliwiayu's guide made him dive into the heavenly water, i.e., the sphere of flux and metamorphosis. The water-spirits, in villages where water flowed around their habitation but wetted nothing, were visited. The water-spirits had different names for things; they called a snake "rope," a wide mouthed fish "basket," etc. (91).[2] Soon Maliwiayu and his guide arrived at the heavenly river

2. For the Mexican parallel see Krickeberg (240, pp. 29, 327).

of the water-goddess. They invoked her, and she appeared in the shape of a lovely mermaid. They followed the water-goddess to her home in the deep. An irate cayman-spirit stood guard, but the goddess fondled him and he changed into a good man.

Here is the beginning of a conscience-examination, for the water-goddess asked if the novice ate any of her pet animals. He said no (probably meaning that he did not do so during his probation period). Then the goddess fell madly in love with him. She took the delighted youth all over her domain and taught him to deal with all the underwater spirits. He was to be allowed to use their magic power.

The supreme water-spirit which appears as a kind of mermaid, half human being and half snake, is the "Great Mother" who bears all Nature. She carries all the magic forces within her. Perhaps the Indian here has an inner perception of something that might be called "living principle," "psychical or astral matter," *orenda* (Iroquois), *wakanda* (Sioux) or *mana* (Melanesia).

Inspired by the water-goddess, they continue. One step into the waves brings Maliwiayu to the other side of the river and the crossing of life and death.

III. ON THE THRESHOLD OF DEATH, THE MORAL WORLD

One more step would sever the youth's body and soul. If his soul were good it would reach Grandfather's place where night never came, if bad it would go to *Ewalumu*'s (darkness-spirit) heavenly garret where day never broke. The right as well as the wrong way was known to *Tukayana*, and he was willing to give Maliwiayu the necessary information.

The deceased then faces the trials of the toad-grandfather, to whom he has to confess whether he ever killed toads (symbol of doing harm), and the village of faith where the dog-grandfather queries him on killing dogs (symbol of faithlessness, seduction, treachery, perfidy).

The penitent human being now arrives at the abode of Innocence where the Indian *Analawali* lives, the great benefactor appointed by Grandfather as keeper of the *Karakuri*, the eternal light. *Analawali* decorates the deceased with this light so Maliwiayu can dwell permanently in the Eveningless Paradise.

One more trial has to be undergone. The *Alawali*-river must be crossed on a bridge of resilient snake-hide. This sparkling river is constantly changing its color like an undulating boa. The worse the people are that step on the bridge, the darker the water grows. Crossing the river is barely possible for the aged, but children, especially babies, fly across.

On a cayman-bench at the bridge entrance sits the big-eared human spirit *Akatombo*, keeping watch for Grandfather. The deceased has to look at himself in *Akatombo*'s round mirror and *Akatombo* screens out the wicked, but beautifully dressed, people that try to cross the bridge. The bad people fall into the water where two gigantic fishes partially swallow them, dismember them and scatter the body parts to the four cardinal points.

The *Alawali* river with the spirit *Akatombo* shows a marked resemblance to an episode of the Guarayo's journey to the land of Grandfather (313, p. 105) where the deceased comes to the "deceptive tree" which tries to lure him to a place of no return.

From these accounts it is clear that these Indians in a trance have a lively sensation of what we call "conscience." The dream vision of *Akatombo* reminds us of the "double" and of the "guardian of the threshold."

Others who are sensitive may feel something like the trance mood. My Oayana friends were greatly afraid of the spirit of a man, who during his life had been a wicked medicine-man. They erected magic barriers as protection against him (91, pp. 98, 117).

The Kaliña call the dream-spirit (*aka*) after it leaves the body *akatombo* (*-to* active, *-mbo*, former). *Akatombo* are the spirits of dead evil-doers and are regarded as malevolent beings who are forever present, waiting to make trouble.

Among the Tupi (312, p. 121)[3] the human soul was called *An* (*a'nga*, spirit, soul, shadow). When separated from the body the soul is called *Angouere* (*-guera*, former) according to Yves d'Evreux, and *Marangioana*, according to Marcgrav. *Marangioana* also means "anything that announces imminent death," a vague concept even to the Brazilians themselves who are apt to faint from dread of this terror. Similarly, the Guarani (340) have *Anay* (*ang*, consciousness; *angai*, evil spirit) which throws a spider's web obstacle in the path of the soul.

IV. THE JUDGE OF THE DEAD IN MYTHOLOGY

The Kaliña guardian of the river of heaven is also called *Kalaipiu*, and according to myth, "a man reborn from the dead," who warns of the coming flood and world conflagration. He is also identical with *Epetembo*, the law-giver. Several mythical magicians correspond, more or less, with these figures: *Harliwanli* (Arawak), *Guyraypoty* (Guarani), *Maire Pochy*, *Yurupari*, *Kurapira*, and *Kapura* (Tupi), and *Kurupi* (Kaliña). *Yurupari* possesses a crystal in which he can see everything that happens anywhere. *Epetembo* has a leg cut off, probably an indication of his separation from the earth before being taken to heaven by the king-vulture spirit. These happenings have been immortalized in constellations (Orion and Taurus) (238, p. 279; 258).

A related figure is, perhaps, the one-legged Maya god *Huracan* (heart of heaven and heart of earth). Certainly, the Mexican god *Titlacaua* (we are his slaves), or *Tezcatlipoca* (*tezcatl*, mirror; *popoca*, smoking: obsidian mirror) another one-legged god, is related. In the night sky he appears as Ursa Major showing a one-legged man much more clearly than the Orion group. In addition the Mexicans made mirrors and the forest tribes of South America probably did not. Thus, it is likely that the myth diffused from Mexico or adjacent regions to South America.

3. The Nambikwara know something similar, cf. C. Lévy-Strauss (266).

Tezcatlipoca is the god of the north where *Mictlan,* country of the dead is located. *Tezcatlipoca* was a great magician, thought to be invisible, who addressed people in the form of a shadow. He also knows the inner thoughts of human beings and punishes wrongs. He plays an important role in the myth of *Quetzalcoatl* (*quetzal,* trogon-bird; *coatl,* snake).

In this myth, *Tezcatlipoca* descends from heaven in the form of a little old man. *Quetzalcoatl* expects him. Omens of the coming destruction of *Quetzalcoatl*'s city *Tollan* appear. *Quetzalcoatl* decides to go to the coast. On his way he rests and looks into a mirror saying, "I am old." Later *Tezcatlipoca* hands him a mirror saying, "Know thyself and look at thyself, my Prince; thou wilt appear in the mirror." *Quetzalcoatl* looking in the mirror is shocked by what he sees. He sets fire to himself and his heart arises again to become the Morning Star.

In other continents, too, a mirror is mentioned in this connection. In Tibet (119, p. 37; 90, p. 34) judgment is meted out by *Shinje-chho-gyal* the "religious king of the dead," who holds a mirror in which the naked soul is reflected while his servant *Shinje* weighs in the balance the good against the bad deeds. The weighing brings to mind the Egyptian judgment of the dead.[4]

The mirror also is part of Japanese sacra. Cobbold wrote (75, p. 2425): "Within the sanctuary of the Shinto temple above the altar, in a conspicuous position, a large mirror is generally placed; and in a box beneath are usually kept a sword and a stone." These three, the mirror, sword and stone, constitute the Japanese regalia, and they are connected with the early legends. In one of the tales about the sacred mirror, *Izangi* (the creator of Japan) exhorts his children to examine themselves in a disc of polished silver to see the impress of evil passions.

4. See Valso, *Encyclopaedia of Religion and Ethics* (Edinburgh, 1908–26), Index under "Mirror," "Doubles," "Hallucination"; in 64, under "Spiegel," "Doppelgänger"; in 152, under "Mirror," "Shadow," "Doubles," "Death." In novels, 289; 315; 174 tells of *Rikombyō* ("ghost sickness") in Japan. Even modern Europeans occasionally see their doubles.

SOME REMARKS ON THE DIVISIONS OF THE GUAYMÍ INDIANS

S. Henry Wassén in collaboration with Nils M. Holmer[1]

On a short visit to Chiriqui in 1947 for archeological purposes, I had the opportunity to meet some members of a *Guaymí* tribe which inhabited the mountains north of San Félix in the eastern part of the province.

These Indians, according to what I was told by Sr. Demetrio Sagel, a merchant at San Félix, in whose house I was lodged with much hospitality, were commonly known as *Guaymies;* those who lived closest to the village were found at a place called Honombí (in Spanish Hatomí), where I visited five Indian houses (Fig. 1). In most of these the men were away working on their plantations and only women and children were left at home. Yet I found a young man by the name of Eugenio (or, as he called himself, *Odji*); he spoke Spanish, but was not very talkative. On further acquaintance, however, he proved more communicative and furnished me with certain information about his tribesmen.

Sr. Sagel further made a distinction between *Guaymies* (i.e., those I visited) and what he called *Sabaneros*, Indians who lived to the east, in the direction of Tolé.

This roused my interest in the division of the *Guaymí* as found in anthropological works. As is well known, the ethnographical facts relating to extant native tribes of Panama, with the exception of the *Cuna*, are both scanty and confused. For the *Guaymí* group, Johnson's recent summary (218) makes a classification. The data presented in this survey are largely based on previous findings and theories, prominent among which are Pinart's. Pinart, as is well known, published several papers on Central American Indians, and according to Johnson (218, p. 52) "Pinart's identification of subtribes of the *Guaymí* is substantially correct." Among these subtribes we find one designated by the name *Bukueta* (Johnson spells it *Bukuete*) (367, 368). Especially in Pinart (367, p. 3) it is perfectly clear that *Bukueta* is an alternative term and equivalent to the tribe name *Murire;* both names are stated to be referred to by the Spanish as *Sabaneros*. Nevertheless, Lehmann in his word lists places certain forms in a column headed *Murire*, others in a column headed *Sabanero*, and this in spite of the fact that he states in the same work (255, p. 153) that the *Murire-Bukueta* are called *Sabaneros* by the Spanish. To Pinart (367), the tribe called *Mové-valiente-norteño* evidently represents at least a linguistic unit. Here Lehmann also places words from this tribe in two different columns.

1. I take this opportunity to express my sincere gratitude to my friend Nils M. Holmer, who has most readily placed his whole knowledge of Chibchan languages at my disposal for the benefit of this paper.—H.W.

During his expedition in 1927 to the Isthmus of Panama Nordenskiöld and his partners also visited a tribal remnant of about 200 persons living in the interior of the country near the Río Calovebora,[2] which flows into the Mosquito Gulf and forms the northern limit between the provinces Bocas del Toro and Veraguas. The Indians in question are named *Bogotá* by Nordenskiöld and according to the report by him of his observations among them (347, chap. xii) he definitely considers them as different from the *Guaymí*. A few quotations will illustrate this:

With the *Guaymí* they (i.e., the *Bogotá*) have neither warlike nor peaceful relations [347, p. 176].

The *Bogotá* Indians themselves assert that their land was given to them by God and that the *Guaymí* are usurpers [347, p. 176].

The *Bogotá* claim that they were in olden times called *Palenques* by the Spanish, a fact which indicates that they once had fortified villages. The palisades were made of palm wood. It is possible that the *Bogotá* belong to those Indian tribes which Columbus contacted when he first discovered these regions. Few as they are, living in mountains only approachable with great difficulty, near a coast with very unsatisfactory harbors, they have remained nearly unknown till our days. As far as I know, we are the first anthropologists to visit their inaccessible houses with the purpose of studying their manners and customs [347, p. 176].

Some of Nordenskiöld's ethnographical observations among these Indians may also be summarized here.

The houses were generally round with earthen floor on which the fireplace was located at one side. The Indians often had several dwellings far away from each other, sometimes as many as four different houses. Plantations belonged to each house and the families moved from one house to the other. As there was a set of household articles in each they did not need to carry much property with them during their movements. Nordenskiöld explains this way of living as a result of the Indian habit of cultivating different plants at different places, or as a possible survival from times of uneasiness. If one house was burned and the plantations destroyed, there was always another left as a reserve.

According to Nordenskiöld, the Indians cultivated maize, bananas, rice, manioc, pejibaye palm or peach palm (*Guilielma utilis* Oerst.), otó,[3] squash, cacao, chili, pineapple, gourds and beans.

Some peculiar ideas related to the cultivation of maize were noted. Unlike other Indians they did not burn the land for the cultivation of maize. "When they cultivate maize, they first cut the brushwood, then the maize is sown and

---

2. Anderson (9, p. 272), quoting an unsigned account of Veraguas, dated 1560, mentions the "valley of *Calobegola*." This form contains the elements *calo, gola*, both common in Guaymí and Cuna. Cf. Cuna *kalu*, "wall," "stronghold," etc. (517, p. 72).

3. Species of *Xanthosoma*. Nordenskiöld (347, p. 178) defines it as *Colocasia esculenta*. The latter—the dasheen or taro—is, according to Paul C. Standley (457, p. 105), "very similar in general appearance and in its uses to the species of *Xanthosoma*, but is easily distinguished by its peltate leaves."

the bigger trees cut down as soon as the maize starts to come up. The Indians are not even allowed to toast their maize. Not a single grain of the maize must be touched by fire, or else there will be a failure of crops. Because of this the *Bogotá* Indians do not even dare to sell their maize to the Negroes for fear that the latter toast it or let some grains fall into the fire, thus bringing the Indians bad luck" (347, p. 177). Twin corncobs were considered to give a good harvest

Fig. 1.—Guaymí woman with her infant in front of house. Photo by Henry Wassén (1947)

and were therefore kept in the houses. "The maize was brought to the people by the Maize mother or one of the maize mothers. She came from the other world chewing at a grain of maize and so eight vessels were filled with maize beer. She had, however, a purulent sore on the elbow and because of that the iguana lizard denied to drink of the beer. The Maize mother was angry and went away and the people had no maize. Now they climbed the ladder which stands between the earth and the heaven and in the latter place the Maize mother gave them flowers which turned into maize and from this maize comes the kind that people now have. Remnants of the ladder are to be seen on a mountain called *Huirigua* in the savannas to the south" (347, pp. 177–78).

The men do the clearing of the land, the women sow the grain (Fig. 2).

Nordenskiöld could not get any definite idea of the importance of hunting among these Indians. Bows and arrows were however used for hunting. Fishing was of little importance. Single-pointed lances, small dip nets, ordinary nets and poison were used.

Children and some of the women wore dresses of bark cloth, and even the men sometimes used long shirts of bark cloth while at work (Fig. 3).

FIG. 2.—Indian burnt clearance north of San Félix. Photo by Henry Wassén (1947)

Among the musical instruments observed by Nordenskiöld were duct-whistles of black wax with two holes (347, Fig. 125; 210, Fig. 231) and friction idiophones consisting of tortoise shells coated with wax (210, pp. 161–63).

The above gleanings from the culture of the Indians whom Nordenskiöld named *Bogotá* could be enlarged with a few others found in his Swedish book and in the Gothenburg Ethnographical Museum catalogue of the collection made during the expedition. The collection consists mainly of bags, baskets, musical instruments, bark clothes, arrows and bows, fire fans and native medicines. The photographs taken during the expedition are also kept in the Gothenburg Ethnographical Museum.

The term *Bogotá* introduced by Nordenskiöld to designate the Indians visited by him at Río Calovebora seems to have been accepted by the Panamanian geographer and ethnologist M. M. Alba C. in several of his works (3, p. 69; 4, p. 18). In the second edition of Alba's *Geografía* (3, p. 60) the form has for some reasons been changed into *bofotá* (it is definitely not a misprint). Conforming to Nordenskiöld's theory, he mentions this group as an independent tribe, along with the *Guaymí, Cuna*, etc. At an interview, however, he expressed

FIG. 3.—"Bogotá" man in shirt of bark cloth. Photo by Erland Nordenskiöld (1927)

his doubts as to the correctness of the name given by Nordenskiöld. On this occasion he also was kind enough to present me with a typed manuscript of a radio talk on the *Guaymí* entitled *El Grupo de los Guaymíes* in which he enumerates five subtribes (and languages); namely the *Chocotá*, the *Cara-Caña*, the *Murrirá*, the *Sabanero* and the *Moló*, and these are also localized. Of these one will recognize the above-mentioned *Murire* (which are located within approximately the same area), the *Sabanero* (cf. above), and possibly the *Moló;* the latter are stated to inhabit the Cricamola region in the province of Bocas del

Toro, where according to most authors the above-mentioned *Mové* tribe is to be found.[4]

In order to bring us closer to a solution of these problems, especially that of Nordenskiöld's *Bogotá*, I have submitted the matter to Professor Nils M. Holmer, of the University of Lund, Sweden, for a linguistic analysis. The linguistic material from these Indians is almost entirely from records by Pinart. In addition to these we possess a vocabulary with short phrases by Nordenskiöld from his expedition to the Río Calovebora (in the library of the Gothenburg Ethnographical Museum, No. 5861), a short word list by the author, and the vocabulary with phrases published by Pinzón.

A comparison of the extant linguistic materials discloses a definite relationship between the dialects which Lehmann (following Pinart) designates as *Murire-Bukueta* and *Sabanero*, on the one hand, and those designated as *Valiente, Mové, Norteño* and *Penonomeño*, on the other hand; there seems, however, to exist a slight difference between Pinart's *Penonomeño* and the other languages in the same group. As far as Nordenskiöld's recordings are concerned they fall very definitely in the former group; curiously, the words noted by the author agree closely with those in the latter group, especially those marked by Pinart as *Penonomeño*. As we have seen above, Pinart positively states that the *Sabanero* are a Spanish designation of the *Murire* or *Bukueta* (the latter constitutes one dialect), and, on the other hand, that the *Mové, Valiente* and *Norteño* likewise constitute one dialect; as for the *Penonomeño*, see above. Although the purport of these statements does not seem to have been realized by modern anthropologists, they are nevertheless confirmed by linguistic evidence. This, at the same time, gives us the solution to the problem of the *Bogotá*. Since practically all of Nordenskiöld's words coincide with Lehmann's *Murire* and *Sabanero*, we must assume that the debatable form *Bogotá* in reality represents the above-mentioned *Bukueta*.[5] Hence, Nordenskiöld is mistaken in thinking that these *Bogotá* are not *Guaymí*. It is significant that certain subgroups have by different authors been opposed to the general term *Guaymí;* cf., e.g., Pinart in *Colección de Lingüística y Etnografía Americanas*, Part IV (San Francisco, 1882), contrasts the *Norteño* as a subdialect to the *Guaymí*. Conversely, the author was informed that the Indians north of San Félix were *Guaymí*, in contrast to the *Sabanero*.[6]

For a classification of the *Guaymí* tribes and languages a comparison of the materials gathered by Nordenskiöld and the author with respective data deriving from Pinart, etc., is no doubt of great importance. If we disregard the three

4. Pinart uses the forms *Mové* and *Moye* and Pinzón (368*a*) uses the forms *Moló* and *Movere-Atate*, of which the latter is stated to be the Indian name.

5. There is a village in western Chiriqui named Boquete. Since Guaymí Indians are still living today not so far from this place, one might assume that the name has a Guaymí origin.

6. As stated by Johnson (218, p. 52), the Guaymí have both migrated and been transplanted to various parts at different times; see also Lehmann (255, p. 152).

dialects which Lehmann lists as *Chumulu*,[7] *Gualaca*[8] and *Changuena*,[9] and perhaps certain others,[10] which generally differ widely from the rest, we may obtain two main groups of *Guaymí:* (1) an Eastern Group (chiefly in the eastern parts of the provinces Bocas del Toro and Chiriqui and including the Indians visited by Nordenskiöld) and (2) a Western Group (chiefly in the central and western parts of the same provinces and including the Indians which the author met north of San Félix).

To prove these postulates, Holmer has made the following comparisons between: (a) part of Nordenskiöld's vocabulary and the *Guaymí Sabanero*, according to the work published by Pinart in *Colección de Lingüística y Etnografía Americanas* and (b) the author's list of words and Pinart's *Vocabulario Castellano-Guaymíe* (Paris, 1892).

Certain pronouns and the numerals are practically identical in *"Bogotá"* and *Murire*.

It thus appears that Eastern *Guaymí* corresponds to the terms *Murire, Bukueta,* and *Sabanero* and Western *Guaymí* to the terms *Valiente, Mové, Norteño,* and the closely related *Penonomeño.* The other languages of western Panama seem to be either dialectal variants of the above standard forms or languages which very much differ from the normal types of *Guaymí.*

Lastly, as a curious detail in this connection, the following brief notes relating to the Aztec settlers in Panama may be added.

In his book (347, p. 176), Nordenskiöld mentions a political union between the *Guaymí* and the *Bogotá.* He says: "During the reign of the second last *Guaymí* chief, who, strangly enough, called himself Montezuma, the *Guaymí* and the *Bogotá* lived in a kind of personal union, which, however, ceased with Montezuma's death." A similar reference was made by Sr. Sagel at San Félix, who informed me that the Indians in these parts were ruled by chiefs belonging to families which, for generations, have been considered to excel other Indians and enjoy better economic conditions (*llevando mejor vida*). These privileged leaders are called *reyes montezumas.* The *Sabanero,* on the other hand, had similar privileged chiefs, called *cires.*

As I have pointed out in my report of the 1947 expedition (516), this is an interesting piece of information, considering the fact that the so-called *Sigua* Indians existed as an Aztec colony in northwestern Panama from the sixteenth century until the beginning of the eighteenth century (278). Pinart has the following interesting note: "Dans les montagnes du Veraguas, au contraire, les

---

7. According to Johnson (218, p. 65), they are Dorasque.

8. According to Lehmann (255), transplanted Dorasque northeast of David, where the village and river of Gualaca are found. Dolega to the west of Gualaca was (218, p. 53) an ancient mission of the Dorasque.

9. Of these, Juan Franco, at the end of the eighteenth century, says that they were "mas bárbaros y valientes que los Guaymies" (366, p. 19).

10. The now extinct Muoi shows many points in common with Lehmann's Murire.

Muites obéissent à un autre grand chef, *Suvala*, fils du célèbre prétendant *Moctezuma*, qui cherche à isoler les Indiens dans les endroits les plus inaccessibles de la Cordillère et à supprimer tout contact avec les étrangères" (367, p. 9).

Did Pinart for this statement depend on observations of his own or did he draw from previous accounts? As early as 1851, Berthold Seeman, in his *The Aborigines of the Isthmus of Panama* (422a, pp. 173–82), mentions that one of

LIST *a*

English	"Bogotá" (Nordenskiöld)[11]	Guaymí Sabanero
ax.	mo	mo
bat.	skuké	scugue
beard.	mané	mane
black.	herere	gerere
calabash.	hogoda	jogota
canoe.	du	du
chicken.	koi	coi
clothes.	nyomé	ñome
deer.	séu	seu
dog.	to	to
ear.	olo (oro)	olo
eye.	huahua	guagava
father.	enú	enu
flea.	skihua	squiba
God.	Chuhué	Chubé
grandfather (cf. thunder).	enusiri	cha-ensulia ('my grandfather')
great.	kueri	queri
green.	lere	leré
head.	chugá	chuga
horse.	ha	ja
house.	u	ju
iguana.	squa	scua
leaf.	gríga	gliga
louse.	ku	cu
maize.	eu	euguba
month, moon.	day	dai
mouth.	ka	ca
net.	déhua	gdebá
nose.	sä (=se)	sé
pineapple.	buá	boa
puma (león).	huredavere	cudde dabere
plantain.	bla	bla
rain.	noy-	noi
red.	daväre (=davere)	dabere
sea.	bre	ble
sick(ness).	-uká	oga
silver.	iqui	gigui
soul.	onyakua	oyaya
sun.	chui	chui
thunder (cf. grandfather).	enúsiri	enusuniglaña
tooth.	dau	dau
water.	chi	chi
white.	kutre	jutré
wind.	ble	mlie
wood (tree).	gli (gri)	gli
yam.	hanya	jaña
yucca.	i	i

11. For typographical reasons Nordenskiöld's forms are somewhat simplified.

the chiefs of the "Savanerics," (of the northern portion of Veraguas), "has adopted the pompous title of King Lora Montezuma, and pretends to be a descendant of the Mexican Emperor." According to Seeman this chief used to send ambassadors to Santiago (Veraguas), to inform the authorities that he was the legitimate lord of the country. To this Seeman (422a, p. 177) added his remark that "although no credit can be attached to the belief that King Lora is a descendant of the great Montezuma, yet there is reason to suppose, and future investigations may tend to corroborate the supposition, that his subjects are a distant branch of the great family of Anahuac." That the "Savanerics" are more or less identical with the Eastern *Guaymí* appears from a comparison of Seeman's short word list (422a, pp. 179–81) with corresponding forms obtained by Nordenskiöld from the "*Bogotá*."

With regard to these statements, I have in the above report (516, p. 156) ventured the supposition that the aforesaid *reyes montezumas* of the present-day *Guaymí* in Chiriqui are somehow connected with the historically attested Aztec colonists in Panama. This supposition would be further corroborated by a short entry in the above-mentioned field notes from the *Bogotá* by Nordenskiöld (347). The entry reads as follows: "The *Guaymí* chief Montezuma ruled both over the Guaymí and the Bogotá. The son Tehua Montezuma has no power of this sort." If this person was identical with Pinart's Suvala (see above), *tehua*

LIST *b*

English	Guaymí (Wassén)[12]	Norteño	Penonomeño
arrow	bugu	bugó	
arrowhead (of wood)	griua		krio (= 'wood')
basket	kudia	kotua	
bow	tue	tugé	
bowstring	ke (ge)	ku, kö	
calabash	si(h)o		sio
chicken	kui	kui	
flute	tolero	tolero	
hook	tin(g)	töñ	
house	hu	ju, u	
maize	iol		yo
metate	ue	uguen, *'pila de barro'* (?)	
moon	tse (tsö)	so	
sun	yono		nono

must evidently be some title of the chief. Such a title is actually found among the Aztec rulers. According to Eduard Seler (423, p. 34), it was given to certain family chiefs, being written *teohua teuhctli* by Seler, which means 'Lord possessor of the gods' (Seler translates "Priesterfürst").

The value of Nordenskiöld's note acquires more weight from the fact that he evidently was acquainted neither with the passage in Seeman or in Pinart nor with Lothrop's sources.

12. Without diacritical marks.

NOTES ON VENEZUELAN ARCHEOLOGY[1]

J. M. CRUXENT

I. A PRELIMINARY ACCOUNT OF THE CAUSEWAYS IN THE STATE OF BARINAS

A. INTRODUCTORY NOTES

Mounds and causeways are common features of different cultures throughout the world. In Venezuela early Spanish chroniclers observed that the Indians raised mounds as an aid in growing certain staples, manihot for instance.

Earthworks in the form of causeways (locally known as *calzadas*) have long since been reported to occur in various regions of the Venezuelan States of Barinas (formerly, Zamora), Portuguesa and Apure. These works are known in Barinas (Fig. 2) under different names, *Turrumotes, Bancos, Terraplenes, Lomos de Perro, Calzadas* and *Caminos de Los Indios*.

B. DESCRIPTION OF THE *calzadas*

Some of the *calzadas* of Barinas, personally known to the authors, will be described.

1. *Calzada de los Mochuelos.*—This structure is located near the settlement of Torunos, and draws its name from the countless nests of *mochuelos* (owl-like birds, *Speotyto cunicularia apurensis* Gill.)[2] tunneled out of its slopes. It has a total length of approximately 1700 meters, a width of between 8 and 27 meters, and a maximum height of about 0.50 meter above the level of the surrounding

---

1. The four memoirs summarized in these notes are part of a single larger work intended to discuss certain fundamentals of the archeology of Venezuela, thus laying the ground for subsequent investigations in this and allied fields. To this end, we have added an account of the peculiar "Tiot-tio" (Memoir II), feeling it may have some bearing on the general subject of petroglyphs and glyphs.

These memoirs bear the following titles:

I. *Las Calzadas de Barinas* ("Barinas Causeways"), by J. M. Cruxent, A. Requena, and B. R. Lewis.

II. *El Tiot-tio* ("The Tiot-tio"), by J. M. Cruxent in collaboration with the Sociedad de Ciencias Naturales La Salle of Caracas.

III. *Las Bateitas de Aguirre, Edo. Carabobo* ("The 'potholes' of Aguirre in the State of Carabobo"), by J. M. Cruxent in collaboration with the staff of the Museo de Ciencias Naturales of Caracas.

IV. *Megalítica y litoglifos de Vigirima, Guacara, Edo. Carabobo* ("Megaliths and Lithoglyphs of Vigirima, Guacara, State of Carabobo") by J. M. Cruxent in collaboration with the Sociedad de Ciencias Naturales La Salle of Valencia (State of Carabobo).

The map (Fig. 1) shows the localities of the subjects of the memoirs.

We acknowledge with thanks the assistance of Dr. Leon Croizat, of the Museo de Ciencias Naturales, Caracas, in preparing these summaries in English from the original Spanish manuscripts.

2. We are indebted to Dr. W. H. Phelps, Sr., for the scientific name of this bird.

llano; it is probable that the original height was greater and became gradually reduced by erosion.

The *calzada* under discussion runs through very gently rolling ground, and is so oriented as to take advantage of a line of higher level, thus helping drainage. It seems clear that this was intentionally done by its builders, considering that the *calzada* is in addition wider at the segments of higher elevation.

The run of this *calzada* is not parallel to the course of the Río Santo Domingo, but there is some indication that its northern end originally pointed toward this

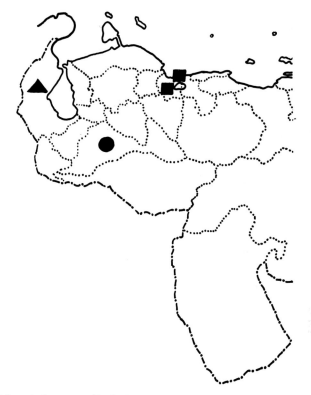

Fig. 1.—Map of the western half of Venezuela, showing the localities discussed in the text. Barinas ("calzadas" district) indicated by circle; Western Zulia ("tiot-tio" region) by triangle; Aguirre and Vigirima ("bateitas" and petroglyphs stations) by square, Aguirre lower left.

watercourse. We are inclined to believe that the *calzada* was once longer than it is now, but was shortened by recent human agencies.

No pottery was found in this *calzada*, but diggings may yield it, considering that the *barrancas* of the Río Santo Domingo are quite rich in artifacts of the kind.

2. *Calzada de Páez (Fig. 3).*—It rises by the *Hato de la Calzada*, some 300 meters west of the main building of this ranch and runs southward perpendicu-

FIG. 2.—Airview of the "calzada" country in the *llanos* of Barinas. The Río Ticoporo at the line of horizon. Photograph by Alfredo Boulton

Fig. 3.—The "calzada de Páez." The difference in level between the *llano* and the top of the structure shown by *A, B.* Photograph by Alfredo Boulton

lar to the Río Ticoporo. Its total length appears to be about 5 kilometers, and it is quite variable in width (13 to 25 meters) and height (1 to 2 meters). Like the *Calzada de los Mochuelos*, this structure tends to adapt itself to a line of major elevations throughout. The diggings that yielded the material for the construction are still clearly visible (Fig. 4) all along its slopes. Fragments of pottery occur here and there, but the major part of the *calzada* seems to be sterile from the archeologist's viewpoint. This structure terminates most probably by the banks of the Río Ticoporo.

3. *Calzada del Chaparral.*—It may be suspected that this structure was intended as a remote prolongation of the *Calzada de Páez* running to the north of the so called *Caño del Oso*. It consists of two main branches running, respectively, north and southwest. The latter has two lesser perpendicular branches, 60 and 80 meters in length. The total length of this *calzada* is about 1500 meters (north branch) and 2000 meters (southwest branch); its width is irregular with an average of some 10 meters; the height varies between 1.50 and 2 meters. Ancient pottery lies on the surface of the *calzada* in spots.

4. *Calzada de Ojo de Agua.*—This is a small structure along the road between Pedraza (Ciudad Bolivia) and the Hato de la Calzada. Its length does not exceed 200 meters; its height reaches here and there to approximately 1.80 meters; the width is irregular throughout. A part of this *calzada* is currently used as a road going to Lomitas.

C. GENERAL CONSIDERATIONS

All the *calzadas* so far studied by the authors of those notes have common characters, suggesting that their main purpose was to secure grounds safe at all times from the inundations, which in this region last up to a period of 6 months beginning with the normal rain-season. The diggings from which material was secured for the construction (Fig. 4) are quite wide as a rule, occasionally to 40 meters which indicates that wooden spades (such as were described by Gumillas in his work *El Orinoco Ilustrado*) might have been used for the purpose.

The *calzadas* in the Venezuelan *llanos* are mentioned by early Spanish writers, such as Juan de Castellanos who relates in his *Elegías de Varones Ilustres de Indias* that the *Conquistador* Cedeño when first entering these immense plains with his men saw *Prolijísima calzada. Que fué más de cien leguas duradera Con señales de antiguas poblaciones Y de labranzas viejos camellones* ("a very long calzada, more than a hundred 'leguas' long bearing vestiges of ancient villages and rows to mark the place of former fields"). Fray Jacinto de Carvajal recalls likewise that he was told by the *Conquistador* Miguel de Ochogavia, who marched southward through the *llanos* to discover the Río Apure, that the Indian Caquetios, following their flight from the region of Coro (Falcón) to the *llanos* of Central Venezuela, had built under the leadership of their *cacique El gran Manaure* certain mounds and earthworks (*Unas explayadas como empinadas ceyuas y hobos, constituydos estos y aquellas en unas eminencias que a manos compussieron las tropas inmenssas de yndios caquetios que se rretiraron por estos llanos quando la venida de los españoles primeros tomaron tierra en Coro, ciudad primera de las Indias, y fueron a poblar con su cacique el gran Manaure la laguna de Caranaca, adonde oy assisten los descendientes de estos).*

The sum total of the evidence, however, is against the possibility that these works were occupied in 1536 by their original builders. The descriptions we have from firsthand witnesses of the protohistoric Indians in the *calzada* region prove them to have been on a very low cultural level, therefore scarcely capable of the organized labor necessary to build these causeways. The food base of these tribes was the products of fishing and hunting and the gathering

Fig. 4.—Diggings (source of the material used in building) alongside the "Calzada de Páez." Photograph by J. M. Cruxent.

of wild fruits and roots. Moreover, when Cedeño first came to the *llanos* he found them inhabited by Indians Jaguas and Caquetios who were at the time engaged in bitter warfare with the invading Caribs, these usually having the better of the fray. This is probably the reason why the missionaries sent to the *llanos* about 1650 found that the Indian settlements of the region were in full decadence and scarcely homogeneous from the ethnic side.

D. POSSIBLE USE OF THE *calzadas*

The authors of these notes incline to the opinion that these earthenworks were built in answer to actual need, but were also employed in different uses.

These uses probably were:

1. *Thoroughfares.*—Although roads and thoroughfares are usually built as far as possible straight, while the *calzadas* are often not so, it appears probable that the *calzadas* could be used for transit, as they indeed are to this day. It is also possible that *calzadas* abutting to a creek or watercourse were intended as an extension of the waterway, considering that it would prove difficult to sail native canoes through the *llanos* because of low waters.

2. *Platforms for actual settlements.*—The quotation previously given from the work of Castellanos who refers to *Señales de Antiguas poblaciones* is emphatic on this score. Remnants of pottery discovered here and there on the *calzadas* also point to the same conclusion. Lands above the high water mark would naturally be sought for dwelling purposes in the rainy season.

3. *Agricultural land.*—It was customary among different Indian tribes and nations throughout the New World to build up earthworks in order to insure the crops against inundations, and also to secure a better medium in which to raise edible tubers and the like. In regions liable to periodical'inundations of the kind normal in the Venezuelan *llanos*, causeways are better than mounds for the purpose. Castellanos who pointedly refers to Cedeño having seen *De labranzas viejos camellones* on these structures implicitly confirms that they were also used for agricultural pursuits.

4. *Hunting preserves.*—It is well known that the *calzada* region of Barinas is rich in game of all kinds. Statistics show that at the end of the last century not less than 100,000 skins of deer were exported yearly from the *llanos*. During the season of high waters, the game congregates on every mound or hillock out of reach of inundation, thus offering an easy mark for the hunter right at a time when food may be scarce and travel anything but easy.

While outlining some of the probable uses of the *calzadas*, the authors of this summary make it clear that it has proved so far impossible to undertake carefully planned and methodically conducted excavations in them, and in their general vicinity. The character of this summary, consequently, is more descriptive than interpretative.

II. THE *Tiot-tio*

This summary has, if possible, a more strictly informative purpose than the remaining three résumés. We are aware that the ramifications of *Tiot-tio* are manifold, and that we have so far done hardly anything beyond learning of its existence.

In this understanding, it seems best to give a brief account how the *Tiot-tio* came to the notice of the author of these notes in the course of an excursion to the district of the Motilone Indians of the Río Negro and Río Shirapa in the State of Zulia, which took him, together with Dr. Luís Carbonell and the graduate student Miguel Shön, to a ranch about an hour's walking distance before reaching the small settlement of Ayapaima.

In the course of a short rest at this ranch, the Indian guide leading the party spoke at first in the local vernacular to its dwellers, then turning this time to one of the Indian women of the ranch, began to address her in a peculiar singsong pointing all the while to certain signs on a piece of paper. We thought at first that a magic formula or the like was being chanted, but we soon learned that, on the contrary, our Indian guide was "reading" a straightforward message to the women. It soon transpired that practices of the sort were current. We had invited, for instance, certain Indian families of the upper Río Negro to spend a few days with us in Ayapaima, and when they came with much ceremony they also took along certain wooden tablets carried by the male members in the party bearing signs which they "read" in their usual style. While it seems sure that facts of the kind could not escape attention on the part of missionaries, geologists, ornithologists, all of whom at some time or other visited this region, still no word of it had ever reached us before.

A. HOW *tiot-tio* IS EMPLOYED

To our present knowledge, *tiot-tio* is used in two main ways, as a direct means for transmitting ordinary messages, and in ceremonial fashion, as follows.

1. *To transmit messages.*—The sender of an intended message draws at first certain signs upon paper or wood calling next the Indian who is to act as messenger. The two squat side by side, and the sender of the message starts chanting, *Tiot-tiooo! Tiot-tiooo! Tiot-tiooo! Tiot-tioooo!* next following with the words of the message itself, while progressively underscoring the signs with his finger. The message repeats in the same chanting tone every thing said by the sender, then departs. Upon reaching his destination, the messenger intones once more, *Tiot-tioo! Tiot-tiooo! Tiot-tiooo! Tiot-tioooo!* next proceeding to deliver the message in the same voice to the addressee.

2. *In ceremonial fashion.*—A party of Indians led by a headmen visits an alien settlement, and, upon reaching its limits, the members of the visiting party arrange themselves single file, proceeding farther very slowly and with repeated genuflexions while holding aloft sticks with signs. Upon being met by the dwellers of the settlement, the visitors point to the *"tiot-tio"* signs and read them in the customary manner.

B. GENERAL REMARKS

The Indians living southwest from Ayapaima beyond the Río Yasa in the settlement of Shirapa (near Río Top-ti-muincha, a tributary of Río Tukukú) apparently know *"tiot-tio"* under some different name, for they identified tablets with signs as *"Ojemaitopo,"* as it was possible for us to learn when presenting the credentials given us by the *cacique* of Ayapaima. We have good reason to suspect that signs more or less similar to, or related with *"tiot-tio,"* are also employed in reference to *totems* or other purposes, but feel it is premature to speak of the subject right now.

As the figure (Fig. 5) reproducing part of the message which aroused our original curiosity about the *"tiot-tio,"* shows, the signs are read right to left beginning with the right end low corner of the sheet or tablet. We experienced considerable difficulty in making ourselves understood by the natives of the region who hardly understand or speak Spanish. We are accordingly not sure that the interpretation we give of the signs is correct in all its details, but it seems that the gist of the message—that part of it at least here reproduced—is to the effect that a donkey had been lost, the return of which to its legitimate owner was pressingly sought. With this, an invitation was being extended to attend the celebration of the *Bird Ot-to-rocó* in the assurance that drinks would

Fig. 5.—Actual tracings of part of "tiot-tio" message. The symbols read approximately as follows: *1, No known meaning; 2, No known meaning; 3,* Down; *4,* Down (*emphatic*); *5, Sign expressing repetition or succession; 6,* Again; *7, 8, 9,* Once more again; *10,* A donkey here; *11,* It is sought in the village; *12, No known meaning; 13,* Field; *14,* Field on the other side; *15,* When you come; *16,* If you do not come it does not make any difference; *17,* The *fiesta* is near; *18,* The *fiesta* of the bird *Ot-to-rocó; 19,* He does not want; *20,* If he wants let us drink; *21,* It is a good *fiesta.* Heavy black is *red;* broken lines *blue* in the original.

be available in friendly company. A provisional interpretation of the signs involved is attached (Fig. 5), each sign with its meaning.

While not improbable that some signs are conventionally understood to convey certain definite names and ideas, still it seems to us at present more probable that the *"tiot-tio"* is intended, usually if not exclusively, as an aid in memorizing a message and thus repeating it without omission to the addressee. It seems further probable that the roots of this means of communication reach deep in time, and that in its present use it has entered a state of decadence already. That there exists a relation between at least some of the signs of the *"tiot-tio"* and standard petroglyphs scattered throughout our regions seems to us very nearly certain.

The Indians probably used wooden tablets as the original stuff to receive *"tiot-tio"* but today use paper and linen and whatever kind of pencil they happen to find available. In at least one case (Upper Irapá) we had the opportunity of securing a wooden tablet with engraved signs of *"tiot-tio."* Prior to the present adoption of pencils, and when pencils are not available, the signs were, and are, written in red tint secured either from *Onoto* (*Bixa orellana*) or *Achote* (*Arrabidea Chica;* fide Pittier, Pls. Us. Venezuela 208. 1926) or perhaps a mixture of both dyes.

Fig. 6.—"Bateitas" in slab. Photograph by J. M. Cruxent

III. THE "POT-HOLES" OF AGUIRRE IN THE STATE OF CARABOBO[3]

Aguirre is a small settlement in the Distrito de Montalban of the State of Carabobo located at the northernmost end of a large valley opening to the west of Bejuma. At this locality, the author found in the course of two excursions in March 1949 not less than thirteen *bateitas* (see Fig. 6, for part of these) mostly

3. Although apt in the descriptive sense, the term "Pot-hole" does not answer the origin of the *bateitas*, as the readers may readily understand. *Bateita* is the diminutive of *batea*, an Americanism of probable Carib extraction, which connotes a more or less definitely canoe-shaped tub or trough currently used in laundering or for other domestic purposes.

hollowed out of hard micaceous gneiss, some on the face of a slab sloping at such an angle that standing upon it proved quite difficult. It is probable that other *bateitas* remain to be discovered in the same general vicinity.

There are marked differences between these structures and the so-called *"pilones"* used throughout the New World for grinding or pulverizing purposes. The four corners of a *bateita* are rounded, most likely because of the method employed in their fabrication. Its walls are patently such as to show that work by percussion was not done at that point. The good state of preservation of the *bateitas* thus far discovered is seemingly due to their having been protected against erosion by an accumulation of soil.

It appears probable that the technique adopted in hollowing out a *bateita* was as follows: First the four corners were marked, and the beginning of a hole made in each, by percussion with a lithic hammer. This done, boring by a hardwood rod rotating some abrasive would begin at the corners until the depth ultimately sought was reached. This achieved, the stone still left in center would be gradually flaked off by percussion with hammer and chisel, the process ending with smoothing and trimming the excavation thus made. It is worth noting that the structural peculiarities of a *bateita* discovered in the *Quebrada de Carmelitas* indicate that the makers of this artifact were more interested in a perfectly horizontal bottom than in holding capacity. This interpretation throws doubt on the hypothesis that the *bateitas* were originally intended to contain liquids. In another of these artifacts at *El Samán*, the bottom consists of two shallow concavities (Fig. 7) which, together with the irrgular outline of the whole structure, tends to discredit the surmise that such a *bateita* could be used for grinding or pulverizing purposes.

It proves very difficult to understand why time and labor were spent by native Americans in an effort to work out lithic excavations of this nature. The offered hypotheses here are purely exploratory, and the author of these notes does not assign higher probability of one over the rest. They are submitted as possible guides for future studies:

1. These *bateitas* may have been used to cook food by stone-boiling in whatever broth or liquid they could be made to hold. It is worth noting, in this respect, that no traces of pottery were found. However, it cannot be forgotten that the above *bateita* from the *Quebrada de Carmelitas* would not fit this purpose.

2. The capacity of the *bateitas* known to date is such that some of them could accommodate a human skeleton of disjointed bones. It is, accordingly, possible that they might have been used for secondary burials. Possibly comparable graves hollowed out of live rock are personally known to the present writer from the vicinity of Olérdola in Spain.

Informed opinion is unanimous that the Olérdola receptacles were intended for funerary purposes. Objections that the *bateitas* of Aguirre are too few in number to fill the need of any large population could be raised, but it should not be forgotten that Olérdola itself gives every indication of having been a sizeable center despite the few receptacles discovered there. It cannot be ruled out, therefore, that the *bateitas* were used only for burial of high-ranking tribal members.

3. *Bateitas* could possibly be employed as crucibles to melt down gold. Gold was melted before the Conquest with the aid of pipes of wood or clay blown through as bellows. *Bateitas* would fit the purpose of crucibles which native industry doubtless found hard to manufacture, even under the best of conditions.

4. These receptacles may have answered religious purposes such as ceremonies in connection with special cult water, or the like.

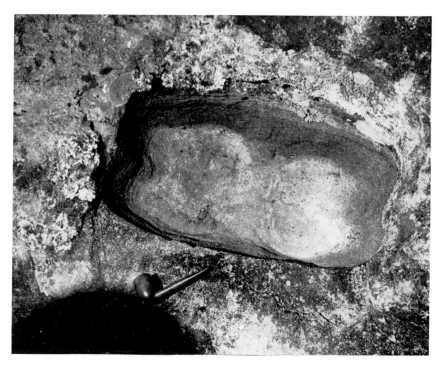

Fig. 7.—"Bateita" at the locality El Samán, with bottom including two separate excavations. Photograph by J. M. Cruxent.

Old Spanish chroniclers give few hints on the *"pilones"* or similar manufactures of the Indians. Padre Las Casas mentions them, remarking that the natives filled them with soil in which they sowed edible plants. We think that if plants were actually so cultivated in *bateitas*, then they served not a current domestic purpose, but rather special uses in connection with magic rites.

Attention is directed to these *bateitas* so that scholars may know of their existence and co-operate in the solution of the problem they offer for study. At present, the writer of these notes feels that a satisfactory explanation of their origin and purpose is not at hand.

IV. MEGALITHS AND LITHOGLYPHS OF VIGIRIMA,
GUACARA, STATE OF CARABOBO

Vigirima, a small settlement north of Guacara, was first recognized as an archeological station of some significance by Dr. Luís R. Oramas, and was as such further referred to by various authors.

The archeological site proper is in the upper reaches of the Valley of Guacara, and consists of two separate stations. Both these stations are easily accessible by the Guacara-Vigirima road, the first station, currently known as *Cerro Pintado* (Painted Hill), is some 8 kilometers north of Guacara: the second station is some 3.5 kilometers beyond the first.

FIG. 8.—Some typical petroglyphs of Vigirima

A. CERRO PINTADO

Cerro Pintado actually consists of two knolls, the lesser in the south, separated from the ridges of the *Cordillera Costanera* by a gulch north of the Lake of Valencia which eventually pours its waters into the *Quebrada Cucharonal*.

From the geological point of view, these knolls consist of a complex of metamorphic rocks with white granite intrusions. They present to the eye rocks and slabs of micaceous schist in a state of more or less marked degradation covered with a multitude of lithoglyphs (see typical examples, Fig. 8), most of which portray a recognizable subject, but of unknown purpose and origin. Walls built of slabs run on the upper ranges of the ridge of the *cordillera* immediately abutting the gulch beyond which rises *Cerro Pintado*.

B. VIGIRIMA

This station is located quite close by the small settlement of Vigirima to the right of the Guacara-Vigirima road, and it is characterized by the presence of a stone wall beginning in the plain, then ascending the first knoll of one of the ridges that hem in the valley.

C. GENERAL NOTES

The lithoglyphs require no comment because their aspect and technique is self-explanatory. They vary greatly in size, from 1560 × 720 millimeters to 100 × 90 millimeters. The walls consist of stones of different height, averaging as much as 120 ×60 centimeters or as little as 40 ×40 centimeters. As the sketch attached shows (see Fig. 9), these stones are mostly slabs arranged in horizontal or vertical patterns, the two often alternating in the construction.

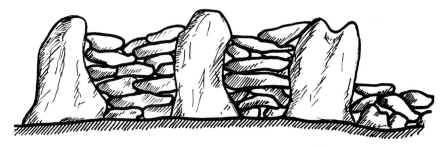

FIG. 9.—General aspects of wall at Vigirima. Notice notched stone standing at right-hand side.

The total length of individual sections of the walls falls approximately within the following limits: 1. *Cerro Colorado*—42, 142, 59, 28 meters; 2.*Vigirima*—234.5 meters of uninterrupted run involving a difference in level between the plain and the hill (see previous description) of some 66 meters.

It is noteworthy that some of the stones at the *Cerro Colorado*, in the 28 meters long wall, are notched above. The notches may have been intended to steady up subsidiary structures by the wall, or they may represent effects of the technique employed in trimming the slabs and setting them in place.

The topography of the walls of *Cerro Colorado* and *Vigirima* is against the possibility that they were intended for military purposes (despite the belief locally prevailing that they are "Spanish trenches"), or to inclose a definite piece of ground. Taking into consideration the short length of the majority of these structures, it is likewise hard to believe that they were meant as boundaries. Dr. Luís R. Oramas wrote that they might have been built in connection with ancient rites and possibly meant to stand, on the whole, as ophidiomorphic figurations. Without rejecting this opinion, we are inclined to think that these walls served a useful purpose in hunting. During a sojourn made with the Piaroa Indians of the Upper Río Parguaza (Edo. Bolívar), we had the opportunity of noticing that these Indians were accustomed to build hedges of fallen logs, lianas, brushwood, etc. to a height of about 0.60 meter and a length exceeding, as a rule, 300 meters. Here and there alongside these hedges, breaches were opened leading across a short way or tunnel to a trap. At morning time the Piaroa women were accustomed to inspect the traps gathering in whatever animal had been led to them by following the hedges.

We have some knowledge of similar methods of trapping used by Indians other than Piaroas, and we should not be surprised if the walls of *Cerro Pintado* and *Vigirima* had been built to help in the hunt of deer, peccaries and the like. However, we do not intend to go on record as saying that this actually was the case. While archeological remains are unknown in the immediate vicinity of the walls, we have located two archeological stations in the gulches by the *Quebrada Cucharonal*, one of them seemingly very promising. It is possible that coming excavations at this site may yield light upon the origin and purposes of the lithoglyphs and walls of *Cerro Pintado* and *Vigirima*.

LA MACROFAMILIA LINGÜÍSTICA WITOTO Y SUS RELACIONES CON LA FAMILIA SABEIA Y OTRAS INDOAMERICANAS

P. J. Marcelino C. de Castellvi

INTRODUCCIÓN

Todo americanista sabe cuanto las ciencias del hombre esperan de la Lingüística Indoamericana. Parece que al presente la urgencia de utilizarla para el propio provecho de la lingüística ha llegado a nuevos extremos y a nuevas exigencias; de modo que se nota en el ambiente el propósito de sacar de los materiales lingüísticos existentes el máximo rendimiento que se pueda obtener. Por esta razón se está resuelto a planear y efectuar nuevas recolecciones complementarias de material, en todos los casos que se trate de lenguas supervivientes que lo permitan.

Para el debido planeamiento de qué aportes tenemos derecho a esperar de la Lingüística Indosuramericana, debe tenerse en cuenta, entre otras, esta triple realidad: (*a*) cuanto ha progresado, (*b*) cuanto indefinidamente progresará y, (*c*) límites ya ciertos que dejan infundadas las esperanzas de progreso.

Para mayor claridad suministraremos algunos ejemplos típicos de cada uno de los tres casos:

de *a*): en esta sección de mayor progreso figuran:

1) *El descubrimiento de lenguas*—(No más en el Cileac contamos más de treinta lenguas antes del todo desconocidas, algunas hasta en su nombre, recogidas por nuestros colegas durante los últimos años).

2) *Un registro mejorado*—cada vez con mayor precisión y técnica.

3) *Una mejor dialectología*—con la necesaria discriminación de dialectos y subdialectos.

4) *Clasificación* de muchas lenguas y dialectos que no habian sido clasificados hasta ahora.

de *b*): entre lo que esperamos, para un futuro inmediato, contamos especialmente la obtención de notación fonética y en registro fonográfico electro-magnético de textos míticos y narrativos de cada uno de los subdialectos indoamericanos más o menos sobrevivientes, en lengua indígena y con su traducción interlíneal, luego análisis gramatical y glosarios.—Estos materiales serán los más eficientes para la clasificación definitiva y completa de muchos dialectos y subdialectos, harán posibles los grandes estudios indolingüísticos y como consecuencia la aplicación de sus resultados a las demás ciencias del hombre.

de *c*): En cambio en tercera realidad no se debe olvidar una serie de lenguas cuyo progreso será siempre muy limitado, pués no cuentan con materiales, sino muy insuficientes recogidos a su tiempo, están ahora extinguidas y por lo que históricamente sabemos, no quedan esperanzas de que nunca se descubra algun

295

antiguo arte o vocabulario, pués pertenecen a ciertas áreas en que jamás se trabajó ni en la evangelización, ni en la explotación industrial, sino apenas de nombre se conocieron, cuando más se las visitó de puro tránsito.

Teniendo en cuenta esta triple situación, juzgamos oportuno buscar a la Lingüística Indoamericana una distribución adecuada y ensayar, a base casi siempre de las existentes, nuevas agrupaciones complementarias de lenguas dentro de cada familia y formando un nuevo tipo peculiar de grandes familias, que en este caso llamamos "Clases" o "Macrofamilias."

Por otra parte creemos ya posible intentar una distribución tricronológica más o menos provisional, pero utilísima, de las misma familias en tres grandes estratos: (1) Epoca Arcaica, (2) Epoca Intermedia, (3) Epoca Moderna.

Respecto a "Familia" lingüística no pretendemos ni mucho menos que se anule su definición tradicional de *"conjunto de dialectos"* más o menos semejantes entre sí que *continúan* una misma lengua común. Sino que a su lado intentamos formar otros grupos: los de *"comunidades de influencias"* que es lo único que en muchos casos permite la lingüística indoamericana. Como son aquellos casos de dialectos extinguidos cuyos materiales disponibles se reducen apenas a cortísimos vocabularios, sin datos gramaticales y plagados de "quid pro quo" o trastrueques de traducción, o llenos de encuestas mal realizadas, sin efectuar comprobación alguna.

Con semejantes materiales se puede a veces alcanzar a demostrar que un dialecto dado es distinto y no se debe identificar con otro alguno de los conocidos en una familia lingüística determinada.

Varios otros casos no permitirán, según toda la técnica de la clasificación genealógica, concluir "comunidad de origen" entre varios dialectos, pero sí podrá llegarse a demostrar siquiera "comunidad de influencias" para varios grandes estratos más o menos contemporáneos, y esto es precisamente lo que utilizamos como dato complementario, en nuestro ensayo de clasificación macrogenealógica de las lenguas de la Gran Colombia (Colombia, Venezuela, Ecuador y Panama) y hemos empezado a aplicar según el mismo sistema a todas las demás familias lingüísticas indoamericanas, distribuidas por países y agrupadas por series "tricronológicas" o sea en las tres grandes épocas que se aceptan generalmente y que se conviene en llamarlas, en algún aspecto, Arcaica, Intermedia y Moderna.

Para evitar equívocos, se convino en el último Congreso Internacional de Antropología de Bruselas que sería preferible distinguir tecnicamente estas 3 épocas y sus indios con los términos griegos ya corrientes en la nomenclatura científica de *eo*, *mio*, y *neo* y también *pleoneo* y *pleistoneo*. En esta forma: Eoindios, Mioindios y Neoindios para 3 épocas hasta la Conquista, Plioneoindios y Pleistoneoindios para la Colonia y la época posterior después de la Independencia.

En el primer grupo como *Eoindios*, clasificamos las lenguas y dialectos que presentan la mayoría de elementos lingüísticos característicos de tribus que encontramos que se conservan en las culturas *protomorfas*. Por lo menos que tengan los estratos fundamentales de este tipo y no de los tipos siguientes mioindios ni neoindios.

En el segundo grupo, *Mioindios*, clasificamos las lenguas de los indígenas de culturas generalmente "amazónicas" y otras con sustratos lingüísticos y culturales superpuestos a la "protomorfis" y todavía sin los protohistóricos llamados de alta cultura.

Son características de este grupo las familias lingüísticas Arawak, Karib, Tupi-Guaraní en sus respectívos estratos.

En el Dialecto Uru de la familia lingüística Arawak propio de indígenas considerados de cultura arcaica o por lo menos anterior a las llamadas "amazónicas" encontróse un sustrato, señalado por Revet, no identificable con otros de la familia Arawak sino con los típicos de dialectos de la familia Capakura que se considera también de cultura más o menos arcaica.

Asimismo en un primer sondeo comparativo de varias familias lingüísticas aisladas, entre ellas el Makrowitoto, correspondientes de hecho a culturas consideradas arcaicas, hemos encontrado nosotros mismos que si no demuestran todavía riguroso parentesco genealógico, por lo menos si concuerdan en varios elementos con dicho sustrato arcaico del Uru (anterior parece al sustrato común Arawak) y también con algun sustrato o influencias de los 3 dialectos hasta ahora conocidos de la familia lingüística Sabela, su vecina occidental.

Desde el punto de vista crítico, debemos amotar enseguida, que en las mentadas comparaciones no se utilizan, es cierto, sino elementos léxicos y solo raramente gramaticales. Ya sabemos la deficiencia demostrativa de semejante comparación léxica, que como sucede a menudo en lenguas sudamericanas, es debida a la escasez de datos gramaticales que hasta el presente no se han recogido. Quizá el hecho de ser muchos los lingüistas que están en ellos sumamente interesados y que anhelan poder pronto utilizarlos, porqué de la recolección de dichos datos gramaticales depende la solución de importantes problemas antropológicos, quizá decimos, una mayor divulgación de tal necesidad de encuestas gramaticales, prácticamente efectuadas, recogiendo simplemente cuentos en lengua indígena, mueva a algún investigador a realizarlas.

Por otra parte, y mientras las esperamos, creemos de la calidad de las comparaciones que si no se acepta ciertamente que pruebe un origen común para el sustrato arcaico en cuestión, por lo menos queda en pie el argumento siquiera negativo, de que según la argumentación lingüística, si no se demuestra la existencia de 3 grandes épocas culturales y parcialmente el parentesco de las familias aisladas, en cambio podemos afirmar que todo concuerda en no contradecirlo y con la tendencia a señalarse cada vez más argumentos a favor, a medida que va prosperando el acopio de materiales y su estudio comparativo.

En el tercer grupo o época de *Neoindios* entran las familias lingüísticas correspondientes a las culturas protohistóricas o llamadas de alta cultura como la Kichua y la Chibcha.

Es verdad que algunos de sus dialectos, por ejemplo el Tunebo de la familia Chibcha parece haber sido impuesto a una tribu de cultura y raza o "getnia" antérior. En este y otros casos análogos no dejaría también de se Neoindia o relativamente moderna, dicha imposición de un dialecto Chibcha a una cultura anterior Eoindia o Mioindia como la Tunebo.

Estamos preparando una clasificación Macrogenealógica y Tricronológica para el "Diccionario de lenguas indoamericanas en la cual se distribuyen los citados estrados (identificables y supuestos de distintas épocas) así:

edad: Neoindia
  clase: Makrochibcha
    família: Chibcha
      sección: Chibcha-Arawak
        subsección: Chibcha Central
          dialecto (*1ª división*): Tunebo (arcaico)
            subdialecto: grupo *a)*—Paleo-Tunebo (de los "Werxaia")
                    —Tunebo-Unkasia
                    —Tunebo-Pedraza
                    —Dobokubi[1]
            grupo *b)*—Tunebo-Tegria
                    —Tunebo-Bokota
                    —Tunebo-Sinsiga
            grupo *c)*—Tunebo-Manare
          dialecto (*2ª división*): Tunebo (Colonial y sin suficientes materiales)
          4 *dialectos extinguidos:*—Subaske
                    —Morkote
                    —Guasika
                    —Sinsiga-Chita

En cambio entre los dialectos y sustratos procedentes de la Edad Eoindia colocamos los mencionados estratos Tunebo que, como señala Loukotka permiten deducir *intrusión* de la familia Arawak.

Si después del requerido estudio comparativo queda demostrado que más bién se relacionan con los más arcaicos (después de completada la prolija tarea de comparar los elementos de los poemas Werxaya del paleotunebo con los pertenecientes a otras familias lingüísticas como "Lagoanas" Kamakan y Kaingan), correspondería entonces dejar sentado definitivamente que semejantes estratos paleotunebos podrían considerarse de la Edad Eoindia y en la forma análoga a los paleoestratos de los dialectos Guambiano, Kaniker y Andaki (y también los 3 Chibcha). Ya que estos sí tienen señalados vestigios de familias lingüísticas "lagoanas" como Masakali. Y el último, el Andaki, incluso tiene vestigios de la Kaingan.

A pesar de tantos distintos estratos que se pueden encontrar en una lengua dada, ya es sabido que en la clasificación genealógica de la técnica lingüística no se acepta de modo alguno que se llame "mezclada" a la misma lengua.

Podrá llamarse "mezclado" solo a tal *léxico* pero no a la lengua en sí, que se

---

1. Recientemente descubierto por nuestro socio el P. Cesareo de Armeliada, clasificada por Rivet en esta división Chibcha y por nosotros entre los arcaicos preferentemente.

distingue ante todo por sus características morfemas. Y desde luego clasificamos una lengua en la familia lingüística a que pertenecen sus morfemas conocidos, más que por su léxico, como enseña ña Glotología tradicional.

Sin deshacer nada, pués, de lo ya adquirido, proponemos que para atender a las realidades de lenguas indosuramericanas extinguidas, se intercalen éstas en otros supergrupos, más o menos definitivos o provisionales, que supongan no necesariamente "comunidad de origen" como sucede en las "familias" lingüísticas en su sentido técnico, sino más bién "comunidad de las mismas influencias recibidas por lenguas aún de distinto origen" y en este sentido formamos y entendemos las Macrofamilias lingüísticas suramericanas, que para evitar equívocos preferentemente se sugiere llamar Clases.

El término griego *Macro* en su sentido usual en la terminología científica incluye (v.gr. en observación macroscópica de la mineralogía en oposición a la microscópica) la idea de examen visual sin aparatos, a simple vista, no según tanto detalle como en la microscópica, pero tampoco de modo que excluya una a la otra. Así también hablamos y decimos *macrocosmos* o sea el conjunto del universo y la palabra no rechaza, sino que incluye y supone en su seno el microcosmos, o pequeño mundo, como tradicionalmente llamamos al hombre.

Presentamos el caso del Makrowitoto[2] como ejemplo de Macrofamilias suramericanas y que no necesariamente tiene el sentido de grupo de familias de un mismo origen, como en ciertas agrupadiones o Macrofamilias norteamericanas, que han contado con suficiente material para su demostración, sino de acuerdo con las insuficiencias a que debemos adaptarnos necesariamente para casos de Suramérica.

El *Makrowitoto* abarca, de este modo, no solo la antígua familia formada por Koch-Gruenberg con unos cinco dialectos y por nosotros completada hasta con más de veinticinco subdialectos, descubiertos unos, y otros empezados a estudiar, con más de 60 documentos lingüísticos de distintos países y la mayoría del Cileac y distribuidos en nuestra agrupación de "subdialectos Menekka, Mekka y Bue," seguidos de subdialectos intermedios" algunos de ellos con estratos "arawakizados" (o con influencias del Arawak); y además se inserta otra *subclase* de dialectos diferenciados, entre ellos el Nonuya y el Okaina y los "Tukanizados" (o con influencias del Tukano) como los dialectos Karapana-Tapuyo e incluso como *subfamilia* el Koeruna (que Loukotka prefirío un tiempo presentarlo como familia provisionalmente aislada y ya extinguida).

Mi propósito es dar las fuentes completas para la lingüística Makrowitoto en varios tomos de una obra o Corpus documental y crítico de etnias indograncolombianas y ayacentes, con el título de *"Pueblos Indígenas de la gran Colombia"* bajo los auspicios del "Instituto Bernardino de Sahagún" de Antropología y Etnología de Madrid (España) y del Centro Cileac de Sibundoy (Colombia).

2. Escribimos aquí con K (Makro) para uniformar la notación de los nombres de familias lingüísticas.

LA CLASE LINGÜÍSTICA MAKROWITOTO

Por el P. J. Marcelino C. de Castellvi con la colaboración del mejor conocedor de los dialectos Witoto, nuestro socio, el P. Javier de Barcelona, descubridor de la clasificación fundamental en Menekka, Mekka y Bue.

clase: Makrowitoto
  familia: Witoto-Menekka
    sección: Aimene-Menekka(Muinane-Witoto) La Chorrera del Igaraparaná
    sección: Menekka

subsección: Muinane-Witoto	El Ultimo Retiro
dialecto: Ifikwene-Jifigi	
dialecto: Dwene	
dialecto: Efagge	
subsección: Muinane de Witoto	Nocaimaní, Atenas y Entreríos
subsección: Muinane del Alto Putumayo	Salado, afluente del Putumayo

  familia: Witoto-Mekka
    sección: Mekka-Muruy

subsección: Mekka del Encanto	río Capaparaná (P. J. de Quito)
subsección: Mekka del Alto Caqueta	
subsección: Mekka del Barro	El Barro, S. Francisco
subsección: Taikene	Entre Tribu Piedras

    sección: Mekka-Ereye

subsección: Dereya	Tribu del Caraparaná (P. Fr. deManresa)
¿*subsección?* Witoto de Solano	Solano (Caquetá)
¿*subsección?* Witoto-Jedua	río Solano (Caquetá) (Preuss)
¿*subsección?* Witoto de Curiplaya	río Caqueta (Kinder)
¿*subsección?* Jairuya	río Tamboryaco, Caquetá (Vraz)

  familia: Witoto-Bue
    sección: Bue

subsección: Bue-Jeya	La Chorrera (P. J. de Barcelona)
subsección: Bue-Encanto	
¿*subsección?* *Nófwikw g*	Tribu "Piedras" (P. M. de Castellvi)
¿*subsección?* Paleowitoto	de las Adivinanzas
¿*subsección?* Hierowitoto	ritual

  familia: Witoto-Arawakizado
    sección: Witoto-Arawakizado

subsección: Kaime	río Apaporis (Koch-Gruenberg)
subsección: Orejon-Witoto	Ambiyacu y Tarapacá (Castelnau)
subsección: Xura	entre Putumayo y Napo (Tessman)
subsección: Meresien	entre Putumayo y Napo (Tessman)
subsección: Seueni	entre Apaporis y Napo? (Koch-Gruenberg)
subsección: Witoto-Tarapaca	Pto. Tarapacá (Pbro. Zawadzky)

  familia: Intermedia
    sección: Witoto-Intermedio (entre Menekka, Mekka y Bue)

subsección: Ifikwene-Kaimito	río Salado (Putumayo) (P. Castellvi)
subsección: Witoto de la Cucha	S. Vicente del Caguan (P. Fr. de Manresa)
subsección: Witoto del Caqueta	rio Caquetá (P. Pinell)
subsección: Witoto-Xatiakua	bajo Caguán (P. Fidel de Barcelona)
subsección: Witoto-Ere	río Eré, Putumayo (Santander, Flavio)
subsección: Witoto (Putumayo-Perú)	(Dr. Farabee)
subsección: Witoto-Orteguaza	proc. del jefe Witoto
subsección: Witoto-Alto Rio Negro	editó (Koch-Gruenberg)

subclase: Diferenciada
  ¿familia?
    sección: Nonuya
      subsección: Nonuya   sabana del Cahuinari (P. Javier de B.)
    sección: Okaina
      subsección: Okaina   quebrada Raisitje, La Chorrera (P. Javier)
    sección: Witoto-Tukanizado
      subsección: Karaparana-Tapuyo   Araracuara, Caquetá (Martius)
    sección: Koeruna
      subsección: Koeruna   cerca del Mirití (Martius)
    sección: ?
      subsección: Jabuyaykiño   Sabaloyaco, Putumayo (P. B. de Igualada)

LES STRUCTURES SOCIALES DANS LE BRÉSIL CENTRAL ET ORIENTAL

Claude Lévi-Strauss

Au cours de ces dernières années, l'attention a été appelée sur les institutions de certaines tribus du Brésil central et oriental que leur bas niveau de culture matérielle avait fait classer comme très primitives. Ces tribus se caractérisent par une structure sociale d'une grande complication comportant divers systèmes de moitiés se recoupant les uns les autres et dotés de fonctions spécifiques, des clans, des classes d'âge, des associations sportives ou cérémonielles et d'autres formes de groupement. Les exemples les plus frappants qui ont été décrits par Colbacchini, Nimuendaju et Lévi-Strauss, après d'autres observateurs plus anciens, sont fournis par les Šerenté, qui ont des moitiés patrilinéaires exogamiques subdivisées en clans; les Canella et les Bororo, avec des moitiés matrilinéaires exogamiques et d'autres formes de groupement; enfin, les Apinayé, avec des moitiés matrilinéaires non-exogamiques. Les types les plus complexes, soit un double système de moitiés subdivisées en clans, et un triple système de moitiés non subdivisées, se rencontrent respectivement chez les Bororo et chez les Canella (78, 341, 342, 343, 261).

La tendance générale des observateurs et des théoriciens a été d'interpréter ces structures complexes à partir de l'organisation dualiste, qui semblait représenter la forme la plus simple (283, 284, 247, 263, 262).[1] C'était suivre l'invitation des informateurs indigènes qui mettaient ces formes dualistes au premier plan de leur description. L'auteur de la présente communication ne se distingue pas, à cet égard, de ses collègues. Toutefois, le doute qu'il entretenait depuis longtemps l'avait incité à postuler le caractère résiduel des structures dualistes dans l'aire considérée (262, 268). Comme on le verra par la suite, cette hypothèse devait s'avérer insuffisante.

Nous nous proposons, en effet, de montrer ici que la description des institutions indigènes donnée par les observateurs sur le terrain—y compris nous-même—coincide, sans doute, avec l'image que les indigènes se font de leur propre société, mais que cette image se réduit à une théorie, ou plutôt une trans-figuration, de la réalité qui est d'une nature toute différente. De cette consta-tation, qui n'avait, jusqu'à présent, été entrevue que pour les Apinayé (176, 247, 265) découle deux importantes conséquences: l'organisation dualiste des populations du Brésil central et oriental n'est pas seulement adventice, elle est souvent illusoire; et surtout, nous sommes amenés à concevoir les structures

---

1. Dès 1940, cependant, Lowie mettait en garde contre les fausses analogies avec les sys-tèmes australiens (284).

sociales comme des objets indépendants de la conscience qu'en prennent les hommes (dont elles règlent pourtant l'existence), et comme pouvant être aussi différentes de l'image qu'ils s'en forment que la réalité physique diffère de la représentation sensible que nous en avons, et des hypothèses que nous formulons à son sujet.

On commencera par l'example des Šerenté, décrits par Nimuendaju (342). Cette population, qui relève du groupe central de la famille linguistique Gê, est distribuée en villages, chacun composé de deux moitiés patrilinéaires exogamiques subdivisées en quatre clans, dont trois considérés par les indigènes comme originels, et un clan supplémentaire attribué par la légende à une tribu étrangère "capturée." Ces huit clans—quatre par moitié—se distinguent par des fonctions cérémonielles et des privilèges; mais ni les clans, ni les deux équipes sportives, ni les quatre associations masculines et l'association féminine qui leur est jointe, ni les six classes d'âge, n'interviennent dans la réglementation du mariage, qui dépend exclusivement du système des moitiés. On s'attendrait donc à rencontrer les corollaires habituels de l'organisation dualiste: distinction des cousins en croisés et parallèles; identification des cousins croisés patrilatéraux et matrilatéraux; et mariage préférentiel entre cousins croisés bilatéraux. Or, ce n'est que très imparfaitement le cas.

Dans un autre travail, dont nous rappelerons très rapidement les conclusions (265), nous avons distingué les modalités fondamentales de l'échange matrimonial en trois formes s'exprimant respectivement dans le mariage préférentiel entre cousins croisés bilatéraux, le mariage entre fils de soeur et fille de frère, et le mariage entre fils de frère et fille de soeur. Nous avons donné à la première forme le nom d'*échange restreint*, exprimant par là qu'elle implique la division du groupe en deux sections, ou un multiple de deux; tandis que le terme d'*échange généralisé*, réunissant les deux autres formes, se réfère au fait qu'elles peuvent se réaliser entre un nombre quelconque de partenaires. La différence entre le mariage matrilatéral et le mariage patrilatéral provient, alors, de ce que le premier représente la forme la plus complète et la plus riche d'échange matrimonial, les partenaires se trouvant orientés une fois pour toutes dans une structure globale et indéfiniment ouverte. Au contraire, le mariage patrilatéral, forme "limite" de la réciprocité, ne lie jamais les groupes que deux à deux, et implique à chaque génération un renversement total de tous les cycles. Il résulte que le mariage matrilatéral s'accompagne normalement d'une terminologie de parenté que nous avons appelée "consécutive": la situation des lignées les unes par rapport aux autres n'étant exposée à aucun changement, leurs occupants successifs tendent à être confondus sous le même terme, et les différences de générations sont négligées. Le mariage patrilatéral entraîne, à son tour, une terminologie "alternative," qui exprime, par l'opposition des générations consécutives et l'identification des générations alternées, le fait qu'un fils se marié dans la direction opposée à celle où son père s'est marié (mais dans la même direction que la soeur de son père), et dans la même direction que celle où le père de son père s'est marié (mais dans la direction opposée à celle de la sœur du père du père). Une situation symétrique et inverse prévaut pour les filles. Une deuxième conséquence s'ensuit: en mariage matrilatéral, on trouve deux termes différents pour qualifier deux types d'alliés: les "maris des sœurs," et les "frères des femmes" qui ne s'identifient jamais. Avec le mariage patrilatéral, cette dichotomie se transpose, au sein même de la lignée, pour distinguer les collatéraux du premier degré, selon leur sexe: le frère et la sœur, qui suivent toujours un destin matrimonial opposé, se différencient par le phénomène, bien décrit par F. E. Williams en Mélanésie, sous le nom de "sex affiliation" (521)[2]; chacun reçoit, à titre privilégié, une fraction du statut de l'ascendant dont il (ou elle) suit le destin matrimonial, ou représente le destin complémentaire. Soit, selon les cas, le fils, de la mère et la fille, du père, ou inversement.

Quand on applique ces définitions au cas des Šerenté, on décèle immédiatement des anomalies. Ni la terminologie de parenté, ni les règles du mariage, ne coïncident avec les exigences d'un système dualiste ou d'échange restreint. Et elles s'opposent entre elles, chaque forme se rattachant à l'une des deux modalités fondamentales de l'échange généralisé. Ainsi, le vocabulaire de parenté offre plusieurs exemples d'appellations consécutives, avec:

fils de la sœur du père = fils de la sœur
fils du frère de la femme = frère de la femme
mari de la sœur du père = mari de la sœur = mari de la fille

Les deux types de cousins croisés sont également distingués. Et cependant, le mariage n'est permis qu'avec la cousine patrilatérale, et exclu avec la cousine matrilatérale, ce qui devrait impliquer une terminologie alternative et non consécutive comme c'est précisément le cas. En même temps, plusieurs identifications terminologiques d'individus relevant de moitiés différentes (mère, fille de la sœur de la mère; frère et sœur, enfants du frère de la mère; enfants de la sœur du père, enfants du frère, etc.) suggèrent que la division en moitiés ne représente pas l'aspect le plus essentiel de la structure sociale. Ainsi donc, un examen, même superficiel, du vocabulaire de parenté et des règles du mariage inspire les constatations suivantes: ni le vocabulaire, ni les règles du mariage, ne coïncident avec une organisation dualiste exogamique. Et le vocabulaire d'une part, les règles du mariage de l'autre, se rattachent à deux formes mutuellement exclusives, et toutes deux incompatibles avec l'organisation dualiste.

Par contre, on trouve des indices suggestifs d'un mariage matrilatéral, en contradiction avec la forme patrilatérale seule attestée. Ce sont: 1) le mariage plural avec une femme et sa fille d'un autre lit, forme de polygynie habituellement associée au mariage matrilatéral avec filiation matrilinéaire (bien que la filiation soit actuellement patrilinéaire); 2) la présence de deux termes réciproques entre alliés, *aimāplĭ* et *izakmŭ* qui laisse à penser que les alliés entretiennent entre eux une relations toujours univoque ("maris de sœurs" ou "frères

2. Sur un problème analogue au Brésil, cf. Lowie (284).

de femmes," mais pas les deux choses simultanément et à la fois). 3) Enfin et surtout, il y a le rôle, anormal dans un système de moitiés, de l'oncle maternel de la fiancée.

L'organisation dualiste se caractérise par une réciprocité de services entre les moitiés, qui sont à la fois associées et opposées. Cette réciprocité s'exprime dans un ensemble de relations particulières entre le neveu et son oncle maternel qui, quel que soit le mode de filiation, appartiennent à deux moitiés différentes. Or, chez les Šerenté, ces relations, restreintes dans leur forme classique à la relation spéciale des *narkwa*, semblent transposées entre le mari ou le fiancé, d'une part et, d'autre part, l'oncle maternel *de la fiancée*. Arrêtons-nous un instant sur ce point.

L'oncle maternel de la fiancée a les fonctions suivantes: il organise et opère l'abduction du fiancé comme préliminaire du mariage; il récupère sa nièce en cas de divorce et la protège contre son mari; il oblige le beau-frère à l'épouser en cas de mort du mari; solidairement avec le mari, il venge sa nièce violée, etc. En d'autres termes, il est, avec le mari de sa nièce, et au besoin contre lui, le protecteur de celle-ci. Or, si le système des moitiés avait vraiment une valeur fonctionnelle, l'oncle maternel de la fiancée serait un "père" classificatoire du fiancé, ce qui rendrait son rôle d'abducteur (et de protecteur, hostile au mari, de la femme d'un de ses "fils"), absolument inintelligible. Il faut donc qu'il y ait, toujours, au moins trois lignées distinctes: celle d'Ego, celle de la femme d'Ego, et celle de la mère de la femme d'Ego, ce qui est incompatible avec un pur système de moitiés.

Au contraire, les services réciproques sont fréquemment rendus entre membres de la même moitié: à l'occasion de l'imposition des noms féminins, les échanges cérémoniels ont lieu entre la moitié alterne de celle des filles, et leurs oncles maternels, qui relèvent de la moitié des officiants; ce sont les oncles paternels qui procèdent à l'initiation des garçons, à la moitié desquels ils appartiennent; lors de l'imposition du nom *Wakedi* à deux garçons, qui est le seul privilège de l'association des femmes, les oncles maternels des garçons accumulent du gibier dont s'emparent les femmes de la moitie alterne, qui est donc la même que celle des oncles en question. En résumé, tout se passe comme s'il y avait une organisation dualiste, mais à l'envers. Ou, plus exactement, le rôle des moitiés s'annule: au lieu qu'elles se rendent des services l'une à l'autre, les services sont rendus au sein de la même moitié, *à l'occasion* d'une activité particulière de l'autre. Il y a donc toujours trois partenaires, et non deux.

Dans ces conditions, il est significatif de rencontrer, sur le plan des associations, une structure formelle qui correspond exactement à une loi d'échange généralisé. Les quatre associations masculines sont ordonnées en circuit. Quand un homme change d'association, il doit le faire dans un ordre prescrit et immuable. Cet ordre est le même qui préside au transfert des noms féminins, qui est le privilège des associations masculines. Enfin cet ordre:

krara → krieriekmū → akemhā → annōrowa → (krara)

et le même, mais inversé, que celui de la genèse mythique des associations, et du transfert, d'une association à l'autre, de la charge de célébrer le cérémonial Padi.

Quand on passe au mythe, une nouvelle surprise se tient en réserve. Le mythe présente, en effet, les associations comme des *classes d'âge* engendrées dans un ordre successif (de la plus jeune à la plus âgée). Or, pour la manufacture des masques, les quatre associations se groupent par paires unies entre elles par une réciprocité de services, comme si elles formaient des moitiés, et ces paires associent des classes, non consécutives, mais alternées, comme si ces moitiés consistaient chacune en deux classes matrimoniales avec échange généralisé, soit (Fig. 1). Cet ordre se retrouve dans les règles de célébration de la fête des morts illustres, ou aikmā.

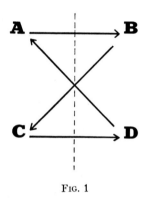

Fig. 1

Ainsi, pour résumer une argumentation dont nous n'avons pu que marquer les articulations essentielles, on retiendra les points suivants:

1. Entre les moitiés exogamiques, les associations et les classes d'âge, il n'y a pas de cloison étanche. Les associations fonctionnent comme si elles étaient des classes matrimoniales, satisfaisant, mieux que les moitiés, aux exigences des règles du mariage et de la terminologie de parenté; sur le plan mythique, elles apparaissent comme des classes d'âge, et dans la vie cérémonielle, elles se groupent dans un système théorique de moitiés. Seuls les clans paraissent étrangers, et comme indifférents, à cet ensemble organique. Tout se passe comme si moitiés, associations et classes d'âge étaient des traductions maladroites et fragmentaires d'une réalité sous-jacente.

2. La seule évolution historique, permettant de rendre compte de ces caractères contradictoires, serait:

a) à l'origine, trois lignées patrilinéaires et patrilocales avec échange généralisé (mariage avec la fille du frère de la mère);

b) introduction de moitiés matrilinéaires imposant:

c) la constitution d'une quatrième lignée patrilocale (le quatrième clan de chaque moitié actuelle, ou "tribu capturée"; le mythe d'origine des associations affirme également qu'elles étaient primitivement trois);

d) un conflit surgissant entre la règle (matrilinéaire) de filiation et la règle (patrilocale) de résidence, entraînant

e) la conversion des moitiés à la filiation patrilinéaire, avec

f) perte concomitante du rôle fonctionnel des lignées qui se transforment en associations, par la mise en oeuvre du phénomène de "résistance masculine" apparu avec l'introduction des moitiés sous leur forme matrilinéaire primitive.

Nous passerons plus rapidement sur les autres exemples, au premier rang desquels figurent les Bororo (78, 261). Tout d'abord, il convient de noter la symétrie remarquable qui existe entre les institutions šerenté et bororo. Les deux tribus ont des villages circulaires, divisés en moitiés exogamiques comptant chacune quatre clans, et une maison des hommes au centre. Ce parallèlisme se poursuit, malgré l'opposition des termes due au caractère, patrilinéaire ou matrilinéaire, des deux sociétés: la maison des hommes bororo est ouverte aux hommes mariés, celle des Šerenté est réservée aux célibataires; c'est un lieu de promiscuité sexuelle chez les Bororo, la chasteté y est impérative chez les Šerenté; les célibataires bororo y entraînent par la violence des filles ou des femmes avec lesquelles ils ont des rapports extra-conjugaux, tandis que les filles šerenté y pénètrent pour y capturer des maris. La comparaison est donc certainement justifiée.

Des travaux récents ont apporté de nouvelles informations sur le système de parenté et l'organisation sociale. En ce qui concerne le premier, les riches documents publiés par le P. Albisetti (5) montrent que, si la dichotomie entre parents "croisés" et "parallèles" se produit bien (comme on peut s'y attendre dans un système à moitiés exogamiques), elle ne reproduit toutefois pas la division en moitiés, mais la recoupe: des termes identiques se retrouvent dans l'une et l'autre moitié. Ainsi, pour se limiter à quelques exemples frappants, Ego identifie les enfants de son frère et les enfants de sa sœur, qui appartiennent pourtant à des moitiés différentes, et si, à la génération des petits-enfants, on trouve la dichotomie aisément prévisible entre "fils et filles" (termes théoriquement réservés aux petits enfants de la moitié alterne d'Ego) d'une part, et "gendres et brus" (termes théoriquement réservés aux petits-enfants de la moitié d'Ego) de l'autre, la distribution effective des termes ne correspond pas à la division en moitiés. On sait que dans d'autres tribus, par exemple chez les Miwok de Californie, de telles anomalies sont précisément l'indice de la présence de groupements différents des moitiés et plus importants que celles-ci. D'autre part, on note, dans le système bororo, des identifications remarquables, comme:

fils du fils du frère de la mère appelé: mari de la fille, pt. fils;
fille de la fille de la sœur du père appelée: mère de la femme, gd. mère;

et surtout:

fils du frère de la mère de la mère, fils du fils du frère de la mère de la mère de la mère appelés: fils;

qui évoquent immédiatement des structures de parenté du type Bank-Ambrym-

Pentecôte, rapprochement confirmé par la possibilité du mariage avec la fille de la fille du frère de la mère dans les deux cas.[3]

Dans le domaine de l'organisation sociale, le P. Albisetti précise que chaque moitié matrilinéaire comprend toujours quatre clans, et que le mariage n'est pas seulement préférentiel entre certains clans, mais doit unir entre elles des sections privilégiées de chaque clan. Chaque clan serait, en effet, divisé en trois sections, matrilinéaires comme le clan: Supérieure, Moyenne, Inférieure. Etant donné deux clans liés par une préférence matrimoniale, le mariage ne peut se faire qu'entre Supérieurs et Supérieurs, Moyens et Moyens, Inférieurs et Inférieurs. Si cette description était exacte (et les informations des Pères salésiens se sont

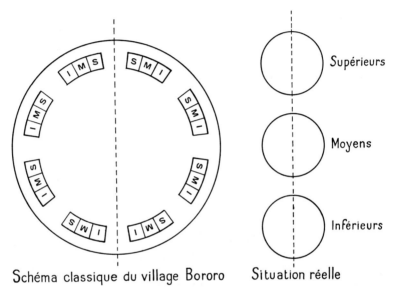

Schéma classique du village Bororo   Situation réelle

Fig. 2

toujours montrées dignes de confiance) on voit que le schéma classique des institutions bororo s'effondrerait. Quelles que soient les préférences matrimoniales qui unissent entre eux certains clans, les clans proprement dit perdraient toute valeur fonctionnelle (nous avons déjà fait une constatation analogue chez les Šerenté), et la société bororo se réduirait à trois groupes endogames: Supérieur, Moyen, Inférieur, chacun divisé en deux sections exogamiques, sans qu'il existe aucun lien de parenté entre les trois groupes principaux, qui constitueraient vraiment trois sous-sociétés (Fig. 2).

Comme la terminologie de parenté semble ne pouvoir être systématisée qu'en fonction de trois lignées théoriques ultérieurement déboublées en six: père de la femme, mère, mari de la fille, liées par un système d'échange généralisé, on

3. Chez les Bororo, toutefois, le mariage reste possible avec la fille du frère de la mère, ce qui indique qu'on ne doit pas pousser trop loin la comparaison.

est conduit à postuler, comme chez les Šerenté, un système primitif tripartite bouleversé par l'imposition d'un dualisme surajouté.

Le traitement de la société bororo comme une société endogame est si surprenant qu'on hésiterait même à l'envisager, si une conclusion analogue n'avait été indépendamment tirée pour les Apinayé, par trois auteurs différents, des documents de Nimuendaju (343). On sait que les moitiés apinayé ne sont pas exogamiques, et que le mariage est réglé par la division du groupe en quatre *kiyé*, selon la formule: un homme A épouse une femme B, un homme B une femme C, un homme C une femme B, etc. Comme les garçons appartiennent à la *kiyé* de leur père et les filles à celle de leur mère, la division apparente en quatre groupes exogamiques recouvre une division réelle en quatre groupes endogames: hommes A et femmes B, parents entre eux; hommes B et femmes C, parents entre eux; hommes C et femmes D, parents entre eux; et hommes D et femmes A, parents entre eux; tandis qu'il n'existe aucune relation de parenté entre les hommes et les femmes groupés dans chaque *kiyé*. C'est exactement la situation que nous avons décrite pour les Bororo sur la base des informations actuellement disponibles, avec cette seule différence que les groupes endogames seraient chez ces derniers au nombre de trois, au lieu de quatre. Certains indices suggèrent une situation du même type chez les Tapirapé (512). Dans ces conditions, on peut se demander si la règle du mariage apinayé, qui prohibe les unions entre cousins, et les privilèges endogames de certains clans bororo (qui peuvent contracter mariage, bien qu'ils relèvent de la même moitié), ne visent pas, par des moyens antithétiques, à remédier de la même façon à la scission du groupe: soit par des exceptions incestueuses, soit par des mariages contraires à la règle, mais que l'éloignement du degré permet moins aisément de déceler.

Il est fâcheux que les lacunes et les obscurités de l'ouvrage de Nimuendaju sur les Timbira orientaux (343) ne permettent pas de pousser aussi loin l'analyse. Toutefois, on ne peut douter qu'on se trouve, ici encore, devant les mêmes éléments d'un complexe commun à toute l'aire culturelle. Les Timbira ont une terminologie systématiquement consécutive, avec:

> fils de la sœur du père = père,
> fille de la sœur du père = sœur du père,
> fils du frère de la mère = fils du frère,
> fille de la fille = fille de la sœur;

et la prohibition du mariage entre cousins croisés (comme chez les Apinayé), malgré la présence des moitiés exogamiques; le rôle de l'oncle maternel de la fiancée, protecteur de sa nièce contre son mari, situation déjà rencontrée chez les Šerenté; le cycle rotatif des classes d'âge, analogue à celui des associations šerenté et des classes matrimoniales apinayé; enfin, leur regroupement par paires de groupes alternés dans les compétitions sportives, comme les associations šerenté dans leurs fonctions cérémonielles, tout cela permet d'affirmer que les problèmes posés ne sauraient être très différents.

Trois conclusions se dégagent de cet exposé, dont on excusera le caractère schématique:

1. L'étude de l'organisation sociale des populations du Brésil central et oriental doit être entièrement reprise sur le terrain. D'abord, parce que le fonctionnement réel de ces sociétés est très différent de son apparence superficielle jusqu'alors seule aperçue, ensuite et surtout, parce que cette étude doit être menée sur une base comparative. Il n'est pas douteux que Bororo, Canella, Apinayé et Šerenté aient systématisé, chacun à leur manière, des institutions réelles qui sont, à la fois, très voisines, et plus simples que leur formulation explicite. Bien plus: les divers types de groupement qu'on rencontre dans ces sociétés: trois formes d'organisation dualiste, clans, sous-clans, classes d'âge, associations, etc., ne représentent pas, comme en Australie, autant de formations dotées d'une valeur fonctionnelle, mais plutôt une série de traductions, chacune partielle et incomplète, d'une même structure sous-jacente qu'elles reproduisent à plusieurs exemplaires, sans jamais parvenir à exprimer, ni à épuiser, sa réalité.

2. Les enquêteurs sur le terrain doivent s'habituer à envisager leurs recherches sous deux aspects différents. Ils sont toujours exposés à confondre les théories des indigènes sur leur organisation sociale (et la forme superficielle donnée à ces institutions pour les faire cadrer avec la théorie), et le fonctionnement réel de la société. Entre les deux, il peut y avoir une différence aussi grande qu'entre la physique d'Epicure ou de Descartes, par exemple, et les connaissances tirées du développement de la physique nucléaire contemporaine. Les représentations sociologiques des indigènes ne sont pas seulement une partie ou un reflet de leur organisation sociale: elles peuvent, comme dans les sociétés plus avancées, la contredire complètement, ou en ignorer certains éléments.

3. On a vu qu'à cet égard, les représentations indigènes du Brésil central et oriental, et le language institutionnel dans lequel elles s'expriment, constituent un effort désespéré pour placer au premier plan un type de structure: moitiés ou classes exogamiques, dont le rôle réel est très secondaire, quand même il n'est pas complètement illusoire. Derrière le dualisme et la symétrie apparente de la structure sociale, on devine une organisation tripartite et asymétrique plus fondamentale,[4] au fonctionnement harmonieux de laquelle l'exigence d'une formulation dualiste impose des difficultés qui sont peut être insolubles. Pourquoi des sociétés, qui sont ainsi entachées d'un fort coefficient d'endogamie, ont-elles un besoin si pressant de se mystifier elles-mêmes, et de se concevoir comme régies par des institutions exogamiques d'une forme classique, mais dont elles n'ont aucune connaissance directe? Ce problème, dont nous avons ailleurs cherché la solution (265), relève de la sociologie générale. Qu'il se pose à propos d'une discussion aussi technique, et d'une aire géographique aussi limitée, que celles qui ont été abordées ici, montre bien, en tout cas, la tendance actuelle des études ethnologiques, et que, désormais, dans le domaine des sciences sociales, la théorie et l'expérience sont indissolublement liées.

---

4. Cette organisation tripartite avait déjà été signalée chez les Aweikóma, mais contestée pour la raison qu'elle aurait été "unique au Brésil" (314).

CARACTERIZAÇÃO DA CULTURA TAPIRAPÉ

Herbert Baldus

Os Tapirapé do Brasil Central moram na parte ocidental da bacia do Araguaia, sendo seus vizinhos: ao norte os Kayapó; ao sul os Akué-Chavante; a oeste índios desconhecidos da bacia do Xingu e a este os Karajá. Atualmente, os neo-brasileiros estão invadindo seu território, vindo do este e sul.

O grupo local a que se refere o presente trabalho foi visitado e estudado pelo Dr. Charles Wagley em 1939 e 1940 e por mim em 1935 e 1947. Habita a bacia do rio Tapirapé, afluente do Araguaia. Há indícios da existência de outro grupo local da mesma tribo, mais ao norte, grupo ainda não visitado por homem branco.

Em outro lugar ventilei as hipóteses acêrca da procedência dessa tribo, apoiando-me principalmente em documentação histórica, para chegar à conclusão de que os Tapirapé vieram do norte para seu atual habitat, morando nêle desde o século XVIII. Aqui quero passar em revista os aspectos etnográficos que considero próprios para a discussão do seu parentesco com outras culturas.

Andar nu, pintado e escarificado, é tão comum entre os índios do Brasil que não representa peculiaridade de determinada cultura tribal. O estojo peniano em forma de funil, usado pelos Tapirapé, parece provir dos Gê. O feitio da tatuagem feminina, os enfeites de penas, a ornamentação das orelhas, o tembetá de quartzo com "botão" na extremidade inferior e os outros ornamentos labiais, a máscara de madeira com penas, a máscara trançada em forma de funil, o ritual de passagem para a maioridade em forma de dança individual do "iniciando," como prova de resistência, e os grupos de comer, distinguem aquêles Tupi de tôdas as outras tribos.

O complexo do tamankurá, a instituição da "criança preferida," a pintura do "iniciando" e seu corte de cabelo, e o costume do cesto de carga ser levado pelo homem e não pela mulher, liga-os aos Karajá. A forma da casa, a sepultura dentro desta, a rêde de dormir, o alto grau de sua lavoura, a importância da mandioca e as diversas formas de sua preparação e consumo, o complexo do *cauî*, a ligação de sêres sobrenaturais, chamados *topŷ*, com o trovão, e, principalmente, a língua, caracterizam-nos como Tupi. Não usam, porém, o tipiti. A diferença talvez mais significativa entre os Tapirapé e os Tupinambá está no padrão de comportamento tribal com suas influências sôbre as diversas esferas da cultura, padrão êsse que era, entre os antigos Tupi do litoral, o do guerreiro, e é, entre os Tapirapé, o do pacífico lavrador. Costume singular, porém, que não se pode enquadrar no comportamento de tribo tìpicamente lavradora, que também distingue os Tapirapé dos Tupinambá e os aproxima de tribos caça-

311

doras, de vida pouco sedentária, é a prática do infanticídio, não deixando o casal tapirapé, viver mais de três de seus filhos e mais de dois do mesmo sexo. A disposição circular das casas da aldeia tapirapé é encontrada também entre os vizinhos gê. Pertencem o arco e a emplumação da flecha, dos Tapirapé, aos tipos chamados por Meyer de "brasileiro oriental." Sua clava redonda e sua lança talvez provenham da cultura karajá. Usam ambos os tipos de moquém estabelecidos por Nordenskiöld. A conservação do têrmo tupi para panela faz supor provir de tempos remotos seu conhecimento de cerâmica. Seu fuso pertence ao "tipo bakairi" da classificação de Frödin e Nordenskiöld. Seu cesto de carga foi incluido por Nordenskiöld, assim como o dos Karajá, no "tipo guarayú," apesar das notáveis diferenças de feitio entre êsses cestos e outros incorporados ao mesmo grupo, como, por exemplo, os das tribos dos formadores do Xingu. Especialidade tapirapé não encontrada, atualmente, entre os seus vizinhos, nem mencionada do Xingu, ou de qualquer outra tribo tupi, são os pequenos cestos de fundo mais ou menos quadrado e bôca redonda. Aliás, o ramo mais importante da indústria tapirapé é a fabricação de trançados, sendo representados todos os três grupos principais em que Max Schmidt dividiu os trançados sul-americanos.

Pelo fato de praticarem couvade, os Tapirapé se parecem não só com os Tupinambá e outros Tupi, mas também com os Karajá, Kayapó e habitantes da parte superior da bacia do Xingu.

A divisão em metades tribais evidenciada por Wagley talvez revele influência gê. Aliás, Lipkind (275) menciona "Moiety" dos Karajá.

O complexo das danças de máscaras, que representa um dos aspectos mais característicos tanto da cultura tapirapé como da cultura karajá, mostra não só grandes semelhanças entre essas culturas, mas também profundas diferenças, havendo, além disso, certos traços tapirapé parecidos com traços dos Tupi do alto Xingu.

Em resumo podemos dizer: a cultura tapirapé é uma cultura tupi que apresenta mais semelhanças com a dos Tupinambá do que com as de outros Tupi até agora conhecidas ou com qualquer outra cultura. Distingue-se, porém, da cultura tupinambá em numerosos aspectos. Pelos prolongados contactos com a cultura karajá desenvolveu parentesco chegado com ela, sendo as diferenças conservadas devidas, na maior parte, a traços tìpicamente tupi. Muito menor é o parentesco com os vizinhos setentrionais, isto é, os Kayapó, embora haja importantes traços similares. Enquanto os Tapirapé tiveram com esta tribo contactos diretos, se bem que geralmente hostis, não se sabe de nenhuma espécie de contactos imediatos com os Akué-Chavante, seus vizinhos ao sul. O que conhecemos da cultura dêstes Gê, mostra-a como sendo ainda mais diversa da cultura tapirapé do que o é a cultura kayapó. As tribos da parte superior da bacia do Xingu, embora se pareçam com os Tapirapé em alguns traços culturais, falando duas delas línguas tupi, distinguem-se tanto dessa tribo da bacia do Araguaia e em aspectos tão importantes, que elas devem ser consideradas culturalmente muito mais afastadas dela do que o são os Karajá e até os Kayapó. Por outro lado, não é possível falar em "província etnográfica do Araguaia" no mesmo sentido em que se falou em "província etnográfica" com referência à área dos formadores do Xingu. Não há, ao que eu saiba, nenhum traço cultural comum a tôdas as tribos da bacia do Araguaia comparável, por sua função caracterizadora, à pequenina peça de indumentária feminina, que permitiu a Eduardo Galvão (134) denominar "área do uluri"a região compreendida entre os rios Batovi e Culuene. Além disso, esta parte da bacia do Xingu apresenta, apesar das diferenças lingüísticas e de algumas especializações industriais dentro dela, homogeneidade cultural predominante, ao passo que entre as culturas do Araguaia prevalecem, relativamente, as diferenças. A cultura tapirapé, como aliás tôdas as culturas vizinhas, a oeste, norte e sul, possui, ainda, traços que não têm similares em qualquer outra cultura.

CACHIMBOS TUPIS-GUARANIS DE PIRASSUNUNGA

Manuel Pereira de Godói

I. CACHIMBO ANGULAR, FIG. 2, *A–D*)

Localidade.—Encontrado na própria Cachoeira de Emas, numa poça com água, areia e cascalhos, excavada na rocha diabásica, que forma uma grande corredeira no Rio Mogi Guassu; no mapa representada sob o número 1 (Fig. 1).

FIG. 1.—Mapa do município de Pirassununga, Estado de São Paulo, Brasil, com a distribuição de cachimbos.

Tipo.—Angular; *sub-tipo:* de porta-boquilha curta, conforme Serrano (426, 29). Ainda, de acôrdo com Serrano (426, 32–33), possue secções circulares e, tanto na base do porta-boquilha, como no corpo do fornilho, acréscimos em forma anelar com entalhes paralelos.

Morfologia.—Quanto às medidas a descrição poderá ser conferida com o diagrama da Fig. 2, *D*.

314

Fornilho.—Altura 30 mm.; larguras da bôca 18 e 21 mm., como mostra a Fig. 2, *C*, pois a bôca do fornilho é irregular nos seus diâmetros. As paredes internas não são perfeitas quanto às medidas e ao pulimento que parece ter sido executado com uma pequena espátula de madeira.

Corpo do fornilho.—Paredes algo grossas por causa do anel de refôrço; a mais larga mede 12,5 mm. O anel de refôrço possue sulcos paralelos verticais e hori-

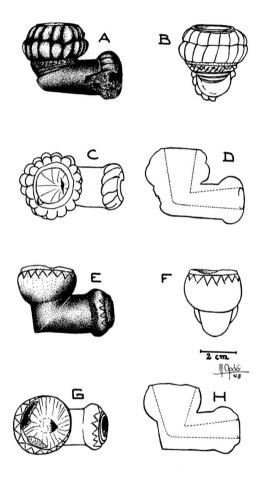

FIG. 2.—*A–D:* Cachimbo angular de argila; procedência: Cachoeira de Emas. *E–H:* Cachimbo angular de argila; procedência: Balsa. *A e E*, vista lateral; *B e F*, vista do corpo do fornilho; *C e G*, vista do fornilho e do porta-boquilha; *D e H*, diagrama.

zontais, assimétricos, o que contribue para a assimetria do conjunto esculpido. Nota-se que os sulcos verticais foram traçados primeiro com o auxílio de um estilete de madeira talvez, e os horizontais, que dividem o refôrço em 32 saliências retangulares, foram feitos com a extremidade circular de um pauzinho que tinha um provável diâmetro de 1,3 mm. Os sulcos horizontais são irregulares na direção e profundidade; o mesmo acontece com os verticais.

Logo abaixo das saliências retangulares há uma cinta com largura irregular, que varia de 5 a 0,4 mm. Nesta cinta há sulcos em forma de X e de traços oblíquos, feitos com estiletes com pontas grossas e finas. Os sulcos ora se aprofundam na argila, ora são superficiais e foram feitos desharmônicamente. Em seguida, no final do corpo do fornilho, aparecem mais duas cintas, irregulares na forma, não completam a volta e são lisas.

Porta-boquilha.—Comprimento 44,5 mm.; larguras 18,5 e 25,5 mm. Os diâmetros do mesmo são variáveis. As paredes externas são pulidas, porém com superfície algo irregular e de grossuras variáveis: de 3,3 a 8,5 mm. Na base existe um anel de refôrço: comprimento 11,8 mm.; largura (só do anel) 3,4 mm. Este possui sulcos quase paralelos e que dão um aspecto de rosca ao anel.

Os sulcos foram feitos com estiletes e ora são superficiais, ora mais profundos e, ainda, cada secção do anel foi alisada no sentido circular e as secções são desharmônicas, pois, os sulcos não são equidistantes e nem traçados, rigorosamente, numa direção. Rematando o acabamento do anel existem dois sulcos, feitos com estilete: um para o lado do corpo do fornilho, bem junto do bordo do anel e outro na base do porta-boquilha, como se pode notar na Fig. 2, *C*, quase circular, traço superficial, circundando a bôca da chaminé. Parte do porta-boquilha e do anel de refôrço estão fragmentados, Fig. 2, *A*, o que permite um melhor estudo da argila e da pouca perfeição do trabalho: existe um orifício, proveniente da falta de homogeneidade da massa e que se comunica com a chaminé, na sua parte inferior, 16 mm. à partir da base da mesma. Todavia, quando o cachimbo era perfeito e estava em uso, tal orifício não prejudicava o ato de fumar, pois, não deveria se comunicar com o exterior.

Boquilha.—Usada e geralmente de madeira que desapareceu com o tempo.

Chaminé.—Cônica e feita com um instrumento, provàvelmente de madeira, de forma idêntica e suas paredes são bem pulidas. A bôca da chaminé não é perfeitamente circular; talvez defeito causado pelo trabalho do oleiro.

No fundo do fornilho e início da chaminé podemos notar a má técnica de pulimento, em virtude da deficiência de meios próprios; assim se a reconhece pelos sulcos da extremidade do instrumento que abriu a chaminé.

Material.—Argila isenta de pedregulhinhos, de areias grossa e de pauzinhos; massa quase homogênia, havendo falhas, pois, há espaços no interior da massa, causados pela deficiência de trabalho.

Após a feitura o cachimbo foi submetido à ação do fogo e curioso: as paredes laterais, no sentido fornilho-chaminé, estão enegrecidas pelo calor menos direto, sinal de queima irregular; as partes restantes apresentam coloração mais clara, índice de fogo direto, quando se procedeu a queima do cachimbo. A mesma técnica aparece para a queima do cachimbo da Fig. 2, *E–H*, o que vem provar que os cachimbos se mantinham numa mesma posição durante o ressecamento pelo fogo.

Pêso.—55,5 gr.

II. CACHIMBO ANGULAR, FIG. 2, *E–H*

Localidade.—Encontrado no leito do Rio Mogi Guassu na passagem denominada Balsa, em extração de areia e pedregulho (149, 38–39).

Tipo.—Angular; *sub-tipo:* de porta-boquilha curta.

Morfologia.—Quanto às medidas a descrição poderá ser conferida pelo diagrama da Fig. 2, *H*.

Fornilho.—Altura 28 mm.; largura na bôca 24,2 mm.; na base 8,5 mm. Cônico e quase perfeito. As paredes internas são bem pulidas e apresentam um acabamento melhor do que o cachimbo anterior e dão a idéia de que foram alisadas com uma diminuta espátula.

Corpo do fornilho.—Paredes grossas em virtude do anel de refôrço; a mais larga mede 8 mm. O anel de refôrço possue um sulco, traçado 2,6 mm. abaixo do bordo do corpo do fornilho, feito com estilete e pouco profundo. Marginando êste sulco há uma cercadura em forma de linha quebrada, construída com um estilete, pouco profunda e não muito regular. Formam-se, assim, figuras de triângulos com a base voltada para cima. O corpo do fornilho é mais bojudo de um lado, Fig. 2, *E*, o que lhe dá assimetria.

A sua parte inferior, lisa e menos larga, acompanha a grossura do portaboquilha, Fig. 2, *F;* termina em ângulo quase reto e não em curva como a fig. 2 *D*. O seu bordo está fragmentado em dois lugares; observa-se, então, o processo de queima e o interior da massa: duas pequenas paredes laterais claras e o interior negro, mostrando a argila que não se queimou bem.

Porta-boquilha.—Comprimento 43 mm.; larguras 20 e 25 mm.; os diâmetros são variáveis. As paredes externas são bem regulares e pulidas; grossura variando de 6,4 a 8,5 mm. Na base há um anel de refôrço: comprimento 10,5 mm. e largura (só do anel) 3,8 mm.; nesta, como se pode notar na Fig. 2, *G*, há um círculo, sulcado com um pauzinho e que circunda a bôca da chaminé. Circundando êste círculo, do mesmo modo como se apresenta no corpo do fornilho, há uma cercadura, sulcada em forma de pequenos triângulos, um colocado ao lado do outro, porém, não muito ordenadamente. O bordo da chaminé, base do portaboquilha, é bem feito, tem 3 mm. de largura e é circular.

Boquilha.—Usada e geralmente de madeira que desapareceu com o tempo.

Chaminé.—Comprimento 29 mm.; larguras 6 e 10,5 mm. Cônica, feita com um instrumento, talvez de madeira, de forma igual e suas paredes são perfeitas e pulidas. Olhando-se o fundo do fornilho pela base da chaminé é possível ver uma *luz* quase circular, prova da amplitude do fornilho, Fig. 2, *H;* caso contrário, Fig. 2, *D*. há pouca *luz*. Bôca circular. No fundo do fornilho e início da chaminé podemos notar a técnica do trabalho e algo de irregular naquelas superfícies, deixado pelos instrumentos que serviram para tal trabalho.

Material.—Argila isenta de pedregulhinhos, de areia grossa e de pauzinhos. Massa homogênia e bem trabalhada. O cachimbo foi queimado e apresenta as partes laterais, sentido fornilho-chaminé, enegrecidas, sinal de queima irregular, fato êsse mencionado na descrição do cachimbo anterior.

O que distingue êste cachimbo dos outros dois mencionados é o pulimento perfeito das suas partes externas e a presença de um verniz que o torna brilhante.

Pêso.—31,8 gr.

III. CACHIMBO TUBULAR CURVADO, FIG. 3, *A–D*

Localidade.—Encontrado em terrenos de cultura na Fazenda do Snr. Fontanari, cêrca de 2 km. distante de Cachoeira de Emas, quase superficialmente, num local que há vários anos vem sendo arado; fragmentado e reconstruído em parte.

Tipo.—Tubular; *sub-tipo:* cônico; *variedade:* curvado.

Morfologia.—A Fig. 3, *D* mostra o diagrama total do cachimbo. A reconstrução do porta-boquilha foi feita com critério; tomei por base a curvatura do

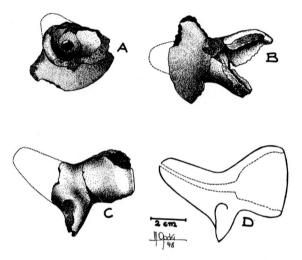

FIG. 3.—Cachimbo tubular curvado de argila; procedência: Fazenda Fontanari. *A*, vista do fornilho; *B*, vista do corpo do fornilho e alça; *C*, reconstrução do porta-boquilha; *D*, diagrama.

seu início, a convergência das linhas do cachimbo e as linhas de fratura. Portanto, o autor pode se referir à Fig. 3, *D* quanto às medidas.

Fornilho.—Altura 29 mm.; largura maior na bôca 31 mm., Fig. 3, *A;* na base, que é arredondada, 10 mm. As paredes internas são bem pulidas e foram alisadas com uma pequena espátula e, com certeza, com as extremidades dos dedos do oleiro.

Corpo do fornilho.—Paredes não muito grossas; medidas: próximos dos bordos 3,5 mm.; da base 7 mm. Bem pulido externamente e sem ornamentação e é mais bojudo, simètricamente, no sentido do comprimento da alça, Fig. 3, *B*. Perto do bordo se torna mais bojudo em tôda a extensão, o que determina a curvatura do bordo para o fornilho, Fig. 3, *B* e *D*. Bordo arredondado e com 2 mm. de largura. Distinto aspecto de funil.

Porta-boquilha.—Comprimento 43 mm.; largura maior 21 mm. e, gradativamente, diminue, Fig. 3, *D*, para ser introduzida na bôca do fumante ou, talvez, numa narina para inhalação nasal. Superfícies das partes presentes pulidas irregularmente e sem ornamentação.

Boquilha.—Talvez fôsse usada, pois, para êsse tipo de cachimbo o portaboquilha servia de boquilha.

Chaminé.—Curva, como mostram as figuras; comprimento 43 mm.; largura no início 5,5 mm.; já na parte fragmentada do porta-boquilha com 3,7 mm. e, provàvelmente, na base deve terminar com 2 mm. Foi construída em sentido diverso do eixo do fornilho, é excêntrica e oval; as medidas se referem aos diâmetros maiores. Suas paredes são irregulares e deve ter sido feita com um pauzinho.

Alça.—Curva e fragmentada, Fig. 3, *B* e *C;* comprimento 46,8 mm.; largura máxima 19,5 mm.; espessura máxima 14,5 mm. É um pouco convexa para o lado do corpo do fornilho e côncava para o do porta-boquilha; paredes lisas. Esta técnica de construção se justifica para a ocasião do uso do cachimbo, pois, então o dedo médio se colocava sôbre a parte convexa, o indicador no lado oposto, sôbre o início do porta-boquilha e o polegar se adaptava perfeitamente na parte côncava. Hoje, ao se repetir esta maneira, se nota uma grande estabilidade e fácil manêjo. Foi adaptada ao corpo do fornilho quando o cachimbo estava sendo modelado e foi pré-fabricada em forma de meia-lua; pode-se notar a técnica de fusão de argila da alça com a do cachimbo. As extremidades eram livres e deveriam ser arredondadas, pois, estão quebradas. Está colocada diametralmente oposta ao sentido do eixo fornilho-chaminé e não possue perfuração ou qualquer sinal que evidencie que o cachimbo possuísse um cordel que permitia ao dono trazê-lo no pescoço.

Material.—Argila tendo em mistura areia, pedregulhinhos, pauzinhos, carvão moído e em pedacinhos; o maior dêstes, visível na superfície superior da alça, mede 3,8 mm. de comprimento. Essa mistura é visível em todo o cachimbo, o que dá um aspecto heterogênio à massa. O cachimbo foi queimado, mas imperfeitamente, pois, se nota manchas escuras no corpo do fornilho, no portaboquilha e na alça.

Pêso.—24,8 gr.

IV. VALOR ETNOGRÁFICO

Nos dez anos de pesquisas pude encontrar sòmente êstes três cachimbos no município de Pirassununga, em terrenos que serviram de habitação aos extintos painguás.

Alguns autores acham que o cachimbo angular não pertence à cultura tupi-guarani pré-colombiana. Acreditam que viajantes da época dos descobrimentos e depois os escravos africanos trouxeram para cá o cachimbo angular e, desde então, tal peça cerâmica se aculturou, sendo fabricada e usada pelos tupis-guaranis. Sôbre esta questão vários autores comentam; o último dêles, Ott (353, pp. 29–41) cita às páginas 38 do seu trabalho as seguintes declarações que vêm corroborar o meu ponto de vista, isto é, o cachimbo angular é elemento cultural ameríndio: "Aliás, hoje em dia, já se admite que, embora o cachimbo angular entre algumas tribos indígenas brasileiras remonte à influência européia, entre outros aborígenes, constitui um elemento cultural puramente ameríndio." Uma das provas apresentdas por Ott (353, p. 38, Figs. 52–54) e decisiva é o encontro de cachimbos angulares em Santarém, Estado do Pará, caindo, dêsse modo, uma teoria que afirmava o desconhecimento do uso do cachimbo no vale do Amazonas pelos seus antigos habitantes indígenas.

Na América do Sul, sobretudo no Chile, já foram encontrados muitos cachimbos angulares, construídos e usados pelos ameríndios numa época bem anterior ao ano de 1500. Bullock (63, p. 148) apresenta vários cachimbos angulares encontrados em Freirinha, Taltal, Puerto Oliva e el Molle, norte do Chile, pertencentes à civilização Chincha-Atacamenha, que viveu entre os anos de 1100 a 1350 d.C. Em Janeiro de 1949 pude estudar 23 cachimbos angulares antigos das tribos chilenas, presentes na coleção etnográfica do Mueso Nacional de História Natural de Santiago, Chile, coletados no sul, centro e norte daquele país e que provam a presença dêles bem antes de 1500 na América do Sul. Graças à gentileza da Dra. Grete Mostny, arqueóloga do citado Museu, o autor obteve várias informações sôbre os mesmos e pôde desenhá-los; a Dra. Grete, para o futuro, irá publicar uma monografia sôbre tão interessantes artefatos de cerâmica e de pedra.

Creio que os cachimbos angulares de Pirassununga pertencem à cultura tupi; a técnica de construção, a forma, a maneira de queimar a argila e como esta se apresenta agora evidenciam o ponto de vista do autor e enriquecem a etnografia brasileira com dados valiosos para estudos futuros.

O cachimbo tubular curvado citado no presente trabalho é o primeiro encontrado na América do Sul. Já foram encontrados vários tipos de cachimbo tubular no Brasil; porém, como êste de alça não há referências, o que lhe dá maior valor e importância.

Serrano (426, p. 31) apresenta um cachimbo tubular, Fig. 4, A, encontrado em Boa Vista, município de São Lourenço, Rio Grande do Sul e Ott (353, p. 63), Fig. 4, B, outro, encontrado no sul da Bahia; ambos de argila.

Todavia, os dois cachimbos não possuem alça, o que destaca bem o tubular de Pirassununga. Nos Estados Unidos muitas tribos fabricavam em pedra mais frequentemente cachimbos tubulares curvados e retos com alça perfurada, a fim de o fumante o trazer no pescoço com o auxílio de um cordel.

Heye (178, pp. 36–37, Figs. 20–22) estuda a cerâmica do sul da California e apresenta vários cachimbos tubulares curvados e retos com alça; todos êles encontrados em urnas funerárias. Gentilmente o *Museum of the American Indian* de New York me ofereceu duas fotografias de cachimbos tubulares feitos em pedra (steatite), um curvado e outro reto; ambos da California, Figs. 5 e 6. Possuem alça perfurada, mas esta está colocada no sentido do eixo fornilho-chaminé, o que se justifica numa construção de pedra. A alça do cachimbo de Pirassununga está colocada opostamente à direção indicada.

V. RESUMO

O autor descreve três cachimbos de argila, encontrados em Pirassununga, Estado de São Paulo, Brasil, nos locais onde viveram os extintos painguás, uma tribo tupi-guarani. Dois cachimbos são angulares com porta-boquilha curta e

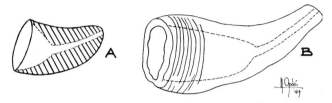

FIG. 4.—*A*, Cachimbo tubular curvado de argila; procedência: Boa Vista, município de São Lourenço, Rio Grande do Sul, seg. Serrano.

FIG. 5.—Cachimbo tubular curvado de pedra; material: steatite; procedência: Point Dume, Los Angeles, California.

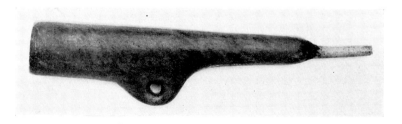

FIG. 6.—Cachimbo tubular reto de pedra com boquilha de osso; material: steatite; procedência: Goleta Slough, Santa Barbara, California.

o terceiro é tubular, curvado e com alça sem perfuração. Os dois primeiros estão completos e o último está fragmentado.

O autor acha que o cachimbo angular é cultura ameríndia e era conhecido na América antes de 1500, época dos descobrimentos.

O cachimbo tubular curvado de Pirassununga é muito importante para a etnografia americana, sobretudo para o Brasil, pois, é o primeiro mencionado na nossa literatura e possue uma alça.

Nos Estados Unidos são conhecidos cachimbos tubulares curvados e retos de pedra com alça perfurada e muito semelhantes ao de Pirassununga.

VI. SUMMARY

The author describes three pottery pipes of Pirassununga, state of São Paulo, Brazil, found where lived the extinct Painguá, a Tupi-Guaraní tribe. Two pipes are angular with a short pipe holder, and one is tubular, curved, and with no perforated flange. The first two are complete, and the last is fragmentary.

The author believes that the angular pipe is an object of Amerindian culture, and was known in America before 1500, the time of discovery.

The tubular curved pipe of Pirassununga is very important to American ethnography, especially to Brazil, since it is the first cited in our literature, and it possesses a flange.

Tubular curved, and straight stone pipes with perforated flange, very similar to the tubular pipe of Pirassununga, are known in the United States.

LOS POBLADORES HISTÓRICOS DE LA REGIÓN DIAGUITA

Antonio Serrano

En el occidente sud-americano florecieron un sinnúmero de manifestaciones culturales vinculadas todas ellas a una cultura básica general, la cultura andina cuyos portadores corresponden a la llamada raza ándida.

Muchas de éstas manifestaciones culturales bajo influencias políticas, religiosas, sociales o simplemente económicas adquirieron una fuerte y definida personalidad como la Tiahuanacota, la nazca, la santamariana, la barreal. En los cuadros arqueológicos las ubicamos como culturas.

Corresponden a núcleos étnicos de los cuales a veces estamos bastante bien informados a través de cronistas y viajeros. En otros casos son anteriores a la conquista y su conocimiento es puramente de origen arqueológico. Algunas persisten hasta nuestros días, transformadas y aculturadas por el contacto con los europeos y aun de otros valores indígenas.

Para nosotros todas estas manifestaciones culturales, llámese así o simplemente culturas, integran una gran civilización a la que en otra oportunidad hemos llamado civilización andina.

La antigua escuela argentina no concebía el estudio de las manifestaciones culturales andinas de nuestro territorio sino como desprendimientos o dependencias de las Perú-bolivianas. Hoy vemos claro que las nuestras como las del territorio perú-boliviano, y más allá las del Ecuador y Colombia, deben ser consideradas en el mismo plano, es decir, como unidades dentro de la civilización andina. Estas unidades son más o menos antiguas, más o menos influenciadas por las vecinas, o las que le precedieron, y aun influenciadas por culturas no andinas especialmente en las zonas periféricas.

Ignoramos de donde han llegado, como y cuando los elementos básicos de la cultura andina. No han ganado simultáneamente todo el territorio andino, sino que en forma paulatina a través de siglos y siglos, fueron expandiéndose a medida que se gestaban formas locales o regionales.

Las evidentes concordancias que descubrimos entre muchas de ellas pueden provenir del fondo común o de mutuas relaciones posteriores.

Lo urgente en América es concretar todas las formas culturales posibles, luego eliminar los denominadores comunes del fondo básico y entonces deducir en base de los elementos locales o regionales, cuáles son los que definen verdaderas culturas y cuales las relaciones de tiempo y espacio de éstas.

Por eso nos place el reciente trabajo discriminatorio realizado por Bennett y dos de sus discípulos sobre el noroeste argentino, no por sus resultados, inad-

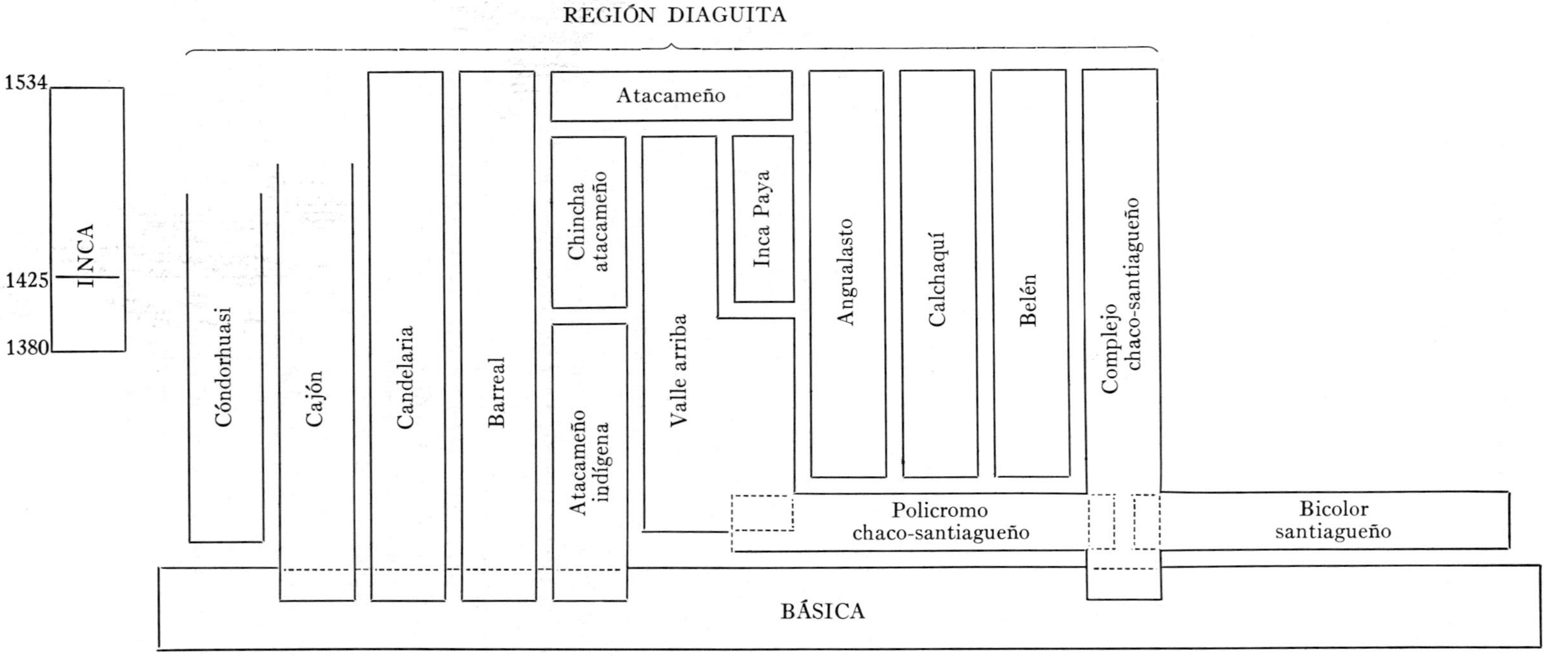

REGIÓN DIAGUITA

Cóndorhuasi

Cajón

Candelaria

Barreal

Atacameño indígena

Chincha atacameño

Atacameño

Valle arriba

Inca Paya

Angualasto

Calchaquí

Belén

Complejo chaco-santiagueño

Policromo chaco-santiagueño

Bicolor santiagueño

BÁSICA

INCA

1534

1425

1380

Fig. 1

misibles en varios de sus puntos finales, sino por el método y el planteamiento del problema.

En la región conocida históricamente como dominio de los diaguitas florecieron varias formas locales que integran en su mayoría las tres mejor caracterizadas de nuestras culturas del noroeste: la santamariana, la barreal y la angualasto. Mejor sería emplear el término de "área" y no de "cultura" porque es evidente que si muchas de las formas que las integran son contemporáneas entre sí, como variantes locales de tribus, otras deben considerarse de cronología distinta.

La alfarería con sus estilos decorativos constituyen el índice discriminatorio de más alto valor. El estudio seriado de estos estilos nos evidencian derivaciones de otros estilos preexistentes o vinculaciones colaterales, con estilos o culturas de la propia región diaguita o de regiones vecinas, tales como Inka o Atacameño en el sentido de Uhle y Kroeber, o Arica en el sentido de Bird.

En muy pocos casos se han constatado superposiciones en el terreno, los que sólo sirven por ahora a ensayos puramente locales.

Las circunstancias señaladas son las únicas que por el momento nos permiten el ensayo de una cronología. Nuestro ensayo toma como base el paso de los españoles por la región, esto en 1534, y el contacto con los incas que fijamos, en 1425. Podrá observarse las relaciones de todas las formas definidas por estilos cerámicos. La Cóndorhuasi, Candelaria, Barreal, Atacameño indígena y parte del complejo chaco santiagueño entroncan en el horizonte básico que admitimos no sólo para la región diaguita, sino para todo el noroeste argentino. Lo consideramos muy antiguo, de alfarerías sin pintar, pero al cual le preceden sin embargo formas culturales muy primitivas, sin alfarería, de instrumentos líticos tallados. Es el hipotético período del salvajismo de Uhle al cual sin duda corresponde el material tallado de los llanos de Catamarca recogidos recientemente por una misión de estudio de la Universidad de Córdoba.

Con el aporte venido de afuera se desarrollan formas culturales bien individualizadas entre sí por los diferentes estilos de su alfarería pintada y la transformación de la básica en estilo como el Candelaria y el propio barreal grabado.

Muchas de estas formas culturales son las que llegan hasta los tiempos históricos como patrimonio de los núcleos que pasaremos a reseñar.

Si bien no nos ocuparemos aquí del problema cronológico reproduciremos nuestro cuadro todavía sujeto a rectificaciones.

La voz diaguita es empleada hoy como gentilicio genérico para designar a los indígenas que a la llegada de los españoles poblaban todo el valle Calchaquí, casi toda Catamarca con su valle de Santa María que es prolongación del Calchaquí, casi toda La Rioja y el norte de San Juan desde el río Jachal.

Para los primeros conquistadores y misioneros todos estos indígenas eran "diaguitas" pero de preferencia hacían uso de gentilicios locales o regionales.

Es evidente que el elemento cultural que servía a los españoles para esta generalización fué el idioma. Se vé claro que para ellos eran diaguitas todos los que hablaban el kakan.

En el mapa adjunto ubicamos los grupos tribales tal como surgen de la documentación histórica. No se trata de los gentilicios que designan a los ocupantes de una aldea, sino a núcleos mayores, por lo general ocupantes de un valle, y es precisamente el "valle" un concepto jurisdiccional y político entre los diaguitas. Sotelo Narváez (1582) refiriéndose a ellos dice "porque aunque tienen caciques y es gente que los respeta son behetrías que no hay más señores en Cada Pueblo o Valle y son muchos Valles y Pueblos pequeños."

Como en general un valle era designado con el nombre de uno de sus pueblos, quizás el asiento del cacique principal, resulta que el gentilicio mayor es igual al de este pueblo, que en muchos casos no es un gentilicio sino un simple toponimio y entre otros el propio nombre de aquel cacique.

No todas las unidades tribales tienen la misma jerarquía numérica y territorial. Aun más, hay gentilicios que incluyen más de una parcialidad como el de calchaquí, capayán, nonogasta.

La independencia de los núcleos tribales ha creado modalidades culturales fácilmente perceptible por el arqueólogo dentro de las formas culturales fundamentales. El propio idioma presentaba formas dialectales anotadas por misioneros.

Los desplazamientos pre o post históricos han creado superposiciones culturales locales, que no pueden tomarse como base para una cronología general del territorio, mientras ellos no se presenten repetidamente.

Los diaguitas pueden ser estudiados en cinco grandes secciones: la septentrional, la central, la meridional, la sud-oriental y la oriental.

En general hay una cierta concordancia entre los núcleos así agrupados y las formas culturales que territorialmente le corresponden.

LOS NÚCLEOS SEPTENTRIONALES

El límite septentrional de los diaguitas puede fijarse en la ciudad prehistórica de La Paya, evidente reducto incásico donde se constata la presencia de por lo menos cuatro manifestaciones culturales: la incásica, la atacameña, la santamariana y la regional de la quebrada del Toro también representada en La Poma. Hay tipos de cerámica que parecen exclusivos y característicos de esta parte del sector norte, como los llamados vasos libatorios y la decoración de los pucos con serpientes de grandes óvalos acompañadas muchas veces por series de triángulos aflecados (llamados "manos"). Este tipo de decoración se vincula aparentemente con motivos predominantes en la cerámica de Santiago del Estero.

Más al sur de La Paya a lo largo del valle Calchaquí las manifestaciones culturales se hacen más uniformes y son de tipo santamariano. Es el tipo de cultura que corresponde a todo el territorio ocupado por los núcleos septentrionales.

LOS PULARES

Se considera a los pulares como la sección más septentrional de los diaguitas. Ocupaban el valle Calchaquí y algunas de sus quebradas orientales hacia Salta.

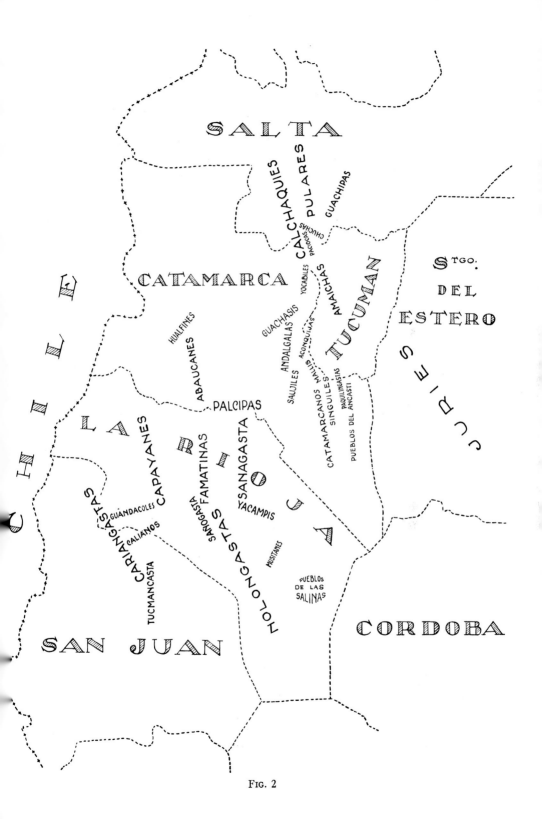

FIG. 2

Su límite sur era la quebrada de los tolombones. Gonzalo de Abreu, en 1577 al hablar del asiento de Salamanao, que quedaba al pie de aquella quebrada dice que estaba "junto a la fuerza de los naturales de un cabo calchaquí chumbicha y otros chiquana pulares y otros muchos de la otra. . . ."

Hablaban la lengua *Kakan*. En los documentos están bien individualizados con respecto a los calchaquíes con los cuales sabían estar de guerra.

Eran pulares además de los así designados, los del pueblo de Escoipe, de Cachi, Pichijao, y Chicoana. Chicoana lo formaban varias parcialidades, entre ellas las de Tupisa y Locloc. Lozano informa que hacia el segundo cuarto del siglo XVII los pulares comprendían ocho pueblos.

El asiento de Chicoana, punto importante en el itinerario de los conquistadores no puede estar en Molinos o sus alrededores, como lo hemos sostenido en nuestro volumen sobre los "Comechingones." Atilio Cornejo con buenos argumentos combate esta tesis, que también es de Levillier, para asentar que "si no estuvo en los valles de Colomé o de Tucuil, con mayor probabilidad, más arriba, en el Luracatao." Esta segunda proposición es más probable, como así también la sostenida por Boman al colocarla en Seclantés, en el mismo valle Calchaquí.

En nuestra opinión actual y tomando como base el itinerario del P. Diego Darío, y la carta de Velazco de 1585 donde dice que Chicoana es, viniendo de Salta, principio del valle y entrada a él, consideramos que estaba en las cercanías de Cachi.

Sugestivo es para una identificación de Chicoana con Cachi que el cacique D. Bartolomé, que se mantuvo fiel a los españoles, figura como del pueblo de Chicoana.

El dominio del cacique Calchaquí no parece que se extendía a través del valle Calchaquí, más al norte de Molinos. Esta sección estaba ocupada por pulares mientras que el dominio de aquel cacique continuaba a través del valle subsidiario de Luracatao. Los tolombones, que era la tribu de Juan de Calchaquí eran "confinantes" de los pulares, según lo afirma el P. Lozano.

LOS GUACHIPAS

Los guachipas eran los indígenas que ocupaban la quebrada de este nombre.

Hacia 1590 el capitán Juan Pedrero de Texo hizo una entrada al valle conquistándolos. Por él sabemos que eran muchos y muy belicosos, pero nada escrito encontramos que permita sospechar si los guachipas son o no diaguitas.

A fines del siglo XVII (1692) "una doctrina de la nación Calchaquí está [ba] asitiada en el valle de los Guachipas" y tenía por jurisdicción "catorce o qui[n]ce leguas caminado a la provincia hasta la estancia de la Pampa Grande" leemos en los documentos para la historia de la Virgen del Valle.

Arqueológicamente la zona de los guachipas, especialmente Pampa Grande se caracteriza por un substratum típicamente Candelaria. Sobre este substratum manifestaciones culturales de tipo santamariano, pero de modalidades propias.

De más hacia el valle de Calchaquí, propiamente de las inmediaciones del pueblo de Guachipas, conocemos algunas alfarerías que no responden a la decoración santamariana y que más bien parecen denunciar un nuevo estilo aunque con un cierto parentesco con La Poma.

Entre los pueblos calchaquíes llevados al valle de los Guachipas después del gran alzamiento, figuran los de Bombolan y Aminaná que por su ubicación en el valle les corresponde una modalidad estilística en sus urnas, que no es la típica y característica de Pampa Grande. Esta es propia de este sector y tendremos que admitir que corresponde a los guachipas si es que así se llamaban los diaguitas que en el siglo XVI ocupaban este valle. Estos diaguitas habrían desalojado a los primitivos habitantes de la región que por su cultura serían tonocotés o lules axios.

Un documento de 1632 que extracta Mons. Cabrera, referente a indios reducidos en Salta nombra a *lules guachipas*. ¿Serán éstos de los guachipas conquistados y encomendados a fines del siglo anterior por el capitán Pedrero Tesco?

LOS CALCHAQUÍES

El nombre de calchaquí con que generalmente son designados los indígenas del valle de este nombre y su continuación meridional, el de Santamaría o Yocabil, proviene según los historiadores coloniales de un cacique que por su valentía y espíritu guerrero se hizo famoso. Se trata de Juan de Calchaquí, cacique principal de los tolombones. Sea por vinculación de sangre o por dominación militar este cacique se convierte en cacique general de los pueblos diaguitas al norte de su valle. No ejercía dominio sobre los pulares, pero sí sobre los pueblos de la quebrada de Luracatao.

Es posible que en un principio no ejerciese dominio sobre los diaguitas al sur de los tolombones y quilmes porque algunos documentos hablan de yocabiles y calchaquíes como de cosas distintas. Lo cierto es que alrededor de este cacique y luego de sus sucesores se aglutinan pueblos vecinos que van a confundirse con el denominativo de Calchaquíes. Los propios *chicoanas* son considerados en algunos documentos como calchaquíes y la parte de amaichas retirados al valle huyendo de sus encomenderos, llamados calchaquí-amaichas.

Con todo consideramos conveniente restringir el nombre de calchaquí para los diaguitas al norte de Santa María es decir a los dependientes del cacicazgo general con asiento en los tolombones.

Como calchaquíes consideramos pues a los quilmes, tolombones, cafayates, luracataos, chuchagastas, sichagasta, tuquigastas (Tacuil o Tacuivil).

LOS TOLOMBONES

Los *tolombones* ocupaban el centro mismo del valle. Era núcleo importante y asiento del Cacique Juan Calchaquí. En los documentos jesuíticos se los llama también *paciocas*. Parcialidades de este núcleo eran los colalaos, tolombones y paciocas.

Según Lozano, el nombre provendría de Tolomba, nombre del valle que ocupaban.

Si bien el antiguo asiento de los tolombones integra el área tipicamente santamariana y los vestigios dominantes corresponden a esta cultura, es frecuente allí la presencia de abundantes alfarerías pertenecientes al característico tipo del valle del Cajón, al oeste del de Calchaquí.

LOS QUILMES

Los quilmes, han sido considerados como una de las tribus más belicosas del valle calchaquí. Según el P. Lozano, vinieron de Chile para no sujetarse a los peruanos, emparentándose con los calchaquíes y convirtiéndose con el tiempo en una parcialidad importante de ellos.

En su antiguo territorio además de la alfarería típicamente santamariana y alguna poca barreal, es frecuente el hallazgo dè alfarerías que corresponde al tipo Candelaria, o a la dominante en el valle del Cajón. No aparecen en cambio piezas que sugieran un indicio de vinculación con las culturas chilenas. Pero para el tiempo de Lozano las provincias de Cuyo eran también parte de Chile. De ahí que algunos autores piensen que estos indios hayan emigrado de la región de Cuyo hacia el valle Calchaquí. Mons. Cabrera por ejemplo, busca su posible origen en los *quilmiquischa* pueblo descubierto en el valle de Famatina por el fundador de la Rioja. Igual cosa piensa este autor de los acalianos en relación a los calianos del Río Bermejo.

LOS YOCABILES

Los yocabiles eran los indios que ocupaban el actual valle de Santa María. La primitiva población indígena de este pueblo se llamaba Encamaná, cuyo cacique hacia principios del siglo XVII era Utimba.

Utimba era también para entonces "cacique principal" del valle de Anguinahao lo que nos indica que yocabiles y anguinahaos deben ser considerados dentro del mismo núcleo.

Este valle estaba a tres leguas de Quilmes junto a Santa María. Entre los pueblos de yocabiles se contaban el de Calian, Angacho, Encamaná, Yocabil, Anguinahao, Guachingasta y Zampacha. No parece probable que el nombre genérico de Yocabil se aplicara en un principio a los núcleos meridionales del actual valle de Santa María (los *ingamaná* por ejemplo).

En 1662 los yocabiles serían unos 300 indios de pelea distribuídos en seis pueblos. Esto llevaría a un cálculo de apenas 1.500 almas.

En algunos documentos se hace expresa indicación de *calchaquíes y yocabiles*, como también de yocabiles y anguinahaos.

LOS AMAICHAS

Los amaichas constituyen sin duda alguna el núcleo más oriental de los diaguitas septentrionales. Ocupaban las faldas orientales del Aconquija, donde fueron conocidos con los nombres locales de *amaichas, anfamas, tafíes,* y *siam-*

bones. El nombre genérico de amaichas para todo este núcleo está expresamente consignado en documentos coloniales. Fueron reducidos muy al principio de la conquista y trasladados al pueblo de los Lules en Tucumán. Con los lules y solcos, que eran de diferente nación, se mezclaron aquí convirtiéndose en valiosos artesanos de carretas y en troperos.

LOS HUALFINES

Hacia fines del siglo XVI y principios del XVII los hualfines ocupaban el valle de este nombre en la provincia de Salta. Su asiento era Hualfingasta (también escrito Gualfingasta y Guassingasta) y Pulpabil. Todo hace pensar que estos hualfines salteños sean originarios de valle de Hualfin en Catamarca. Más aún, estos parecen ser parte de los indios advenedizos de Londres que los españoles encontraron en el valle calchaquí en son de guerra contra sus pobladores. Ramírez de Velasco en carta de 1588 dice que a 20 leguas de Chicoana encontró "una ranchería al parecer de hasta 400 indios [ad] benediços de los de Londres los quales estaban fortificados por la guerra que traen en calchaquí."

Atemorizados por las represalías de las autoridades españoles abandonan su quebrada salteña y van a ocupar su probable primitivo asiento, esto es el valle de Hualfin en Catamarca, lo que acontece alrededor del año 1640. Su presencia despierta el temor de abaucanes y otras parcialidades vecinas, y quizás esto haya sido la causa de su reaparición en Salta, pues en 1659 figuran nuevamente en la quebrada de Hualfin sembrando en los llanos vecinos de Angastaco.

LOS LURACATAOS

Ocupaban la quebrada de este nombre siendo su asiento Luracatao. Este pueblo estaba defendido por un fuerte, famoso en la época de la conquista, llamado Elencot.

LOS CHUSCHAS

Los chuschas estaban al norte de los tolombones. Sus dos más importantes asientos eran Chuschagastas y Cafallate.

LOS NÚCLEOS CENTRALES

El territorio de los núcleos centrales constituye el sector arqueológico más complejo de toda la región diaguita. Con todo predomina allí como forma cultural generalizada la barreal y en ciertos valles la de tipo Belen. En este sector está sin duda el centro de la cerámica tipo Condorhuasi y sus derivados; la de las urnas tipo Villavil, que parece constituír un desarrollo local de la angualasto. La matalurgia y el trabajo del tallado de la piedra alcanzan aquí su más alto desarrollo.

En la zona oriental de este territorio son frecuentes las cerámicas más típicas de la cultura chaco-santiagueña; especialmente en Adalgalá y los valles al norte de Catamarca. Por el Alto en el Ancaste y por el pucará del Aconquija, los pueblos de la llanura santiagueña mantendrían sus relaciones de intercambio con los núcleos centrales proveedores sin duda de las piezas metálicas que aparecen en sus yacimientos.

En este territorio estuvo originariamente la famosa provincia de la Zuraca, donde los incas explotaban minas.

En documentos coloniales, los españoles para distinguir estos núcleos centrales de los diaguitas de Calchaquí y La Rioja, los llamaban "diaguitas de Londres."

Si bien Londres fué fundado en le valle de Quimivil, se entendía por "valle de Londres" hacia 1607, segun se deduce de carta del capitán Gaspar Doncel los llanos de Belen, Pacipas y parte de Tinogasta. Entraban pues en esta designación los pacipas, los abaucanes.

Los pueblos de los "diaguitas de Londres" que cita Doncel son los siguientes: Malle, Pipanaco, Colpes, Pissapanaco, Sabuel, Xijan, Yuctava, Amoyamba, Pacipa, Orcagasta, Amangasta, Pituil, Paymogasta, Tinogasta, Quilmevid, Famaytil.

LOS ANDALGALÁS

Andalgalá constituía uno de los centros indígenas más importantes viniendo del valle de Calchaquí. Este núcleo daba nombre al valle, y a los pueblos vecinos tanto al norte como al sur, y cuyas ruinas se observan todavía. La cultura que aquí predomina es la de tipo barreal.

Fundado el fuerte de Andalgalá se redujeron a su alrededor una serie de tribus de varias partes de la jurisdicción del Tucumán, cuyos nombres se han mantenido en la toponimia, y las que por ocupar este valle se les confundía a partir de 1633 bajo el nombre genérico de *Andalgaláes*.

Pueblos que posiblemente constituyeron núcleos orientales de los andalgalás fueron los *aconquijas* y *mallis*.

El P. Larrouy con buenos argumentos sostiene que Conando fué el mismo Andalgalá.

LOS INDIOS DEL VALLE DE CATAMARCA

Los diaguitas que poblaban el antiguo valle de Catamarca no recibieron un nombre general. Sin embargo al referirse a su dialecto el P. Barzana lo llama "catamarcano" y un documento de 1594 referente a indios del sud este de La Rioja el de "capayan."

El antiguo valle de Catamarca era más amplio que el actual pues comprendía hacia el norte los pequeños valles de Paclin, Singuil y el Rodeo.

En el valle de Paclin estaban los pueblos de Paquilingasta, Yocangasta y Ocangasta.

En el de Singuil, Singuil, Colpes y Pomangasta.

LOS FAMATINAS

Los famatinas ocupaban el actual valle de este nombre. Según el título de repartimiento del fundador de La Rioja (1591) eran pueblos de este valle *Anquilpate, Quilacolquicha, Pohonogasta, Jungunigasta, Famatina, Anguinahao, Quimamalinja* y *Ambaragasta*.

La cultura que predomina en el valle es el tipo barreal. En Huaco, que evidentemente es una reducción, predominan dispersos fragmentos de cerámica de tipo Angualasto.

LOS CAPAYANES

Los capayanes constituían con los *mocaybiles* y *guandacoles* los grupos más sud occidentales de los diaguitas.

Por *capayanes* entendían los hombres de la conquista a los pueblos indios que se extendían al occidente del cordón del Famatina y al oriente de las sierras de Umango y Villa Unión, más el valle del Jagüel que según la expresión de Doncel en su carta de 1607 "está en el propio valle de los Capayanes."

No parece que los españoles de la primera Londres (1558) hayan tenido trato directo con los capayanes, no obstante que su territorio formaba parte de su jurisdicción y que el valle del Jagüel estaba en el camino a Copiapó, en Chile.

Ramirez de Velasco, fundador de La Rioja, intenta en 1588 desde Famatira donde se encontraba, entrar al valle de los capayanes. Por no haber paso o carecer de guías desistió de sus propósitos, pero lo cierto es que al fijar tres años más tarde los límites de la jurisdicción de la ciudad por él fundada, incluye explícitamente el valle de los capayanes. La conquista de este valle no es anterior al 1600, año que se propone realizarla el capitán Juan Bautista Muñoz "por lo mucho que importa que se vea y conquiste la gente del dicho valle de los capayanes y se descubran los minerales de oro y plata y todos metales de que se tiene noticias hay en el dicho valle y su comarca . . ." según se lee en actas capitulares de la ciudad de La Rioja.

Para 1607 había en los *capayanes* los siguientes pueblos: *Vinchina, Cocayambis, Sano, Acampis, Mocaybin, Dilaha, Anguinan, Cabuy,* y *Caguey.*

ABAUCANES

Los abaucanes vivían en el valle de este nombre, en la provincia de Catamarca. Además de los abaucanes que vivían en Tinogasta, y los *tinogastas*, serían abaucanes los indios de los pueblos du Batugasta, Fiambalá y Saujil.

LOS PACIPAS

Los *Pacipas* eran los diaguitas que ocupaban el valle del actual río Colorado, conocido por Valle Vicioso y también por el valle de los pacipas.

Cuando Gerónimo Luis de Cabrera pacifica este valle saca de él, según el P. Lozano, 1.200 almas. Se trata pues de un núcleo numeroso.

Entre sus pueblos se contaban además del de Pacipa los de Yuctava y Araupatis pero muy probablemente también los de Amoyamba, Orcagasta y Amangasta.

Todos estos pueblos formaban parte del llamado valle de Londres.

Cuando el gobernador Francisco de Aguirre lleva socorro a los españoles de Chile cruza el Valle Vicioso y le salen "muchos yindios e caciques diaguitas de paz."

LOS NÚCLEOS MERIDIONALES

LOS CARIANGASTAS

En el título que se le otorga en 1591 al fundador de San Juan; Juan Jufré, se le nombra teniente de gobernador y capitán general de las "provincias de Cuyo e Cariangasta, que por otro nombre se llama Tacuma y de Nolongasta y Famatina."

En el valle de Mocna estaba Tucumancasta. Calian era "apellido" del Río Bermejo y Cariangasta sin duda era el asiento o valle de los indios *calianos* o *galianos*. Su ubicación probable es a la entrada del valle de los capayanes y casi vecino a los guandacoles. Pero la provincia en sentido amplio debió ocupar toda la cuenca del Río Blanco hasta más al sur de Jachal y la del Bermejo. Un proceso contra indios que participaron en el levantamiento general de 1632, nos pone el corriente de algunos "apellidos" que evidentemente son nombre de tribus. Por ejemplo: Ahagasta en el valle de Angaco; en el Bermejo además de *Calian, Utunucasta, Quicha han, Sapujil, Amacasta.*

La cultura que predomina en el antiguo territorio de los cariangastas es del tipo angualasto.

LOS SAÑOGASTAS

Los sañogastas estaban al sur de La Rioja, en el pequeño valle llamado de Sañogasta porque éste era el más importante. Además de éste figuran en 1591, los pueblos de *Ampaccascha, Cavilanmipa* y *Sipisgasta.*

La cultura que aquí predomina es el tipo angualasto.

LOS MOCALINGASTAS

Según Lozano, los *mocalingastas* "era un gentío situada a las espaldas del valle calchaquí." Eran pacíficos y se dedicaban a la cría de ganado. En alguna oportunidad los del pueblo de Batungasta los asaltaron y robaron. Los calchaquíes apenas tenían vagas referencias de ellos.

Parece que estos mocalingasta de Lozano sean los mismos del pueblo de Mocaybin encomendados a Gaspar Doncel que escribía sobre ellos en 1607 "tiene indios de visita treinta y por otra parte me dicen que no llegan a veinticinco, por estar casi en los términos de San Juan de la Frontera y tan a trasmano no se sabe de cierto lo que hay más de que estaban encomendados en las monjas de Santiago de Chile."

Si nuestras conjeturas son exactas, los mocalingastas serían indios de Guandacol.

LOS SANAGASTAS

Una prolija discriminación de antecedentes nos convence que la "provincia de los sanagastas" descubierta y conquistada por el fundador de La Rioja no es otra cosa que el actual valle de este nombre y los que le siguen hacia el norte al oriente del Velasco, hasta las costas de Arauco por los menos. Incluye también el valle de La Rioja que era el de los *yacampis.*

Era esta provincia circunvecina a la de Londres y si bien su conquistador dice que sus naturales "no habían sido descubiertos por "xpianos" [cristianos] afirma en otra oportunidad que los del valle de sanagasta "an servido."

Los *sanagastas* incluyendo a los *yacampis* serían "al parecer diez o doce mil yndios gente gallarda y vien vestida" según la expresión del propio Ramírez de Velasco.

En trabajos anteriores hemos dado a la provincia de sanagasta una mayor extensión de la que aquí le asignamos. Creemos conveniente ajustar los límites de esta provincia a los de su designación histórica, si bien es cierto que la cultura "sanagasta" se extiende fuera de ellos hasta más allá de Guandacol y Río Jachal en San Juan.

El nombre general de estos indígenas debe provenir de los del pueblo de Sanagasta, en el valle del mismo nombre. Estos figuran alzados con abaucanes y hualfines después del gran alzamiento de los diaguitas.

Sanagasta en sentido limitado deben ser los *cilpigastas* y *cochangastas* si es que no eran *yacampis*.

LOS NÚCLEOS ORIENTALES

LOS DIAGUITAS DE ANCASTI

Las faldas orientales de la antigua "sierra de Sangiago," de Guayamba o de Quimilpa, hoy llamada de Ancasti y de El Alto, fueron asiento de numerosos pueblos diaguitas de los cuales muy poco sabemos.

De estos diaguitas nos ha dejado una breve referencia Sotelo Narváez en su ya clásica carta de 1582. Dice este autor . . . "viven en la sierra, la cual tiene falta de aguas, viven de manantiales pequeños y Riachuelos y Xagueyes, sutentanse como los demas, y siembran de temporal y algún poco de regadío. Estos siempre visten a fuer de los diaguitas y hablan su lengua. Es gente de mas razón (que los de Santiago, de los llanos) y tienen más ganados de los dichos como los del Perú.

Hacia 1550 Juan Nuñez del Prado conquistó el pueblo de Alibigasta y sus vecinos. Para entonces eran caciques principales de Alibigasta Chupan y Guenchica.

Próximos a Alibigasta estaban los pueblos de Choya, Collagasta, Anjuli y Simogasta. Más al noroeste hacia las faldas y primeras estribaciones de El Alto, los pueblos de Guayamba, Alijilan y Quimilpa.

Es poco lo que sabemos de la arqueológia de esta región. En general corresponde a la arqueología de los yacimientos chaco santiagueños pero aquí no aparecen los recipientes con representaciones antropomorfas en relieve, y al parecer las asas cónicas.

Hay grandes urnas funerarias lisas, muchas veces con esas aplicaciones en relieve cortadas a trechos que los Wagner han llamado sin razón "barritas ofídicas." Es abundante la cerámica eskeimórfica fina que tanto caracteriza los yacimientos arqueológicos de Santiago del Estero. Hay hachas de piedra de media garganta y puntas de flechas de piedra; son frecuentes las pequeñas bolas elipsoidales e igualmente una cerámica tosca, gruesa, decorada con dibujos geométricos negros, bordeados de blanco. Este tipo de cerámica ya llamó la atención de los hermanos Wagner reconociendo que es esporádica y poco frecuente en los yacimientos de la mesopotamia santiagueña. En los yacimientos de esta región suele encontrarse cerámica de la cultura barreal.

LOS DIAGUITAS DEL RÍO DULCE

Al oriente de estos pueblos se extiende una llanura boscosa, sin agua, que va a enmarcar la sierra de Guasayan en Santiago del Estero. Este interlad serrano constituía el límite entre las provincias de los juries y de los diaguitas. En las primeras estribaciones occidentales de la sierra de Guasayan está Conso, el antiguo Concho del itinerario de Rojas, que no debemos confundir con el Soconcho del Río Dulce.

Lozano precisa bien el límite entre las dos provincias cuando nos dice que los compañeros de Rojas después de caminar de Concho a Macajar que era parte de lo que después se llamó provincia de los juries "por nombrarse así los naturales del país ... como diaguitas los otros por donde habian transitado."

Los límites de la provincia de los juries ha sido precisada en trabajos anteriores. Se extendía a lo largo de casi todo el río Dulce y ambas faldas de la Sierra de Guasayan.

La documentación es precisa al consignar que la lengua hablada por los indígenas de esta provincia era el *kakan*. Barzana ya lo dice: "los pueblos casi todos que sirven a Santiago, así los poblados en el río del Estero como otros que estan en la sierra"; "el tonocote casi todos los del Salado y tan sólo 'cinco o seis del río del Estero.' "

El conocimiento de la arqueología de la región diaguita prueba la no uniformidad cultural de este pueblo a la par que de la discriminación histórica se induce que para los españoles eran diaguitas todos los que hablaban la lengua kakana.

En este caso están los juries, antropológica y culturalmente vinculados a los núcleos occidentales.

A estos juries corresponde una buena parte del contenido de la llamada "civilización chaco santiagueña." Este contenido no ha sido aun bien discriminado.

En el momento histórico de la conquista los núcleos sedentarios y agricultores de juries del Río Dulce estaban amenazados de desaparecer por la guerra de exterminio que sobre ellos venía ejerciendo los lules. Esta guerra no era sólo en busca de sus cosechas y ganados, sino también de sus mujeres. Todo esto está consignado en documentos históricos de la primera hora.

La arqueología de la zona occidental de la sierra de Guasayan, no frecuentada por los lules, es menos compleja que la del Río Dulce. No aparecen aquí cierto tipo de urnas y de representaciones plásticas que son abundantes en la cuenca de este y aun en la del Río Salado. No tampoco conocemos la existencia de narigueras cilíndricas que caracterizan ciertas representaciones plásticas del Río Dulce.

Todos estos elementos ausentes en el interlad de las sierras de El Alto-Ancasti y Guasayan serían exóticos con respecto a la cultura autóctona del antiguo territorio jurí. La caracterización de esta cultura estaría dada en particular por el estilo decorativo ornitogénico de sus cerámicas pintadas.

LOS NÚCLEOS SUD-ORIENTALES

La provincia indígena de Nolongasta estaba adjudicada junto con las de Famatina y Cariangasta a Juan Jufré en su título de teniente de gobernador. Nolo era un pueblo en el actual Nonogasta al sur de Chilecito.

Es evidente que este asiento es el que ha dado nombre a la provincia de los *nolongastas* u *olongastas* como también se les llamaba en Cuyo y Córdoba.

Según Mons. Cabrera olongastas era la designación de los aborígenes de La Rioja y de todos los diaguitas en general. Esta generalización no surge claramente de la documentación conocida. La provincia de los nolongastas del título de Jufré no era otra que el valle de Chilecito y quizás las tierras al sur de éste y al oriente de la sierra de la Huerta, incluyendo los pueblos de la sierra de los llanos.

El argumento lingüístico que aprovecha Canals Frau para indentificar a la tierra de los olongastas con los llanos es exacto pero disentimos con él al separarara estos indios del área del habla kakán y crear una unidad lingüística tan sólo en base de la desinencia *san* de unos pocos toponimios.

Si hemos de consagrar el nombre de *olongastas* o *nolongastas* para los núcleos sub-orientales del territorio diaguita convendrá distinguir a los del valle de Chilecito de los de los Llanos. En el territorio de los primeros predomina al parecer los elementos de la cultura angualasto; elementos de la barreal y una influencia incásica bien pronunciada en las tamberías del inca.

Los núcleos indígenas que con propiedad debemos estudiar aquí, como sud-orientales, son los de los llanos.

Estos pueblos eran también agricultores pero en escaso grado, alimentándose especialmente de algarroba y de maíz y zapallos que cultivaban.

Los *atiles* estaban al occidente de la Sierra de los Llanos entre sitios y aguadas en cuyas designaciones entra la desinencia *san* tan característica de los olongastas.

En carta del gobernador Albornoz, de 1633, referente al gran alzamiento, al referirse a estos atiles, sin nombrarlos se los llama "indios de los llanos."

Muy próximos a los atiles vivían los *silinguis* y los del pueblo de Malanzan.

Hacia el norte en la misma punta de la sierra de los Llanos, estaban los pueblos de Catuno y Salangasta de los cuales sabemos por un documento de 1594 que su idioma era el dialecto capayan o catamarcano del cacan.

LOS MUSITIANES

Entre la Punta de la Sierra de los Llanos y Padquiad, vivián los musitianes, que como sus vecinos meridionales salanagasta hablaban la lengua capayan. Entre sus pueblos se citan Guaycama, Timala y Musitian.

Tal es en síntesis el panorama étnico que a la llegada de los españoles presentaba el territorio diaguita.

Ya hemos dicho que no todo lo encontrado en este territorio debe ser tomado como perteneciente a los grupos históricamente conocidos.

Un antiguo estrato cultural es admisible en base a ciertos elementos que contrastan en el conjunto del contenido patrimonial de este pueblo. Elementos característicos y dominantes en el patrimonio de pueblos vecinos nos indican vinculaciones culturales en unos casos y en otros relaciones circunstanciales. Dentro del propio territorio notamos aportes interculturales los cuales nos prueban que en un determinado momento determinados núcleos se frecuentaban.

Hay sectores como el chaco santiagueño donde la convergencia de elementos culturales es grande, y dificultosa su discriminación.

Capítulo importante que no debemos descuidar, pues ayudará a la interpretación de la dispersión de ciertos elementos lingüísticos y materiales, es el referente a los desplazamientos o desnaturalizaciones realizadas por los españoles. Estos desplazamientos han sido hechos a zonas vecinas unas veces; otras a zonas alejadas pero interterritoriales y en no pocos casos a territorios lejanos, como el de los quilmes y acalianos llevados a los alrededores de Buenos Aires. Cuando en 1616 Juan Porcel de Padilla funda en Tarija, Bolivia, su ciudad Nueva Vega de Granada, tenía en sus fincas numerosos indios copiapóes y diaguitas.

Hacia Córdoba fueron numerosos los desplazamientos realizados desde la primera hora de la conquista.

Mas dificultoso que determinar las relaciones de espacio de las modalidades culturales referidas anteriormente, es la de fijar sus relaciones de tiempo. No existen suficientes hallazgos estratigráficos que permitan fijar una cronología general del territorio. Los conocidos se refieren a una o dos localidades y parecen mas bien corresponder a desplazamientos locales de tribus vecinas. Son insuficientes para un ensayo general. En el estado actual de nuestros conocimientos todo ensayo de cronología debe basarse en las interferencias mutuas y en las influencias de estilo, aprovechando datos indirectos de caracter histórico.

LA MANCHA MONGÓLICA EN LOS ABORÍ-GENES DEL ECUADOR

Antonio Santiana

Con el objeto de establecer el grado de frecuencia i otras características de la mancha mongólica, hemos procedido a su examen en numerosos individuos pertenecientes a varios grupos de la población ecuatoriana. Según nuestro saber esta es la primera investigación que se hace en nuestro pais sobre tal caracter morfológico. Los individuos examinados se distribuyen en las diversas localidades de la siguiente manera:

Provincia de Imbabura (Población Aborigen)		Quito (Capital) (Población Total)	
Otavalo	245	Indios	23
Espejo	43	Mestizos	345
San Pablo	111	Blancos	51
Atuntaqui	59	Negros	4
San Rafael	78		
Total	536	Total	423

La mayoría de estos eran recién nacidos o se encontraban en los dos primeros años de la vida. Por otra parte examinamos 92 indios adultos para estudiar el fenómeno de la pigmentación cutánea desde un punto de vista general, con lo que el número de individuos examinados por nosotros se eleva a 1.051.

I. MATERIAL I MÉTODOS

Dada la abundancia del elemento indígena en·la citada región (norte del Ecuador), como también su homogeneidad étnica i morfológica, la selección racial de los individuos fué muy fácil. Después hicimos este examen en la población de Quito, sobre el material de maternidad o sea en recién nacidos, cuyo diagnóstico racial se hizo partiendo de las características físicas de la madre. De su exactitud, en cuanto a los niños clasificados como "mestizos," podemos estar seguros, no así en lo que se refiere a los llamados "blancos" i de hecho el número de casos con mancha mongólica encontrados entre ellos ya sugiere la influencia del mestizaje.

Los exámenes fueron hechos en lugares bien iluminados por el sol, anotándose los resultados, en cada caso, en una hoja impresa donde consta la figura del dorso con sus principales referencias anatómicas. Se tomó, localizándola debidamente, una copia de la mancha, desechándose el procedimiento fotográfico. Para determinar su superficie se midieron los dos diámetros principales i en cuanto al color las diversas tonalidades fueron referidas a los dos colores fundamentales de la mancha, el verde i el gris azulado. La intensidad de la pigmentación se refirió a tres grados solamente. Después del examen se hizo entre los indios un interrogatorio para establecer su folklore. Por último, en cerca de un centenar de indígenas adultos se practicó un examen generäl de los tegumentos i de la cavidad bucal para determinar las características de su pigmentación cutánea.

Los resultados obtenidos constan en el Cuadro que acompaña a este trabajo, donde sus variaciones se expresan en función con la edad, que varía en una escala comprendida entre 0-10 años. Creemos que siendo la mancha mongólica una formación transitoria, que varía en estrecha relación con la edad, es indispensable estudiar sus características en función de la misma. Por último, mediante curvas, hemos representado las relaciones existentes entre las cifras que corresponden a cada característica i las relaciones que existen entre estas.

II. LOS RESULTADOS OBTENIDOS

A. FRECUENCIA DE LA MANCHA MONGÓLICA

Conforme a lo aseverado por otros investigadores (331, 294, 69, 137) nosotros la hemos encontrado con una frecuencia mayor en los indios que en los mestizos i blancos:

RAZA	INDIVIDUOS EXAMINADOS	INDIV. CON MANCHA MONGÓLICA	
		No.	Por Ciento
Indios........	559	471	84,25
Mestizos......	345	254	73,62
Blancos.......	51	9	17,64

Es al parecer más frecuente en el hombre que en la mujer:

Raza	Hombres (Por Ciento)	Mujeres (Por Ciento)
Indios.............	85	82
Mestizos...........	77	71
Blancos...........	19	16

Por último, en los aborígenes, en los que se estudiaron sus variaciones de frecuencia según la edad, aquella disminuye conforme aumenta esta, para desaparecer más tarde de lo que generalmente se ha indicado en los aborígenes americanos:

HOMBRES		MUJERES	
Años	Por Ciento	Años	Por Ciento
0– 2	96,5	0– 2	97,2
2– 4	86,2	2– 4	71,4
4– 6	80,8	4– 6	53,0
6– 8	75,0	6– 8	56,5
8–10	63,8	8–10	9,09

Es lo más probable que en los mestizos i blancos desaparece más temprano, quizás entre los 2-3 años de edad.

B. CARACTERES DESCRIPTIVOS

No siendo siempre bien definidos su examen es difícil. Observamos los siguientes:

1. *Localización.*—En el indio (véase Fig. 1) se asienta con frecuencia sobre la línea media en la región sacrococcígea (Indios: Hombres 56,2%, Mujeres 34,4%). En los grupos restantes la frecuencia de esta localización disminuye (Mestizos 17,3%, Blancos 11%). A menudo asciende hacia la región lumbar o desciende a la región glútea, en ambos lados a la vez o en uno de ellos solamente. En un menor número de casos llega a la región escapular o desciende hasta los muslos. Excepcionalmente la hemos encontrado en el abdomen, la frente o sobre las rodillas. Cuando la edad aumenta queda de ella un vestigio en la región coccígea, visible a veces durante la juventud.

2. *Forma.*—En el elemento aborigen i en ambos sexos su forma es con frecuencia circular (37,5%) i ovoide (22,7%), siguiéndole la forma irregular (27,6%), que es más frecuente en la mujer (37,5%) que en el hombre (21,3%). En mestizos de ambos sexos es por el contrario la forma irregular la más frecuente (38,5 %), siguiéndole las formas circular (26,7%) i ovoide (16,1%). El pequeño número de casos observados en blancos i negros no permite sacar conclusiones. Se observa que cuando la mancha es circular u ovoide es única; cuando es irregular, tiende a ser múltiple. El vertigio regresivo de la misma adopta generalmente una forma lineal, vertical i media, u ovoide i está siempre colocado en el pliegue interglúteo (cuando se distiende esta hacia los lados con la mano, la forma líneal vuélvese ovoide).

3. *Color.*—Durante los dos primeros años de la vida la tonalidad más frecuente es un color verde obscuro tirando a aceituna; esto ocurre en el indio tanto en el hombre (73,2%) como en la mujer (80,4%). A partir del tercer año adquiere la mancha de un modo progresivo una tonalidad azulina i grisácea (gris de pizarra), obscura en los primeros tiempos i clara posteriormente. Cuando su color es verdoso tiene límites bien definidos; si es gris, estos son difusos. El color gris predomina en el elemento aborigen desde el segundo año, haciéndose casi exclusivo a partir de los seis años de edad. En cambio en el mestizo predomina en ambos sexos la tonalidad grisácea ya desde el nacimiento (verde 32,2%), gris 67,7%), lo que al parecer ocurre también en el blanco. Su coloración no siempre es homogénea: en el seno de la mancha principal se diferencian zonas de pigmentación más acentuada o más clara; por ejemplo, en el seno de una mancha gris hay islotes de coloración verdosa e islotes apigmentarios. A veces tiene un tinte equimótico, tonalidad que se aprecia con frecuencia en la región frontal que está siempre más pigmentada que el resto de la cara.

4. *Superficie.*—En el indio la superficie de la mancha se reduce conforme aumenta la edad. Este carácter no presenta una diferencia sexual bien marcada (Hombres 23 c.c., Mujeres 27 c.c.). En el mestizo su superficie es igual que en el

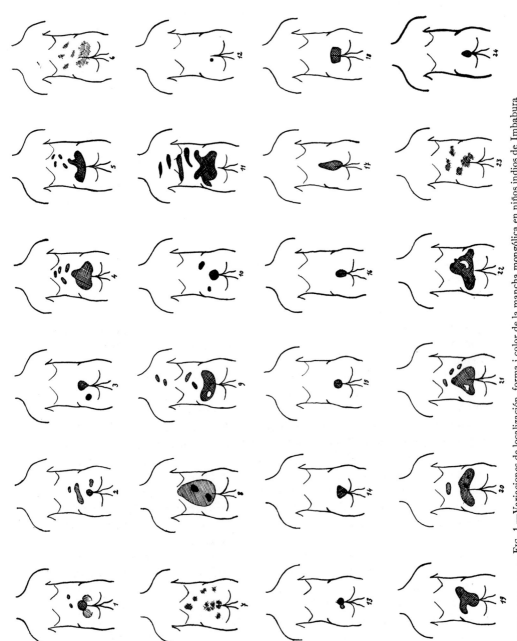

Fig. 1.—Variaciones de localización, forma i color de la mancha mongólica en niños indios de Imbabura

indio (25 c.c.) i en el blanco algo menor (21 c.c.). Cuando las manchas son múltiples tienen generalmente una extensión menor que la mancha principal, de localización sacrococcígea. Todo vestigio de la mancha desaparece en el indio entre los 8-20 años i en el mestizo después del segundo año de la vida.

La reducción de su superficie se opera de la periferia al centro, hasta cierto límite; después desaparece globalmente. Su vestigio queda siempre localizado en la región sacrococcígea.

5. *Límites.*—Los límites de la mancha mongólica pueden estar bien definidos o esta puede confundirse gradualmente con las regiones vecinas. La primera modalidad es más frecuente en el Indio durante los dos primeros años de la vida (Hombres 57,7%, Mujeres 59,4%) en tanto que la otra se acentúa definitivamente desde el tercer año de la vida. En el Mestizo la forma difusa predomina ligeramente ya en el recién nacido (Hombres 51,8%, Mujeres 50,6%) lo que en el blanco aún se acentúa. Es evidente el carácter regresivo de la segunda modalidad.

6. *Intensidad de la pigmentación.*—Distinguimos tres modalidades, acentuada, mediana i ligera. En el indio la primera es la más frecuente en los dos primeros años de la vida, en uno i otro sexo (Hombres: acentuada 47%, mediana 34%, ligera 18%; Mujeres: acentuada 46%, mediana 39%, ligera 13%). A partir del tercer año las modalidades mediana i ligera alcanzan un predominio que se acentúa desde el sexto año de la vida en uno i otro sexo. Es probable que en el mestizo i el blanco tenga lugar la misma evolución aunque en menor tiempo.

C. PIGMENTACIÓN DEL INDIO ADULTO

Con el objeto de determinar sus principales características, hemos practicado el examen de 92 individuos, hombres, de la región de Imbabura.

Se revela una gran actividad reaccional de la piel en sentido pigmentario. Ya la acción de la luz solar i de la intemperie producen una coloración más acentuada en las extremidades (Fig. 2). Ciertos agentes mecánicos que actúan con una presión continuada o repetida con frecuencia, por golpes o frotamientos, producen también un cambio permanente de coloración de la piel. Tal es el cinturón pigmentario suprapélvico debido a la acción de la faja con que el indio sostiene sus pantalones (Fig. 3), tal la pigmentación más obscura de la región glútea i de la rodilla (Fig. 4), del codo i de los trocánteres (Fig. 3).

Al lado de esto debemos señalar la gran frecuencia con que en el cuerpo del indio aparecen "lunares," a veces gigantescos, la efélides i los llamados "paños," que se caracterizan por manchas obscuras extensas e irregulares, de contornos bien limitados, que ocupan grandes regiones de la cara i en particular los carrillos (Fig. 5). El origen de estas formaciones es endógeno i aparecen en la edad adulta i se cree que están en relación con ciertos trastornos hepáticos de origen alcohólico o alimenticio.

También se producen extensas placas negruscas de límites bien definidos en la cara dental de los carrillos i sobre las encías, exclusivamente en el adulto i el viejo, las que se atribuyen por los médicos a una acción hepática i suprarrenal de carácter pigmentario i debida a los hábitos alcohólicos inveterados del indio i en especial a la chicha fermentada que consume en grandes cantidades, de poder francamente tóxico. Por fin, las enfermedades cutáneas caracterizadas por erupciones puntiformes, que en el indio son tan frecuentes i evolucionan sin tratamiento, dejan una huella pigmentaria que consiste en una zona central blanquesina rodeada de un reborde obscuro.

D. FOLKLORE

Con el objeto de establecer el concepto popular i especialmente el del indio sobre el carácter pigmentario que hemos estudiado, practicamos un interroga-

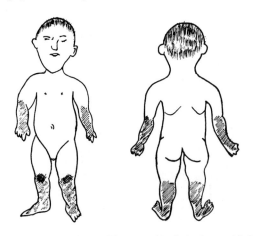

Fig. 2.—Indios adultos. Pigmentación de las extremidades

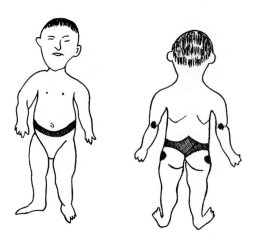

Fig. 3.—Indios adultos. Faja pigmentaria. Puntos pigmentarios en el codo i trocánteres

torio que arrojó un conjunto de respuestas de las cuales las más interesantes i numerosas son las siguientes:

Tenemos, porque somos indios.
Porque nuestros padres fueron indios.
Porque los de nuestra raza la tienen.
Porque es así nuestra sangre.
Desaparece cuando la sangre se purifica.
Porque se hace sentar en brazos a los niños tiernos i entonces se les quiebra el rabo.
Porque se les golpea.
Porque el marido golpea a la madre cuando está en cinta.
Porque la madre come nabos.
Por espanto.

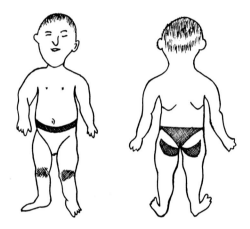

Fig. 4.—Indios adultos. Faja pigmentaria i puntos pigmentarios en la rodilla i región glútea.

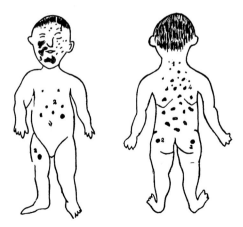

Fig. 5.—Indios adultos. Diversas pigmentaciones cutáneas

Porque Dios así lo ha dispuesto
Cuando la madre sufre golpes en el vientre mientras trabaja.
Porque se cayó la madre.
También la tuvo su padre.
Ya en el vientre materno la tenía.
Dios hace así.
De gana es asi [sin objeto].
No sé.
Porque les tienen echados.
Así nacemos porque somos runas [indio, en el concepto popular].
Aunque se les baña, quedan así.
Cuando el parto es tardío.
Todas las familias la tienen.
Porqué será?

Entre los otros grupos de la población existe la creencia de que se trata de un rasgo físico que denuncia en el que lo posee su ascendencia aborigen.

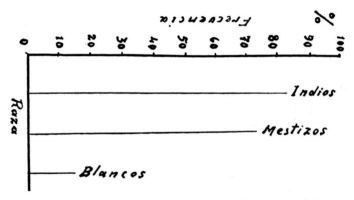

Fig. 6.—Frecuencia de la mancha mongólica en indios, mestizos i blancos

III. DISCUSIÓN

Los datos obtenidos por nosotros demuestran que, conforme a lo sostenido por otros investigadores, la mancha mongólica constituye un caracter físico de significación racial, encontrándose en el indio, como en las razas mongoloides, en alto porcentaje de frecuencia (Fig. 6), en menor número de casos en mestizos i por fin en blancos.

Considerada su evolución en el indio i separadamente en los dos sexos, su frecuencia disminuye progresivamente conforme avanza la edad (Fig. 7). Su evolución es tal que si en el momento del nacimiento presenta el mismo grado de frecuencia en los dos sexos al llegar el hombre a los 10 años la presenta todavía en un 63% en tanto en la mujer baja al 9 por ciento. De esto resulta que considerada la frecuencia de la mancha entre los 0-10 años, sin distinguir las variaciones de edad, se presenta con un porcentaje más alto en el hombre (85) que en la mujer (82). La evolución regresiva de la mancha mongólica es pues más rápida en la mujer que en el hombre en el que persiste más, lo que constituye una característica sexual.

Una interrelación entre la forma de la mancha mongólica i su localización no se manifiesta siempre, pero en el elemento indígena se revela, al menos en un carácter, una dependencia recíproca que consiste en que las formas circular i ovoide tienen siempre una localización sacrococcígea. En efecto su evolución es paralela lo que significa que la forma circular, que tiene esta localización, es la que más persiste i, de hecho, todo vestigio de la mancha tiene forma redondeada i localización sacrococcígea (Fig. 8).

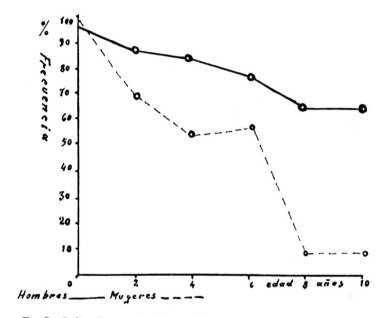

FIG. 7.—Indios. Frecuencia de la mancha mongólica según el sexo i la edad

Después de la raza la edad es el factor que más influye sobre la mancha mongólica i sus rasgos distintivos. Por ello todo estudio de este fenotipo deberá tener en cuenta su evolución de acuerdo con estos factores. La figura No. 9 demuestra que su superficie se reduce conforme aumenta la edad, aunque esto tiene lugar sólo hasta cierto límite, i lo mismo ocurre con la pigmentación verdosa, la intensidad acentuada i los límites definidos, cuya presencia disminuye conforma aumenta la edad. Al contrario (Fig. 10) otros carácteres, como el color gris de la mancha, los límites mal definidos i la ligera intensidad pigmentaria presentan en los individuos una frecuencia que aumenta con la edad. Existe pues una relación inversa entre el un grupo de carácteres i el otro, lo que se debe al hecho de que los segundos reemplazan a los primeros, de cuya evolución regresiva son la consecuencia: así la tonalidad gris sucede a la colora-

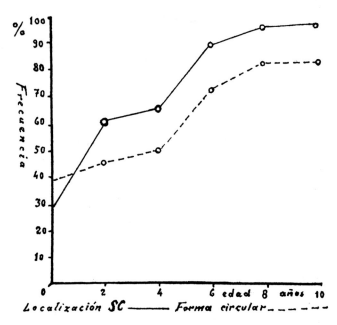

FIG. 8.—Mancha mongólica. Indios. Relaciones entre la localización sacrococcígea i la forma circular. Su evolución es paralela.

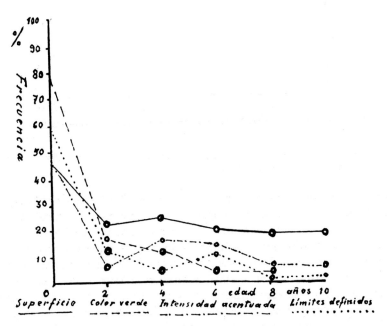

FIG. 9.—Mancha mongólica. Indios. Relaciones entre la superficie, color verde, intensidad acentuada i límites definidos. Su evolución es semejante.

ción verdosa, los límites difusos a los límites definidos i la ligera intensidad pigmentaria de la segunda infancia a la intensa pigmentación de los primeros tiempos. La regresión de la mancha mongólica se exterioriza, en resumen, por una reducción de su superficie, un cambio de coloración, la pérdida de su intensidad pigmentaria i por su insensible continuidad con la región circundante, que la asimila progresivamente.

Hace algún tiempo hemos estudiado en los aborígenes de Imbabura otro carácter tegumentario, la distribución pilosa (412), cuyas relaciones con la

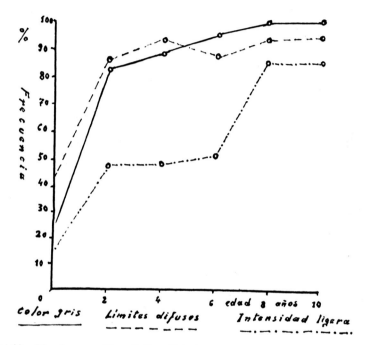

FIG. 10.—Mancha mongólica. Indios. Relaciones entre el color gris, límites difusos e intensidad ligera. Su evolución es semejante.

mancha mongólica importa considerar. Como la distribución pilosa de tipo infantil feminoide, la mancha mongólica constituye una característica racial propia de los aborígenes americanos aunque no exclusiva de ellos. Así como la distribución pilosa ofrece en los aborígenes americanos diferencias sexuales que a pesar de ser poco marcadas son bien evidentes i que se traducen por un mayor volumen de la pilosidad en el hombre, así la mancha mongólica ofrece tales diferencias en el sentido de una persistencia más sostenida en el hombre. Hemos visto que casi todas las características de la mancha mongólica—excepto la localización i la forma—evolucionan con la edad mediante cambios que en último término conducen a su desaparición, del mismo modo que ciertos rasgos de la distribución pilosa evolucionan en relación con la edad en sentido positivo o

TABLE 1

FRECUENCIA DE LA MANCHA MONGÓLICA (EXPRESADA EN CIFRAS ABSOLUTAS I PORCENTAJES) I DE ALGUNAS DE SUS CARACTERÍSTICAS EN SUS RELACIONES CON LA EDAD, EL SEXO I LA RAZA

RAZA	EDAD	INDIVIDUOS EXAMINADOS	INDIVIDUOS CON LA MANCHA	SUPERFICIE MEDIA (CENTS.)	COLOR		LÍMITES		INTENSIDAD DE LA PIGMENTACIÓN		
					Verde	Gris	Definidos	Difusos	Acentuada	Mediana	Ligera
Indios:											
Hombres...	0–2 años	147	142 / 96,5	39,57	104 / 73,2	38 / 26,7	82 / 57,7	60 / 42,2	67 / 47,1	49 / 34,5	26 / 18,3
	2–4	51	44 / 86,2	24,9	7 / 15,9	37 / 84,0	6 / 13,6	38 / 86,3	2 / 4,54	23 / 52,2	19 / 43,1
	4–6	47	38 / 80,8	14,46	4 / 10,5	34 / 89,4	..... /	38 / 100	..... /	9 / 23,6	29 / 76,3
	6–8	48	36 / 75,0	18,06	..... /	36 / 100	..... /	36 / 100	..... /	12 / 33,3	24 / 66,6
	8–10	47	30 / 63,8	17,91	..... /	30 / 100	3 / 10,0	27 / 90,0	3 / 10,0	6 / 20,0	21 / 70,0
Total....		340	290 / 85,29	23,0	115 / 39,6	175 / 60,3	91 / 31,3	199 / 68,6	72 / 24,8	99 / 34,1	119 / 41,0
Mujeres...	0–2 años	147	143 / 97,2	43,25	115 / 80,4	28 / 19,5	85 / 59,4	58 / 40,5	67 / 46,8	56 / 39,1	20 / 13,9
	2–4	21	15 / 71,4	18,9	3 / 20,0	12 / 80,0	2 / 13,3	13 / 86,6	1 / 6,66	6 / 40,0	8 / 53,3
	4–6	17	9 / 53,0	34,5	1 / 11,1	8 / 88,8	1 / 11,1	8 / 88,8	3 / 33,3	4 / 44,4	2 / 22,2
	6–8	23	13 / 56,5	22,4	1 / 7,69	12 / 92,3	3 / 23,0	10 / 76,9	..... /	8 / 61,5	5 / 38,4
	8–10	11	1 / 9,09	19,0	..... /	1 / 100	..... /	1 / 100	..... /	..... /	1 / 100
Total....		219	181 / 82,6	27,6	120 / 66,2	61 / 33,7	91 / 50,2	90 / 49,7	71 / 39,2	74 / 40,8	36 / 19,8
Total ambos sexos		559	471 / 84,2	25,3	235 / 49,8	236 / 50,1	182 / 38,6	289 / 61,3	143 / 30,3	173 / 36,7	155 / 32,9
Mestizos:											
Hombres...	0–1 mes	137	106 / 77,3	25,06	37 / 34,9	69 / 65,0	51 / 48,1	55 / 51,8	38 / 35,8	50 / 47,1	18 / 16,9
Mujeres...	0–1 mes	208	148 / 71,1	26,70	45 / 30,4	103 / 69,5	73 / 49,3	75 / 50,6	63 / 42,5	53 / 35,8	32 / 21,6
Total ambos sexos		345	254 / 73,6	25,8	82 / 32,2	172 / 67,7	124 / 48,8	130 / 51,1	101 / 39,7	103 / 40,5	50 / 19,6
Blancos:											
Hombres...	0–1 mes	26	5 / 19,2	26,2	2 / 40	3 / 60	2 / 40	3 / 60	1 / 20	2 / 40	2 / 40
Mujeres...	0–1 mes	25	4 / 16,0	17,5	..... /	4 / 100	..... /	4 / 100	..... /	125 / 31,2	3 / 75
Total ambos sexos		51	9 / 17,6	21,8	2 / 22,2	7 / 77,7	2 / 22,2	7 / 77,7	1 / 11,1	3 / 33,3	5 / 55,5
Negros...	0–1 mes	4	3 / 75,0	9,3	..... /	3 / 100	2 / 6,66	1 / 33,3	2 / 6,66	1 / 33,3	..... / .....

TABLE 2

LOCALIZACIÓN I FORMA DE LA MANCHA MONGÓLICA (EXPRESADA EN CIFRAS ABSOLUTAS I PORCENTAJES) EN SUS RELACIONES CON LA RAZA, EL SEXO I LA EDAD

RAZA	EDAD	LOCALIZACIÓN					FORMA			
		Dorsal	Lumbar	Sacro-coccígea	Sacro-glútea	Total	Ovoide i elipsoide	Irregular	Circular	Geométrica
Indios:										
Hombres....	0–2 años	.....	28	47	25	42	20	70	44	8
		.....	19,6	33,0	17,6	29,4	14,0	49,2	30,9	5,63
	2–4	.....	7	29	5	3	20	6	16	2
		.....	15,9	65,8	11,3	6,81	45,4	13,6	36,3	4,54
	4–6	1	3	32	2	.....	22	3	12	1
		2,63	5,89	84,2	5,26	.....	57,8	7,89	31,5	2,63
	6–8	.....	.....	32	4	.....	9	.....	27	.....
		.....	.....	88,8	11,1	.....	25,0	.....	75,0	.....
	8–10	.....	.....	28	2	.....	10	.....	19	1
		.....	.....	93,3	6,6	.....	33,3	.....	63,3	3,33
Total......		1	38	168	38	45	81	79	118	12
		0,34	13,0	73,4	13,1	15,4	27,8	27,1	40,6	4,13
Mujeres.....	0–2 años	6	21	47	20	49	25	75	35	8
		4,18	14,6	32,7	13,9	34,1	17,3	52,3	24,4	5,58
	2–4	.....	1	10	2	2	4	3	8	.....
		.....	6,66	66,6	13,3	13,3	26,6	20,0	53,3	.....
	4,6	.....	1	4	3	1	2	1	6	.....
		.....	11,1	44,4	33,3	11,1	22,2	11,1	66,6	.....
	6–8	.....	.....	13	.....	.....	4	.....	9	.....
		.....	.....	99,9	.....	.....	30,7	.....	69,2	.....
	8–10	.....	.....	1	.....	.....	.....	.....	1	.....
		.....	.....	100	.....	.....	.....	.....	100	.....
Total......		6	23	75	25	52	35	79	59	8
		3,30	12,7	34,2	13,8	63,3	19,2	43,5	32,5	4,40
Total ambos sexos		7	61	243	63	97	116	158	177	20
		1,47	12,9	51,5	13,3	20,5	24,6	33,5	37,5	4,24
Mestizos:										
Hombres....	0–1 mes	.....	11	22	18	55	20	58	26	2
		.....	10,3	20,7	16,9	51,8	28,7	54,6	24,5	1,88
Mujeres....	0–1 mes	.....	27	23	24	74	27	66	42	13
		.....	18,2	15,4	16,20	49,9	18,15	44,5	28,3	8,78
Total ambos sexos			38	45	42	129	47	124	68	15
			14,9	17,6	16,4	50,7	18,4	48,7	26,7	5,89
Blancos:										
Hombres....	0–1 mes	.....	1	1	1	2	.....	.....	5	.....
		.....	20,0	20,0	20,0	40,0	.....	.....	100	.....
Mujeres......	0–1 mes	.....	.....	.....	1	3	1	2	.....	1
		.....	.....	.....	25,0	75,0	25,0	50,0	.....	25,0
Total ambos sexos			1	1	2	5	1	2	5	1
			11,1	11,1	22,2	55,5	11,1	22,2	55,5	11,1
Negros........	0–1 mes	.....	1	1	.....	1	1	1	1	.....
		.....	33,3	33,3	.....	33,3	33,3	33,3	33,3	.....

negativo. Tales relaciones con la edad hacen que la mancha mongólica, como la pilosidad, evolucionen como un todo, como una unidad, lo que probablemente se realiza a travez de interrelaciones endocrinas en los territorios cutáneos aptos para reaccionar con la producción de formaciones pigmentarias. Por último, la mancha mongólica, como el sistema piloso, constituye una formación *rudimentaria*, muy variable en sus caracteres i hasta en su misma existencia. Así los indios del Ecuador, como en general los aborígenes americanos, presentan dos características muy propias en su sistema tegumentario i en innegable correlación una con otra: la mancha mongólica, de lenta evolución regresiva, i la distribución pilosa, de naturaleza atrófica i de tipo infantil feminoide.

Aquí quiero presentar los debidos agradecimientos a mi distinguido amigo, el Prof. Robert Hoffstetter, por su colaboración al Cuadro que acompaña a este trabajo, como también por su excelente estudio matemático de mi trabajo *Los Grupos sanguineos de los indios del Ecuador*, que acaba de publicar en México, en compañía del Prof. J. Martelly, de la Misión Francesa Universitaria en el Ecuador.

THE ANTIQUITY OF MAN IN THE ARGENTINE AND THE SURVIVAL OF SOUTH AMERICAN FOSSIL MAMMALS UNTIL CONTEMPORARY TIMES

Kazimierz Stołyhwo

I. INTRODUCTION

Since the existence of prehistoric man in late Paleolithic times in North America has already been established from the investigations of Jenks (213) and Helmuth de Terra, then it is to be expected that the adjacent continent of South America, which has a direct connection with North America, should likewise reveal settlements of prehistoric man dating more or less from the same period of time.

II. PATHS OF IMMIGRATION TO THE AMERICAN CONTINENT

The penetration of man into the American Continent may have taken place by two paths; one of these, according to Hrdlička (193), led from Asia through the Bering Straits on to the North American Continent. By this route, waves of immigration of prehistoric man penetrated to America, chiefly in the Neolithic Age. They must, however, have also arrived even earlier, in the late Paleolithic Age, according to the discoveries of Jenks in Minnesota (213, 214) and de Terra in Mexico.

These waves of immigrating Asiatic peoples gradually spread out over the enormous space of the double American continent, reaching as far as Tierra del Fuego. The researches of certain scholars have attempted to show the possiblity of migration to the American Continent by yet another route (132). Uhle, regarding the hypothesis of Hrdlička as quite correct, accepts the possibility of the existence of an autochthonic, and considerably older American population, not only on account of the protomorphism of the American race suggested by Stratz, but also on account of its unusual variety of nationalities, tribes, languages, and civilizations. What then is the origin of this autochthonic American population, and by which route did it reach the continent of South America?

According to Frenguelli (132) the problem of the connections existing between certain American cultures and those of the Pacific was advanced by Moreno and subsequently carried further by the investigations of Rivet (391, 392, 393) and Imbelloni (205, 206). A number of scholars such as Cora, Hale, Haddon, Passarge, Steinmann and Vallaux opposed the possibility of the immigration of peoples from Oceania to America because of the difficulties connected with the crossing of the southern part of the Pacific. Yet, on the basis of the hypothesis of Mendez Correa, who points out that in Antarctic territory there formerly existed a chain of islands which could be comparatively easily crossed from the continent of Australia to that of South America, we may assume that it was just by this southern route that the South American continent was also conquered by prehistoric man. The researches of Rivet and Imbelloni are in the fullest agreement with this assumption, as they demonstrate numerous and undeniable morphological, ethnographic and linguistic links between the autochthons of America and those of Oceania, i.e., the Australians and especially the Malayo-Polynesians. At present, according to Imbelloni, we cannot deny that a more or less significant part of the cultural patrimony of the American autochthons depends directly on the immigrations from the Pacific islands to the western shores of America.

The work of Imbelloni (204, 206) gained the full approval of P. W. Schmidt, who in his previous work had also defended the conception of cultural connections between Oceania and South America.

Thus, then, in my opinion we must accept that on the continents of both Americas there existed two chief currents of migration of primitive man, of which one moved from north to south and the other from south to north. There must have been interaction between these conflicting currents. The northern current must surely have been stronger than the southern, because the Bering Strait gave an easier access to the American continent from Asia. Consequently the northern current of immigration appears to have been victorious and had a very strong influence on the whole population of the American continent. Which of these currents is the older is now difficult to judge. In any case Frenguelli (132) affirms that the pampas strata contain the remains of ancient men, the age of which considerably exceeds the epoch foreseen by the chronological calculation of Uhle and Hrdlička. Later discoveries of prehistoric man in North America, e.g., those made by Jenks, augment, it is true, the antiquity of man in North America.

According to Suk (479) the above discovery was made on the territory of the glacial lake "Pelican," the age of which has been determined by geologists as 20,000 years. On the strength of Jenks (213, 214), it may also be assumed that the skull of the skeleton has mongoloid characteristics. This fact demonstrates that North America had already human settlements originating from Asia on its territory at the end of the Ice Age. The period of the end of the Ice Age however is a period incomparably later than the old pampas strata, which, according to Frenguelli (132), contains the remains of the ancient population of the Argentine. But the pampas formation supposedly goes back to the Tertiary or the beginning of the Pleistocene!

III. THE PSEUDO-ANTIQUITY OF MAN IN THE ARGENTINE

The assertion by the distinguished Argentine archeologist Frenguelli that in the pampas strata in the Argentine there are human remains earlier than those in North America raises the question of validity from a point of view of anthropological research. All the pseudo-discoveries of the Pleistocene and Tertiary in

South America raise very serious doubts as to their scientific value. The hypothesis of Ameghino on the descent of man from American apes, as well as his proofs of the existence of man or his predecessors on Argentine territory in the Pleistocene or even in the Tertiary, have not withstood the severe criticism of a number of scholars. Almost all the human remains described by Ameghino or his followers as fossil human remains show distinct traces of artificial deformation, which decisively denies their great antiquity. It is not strange, therefore, that in the scientific literature (even to a certain extent in the Argentine) a completely skeptical attitude now prevails as to the problem of fossil man in the Argentine. This problem, as Frenguelli (132) writes, has not yet reached a satisfactory solution. This state of affairs is largely caused by the lack of definitive contextual data on the archeological, paleontological, and geological aspects of the above discoveries of prehistoric man.

On the basis of my former researches on fossil man in the Argentine (470, 471, 472, 473), as well as on the strength of my direct observations carried out in 1932 on the material in the Museo Nacional in Buenos Aires and La Plata, I came to the conclusion that all the discoveries of human remains hitherto made in the pampas strata in the Argentine are not of very great antiquity. These human remains originate in historic or proto-historic times, hence up to the present there is no confirmation of the existence of fossil-pleistocene man in South America.

Hence the question arises: how can the genesis of faults in the determination of the antiquity of these human remains by Ameghino and his followers be explained? It may be that these remains are only intrusions in the ancient pampas strata in which they were buried, e.g., during a funeral ceremony. As we know, the pampas strata are distinguished by their exceptional plasticity, which makes it extremely difficult to recognize, after a certain period has elapsed, whether the given stratum has already been dug up. It may be, therefore, that the human remains described by Ameghino and his followers were buried even in the very old pampas strata, though their origin is of much later date.

IV. THE ANTIQUITY OF THE PAMPAS STRATA

The great antiquity of the pampas strata also raises serious doubts. Hence the necessity for a thorough geological, paleontological and archeological examination of these strata. The investigations of Frenguelli (132) indeed led to a considerable lessening of the antiquity of the pampas formation. The supposition arises that this age decrease advocated by Frenguelli is still insufficient. It is difficult, moreover, to agree with his opinion that human life in the pampas strata has been proved for the earliest Pleistocene and that it has continuity until the present day. This requires more confirmation. It should be kept in mind that a too ready assumption of the great age of the series of discoveries of human remains described by Ameghino and by his pupils and followers has only the justification that in these same strata have been found the remains of animals already extinct, and which were characteristic of the Tertiary and Pleistocene. This would be a very important justification or even decisive, if the archaism of these animal remains were a completely proved case. This however is not so.

V. THE ARCHAISM OF PAMPAS MAMMALS

Frenguelli (132) writes, quite correctly, that the errors in the chronology of the formation of the pampas are accompanied by various factors, such as the archaic character of the mammals of this region, the frequent and apparently profound changes in the faunal association and the morphological conditions of the surface of the pampas, as well as the absence of marks of glaciation over the whole area of the pampas. It should also be stressed that the fauna of the Mollusca of the pampas formation is of a *modern* character and that in it appear elements of *contemporary* fauna, *beginning from the oldest of its strata.*

These facts indicate the possibility of a still more intensive diminution of the antiquity of the strata of the pampas formation. A critical investigation should be made with the aim of seeing whether the archaism of the pampas mammals forms a proper basis for the conclusion of the great age of the pampas formation. I am supported in this case by my own observations on the human and animal remains which were found in 1900 by Hauthal in the cave Eberhardt de Última Esperanza in southern Patagonia. Thanks to Professor Angel Cabrera I had an opportunity of becoming acquainted with the interesting material preserved in the Museo Nacional in La Plata which gave me considerable help in my comprehension of the problem of the antiquity of man in South America. In the cave Última Esperanza were found two human metacarpal bones, which Lehmann-Nitsche (256) described as Metacarpus III from a right hand and Metacarpus IV from the same hand, probably belonging to the same individual. These bones are in a good state of preservation and have a very fresh completely contemporary appearance. I am in complete agreement with the opinion of Lehmann-Nitsche on this matter. Lack of great age is especially apparent in those parts where the lamina externa is destroyed, making the spongy substance visible. Lehmann-Nitsche (258) writes that "whoever examined these bones not knowing their origin, could not imagine that they belong to such a distant epoch" as is presumed by certain authors. In this cave was also found a human metatarsal bone, which Lehmann-Nitsche described as Metatarsus III of the right foot. The surface of this bone is considerably macerated but, as Lehmann-Nitsche writes, "on the head of this bone nearly half of the cartilaginous surface is preserved."

All these human bones are delicate, slender, and in the opinion of Lehmann-Nitsche, probably belonged to one female. If we appraise these human remains objectively and impartially, and if we take into consideration the behavior of the metatarsus superficies cartilaginosa, we are forced to the conclusion that they are contemporary remains and not at all ancient. I myself cannot imagine how even under the most favorable cave conditions the superficies cartilaginosa could have been preserved on a bone said to belong to the Quaternary, let alone the Tertiary. The archeological finds in this cave support this assumption in a marked manner. Two bone instruments have been found, of which one was made out of the metacarpus of a representative of the Equidae. The second was made out of the elbow (cubitus) of a bird. Their ends are smoothed and polished. They are certainly awls or something of a similar nature. In the same cave also were found a fragment of a flint knife and pieces of leather used by man. The character of these artifacts—judging from the description of Lehmann-Nitsche (257)—does not support a supposition of great age, as similar objects are used by contemporary Indians in South America.

And so the archeological discoveries in Última Esperanza are not indicators of great antiquity of man in this region. And yet in spite of this, these human remains have been pronounced very ancient by some Argentine scholars on the strength of the fact that together with the finds mentioned above were excavated animal remains which were known as fossil forms characteristic of the ancient Argentine pampas. According to Roth (1902), the remains of *Felis listai* have been found. But let us look at the character of these animal remains. Does it support Ameghino's assumption of the great antiquity of these finds?

Roth (402) in a description of these animal remains gives this detail among others: "*La garra No. 1526 conserva la segunda y tercera falanje y un poco de cuero*" (The claw No. 1526 preserves the second and third phalanges and a little skin). The following conclusion may be drawn from this: if in the cave conditions a piece of skin belonging to the fourth claw of the forepaw of *Felis listai* could be preserved, then surely the remains of this clawed beast are not so very ancient. In any case they cannot possibly date from the Tertiary or Quaternary. Again, Lehmann-Nitsche (256) writes on the matter of the remains of *Felis listai* from Última Esperanza that the bone of *Felis listai* marked No. 1532 is *muy fresco*, i.e., has the appearance of a very fresh bone of recent origin, which is indicated by the fact that on the surface of this joint-bone the cartilage was still preserved, and, besides this, there are still numerous remains of the periosteum and muscles. This fact bears distinct testimony that *Felis listai* still existed in comparatively recent times. In any case, Roth (402) affirms that the assertion of Ameghino that these remains were contemporary with the Megatherium of the ancient pampas is not correct. In the same cave were afterwards found remains of Canis closely approaching those of *Canis avus*, which according to Burmeister corresponds to the pampas formation. According to Roth (402) there is no doubt that the two instruments made of the tibia of a dog and the piece of leather which were found later in 1901 in the same cave belong to this species of *Canis avus*. As regards the tanning method of this piece of leather of *Canis avus* (found in the cave Última Esperanza), Lehmann-Nitsche (256) writes that it exactly corresponds to the method of tanning skins now in use among the Chon Indians, the contemporary inhabitants of Tierra del Fuego, who are erroneously named Onas.

If in the Última Esperanza cave a piece of leather of *Canis avus* has been preserved, the method of tanning of which corresponds exactly to that now used by the Chon Indians, then we have striking evidence that *Canis avus* still lived not so very long ago in South America.

Doubtless the most interesting of the animal remains found in the Última Esperanza are those of *Grypotherium darwinii* (var. *domesticum*). Besides the bones of this animal, there were also found in this cave three pieces of its skin, and some handfuls of hair. The structure and shape of the bones of this toothless animal from the cave exactly correspond, according to Nordenskiöld and Roth, to the structure of *Grypotherium darwinii* from the pampas formation. A difference can be observed only in the size of this sloth, i.e., the Grypotherium from the cave shows a much smaller development as compared with *Grypotherium darwinii*.

It seems however that *Grypotherium domesticum* was not at all dwarfed, since the discoveries of Nordenskiöld and the new finds by Hauthal indicate that in this region lived individuals of *Grypotherium domesticum* of the same size as *Grypotherium darwinii* of the pampas formation. In consequence of this Roth expresses the conviction that the Grypotherium from Última Esperanza cannot constitute a separate species from *Grypotherium darwinii*. We can only speak in this case of different races within the range of *Grypotherium darwinii*.

Still another question now arises: can we identify the grypotherium from the cave with *Neomylodon listai*, as was done by Ameghino? Roth (402) asserts decidedly that it would not be correct. Both Lehmann-Nitsche and Hauthal have demonstrated quite convincingly that the different descriptions of *Neomylodon listai* given by Ameghino do not agree at all with the remains of the Grypotherium found in the cave of Última Esperanza. Roth expresses the conviction that the Grypotherium of the Última Esperanza was an animal domesticated by man, and this is why he supplements the name of this toothless animal by "var. *domesticum*," in order to distinguish it from the *Grypotherium darwinii* originating in the pampas formation.

It seems to me that Roth's assertion that the Grypotherium of the Última Esperanza was an animal domesticated by man may raise serious doubts. Professor Nehring of Berlin has also opposed this statement. I think that at most it might have been an animal tamed by man. But Lehmann-Nitsche (256, 257) said in effect that he did not deny the possibility that the Grypotherium might have been a domestic animal. This however is of quite secondary importance. The most important thing about this discovery for us is the fact that in relatively recent times there lived in the cave Última Esperanza a Grypotherium of a size even greater than *Mylodon robustus*. This is indicated by the dimensions of the scapula of the Grypotherium found in this cave. It should be stressed that the bones of the Grypotherium found in the cave do not on the whole show any fossilization. Roth indeed writes that some of these bones reveal *estado fosil*. This fact does not at all prove their great age, as we know that sometimes in suitable conditions a fossilization of bones may start in caves even in contemporary times. Indeed Lehmann-Nitsche when examining the bones of the Grypotherium of the Última Esperanza found in many of the bones of this animal a completely fresh state, e.g., he writes of bone No. 1549 that it has *la superficia cartilaginosa muy fresca* (256). On the basis of his examinations of these bones, Lehmann-Nitsche came to the conclusion that *Grypotherium darwinii* was eaten by man both raw and roasted (*crudo y asado*).

On the basis of these facts, and on that of the discoveries in the cave Última Esperanza of the skin and hair of the Grypotherium which in cave conditions could in no way have been preserved since the Tertiary or even the Quaternary, we may assert that this animal still lived in Patagonia in comparatively recent times.

In the Última Esperanza were at last found the remains of *Onohippidium saldiasi*, also characteristic of the pampas formation, but which survived in South America, as we see from the above, to nearly or quite modern times. The discovery of animals in the cave Última Esperanza therefore gives clear evidence of the persistence, i.e., of the survival, of certain animal forms hitherto considered as characteristic of the period from the Tertiary to almost contemporary times. On the basis of the above observations of these animal and human finds in the cave Última Esperanza, we cannot by any means conclude that they are of great antiquity.

A series of discoveries demonstrated by Frenguelli in 1932 in the course of his report (132) at the International Assembly of American Scholars in La Plata also attests to the possibility of the survival of certain fossil animal forms in South America until contemporary times.

Frenguelli (132) namely showed a mandible of *Doedicurus kokenianus* from the Lujanensian stratum of the river Quequén Salado (Buenos Aires), which had not only preserved a great part of its organic substance, as the skeleton of a contemporary animal found after a certain time in bad atmospheric conditions is preserved, but had also preserved its covering of skin.

Frenguelli also indicated the survival of Toxodon in the contemporary loess of Córdoba. Finally he presented the skull of Eumylodon from the collection of the Natural History Museum in Buenos Aires, which had only recently been found in the contemporary sand dunes on the bank of the river Sauce Chico in the Tornquist District (Buenos Aires). Frenguelli also recalled the exceptionally interesting find made by Uhle, who had discovered the skeleton of a mastodon in the contemporary strata in Alaugasi (Ecuador) together with some pottery, which if not exactly appropriate to the second or third century of our era, as Uhle supposes, then in any case in the opinion of Frenguelli may be compared to the pottery which is found, according to Doering, in the Argentine in the archeological humus in the Aimarensian strata.

The fact of the existence of the mastodon in the third century A.D. in the territory of Ecuador, if this should result from the discovery of Uhle, is more than striking. If however it is possible to accept this fact, then we may fully agree with Frenguelli, that the archaic character of the pampas mammals does not necessarily constitute a criterion of chronology (132). I therefore suppose that consequent on this opinion, more radical conclusions might be drawn. It may be assumed that at least some of the pampas strata can be shown to be similar to those of the present time, if we use the criterion of the archaic mammals, which have survived until the present in the Argentine. Since we take our stand on this fact—the survival until almost contemporary times of a series of fossil forms, characteristic of the pampas formation, as the paleontological material in the cave of Última Esperanza proves—it is no longer strange that in certain cases fundamental errors can be made in the determination of the antiquity of the stratum investigated and of the human remains found in it. This is my understanding of how the problem of the pseudo-great antiquity of man in the Argentine arose, since a whole series of "facts" argue supposedly in favor of this hypothesis. We see then that the proper grasp of this situation is not at all a simple matter. Anthropology has here unfortunately been given up to the mercy, or lack of it, of paleontologists and geologists and their errors in the sphere of the stratification of the strata investigated. A renewed and thorough examination of the age of the pampas strata and their parallels among European strata is therefore indispensable, because the solution of the problem of the antiquity of man in the Argentine is dependent above all on an exact interpretation of the chronology of the pampas strata.

Summing up the results of the considerations hitherto made with the aim of clearing up the problem of the great antiquity of man in Argentine territory and in South America in general, we must at present take up a negative position in this matter. We cannot moreover at this time accept a preconceived idea that prehistoric man existed in South America, because this has been already ascertained in North America. In this matter, it behooves us to wait for the results of the revised valuation of the antiquity of the pampas strata as well as for new discoveries of prehistoric man in South America, which may lie in the future. The possibility of this kind of discovery is indicated by the fact of the existence of the two paths by which man reached the continent of America. The northern route was doubtless in use from the earliest times, and we already know that it provided North America with prehistoric peoples from Asia. The Bering Strait, especially during the Ice Age, was a convenient bridge between Asia and America, which did not require very much knowledge of seafaring, and this was why the North American route of immigration could be established earlier and develop more vigorously than the South American path of immigration. The North American path could, for that matter, gradually supply South America with prehistoric peoples. However, the southern path of human immigration in America probably had its beginning at a later date, when the art of sailing in the regions of the Pacific cultures had already reached a higher standard, permitting struggles with greater sea-distances.

The confirmation of the persistence until the present day of various forms of archaic mammals, characteristic of the pampas formation, is extremely interesting. It brings the possibility of a marked decrease in the age both of this formation, and in the human remains found in the Argentine and described as incalculably ancient.

PHYSIOLOGICAL ANTHROPOLOGY OF THE DWELLERS IN AMERICA'S HIGH PLATEAUS

Carlos Monge M.

I. INTRODUCTION

What characterizes life in the high plateaus is the ability of the body to be equilibrated with an oxygen atmosphere which is only a third or a half of the oxygen pressure at sea level. In those environments of rarefied air many millions of people have lived, worked and reproduced since prehistoric times. They are acclimatized. Furthermore, there is a continuous migration of people who either go up to the altitude or down to sea level, people who have to adapt themselves to a new environment. To be fully acclimatized to the altitude the organism from sea level has to call forth its emergency adjustments and then build up a new set of biological devices to reach the balanced state of the native. He has to be adapted first. Adaptation leads to acclimatization. Then, acclimatization may be congenital or acquired.

Respiration at sea level is accomplished within an excess of oxygen in the air, the oxygen pressure being 153 mm. Contrariwise in the altitude there is a permanent oxygen want, with oxygen pressure as low as 75 mm. or even less in places where man actually lives (Bowman). The human motor, like the airplane supercharged engine, has to get enough oxygen from a rarefied atmosphere to supply the requirements of the organism—at rest, under stress, and finally to maintain an adequate supply for every change of altitude, because life, in fact, evolves geographically in a vertical sense. Therefore, as I stated some time ago, Physical Anthropology does not suffice to ensure a whole understanding of altitude man. The fundamental basis must be found in the physiological dynamics of altitude life equilibrium: Physiological Anthropology.

We can anticipate that the anthropological studies carried out up to this point have made us conclude that: (1) the physiological systems of every function of the body are different at diverse altitudes for acclimatized men. Their integration measures the fitness of the body to stand the altitude; (2) there is a process of physiological adaptations to overcome the climatic aggression which men going up or down have to endure; (3) there may be a gradient of physiological dynamics which allow men to adapt themselves at once to the stress brought on by rapid changes of altitude and oxygen pressure, an experience unknown to sea level man who lives in a superoxygenated steady atmosphere.

The above mentioned characteristics would mean that altitude men belong to a climatic variety of human race as Piery inclines to believe, or to a physiological variety as Cannon thought likely.

Acclimatization can be lost for causes unknown or men cannot get acclimatized. In both cases chronic mountain sickness, a disease described in 1928 (Monge), supervenes, curing only with the descent to a lower land or to sea level. Furthermore, in certain inapparent forms of the disease the soma might get adapted but the individual does not procreate. Thus in the altitude the unfit are eliminated through a process of natural selection.

II. ANDEAN MAN

We will review briefly the biological characteristics of Andean man when studied at altitudes of 10,170 feet with an oxygen partial pressure of 104 mm. (Huancayo), 12,230 feet with an oxygen partial pressure of 96 mm. (Oroya), and 14,900 feet with an oxygen partial pressure of 89 mm. (Morococha).

I will here summarize only a few of the outstanding physiological characteristics of altitude dwellers as compared with the normal data of men studied at sea level.

The main characteristics of the respiratory function of the lung in the altitude are as follows:

A remarkable thoracic development and a great extension of the chest. There is functionally a very high total capacity of the lung and an absolute and relative increase of residual air which suggest "a true physiological emphysema" (Hurtado), which favors the diffusion of the respiratory gases. Morphologically it has been found as hyperplasia of the capillary bed (Monge, Mori-Chávez), a fact related to the old observation of D'Orbigny about the great size of altitude lungs.

Boothby has shown that acclimatization at 6,200 feet raises the alveolar air's pO_2 and diminishes the pCO_2. We have plotted the data obtained in the Andes by several investigators and found out that the values for native men surpass the Boothby values as follows: According to Boothby the alveolar air pressure at 16,000 feet in acclimatized men is:

Boothby: pO_2 : 45 mm.   and pCO_2 : 29 mm.
We found: pO_2 : 50 mm.   and pCO_2 : 26 mm. in our revision.

That proves the enormous capacity of the Andean when facing a diminished oxygen pressure. In fact Peruvian aviators go up as high as 24,000 feet without feeling any ill effects due to lack of oxygen masks, while foreign war regulations require that air crews use oxygen masks above 10,000 feet altitude.

In regard to the respiratory function of the blood we can make the following observations:

Some blood constituents such as the oxygen arterial saturation, carbon dioxide and bicarbonates show decreased values but the pH is maintained within normal limits with only a slight tendency to the alkalosis (Barcroft, Dill, Guzmán Barrón, Monge, The High Altitude Expedition to the Andean Region of Chile, Hurtado and Aste-Salazar).

Other blood constituents have an increased concentration in the altitude (Table 1). It is the case of the hemoglobin, bilirubin, pyruvic acid and lactic acid. In this regard hemoglobin for instance, from a sea level value of 16 grams per cent goes up to 16.85 grams at 10,170 ft.; 18.82 grams at 12,230 ft. and finally in Morococha at 14,900 feet, has a value of 20.76 grams per cent. As the total blood volume is also increased the absolute amount of those constituents

TABLE 1

HEMATOLOGY AND BIOCHEMISTRY	LIMA MEN FROM SEA LEVEL	HUANCAYO NATIVES (Altitude 10,170 ft.)	OROYA NATIVES (Altitude 12,230 ft.)	MOROCOCHA NATIVES (Altitude 14,900 ft.)
Red blood cells.......... (mill. per cu. mm.)	5.14	5.65	5.67	6.14
Hemoglobin............ (grs. per 100 ml.)	16.00	16.85	18.82	20.76
Hematocrit............. (red cells per cent)	46.80	50.36	54.10	59.90
Reticulocytes........... (per cent)	0.5	0.47	0.8	1.5
Total bilirubin.......... (mgrs. per 100 ml.)	0.72	0.84	1.47	1.56
Direct bilirubin......... (mgrs. per 100 ml.)	0.37	0.16	....	0.46
Indirect bilirubin........ (mgrs. per 100 ml.)	0.35	0.68	....	1.10
Blood volume........... (liters)	5.21	5.36	6.15	6.98
Plasma volume.......... (liters)	2.82	2.55	2.76	2.65
Red cell volume......... (liters)	2.34	2.79	3.36	4.29
Total hemoglobin........ (grs.)	788.00	905.01	1150.00	1464.00
Glucose............... (mgrs. per 100 ml.)	105.0	64.0	78.0	82.0
Lactic acid............. (mgrs. per 100 ml.)	11.0	12.76	12.59	14.07
Pyruvic acid............ (mgrs. per 100 ml.)	1.37	1.52	2.16	2.13
Air Oxygen Partial pressure	150 mm.	104 mm.	96 mm.	89 mm.

is actually higher than their absolute amount at sea level. What is really demonstrative though, is the rate of increase of the total hemoglobin which from 788 grams at sea level increases to 905, 1,150 and finally 1,464 grams at 10,170, 12,230 and 14,900 feet, respectively.

It should be observed that the values of total plasma are constant and one successively finds 2.82 liters, 2.55, 2.76 and 2.65 liters from sea level to 15,0C0 ft. Consequently the increase in blood volume is on account of the morphologic constituents of blood (Hurtado, Merino, Delgado, Monge and associates).

If we examine individually the systems formed by total hemoglobin and total

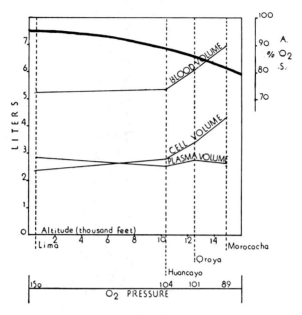

FIG. 1

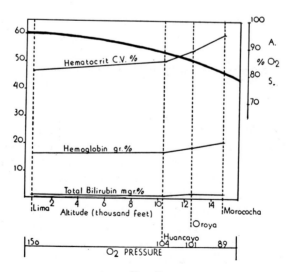

FIG. 2

blood plasma and cell volumes first (Fig. 1); by the hemoglobin, hematocrit and bilirubin percentiles, second (Fig. 2); and by the different kinds of bilirubin, third (Fig. 3) we find that at 10,170 feet the position of the systems is already changed as compared with the sea level systems. The changes are more marked at 12,230 feet and even more at 14,900 feet where the values reach unusual proportions and yet they are normal.

We can sum up in a few words a very important observation: a sea level man to become an Andean man has to build up two more liters of blood, 676 grams of hemoglobin, and has to raise the concentration of his blood bilirubin 100

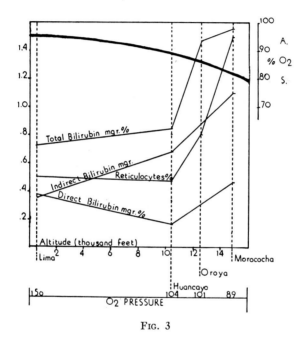

FIG. 3

per cent and his blood pyruvic acid concentration 80 per cent. Furthermore, he has to stabilize his acid-base balance with a diminished amount of carbon dioxide and bicarbonates to maintain his blood pH within normal limits. (Barcroft, High Altitude Expedition, Monge, Hurtado, Aste-Salazar.)

The circulatory system in order to balance the chronic oxygen deficiency goes through very deep modifications, some of which will be shown:

The heart rate tends to be markedly slow in the altitude. Bradycardia is the rule. A paradoxical bradycardic phase occurs in 50 per cent of all cases studied, after a moderate work (700 kilogrammeters). The venous pressure is increased and the arterial tension slightly lower than at sea level (Torres). The systolic output is equal to that of sea level, the cardiac index reaches 2.3 liters per minute, 12 per cent higher than at sea level (Rotta). Electrocardiographic observations show: a shift of the pacemaker, inverted or wandering P wave, shortness of PR and displacement of ST after moderate exercise at 10,000 feet (Monge, Sáenz) (see Fig. 4). The normal altitude electrocardiogram resembles the sea level electrocardiogram with slight changes only in the extreme limits. Thus the ST segment is higher than at sea level and chiefly in the precordial leads V2 and V3. The size of the electrical axis A.QRS is markedly greater and the T wave axis is frankly smaller than at sea level. The heart electric position shows a slight predominance of the horizontal upon the vertical (389). All these changes are rather pronounced at 14,900 feet. There is often a right axis deviation (403, 404).

An enlargement of the diameters of the heart is present as compared with the sea level values (231, 316, 403, 404, 6, 325, 318). At 10,170 ft. this enlargement is quite less marked (318, 319, 325). At 14,900 feet a frequent radiologic pattern is the one showing a 20 per cent increase of the transverse diameters, found in 69 per cent of the cases studied (403, 404). As far as the vegetative nervous system is concerned, clinical tests carried out by Pesce, Monge and Aste have proved that there is an increase of the sympathetic and parasympathetic tonus. Actually, altitude men at 15,000 feet are capable of resisting a dose of 3 milligrams of atropin without ill effects (Pesce). The vagal hypertonia explains the paradoxical bradycardic pulse rate after moderate exercise. However, this is a handicap for the newcomers to an altitude because their hearts are compelled to work stretching their fibers to the utmost. Certain cases of sudden death of newcomers to altitude might be explained by this kind of stress brought upon the cardiac contraction.

Among many other modifications of the altitude organism we might include the finding of Arellano showing a 10 per cent increase of the spinal fluid pressure.

Clinical tests have shown that the Andean has all the characteristics of an athlete; of a long distance runner we might add. In fact, the sport of skiing is played at 17,000 feet in Chacaltaya, Bolivia and normal deliverances occur at 16,000 ft.

From the observations of deficient respiratory patterns to different altitudes it is clearly seen that there is a gradient of physiological balanced systems to adjust the internal milieu and the external altitude environment. These mechanisms, unnecessary at sea level have to be *learned* by sea level men when changing altitude environments.

III. ADAPTATION OF ANDEAN MAN TO LOW ALTITUDE

We have been able to perform a methodical investigation on subjects descending from the altitude. The research was carried out in a group of twelve soldiers carefully selected. We took them from their home (Huancayo) at 10,170 feet with an oxygen partial pressure of 104 mm. to 14,900 feet (Morococha) with an oxygen partial pressure of 89 mm., where they stayed for 15 days and then brought down to sea level (Lima) where they have been closely followed for six

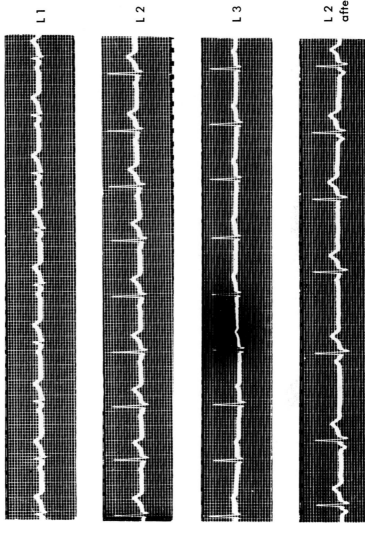

L 1

L 2

L 3

L 2
after exercise

FIG. 4

months. Biochemical, hematologic and respiratory studies were performed as well in each of the three places. Some of the results obtained are summarized in Table 2 and Figures 5, 6, and 7, which show the following facts:

a) The 15 day period of stay at 14,900 feet, after an ascent of about 5,000 feet, has affected the building up of hemoglobin which shows an increase of 100 grams. On the other hand, the blood destruction when the subjects were taken

TABLE 2

HEMATOLOGY AND BIOCHEMISTRY	HUANCAYO NATIVES (Altitude 10,170 ft.)	MOROCOCHA MEN FROM HUANCAYO	LIMA MEN FROM HUANCAYO		
			1st Week	3d Week	8th Week
Red blood cells.......... (mill. per cu. mm.)	5.65	6.05	5.57	5.37	4.70
Hemoglobin............. (grs. per 100 ml.)	16.85	17.98	16.49	15.95	14.30
Hematocrit.............. (red cells per cent)	50.36	54.43	50.67	49.46	43.10
Reticulocytes............ (per cent)	0.47	1.94	0.77	0.25	0.4
Total bilirubin........... (mgrs. per 100 ml.)	0.84	0.84	0.91	....	0.83
Direct bilirubin.......... (mgrs. per 100 ml.)	0.16	0.38	0.26	....	0.33
Indirect bilirubin......... (mgrs. per 100 ml.)	0.68	0.46	0.65	....	0.50
Blood volume............ (liters)	5.36	5.58	5.55	5.49	5.17
Plasma volume........... (liters)	2.55	2.29	2.66	2.67	2.80
Red cell volume.......... (liters)	2.79	3.25	2.87	2.79	2.35
Total hemoblobin........ (grs.)	905.01	1002.42	894.32	867.26	737.99
Glucose................. (mgrs. per 100 ml.)	64.0	73.0	80.0	85.0	85.0
Lactic acid.............. (mgrs. per 100 ml.)	12.76	14.30	11.5	12.78	10.36
Pyruvic acid............. (mgrs. per 100 ml.)	1.52	1.44	....	2.24	2.20
Air Oxygen Partial Pressure	104 mm.	89 mm.	150 mm.	150 mm.	150 mm.

down to Lima has been considerable because at the end of the eighth week the absolute value of hemoglobin decreased in 300 grams falling below the normal values for sea level dwellers.

b) The amount of pyruvic acid at the altitude is markedly increased and continues to be so at sea level without reaching the low pyruvic acid values of sea level dwellers after the eighth week of observation.

c) The acid basic balance, studied in venous blood, shows a shift to the acidity zone as a tendency to the metabolic acidosis during the stay at 14,900 feet.

At sea level the deviation was rather marked towards the zone of respiratory acidosis.

d) The changes of the basal metabolism are shown in Figure 8. We appreciate that the respiratory quotient tends to increase in the later determinations at sea level.

e) The electrocardiographic changes reveal profound disturbances of the electric potentials and currents such as: the elevation of the ST segment which in some cases at 15,000 feet appears particularly in lead V2 (Fig. 9). Frequently

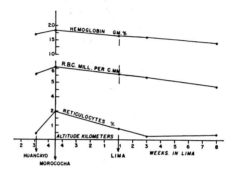

FIG. 5

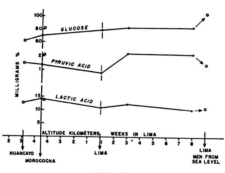

FIG. 6

a dyphasic T wave is found. With the descent to sea level marked variations of the phase of ventricular repolarization appear, the T wave returns to its normal appearance and the ST segment returns to its normal level. Then, an increase in the amplitude of the QRS and T waves appears chiefly in the precordial leads. This fact together with the frequent shift to the left of the electrical axis and the tendency of the heart to change its position towards the horizontal would favor the hypothesis that in the altitude there is a state of hyperactivity of the right ventricle, a state which is unnecessary at sea level and which gives origin to the mentioned changes (6).

f) Radiologically an enlargement of the heart has been found on arriving at 14,900 feet. During the stay in Lima the heart diameters tended to increase during four months and then showed a regression to the normal values of sea level (318).

In brief, a native of the Andes to become a sea level man has to go through a succession of physiological changes which a sea level man has never suffered. In our experiences, six months were not enough to bring about normality from the viewpoint of cardiac adjustment as measured by the electrocardiographic and radiologic patterns. There was no clinical evidence of impaired health

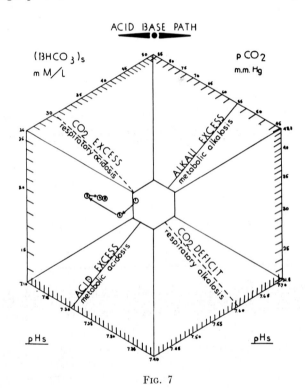

Fig. 7

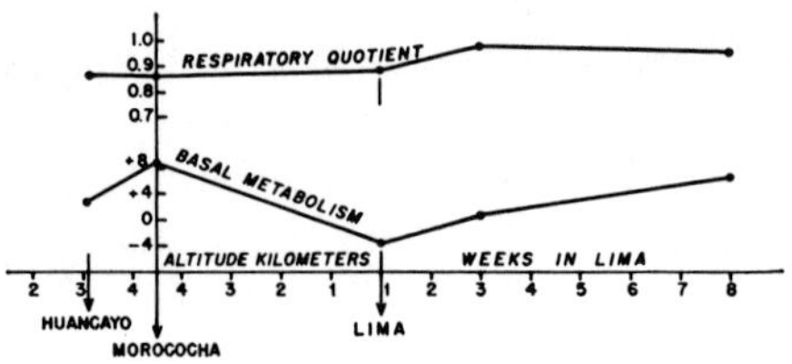

Fig. 8

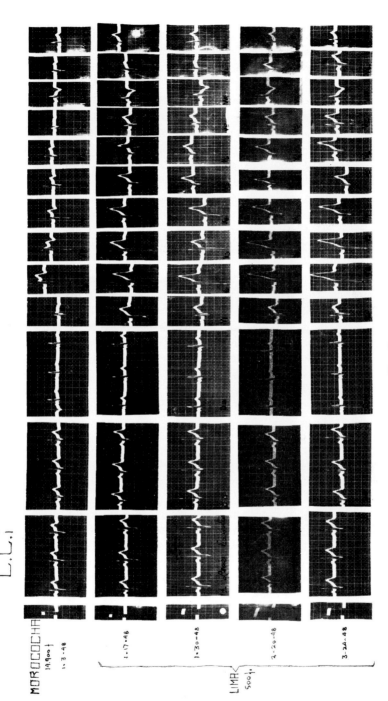

Fig. 9

condition. However, we must consider the adaptive period as a concealed disease which originates a handicap for the work output and predisposes to diseases of the respiratory tract.

IV. ADAPTATION TO HIGH ALTITUDE

It should be remarked here that we have not been able to carry out a methodical research on the progression of adaptation to the highlands. Our observations are only fragmentary, and most of the data is not yet published. Recently Hurtado and Aste-Salazar in a study on arterial blood gases and acid balance at sea level and at high altitudes have demonstrated that the properties of the arterial blood under the influence of a low pressure environment are largely determined by the length of the exposure in addition to the level of pressure. We have studied rather the physiology of reproduction at different altitudes. Clinical observations, for instance have proved since 1928 that certain young married couples were unable to reproduce in the high plateaus (319). In animals, up to 10,000 feet it can be stated that there is no visible impairment of reproduction and in the cases where fertility is impaired a process of recovery is the rule. Moore at 14,500 feet has found subnormal performance reproduction on account of cannibalism and faulty lactation. At 14,900 feet we have found permanent infertility and deterioration of the germinal epithelium in white rats notwithstanding the fact that the increase in weight of the altitude rats was as normal as the increase in weight of rats at sea level. Therefore, we see that the individual was acclimatized, the species, was not. These facts have a definite importance when seen from the industrial viewpoint by its reflection on the problems of animal husbandry.

V. SUMMARY

All the above mentioned observations as well as the researches carried out by the staff of the Institute of Andean Biology make possible for us to establish the following facts:

High altitude man from the anthropological point of view presents racial and physiologic characteristics different from those of sea level man. The altitude man to be acclimatized to sea level and conversely the sea level man to become acclimatized to altitude have to develop a succession of functional changes to overcome the climatic aggression. In both cases the organism develops a gradient of dynamic systems whose integration constitutes the ability of the body to stand the adverse conditions of the environment (excess or deficit of oxygen). There is a transitional zone of tolerance to the altitude for the sea level individual below which he maintains an optimum of physical fitness, above that line his efficiency is impaired and there is yet an upper limit of tolerance above which chronic mountain sickness supervenes. In the case of altitude man there is a lower limit of tolerance below which he might show either a diminished capacity for work or a predisposition to disease until acclimatization is acquired.

Altitude races are so deeply affected by the telluric environment that in the organization of their societies a bio-climatic determinism had necessarily to be an activating force. Since the time of the Incas the system of internal colonization, the migrations in mass (Mitimaes) and the war strategy were based on a climatic foundation: men should go to places of the same altitude of their home or were to return to the place of origin after a definite period of time. Thus, to conquer the low lands the Incas had two armies to relieve each other every other month to avoid the climatic aggression (Garcilaso).

The biologic effect of the high plateaus and their anoxic environment have a profound influence upon the individual, the race and the sociological behavior of altitude peoples, a fact that leads to the necessity of studying "Altitude Anthropology," and its social implications.

ANCIENT MAN IN SOUTH AMERICA

Theodore D. McCown

The XVIIIth International Congress of Americanists met in London in 1912. The subject of ancient man in the New World received considerable attention but of a rather different character from that accorded it two years earlier when the first session of the Seventeenth Congress met in Buenos Aires. Aleš Hrdlička was present at the meetings in London. His and Bailey Willis' expedition to South America had taken place during May, June and July of 1910 and the manuscript of what was to be the Bureau of American Ethnology's Bulletin 52, *Early Man in South America*, was ready for the printer in June of 1911. The Bulletin appeared in 1912 (197), whether before or after the May meetings of the Congress I have been unable to determine, but Hrdlička was never one to conceal his views and the general trend of his ideas and conclusions was already known. There was, nevertheless, great interest in the paper he presented on the afternoon of May 28, entitled "Early Man in South America" (192). In this he summarized the nature of the evidence and the reasons for his conclusions regarding the Brazilian and Argentinian discoveries of ancient man from the period of Lund's work in Minas Gerais to the 1910 discovery of *Homo caput inclinatus*. The twenty-six occurrences he presented in a table which itemized by columns the essential information, or lack of it, relating to each specimen or discovery. This table is not reproduced in Bulletin 52 but would have added to the value of that memoir.

The passage of close to forty years has dulled somewhat the appreciation of most of us of the precise nature of the problem with which Holmes, Hrdlička and Willis were faced. In general terms it was: How ancient is Man in the New World? but it had two specific formulations. One was that Tertiary man indubitably existed, more particularly, in Argentina; and the other was that his Quaternary, that is, Pleistocene, descendants connected Tertiary man with Recent man and thereby strengthened the proof of Tertiary man's existence.

This is not the place or time to discuss the nature of the intellectual climate in which flourished the views of the proponents of Tertiary hominids. That climate was partly general, partly special to Ameghino and his followers. To Hrdlička, but particularly to Bailey Willis, must go the genuine scientific merit of having shown the grave and insurmountable defects of what was offered as evidence for the existence of Tertiary man. I emphasize the part Willis played in the investigation even though his report in Bulletin 52 is shorter than those of Holmes and Hrdlička. Willis' comments and analysis of the stratigraphic sequence, or lack of it, for the Tertiary and Quaternary of southern South

America are invaluable and fundamental and it is a pity that more attention has not been paid to his definition of the problem and his suggestions of how a solution might be reached (197).

Hrdlička in his London paper carefully hammered home the nails of faulty archeological and paleontological context in placing the coffin-lid on Tertiary man, but when he screwed down the lid it was with the screws of the morphological modernity of the human remains themselves. This latter argument was used decisively by him also in settling the claims of the supposed Pleistocene specimens. It is interesting to note that the then Professor Arthur Keith, who was an attentive listener to this paper, voiced some reservations as to the principle involved, remarking that ". . . it was possible that the modern form may be very much more ancient than we suppose at present . . ." (224). Dr. T. D. Stewart of the United States National Museum has recently summarized the development and background of Hrdlička's views that the data of human morphology could be pretty directly translated into chronological equivalents (469). Constant reiteration of this theme, with variations, expunged any early reservations he may have had. But it is necessary to keep two sets of facts in mind. First, it was and is generally believed by the laity and by many archeologists that if the paleontologist can successfully date geological formations on the basis of the morphology of the contained fossils, the physical anthropologist will quite naturally be able to do the same thing with his human fossils. Second, Hrdlička always did pay attention to the geological and archeological context of the fossil human discoveries. He never, to my knowledge, left that flank unprotected and it has to be remembered that no New World fossil human bones studied by him or found during his lifetime had an absolutely unequivocal and undisputed Pleistocene context.

The problem of Tertiary man in the New World and the supposed absolute independence of hominid evolution in that area no longer is raised to seriously trouble the scientific anthropologist and to muddy the waters of the still real question of how ancient is man in the Western hemisphere. The matter has been redefined and now concerns the accurate assessment of the evidence for man in the Pleistocene period. In more detail, the problem revolves around the determination of a Pleistocene-Recent boundary which will prove workable within North America and as between North and South America and then of sifting the evidence as to how far back into the Pleistocene are man's settlements and his bones to be found. This definition of the problem had been reached and very widely accepted twelve years ago at the time of the "Symposium on Early Man," held in Philadelphia. The success which has attended the efforts of a whole group of workers in the past fifteen years has been, in part, a measure of this sharpened definition. Hrdlička had reached by 1937 a point where it seems to me that he really no longer believed there was a problem and the sharper phrasing of it had little meaning to him. It also seems to me that backward-looking as were his views, in one respect they were right. It is exceptionally difficult to rehabilitate or resuscitate the older discoveries and to use them in any effective way to support the more recently made finds. The associations, the context, of the older material is so patently faulty that the study of it is mainly profitable in teaching oneself how not to find a fossil human.

South of Panama there was a lull of almost a decade in the reports of new fossil humans after 1912. This is not to ignore two discoveries made in 1910 and 1911 respectively which were not considered in Bulletin 52. Juan Ambrosetti had brought to the London Congress two incomplete skulls which are variously known as the Guerrero or Banderaló crania (7). Keith joined with Hrdlička in being unable to see that they differed from recent American Indian crania. The claims for their antiquity have never been pressed, partly because Florentino Ameghino's death prevented his publication of them.

The ancient man of Cuzco, recovered by Professor Hiram Bingham's expedition to the southern Andes of Peru, was subjected to the sharpest scrutiny by Bingham and his colleagues with an ultimately adverse opinion as to the high antiquity of the remains (194).

These examples are a kind of postscript requiring no answer, as far as the story of ancient man in South America is concerned.

Some new discoveries have been reported since 1918 from Argentina. Several come from Santa Fé province (Arroyo Cululú in 1918; Esperanza in 1919; Laguna Melincué in 1919), from Córdoba, especially the Gruta de Cadonga (1939) and from Miramar, 1920. Elsewhere there is the Punin skull from Ecuador, found in 1923, the Palli Aike and Cerro Sota discoveries made by Junius Bird during his second expedition of 1934–1937, and the revived interest in the bone caves of Minas Gerais beginning in the 1930's, of which the Confins discovery is the best known. The spate of ancient fossil human remains which flowed in the final decade of the nineteenth and the initial decade of the twentieth centuries has slowed to a trickle.

The discoveries in Argentina which merit attention are the Esperanza skeleton (505), the molar teeth from Miramar (506) and the Cadonga cave (68, 61). The first two have been well described by Professor Vignati. A careful study of the published evidence fails to convince me that the assertions of the contemporaneity of the human remains with the ancient deposits from which they were removed can be substantiated. The circumstances of the finding of the Esperanza skeleton are very like those which characterized the older discoveries. The human teeth from Miramar are not a much better case, and, in addition, the horizon from which they are supposedly derived may be either Pliocene or Pleistocene depending on which geological or paleontological authorities one follows.

The fragmentary child's skull from the Gruta de Cadonga has not, to my knowledge, been described fully but the preliminary report speaks of cranial deformation and makes no claim for a distinctive, non-*sapiens* morphology. The importance of the site is that it is an example of what careful work can outline with regard to an archeological and paleontological context in stratigraphic sequence and in addition provide evidence of climatic fluctuations. This sequence is still a "floating" one, not yet relatable to Bird's sequences from the Straits of Magellan, for instance, but it is a hopeful augury of other good things to come.

The Punin skull lacks archeological or paleontological context although Harold Anthony clearly indicates his belief in its Pleistocene age on the basis of the fossil mammals found near by (12). His description of the find spot mentions a seep of water and it is not apparent that any detailed investigation was made to determine whether this might have indicated a filled tributary of the Quebrada Chalan containing later redeposited material. The accelerated rate of erosion he mentions as characterizing the Punin area makes mandatory the kind of an investigation which will exclude the possibility contained in my suggestion, if we are to go on and accept a high antiquity for the specimen.

The Punin calvarium is frequently cited as the most convincing evidence for the presence of an Australian-like or Tasmanian-like racial element in the New World. Its supposed antiquity is regarded as corroborative evidence by such theorists. It has long been evident to me that the conceptual framework used by Sullivan and Hellman in interpreting the racial nature of the Punin skull was faulty (480). They were of the opinion that the ideal method of allocating the skull to its proper racial niche would have been to know nothing of its context. This implies a concept of fixity of physical patterns, of gene-complex aggregates, so that no matter where or when these latter are found, they result from processes of a historico-genetic nature that are always the same. Such a general proposition, I submit, is incapable of proof by any yet available anthropological or genetic data, although I am well aware that in some limited cases there is evidence of great stability of gene patterns for some hundreds of human generations.

It is by no means evident just what these authors mean by "Australoid." They emphasize that metrically and, to a somewhat lesser degree morphologically, the Punin skull comes closest to the "norms" for unspecified series of Australian, Tasmanian and New Guinea crania. Whether they mean mode, average or what in using the term "norm" is not clear. If their basic proposition, the fixity of physical patterns, is a matter of opinion, and we reject it, and this Ecuadorian skull be a deviant from the mode of the population from which it came, there is little significance, in terms of racial origins, in comparing it with Australians or Tasmanians.

The rarity of this type of skull in America is emphasized and the American "norms" it most closely approaches are the Lagoa Santa, Paltacalo and Pericue crania. These collectively are the nucleus of the Lagoa Santa "race." The unity of the Lagoa Santa material proper rests quite heavily on its supposed antiquity, a matter about which there is still room for speculation. The Paltacalo material has been approximated to the Lagoa Santa by a process of selection which could not fail to emphasize the physical resemblances between them. The

Pericue material is pre-Columbian but otherwise floating in time and is further quite limited as yet in number of specimens. The Lagoa Santa "race" is an exceedingly ingenious logical fabrication but it is not demonstrable that it has any biological reality.

No demonstration has yet been made that the Punin skull falls outside the ranges of variation for aboriginal American populations, imperfectly known though these are. I think that Sullivan and Hellman further wrongly conceived their problem when they are emphatic that it hinges on whether or not one accepts one or the other of the antitheses of the unity or of the plurality of origin of the New World peoples. The plurality of gene patterns in *Homo sapiens* of the Old World is a definite fact, and this at a time when we have no evidence that immigration into the New World had begun. Hence homogeneity or diversity of the physical patterns of American populations as evidence of unity or plurality of origin are concepts whose meaning can be fully understood only in relation to space and time. Consequently it is of the greatest importance that the physical anthropologist know that this skull comes from Ecuador and of even greater importance that he know that it lived or died at a particular time. Lastly the important facts which allow the physical anthropologist to estimate population variability are not determinable from single specimens. We shall seldom, if ever, find cemeteries of the most ancient inhabitants of America, hence the physical anthropologist cannot blithely and easily find immediate answers to all the questions he can pose.

The human specimens recovered by Bird have both archeological and faunal context (29). The modest claims for their antiquity should not impel anyone to lessen their estimate of the importance of these finds. Regrettably undescribed as yet, it would be inappropriate for me to anticipate Dr. Shapiro's and Mr. Bird's forthcoming study, but their courtesy in permitting me to see the specimens on several occasions will not be hardly used if I say that considering the present and recent past aboriginal populations of the region, I would not have expected to find what Bird did uncover in the way of human beings.

The Brazilian area of Minas Gerais has received some attention in the last twenty years (303). The best known discovery is from the Lapa de Confins (513, 514). But the chronology is uncertain, being of the vague sort which depends on the association of man with extinct mammals and which admits the possibility of a late survival of the animals. Paul Rivet in his summarizing work, *The Origins of American Man* (395), cites the opinion of Professor Padberg-Drenkpol of the Rio de Janeiro National Museum that it is doubtful if the human remains from the caves of Minas Gerais come from the red deposits containing a fossil or part-fossil fauna; that their provenience is the more recent black-colored deposits. Furthermore, the Brazilian situation is beclouded by the Fata Morgana of the Lagoa Santa "race."

In concluding what I know is a pessimistic review of the South American situation on the osseous remains of ancient humanity I want to make it quite clear that I am not assuming the role of a present day Hrdlička. The physical anthropologist cannot translate human morphology into human chronology in any way that will make sense to the archeologist and his understanding and use of time series. If the archeologist thinks he can buttress a weak or faulty archeological situation with the help of a physical anthropologist, he is fooling himself in a dangerous manner. It behooves the archeologist to have clear-cut evidence of the total archeological context of the human remains before he calls on the physical anthropologist. Otherwise, the physical anthropologist is wasting his time on these ancient man problems. The cultural, environmental, geological and paleontological contexts of nearly all the South American discoveries are either nonexistent or so weak and faulty that in my opinion a great many physical anthropological man-hours have gone for nought. The situation shows signs of improvement. The Tertiary Hominid mirage is gone, a *Homo sapiens* character of the human remains is no longer grounds for ruling out a putative antiquity, the more abundant current North American work sets a time frame-of-reference from the present back to the second interstadial of the Fourth glacial period, and climatic sequences are obviously better, if by no means simple, methods of establishing regional and inter-regional chronologies than are the uncertainties of late Pleistocene comparative mammalian paleontology. Finds will probably always be rare and they must always be tested exhaustively to rule out the possibility of later burial into an older deposit, or of redeposition of more ancient materials. Fossilization is a poor criterion of age but newer techniques of organic or radioactive analysis have promise. The future seems to me to be distinctly brighter than the past.

EL TIPO ANTROPOLÓGICO DEL INDIO SUDAMERICANO
OBSERVACIONES GENERALES

Martin Gusinde

El afortunado americanista, el benemérito Dr. Paul Rivet, al tratar la antigüedad del hombre en América del Sur, llegó a las siguientes conclusiones: "El hombre americano no es autóctono; venido del Antiguo Continente, no aparece en el Nuevo Mundo antes del Cuaternario final, después del retroceso de los grandes glaciares; y sólo pudo llegar a él utilizando vías de acceso iguales a las existentes hoy día, puesto que América tenía, desde esta época lejana, sus contornos actuales" (395). La inmensa mayoría de los americanistas, sin duda alguna, está de acuerdo con dichas conclusiones.

Siendo así, pueden dejarse a un lado las interpretaciones del gran paleontólogo Florentino Ameghino, referentes al origen del hombre en la Argentina. Por lo que toca al hombre norte-americano, los hallazgos provenientes de Folsom (rincón nordeste de New Mexico) dan a conocer con claridad convincente que, al comenzar la retirada de los inmensos heleros, esos artefactos han sido confeccionados por seres humanos; y estos últimos, por consiguiente, han vivido en el período pleistoceno (397, 398). Nada se sabe del tipo racial y de los carácteres físicos de los hombres en el período cultural de Folsom; a pesar de que el así llamado "Folsom complex" parece haberse esparcido sobre una área de muy vasta extensión, prefiriendo la región Este del Continente.

Algunos autores defienden la prioridad geológica de los hallazgos de Yuma provenientes del Este del estado de Colorado. Pero, sea como fuera, restos oseos del hombre no han sido descubiertos ni juntos con los artefactos de Yuma ni con los de Gypsum Cave, de Ventana Cave en Castle Mountains y de otros lugares. Tal es así que en América del Norte no se han descubierto esqueletos y cráneos humanos en condiciones que con seguridad revelen su edad geológica. La sola circunstancia de que se descubrió artefactos así llamados prehistóricos juntos con huesos de ciertas especies animales hoy extinguidas, no impide de manera alguna el suponer que aquellos representan obras del indio de la época actual; pues, todo el mundo lo sabe que dichas especies animales han desaparecido más o menos recientemente. Las circunstancias que en favor de una considerable antigüedad del hombre en América del Norte han sido resaltadas, carecen del eficaz apoyo de parte de la geología; y sólo puede admitirse con seguridad suficiente que el hombre apareció hacia el final del Cuaternario, es decir, después del retroceso glaciar (397, p. 542).

En América del Sur se presenta una situación apenas diferente de la arriba analizada. En decenios anteriores han sido descubiertos muchos artefactos y algunas calaveras, a los cuales, casi generalmente y por motivos variados, se les ha atribuído una edad excesivamente elevada. Sin examinar minuciosamente el terreno o sea las condiciones geológicas en que esos hallazgos se habían conservado, calculábase la antigüedad de ellos por la mera impresión que su forma exterior y ciertas particularidades ejercían sobre quien había tenido la dicha de descubrirlos: es decir, se juzgaba por las solas apariencias. Conforme a este modo de proceder se le había atribuído una edad harto excesiva ya al cráneo de Punín en el Ecuador, preconizándolo como el hombre más antiguo de América. A mi juicio, dicho cráneo representa nada más que uno de los tipos groseros y toscos que no son raros en toda la América del Sur. En nuestros días aún no falta quien sigue el mencionado procedimiento del todo inadecuado y erróneo;[1] y ya es el timpo para atenerse a métodos objetivos y a abstenerse de juicios que carecen de base sólida y real. Mientras que no se haya establecido una concordancia de las capas geológicas en el Nuevo Mundo con esas en el Viejo Mundo, no debe sincronizarse ni coordinarse como productos del mismo período cultural ni calificarlos como contemporáneos los artefactos excavados allá y acá, por más que en su sola forma se asemejen o se igualen.

Parece un hecho casi comprobado, que el hombre sud-americano no ha desarrollado sus artefactos progresivamente en largos períodos; utensilios de factura paleolítica y de factura neolítica europea se presentan en América a veces no sólo como productos de una sola época, sino también como objetos que aun hoy mismo se confecciona de un modo y otro. La forma propiamente tal de un objeto de hueso o de piedra no decide aquí sobre la época, sea antigua o sea reciente, a manera de un fósil. Max Uhle, "que ha realizado un buen estudio del conjunto de la prehistoria americana, llega a la conclusión de que el hombre de América del Sur, como el del Antiguo Continente, tuvo una industria paleolítica antes de utilizar los utensilios de piedra pulimentada, mas sin que ello implique, según afirma con insistencia, que dicha industria posca una antigüedad comparable a la industria similar y correspondiente de Europa" (395, p. 67). Del mismo modo opina Roberts (398, p. 428) quien dice: "Such similarities to European types as may occur have no chronological significance and should not be used as criteria for dating New World material."

Por consiguiente, utensilios de cualquier forma o material, no determinan ni comprueban unívocamente el período de cultura, en que han vivido los animales y los hombres, de los cuales se descubrió restos oseos acompañando a esos en cualquier capa de terrenos. Tal es así que sólo al geólogo se le toca determinar la edad absoluta del terreno que guarda reminiscencias de una población hoy desaparecida. Hasta la fecha, nuestros conocimientos de las formaciones de la capa terrestre en América del Sur son aun muy incompletos y por parte harto inseguros; los especialistas no han logrado todavía establecer una relación

---

1. Me refiero al juicio que Leo Pucher ha emitido, hace sólo tres años, sobre el así llamado "Homo ivoensis," desenterrado en el departamento de Tarija en Bolivia y descrito por el nombrado autor. Véase L. Pucher (372, pp. 351–87).

cronológica más o menos verídica de los períodos geológicos en el Viejo y Nuevo Mundo.

Frente a los hechos arriba establecidos, a nadie se le escapan las dificultades en determinar la edad de restos óseos humanos que han sido excavados en cualquier terreno. Hasta hace sólo pocos años, se les había atribuído una edad de muchos miles de años a los conchales llamados "sambaquís," que son enormes montículos formados por conchas y ciertos desperdicios de cocina acumulados a larga extensión en la costa oriental del Brasil, como también a otro conchal cerca del puerto de Taltal en el Norte de Chile; por consiguiente asimismo a los restos oseos humanos allí enterrados. Uhle (501) ha calificado los hallazgos de Taltal como neolíticos y Serrano (427) llegó a la inesperada conclusión siguiente: "A sambaquí is not always a kitchen midden (kjökkenmöddinger); a large majority of the sambaquís are nothing more than natural deposits of mollusks which the receding ocean left on the shore." Como formación del mismo origen, es decir, una acción del océano que ha retrocedido algo, he considerado yo los enormes estratos en las costas de la parte central de Chile. Lo que Serrano opina acerca de los sambaquís brasileros tiene su valor también para los conchales chilenos, es decir, que "the origin and antiquity of the sambaquís is purely a geological problem, and it is a waste of time to maintain that native artifacts found in them are of the same age, merely because of having been discovered there. . . . Artifacts in the most ancient sambaquís, which are farthest from the sea, correspond to the primitive culture of Lagoa Santa, while the most modern are analogous to the classic archeological culture of coastal region, with its carefully polished stone articles" (427). Presentan dichos depósitos en el Este del Brasil diferentes fases de cultura; hecho importante comprobado por el mismo autor. En cuanto a la gente, al cual el nombrado investigador atribuye los objetos descubiertos en esos conchales, decide él mismo lo siguiente: "The paleo-American is the racial element that produced the culture of the southern sambaquís; this element is now divided by Imbelloni into *raza lágida* and *raza fuéguida*" (427).[2]

Pregúntase ahora por los caracteres exteriores y las cualidades físicas de los indígenas extinguidos, de quienes se han conservado algunos restos oseos en los conchales y en otras partes de América del Sur. Por justa razón que se comprende, dejamos aquí a un lado las opiniones que sobre el origen del hombre americano se han emitido en decenios anteriores.[3] Hoy en día apreciamos los cráneos de la así llamada raza de Lagoa Santa de una manera diferente a la que se había emitido poco después de haberlos descubierto. Acentuamos, sobre todo, la falta de la uniformidad de los caracteres físicos que imprescindiblemente debe exigirse de un grupo considerado como una raza. Basándose sobre su examen de algunos cráneos excavados en los sambaquís brasileños y hoy conservados en

2. La extensión geográfica del tipo racial láguido ha sido comprobado recién por Salvador Canals Frau (64, pp. 3–27).

3. Compárese al respecto Paul Rivet (393).

el Museo Paulista de São Paulo, Mendes Correa afirma sin restricción: "La comparaison de nos resultats avec ceux de Lacerda, Krone, Rivet et Lebzelter nous montre de suite qu'il n'y a pas, comme on l'a supposé, une 'race des sambaquís" (307). Pocos años antes, Lebzelter ya ha declarado, a raíz de haber examinado y descrito cuatro cráneos desenterrados en los sambaquís de Iquapé, lo siguiente: "Wir können diese Sambaquischädel zur sogenannten Lagoa-Santa-Rasse P. Rivet's zählen, wobei allerdings zuzufügen ist, dass ich diese Lagoa-Santa-Rasse, wie sie P. Rivet definiert, nicht für ganz einheitlich halte. Sie besteht aus einer sehr wenig spezialisierten mesokephalen Rasse (vielfach als 'paläo-amerikanische Rasse' bezeichnet), der im höheren oder geringeren Grade ein fueguides Rassenelement beigemischt ist" (254). Anteriormente, algunos antropólogos han supuesto que los caracteres físicos de la raza de Lagoa Santa aparecen en cráneos de grupos ya extinguidos y en varios pueblos esparcidos sobre toda la América del Sur (391).

¿Quáles son esas propiedades y de qué naturaleza? A mi parecer, el antropólogo argentino J. Imbelloni ha sido el primero en descubrir dos diferentes razas en aquel conjunto, que el antropólogo alemán E. von Eickstedt (115) había determinado como la raza de Lagoa Santa. Imbelloni separa los "Laguides, Laguiden (Berghöhlentypus) von Eickstedt, Race de Lagoa Santa de De Quatrefages, Sous-race Paléo-américaine de Deniker, Formazione Brasiliana Orientale de Biasutti" del grupo de los "Fuéguides, Lagiden (Küstentypus) von Eickstedt, Formazione Austroamericana de Biasutti" (208). Después de haber circunscrito geográficamente los así llamados Fuéguidos y los Láguidos, incluso "les peuples Fuégoïdes et Lagoïdes," Imbelloni describe también las cualidades físicas de cada una de estas secciones y concluye diciendo: "Si l'on compare les caractères homologues [énumerés], on voit clairement qu'on ne peut confondre le modèle morphologique des Fuéguides avec celui des Laguides" (208, p. 302). Pero, a pesar de las diferencias establecidas por dicho antropólogo, concede él mismo en seguida, "qu'il y a un certain nombre de caractères ... qui indiquent— avec d'autres éléments constructifs d'une evidente primitivité—un grand rapprochement entre les Laguides et les Fuéguides."

Bien sabido es, cuántas dificultades se oponen al quien intenta avaluar las cualidades físicas de un cráneo o de un tipo antropológico; y no debe estrañar, por lo tanto, que las opiniones acerca del mismo objeto divergen, de vez en cuando, hasta el grado de una declarada contradicción. Permítaseme la declaración franca de que no puedo conformarme con la calificación de los así llamados Fuéguidos y Láguidos arriba expuesta. Consta que los renombrados antropólogos Eickstedt e Imbelloni han emitido su opinión científica acerca de esos dos grupos raciales poco antes de publicarse mi obra monográfica sobre la antropología de los indios de la Tierra del Fuego (159); es ésta, hasta ahora, la descripción más completa de las cualidades antropológicas y morfológicas de dichos indígenas. Únicamente pocos rasgos importantes que caracterizan esencialmente el tipo físico de estos indios, quiero dibujar aquí.

Por la altura total del cuerpo, los Sélk'nam (Onas) se diferencian notablemente de las otras dos tribus, llamadas Yámana y Halakwúlup; mientras que en la formación del cráneo, en sus medidas e índices, no se manifiestan diferencias en gran escala. Los cráneos de las tres tribus representan el mismo tipo morfológico racial, muy bien caracterizado e individual. Se acentúa, entre los contornos lofocefálicos y otras particularidades, el peso enorme, debido al tamaño total y a las gruesas osificaciones ostensibles; además, la expresión de una construcción tosca y maciza; finalmente, un notable conjunto de formas netamente primitivas. Varias de estas últimas demuestran una especialisación tan avanzada, que no faltaron quienes admitían y defendían una relación genética de nuestros Fueguinos con los Australianos. Rechazando tal explicación y en contraposición decidida, he creado el término "australiforme"; que no quiere decir más que una semejanza o identidad únicamente de la forma externa, lejos de un parentesco directo y cercano. Las medidas absolutas y relativas que en dos largas series de cráneos fueguinos y australianos he determinado, manifiestan evidentemente el origen genético independiente de cada uno de dichos grupos indígenas.

Tan poco exacta como se presenta la división racial del hombre sud-americano en Andidos, Amazónidos, Pámpidos, Láguidos y Fuéguidos (según Eickstedt e Imbelloni), tan incorrecta e insuficiente aparece la tentativa de atribuir a cada cual de esas cinco razas su cultura propia; pues, esas clasificaciones no toman en consideración las inmensas variaciones particulares y locales tanto en el tipo racial cuanto en el carácter cultural de las numerosas tribus que pueblan el vasto continente sud-americano. Las diferencias morfológicas que en tantos grupos de indios se observan, las califico de importancia solamente secundaria; *y esos grupos no me parecen ser más que tipos antropológicos locales.* Común a todos ellos son los rasgos esenciales del hombre americano, en su mayoría de origen mongoloide. En las tribus que pueden verificarse como los primeros invasores y los más antiguos pobladores de América del Sur, se han desarrollado y acentuado verdaderos caracteres primitivos tanto más, en cuanto esas gentes se vieron obligados a retirarse y a mantenerse en regiones muy inhospitalarias, como lo son la Tierra del Fuego y el Este del Brasil. Allá la selección rigorosa aniquilaba todas las formas y cualidades menos resistentes, y permitía el sobrevivir solamente a los individuos robustos y bien adaptados al ambiente.

Aunque bien puede admitirse que el tipo racial fueguino y el tipo de Lagoa Santa sea calificado como "paleo-americano," aquel con más razón que éste, conviene no olvidar que ambos viven aun hoy mismo como contemporáneos de todos los demás tipos morfológicos en América del Sur. Los caracteres primitivos aun de avanzada expresión no representan un criterio absoluto para establecer una edad muy elevada de las tribus que por tales se distinguen; a lo sumo indican cierta prioridad en ocupar el suelo sud-americano. No debe olvidarse finalmente, que la invasión de los primeros pobladores se ha efectuado sólo hace unos pocos miles de años.[4] En tal reducido transcurso de tiempo, las cualidades morfológicas de los indígenas no pueden haber sufrido notables alteraciones ni cambios esenciales; los rasgos típicos que distinguen a los Fueguinos contemporáneos y a los pobladores de los sambaquís de los demás indígenas, esos mismos rasgos, más o menos, caracterizaban a dichas tribus ya al pisar por vez primera el suelo en su ambiente actual.

Creo haber establecido que los indígenas sud-americanos forman cierto número de tipos locales por sus propias y variadas cualidades morfológicas, sin que estas últimas alteren el carácter racial decisivo del hombre americano. Uno y otro de esos tipos se distinguen por un aumento notable de atributos netamente primitivos, sin que tales particularidades pregonen una prioridad significativa de su existencia en el Nuevo Mundo.

4. Dice Roberts (398, p. 430) al respecto: "There is nothing in the human physical types that would conflict with a 10,000- to 15,000-year age for the first occupation of the New World." Me parece a mí, que la mitad de ese espacio de tiempo bastará para hacer comprender la repartición de tantos pueblos y tribus que se han arraigado, que han vivido y que aun viven en el suelo sud-americano.

BIBLIOGRAPHY

1. ADAMSON, THELMA. "Chehalis Ethnographic Notes." Unpublished MS.
2. AGINSKY, B. W. "Culture Element Distributions. XXIV. Central Sierra," *University of California Anthropological Records* (Berkeley), VIII (1943), 393–468.
3. ALBA C., M. M. *Etnología y población histórica de Panamá.* Panama: Imprenta Nacional, 1928.
4. ———. *Geografía descriptiva de la República de Panamá.* Panama: Benedetti Hermanos, 1929.
5. ALBISETTI, PADRE C. "Estudos e notas complementares sôbre os Boróros orientais," *Contribuições missionarias, publicações de Sociedade Brasileira de Antropologia e Etnologia* (Rio de Janeiro), Nos. 2 and 3 (1948).
6. ALZAMROA, R., and MONGE, C. "Algunas observaciones del electrocardigrama humana consecutivas a los cambios climáticos de altitud." Instituto de Biología Andina (to be published).
7. AMBROSETTI, JUAN B. "Nuevos restos del hombre fosil argentino," *Proceedings of the XVIIIth International Congress of Americanists,* pp. 5–8. London, 1913.
8. AMES, OAKES. *Economic Annuals and Human Cultures.* Cambridge: Botanical Museum of Harvard, 1939.
9. ANDERSON, C. L. G. *Old Panama and Castilla del Oro.* Boston: Page Co., 1914.
10. ANDRES-BONN, F. "Die Himmelsreise der caraïbischen Medizinmänner," *Zeitschrift für Ethnologie* (Berlin), LXX (1938), 331–42.
11. ANGULE, JAIME DE. "The Background of the Religious Feeling in a Primitive Tribe," *American Anthropologist,* XXVIII (1926), 352–60.
12. ANTHONY, HAROLD. *The Punin Calvarium.* Edited by L. R. SULLIVAN and M. HELLMAN. ("Anthropological Papers of the American Museum of Natural History," Vol. XXIII.) New York, 1925.
13. ARELLANO, A. "El Liquido céfalo-raquideo en la altura: Verificación de un caso de enfermedad de Monge," *Revista de neuro-psiquiatría* (Lima), II (1939), 246–53.
14. ASTE-SALAZAR, H. "Exploración funcional del sistema nervioso vegetativo extracardiaco del andion," *Anales de la Facultad de Medicini* (Lima: Universidad Nacional Mayor de San Marcos de Lima), Vol. XIX (1936).
15. BALDUS, HERBERT. "Os Tapirape," *Revista do Arquivo Municipal* (São Paulo), XCVII (1944), 45–54.
16. BANDELIER, ADOLF and FANNY R. *The Journey of Alvar Nuñez Cabeza de Vaca from Florida to the Pacific, 1528–1536.* Translated by FANNY BANDELIER. New York: Allerton Book Co., 1922.
17. BARBEAU, CHARLES MARIUS. *Huron-Wyandot Mythology.* ("Memoirs of the Ottawa Department of Mines," No. 80.) Ottawa, 1915.
18. ———. "The Hydra Reborn in the New World," *Art Quarterly* (Detroit), XII (1949), 156–64.
19. BARCROFT, J. *The Respiratory Function of the Blood,* Parts I and II. Cambridge: At the University Press, 1925–28.
20. BARNETT, H. G. "Culture Element Distributions. VII. Oregon Coast," *University of California Anthropological Records* (Berkeley), I (1937), 155–204.

21. ———. "The Coast Salish of Canada," *American Anthropologist*, XL (1938), 118–41.

22. ———. "Culture Element Distributions. IX. Gulf of Georgia Salish," *University of California Anthropological Records* (Berkeley), I (1939), 221–95.

23. BEALS, R. L.; BRAINERD, G. W.; and SMITH, W. *Archaeological Studies in Northeast Arizona.* ("University of California Publications in American Archaeology and Ethnology," Vol. XLIV, No. 1.) Berkeley, 1945.

24. BELLOC, HILAIRE. *The Old Road.* London: A. Constable & Co., Ltd., 1911.

25. BENEDICT, RUTH F. *The Concept of the Guardian Spirit in North America.* ("Memoirs of the American Anthropological Association," No. 29.) Lancaster, Pa., 1923.

26. ———. *Patterns of Culture.* New York: Houghton Mifflin Co., 1934.

27. BENNETT, JOHN W. "Middle American Influences on the Culture of the Southeastern United States," *Acta Americana* (Ann Arbor, Mich.), II (1944), 25–50.

28. BENNETT, WENDELL C., and ZINGG, ROBERT M. *The Tarahumara.* Chicago: University of Chicago Press, 1935.

29. BIRD, JUNIUS. "Antiquity and Migrations of the Early Inhabitants of Patagonia," *Geographical Review* (New York), XXVIII (1938), 250–75.

30. ———. "The Alacaluf." In STEWARD, JULIAN (ed.), *Handbook of South American Indians*, I, 55–80. (Bulletin of the United States Bureau of American Ethnology, No. 143.) Washington, D.C., 1946.

31. BIRKETT-SMITH, KAJ, and DELAGUNA, FREDERICA. *The Eyak Indians of the Copper River Delta, Alaska.* Copenhagen: Levin & Munksgaard, 1938.

32. BLOM, FRANS, and LA FARGE, OLIVER. *Tribes and Temples.* 2 vols. ("Middle American Research Series Publications," No. 1.) New Orleans: Tulane University, 1926.

33. BLOOMFIELD, LEONARD. "A Set of Postulates for the Science of Language," *International Journal of American Linguistics* (Baltimore), XV (1949), 195–202.

34. BOAS, FRANZ. "Second General Report on the Indians of British Columbia," *Report of the 60th Meeting of the British Association for the Advancement of Science, 1890,* pp. 562–715. London, 1891.

35. ———. "Third General Report on the Indians of British Columbia," *Report of the 61st Meeting of the British Association for the Advancement of Science, 1891,* pp. 408–47. London, 1892.

36. ———. "The Doctrine of Souls and of Disease among the Chinook Indians," *Journal of American Folklore* (New York), VI (1893), 39–43.

37. ———. "The Indian Tribes of the Lower Fraser River," *Report of the 64th Meeting of the British Association for the Advancement of Science, 1894,* pp. 453–63. London, 1894.

38. ———. *Indianische Sagen von der nord-pacifischen Kueste Amerikas.* Berlin: A. Asher & Co., 1895.

39. ———. "The Social Organization and the Secret Societies of the Kwakiutl," *Report of the United States National Museum, 1895,* pp. 311–738. Washington, D.C., 1897.

40. ———. "The Decorative Art of the Indians of the North Pacific Coast," *Bulletin of the American Museum of Natural History* (New York), IX (1897), 123–76.

41. ———. "The Tribes of the North Pacific Coast," *Annual Archaeological Report, 1905: Appendix to the Report of the Minister of Education, Ontario,* pp. 235–49. Toronto, 1906.

42. ———. "Decorative Designs of Alaskan Needlecases," *Proceedings of the United States National Museum* (Washington, D.C.), XXXIV (1908), 321–44.

43. BOAS, FRANZ. *Handbook of American Indian Languages*, Part I, pp. 559–678. (Bulletin of the United States Bureau of American Ethnology, No. 40.) Washington, D.C,. 1911.

44. ———. "Tsmishian Mythology," *Annual Report of the United States Bureau of American Ethnology* (Washington, D.C.), XXXI (1916), 29–1037.

45. ———. "Ethnology of the Kwakiutl," *Annual Report of the United States Bureau of American Ethnology* (Washington, D.C.), XXXV (1921), 43–1481.

46. ———. "The Social Organization of the Tribes of the North Pacific Coast," *American Anthropologist*, XXVI (1924), 324–32.

47. ———. *Primitive Art*. ("Instituttet for Sammenlignede Kulturforskning," Serie B-VIII.) Oslo: H. Aschehoug & Co., 1927.

48. ———. *The Religion of the Kwakiutl Indians*. ("Columbia University Contributions to Anthropology," Vol. X.) 2 vols. New York, 1930.

49. ———. *Race, Language, and Culture*. New York: Macmillan Co., 1940.

50. ———. *The Mythology of the Bella Coola Indians*. ("Memoirs of the American Museum of Natural History," Vol. II.) New York, 1948.

51. BOLTON, H. E. "The Spanish Occupation of Texas, 1518–1690," *Southwestern Historical Quarterly* (Austin), XVI (1912), 1–26.

52. BOOTHBY, W. M. "Effect of High Altitudes on the Composition of Alveolar Air: Introductory Remarks," *Proceedings of the Staff Meetings of the Mayo Clinic* (Rochester, Minn.), XX (1945), 209–13.

53. BOROVKA, GREGORY. *Scythian Art*. New York: Frederick A. Stokes Co., 1928.

54. BOSSERT, HELMUTH THEODOR. *Altkreta*. 2d ed. Berlin: Wasmuth, 1923.

55. BOWMAN, I. *Los Andes del sur del Peru*. ("Editorial la Colmena.") Arequipa, Peru, 1938.

56. BRAND, DONALD D. "The Origin and Early Distribution of the New World Cultivated Plants," *Agricultural History* (Chicago and Baltimore), XIII (1939), 109–17.

57. BREHM, BRUNO. "Der Ursprung der germanischen Tierornamentik." In STRZYGOWSKI, JOSEF, and OTHERS, *Der Norden in der bildenden Kunst Westeuropas: Heidnisches und Christliches um das Jahr 1000*, pp. 37–95. Vienna: Krystall-Verlag, 1930.

58. BRINTON, DANIEL. "Nagualism," *Proceedings of the American Philosophical Society* (Philadelphia), XXXIII (1894), 11–73.

59. BROWN, ROBERT (ed). *The Adventures of John Jewitt*. London: Clement Wilson, 1896.

60. BRYAN, KIRK. "Pre-Columbian Agriculture in the Southwest, as Conditioned by Periods of Alluviation," *Annals of the Association of American Geographers* (Lancaster, Pa.), XXXI, No. 4 (1941), 219–42.

61. ———. "Recent Work on Early Man at the Gruta de Cadonga in the Argentine Republic," *American Antiquity* (Salt Lake City), XI (1945), 58–60.

62. BÜHLER, KARL. *Sprachtheorie*. Jena: G. Fischer, 1934.

63. BULLOCK, DILLMAN S. "Algunos tipos de cachimbas antiguas chilenas," *Boletín del Museo Nacional de Historia Natural* (Santiago, Chile), XXII (1944), 147–52, Figs. 1–5.

64. CANALS FRAU, SALVADOR. "Paleoamericanos (Láguidos) en la Mesopotamia Argentina en la epoca colonial," *Anales del Instituto de Etnografía Americana de la Universidad Nacional de Cuyo* (Mendoza, Argentine Republic), I (1940), 3–27.

65. CANDOLLE, ALPHONSE DE. *Origin of Cultivated Plants*. New York: D. Appleton & Co., 1885.

66. ———. *Géographie botanique raisonnée*. Paris: Librairie de Victor Masson, 1855.

67. CARTER, GEORGE F. *Plant Geography and Culture History*. ("Viking Fund Publications in Anthropology," No. 5.) New York, 1945.
68. CASTELLANOS, ALFREDO. *Antigüedad geológica del yacimiento de los restos humanos de la Gruta de Cadonga (Córdoba)*. ("Publicación Instituto de Fisiographía y Geología, Universidad Nacional de Litoral," No. 14.) Córdoba, 1943.
69. CASTEÑADA-LORGRETTA, D. "Thèse de Mexico City, 1937," in LELEU, R. G. (ed.), *Au sujet de la tâche bleue mongolique*. Thèse de Medécine, Paris, 1943.
70. CASTETTER, EDWARD F., and ERWIN, A. T. *A Systematic Study of Squashes and Pumpkins*. (Bulletin of the Agricultural Experiment Station, Iowa State College of Agriculture, No. 244.) Ames, Iowa, 1927.
71. CHILDE, V. GORDON. *What Happened in History*. New York: Penguin Books, 1946.
72. CHRISTIAN, VIKTOR. "Vorderasiatische Vorläufer des eurasischen Tierstiles," *Wiener Beiträge zur Kunst- und Kulturgeschichte Asiens* (Vienna), XI (1937), 11–31.
73. CLEMENTS, FORREST E. *Primitive Concepts of Disease*. ("University of California Publications in American Archaeology and Ethnology," Vol. XXXII, No. 2.) Berkeley, 1932.
74. CLINE, WALTER. "Religion and World View." In SPIER, L. (ed.), *The Sinkaietk or Southern Okanagon of Washington*, pp. 131–82. ("General Series in Anthropology," No. 6.) Menasha, Wis., 1938.
75. COBBOLD, G. A. *Religion in Japan*. London: Society for Promoting Christian Knowledge, under direction of Tract Commission, 1894.
76. CODERE, HELEN. "The Swaixwe Myth of the Middle Fraser River," *Journal of American Folklore* (New York: G. E. Stechert & Co.), LXI (1948), 1–18.
77. ———. "The Harrison Lake Physical Type." In SMITH, MARIAN W. (ed.), *Indians of the Urban Northwest*, pp. 175–84. New York: Columbia University Press, 1949.
78. COLBACCHINI, ANTONIO A. *I Bororos orientali*. Turin, 1925.
79. COLLIER, DONALD. "Conjuring among the Kiowa," *Primitive Man* (Washington, D.C.), XVII (1944), 45–49.
80. COLLINS, HENRY B., JR. *Archaeology of St. Lawrence Island, Alaska*. ("Smithsonian Miscellaneous Collection," Vol. XCVI, No. 1.) Washington, D.C., 1937.
81. COLLINS, JUNE M. "Description of the Chemakum Language." In SMITH, MARIAN W. (ed.), *Indians of the Urban Northwest*, pp. 147–60. New York: Columbia University Press, 1949.
82. COLTON, H. S. "The Rise and Fall of the Prehistoric Population of Northern Arizona," *Science* (New York), LXXXIV (1936), 337–43.
83. COMAS, J. *La Antropología física en México y Centro América*. Mexico, D.F.: Talleres de la Editorial Stylo, 1943.
84. CONTRERAS, L. "Estudios sobre metabolismo básico en Huancayo (10.170 pies)." In preparation, 1949.
85. COOPER, J. M. "The Shaking Tent Rite among Plains and Forest Algonquins," *Primitive Man* (Washington, D.C.), XVII (1944), 60–84.
86. ———. "Area and Temporal Aspects of Aboriginal South American Culture," *Smithsonian Report for 1943*, pp. 429–62. Washington, D.C., 1944.
87. CURTIS, EDWARD S. *The North American Indian*, Vol. IX. Cambridge: At the University Press, 1913.
88. CUSHING, FRANK H. "Preliminary Notes on the Origin, Working Hypothesis, and Primary Researches of the Hemenway Southwestern Archaeological Expedition," *Congrès International des Américanistes, Compte-rendu de la septième session, 1888*, pp. 151–94. Berlin, 1890.

89. DAVENPORT, HERBERT (ed.). "The Expedition of Panfilo de Narvaez, by Gonzalo Fernandez Oviedo y Valdez," *Southwestern Historical Quarterly* (Austin, Tex.), XXVII (1924), 120–39.

90. DAVID-NEEL, A. *Magic and Mystery in Tibet.* New York: C. Kendall, 1932.

91. DE GOEJE, C. H. De Inwijding tot Medicijnman bij de Arawakken (Guyana) in Tkst en *Mythe.* ("Bÿdr.," Vol. LV, "Ned Indië," No. 101.) 's Gravenhage, 1942.

92. ———. "Philosophy, Initiation, and Myths of the Indians of Guiana and Adjacent Countries," *International Archiv für Ethnography* (Leiden: J. Brill), XLIV (1943), 1–136.

93. ———. *Zondvloed en Zondeval bij de Indianen van West-Indie. Mededeling*, Vol. LXXIX. ("Indisch Instituut, Afdeeling Volkenkunde," No. 28.) Amsterdam, 1948.

94. DE GROOT, A. W. "Structural Linguistics and Word Classes," *Lingua* (Haarlem), I, No. 4 (1948), 427–500.

95. DE J. PINZÓN, Francisco. "Indios de Cricamola y Península Valiente," *Organo de la Universidad de Panamá* (Panama), No. 25 (1946), pp. 127–40.

96. DE LEÓN, ALONSO. "Historia de Neuvo León." In GARCÍA, GENARO (ed.), *Documentos para la historia de México*, pp. 34–40. Mexico City: Vda de C. Bouret, 1909.

97. DELGADO, E. "La Bilirubinemia. Tesis de Lima," *Anales de la Facultad de Medicina* (Lima: Universidad Nacional Mayor de San Marcos de Lima), Vol. XXXII (1949).

98. DILL, D. B.; TALBOTT, J. H.; and CONSOLAZIO, W. V. "Blood as a Physico-chemical System. XII. Man at High Altitude," *Journal of Biological Chemistry* (Baltimore), MXVIII, No. 3 (1937), 649–66.

99. DIXON, ROLAND B. "The Shasta," *Bulletin of the American Museum of Natural History* (New York), XVII, Part V (1907), 383–495.

100. D'ORBIGNY, A. *L'Homme américain.* 2 vols. Paris: Pitois-Levrault, 1839.

101. DORSEY, GEORGE AMOS. "The Dwamish Indian Spirit Boat and Its Use," *Bulletin of the University of Pennsylvania Free Museum of Science and Art* (Philadelphia), III (1902), 227–38.

102. DOUGLAS, W. B. "Land of the Small House People," *El Palacio* (Santa Fe), IV (1917), 3–23.

103. DOUGLASS, FREDERIC H. *Indian Art of the United States.* New York: Museum of Modern Art, 1941.

104. DRIVER, HAROLD E. *Wappo Ethnography.* ("University of California Publications in American Archaeology and Ethnology," Vol. XXXVI, No. 3.) Berkeley, 1936.

105. ———. "Culture Element Distributions. VI. Southern Sierra Nevada," *University of California Anthropological Records* (Berkeley), I, No. 2 (1937), 53–154.

106. ———. "Culture Element Distributions. X. Northwest California," *University of California Anthropological Records* (Berkeley), I, No. 6 (1939), 297–434.

107. DRUCKER, PHILIP. "Kwakiutl Dancing Societies," *University of California Anthropological Records* (Berkeley), II (1940), 201–30.

108. ———. "Culture Element Distributions. V. Southern California," *University of California Anthropological Records* (Berkeley), I, No. 1 (1937), 1–52.

109. ———. *The Tolowa and Their Southwest Oregon Kin.* ("University of California Publications in American Archaeology and Ethnology," Vol. XXXVI, No. 4.) Berkeley, 1937.

110. ———. "Culture Element Distributions. XVII. Yuman-Pima," *University of California Anthropological Records* (Berkeley), VI, No. 3 (1941), 91–230.

111. ———. *Archaeological Survey of the Northern Northwest Coast.* (Bulletin of the

United States Bureau of American Ethnology, No. 133.) Washington, D.C., 1943.

112. ———. "Culture Element Distributions: Northwest Coast." Unpublished MS.

113. DUBOIS, CORA A. *Wintu Ethnography*. ("University of California Publications in American Archaeology and Ethnology," Vol. XXXVI, No. 1.) Berkeley, 1935.

114. DU SOLIER, WILFRIDO; KRIEGER, ALEX D.; and GRIFFIN, JAMES B. "The Archaeological Zone of Buena Vista, Huaxcama, San Luis Potosí, Mexico," *American Antiquity* (Salt Lake City), XIII (1947), 1–32.

115. EICKSTEDT, E. VON. *Rassenkunde und Rassengeschichte der Menschheit*. Stuttgart: F. Enke, 1934.

116. EMMONS, G. T. "Petroglyphs in Southeastern Alaska," *American Anthropologist*, X (1908), 221–30.

117. ESPINOSE Y TELLO, J. *A Spanish Voyage to Vancouver and the Northwest Coast of America in 1792*. Introduction and translation by CECIL JANE. London: Argonaut Press, 1930.

118. ESSENE, FRANK. "Culture Element Distributions. XXI. Round Valley," *University of California Anthropological Records* (Berkeley), VIII, No. 1 (1942), 1–98.

119. EVANS-WENTZ, W. Y. *The Tibetan Book of the Dead*. London: Oxford University Press, 1927.

119a. FERNÁNDEZ DE NARVARRETE, MARTÍN. *Collección de los viajes y descubrimientos, que hicieron por mar los españoles, desde fines del siglo XV*, Vol. III. Madrid, 1929.

120. FIELD, H. "Early Man in Mexico," *Man* (London), XLVIII (1948), 17–19.

121. FLANNERY, R. "The Gros Ventre Shaking Tent," *Primitive Man* (Washington, D.C.), XVII (1944), 54–59.

122. FLANNERY, REGINA. *An Analysis of Coastal Algonquin Culture*. ("Catholic University of America Anthropological Series," No. 7.) Washington, D.C., 1939.

123. FORD, J. A., and WILLEY, GORDON R. "An Interpretation of the Prehistory of the Eastern United States," *American Anthropologist*, XLIII (1941), 325–63.

124. FORDE, C. DARRYL. *Ethnography of the Yuma Indians*. ("University of California Publications in American Archaeology and Ethnology," Vol. XXVIII, No. 4.) Berkeley, 1931.

125. FRACHTENBERG, LEO J. "Quileute Ethnography." Unpublished MS.

126. FRANCHERE, GABRIEL. "Narrative of a Voyage to the Northwest Coast of America," in THWAITES, R. G. (ed.), *Early Western Travels*, II, 167–440. Cleveland, Ohio: A. H. Clark Co., 1904.

127. FREELAND, L. S. *Pomo Doctors and Poisoners*, pp. 57–73. ("University of California Publications in American Archaeology and Ethnology," Vol. XX.) Berkeley, 1923.

128. ———. *Language of the Sierra Miwok*. ("Indiana University Publications in Anthropology and Linguistics, Memoirs of the International Journal of American Linguistics," Suppl. to XIV, No. 3, 1–194.) Baltimore, 1948.

129. FREEMAN, GEORGE F. *Southwestern Beams and Teparies*. ("Bulletin of Agricultural Experiment Station, University of Arizona," No. 68.) Tucson, 1912.

130. FRENGUELLI, J. "El Problema de la antigüedad del hombre en la Argentina," *Actas y trabajos científicos del XXV Congreso Internacional des Americanistas, session 25, La Plata, 1932*, pp. 1–23. Buenos Aires: "Coni," 1934.

131. FREUD, SIGMUND. *Totem und Tabu*. Leipzig: Internationaler psychoanalytischer Verlag, 1922.

132. FRIEDERICI, GEORG. *Der Charakter der Entdeckung und Eroberung Amerikas durch die Europäer*. Stuttgart: Verlag Friedrich Andreas Perthes A.G., 1924–36.

133. FRIES, CHARLES C., and PIKE, KENNETH L. "Coexisting Phonemic Systems," *Language* (Baltimore), XXV (1949), 29–50.

134. GALVAO, EDUARDO. *Apontamentos sôbre os Indios Kamaiurá*, p. 47. ("Publ. av. do Museo Nacional," Vol. V.) Rio de Janeiro, 1949.

135. GARFIELD, VIOLA. "Tsimshian Clan and Society," *University of Washington Publications in Anthropology* (Seattle), VII (1939), 167–349.

136. GAUL, JAMES H. "Observations on the Bronze Age in the Yenisei Valley," *Papers of the Peabody Museum* (Cambridge, Mass.), XX (1943), 149–86.

137. GESSAIN, ROBERT. "Contribution à l'étude des Tepehua de Huehuetla (Hidalgo, Mexico). La Tache pigmentaire congénitale," *Journal de la Société des Américanistes*, N.S., Vol. XXXVI (1947), 145–68.

138. GIDDINGS, J. L. "Early Flint Horizons on the North Bering Sea Coast," *Journal of the Washington Academy of Sciences* (Menasha, Wis.), XXXIX (1949), 85–90.

139. GIFFORD, E. W. *The Kamia of Imperial Valley*. (Bulletin of the United States Bureau of American Ethnology, No. 97.) Washington, D.C., 1931.

140. ———. *The Northfork Mono*. ("University of California Publications in American Archaeology and Ethnology," Vol. XXXI, No. 2.) Berkeley, 1932.

141. ———. *The Cocopa*. ("University of California Publications in American Archaeology and Ethnology," Vol. XXXI, No. 5.) Berkeley, 1933.

142. ———. *Northeastern and Western Yavapai*. ("University of California Publications in American Archaeology and Ethnology," Vol. XXXIV, No. 4.) Berkeley, 1936.

143. ———. "Culture Element Distributions. XII. Apache-Pueblo," *University of California Anthropological Records* (Berkeley), IV (1940), 1–208.

144. GRIFFIN, JAMES B. "The De Luna Expedition and the 'Buzzard Cult' in the Southeast," *Journal of the Washington Academy of Sciences* (Menasha, Wis.), XXXIV, No. 9 (1944), 299–303.

145. GILMORE, MELVIN R. *The Ethnobotanical Laboratory at the University of Michigan*. ("Occasional Contributions from the Museum of Anthropology of the University of Michigan," No. 1.) Ann Arbor: University of Michigan Press, 1932.

146. GLADWIN, H. S. *Methods and Instruments for Use in Measuring Tree Rings*. ("Gila Pueblo Archaeological Foundation, Medallion Papers," Vol. XXVII.) Globe, Ariz., 1940.

147. ———. *The Chaco Branch: Excavations at White Mound in the Red Mesa Valley, Arizona*. ("Gila Pueblo Archaeological Foundation, Medallion Papers," Vol. XXXIII.) Globe, Ariz., 1945.

148. GODDARD, P. E. *Indians of the Northwest Coast*. ("Handbook Series of the American Museum of Natural History," No. 10.) New York, 1924.

149. GODÓI, MANUEL PEREIRA DE. *Los extinguidos painguá de la cascada de Emas*. ("Publicação do Instituto de Arquelogia, Lingüística y Folklore 'Dr. Pablo Cabrera,'" Vol. XIV.) Córdoba, Argentina: Universidad Nacional de Córdoba, 1946.

150. GOLDSTEIN, M. S. *Demographic and Bodily Changes in Descendants of Mexican Immigrants with Comparable Data on Parents and Children in Mexico*. Austin, Tex.: Institution of Latin-American Studies, 1943.

151. GRAY, ASA, and TRUMBULL, J. HAMMOND. "Review of De Candolle's *Origin of Cultivated Plants*," *American Journal of Science* (New Haven), CXXV (1883), Part I, pp. 241–55; Part II, pp. 370–79; CXXVI, Part III, 128–38.

152. GRAY, LOUIS H., and MOORE, GEORGE F. (eds.). *The Mythology of All Races*, Parts I–XI. Boston: Marshall Jones Co., 1916–32.

153. GREGORY, H. E. *The Navajo Country*. ("United States Geological Survey, Water-Supply Papers," No. 380.) Washington, D.C., 1916.

154. GUINDON, ARTHUR. *En Mocassins*. Montreal, 1920.

155. GUNTHER, ERNA. "Klallam Ethnography," *University of Washington Publications in Anthropology* (Seattle), I (1927), 171–314.
156. ———. "Culture Element Distributions: Puget Sound." Unpublished MS.
157. GUSINDE, MARTIN. *Urmenschen in Feuerland.* Berlin: P. Zsolnay, 1946.
158. ———. *Die Feuerland-Indianer.* I. Die Selk'nam; II. Die Yamana. Mödling: Verlag der internationalem Zeitschrift *Anthropos, 1931.*
159. ———. *Anthropologie der Feuerland-Indianer.* Mödling: Verlag der internationalem Zeitschrift *Anthropos,* 1939.
160. GUZMÁN BARRÓN, E. S.; DILL, D. B.; EDWARDS, H. T.; and HURTADO, A. "Acute Mountain Sickness," *Journal of Clinical Investigation* (Baltimore), XVI (1937), 541–46.
160*a*. HAEBERLIN, HERMANN. "SbEtEdá q: A Shamanistic Performance of the Coast Salish," *American Anthropologist,* XX (1918), 249–57.
161. HAECKEL, JOSEF. "Zweiklassensystem, Männerhaus und Totemismus in Südamerika," *Zeitschrift für Ethnologie* (Berlin), LXX (1938), 426–54.
162. HALE, HORATIO. *The Development of Language.* Toronto, 1888.
163. HALL, E. T. *Early Stockaded Settlements in the Governador, New Mexico: A Marginal Anasazi Development from Basket Maker III to Pueblo I Times.* New York: Columbia University Press, 1944.
163*a*. HALLOWELL, I. J. "Some Psychological Characteristics of the Northeastern Indians." In JOHNSON, F. (ed.), *Man in Northeastern America,* pp. 217–23. Andover, Mass.: Phillips Academy, The Foundation, 1946.
164. *Handwörter des deutschen Aberglaubens,* Vol. IX. Berlin: Arsgunter besonder von E. Hoffmann-Krayer, 1938–41.
165. HARRINGTON, JOHN P. "Culture Element Distributions. XIX. Central California Coast," *University of California Anthropological Records* (Berkeley), VII, No. 1 (1942), 1–46.
166. ———. "Yunka, Language of the Peruvian Coastal Culture," *International Journal of American Linguistics* (Baltimore), XI (1945), 24–30.
167. ———. "Matako of the Gran Chaco," *ibid.,* XIV (1948), 25–28.
168. HARRINGTON, M. R. *Gypsum Cave, Nevada.* ("Southwest Museum Papers," No. VIII.) Los Angeles, 1933.
169. HARRIS, ZELLIG. "Structural Restatements I, II," *International Journal of American Linguistics* (Baltimore), XIII (1947), 47–58, 175–86.
170. HASTINGS, JAMES (ed.). *Encyclopedia of Religion and Ethics.* Edinburgh: T. & T. Clark, 1908–26.
171. HASWELL, ROBERT. "Log of the First Voyage of the Columbia." In HOWAY, F. W. (ed.), *Voyages of the Columbia to the Northwest Coast of America,* pp. 3–107. Boston: Massachusetts Historical Society, 1941.
172. HAURY, E. W. "Climate and Human History," *Tree-Ring Bulletin* (Flagstaff, Ariz.: Museum of Northern Arizona), I (1934), 13–15.
173. ———. *The Excavation of Los Muertos and Neighboring Ruins in the Salt River Valley, Arizona.* ("Peabody Museum of American Archaeology and Ethnology, Papers," Vol. XXIV, No. 1.) Cambridge, Mass., 1945.
174. HEARN, LAFCADIO. *The Romance of the Milky Way and Other Studies and Stories.* Boston and New York: Houghton Mifflin Co., 1905.
175. HEDRICK, U. P. (ed.). "Sturtevant's Notes on Edible Plants," *Report of the New York Agricultural Experiment Station for the Year 1919,* Part II. (Albany, 1919).
176. HENRY, J. "Compte-rendu de Nimuendaju, *The Apinaye,*" *American Anthropologist,* XLII (1940), 337–38.
177. HERSKOVITS, MELVILLE. *Man and His Works.* New York: Alfred A. Knopf, 1948.

178. HEYE, GEORGE G. *Certain Aboriginal Pottery from Southern California*, pp. 1–46, Pls. I–XXI, Figs. 1–25. ("Indian Notes and Monographs," Vol. VII.) New York: Museum of the American Indian, Heye Foundation, 1919.

179. HIBBEN, FRANK C. "The Gallina Phase," *American Antiquity* (Salt Lake City), IV (1938), 131–36.

180. ———. *Evidences of Early Occupation in Sandia Cave, New Mexico, and Other Sites in the Sandia-Manzano Region*, pp. 1–44. ("Smithsonian Miscellaneous Collections," Vol. XCIX, No. 23.") Washington, D.C., 1941.

181. ———. "The Gallina Architectural Forms," *American Antiquity* (Salt Lake City), XIII (1948), 32–36.

182. ———. "The Pottery of the Gallina Complex," *ibid.*, XIV (1949), 194–202.

183. HILL-TOUT, C. "Notes on the Sk quomik of British Columbia, a Branch of the Great Salish Stock of North America," *Report of the British Association for the Advancement of Science*, pp. 427–544. London, 1900.

184. HODGE, F. W. "The Early Navajo and Apache," *American Anthropologist*, VIII (1895), 223.

185. ———. "The Narrative of Alvar Nuñez Cabeca de Vaca." In HODGE, F. W., *Spanish Explorers in the Southern United States*, pp. 1–126. New York: Charles Scribner's Sons, 1907.

186. HOFFMAN, WALTER JAMES. "The Graphic Art of the Eskimos," *Annual Report of the Bureau of American Ethnology, for 1894–1895*. Washington, D.C., 1897.

187. HOLMBERG, UNO. "Über die Jagdriten der nördlichen Völker Asiens und Europas," *Journal de la Société finno-ougrienne* (Helsinki), XLI (1925–26), 1–53.

188. ———. "Der Baum des Lebens," *Annales Academiae Scientiarum Fennicae.* (Helsingfors, Helsinki), Series B, XVI (1923), 14–27.

189. HOLMER, NILS M. "Outline of Cuna Grammar," *International Journal of American Linguistics* (Baltimore), XII (1946), 185–97.

190. ———. "Critical and Comparative Grammar of the Cuna Language," *Ethnologiska Studier* (Göteborg), XIV (1947), 1–219.

191. HOOPER, LUCILLE. *The Cahuilla Indians.* ("University of California Publications in American Archaeology and Ethnology," Vol. XVI, No. 6.) Berkeley, 1920.

191a. HOWARD, E. B., and HACK, E. T. "The Finley Site," *American Antiquity* (Salt Lake City), VIII (1942), 224–41.

192. HRDLIČKA, ALĔS. "Early Man in South America," *Proceedings of the XVIIIth International Congress of Americanists, London, 1912*, pp. 1–23. London, 1913.

193. ———. "The Genesis of the American Indian," *Proceedings of the XIXth International Congress of Americanists*, pp. 559–68. Washington, D.C., 1915.

194. ———. *Recent Discoveries Attributed to Early Man in America* (Bulletin of the United States Bureau of American Ethnology, No. 66.) Washington, D.C., 1918.

195. ———. "Anthropological Survey in Alaska," *46th Annual Report of the United States Bureau of American Ethnology, for 1928*, p. 29. Washington, D.C., 1930.

196. ———. *The Skeletal Remains of Early Man.* ("Smithsonian Miscellaneous Collection," Vol. LXXXIII, No. 3033.) Washington, D.C., 1930.

196a. ———. *Practical Anthropometry.* Philadelphia: Wistar Institute of Anatomy, 1939.

197. HRDLIČKA, ALĔS; HOLMES, W. H.; WILLIS, B.; WRIGHT, F. E.; and FENNER, C. N. *Early Man in South America.* (Bulletin of the United States Bureau of American Ethnology, No. 52.) Washington, D.C., 1912.

198. HULBERT, ARCHER B. "The Indian Thoroughfares of Ohio," *Ohio Archaeological and Historical Quarterly* (Columbus, Ohio), VIII (1900), 263–95.

199. ———. *Historic Highways of America.* Cleveland, Ohio: A. H. Clark Co., 1902–5.

200. HURTADO, A. "Respiratory Adaptation in the Indian Natives of the Peruvian Andes," *American Journal of Physical Anthropology* (Philadelphia), XVII (1932), 137–65.

201. ———. *Aspectos fisiológicos i patológicos de la vida en la altura.* Lima: Rimac, 1937.

202. HURTADO, A.; MERINO, C.; and DELGADO, E. "Influence of Anoxemia on the Hemopoietic Activity," *Archives of Internal Medicine* (Chicago), LXXV, No. 5 (1945), 284–323.

203. HUSCHER, B. H. and H. A. "The Hogan Builders of Colorado," *Southwestern Lore* (Gunnison, Colo.), IX, No. 11 (1943), 1–92.

204. IMBELLONI, J. "Le Relazione di parentela dei popoli Andini secondo il 'sistema classificatore' proprio degli Oceanici," *Atti del XXII Congresso Internazionale degli Americanisti, 1926,* pp. 407–20. Rome, 1928.

205. ———. "On the Diffusion in America of Patu, Onewa, Okewa, Patu Parava, Miti, and Other Relatives of the Mere Family," *Journal of the Polynesian Society* (New Plymouth, New Zealand), XXXIX (1930), 321–45.

206. ———. "Toki: La primera cadena isoglosemática establecida entre las islas del Oceano Pacífico y el Continente Americano," *Revista de la Sociedad "Amigos de la Arquelogía"* (Montevideo), V (1932), 3–25.

207. ———. "Der Zauber 'Toke,'" *Verhandlungen des XXIV Internationalen Amerikanisten-Kongresses, Hamburg, 1930,* pp. 228–42. Hamburg: Friederichsen, de Gruyter & Co., 1934.

208. ———. "Fuéguides et Laguides," *Zeitschrift für Rassenkunde* (Stuttgart), V (1937), 295–315.

209. ———. "De la estatura humana. Su reivindicación como elemento morfológico y classificatorio," *Runa* (Buenos Aires), I, Nos. 1–2 (1948), 196–243.

210. IZIKOWTIZ, K. G. *Musical and Other Sound Instruments of the South American Indians.* Göteborg: Elanders Boktryckeri Aktiebolag, 1935.

211. JACOBS, MELVILLE. "Culture Element Distributions: Kalapuya." Unpublished MS.

212. JAKOBSON, ROMAN. *Kindersprache, Aphasie, und allgemeine Lautgesetze.* Uppsala, 1941.

213. JENKS, A. E. "Pleistocene Man in Minnesota," *Science* (New York), LXXV, No. 1953 (1932), 607–9.

214. ———. "Minnesota Pleistocene Homo," *Proceedings of the National Academy of Science* (Washington, D.C.), XIX, No. 1 (1933), 1–6.

215. JOCHELSON, W. "Past and Present Subterranean Dwellings of the Tribes of North Eastern Asia and North Western America," *Proceedings of the XVth International Congress of Americanists, Quebec, 1907,* pp. 115–28. Quebec: Dussault & Proulx, 1907.

216. ———. "The Koryak." In BOAS, FRANZ, *The Jessup North Pacific Expedition,* Part II, pp. 383–842. ("Memoirs of the American Museum of Natural History," Vol. VI.) New York: G. E. Stechert, 1908.

217. ———. *Peoples of Asiatic Russia.* New York: American Museum of Natural History, 1928.

218. JOHNSON, FREDERICK. "Central American Cultures, an Introduction." In STEWARD, JULIAN H. (ed.), *Handbook of South American Indians,* IV, 51–68. (Bulletin of the United States Bureau of American Ethnology, No. 143.) Washington, D.C., 1948.

219. JONES, W. *Ojibwa Texts.* ("Publications of the American Ethnological Society," Vol. VII.) Leiden, 1917–19.

219a. JONES, VOLNEY H. "The Plant Material from Winona and Ridge Ruin." In McGREGOR, JOHN C. (ed.), *Winona and Ridge Ruin*, Appendix 2, pp. 295–300. (Bulletin of the Museum of Northern Arizona, No. 18.) Flagstaff, Ariz., 1941.
219b. JOYCE, T. A. *Mexican Archaeology.* London: P. L. Warner, 1920.
220. KANTOR, HELENE J. "The Shoulder Ornament of Near Eastern Lion," *Journal of Near Eastern Studies* (Chicago), VI (1947), 250–74.
221. KARDINER, ABRAM. *The Individual and His Society.* New York: Columbia University Press, 1939.
223. KARLGREN, BERNHARD. "Ordos and Huai." In *New Studies on Chinese Bronzes*, pp. 97–112. (Bulletin of the Museum of Far Eastern Antiquities, Vol. IX.) Stockholm, 1937.
224. KEITH, ARTHUR. "Discussion of Paper," *Proceedings of the XVIIIth International Congress of Americanists, 1912*, p. xxxix. London: Harrison & Sons, 1913.
225. KEITHAHN, E. L. "The Petroglyphs of Southeastern Alaska," *American Antiquity* (Salt Lake City), VI (1940), 123–32.
226. KELLEY, CHARLES FABENS. "Exhibition of the Brundage Collection of Chinese Bronzes at the Art Institute of Chicago," *Oriental Art* (London), II, No. 1 (1949), 11–15.
227. KELLEY, ISABEL T. "Chemehuevi Shamanism." In *Essays in Anthropology in Honor of Alfred Louis Kroeber*, pp. 129–42. Berkeley: University of California Press, 1936.
228. ———. "Southern Paiute Shamanism," *University of California Anthropological Records* (Berkeley), II, No. 4 (1939), 151–68.
229. KELLEY, J. CHARLES. "The Cultural Affiliations and Chronological Position of the Clear Fork Focus," *American Antiquity* (Salt Lake City), XIII (1947), 97–109.
230. ———. "Jumano and Patarabueye; Relations at La Junta de los Rios." Ph.D. thesis, Harvard University, 1947.
231. KERWIN, A. J. "Observation of the Heart Size of Natives Living at High Altitudes," *American Heart Journal* (St. Louis), XXVIII (1944), 69–91.
232. KIDDER, A. V. *An Introduction to the Study of Southwestern Archaeology (with a Preliminary Account of the Excavations at Pecos.)* New Haven: Yale University Press, 1924.
233. KIRCHHOFF, PAUL. "Food-gathering Tribes of the Venezuelan Llaños." In STEWARD, JULIAN H. (ed.), *Handbook of South American Indians*, IV, 445–68. (Bulletin of the United States Bureau of American Ethnology, No. 143.) Washington, D.C., 1948.
234. KISELEV, S. V. *Drevniaia Istoriia Iuzhnoi Sibiri.* ("Materialy i Issledovania po Arkheologii, SSSR," No. 9.) Moscow: Akademia nauk SSSR. Institut Istorii material'noj kultury, 1949.
235. KISSELL, MARY LOIS. *Basketry of the Papago and Pima.* ("Anthropological Papers of the American Museum of Natural History," Vol. XVII.) New York, 1916.
236. KLEMENTS, D. *Drevnosti Minusinskago Muzeia; Pamiatniki Metallischeskikh Epokh.* ("Antiquities of the Minusinsk Museum; Monuments of the Metal Ages.") Tomsk, 1886.
237. KLUCKHOHN, CLYDE. *Mirror for Man.* New York and Toronto: McGraw-Hill Book Co., Inc., 1949.
238. KOCH-GRÜNBERG, T. *Vom Roraima zum Orinoco.* 5 vols. Berlin and Stuttgart: D. Reiner, 1917–28.
239. KRAUSE, A. *Die Tlinkit Indianer.* Jena: H. Costenoble, 1885.

240. KRICKEBERG, W. *Märchen der Azteken und Inkaperuaner Maya und Muisca.* Jena: E. Diederichs, 1928.

241. KRIEGER, ALEX D. "An Inquiry into Supposed Mexican Influence on a Prehistoric 'Cult' in the Southern United States," *American Anthropologist,* XLVII (1945), 483–515.

242. ———. *Culture Complexes and Chronology in Northern Texas.* ("Publications of the University of Texas," No. 4640.) Austin, Tex., 1946.

243. ———. "Importance of the 'Gilmore Corridor' in Culture Contacts between Middle America and the Eastern United States," *Bulletin of the Texas Archaeological and Palaeontological Society* (Abilene, Tex.), XIX (1948), 155–78.

244. KROEBER, A. L. *Handbook of the Indians of California.* Washington, D.C.: Government Printing Office, 1925.

245. ———. *The Patwin and Their Neighbors.* ("University of California Publications in American Archaeology and Ethnology," Vol. XXIX, No. 4.) Berkeley, 1932.

246. ———. *Cultural and Natural Areas of Native North America.* ("University of California Publications in American Archaeology and Ethnology," Vol. XXXVIII.) Berkeley, 1939.

247. ———. "The Societies of Primitive Man," *Biological Symposia* (Lancaster, Pa.), VIII (1942), 205–16.

248. ———. *Anthropology.* New York: Harcourt, Brace & Co., 1943.

249. LANGDON, BESS D. "Additional Notes on the Tillamook." Unpublished MS.

250. LANTIS, MARGARET. "The Alaskan Whale Cult and Its Affinities," *American Anthropologist,* XL (1938), 438–64.

251. ———. *Alaskan Eskimo Ceremonialism.* ("Monographs of the American Ethnological Society," Vol. XI.) New York, 1947.

252. LARSEN, HELGE, and RAINEY, FROELICH. *Ipiutak and the Arctic Whale Hunting Culture.* ("Anthropological Papers of the American Museum of Natural History," Vol. XLII.) New York, 1948.

253. LASKER, GABRIEL. "Migration and Physical Differentiation: A Comparison of Immigrant with American-born Chinese," *American Journal of Physical Anthropology* (Philadelphia), IV (1946), 273–300.

254. LEBZELTER, VIKTOR. "Altindianische Schadel aus den Sambaquís von Iguapé bei Santos," *Mitteilungen der Anthropologischen Gesellschaft* (Vienna), LXIII, No. 8 (1933), 326–33.

255. LEHMANN, WALTER. *Zentral-Amerika,* Part I: "Die Sprachen Zentral-Amerikas." Berlin: D. Reimer, 1920.

256. LEHMANN-NITSCHE, R. "L'Homme fossile de la formation pampéene," *Compte-rendu du Congrès International d'Anthropologie et d'Archéologie Préhistorique, XII, 1900,* pp. 143–48. Paris: Mason et Cie, 1902.

257. ———. "Nuevos objetos de industria humana encontrados en la caverna Eberhardt en Última Esperanza," *Revista del Museo de La Plata* (Buenos Aires), XI (1902), 1–16.

258. ———. "Las Constellationes del Orión y de las Híadas," *Revista del Museo de La Plata* (Buenos Aires), XXVI (1921), 17–68.

259. LEIGHTON, D., and KLUCKHOHN, C. *Children of the People.* Cambridge: Harvard University Press, 1947.

260. LESSER, ALEXANDER. *The Pawnee Ghost Dance Hand Game.* ("Columbia University Contributions to Anthropology," Vol. XVI.) New York, 1933.

261. LÉVI-STRAUSS, C. "Contribution à l'étude de l'organisation sociale des Indiens Bororo," *Journal de la Société des Américanistes* (Paris), N. S., XXVIII (1936) 269–304.

262. Lévi-Strauss, C. "Reciprocity and Hierarchy," *American Anthropologist* (Menasha, Wis.), N.S., XLVI (1944), 266–68.
263. ———. "On Dual Organization in South America," *América indígena* (Mexico City), IV, No. 1 (1944), 37–47.
264. ———. "L'Analyse structurale en linguistique et en anthropologie," *Word* (New York), I (1945), 33–53.
265. ———. "La Vie familiale et sociale des Indiens Nambikwara," *Journal de la Société des Américanistes* (Paris), XXXVII (1948), 1–131.
266. ———. "Sur certaines similarités morphologiques entre les langues Chibcha et Nambikwara," *Actes du XXVIIIᵉ Congrès International des Américanistes, Paris, 1947*, pp. 185–92. Paris, 1948.
267. ———. *Les Structures élémentaires de la parenté.* Paris: Presses universitaires de France, 1949.
268. ———. "La Notion d'archaïsme en ethnologie," *Les Annales* (in press).
269. Li Fang-Kuei. "Chipewyan." In Hoijer, Harry; Bloomfield, L.; Haas, M. R., *et al.* (eds.), *Linguistic Structures of Native America*, pp. 398–423. ("Viking Fund Publications in Anthropology," No. 6.) New York, 1946.
269a. *Life* (New York), September, 1922.
270. Linnaeus, Carolus. *Species plantarum.* 2 vols. Stockholm: Holmiae, imprensis L. Salvi, 1753.
271. Linton, Ralph. *The Study of Man.* New York: D. Appleton–Century Co., Inc., 1936.
272. ———. "Nomad Raids and Fortified Pueblos," *American Antiquity* (Salt Lake City), X (1944), 28–32.
273. ———. *The Cultural Background of Personality.* New York and London: D. Appleton–Century Co., Inc., 1945.
274. Lipkind, W. "The Caraja." In Steward, Julian H. (ed.), *Handbook of South American Indians*, III, 179–92. (Bulletin of the United States Bureau of American Ethnology, No. 143.) Washington, D.C., 1948.
275. Loehr, Max. "Das Rolltier in China," *Ostrasiatische Zeitschrift* (Berlin), XXIV (1938), 137–42.
276. Lopatin, Ivan A. *Social Life and Religion of the Indians of Kitimat, British Columbia.* ("University of Southern California Social Science Series," No. 26.) Los Angeles, 1945.
277. Lothrop, S. K. *The Indians of Tierra del Fuego.* New York: Museum of the American Indian, Heye Foundation, 1928.
278. ———. "The Sigua: Southernmost Aztec Outpost," *Proceedings of the VIIIth Scientific Congress* (Washington, D.C., Department of State), II (1942), 109–16.
279. Lowie, R. H. "The Religion of the Crow Indians," *Annual Reports of the American Museum of Natural History* (New York), XXV (1922), 313–444.
280. ———. *Primitive Religion.* London: G. Routledge & Sons, Ltd., 1924.
281. ———. "On the Historical Connection between Certain Old World and New World Beliefs," *Compte-rendu de la XXIᵉ session du Congrès International des Américanistes, Göteborg en 1924, deuxième partie*, pp. 546–49. Göteborg, 1925.
282. ———. "Religious Ideas and Practices of the Eurasiatic and North American Areas." In Evans-Pritchard, E. E.; Firth, R.; Malinowski, B.; and Schapera, I. (eds.), *Essays Presented to C. G. Seligman*, pp. 113–43. London: K. Paul, Trench, Trubner & Co., Ltd., 1934.
283. ———. "American Culture History," *American Anthropologist*, N.S., XLII (1940), 409–28.
284. ———. "A Note on the Northern Gê Tribes of Brazil," *ibid.*, XLIII (1941), 188–96.

285. ———. "A Note on the Social Life of the Northern Kayapo," *ibid.*, XLV (1943), 633–35.
286. ———. *Primitive Religion.* ("Black and Gold" ed.) New York: Liveright, 1948.
287. LOWIE, R. H.; HARRIS, Z. S.; and VOEGLIN, C. S. *Hidatsa Texts.* Indianapolis: Indiana Historical Society, 1939.
288. LUMHOLTZ, CARL. *Unknown Mexico.* 2 vols. New York: Charles Scribner's Sons, 1902.
289. LYTTON, EDWARD BULWER-. *Zanoni.* Boston: Little, Brown & Co., 1893.
289a. MACALISTER, R. A. S. *A Text Book of European Archaeology.* Cambridge, Eng., 1921.
290. MacCURDY, GEORGE GRANT. *A Study of Chiriquian Antiquities.* ("Memoirs of the Connecticut Academy of Arts and Sciences," Vol. III.) New Haven, 1911.
291. MALINOWSKI, BRONISLAW. *A Scientific Theory of Culture and Other Essays.* Chapel Hill: University of North Carolina Press, 1944.
292. MANGLESDORF, P. C., and SMITH, C. E., Jr. "New Archaeological Evidence on Evolution in Maize," *Botanical Museum Leaflets* (Cambridge), XIII, No. 8 (1949), 213–47.
293. MANOUVRIER, L. "La Détermination de la taille d'après les grands os des membres," *Mémoires de la Société d'Anthropologie de Paris* (Paris), 2d ser., IV (1893), 351.
294. MARDONES, B. CARLOS. "Observaciones somatológicas e histológicas cerca de la mancha mongólica en la población chilena," *Boletín de la Sociedad Biología de Concepción* (Chile), XI (1937), 25–44.
294a. MARKAHAM, C. R. (ed. and trans.). *Narrative of the Proceedings of Pedrarias Davila.* ("Hakluyut Society," Vol. XXXIV.) London, 1865.
295. MARTENS, GEORG VON. *Die Gartenbonnen: Ihre Verbeitung, Cultur, und Benenutzung.* Ravensburg: E. Ulmer, 1869.
296. MARTIN, PAUL S.; QUIMBY, GEORGE I.; and COLLIER, DONALD. *Indians before Columbus.* Chicago: University of Chicago Press, 1947.
297. MARTIN, PAUL S.; RINALDO, J. B.; and ANTEVS, E. *Cochise and Mogollon Sites, Pine Lawn Valley, Western New Mexico.* ("Fieldiana: Anthropology, Chicago Natural History Museum," Vol. XXXVIII, No. 1.) Chicago, 1949.
298. MARTIN, R. *Lehrbuch der Anthropologie in systematischer Darstellung.* Jena: G. Fischer, 1928.
299. MARTINEZ, E. J. "Diario de la Navegación, 1789." MS, que obsta en el Depósito Hidrográfico de Madrid. Copy and English translation by H. I. PRIESTLY in Bancroft Library, Berkeley.
300. MASON, J. ALDEN. "Further Remarks on the Pre-Columbian Relationships between the United States and Mexico," *Bulletin of the Texas Archaeological and Palaeontological Society* (Abilene, Tex.), IX (1937), 120–29.
301. MASON, OTIS T. *Handbook of the American Indians North of Mexico.* Edited by FREDERICK WEBB HODGE. (Bulletin of the United States Bureau of American Ethnology, No. 30.) Washington, D.C., 1910.
302. MATHIASSEN, THERKEL. *Material Culture of the Iglulik Eskimo.* Copenhagen: Gyldendal, Nordiskforlag, 1928.
303. MATTOS, ANIBAL. "Lagoa Santa Man." In STEWARD, JULIAN H. (ed.), *Handbook of South American Indians*, I, 399–400. (Bulletin of the United States Bureau of American Ethnology, No. 143.) Washington, D.C., 1946.
304. McILWRAITH, T. F. *The Bella Coola Indians.* 2 vols. Toronto: University of Toronto Press, 1948.
305. McNEISH, RICHARD S. "A Preliminary Report on Coastal Tamaulipas, Mexico," *American Antiquity* (Salt Lake City), XIII (1947), 1–15.

306. MEARES, J. Extracts from *Voyages Made in the Years 1788 and 1789 from China to the Northwest Coast of America*. London: John Meares Press, 1791.

307. MENDES-CORREA, A. A. "Nouvelle hypothèse sur les peuplement primitif de l'Amérique du Sud," *Annales de Faculdade de Sciencias de Porto* (Porto), Vol. XXV (1928).

308. ———. "Crânes des Sambaquís du Brésil," *L'Anthropologie* (Paris), L (1941–46), 331–64.

309. MERA, H. P. "Ceramic Clues to the Prehistory of North Central New Mexico," *Bulletin, Laboratory of Anthropology, Technical Series* (Santa Fe), No. 8 (1935), pp. 8–12.

310. ———. "Some Aspects of the Largo Cultural Phase, Northern New Mexico," *American Antiquity* (Salt Lake City), III (1938), 236–43.

311. MERHART, GERO VON. *Bronzezeit am Jenissei*. Vienna: Schroll, 1926.

312. MÉTRAUX, A. *La Religion des Tupinamba*. Paris: E. Leroux, 1928.

313. ———. *The Native Tribes of Eastern Bolivia and Western Matto Grosso*. (Bulletin of the United States Bureau of American Ethnology, No. 134.) Washington, D.C., 1942.

314. ———. "Social Organization of the Kaingang and Aweikóma," *American Anthropologist*, XLIX (1947), 148–51.

315. MEYRINK, G. *Der Golem, Roman*. Leipzig: K. Wolff, 1915.

316. MIRANDA, A., and ROTTA, A. "Medidas del corazón en nativos de la altura," *Anales de la Facultad de Medicina* (Lima: Universidad Nacional Mayor de San Marcos de Lima), Vol. XXVII (1944).

317. MONGE, CARLOS. "El Sistema nervioso vegetativo del Hombre de los Andes," *Jornal Neuro-Psiquiatría* (Panama), Vol. XI (1939).

318. ———. *Climatophysiologie et climatopathologie*. ("Traite de climatologie biologique et médicale.") Paris: Masson & Cie, 1934.

319. ———. "High Altitude Disease," *Archives of Internal Medicine* (Chicago), LIX (1937), 32–40.

320. ———. "Life in the Andes and Chronic Mountain Sickness," *Science* (Cambridge), XCV, No. 2456 (1942), 79–84.

321. ———. "Chronic Mountain Sickness," *Physiological Reviews* (Baltimore), XXIII (1943), 166–84.

322. ———. "La Enfermedad do los Andes: Sindromes eritremicos," *Anales de la Facultad de Medicina* (Lima: Universidad Nacional Mayor de San Marcos de Lima), Vol. XXVII (1944).

323. ———. *Acclimatization in the Andes*. Baltimore: Johns Hopkins Press, 1948.

324. MONGE C.; CONTRERAS, L.; VELÁSQUEZ, T.; REYNAFARJE, C.; MONGE C., JR.; and CHÁVEZ, R. "Physiological Adaptations of Dwellers in the Tropics," *Proceedings of the IVth International Congress of Tropical Medicine and Malaria*, pp. 136–47. ("United States Department of State Publications, International Organization and Conference Series," Vol. I, No. 5.) Washington, D.C., 1948.

325. MONGE C.; ENCINAS, E.; HERAUD, C.; HURTADO A.; and CERVELLI, M. "Estudios fisiológicos sobre el hombre de los Andes," *Anales de la Facultad de Medicina* (Lima: Universidad Nacional Mayor de San Marcos de Lima), Vol. XXXII (1948).

326. MONGE C., JR. "Glucosa, acido láctico i acido pirúvico a nivel del mar i en la altura: Tesis de Lima," *Anales de la Facultad de Medicina* (Lima: Universidad Nacional Mayor de San Marcos de Lima), Vol. XXXII (1949).

327. MOOK, MAURICE A. "The Aboriginal Population of Tidewater Virginia," *American Anthropologist*, XLVI (1944), 203–4.

328. MOONEY, JAMES. *The Aboriginal Population of America North of Mexico*, pp.

1–40. ("Smithsonian Miscellaneous Collection," Vol. LXXX, No. 7.) Washington, D.C., 1928.

329. MOORE, CLARENCE B. "Antiquities of the Ouachita Valley," *Journal of the Academy of Natural Sciences* (Philadelphia), XIV (1909), 1–170.

330. MOORE, C. R., and PRICE, D. "A Study at High Altitude of Reproduction, Growth, Sexual Maturity, and Organ Weights," *Journal of Experimental Zoölogy* (Philadelphia), CVIII, No. 2 (1948), 171–216.

331. MORALES, VILLAZÓN NESTOR. "Estudio de la mancha sacro mongólica en La Paíz," *Proceedings of the Second Pan-American Scientific Congress* (Washington, D.C.), I, No. 1 (1917), 347–49.

332. MORI-CHÁVEZ, P. "Manifestaciones pulmonares del conejo del llano transportado a la altura," *Annales de la Facultad de Medicina* (Lima: Universidad Nacional Mayor de San Marcos de Lima), Vol. XIX (1936).

333. MORICE, A. G. "The Canadian Denes," *Annual Archaeological Report: Appendix to the Report of the Minister of Education, Ontario*, pp. 187–219. Toronto, 1905.

334. MORRIS, E. H. *Archaeological Studies in the La Plata District, Southwestern Colorado and Northwestern New Mexico.* ("Carnegie Institution of Washington Publications," No. 519.) Washington, D.C., 1939.

335. MOSER, CHARLES (Rev.). *Reminiscences of the West Coast of Vancouver Island.* Victoria, B.C.: Acme Press, Ltd., 1926.

336. MOZIÑO SUÁREZ DE FIGUEROA, J. M. *Noticias de Nutka.* Mexico City, 1913.

337. MURDOCK, G. P. *Social Structure.* New York: Macmillan Co., 1949.

338. NELSON, EDWARD WILLIAM. "The Eskimo about Bering Strait," *18th Annual Report of the United States Bureau of American Ethnology for 1896–1897*, Part I. Washington, D.C., 1899.

338a. NEWELL, H. PERRY; and KRIEGER, ALEX D. *The George C. Davis Site, Cherokee County, Texas.* ("Memoirs of the Society for American Archaeology," No. 5.) Menasha, Wis., 1949.

339. NIBLACK, A. P. "The Coast Indians of Southern Alaska and Northern British Columbia," *Annual Report of the United States National Museum, 1888*, pp. 256–386. Washington, D.C., 1890.

340. NIMUENDAJÚ UNKEL, CURT. "Religion der Apapocuva-Guarani," *Zeitschrift für Ethnologie* (Berlin), XLVI (1914), 284–403.

341. ———. *The Apinayé.* ("Catholic University of America Anthropological Series," No. 8.) Washington, D.C., 1939.

342. ———. *The Šerênte.* ("Publications of the Frederick Webb Hodge Anniversary Publication Fund," Vol. IV.) Los Angeles, 1942.

343. ———. *The Eastern Timbira.* ("University of California Publications in American Archaeology and Ethnology," Vol. XLI.) Berkeley, 1946.

344. ———. "Social Organization and Beliefs of the Botocudo of Eastern Brazil," *Southwestern Journal of Anthropology* (Albuquerque), II (1946), 93–115.

345. NORDENSKIÖLD, ERLAND. *Comparative Ethnographical Studies*, Vol. III. Göteborg: Elanders Boktryckerei Aktiebolag, 1924.

346. ———. "Cuna Indian Religion," *Proceedings of the XXIIIrd International Congress of Americanists, 1928*, pp. 668–78. Lancaster, Pa., 1930.

347. ———. *Indianerna på Panamanäset*, chap. xii. Stockholm, 1928.

348. NUTTAL, ZELIA. "Comparison between Etowan, Mexican, and Mayan Designs." In *Etowah Papers*. New Haven: Yale University Press, 1932.

349. OBERG, KALERVO. *The Terena and the Caduveo of Southern Mato Grosse, Brazil.* ("Smithsonian Institute of Social Anthropology Publications," No. 9.) Washington, D.C., 1949.

350. OLSON, R. L. "The Quinault Indians," *University of Washington Publications in Anthropology* (Seattle), VI (1936), 1–190.
351. OPLER, M. E. *Myths and Legends of the Chiricahua Apache.* ("Memoirs of the American Folk Lore Society," Vol. XXXVII.) Boston, 1942.
352. OSGOOD, C. *The Ethnography of the Tanaina.* ("Yale University Publications in Anthropology," No. 16.) New Haven, 1937.
353. OTT, C. F. "Contribuição a arqueologia baiana," *Boletim do Museu Nacional* (Rio de Janeiro), N.S., *Antropologia,* No. 5 (1944), pp. 1–73, Figs. 1–57, 1 map.
354. OWEN, M. A. *Folk-Lore of the Musquakie Indians of North America.* London: D. Nutt, Folk Lore Society, 1904.
355. PARK, W. Z. "Paviotso Shamanism," *American Anthropologist,* XXXVI (1934), 98–113.
356. ———. *Shamanism in Western North America.* ("Northwestern University Studies in the Social Sciences," No. 2.) Evanston, Ill., 1938.
357. PARSONS, ELSIE CLEWS. *Notes on Ceremonialism at Laguna.* ("Anthropological Papers of the American Museum of Natural History," Vol. XIX, Part 4.) New York, 1920.
358. ———. *Mitla, Town of the Souls.* Chicago: University of Chicago Press, 1936.
359. ———. *Pueblo Indian Religion.* 2 vols. Chicago: University of Chicago Press, 1939.
360. PENARD, A. P. *Het Pujai-Geheim der Surinaamsche Caraiben.* ("Bydr. T.L.," Vol. V, "Ned Indie," No. 84.) The Hague, 1929.
361. PETITOT, ÉMILE F. S. "La Femme au serpent, légende des Déné Chippewayans," *Mélusine* (Paris), II (1884–85), 19–21.
361a. PETITT, G. A. *Primitive Education in North America.* Berkeley: University of California, 1946.
362. PHILLIPS, PHILIP. "Middle American Influences on the Archaeology of the Southeastern United States." In *The Maya and Their Neighbors,* pp. 349–67. New York: D. Appleton–Century Co., 1940.
363. PHILLIPS, PHILIP; FORD, JAMES A.; and GRIFFIN, JAMES B. "Archaeological Survey in the Lower Mississippi Alluvial Valley, 1940–1947," *Papers of the Peabody Museum of American Archaeology and Ethnology,* Vol. XXV (1951).
364. PIERY, M. "Modern Medical and Biological Climatology," *Proceedings of the Royal Society of Medicine* (London), XXXI, Part II (1938), 1039–44.
365. PIKE, KENNETH L. "Grammatical Prerequisites for Phonemic Analysis," *Word* (New York), III (1947), 155–72.
366. PINART, ALPHONSE L. *Colección de lingüística y etnografía americanas,* Part IV. "Noticias de los Indios del departamento de Veragua y vocabularios." San Francisco: A. L. Bancroft, 1882.
367. ———. "Les Indiens de l'état de Panama," *Revue d'ethnographie* (Paris), VI (1887), 33–56, 117–32.
368. ———. *Vocabulario castellano-Guaymie.* Paris: E. Leroux, 1892. PLOETZ, HERMANN, and MÉTRAUX, A. "La Civilisation matérielle et la vie sociale et religieuse des Indiens Ze du Brésil méridional et oriental." *Revista Inst. Etnol. Univ. Nac. Tucumán* (Tucumán), I (1930), 107–238.
368a. PINZÓN, FRANCISCA I. DE. "Indios de Cricamola y Península Valiente," *Universidad* (Panama), XXV (1946), 127–40.
369. POOLE, FRANCIS. *Queen Charlotte Islands.* Edited by John W. Lyndon. London: Hurst & Blackett, 1872.
370. POWERS, WILLIAM E. "Basin and Shore Features of the Extinct Lake San Augustin, New Mexico," *Journal of Geomorphology* (New York), XI (1939), 345–57.

371. PROKOSHEV, N. A. "Iz Materialov po Izucheniĩu Anan'inskoĭ Epokhi v Pri-kam'e" ("Some Materials for the Study of the Anan'ino Epoch on the Kama"), *Sovetskaĩa Arkheologiĩa* (Moscow), X (1948), 183–202.
372. PUCHER, L. *El Homo ivoensis* ("Universidad de San Francisco Xavier," Vol. XIV, Nos. 33 and 34.) Sucre, Bolivia, 1946.
373. QUIMBY, G. I. *Prehistoric Art of the Aleutian Islands.* ("Fieldiana: Anthropology, Chicago Natural History Museum," Vol. XXXVI.) Chicago, 1948.
374. RANK, GUSTAV. "Das System der Raumverteilung in der Nordeurasischen Behausung." MS (to be published in Stockholm).
375. RADIN, PAUL. *Indians of South America.* New York: Doubleday, Doran & Co., Inc., 1942.
376. ———. *Winnebago Hero Cycles.* Baltimore: Waverly Press, 1948.
377. RASSMUSSEN, KNUD. *Intellectual Culture of the Iglulik Eskimos.* Copenhagen: Gyldendal, 1929.
378. RAY, VERNE F. *The Sanpoil and Nespelem: Salishan Peoples of Northeastern Washington.* ("University of Washington Publications in Anthropology," Vol. V.) Washington, D.C., 1933.
379. ———. *Cultural Relations in the Plateau of North America.* ("Publications of the Frederick Webb Hodge Anniversary Publication Fund," Vol. III.) Los Angeles, 1939.
380. ———. "Historic Backgrounds of the Conjuring Complex in the Plateau and the Plains." In SPIER, LESLIE; HALLOWELL, IRVING; and NEWMAN, STANLEY S. (eds.), *Language, Culture, and Personality: Essays in Memory of Edward Sapir,* pp. 204–16. Menasha, Wis.: Sapir Memorial Publication Fund, 1941.
381. ———. "Culture Element Distributions. XXII. Plateau," *University of California Anthropological Records* (Berkeley), VIII, No. 2 (1942), 99–262.
382. REAGAN, F. "Pictographs of Ashley and Dry Fork Valleys in Northwestern Utah," *Transactions of the Kansas Academy of Sciences* (Topeka), XXXIV (1931), 168–216.
383. ———. "Some Notes on the Snake Pictographs of Nine Miles Canyon, Utah," *American Anthropologist,* XXXV (1933), 550–51.
384. Reed, E. K. "The Abandonment of the San Juan Region," *El Palacio* (Santa Fe), LI (1944), 61–73.
385. REICHARD, GLADYS A. "Coeur d'Alene." In *Handbook of American Indian Languages,* III, 515–707. New York, 1938.
386. ———. "An Analysis of Coeur d'Alene Myths," *Memoirs of the American Folk Lore Society* (Boston), XLI (1947), 98–103.
387. RITCHIE, WILLIAM A. "A Perspective of Northeastern Archaeology," *American Antiquity* (Salt Lake City), IV (1938), 94–112.
388. ———. *The Pre-Iroquoian Occupations of New York State.* ("Rochester Museum Memoirs," No. 1.) Rochester, N.Y., 1944.
389 RÍOS, C. "Contribución al estudio de la electrocardiografía en la altura." Tesis de Lima, 1948. (To be published.)
390. RIVERS, W. H. R. *Social Organization.* Edited by W. J. PERRY. New York: A. A. Knopf, Inc., 1924.
391. RIVET, PAUL. "La Race de Lagoa Santa chez les populations pré-colombiennes de l'Equateur," *Bulletins et mémoires de la Société d'anthropologie de Paris* (Paris), 5th ser., IX (1908), 209–68.
392. ———. "Les Mélanéso-polynésiens et les australiens en Amérique," *Anthropos* (Mödling: St. Gabriel), XX (1925), 51–54.
393. ———. "Les Origines de l'Homme Américain," *L'Anthropologie* (Paris), XXXV (1925), 283–319.

394. RIVET, PAUL. "La Famille linguistique Timote (Venezuela)," *International Journal of American Linguistics* (Baltimore), IV (1927), 137–67.

395. ———. *Los Orígenes del Hombre Americano*. Mexico City. Cuadernos Americanos, 1943.

396. RIVET, P.; KOK, P.; and TASTEVIN, C. "Nouvelle contribution à l'étude de la langue Maku," *International Journal of American Linguistics* (Baltimore), III (1925), 133–93.

397. ROBERTS, FRANK H. H. "The Folsom Problem in American Archaeology," *Smithsonian Report for 1938*, pp. 531–46. Washington, D.C., 1939.

398. ———. "The New World Paleo-Indian," *Smithsonian Report for 1944*, pp. 403–34. Washington, D.C., 1945.

399. ROGERS, MALCOLM J. *Early Lithic Industries of the Lower Basin of the Colorado River and Adjacent Desert Areas*. ("San Diego Museum Papers," No. 8.) Los Angeles, 1939.

400. ROGERS, SPENCER L. "Disease Concepts in North America," *American Anthropologist*, XLVI (1944), 559–64.

400a. ROHEIM, CEZA. "The Divine Child," *Journal of Clinical Psychopathology* (Woodbourne, N.Y.), IX (1948), 309–23.

401. ROQUEFEUIL, M. CAMILLE DE. *A Voyage round the World between the Years 1816–1819*. London, 1823.

402. ROTH, W. E. "An Introductory Study of the Arts, Crafts, and Customs of the Guiana Indians," *38th Annual Report of the United States Bureau of American Ethnology*, pp. 25–745. Washington, D.C., 1924.

403. ROTTA, A. *La Circulación en las grandes alturas*. (Tesis de doctor.) Lima: Librería e Imprenta Gil, S.A., 1938.

404. ———. "Physiologic Condition of the Heart in the Natives of the High Altitudes," *American Heart Journal* (St. Louis), XXXIII (1947), 669–76.

405. ROUSE, IRVING R. "Styles of Pottery in Connecticut," *Bulletin of the Massachusetts Archaeological Society* (Cambridge, Mass.), III (1945), 1–8.

406. ———. "Ceramic Traditions and Sequences in Connecticut," *Bulletin of the Archaeological Society of Connecticut* (New Haven), No. 21 (1947), pp. 10–25.

407. ROWE, JOHN H. "Inca Culture at the Time of the Spanish Conquest." In STEWARD, JULIAN H. (ed.), *Handbook of the South American Indians*, II, 183–330. (Bulletin of the United States Bureau of American Ethnology, No. 143.) Washington, D.C., 1946.

408. ROWLEY, GRAHAM. "The Dorset Culture of the Eastern Arctic," *American Anthropologist*, XLII (1940), 490–99.

409. SAENZ, R. "Electrocardiograma en la altura," *Anales de la Facultad de Medicina* (Lima: Universidad Nacional Mayor de San Marcos de Lima), XXII (1939), 237.

410. SALMONY, ALFRED. *Sino-Siberian Art in the Collection of C. T. Loo*. Paris: Loo, 1933.

411. ———. "Sarmatian Gold Collected by Peter the Great. III. The Early Group with Winged Circle Sockets," *Gazette des beaux-arts* (Paris), 6th ser., XXXIII (1948), 321–26.

412. SANTIANA, ANTONIO. "La Distribución Pilosa como caracter racial: Su modalidad en los Indios de Imbabura (Eduador)." MS, 1941.

413. SAPIR, EDWARD. "Religious Ideas of the Takelma Indians of Southwestern Oregon," *Journal of American Folklore* (New York), XX (1907), 33–49.

414. ———. "The Social Organization of the West Coast Tribes," *Proceedings and Transactions of the Royal Society of Canada* (Ottawa), 3d ser., IX (1915), 355–74.

415. ———. "Southern Paiute, a Shoshonean Language," *Proceedings of the American Academy of Arts and Sciences*, Vol. LXV (Boston, 1931).

416. ———. "Cultural Anthropology and Psychiatry," *Journal of Abnormal and Social Psychology* (Boston), XXVII (1932), 229–42.

417. ———. "La Réalité psychologique des phonèmes," *Journal de psychologie* (Paris), XXX (1933), 247–65.

418. SAUVAGEOT, AURELIEN. "Eskimo et Ouralien," *Journal de la Société des Américanistes de Paris* (Paris), XXI (1924), 296–97.

419. SAYLES, E. B. and ANTEVS. *The Cochise Culture.* ("Gila Pueblo Archaeological Foundation, Medallion Papers," No. XXIX.) Globe, Ariz., 1941.

420. SCHMIDT, MAX. *Indianerstudien in Zentralbrasilien.* Berlin: D. Reimer (E. Vohsen), 1905.

421. SCHOOLCRAFT, HENRY R. *Algic Researches.* (First series of "Indian Tales and Legends"; no more published.) New York: Harper & Bros., 1839.

422. ———. *The Myth of Hiawatha and Other Oral Legends, Mythologic and Allegoric, of the North American Indians.* Philadelphia: J. B. Lippincott & Co., 1856.

422a. SEEMAN, BERTHOLD. *The Aborigines of the Isthmus of Panama.* ("Transactions of the American Ethnological Society," Vol. III.) New York, 1953.

423. SELER, EDUARD. *Die mexikanischen Bilderhandschriften Alexander von Humboldt's in der Königlichen Bibliothek zu Berlin.* Berlin: Hopfer, 1893.

424. SELTZER, C. C. *Racial Prehistory of the Southwest and the Hawikuh Zunis.* ("Papers of the Peabody Museum of Archaeology and Ethnology," Vol. XXIII.) Cambridge: Harvard University Press, 1944.

425. SEMPER, GOTTFRIED. *Der Stil in den technischen und tektonischen Künsten.* 2 vols. Munich: F. Bruckmann, 1878.

426. SERRANO, ANTONIO. "Arqueologia brasileira: Subsídios para a arqueologia do Brasil meridional," *Revista do Arquivo Municipal* (São Paulo), XXXVI (1937), 3–42.

427. ———. "The Sambaquís of the Brazilian Coast." In STEWARD, JULIAN H. (ed.), *Handbook of South American Indians*, I, 401–97. (Bulletin of the United States Bureau of American Ethnology, No. 143.) Washington, D.C., 1946.

428. SHAPIRO, H. L. *Migration and Environment.* London: Oxford University Press, 1939.

429. SKINNER, A. "Notes on the Eastern Cree and Northern Saulteaux," *Anthropological Papers of the American Museum of Natural History* (New York), IX, Part I (1911), 1–116.

430. ———. "Notes on the Florida Seminole," *American Anthropologist*, XV (1913), 63–77.

431. ———. "Chronological Relations of the Coastal Algonquin Culture," *Proceedings of the XIXth International Congress of Americanists, 1915*, pp. 52–58. Washington, D.C., 1917.

432. SMITH, CARLYLE S. "Clues to the Chronology of Coastal New York," *American Antiquity* (Salt Lake City), X (1944), 87–89.

433. ———. "Notes on the Archaeology of Long Island," *Bulletin of the Massachusetts Archaeological Society* (Cambridge, Mass.), IV (1944), 56–59.

434. ———. "An Outline of the Archaeology of Coastal New York," *Bulletin of the Archaeological Society of Connecticut* (New Haven), XXI (1947), 3–9.

435. ———. *The Archaeology of Coastal New York.* ("Anthropological Papers of the American Museum of Natural History," Vol. XLIII, Part 2.) New York, 1950.

436. SMITH, DOROTHY A., and SPIER, LESLIE. "The Dot and Circle Design in Northwestern America," *Journal de la Société des Américanistes de Paris* (Paris), XIX (1927), 47–55

437. SMITH, GRAFTON ELLIOT. *The Evolution of the Dragon*. London and New York: Longmans, Green & Co., 1919.
438. SMITH, H. I. "A List of Petroglyphs in British Columbia," *American Anthropologist*, XXIX (1927), 605–10.
439. ———. "Aboriginal Pictographs on the Pacific Coast of Canada." Unfinished MS, National Museum of Canada, Ottawa.
440. SMITH, MARIAN W. *The Puyallup-Nisqually*. New York: Columbia University Press, 1940.
441. ———. "The Coast Salish of Puget Sound," *American Anthropologist*, XLIII (1941), 197–211.
442. ———. "House Types of the Middle Fraser River," *American Antiquity* (Salt Lake City), XII (1947), 255–67.
443. ———. "Archaeology of the Columbia-Fraser Region." In SMITH, MARIAN W. (ed.), *Indians of the Urban Northwest*. New York: Columbia University Press, 1949.
444. ———. *The Archaeology of the Columbia-Fraser Region*. ("Memoirs of the Society for American Archaeology," Vol. XV, No. 4, Part 2.) Menasha, Wis., 1950.
445. SPARKMAN, P. S. *The Culture of the Luiseno Indians*. ("University of California Publications in American Archaeology and Ethnology," Vol. VIII, No. 3.) Berkeley, 1908.
446. SPAULDING, ALBERT C. "Northeastern Archaeology and General Trends in the Northeastern Forest Zone." In JOHNSON, FREDERICK (ed.), *Man in Northeastern North America*, pp. 143–67. ("Papers of the Peabody Foundation for Archaeology," Vol. III.) Andover, Mass.: Phillips Academy, 1946.
447. SPECK, FRANK G. *Ethnology of the Yuchi Indians*. ("Anthropological Publications of the Pennsylvania University Museum," Vol. I, No. 1.) Philadelphia, 1909.
448. SPENCER, B., and GILLEN, F. *The Native Tribes of Central Australia*. London and New York: Macmillan Co., 1899.
449. SPIER, LESLIE. *Klamath Ethnography*. ("University of California Publications in American Archaeology and Ethnology," Vol. XXX.) Berkeley, 1930.
450. ———. *Yuman Tribes of the Gila River*. Chicago: University of Chicago Press, 1933.
451. ———. *The Prophet Dance of the Northwest and Its Derivatives: The Source of the Ghost Dance*. ("General Series in Anthropology," No. 1.) Menasha, Wis., 1935.
452. SPIER, LESLIE, and SAPIR, EDWARD. *Wishram Ethnography*. ("University of Washington Publications in Anthropology," Vol. III, No. 3.) Seattle, 1930.
453. SPINDEN, HERBERT J. *The Nez Percé Indians*. ("Memoirs of the American Anthropological Association," No. 2, Part 3.) Menasha, Wis., 1908.
454. ———. "The Population of Ancient America," *Geographical Review* (New York), XVIII (1928), 641–60.
455. ———. *Ancient Civilizations of Mexico and Central America* ("Handbook Series of the American Museum," No. 3.) New York: American Museum Press, 1928.
456. SPITSYN, A. "Shamanskiia Izobrazheniia" ("Shaministic Representations"), *Zapiski Otdeleniia Russkoi i Slavianskoi Arkeologii Imperatorskago Russkago Arkelogichenskago Obschestrva*, VIII (1906), 29–145.
457. STANDLEY, PAUL C. *Flora of the Panama Canal Zone*. Washington, D.C.: Government Printing Office, 1928.
458. STERN, BERNHARD J. *The Lummi Indians of Northwestern Washington*. New York: Columbia University Press, 1934.

459. STEVENSON, M. C. "The Sia," *11th Annual Report of the United States Bureau of American Ethnology*. Washington, D.C., 1890.

460. STEWARD, JULIAN H. *Ethnography of the Owens Valley Paiute*. ("University of California Publications in American Archaeology and Ethnology," Vol. XXXIII, No. 3.) Berkeley, 1933.

461. ———. *Basin-Plateau Aboriginal Sociopolitical Groups*. (Bulletin of the United States Bureau of American Ethnology, No. 120.) Washington, D.C., 1938.

462. ———. "Culture Element Distributions. XIII. Nevada Shoshone," *University of California Anthropological Records* (Berkeley), IV, No. 2 (1941), 209–360.

463. ———. "Culture Element Distributions. XXIII. Northern and Gosiute Shoshoni," *ibid.*, VIII, No. 3 (1943), 263–392.

464. ———. "The Cirum-Caribbean Tribes: An Introduction." In STEWARD, JULIAN H. (ed.), *Handbook of South American Indians*, IV, 1–15. (Bulletin of the United States Bureau of American Ethnology, No. 143.) Washington, D.C., 1948.

464a. STEWART, K. M. "Spirit Possession in Native America," *Southwestern Journal of Anthropology* (Albuquerque), II (1946), 323–39.

465. STEWART, OMER C. "Culture Element Distributions. XIV. Northern Paiute," *University of California Anthropological Records* (Berkeley), IV, No. 3 (1941), 361–446.

466. ———. "Culture Element Distributions. XVIII. Ute-Southern Paiute," *ibid.*, VI, No. 4 (1942), 231–360.

467. STEWART, T. D. *Anthropometric Observations on the Eskimos and Indians of Labrador*. ("Field Museum of Natural History Anthropological Series," Vol. XXXI, No. 1.) Chicago, 1939.

468. ———. "Noticias sobre esqueletos prehistóricos hallados en Guatemala," *Antropología e historia de Guatemala* (Guatemala City), I, No. 1 (1949), 23–34.

469. ———. "The Development of the Concept of Morphological Dating in Connection with Early Man in America," *Southwestern Journal of Anthropology* (Albuquerque), V (1949), 1–16.

470. STOŁYHWO, K. "Contribution à l'étude de l'homme fossile sudaméricain de son prétendu précurseur le Diprothomo platensis," *Bulletin et mémoires de la Société d'anthropologie* (Paris), 6th ser., II (1911), 158–68.

471. ———. "Diprothomo platensis predpotagaejemyj predszestwiennik czelowieka," *Izvêstiâ Warszavskogo Universitieta* (Warsaw, 1912), pp. 1–9.

472. ———. "Wrazenia ze Zjasdu Miedzynarodowego Amerykanistow w La Plata w 1932 r," *Przeglad Antropologiczny* (Poznán), VII (1933), 3–4.

473. ———. "W sprawie czlowieka kopalnego w Argentynie," *ibid.*, VIII (1934), 1–5.

474. STOUT, D. B. "Further Data on Ablinism among the San Blas Cuna, Panama," *American Journal of Physical Anthropology* (Philadelphia), IV (1946), 483–90.

475. ———. "Land Tenure and Other Property Concepts among the San Blas Cuna," *Primitive Man* (Washington, D.C.), XIX (1946), 63–80.

476. ———. *San Blas Cuna Acculturation: An Introduction*. ("Viking Fund Publications in Anthropology," No. 9.) New York, 1947.

477. STRONG, W. DUNCAN. "The Occurrence and Wider Implications of a 'Ghost Cult' on the Columbia River, Suggested by Carvings in Wood, Bone, and Stone," *American Anthropologist*, XLVII (1945), 244–61.

478. STRONG, W. D.; SCHENCK, W. E.; and STEWARD, J. H. *Archaeology of the Dalles Deschutes Region*. ("University of California Publications in American Archaeology and Ethnology," Vol. XXIX, No. 1.) Berkeley, 1930.

479. SUK, V. "Prwvni pleistocenni kostra človeka z Ameriky," *Biologicke Listy* (Praha), XVIII (1933), 1–3.

480. SULLIVAN, L. R., and HELLMAN, M. "The Punin Calvarium;" *Anthropological Papers of the American Museum of Natural History* (New York), XXIII (1925), 309–37.

481. SWADESH, MORRIS. "The Linguistic Approach to Salish Prehistory." In SMITH, MARIAN W. (ed.), *Indians of the Urban Northwest*, pp. 161–74. New York: Columbia University Press, 1949.

482. SWAN, J. G. *The Indians of Cape Flattery*. ("Smithsonian Contributions to Knowledge," Vol. XVI, No. 220.) Washington, D.C., 1868.

483. SWANTON, J. R. "Social Condition, Beliefs, and Linguistic Relationship of the Tlingit Indians," *26th Annual Report of the Bureau of American Ethnology*, pp. 391–486. Washington, D.C., 1908.

484. ———. *Tlingit Myths and Tents*. (Bulletin of the United States Bureau of American Ethnology, No. 39.) Washington, D.C., 1909.

485. ———. *Contributions to the Ethnology of the Haida*. ("Memoirs of the American Museum of Natural History," Vol. VIII.) Leiden, 1909.

486. TALLGREN, A. M. *Collection tovostine des antiquités préhistoriques de Minoussinsk*. Helsingfors: Société finlandaise d'archéologie, 1917.

487. ———. "Études archéologiques sur la Russie orientale durant l'ancien âge du fer," *Eurasia septentrionalis antiqua* (Helsinki), VII (1932), 7–32.

488. TEIT, JAMES. *Traditions of the Thompson River Indians of British Columbia*. ("Memoirs of the American Folk Lore Society," Vol. VI.) Boston, 1898.

489. ———. "The Thompson Indians of British Columbia," *Memoirs of the American Museum of Natural History* (New York), II (1900), 165–392.

490. THALBITZER, W. "Parallels within the Culture of the Arctic Peoples," *Annales de XX Congresso Internacional de Americanistas*, I, 283–87. Rio de Janerio, 1922.

491. ———. *Uhlenbeck's Eskimo-Indo-European Hypothesis: A Critical Revision*, pp. 66–96. ("Études Linguistiques, 1944," "Travaux du Cercle Linguistique de Copenhague," Vol. I.) Copenhagen, 1945.

492. THOMPSON, STITH. *European Tales among North American Indians: A Study in the Migrations of Folk Tales*. ("Colorado College Publications, General Series," Nos. 100–101.) Colorado Springs, 1919.

493. ———. "Tales Borrowed from Europeans." In his *Tales of the North American Indians*, chap. viii. Cambridge: Harvard University Press, 1929.

494. ———. *Motif-Index of Folk-Literature*. ("Indiana University Studies," Vol. XIX.) Bloomington, 1936.

495. ———. *The Folk Tale*. New York: Dryden Press, 1946.

496. TORRES, H. "La Presión arterial en al altura," *Anales de la Facultad de Medicina* (Lima: Universidad Nacional Mayor de San Marcos de Lima), XX (1938), 406.

497. TURNER, L. M. "Ethnology of the Ungava District, Hudson Bay Territory," *11th Annual Report of the United States Bureau of American Ethnology*. Washington, D.C., 1894.

498. TURNEY-HIGH, H. H. *The Flathead Indians of Montana*. ("Memoirs of the American Anthropological Association," No. 48.) Menasha, Wis., 1937.

499. ———. *Ethnography of the Kutenai*. ("Memoirs of the American Anthropological Association," Vol. LXIV.) Menasha, Wis., 1941.

500. TYLOR, E. B. *Researches into the Early History of Mankind and the Development of Civilization*. London: J. Murray, 1865.

501. UHLE, MAX. *Sobre la estación paleolítica de Taltal*, pp. 31–50. ("Publicaciones del Museo de Etnología y Antropología de Chile," Vol. I.) Santiago, Chile, 1917.

502. UHLENBECK, C. C. "La Langue Basque et la linguistique générale," *Lingua* (Haarlem), I (1948), 59–76.

503. ———. "Additional Blackfoot-Arapaho Comparisons," *International Journal of American Linguistics* (Baltimore), VI (1931), 227–71.

504. VELASQUEZ, T. "El Metabolismo basal en la altura" (Tesis de Lima), *Anales de la Facultad de Medicina* (Lima: Universidad Nacional Mayor de San Marcos de Lima), XXX (1947), 194.

505. VIGNATI, M. A. "El Hombre fosil de Esperanza. Notas preliminares," *Revista del Museo de La Plata* (Buenos Aires), III (1934), 7–75.

506. ———. "Descripción de los malares humanos fosiles de Miramar (province de Buenos Aires)," *Revista del Museo de La Plata* (Buenos Aires), No. 1 (1941), pp. 271–358.

507. VILLA ROJAS, ALFONSO. *The Maya of East Central Quintana Roo.* ("Carnegie Institution of Washington Publications," No. 559.) Washington, D.C., 1945.

508. VISSER, H. F. E. *Asiatic Art.* New York: Beechhurst Press, 1946.

509. VOEGELIN, CHARLES F. *Tubatulabal Grammar,* pp. 55–189. ("University of California Publications in American Archaeology and Ethnology," Vol. XXXIV.) Berkeley, 1936.

509a. VOEGELIN, C. F., and HARRIS, Z. S. "Linguistics in Ethnology," *Southwestern Journal of Anthropology* (Albuquerque), I (1945), 455–65.

510. ———. "The Scope of Linguistics," *American Anthropologist*, XLIX (1947), 588–600.

511. VOEGELIN, ERMINIE W. "Culture Element Distributions. XX. Northeast California," *University of California Anthropological Records* (Berkeley), VII, No. 2 (1942), 47–252.

512. WAGLEY, CHARLES, and GALVÃO, E. "The Tapirapé." In STEWARD, JULIAN H. (ed.), *Handbook of South American Indians*, III, 167–92. (Bulletin of the United States Bureau of American Ethnology, No. 143.) Washington, D.C., 1948.

513. WALTER, H. V. *The Prehistory of the Lagoa Santa Region.* Minais Geraies, Brazil, 1948.

514. WALTER, H. V.; CATHOUD, A.; and MATTOS, A. "The Confins Man—a Contribution to the Study of Early Man in South America." In MacCURDY, G. G. (ed.), *Early Man*, pp. 341–48. Philadelphia: J. B. Lippincott Co., 1937.

515. WARING, A. J., JR., and HOLDER, PRESTON. "A Prehistoric Ceremonial Complex in the Southeastern United States," *American Anthropologist*, XLVII (1945), 1–34.

516. WASSÉN S., HENRY. *Illustrerad rapport över resa i Central- och Sydamerika 1947*, pp. 155–56. ("Göteborgs Musei Arstryck," 1948.) Göteborg, 1949.

517. ———. *Contributions to Cuna Ethnography.* ("Ethnologiska Studier," No. 16.) Göteborg: Elanders Boktryckeri Aktiebolag, 1949.

518. WATERMAN, T. T. "The Paraphernalia of the Duwamish 'Spirit Ceremony,'" *Indian Notes*, pp. 129–48. ("Museum of the American Indian, Heye Foundation," Vol. VII.) New York, 1919.

519. WERNER, EDWARD T. C. *Myths and Legends of China.* London: G. G. Harrap & Co., Ltd., 1922.

520. WIKE, J. "Field Notes on Southeastern Vancouver Island." Unpublished MS.

521. WILLIAMS, F. E. "Sex Affiliation and Its Implications," *Journal of the Royal Anthropological Institute* (London), LXII (1932), 51–81.

522. WILLOUGHBY, CHARLES C. *Antiquities of New England Indians.* Cambridge, Mass.: Peabody Museum of American Archaeology and Ethnology, 1935.

523. WISSLER, CLARK. *The American Indian.* New York: D. C. McMurtrie, 1917.

524. ———. *North American Indians of the Plains.* ("Handbook Series of the American Museum of Natural History," No. 1.) New York, 1920.

525. WITTMACK, LUDWIG. "Bohnen aus Altperuanischen Gräbern," *Verhandlungen des Botanischer Vereins der Provinz Neu Brandenburg, Sitzungsberichte*, XXI, 176–84. Berlin, 1879.

526. ———. "Das Vaterland der Bohnen und Kürbis," *Tageblatt der 53 Versammlung Deutscher Naturforscher und Aertze zu Danzig*, pp. 205 ff. Danzig, 1880.

527. ———. "Antike Sämereien aus der Alten und Neuen Welt," *Nachrichten aus dem Klub der Landwirte zu Berlin* (Berlin), No. 115 (1881).

528. ———. "Die Heimat der Bohnen und der Kürbisse," *Berichte der Deutschen Botanischer Gesellschaft* (Berlin), VI (1888), 374–80.

529. ———. "Die Nutzpflanzen der Alten Peruaner," *Compte-rendu de la septième session de la Congrès International des Américanistes*, pp. 325–48. Berlin, 1888.

530. ———. "Our Present Knowledge of Ancient Plants," *Transactions of the Academy of Science of St. Louis* (St. Louis), XV (1905), 1–15.